*What They Said*
*in 1969*

# What They Said In 1969

## The Yearbook of Spoken Opinion

●

Compiled and Edited by

ALAN F. PATER

and

JASON R. PATER

**MONITOR BOOK COMPANY, INC.**

*To*

*The Newsmakers of the World . . .*

*May they never be at a loss for words*

# Acknowledgments

Among the sources used in compiling WHAT THEY SAID IN 1969 were many of the world's major newspapers, periodicals and broadcast news services, certain material from which appears in this volume under the "Fair Use Doctrine." Although it is not feasible to list all of the sources here, the editors wish to gratefully acknowledge the following domestic news organizations for their special cooperation:

*Nation's Business; Los Angeles Herald-Examiner; Los Angeles Times; The New York Times* (© 1969 The New York Times); *The Sporting News; TV Guide* (© 1969 Triangle Publications, Inc.)

Some of the quotations included in this book were excerpted from interviews published in *U. S. News & World Report* and *The Christian Science Monitor,* as follows:

Copyright 1969 by *U. S. News & World Report* . . .

James E. Allen, Jr., p. 43 (June 30); George W. Anderson, Jr., pp. 124, 253; Raymond Aron, p. 440; Joseph M. Barr, p. 179; Winton M. Blount, p. 87; Willy Brandt, p. 76; Alastair Buchan, pp. 77, 126, 255; Ellsworth Bunker, p. 226; Arthur F. Burns, p. 166 (July 14); Sheldon S. Cohen, p. 179; Luis A. Ferre, p. 202; Joseph Fromm, p. 259; Minoru Genda, pp. 209, 229; John L. Harrington, p. 121; S. I. Hayakawa, p. 344; Lewis B. Hershey, p. 132; W. Sprague Holden, p. 102; Sidney Hook, pp. 50, 66 (May 19); Roy Innis, p. 9; Harry S. Johnson, p. 304; David M. Kennedy, p. 103; Warren P. Knowles, p. 52; James D. Koerner, p. 52; Nguyen Cao Ky, p. 236; Melvin R. Laird, p. 135 (April 7); Lyman L. Lemnitzer, pp. 136, 443; Mike Mansfield, pp. 94, 160; Ferdinand E. Marcos, p. 212 (March 31); Floyd B. McKissick, p. 173; George W. Mitchell, p. 105; Thomas H. Moorer, pp. 139, 240; John H. Morsell, p. 106; Karl E. Mundt, p. 161; Thomas O. Paine, p. 407 (July 7); Chung Hee Park, p. 214 (Aug. 25); Joseph E. Ragen, p. 39; David C. Richardson, p. 445; James M. Roche, p. 24; George W. Romney, p. 175; George P. Shultz, p. 108; John Stennis, p. 147 (July 14); Franz-Josef Strauss, p. 270; Stuart Symington, p. 148 (July 14); Edward Teller, p. 149; Jerome B. Wiesner, p. 151 (May 26); Stanley F. Yolles, p. 309.

Copyright 1969 by The Christian Science Publishing Society (all rights reserved) . . .

Woody Allen, p. 341; Sir Frederick Ashton, p. 352; Alfredo Ovando Candia, p. 201; John Conyers, Jr., p. 3; Jean Dalrymple, p. 379; John Gardner, pp. 7, 168; H. R. Haldeman, p. 80; Edgardo M. Jarrin, p. 203; Urho K. Kekkonen, p. 262; Darius Milhaud, pp. 334, 364; Charles Morgan, Jr., p. 161; David A. Morse, p. 105; Rogers C. B. Morton, p. 32; Barbara Walters, p. 371; Samuel W. Yorty, p. 99.

# Table of Contents

# *Preface*

Words can be powerful or subtle, humorous or maddening. They can be vigorous or feeble, lucid or obscure, inspiring or despairing, wise or foolish, hopeful or pessimistic . . . they can be fearful or confident, timid or articulate, persuasive or perverse, honest or deceitful. As tools at a speaker's command, words can be used to reason, argue, discuss, cajole, plead, debate, declaim, threaten, infuriate, or appease; they can harangue, flourish, recite, preach, discourse, stab to the quick, or gently sermonize.

When casually spoken by a stage or film star, words can go beyond the press-agentry and make-up facade and reveal the inner man or woman. When purposefully uttered in the considered phrasing of a head of state, words can determine the destiny of millions of people, resolve peace or war, or chart the course of a nation on whose direction the fate of the entire world may depend.

Until now, the *copia verborum* of well-known and renowned public figures—the doctors and diplomats, the governors and generals, the potentates and presidents, the entertainers and educators, the bishops and baseball players, the jurists and journalists, the authors and attorneys, the congressmen and chairmen-of-the-board—whether enunciated in speeches, lectures, interviews, radio and television addresses, news conferences, forums, symposiums, town meetings, committee hearings, random remarks to the press, or delivered on the floors of the United States Senate and House of Representatives or in the parliaments and palaces of the world—have been dutifully reported in the media, then filed away and, for the most part, forgotten.

The editors of WHAT THEY SAID believe that consigning such a wealth of thoughts, ideas, doctrines, opinions and philosophies to interment in the morgues and archives of the Fourth Estate is lamentable and unnecessary. Yet the media, in all their forms, are constantly engulfing us in a profusion of endless and increasingly voluminous news reports. One is easily disposed to disregard or forget the stimulating discussion of critical issues embodied in so many of the utterances of those who make the news and, in their respective fields, shape the events throughout the world. The conclusion is therefore a natural and compelling one: the educator, the public official, the business executive, the statesman, the philosopher—everyone who has a stake in the complex, often confusing trends of our times—should have material of this kind readily available.

These, then, are the circumstances under which WHAT THEY SAID was conceived. It is the culmination of a year of listening to the people in the public eye; a year of scrutinizing, monitoring, reviewing, judging, deciding—a year during which the editors resurrected from almost certain oblivion those quintessential elements of the year's *spoken* opinion which, in their judgment, demanded preservation in book form.

WHAT THEY SAID is a pioneer in its field. Its *raison d'etre* is the firm conviction that presenting, each year, the highlights of vital and interesting views from the lips of prominent people on virtually every aspect of contemporary civilization fulfills the need to give the *spoken* word the permanence and lasting value of the *written* word. For, if it is true that a picture is worth 10,000 words, it is equally true that a verbal conclusion, an apt quote or a candid comment by a person of fame or influence can have more significance and can provide more understanding than an entire page of summary in a standard work of reference.

The editors of WHAT THEY SAID did not, however, design their book for researchers and scholars alone. One of the failings of the conventional reference work is that it is blandly written and referred to primarily for facts and figures, lacking inherent "interest value." WHAT THEY SAID, on the other hand, was planned for sheer enjoyment and pleasure, for searching glimpses into the lives and thoughts of the world's celebrities, as well as for serious study, intellectual reflection and the philosophical contemplation of our multifaceted life and mores. Furthermore, those pressed for time, yet anxious to know what the newsmakers have been saying, will welcome the short excerpts which will make for quick, intermittent reading—and rereading. And, of course, the topical classifications, the speakers' index, the subject index, the place and date information—documented and authenticated and easily located—will supply a rich fund of hitherto not readily obtainable reference and statistical material.

Finally, the reader will find that the editors have eschewed trite comments and cliches, tedious and boring. The selected quotations, each standing on its own, are pertinent, significant, stimulating—above all, relevant to today's world, expressed in the speakers' own words. And they will, the editors feel, be even more relevant tomorrow. They will be re-examined and reflected upon in the future by men and women eager to learn from the past. The prophecies, the promises, the "golden dreams," the boastings and rantings, the bluster, the bravado, the pleadings and representations of those whose voices echo in these pages (and in those to come) should provide a rare and unique history lesson. The positions held by these luminaries, in their respective callings, are such that what they say today may profoundly affect the future as well as the present, and so will be of lasting importance and meaning.

ALAN F. PATER

JASON R. PATER

*Beverly Hills, California*

# Editorial Treatment

## ORGANIZATION OF MATERIAL

(A) The topics are arranged alphabetically within each of three major sections: Part 1—"The United States"; Part II—"The World"; Part III—"General." In this way, the reader can promptly locate all quotations pertaining to particular fields of interest.

(B) Under each topic, the speakers' names are in alphabetical order.

(C) Where there are two or more excerpts by one speaker under the same topic, *spoken on different occasions*, these appear chronologically; in those instances where they were spoken at the *identical time and place*, the documentation is given after the final statement.

## SPEAKER IDENTIFICATION

The rank, position, occupation, profession or title of the speaker is given as it was in effect at the time the statement was made. The same speaker may be shown with a different position or rank in continuing statements within the same subject category or elsewhere in the book. This arises from the fact that such position or rank may have changed during the course of the year. Also, in the case of a speaker who may hold more than one office or post simultaneously, the designation most relevant to the particular quotation is used.

## THE QUOTATIONS

All statements are quoted verbatim, as they were delivered originally or as reported in the media, except in those cases where the editors have eliminated extraneous or overly-long portions. In such cases, *ellipses* are always inserted, and in no case has the meaning of any quotation been altered.

## DOCUMENTATION

Specific details of place, date and circumstance have been supplied with each quotation, where such information was available. Where the actual date of utterance was unknown or obscure, *"pub."* (published) indicates the date of its appearance in the print media (newspapers, magazines) or the date of its broadcast over radio or television.

## THE INDEXES

(A) Arranged alphabetically in the *Speakers' Index,* with their respective page numbers, are the names of all speakers whose quotations appear in the book. This will be of use to those wishing to locate *all* of the quotations of a particular speaker, regardless of topic.

(B) For detailed study and research, the *Subject Index* provides an in-depth listing of all subjects and individuals mentioned or discussed in the quotations throughout the book, along with page numbers of their locations.

## THE QUOTE OF THE YEAR

Each year, from the tens of thousands of verbal statements made by the world's notable personalities, the editors of WHAT THEY SAID will select the one quotation they feel most affected the lives and emotions of the people of all nations, or that may most affect man's future. "The Quote of the Year" will, we hope, always reflect the *best* man has to offer—his achievements toward a *better* world.

●

WHAT THEY SAID is the result of a year-long and continuing survey of the world's major news media—print and broadcast. Since errors can occur, the editors have made determined efforts to authenticate not only the quotations themselves, but also the spelling of names and places and the accuracy of identifications and documentation. If, despite our vigilance, some errors have intruded (whether ours or those of the news source), we ask for understanding of the monumental task we face in compiling the vast numbers of details inherent in a work of this kind; and we offer assurance that every precaution will continue to be taken for succeeding editions.

●

There has been no conscious editorial bias in the selection of the quotations, the choice of speakers or in the manner of editing. Relevance of the statements and the status of the speakers have been the exclusive criteria for inclusion, without regard to the personal beliefs and views of the editors. Furthermore, every effort was made to include a multiplicity of opinions and ideas by a wide cross-section of speakers on each topic. Nevertheless, if there appears to be, in some instances, a preponderance of material favoring one point of view over another, it is simply the result of there having been a preponderance of those views expressed during the year.

# *The Quote of the Year*

"Houston, Tranquility Base here. The Eagle
has landed!"

*—United States Astronaut* NEIL A. ARMSTRONG;
*aboard Apollo 11, upon landing
on the moon, July 20, 1969.*

# PART ONE

# The United States

**Ralph D. Abernathy**
*Chairman, Southern Christian*
*Leadership Conference*

We don't have a black man to represent the black people of the nation on the (President's) cabinet, and to me that is a backward step.

*New York, Jan. 14.*

**Morris Abram**
*President, Brandeis University*

The black students . . . use it (the word "racism") as an epithet, but it has no precise meaning. Generally, it means the world . . . acting upon them in a way they don't like. And they will admit at the same time that the university they label racist actually has treated them well; it has made incredible efforts to give them not only equality but preference. Yet they still say it's racist. But when I use the word, I would mean something entirely different. I would mean a malignant purpose; discrimination by word or deed or thought against people on account of race.

*Interview, pub. Jan. 27.*

The Jew is never really safe in either a right-wing or left-wing society. Although he may prosper, temporarily, in either, he lives always at the lip of a precipice. The Jew is caught in the middle.

*Before Union of Hebrew Congregations,*
*Miami Beach, pub. Oct. 31.*

**Spiro T. Agnew**
*Vice President of the United States*

This Administration favors integration but not mandatory, artificially contrived social acceptance. I mean that on a subject as delicate as busing, for example, if you don't want artificially contrived integration brought about in a disruptive manner,

then those people who are in charge of the state and local governments have got to stop gerrymandering school districts.

I'm against busing of . . . children to other neighborhoods simply to achieve an integrated status of a larger geographic entity.

*At Southern Governors Conference,*
*Williamsburg, Va., Sept. 16.*

**Ivan Allen, Jr.**
*Mayor of Atlanta*

The white man in the South has never been willing to face the Negro issue in terms of full equal rights. He can't understand why there is not complete satisfaction (on the part of the Negro) at what's been done. Therefore, there is this violent reaction to riots and demonstrations.

*Interview, pub. March 24.*

**Richard D. Allen**
*Chairman, Economic Resources*
*Corporation*

It's time for the black community to ease the pressure . . . to stand back and see if White America is as sincere as I think it is when it says it wants to do something about the problems . . . Black America, to survive in the mainstream of business, must accept the help that White America is now ready to give. I'm trying to get over to the brother that he must be less hostile.

*Interview, Los Angeles, pub. April 7.*

**Lucius D. Amerson**
*Sheriff, Macon County, Alabama*

I think it is more significant for a Negro to be sheriff than to be a congressman. A sheriff works with trouble at the grassroots level, where he is dealing with the nitty-gritty. He's right on the battlefront,

(LUCIUS D. AMERSON)

and Negroes see that he is handling the job . . . Negroes in Congress or the Cabinet help, but you've got to prove on the local level that you can do the job to break down psychological barriers.

*Interview, Atlanta, pub. Feb. 17.*

**Arthur Ashe**
*Tennis Player*

It is tragically true that black people in the United States have been indoctrinated to the point where they do feel inferior. When black children of five and six were asked to draw themselves in schools it was found that they always, but always, drew themselves as white. They had been brainwashed for generations. That's why we have to keep shouting from the rooftops that black is beautiful.

*Wimbledon, England, pub. July 7.*

**James Baldwin**
*Author*

What we called the civil rights struggle can be said to have been buried with Martin Luther King. Because as of that event . . . and with the arrival of the new Administration, it began to be very clear to black people in the United States that what *Time* magazine calls "the troubled American" is not going to listen, does not want to know, does not want to hear the truth about the situation of the American black.

*Interview, Istanbul, pub. Dec. 17.*

**Roger Baldwin**
*Political Reformer*

Rights are not won on paper. They are won only by those who make their voices heard—by activists and militants. Silence never won rights. They are not handed down from above; they are forced by pressures from below.

*Brandeis University, pub. June 9.*

**Hugo L. Black**
*Associate Justice, Supreme Court of the United States*

"All deliberate speed" (used in connection with school desegregation) has turned out to be only a soft euphemism for "delay." I would do away with that phrase completely . . . There is no longer the slightest excuse, reason or justification for further postponement of the time when every public school system in the United States will be a unitary one, receiving and teaching students without discrimination on the basis of their race or color.

*Washington, pub. Sept. 9.*

**Charles F. Bound**
*Vice president, Morgan Guaranty Trust Company of New York*

Equal opportunity—often, any opportunity—for black people and other minority groups has been decidedly limited in the past. Thank God the top business and financial leaders, one after another, are coming out loud and clear and stating for all to hear that, for a solution to be reached, the private sector must get in the act to its eyebrows and apply its talents, skill, knowhow and time, as well as resources, to find solutions.

*Before the Book Clinic, American Institute of Graphic Arts, New York, April 10.*

**Thomas Bradley**
*Los Angeles City Councilman*

. . . I believe in cultural pluralism and the need of minority groups to develop self-pride and identity, but that does not mean we can or should exclude relationships with other groups. Separatism won't work. No group, and no nation, can go it alone.

*Interview, Los Angeles, Feb. 8.*

**Thomas P. Brady**
*Associate Justice, Supreme Court of Mississippi*

So long as we live, so long shall we fight for segregation. And we shall be victorious.

*Pub. Aug. 31.*

**Ralph J. Bunche**
*Under Secretary for Special Political Affairs of the United Nations*

. . . I would say that to break the back of racism in the United States, which means putting an end to the racial-conflict situation—a conflict situation, incidentally, which if it continues along its present course could mean ultimately a chronic condition of racial conflict, even guerilla warfare, in this society—it is imperative to have a massive mobilization of will and effort in the same way and on the same scale that there has to be a massive mobilization of will and effort to fight and win a war. In this, all levels of government—local, state and national—the institutional life of the country and all of its people have to be involved and committed. In other words, there is a war that has to be won against racism, which can only be won through this kind of determined and courageous effort.

*United Nations, N.Y., pub. Sept. 16.*

There is little black confidence in Nixon, in Attorney General Mitchell or in Vice President Agnew . . . The Administration must wage war against racism on the same scale as the Vietnam war, or some $30 billion a year.

*Television interview, Dec. 28.*

**Ray Charles**
*Singer, Musician*

We (the black people) have to realize that it is to the advantage of all of us— black and white—to be of the best quality, in our thoughts, in our minds, in our hearts, in our actions and in what we produce. If we're really going to be a power, we have to remain on a competitive level with everybody. If a man in a hospital needs blood, he wants to get it from whoever has the type he needs. Similarly, someone might say to me, "Well, here's a guy going to open a store up the street, and he's going to have all kinds of lousy goods, but he's colored; and there's another guy up the street who's going to have nicer goods, for the identical price." If somebody asked who I'd buy from, well, I'd say I'd buy from the white guy. It's as simple as that. Color has nothing to do with it.

*Interview, Los Angeles, pub. Aug. 24.*

**Shirley Chisholm**
*United States Representative, D-N.Y.*

. . . The Communists have tried for years to use us (the Negroes) to their advantage, but we have not succumbed.

The Communists have claimed that American society has failed the black man, yet he has resisted and still measures America in terms of its potential. We have been so patient and loyal . . . and what has it gotten us? We want our full share now.

*Interview, Washington, pub. April 28.*

**William Clay**
*United States Representative, D-Mo.*

We will see our greatest day when we no longer expect a man to be born in a segregated hospital, reared in a segregated school, married in a segregated church, die and be buried by a segregated undertaker in a segregated cemetery—and wake up in an integrated heaven.

*Washington, pub. Nov. 23.*

**Eldridge Cleaver**
*Information Minister,*
*Black Panther Party*

If everyone who is oppressed were involved, the Government would fall in a couple of days. It's only a question of arousing people to a point of wrath. Many complacent regimes thought they would be in power eternally—and awoke one morning to find themselves up against the wall. I expect that to happen in the United States in our lifetime.

*Interview, Moscow, pub. Oct. 24.*

**John Conyers, Jr.**
*United States Representative, D-Mich.*

There are, no doubt, vast numbers of Americans who feel that the Voting Rights Act solved all the problems of Negroes who wanted to register in the South. But I want them to know—just as the many persons who have worked and are still working on voter registration in the South know—that there is still intimidation, there are still illegal elections, and there are still persons who are illiterate due to traditional patterns of segregation, and that if the Voting Rights Act is not extended and adequately enforced, many black Americans will be doomed to second-class citizenship.

*Pub. Jan. 23.*

The story of the American black man is tremendously exciting today. Today,

(JOHN CONYERS, JR.)

fewer and fewer people are ashamed of being black than ever before. We're in the process of purging ourselves of all the brain-washing effects that we've been fed over the centuries.

*Interview, New York, pub. Sept. 8.*

**Bill Cosby**
*Actor, Comedian*

I'm not a believer in the black people taking up arms and going to war against the white people of this country. Number one, they would never win. Number two, it's a fast way of annihilating ourselves.

*Interview, pub. Oct. 4.*

**Walter Cronkite**
*News Commentator,*
*Columbia Broadcasting System*

The black American knows intuitively that his time of acceptance depends less on his own efforts than on the conscience of other ethnic groups who are affluent and secure and don't care to look behind them . . .

*Radio broadcast, March 17.*

**Marvin Davies**
*Florida Field Secretary,*
*National Association for the*
*Advancement of Colored People*

Our (Negro) women need to produce more babies, not less. Our problems are mainly economic ones, and until we comprise 30 to 35 per cent of the population, we won't be able to really affect the power structure in this country.

*Pub. July 19.*

**Charles C. Diggs, Jr.**
*United States Representative, D-Mich.*

The denial of entry into the construction trades in 1969 of black men on the sweat and the skills of whose forebears the South was built centuries ago reveals the shame anew that, while men sought freedom, they enslaved; while they concentrate their concern on the exploration and utilization of all environmental resources, they bury their greatest human wealth because it is black.

*Before the House, Washington, Sept. 19.*

**Milovan Djilas**
*Author; former Vice President*
*of Yugoslavia*

. . . as to the charge that the United States is the most racist country in the world, it's another ignorant statement. It's the first country in the world that is trying to resolve the race problem on an equitable basis. There isn't any other country making a comparable effort on so large and decisive an issue.

*Interview, Belgrade, pub. Sept. 15.*

**Anthony Downs**
*Consultant, President Lyndon B.*
*Johnson's Riot Commission Report*

There is a great error in the minds of whites that, since we have been talking about solving problems, we've actually been getting it done. And the sudden quiet in the ghetto only underscores that feeling. There's been a tremendous substitution of rhetoric for fact—like black capitalism —which is a myth. There is an attitude of hope because people have been discussing these questions, but no bread has appeared on the table—and that's dynamite.

*Pub. March 17.*

**Will Durant**
*Author, Historian*

I believe that we shall solve, or dissolve, within the limits of our nature, one after another of the problems that harass us today. Already our government, through a maze of difficulties, is seeking to end a disastrous war (in Vietnam). Our ethnic minorities will enter in ever greater number into our high schools, colleges and universities; they will get the courses that their pride may claim, and those that their adjustment to technology requires; they will rise in industry, in the professions, in the arts and sciences, and in public office; they will become established parts of the American scene as did our German-Americans, our Irish-Americans, our Polish-Americans, our Jewish-Americans—even a French-Canadian-American like me. And, like their predecessors, they will lower their birth rate as they raise their income; and the urban ghettoes will relieve their pressure and their poverty by following a hundred outlets into American life. It will take more time and patience than before, but it will come, or America will lose its meaning in the history and aspirations of humanity.

*Graduation exercises, The Buckley School, Los Angeles, pub. June 16.*

**Jack Edwards**
*United States Representative, R-Ala.*

I think this decision (U.S. Supreme Court ruling for immediate school desegregation) is going to destroy the school systems of many areas. It is already happening in many parts of the South. The white kids who can't afford private schools are dropping out. The public school system will become a colored school system. It is almost impossible now to get any bond or school tax through.

*Pub. Oct. 31.*

**James Charles Evers**
*Negro Candidate for Mayor of Fayette, Miss.*

If one of them (whites) is caught speeding, I'll look at that state law, which has a maximum fine of $105. I'll read it to him and he can either pay $105 or work it off at $3 a day (in jail). We got a lot of work needing done and they'll get enough bread and water not to starve. Unfair? That's just how those whites taught us niggers to behave.

*Interview, Fayette, pub. May 12.*

They have beat us, cussed us, killed our brothers and our friends, but we keep coming on. All we got to do now is lock arms, blacks and whites, and let the black and white extremists know that we gonna make America work. So if our country is not going to work, then where do we go? What do we do? We *got* to make it work.

*Campaign speech, Fayette, pub. May 15.*

I'm not going to do to you (white people) what's been done to us (black people). I'm not going to allow a white policeman to throw you in jail if you're passing through, the way we have been

thrown in jail, or to shoot you if he feels like it. But we are going to make very sure you don't do it to us.

*As Mayor-elect, before Women's Democratic Club, Washington, May 26.*

I can guarantee you there will be no more hate talk in this town and no more guns carried around to destroy just because of differences between men . . . and no more clownin' and cursin' people and showin' disrespect for people—and if you do, you gonna pay for it.

*At his inauguration as Mayor, Fayette, July 7.*

The time for picketing and boycotting and raising hell has about passed (for Negroes). We got to do our fighting on the inside, with the ballot and the dollar. We got to keep our head and not let some groups get us so frustrated we lose sight of our goals. We can't lose our cool and riot and destroy what we've gained. Oh yes, we've accomplished something. And we're going to be part of this country. Nobody can stop us, not even the Nixon Administration. We've had worse opposition than that.

*As Mayor, Fayette, pub. Oct. 26.*

**James Farmer**
*Assistant Secretary for Administration, Department of Health, Education and Welfare of the United States*

I think it is important that the minorities know Government holds opportunities for them. It is important we get in the government and not stand outside and criticize . . .

*News conference, Washington, Feb. 12.*

I'm not an ambassador from the Administration to the black community, but the other way—an ambassador from the black community to the Administration —maybe a little of each.

*Washington, Feb. 16.*

The crucial issues are voting, law enforcement and control of the courts. The enemies of civil rights will zero in on these issues. Racists control the courts of

(JAMES FARMER)

the South and law enforcement, and, if they reduce black voting, they have it made. These are the issues we have to battle.
*Pub. Oct. 13.*

**Mia Farrow**
*Actress*

Right now I'm in love with someone, and it wouldn't make the slightest difference if he was black. Someday it will have to happen that one and one will make two. Just two—no other thing about color or anything else. That's utopia.
*Interview, New York, pub. Feb. 7.*

**Leonard Fein**
*Associate Director, Harvard-M.I.T.*
*Joint Center for Urban Studies*

I may be dead wrong on this, but I sense that blacks say to themselves: "Look, the Jews have gotten it in the neck, too, yet they've been extraordinarily successful . . ." How do I explain their success and black non-success? They're certainly not going to conclude that Jews are better than black people. But there is a convenient alternative explanation. Just assert that the Jews were successful only by cheating, and that the people they cheated were black. So, in one fell swoop, you explain both Jewish success and black non-success . . .
*Interview, New York, pub. Jan. 31.*

Not every conflict of interest arises out of anti-Semitism, just as not every conflict arises out of racial bigotry. To permit the argument to be so trivialized, to permit blacks who seek change to allege that it is Jewish bigotry which impedes change, or to permit Jews who resist change to allege that it is anti-Semitic blacks who seek it, is to insure an intolerable confrontation.
*Before Synagogue Council of America,*
*Columbia University, pub. March 16.*

**W. H. Ferry**
*Vice president, Center for the*
*Study of Democratic Institutions*

As middle-class America looks across the tracks to blacktown, it does not understand what it sees there. But it is clear enough, I think, that middle-class America does not see human beings like themselves. It sees people different in hue, outlook, manners, dress, mal-educated, badly housed and poor. People who are angry and demanding and, therefore, dangerous. Most important, it sees people who consistently display the most reprehensible of traits—ingratitude. Blacks are never sufficiently grateful for the kindness and favors done them by whitetown.
*Pub. Oct. 19.*

**Robert H. Finch**
*Secretary of Health, Education and*
*Welfare of the United States*

The (school integration) law is on the books, and we're going to enforce it nationally, not just in the South. You've got de facto segregation in every part of this country, and we're going to go after it . . . I know I'm basically a political animal, but, in view of the explosive nature of the issue, I can't play any political game with the whole issue of compliance. Any indication that there's politics in this would be disastrous.
*Washington, Feb. 10.*

If you look at the Supreme Court decision, segregation in fact is not prohibited by law. What is prohibited by law is deliberate discrimination. If segregation in fact were prohibited by law, what are you going to do with all the solid Negro schools in solid Negro areas in Northern cities?
*Washington, pub. Feb. 27.*

**Arthur A. Fletcher**
*Assistant Secretary of Labor*
*of the United States*

Negroes are as emotionally, politically prejudiced against Republicans as Wallaceites are against Negroes. This is where the Negro community has got to develop some sophistication. They should be presenting their agenda to the White House and pressing for action just as they did under Kennedy and Johnson . . . Needs of the black people are not going to wait four or eight years for a change of Administration.
*Interview, pub. Oct. 5.*

. . . This Administration is not going to spread itself thin over the whole range of civil rights activities. It's going to concentrate on economic opportunities. We got so hung up on the idea that civil rights was a social problem that we failed to see the connecting links. We've got to talk economics.

*Interview, pub. Oct. 5.*

**Henry Ford II**
*Chairman, Ford Motor Company*

There has been a great deal of discussion about whether or not it is proper to discriminate in favor of minorities in order to make up for generations of discrimination against them. In my opinion, much of this argument is academic. There is still a long way to go in eliminating discrimination *against* before we have to start worrying too much about discrimination *for*.

*Before Yale Political Union,
Yale University, pub. April 30.*

The hidden revolution can be measured by the slow but constant falling away of such barriers to brotherhood as bias and suspicion and ignorance. It can be measured by new glimmers of understanding in the white consciousness of the hurdles that must be overcome by black men. It can be measured by a growing realization that ghetto life, poor schooling and continuing frustration can trap even people of high potential into an existence that is only a shadow of what they could achieve if they had a chance.

*At Brotherhood Testimonial Dinner,
National Conference of Christians
and Jews, Beverly Hills, Calif., June 5.*

**James Forman**
*Founder-Director, National Black
Economic Development Conference*

We must be committed to taking the wealth away from the rich and distributing it to the people . . . We have resisted the white man's intention of making us slaves, now we must resist any attempts to make us capitalist.

*At Black Economic Development
Conference, Detroit, April 29.*

**John W. Gardner**
*Chairman, Urban Coalition*

To bring full justice and equality to black people is the historic assignment of this generation. We cannot evade that assignment and preserve the kind of nation we care about. Everything we believe in—the phrases in our founding documents, the words on the monuments—says that every individual is of value. Our past record of dealing with black Americans says something very different. A reckoning was bound to come, and it has come in this generation. It will not be resolved by violence or hatred or bitterness or police suppression. It will be resolved only by patient, determined efforts on the part of the great, politically moderate majority of whites and blacks.

*The Godkin Lectures, Harvard
University, pub. Sept. 23.*

The effort to correct our past errors with black Americans is going to take time and we must stay with it. We suffer very badly as a nation from the habit of seizing on a cause or an enthusiasm at one moment and then, before giving it a really thorough effort, rejecting it because we're sick of it or we've made some mistakes or we're disillusioned or discouraged. It's true of Head Start, it's true of black entrepreneurship, it's true of the Job Corps, it's true of just about every experiment you can think of.

*Interview, pub. Sept. 30.*

**Harry Golden**
*Author*

White racism is still the curse of America. We've lost a war to the Negro, trying to keep him invisible. Well, he's no longer invisible. He's burning our cities, and we must begin to pay the indemnities due him. Congress must appropriate huge sums of money for housing, jobs and education. Believe me, we'll get it back. When the 22 million Negroes in this country take their rightful place in our society, they'll contribute great intellectual, cultural and economic wealth.

*Interview, Beverly Hills, Calif.,
pub. Aug. 16.*

**Henry B. Gonzalez**
*United States Representative, D-Tex.*

I do not believe that violence is necessary to obtain justice, and I do not believe that hatred is necessary either. I do not believe there is any reason why despair should be so great that reverse racism can be justified. Yet reverse racism and reverse racists exist and their voices are loud.

*Pub. June 2.*

**David Gottlieb**
*Senior Research Professor,*
*College of Human Development,*
*Pennsylvania State University*

He (the Negro) wants a change of status, and he wants it now. He wants out of the slums. He wants out of unemployment. He wants out of a physical setting which restricts mobility and maximizes feelings of personal defeat. Given a choice and a similarity of opportunities, many would gladly change places with the disenchanted of Harvard, Vassar and Yale.

*Pub. March 11.*

**Edith Green**
*United States Representative, D-Ore.*

I seriously question busing for social reform—taking a youngster from a disadvantaged home in a ghetto area . . . transporting him to another school where he spends five or six hours of the day and then is picked up and taken back to the same disadvantaged home, the same tenement area. I have serious questions of how much we're really helping that child.

*Interview, pub. Oct. 13.*

**Dick Gregory**
*Comedian and Civil Rights Leader*

To my white brothers and sisters: the black folks in America don't dislike you; they don't hate you. We hate your stinking white, corrupt, racist system.

*Washington, March 4.*

**Nathan Hare**
*Chairman, Black Studies Department,*
*San Francisco State College*

To solve the problems of American society, (Afro-Americans) must first black-wash—revamp—the existing educational system and revolutionize America's youth —black, yellow, brown and white . . . The Bible says there is a time for everything. I think this is a time for hate.

*Pittsburgh, Jan. 15.*

**Louis R. Harlan**
*Professor of History,*
*University of Maryland*

One hundred pages of cotton candy about Jackie Robinson does not teach the realities ghetto students need to cope with the world. We need to present a black past that has villains as well as heroes.

*Washington, pub. Feb. 9.*

**S. I. Hayakawa**
*President, San Francisco State College*

To use a phrase I detest, but which in this instance is all too descriptive, white revolutionaries, by their largess, are making "house niggers" of their black allies. And when the crackdown on revolutionary activities comes, it will be the blacks who will go to prison, not the whites who fed them, taught them their Marxism and egged them on.

*Before Senate subcommittee on campus disorders, Washington, May 13.*

**Herbert Hill**
*Director of Labor, National*
*Association for the Advancement*
*of Colored People*

Either black men work, or nobody works.

*News conference, Pittsburgh, Aug. 28.*

**Ben Holman**
*Director, Community Relations Service,*
*United States Department of Justice*

I've personally found that I've drifted away from the integration goal, and I think I'm mirroring the attitude of a lot of blacks in this country. How can you really have integration when 85% of the country doesn't want it?

*Interview, Washington, pub. Nov. 6.*

. . . I think what the goal should be in this country is not some sort of vague, illusory melting pot in which we're all mixed like salt and pepper, but a multi-racial society in which we have black neighborhoods and black communities, and still live as one nation . . . If I had my way, I would simply drop the word integration.

*Television interview, New York, Nov. 16.*

**Hubert H. Humphrey**
*Former Vice President*
*of the United States*

It would be a tragedy if the American city were simply abandoned to the blacks as more and more whites move to the suburbs. It would be an even greater tragedy if, by neglect of the city, we practiced the cruelest form of discrimination—that of apartheid, the deliberate separation of the races.

*Macalester College, St. Paul, Minn.,*
*Feb. 23.*

**Roy Innis**
*Director, Congress of Racial Equality*

We are against the policy of integration and assimilation being offered by Mr. (Roy) Wilkins. We say the civil rights movement is dead.

*News conference, New York, Jan. 21.*

If they (the Negro students) are going to live in a white world, they had better learn what the white boys are learning.

*Pub. Jan. 24.*

President Nixon uses this obnoxious term, "black capitalism." This term turns off a lot of our bright young men. When they hear "black capitalism" they think of black exploitation . . . Integration? That is off our list of priorities altogether. Integration is just a dream that may come true down the road someplace. I have no particular desire for it.

*Interview, pub. Feb. 24.*

**J. H. Jackson**
*President, National Baptist Convention*

We cannot blame President Nixon for a slowdown in integration until we have blamed separatist blacks seeking black segregation . . . Many of the Negroes today are teaching the same gospel as the Ku Klux Klan. And that has to stop.

*News conference, New York, July 1.*

**Jesse Jackson**
*Director, Operation Breadbasket*

America is pluralistic. There is talk about it being a melting pot. But it really is more like vegetable soup. There are separate pieces of corn, meat and so on, each with its own identity. The blacks have been pushed down to the bottom of the pot. We are going to come up and be recognized or turn the pot over.

*News conference, Chicago, pub. June 2.*

**William Loren Katz**
*Author, Editor, Consultant on Education*

Certainly black people should know about the contributions that black individuals and black groups have made in the building of America. This is terribly important for their pride, their self-image, their self-esteem. But it's perhaps even more important for white people to know. For if you believe that a man has no history worth mentioning, it's easy to assume that he has no humanity worth defending. Let's face it: we have a major racial problem in this country—and the only way we'll finally eradicate it is through education. Nothing else will destroy the stereotypes and myths that have been built up through the years.

*Interview, pub. July.*

**Theodore J. Kolish**
*Chairman, Metropolitan Executive*
*Committee, American Jewish Congress*

The surest way of arousing hostility between racial and religious groups is to forecast that it will occur.

*New York, March 25.*

**William M. Kunstler**
*Civil Rights Lawyer*

I believe the psychological war going on between the races in this country is based on a simple feeling in the gut of every white man that he is superior to all black people. White people can deny this and say, "Not me, I have many friends who are black, I go to NAACP dinners." But it's a hard fact of life—and any white person, including myself, who says this feeling is not so is deluding himself.

I don't think that we can point our finger at Nazi Germany and say that we

(WILLIAM M. KUNSTLER)

are any better than it in the way we have treated racial minorities in this country. We made black men slaves and we breed animals. Germany had its highly dramatic and awful decadence between 1935 and 1945, but our dehumanization of minorities has gone on for centuries.

*Interview, pub. July 25.*

**Ruby Martin**
*Former Director, Office for Civil Rights, Department of Health, Education and Welfare of the United States*

If the Administration policy is to give new authority to states and local governments, I think we black people are in for a great deal of difficulty. I wish the Nixon Administration had spent more time studying what happens to black people when authority is turned over to states and localities.

*Pub. Sept. 21.*

**Hans Massaquoi**
*Managing Editor, "Ebony" Magazine*

At one time it didn't matter to me whether I was called Negro or black. But now it does matter and I prefer to be called black. As I read copy, I am aware that when certain writers say "Negro" they are describing someone they *see* as a Negro—an Uncle Tom.

*Pub. June 30.*

**Tom Mboya**
*Minister for Economic Planning and Development, Republic of Kenya*

I was once asked whether I support the movements of Afro-Americans from the United States to Africa. My answer was, no. I do not believe that there should be a movement. I do not believe that we should run away from the struggle.

*New York, pub. March 23.*

**George Meany**
*President, American Federation of Labor-Congress of Industrial Organizations*

As far as the black, non-white minority is concerned, there is no question that they still have a long way to go—but there is no question that they have come a long way. They are going up—but the black militants don't want to hear about that. They don't want to know what happened yesterday or the day before—they want some instant solutions for all these problems. And, of course, they are not going to get it.

*Interview, Washington, Aug. 28.*

**John N. Mitchell**
*Attorney General of the United States*

I want to encourage our Negro citizens to take out their alienations at the ballot box, and not elsewhere. I want them to know that their ballot is important and will be significant in determining the policies of the officials who govern.

*Testimony before House Judiciary Subcommittee, Washington, July 1.*

My personal view is that all adult citizens, who are of sound mind and who have not been convicted of a felony, should be free to, and be encouraged to, participate in the electoral process. The widespread and increasing reliance on television and radio brings candidates and issues into the homes of almost all Americans. Under certain conditions, an understanding of the English language, and no more, is our national requirement for American citizenship. Perhaps more importantly, the rights of citizenship, in this day and age, should be freely offered to those for whom the danger of alienation from society is most severe—because they have been discriminated against in the past, because they are poor and because they are undereducated. As responsible citizenship does not necessarily imply literacy, so responsible voting does not necessarily imply an education. Thus, it would appear that the literacy test is, at best, an artificial and unnecessary restriction on the right to vote.

*Pub. Aug. 18.*

**Archie Moore**
*Former World Lightheavyweight Boxing Champion*

I am a Negro and proud to be one. I am also an American and proud of that. Granted, the Negro still has a long way to go to gain a fair shake with the white man in this country. But believe this: If we resort to lawlessness, the only thing we can hope for is bloodshed and the end of our dreams.

*San Diego, pub. Feb. 24.*

**John Morsell**
*Assistant Executive Director,*
*National Association for the*
*Advancement of Colored People*

Adam Clayton Powell is the vicar for the man who always (wants) to spit in Mr. Charlie's face. They love him for that, but they don't expect him to do anything solid.

*Pub. April 4.*

**Stanley Mosk**
*Associate Justice, Supreme*
*Court of California*

The rights of our society do not extend to adults only but also to . . . students. It would be ironic to allow rights to criminals but deny them to students because of age. If we prove we desire the inclusion of young people in our society, they will relate and respond. Back of that facade of rudeness, they are fundamentally thinking of the right things—defending the environment, preserving individuality and performing services.

*Fairfield, Calif., Aug. 27.*

**Slawomir Mrozek**
*Polish Playwright in Exile*

What draws me to the United States is the feeling that it (the country) is at a sort of a Shakespearean crossroads. People are ready to kill a Negro—or be killed for a Negro. Whereas in Europe, everyone shakes hands with a Negro, but racism is concealed and the anti-racists just make loud noises.

*Pub. Jan. 26.*

**Gunnar Myrdal**
*Swedish Economist and Sociologist*

I don't think America can stand a de facto apartheid for too much longer. I don't think that America can live with this type of society. It is against the vision of America.

*Before House Subcommittee on*
*Urban Growth, Washington, Oct. 30.*

**Richard M. Nixon**
*President of the United States*

My task force on education pointed up that I was not considered . . . as a friend by many of our black citizens in America. I can only say that, by my action as President, I hope to rectify that.

*News conference, Washington, Feb. 6.*

. . . There are two extreme groups. There are those who want instant integration and those who want segregation forever. I believe that we need to have a middle course between those two extremes. That's the course on which we're embarked. I think it is correct . . . We are for it (desegregated education), but we are going to avoid extremes.

*News conference, Washington,*
*pub. Oct. 3.*

The Supreme Court has spoken decisively on the timing of school desegregation. There are, of course, practical and human problems involved. With all of us working together in full respect for the law, I am confident we can overcome these problems. I intend to use the leadership resources of the executive branch of government to assist in every possible way in doing so.

*Washington, Oct. 30.*

**George Pierre**
*Chief of the Colville Confederated*
*Tribes of Washington State*

Through the years, since Congress created the office of Commissioner in 1832, the operation of the Bureau of Indian Affairs has been by trial and error and has repeatedly reflected ignorance, arrogance and often total indifference for Indians . . . At first, the policy was that "the only good Indian is a dead Indian."

*Pub. Jan. 3.*

**Stephen Pollak**
*Former Assistant Attorney General,*
*Civil Rights Division, Department of*
*Justice of the United States*

Many of these local school boards (in the South) will desegregate only if they are convinced the government means

(STEPHEN POLLAK)

business. The more they see evidence of waffling, the more they're going to drag their feet.

*Pub. Sept. 15.*

**Wesley A. Pomeroy**
*Associate Administrator, Law
Enforcement Assistance Administration,
Department of Justice
of the United States*

If the black people really want to control the police department, why don't they join them? Every police department is making affirmative efforts to attract Negroes. How do they propose we do it . . . take white people and dye them black?

*Interview, Jan. 5.*

**Adam Clayton Powell**
*United States Representative, D-N.Y.*

Don't go out with any shadow of second-class citizenship. That's the shadow your mothers and fathers walked under. Go out saying: "I am a man. I am a woman, made in the image of God, and I'm going to walk like God intended me to walk . . ." Think big. The world does not belong to (President) Nixon and Chief (Justice Warren) Hamburger—I mean, Chief Burger. The world doesn't belong to the Pentagon.

*Address to graduating class,
Benjamin Franklin High School,
New York, June 24.*

(The Vietnam war is) a white man's war against colored people. If we're gonna fight, the fight's gonna be here, and Charlie is scared to death. Charlie knows that he has trained in Vietnam a sophisticated group of black men who know all the angles of guerilla warfare . . . And these cats are coming back home . . . some of 'em are already here.

*Norfolk State College, Norfolk, Va.,
Oct. 13.*

**A. Philip Randolph**
*Civil Rights Leader; member,
Executive Council, AFL-CIO*

. . . We must reject confrontationism and together reaffirm the necessity for democratic means of political protest. We must reject violence, and together reaffirm the power and the wisdom of non-violence. And we must reject racial separatism, and together—with the conviction that one day our nation can cease to be divided within itself—reaffirm our abiding faith in integration. We cannot reject these principles without also denying ourselves the possibility of freedom.

*New York, May 6.*

**Henry H. Rapaport**
*National President,
United Synagogues of America*

The trouble starts when a black militant, trained or not, wants a position someone else has, but he is not willing to claw his way up to the higher economic status he seeks.

*Los Angeles, March 6.*

**John R. Rarick**
*United States Representative, D-La.*

If the Constitution of the United States forbids a state to assign pupils to a school solely because of their race, it makes no difference whether the object of such assignment is segregation or forced integration under the newly invented "Doctrine of Racial Proportion." If government has no power to forcefully segregate, it has no power to forcefully integrate.

*Before the House,
Washington, Oct. 29.*

**Warren Robbins**
*Director, Frederick Douglass
Institute of Negro Arts and History,
and the Museum of African Art,
Washington*

The widespread myth that the Negro American has had no past other than slavery and savagery has constituted one of the most tragic—and unnecessary—stumbling blocks in his thinking about himself, while, at the same time, it has been a prime source of racial prejudice.

*Pub. Feb. 24.*

**Thomas F. Roeser**
*Assistant to the Secretary of Commerce
of the United States*

I am discouraged when I see—and I occasionally do—black people writing off the Nixon Administration. I think prob-

ably it's more a case of black people writing off the Nixon Administration than it is the Nixon Administration writing off black people.
*Before Cosmopolitan Chamber of Commerce, Chicago, Sept. 30,*

**George W. Romney**
*Secretary of Housing and Urban Development of the United States*

It is contrary to everything this country stands for to have zoning laws that exclude poor people from areas of the country. We cannot continue this mistaken idea . . . that there is an advantage in living in enclaves where we only associate with people with the same economic, social and racial backgrounds. That's got to go.
*At United States Conference of Mayors, Pittsburgh, June 16.*

**Diana Ross**
*Singer*

If I'm any kind of symbol to black kids —and I *don't* mean sex symbol—it's that when they see me dancin' the Popcorn with my fella, my little ponytail flyin', they say, "Hey, that Diana, she's groovy. She's regular, she's one of us. If she can make it, so can we."
*Interview, pub. Sept. 23.*

**Alice Rossi**
*Lecturer in Sociology, Johns Hopkins University*

Bagels and lox for breakfast, soul food for lunch and lasagna for dinner are great —but no Jews, blacks or Italians on the professional or neighborhood turf!
*At meeting of American Sociological Association, San Francisco, pub. Sept. 3.*

**Bayard Rustin**
*Civil Rights Leader; executive director, A. Philip Randolph Institute*

Negro leaders have a moral obligation to fight against anti-Semitism. Jews have been in the forefront of the civil (rights) fight and probably made more of a contribution than any single group. We cannot be timid and we cannot be silent. Negro children, who themselves have been brutalized by racism, ought not to be further brutalized by teaching them anti-Semitism and religious prejudice.
*Interview, pub. Jan. 26.*

The Ku Klux Klan said for years that only white teachers could teach white children. Some black students must be having nervous breakdowns when they now echo the KKK and say only blacks can teach blacks. These people must know nothing can be learned effectively in a segregated school system, black or white.

There is nothing more beautiful about black than about white. I know a black family in the ghetto in New York which pays $100 a month for one rat-infested room, and they pay it to a black landlord. That is what a black man is doing to a black man and that ain't beautiful.
*Los Angeles, March 29.*

. . . The fundamental mistake of the black nationalist movement is that it does not comprehend that class ultimately is a more driving force than color and that any effort to build a society for American Negroes that is based on color alone is doomed to failure.
*Pub. May 16.*

**Betty Shabazz**
*Widow of Malcolm X, Black Muslim Leader*

Whites don't understand blacks. They never have. Frederick Douglass used to say that he was amazed that the white master could be so dumb as to think his slaves were singing because they were happy. The slaves were singing as a kind of tranquilizer. Life was so bitter and cruel that, if they did not sing, they might not have survived . . . But blacks will survive, and we will improve our status. If we're not allowed to improve, then nobody is going to improve.
*Interview, Mount Vernon, N.Y., pub. March 4.*

**Robert M. Shelton**
*Imperial Wizard of the Ku Klux Klan*

A silent majority has realized that it is no longer a question of bad government. It's a question of impossible government, and we are chained to the infested black

(ROBERT M. SHELTON)

carcass that's dragging us down to the low morals and disruption that's in this nation today. I'm going back into the field again as head of the Klan organization and we're going to start one of the largest crusades this country has ever seen.

*Texarkana, Tex., Nov. 17.*

### Stephen G. Spottswood
*Chairman, Board of Directors,*
*National Association for the*
*Advancement of Colored People*

Our struggle for full and equal citizenship is made harder and the course more difficult by the emerging policies of the Nixon Administration. Stripped of its rhetoric, the clear message from Washington is, "If you are black, stay black."

*Pub. July 6.*

### Johannes F. Spreen
*Police Commissioner of Detroit*

I have some 200 job openings, and if I get 200 blacks I'll put them in right now. But we want to make sure everyone is qualified, and if we get 200 whites, we'll put them in, too. The color is blue—police blue—but we're encouraging and trying to get the blacks in. The trouble is a lot of them aren't interested because they're afraid of being called "Uncle Toms," or "pigs," or joining a so-called racist, oppressive police force . . . And jobs are easier in industry.

*Detroit, Aug. 29.*

### John Stennis
*United States Senator, D-Miss.*

If it is true, as advocates of integration claim, that segregation deprives the Negro students of an equal education, millions of Negro students in the *North* are being deprived of their rights.

*Before the Senate, Dec. 8.*

### George C. Wallace
*Former Governor of Alabama;*
*1968 Presidential candidate*

I expected such a decision (U.S. Supreme Court ruling for immediate school desegregation). This court is no better than the Warren Court, and the time is fast approaching when the people of this country are going to—within the law —take back the control of the education of their children.

*Jackson, Miss., Oct. 30.*

### Earl Warren
*Former Chief Justice*
*of the United States*

We are now at the decision-making point where we must decide whether we are to honor the concept of a plural society which gains strength through diversity, or whether we are to have bitter fragmentation that will result in perpetual tension and strife. If we really believe in the former, we will pocket our prejudices and accord to every American that which is his due—absolute equality under the law—and his right to life, liberty and the pursuit of happiness. Nothing short of that will solve our problems. An if we do not solve them speedily, future for our children and their child will not be bright.

*New York, O ation,*
*ne 6.*

### Dionne Warwick
*Singer*

I don't believe in black militancy totally unnecessary. It demeans e ple thing a black person is capable of ac ve ing. The black militant is wrong to e black people don't have any opportu today. More black people are gettin ahead than ever before . . .

*Interview, pub. Sept. 14.*

### Roy Wilkins
*Executive Director, National*
*Association for the Advancement*
*of Colored People*

We must be for change, yes. Reform, yes. Sharp alteration in methods, yes. Acceleration, yes. But separatism, no.

*New York, Jan. 13.*

We have suffered too many heartaches and shed too many tears and too much blood in fighting the evil of racial segregation to return, in 1969, to the lonely and dispiriting confines of its demeaning prison.

*Interview, pub. Jan. 16.*

It's almost enough to make you vomit. This is not a matter of too little too late; rather, this is nothing at all.

*Address at convention of NAACP, referring to the Nixon Administration postponement of the September deadline for integration in some school districts. Jackson, Miss. July 3.*

I think the President (Nixon) is not really regarding the presidency as an opportunity to flaunt his partisanship, but it argues that, whereas he might be a liberal in visiting Romania, he is peculiarly insensitive to the problem knocking right here on his doorstep.

I think Mr. Mitchell (U.S. Attorney General John N. Mitchell) is undoubtedly a good lawyer, a fine New York corporation lawyer; but what he knows about ~ial issues and about handling 200 mil- ~eople in the country is nothing.

*Television interview, New York, Aug. 20.*

. The fight for the unsegregated . will go on. When it's won, the youths are marching now will realize that 's going to be beer, and double- ~rs with the Yankees, and ice cream, ~ mortgages and taxes, and all the ~s that whites have in their world— . tedium, too. It's not going to be ~aven.

*Interview, pub. Sept. 28.*

### Franklin H. Williams
*Director, The Urban Center, Columbia University*

It is bad enough to be poor today— but to be poor *and* Black is to be in double jeopardy. If we are to move forward toward justice, it must be justice for all of us, rich or poor, White or Black. America is going to have to put it on the line, and root out the racism permeating our society. Blacks will not wait much longer. The burden of blame for the past—and the burden of proof for the future— belong to White America.

*At Conference on Crime and the Press, Syracuse University, Jan. 12.*

### Nancy Wilson
*Singer*

The problem in the ghetto is defeat. Eight-year-old kids already figure, "Why should I bother?" It's tragic. Somebody has to tell them about the scholarships that are available, that they can stand up and speak out if they don't like things. I'm not talking about burning up something; a militant with no program is just another cat yelling on the corner. I'm talking about seeking knowledge and not accepting something just because somebody told you so.

*Pub. May 11.*

### Andrew J. Young, Jr.
*Executive vice president, The Southern Christian Leadership Conference*

There can be no general dramatizing of the problem (civil rights) in hopes that the nation will respond. They won't. They may promise, they may play games, but there will be no concessions granted; they must be taken.

*At SCLC Conference, Charleston, S.C., Aug. 17.*

### Whitney M. Young, Jr.
*Executive Director, National Urban League*

The trouble is that blacks are so visible. You hire one secretary and it looks like a lot of integration.

*Pub. June 9.*

So long as national power and the nation will continue to be directed at ends other than the assurance of full equality, the ghettos will become festering, running sores of bitterness and resentment. The gap between the races will become greater. Oppression will increase. And the gathering storm of outrage and tensions will burst upon the land.

*New York, Nov. 19.*

# Commerce, Industry and Finance

**Ralph Ablon**
*President, Ogden Corporation*

The nation's most important industries were created by merger and acquisition. Without them, we would probably still have to rely on the stagecoach lines, which would undoubtedly have been nationalized, and be talking about training programs for the horses to solve the problems in that system.
*New York, Feb. 5.*

**Charles F. Adams**
*President, MacManus, John & Adams, Inc.*

Youth is an easy sale and a safe bet . . . Perhaps advertising people have come to the conclusion that middle age is obscene.
*Interview, Pub. Aug. 8.*

**William M. Allen**
*President, The Boeing Company*

We are living under the effects of what I sincerely believe is a widely held misconception: that the defense industry is a "kept" industry, eating at the public trough; that there is something basically un-American about profits on Government business; that defense contractors should be regarded with suspicion.
*Pub. April 21.*

**Lawrence A. Appley**
*President, American Management Association*

I think in the 1980's there are going to be fewer people in offices. Offices are a tremendous waste of time for chief executives and they create 60 per cent of all the work that takes place in them. I can be away from my office for three weeks, and things get done. But if I come in for one day, everything stops. Everyone wants to ask me what to do. In most cases, the boss is busy because he is in. He should be out where the rubber hits the road, working with people and watching them.
*Interview, pub. June.*

**C. Canby Balderston**
*Former vice chairman,*
*Federal Reserve System*
*of the United States*

My concern has been accentuated recently by the surprising reports of improvement in profitability that stem from accounting gymnastics. The real peril is that if procedural gimmicks hide the truth, they may lead to eventual disillusion among investors. The country's savin are too precious for them to be frit away.
*Before District of Col*
*Bankers Assoc*
*White Sulphur Springs, Va., J*

**William Bernbach**
*President, Doyle-Dane-Bernbach*

We've had some weird-looking peop working for us. But if they do the job, hire them. You can overcome all prejudi in this world if you make money for some one. They'll forgive your religion and everything. That's really the answer.
*Pub. Dec. 18.*

**William Blackie**
*Chairman, Caterpillar Tractor Company*

There is a current danger that money— especially in international affairs—is being regarded more as an end than a means. The whole monetary system is an instrument for the achievement of purposes which have to do with the welfare of people. The end purpose of the monetary system is not and should not be made money itself or the preservation of historical parities which can become outmoded by changing times. Rather, it should be the preservation of real values, and these involve people and their needs or desires for employment, for goods and services which contribute to their welfare, and for a sense of security, which at times seems more threatened than strengthened by efforts to overcome international monetary instability.

*At World Trade Symposium,*
*Springfield, Ill., pub. April 9.*

**Charles G. Bluhdorn**
*Chairman, Gulf & Western Industries*

If we are chiselers, we are chiselers for our stockholders. I want a dollar for a dollar—or, better yet, $1.10.

*Pub. March 7.*

**Edward L. Bond**
*Chairman, American Association of Advertising Agencies*

If the truth were to be told, advertising is every boyhood dream come true—as colorful as the circus, as exciting as the rodeo, as full of promise as the road shows come to town.

*Before American Association of Advertising Agencies,*
*White Sulphur Springs, Va., April 24.*

**Alfred Brittain, III**
*President, Bankers Trust Company of New York*

In raising the prime rate (to 8½%), we acted reluctantly but deliberately, because rapidly rising interest rates in the open market were causing business corporations to shift more of their borrowings to the banks. The increase in our prime rate was therefore unavoidable, if we were to protect the ability of our bank to meet its commitments to its borrowers and to preserve the availability of funds for lending to small business, real estate and the consumer.

*Before House Banking Committee,*
*Washington, June 20.*

**W. Herman Browne**
*Chairman, Moore Business Forms*

. . . I feel generally that we should have a minimum of government interference in business, but there does seem to be a need in some areas for satisfactory spelling out of what the rules of the game should be, and perhaps we just have to live with more government regulations.

*Interview, Toronto, pub. November.*

**Hamer H. Budge**
*Chairman, Securities & Exchange Commission of the United States*

Those who are engineering the present wave of (corporation) take-overs appear to find short-term profits so tempting that they ignore life-long risks.

*Before House Commerce Committee,*
*Washington, Feb. 25.*

**Miles Colean**
*Economist*

An exposure to equities is like the taste of blood to a young lion.

*Washington, pub. Aug. 29.*

**Fairfax M. Cone**
*Former Chairman,*
*Foote, Cone & Belding*

I see advertising as trying to tell somebody something, and, if I'm trying to tell someone something, I don't get out a brass band, and I don't put on a clown suit.

*Interview, New York, pub. Nov. 2.*

**Joseph F. Cullman, III**
*Chairman, Philip Morris, Inc.*

The right to advertise—an essential commercial right—is destroyed if a manufacturer is required in every advertisement to disparage his product. No businessman will spend his company's money for a self-defeating purpose.

*Pub. June 2.*

**Donald E. Farrar**
*Associate Professor of Finance,*
*Columbia University*

There is the possibility that the institutions' role in the market could be dangerous. All the trends do seem to point toward further growth of the types of behavior that have concerned people—lots of trading, the tendency to adopt riskier issues. This isn't necessarily bad, but at the same time it does have an impact on the market.

*New York, pub. Jan. 19.*

**Harvey S. Firestone, Jr.**
*Former Chairman,*
*Firestone Tire & Rubber Company*

Fundamentally, I believe that "free trade" is the soundest economic policy for this country. The United States historically has been a great exporting country, and this has contributed substantially to our industrial growth and strength. It is basically unsound to think that any country can set up tariff barriers against other countries' products, and at the same time expect to trade freely with its own products in the markets of these same countries.
*Interview, pub. August.*

**Milton Friedman**
*Professor of Economics,*
*University of Chicago*

The fact is that the world is now on a dollar standard. Those are words nobody likes to speak . . . European central bankers can say they are on a gold and not a dollar standard, and so they are—as long as they don't ask for gold, they are on gold.
*Geneva, pub. May 21.*

**John Kenneth Galbraith**
*Professor of Economics,*
*Harvard University*

We must, as grownup people, abandon now the myth that the big defense contractors are something separate from the public bureaucracy. They must be recognized for what they are—a part of the public establishment. (Nationalization) would insure that such firms are held to strict standards of public responsibility.
*Pub. June 9.*

I'm sure a (stock market) crash like 1929 will happen again. The only thing is that one doesn't know when. All it takes for another collapse is for the memories of the last insanity to dull.
*Pub. Oct. 28.*

**H. S. Geneen**
*Chairman, International Telephone*
*& Telegraph Company*

It is more than a coincidence that the two losing nations of the last world war,

Germany and Japan, today lead in economic enterprise and in growth of world trade. It is more than a coincidence that the governments of both these countries work very closely in support of their businessmen—a lesson they learned during the period of adversity, following the war, in which they rose to their present competitive strengths. We can win that competitive struggle tomorrow as we did yesterday, but we must not be hampered with artificial strictures against diversification or size. We must not be hampered by yesterday's myths in concentrating on today's needs.
*Before American Bar Association,*
*New York, Oct. 23.*

**Andrew E. Gibson**
*Maritime Administrator*
*of the United States*

Unlike the last Administration, we believe in sea power. This Administration recognizes the largest trading nation in the world needs a commercial fleet to carry out commercial policy.
*Interview, pub. Oct. 12.*

**Harold V. Gleason**
*President, Franklin National Bank*
*of New York*

. . . one man, no matter how brilliant, can't be a successful corporation. A successful corporation is a group effort. The man at the top can help shape and define the company's goals; he can create an environment that gets people working together creatively; and he can act as umpire. He might know it all, but he can't run it all alone.
*Pub. Sept. 14.*

**Carl E. Hathaway**
*Vice president, Morgan Guarantee*
*Trust Company of New York*

A cult of equity has arisen: Buy because there's not enough to go around—the most dangerous and capricious reason to buy stock.
*New York, pub. Jan. 24.*

**Daniel J. Haughton**
*Chairman, Lockheed*
*Aircraft Corporation*

Protectionism—whether by high tariff

barriers or by the host of nontariff barriers we now see springing up—is no answer at all. It pushes us toward more inflation, it reduces the benefits of competition, it increases cost to the consumer, and it dims our image abroad and strains our international relations at the very time that we are making an effort to improve them. With our Government continuing to work diligently to establish better international relations on the diplomatic level, it makes little sense for us to tear them down in terms of trade.

*Before Aerospace Industries Association, Washington, pub. April 13.*

**Alfred Hayes**
*President, Federal Reserve Bank of New York*

We in the Federal Reserve like to emphasize that the System is not independent *of* the Government, but independent *within* the Government.

*Pub. March 2.*

**Sol Hurok**
*Impresario*

Everybody's merging. It's the style. If you can't grow bigger, you have to get smaller. If you can't expand, suspend.

*Pub. March 10.*

**Yoshizane Iwasa**
*Head of Fuji Bank, Ltd., Tokyo*

Protectionism is a contagious disease. A case of "creeping protectionism" in United States-Japan relations would quickly spread—infecting the world with the virus of economic anarchy and warfare that proved so deadly in the nineteen-thirties. To retreat once again in the nineteen-seventies could be even more disastrous because it would mean abandonment of two-thirds of mankind in the less-developed countries to economic stagnation and anarchy.

*At conference of Far East-American Council, New York, Oct. 6.*

**Ray Jallow**
*Vice president and chief economist, United California Bank*

It is becoming crystal clear that inflation will not be checked by raising interest rates on the part of monetary authorities or the banking industry. It is time for banks to effectively and earnestly reduce their lending, and they must consistently say "No" to every loan that is intended to be used for speculative or non-productive purposes. It is up to banks to ration their credit before somebody else imposes it on them.

*Los Angeles, April 10.*

**Ernest A. Jones**
*Chairman, MacManus, John & Adams, Inc.*

The use of cigarets is a medical question; the arbitrary banning of their advertising—however vapid or insipidly stupid it may be—is a constitutional question. If the voice of legitimate business can be stifled in this manner, I wonder what product or service will be next obliterated by a statistical shadow. For any successful unopposed move will be repeated, expanded, extended.

*Pub. May 12.*

**Matthew Josephson**
*Author, Historian*

Today's Horatio Alger capitalists just go out and get a contract from the military-industrial complex. They're virtually faceless partisans of state capitalism. Even the conglomerateurs—those who put one and one companies together and come out with three, four or five—are awfully tame compared with such flamboyant characters as Jay Gould and J.P. Morgan.

*Interview, New York, pub. Dec. 1.*

**David M. Kennedy**
*Secretary of the Treasury of the United States*

Calm study in cooperation with our friends—not unilateral actions or disruptive changes in the vital role of the dollar and gold—must remain the foundation of real reform and progress in the international financial system.

*Pub. Feb. 3.*

**Miles W. Kirkpatrick**
*Antitrust Lawyer*

The underlying antitrust paradox has not been fully explored. Increased effic-

(MILES W. KIRKPATRICK)

iency is certainly one of the hallmarks of industrial progress and must not be impeded over the long run by antitrust laws. On the other hand—and efficiency has this double edge—by its very success, it can crush competition.

*At antitrust conference of National Industrial Conference Board, New York, March 6.*

**Alexandre Lamfalussy**
*Managing Director, Banque de Bruxelles*

The power, organization and innovating capacity of American industry make such a formidable competitor for the rest of the world that the latter could hardly accept a devaluation of the dollar relatively to all the other currencies. If the dollar was to lose its gold parity, the large majority of countries would be obliged to follow the dollar in order to protect their competitive positions.

*Pub. Nov. 17.*

**Charles Y. Lazarus**
*President, American Retail Association*

The fact seems to be that business, particularly retailers, has hardly been talking to government. When it has talked, it has been primarily as an antagonist. We've got to work with government.

*San Francisco, March 12.*

**Leon Levy**
*President, Oppenheimer Fund, Inc.*

The take-over syndrome is not likely to reverse itself, but its character may change. Some of the targets of takeovers may be conglomerates that have failed to do a good job with the properties they have acquired. They may be devoured by the same techniques they used to acquire other companies.

*New York, pub. Jan. 26.*

**Walter J. Levy**
*Oil consultant*

A tariff system may look good in theory for some industries; but for the oil industry, in practice, it would be completely unmanageable. The present quota system can certainly be improved; but a tariff would create many, many more problems than it solved . . . I do not mean to im-

pugn the motives of those who are advocating a tariff solution. They believe they are right. However, all my knowledge and experience in this complicated industry tells me they are wrong.

*Interview, New York, pub. Dec. 14.*

**David E. Lilienthal**
*Chairman, Development and Resources Corporation*

There are plenty of farmers in the world who cannot read, but very few who cannot count.

*Nairobi, Kenya, pub. Feb. 3.*

**James J. Ling**
*Chairman, Ling-Temco-Vought*

Very few concepts have had as little critical analysis and undergone fewer changes in the past 80 years than antitrust, even though today's world was largely unpredictable in 1890. All of the patches that have been added to the antitrust quilt during that period have been cut from the same bolt of cloth—a vague, semi-emotional feeling that bigness is bad or dangerous or the associated ill-formed concept that economic concentration is bad or dangerous. I cannot believe the Populist philosophy can really exist in the full light of today's totally different atmosphere and environment.

*Before American Bar Association, Aug. 12.*

**L. B. Lundborg**
*Chairman, Bank of America*

The curtailing of credit stems from a lot more than efforts to control inflation, and long-term priorities gearing government policies and programs, here and abroad, to what we can pay for will be needed to achieve lasting stability.

*Pub. September.*

**Sherman J. Maisel**
*Member, Federal Reserve Board*

I am often appalled, amazed, amused or horrified at what broad conclusions can be constructed on narrow foundations when I read news accounts interpreting the monetary statistics that the Federal Reserve publishes each week.

*At economics seminar, University of Michigan, pub. March 11.*

**Ross L. Malone**
*Vice president and general counsel,*
*General Motors Corporation*

Concentration in an industry, in and of itself, does not constitute a violation of antitrust laws or a basis for divestiture, and I suggest that any interpretation or modification of the law which would have that result is undesirable.

*At antitrust conference of National*
*Industrial Conference Board,*
*New York, March 6.*

**William McChesney Martin, Jr.**
*Chairman, Federal Reserve Board*

It is not too much to hope that businessmen . . . are having second thoughts about the wisdom of counting on a continued inflationary boom to justify unrestrained spending on plant and equipment . . . I believe that it would be a mistake for businessmen to count on being bailed out by inflation in the years to come for investment errors they make in 1969.

*Before House Banking Committee,*
*Washington, June 30.*

**Charles B. McCoy**
*President,*
*E.I. du Pont de Nemours & Company*

There is nothing mutually exclusive about making a profit and serving the needs of society. Personally, I have no doubt that the companies that will be the most profitable in the long run will be those that serve society best . . . Society will reward those that help unclog our highways, rebuild and revitalize our cities, cleanse our streams and conquer poverty and disease—not those whose pursuit of the dollar blinds them to such needs.

*Union, N.J., Sept. 5.*

**Richard W. McLaren**
*Assistant Attorney General,*
*Anti-Trust Division,*
*Department of Justice*
*of the United States*

Republican administrations have been characterized by vigorous antitrust enforcement—and the Nixon Administration will be no exception.

*Pub. Feb. 3.*

. . . I want to make it crystal clear that I am not opposed to all mergers, and that I do not subscribe to the idea that "bigness is badness . . ." The point I make is that the economy of the country is undergoing a radical restructuring. Are the underlying reasons for the change valid ones? Will the revamped economy be a more efficient and competitive one? Or are we getting aggregation of business units irrespective of economies of scale?

*Before House Ways and Means*
*Committee, Washington, March 12.*

When an economy is dominated by 200 large companies—a very real threat—individual initiative and free enterprise are circumscribed . . . I don't buy the argument that business has no conscience. Maybe the call for restraint will be heard. The "in" thing of late has been merger and acquisition. Maybe if we can make it an "out" thing, the law won't have to overreact.

*Pub. March 24.*

I realize that a lot of people think it is very odd that we have a very tough anti-merger policy. And they say, "If you're going to be tough on mergers . . . why don't you get tough with people who have already had their growth and now are in dominant positions . . ." (The answer is) you aren't destroying something when you keep two companies from getting together. But you may be destroying something when you go to bust somebody up . . . I think I rationalize the thing on this basis: If we were able to hold down the level of concentration, to hold where we are, to hold even, as opposed to more big mergers, at least we're giving competition a chance to erode the position of the already big companies.

*Interview, Washington, pub. Aug. 18.*

**Arjay Miller**
*Vice chairman, Ford Motor Company*

It should be made clear to the American people that business cannot and should not attempt to solve all of our present social ills . . . it is no more reasonable to expect business to do everything than it is to expect government to do everything.

*At Stanford Business Conference,*
*Stanford, Calif., Feb. 19.*

**Otto Miller**
*Chairman, Standard Oil Company*
*of California*

We are living in turbulent times. The oil industry does business with everybody. It is only natural that some of the problems of society at large should rub off on the industry, and some general and specific disaffection be aimed toward it. Oil is a very complex business. It is not, unfortunately, very well understood by the public.

*Interview, pub. Dec. 7.*

**John N. Mitchell**
*Attorney General of the United States*

There has been some question as to whether under existing law we have the authority to attack the pure conglomerate —a corporation which acquires another in an apparently unrelated field of business. My view is that, when in doubt, I will give the benefit to the American consumer.

*Before Fordham University Alumni*
*Association, New York, March 8.*

**Walter F. Mondale**
*United States Senator, D-Minn.*

The Communist countries of Eastern Europe are not hurt (by the United States embargo). They can obtain what they need from other free world countries. Only the American businessman and the U.S. balance of payments are substantially hurt. Basically, we deny ourselves the right to compete.

*Before the Senate,*
*Washington, Oct. 22.*

**George Moore**
*Chairman, First National*
*City Bank of New York*

Any bank management reaching out into non-financial fields risks losing its competitive sharpness in banking, as well as having its hands full in a business where it lacks know-how. I would be happy to see one of our competitors try it.

*Pub. Feb. 3.*

**Rupert L. Murphy**
*Commissioner, Interstate Commerce*
*Commission of the United States*

Fair and unrestrained competition is a good regulation of rates; unfair and unrestrained competition can be madness.

*University of Alabama, May 14.*

**Richard M. Nixon**
*President of the United States*

I believe that the interests of the United States and the interests of the whole world will best be served by moving toward freer trade rather than toward protection. I take a dim view of this tendency to move toward quotas and other methods that may become permanent, whether they are applied here or by nations abroad.

*News conference, Washington, Feb. 6.*

. . . I believe that the (oil) depletion allowance is in the national interest because I believe it is essential to develop our resources . . .

*Pub. Sept. 20.*

**David Ogilvy**
*Chairman, Ogilvy & Mather*
*International, Inc.*

The new breed (of advertising people) has no regard for how well an ad sells the product. These pseudo-intellectuals who are now flocking to advertising, these callow, half-baked, overpaid young men and women haven't the slightest interest in how the consuming public reacts to stimuli any more than abstract painters have. They are departing from tested formulae and going to things that are very doubtful.

*Pub. Aug. 18.*

There has arisen this school of self-conscious, intellectually pretentious advertising which spawns these boutique advertising agencies, and I believe that almost all the time their work is incomprehensible to the great American middle class. Most of the people who are writing advertising today have never had to sell anything to anybody. They've never seen a consumer.

*Interview, pub. Oct. 10.*

**Wright Patman**
*United States Representative, D-Tex.*

I think it is a sad state of affairs when an Administration sends us bankers to comment on banking legislation.

*Before House Banking Committee,*
*Washington, April 17.*

There is no doubt in my mind, and I do not believe there should be any doubt in anyone's mind who examines the facts, that at the very least there is a serious suspicion that most of the major banks in this country did conspire to fix the prime rate of interest on June 9.

*Before House Banking Committee, Washington, June 21.*

I am convinced that the banking industry had a firm agreement with President Nixon before he was elected that it would not be subjected to official questioning on its economic decisions—that there would be no "jawboning or moralsuasion" used to hold down interest rate increases. Nothing else can adequately explain the weak, indifferent attitude that has been taken by Secretary of the Treasury David M. Kennedy on these interest rate increases . . . Today's economy—with the highest interest rates in the nation's history—is largely the result of banking and monetary policy written *by* special interests *for* special interests.

*Before National Press Club, Washington, July 31.*

## Thomas F. Patton
*Chairman, Republic Steel Corporation*

The United States, the greatest producer of steel, is now the greatest importer of steel. I am very conscious of the fact that freer trade among nations is better for the world. Nevertheless, when a basic domestic industry's very survival is threatened by too big a percentage being taken over by a foreign product, then I think it is in the interest of our nation and its people that some restriction be placed on the tonnage of that product that can be imported. If a major war comes, God help this country if we don't have a strong, healthy steel industry.

The X factor is that little something special that you find in the human qualities of a corporation. You can have the finest plants and the best raw materials and all of the finances that you can possibly want; but if you don't have the proper human beings to manage so that they will produce income and goods of a quality that can be sold to customers at a profit, you don't

have that X factor, that human factor. You have nothing.

*Interview, pub. October.*

## Charles H. Percy
*United States Senator, R-Ill.*

Other Western nations think it is incredible that we're letting them have all this business (from communist countries). We turn down millions and millions of dollars' worth. They think we're certainly naive.

*Before the Senate, Washington, Oct. 22.*

## Alph B. Peterson
*Chairman, Benrus Corporation*

Advertising is not spending; it's an investment to get a piece of the mind of millions of Americans.

*Pub. April 11.*

## Peter G. Peterson
*Chairman, Bell & Howell Company*

One of the things that is kind of shocking, or perhaps disappointing, is that most of the time innovations do not take place within the industry in which one would have expected them to take place.

*Interview, Chicago, pub. Jan. 12.*

## Rudolph A. Peterson
*President, Bank of America*

The dollar will continue to be the fundamental trading and reserve currency. I cannot see how it can be otherwise, for the dollar—backed by the industrial strength of the United States—is still, and will continue to be, in the most fundamental way, the world's strongest currency.

*At Australian Finance Conference, Sydney, pub. March 17.*

## Chester L. Posey
*Vice chairman, McCann-Erickson, Inc.*

. . . I believe that advertising is an investment where risk taking is inordinately rewarded and where the penalty for failure is not correspondingly severe.

*Before National Association of Advertisers, Coronado, Calif., pub. March 24.*

**K. A. Randall**
*Chairman, Federal Deposit
Insurance Corporation*

We must make certain that minority enterprise is successful . . . because ultimately its chief value is symbolic, and I believe we cannot afford the failure of this symbol . . . There is widespread cynicism in the ghettos now about the sincerity of the so-called white power structure in allowing minorities to have a "piece of the action." I do not like to contemplate what that cynicism will turn into if our present efforts are a flop.
*Before New Jersey Bankers Association,
Atlantic City, N.J., May 23.*

**Thomas R. Reeves**
*Senior vice president,
Investors Diversified Services*

. . . The stock market represents the simplest, most orderly and most effective way to put savings to work. People who use stocks in a consistent and thoughtful way can't help but prosper over the long pull because they are betting on the future growth of the country—and that is as sound a bet as I know how to make.
*New York, pub. Feb. 3.*

**J. L. Robertson**
*Vice chairman, Federal Reserve Board*

We appear to be drifting toward a repetition of serious errors that the banking industry fell into in the 1920s. For example, the one-bank holding-company loophole threatens to take us back into the kind of situation that only students of history and a few old fogies remember.
*Pub. Feb. 5.*

**James M. Roche**
*Chairman, General Motors Corporation*

At General Motors, we realize we are an important influence in the scheme of things . . . Maybe that's why some people regard us as a menace. General Motors is a corporation that's owned by 1.4 million stockholders. We have 750,000 employes worldwide, nearly 15,000 dealers and 128,000 other retail outlets that sell our products. There are a lot of people to whom we're responsible and we just don't do some of the things that are attributed to us. Some critics seem to think that all we have to do is call up Washington and say, "You do this and you do that," and it will be done. If anybody believes that is the case, just ask some of us who are invited to Washington occasionally.
*Interview, Washington, pub. Feb. 10.*

The size of General Motors is not the cause of its success, but the consequence of success.
*At stockholders meeting,
Detroit, May 23.*

**George A. Roeder, Jr.**
*Vice chairman, Chase Manhattan Bank*

Forbidding banks to pursue the natural expansion of their activities in modern times (to insurance, travel agencies, accounting, data processing, etc.) is unreasonable. It is analogous to limiting dairy-product companies to the selling of only milk, petroleum companies to only kerosene and drug stores to only drugs.
*Pub. Dec. 21.*

**George T. Scharffenberger**
*President, City Investing Company*

Unless conglomerate management builds on sound components and manages its units effectively, the mere acquisition of companies is probably an effective road to economic disaster. The real key to conglomerate success is the internal growth which acquisitions only make possible.
*Panel discussion, New York, Jan. 24.*

**Robert F. Six**
*President, Continental Airlines*

You've got to gamble in this business, try new approaches. I'd rather go for the fast nickel than the slow buck. The carriage trade is not large enough to support the airlines of America. This is not a luxury business. Anyone who tells you that the way to make money in this business is to charge higher prices to fewer passengers doesn't know his rear end from a hole in the ground.
*Interview, Honolulu, pub. Oct. 12.*

**Donald Sneed, Jr.**
*President, Unity Bank &*
*Trust Company of Boston*

We're more than a bank. If we have to say No to a customer, we say, "No, because . . ."

*Pub. Feb. 28.*

**George Spatta**
*Honorary Chairman,*
*Clark Equipment Company*

. . . universities don't teach our kids how our capitalistic system works. We are a nation of employees. We all work for somebody. 75 or 80 million of us. Yet nobody tells our kids how our system works, the means by which we make our living. Take the 500 top corporations. They have several hundred billion in capital, they hire 15 million people, and they only make a nickel on the dollar. Just think, some of these stupid kids want to destroy this Establishment. I'm going to tell them this, but I'm afraid they may laugh me right out of the building.

*Interview, pub. December.*

**Maurice H. Stans**
*Secretary of Commerce*
*of the United States*

There is not enough money in the Treasury of the United States or knowledge and wisdom in the Federal Government for it to be even an unequal partner (in helping minority groups in business). The ultimate solution, the question of whether the enterprise succeeds or fails, lies in the private sector. If you cannot do it, it will not be done. You have the power and the resources and the knowledge and the experience. All you need is the inclination.

*Before International Downtown*
*Executives Association,*
*Washington, Sept. 19.*

For progress in the '70s, we must find ways to reduce taxes on corporations and permit the capital growth that is necessary. After all, it is American enterprise that has given us everything we have now. If we encourage it, it can give us about anything we want.

*Washington, pub. November.*

**Donald J. Stocking**
*Denver Regional Director,*
*Securities & Exchange Commission*
*of the United States*

You don't buy a stock because it has real value. You buy it because you feel there is always a greater fool down the street ready to pay more than you paid.

*Pub. March 24.*

**Erwin R. Tichauer**
*Biochemist, New York University*

Efficiency is the by-product of comfort. The enterprise that manufactures no sore backs, shoulders, wrists or behinds is at a competitive advantage over one with suffering workers.

*Pub. May 2.*

**William S. Vaughn**
*Chairman, Eastman Kodak Company*

The responsibility of business has expanded to the point where it can now be said that the business of business is human development. The laws of economic engineering still stand, to be sure, but the frontiers of that largely unexplored land of human engineering are just opening up. Looking ahead into the 70s, and following, I am inclined to think the corporation that is not in the business of human development may not be in any business. At least, not for long.

*At International Industrial Conference,*
*San Francisco, Sept. 17.*

**William Verity**
*President, Armco Steel Corporation*

Wage and price controls have a dismal past and an even bleaker future. I oppose them in principle and detest them in practice. Our market system and our collective bargaining procedures contain imperfections and abuses, but these can, and will, be corrected by competitive reality. Frankly, I can conceive of no greater disservice to economic progress than the imposition of price and wage controls.

*Pub. June 8.*

## Peter C. Vink
*President, North American*
*Philips Corporation*

The key to success in business is understanding of the world about you and then making products to fit the needs of the times. A person who looks inward is bound to try to make the times try to fit his company's products.

*Interview, pub. Oct. 26.*

## Robert H. Volk
*President, Unionamerica, Inc.*

One problem one-bank holding companies have is the misunderstanding that if it's big, it's bad. In our economy you need large companies and their large capital to progress. After all, you can't build an L-1011 (Lockheed's giant new airliner) in your garage.

*News conference,*
*Los Angeles, June 17.*

## Arthur K. Watson
*Chairman,*
*International Business Machines*
*World Trade Corporation*

. . . the real wave of the future is not Marxism, but free enterprise. It is not centralization, but decentralization. It is not the public sector, but the private sector. And, finally, it is not the nation-state, but internation.

*Before Congress of International*
*Chamber of Commerce,*
*Istanbul, June 2.*

## Thomas J. Watson, Jr.
*Chairman, International*
*Business Machines*

Bigness alone is no assurance of success. Industry is ideas and innovation, and creative ideas can be achieved anywhere by anybody. There are some 500 companies in peripheral support areas of the computer industry just because of that fact.

*Before IBM stockholders,*
*Santa Monica, Calif., April 28.*

## Mary Wells
*President, Wells, Rich & Green,*
*Advertising Agency*

I think cigarette advertising on TV and radio will continue. If a product can be sold in this country, a company should be able to advertise it. This really burns me up. It's unfair (banning cigarette advertising), un-American and undemocratic. It's a sad, terrifying kind of thing, the beginning of a dangerous precedent.

*Pub. Aug. 18.*

## David L. Yunich
*President, R. H. Macy, Inc., New York*

The merchant (in the 21st century) will be more of a showman than he is today, more creative, more innovative, more concerned with how he presents his message to his customers. Rather than be a buyer-and-seller, rather than a department manager, tomorrow's merchant will be an impresario.

*At conference of Sales Promotion*
*Executives Association,*
*New York, pub. June 1.*

**Ansel Adams**
*Photographer*

The big enemy now is not the dam and highway builders. It's the damn unconcerned people. People want to take all their comforts, everything, into the wilderness. All they want is a different view out their trailer window.
*Pub. April 14.*

**Donald W. Aitkin**
*Astrophysicist, Stanford University*

When we attach so much value to traveling in air-conditioned cars speeding on freeways; to eating artificially colored and flavored food; to ridding ourselves of insects by pushing the button on a spray can—then it is increasingly impossible for humans to understand man's place in nature and to appreciate the complexity and fragility of the ecological web that lets us live.
*At John Muir Institute Conference, Aspen, Colo., pub. Sept. 22.*

**Robert Barsky**
*Deputy Air-Pollution Officer, Air Pollution Control District of Los Angeles County*

If the auto industry had started in 1955 to put effective devices on automobiles, we wouldn't have a smog problem today. The position of the automobile industry is that there isn't any pollution; if there is, they didn't cause it, and if there was, they fixed it.
*Los Angeles, pub. Oct. 19.*

**Max Black**
*Professor of Philosophy, Cornell University*

Science cannot bridge the morality gap. Man cannot kill the great lakes with his effluent, then expect an engineer or a scientist to come up with a pill and make the water clean again. He must recognize the consequences of his actions.
*Pub. Dec. 28.*

**David Brower**
*Executive Director, Sierra Club*

We are fighting the good fight, the war against man's own ignorance and cleverness. Against his ignorance, because he's got to stop piling people up deeper. Against his cleverness, because he's got to control rampant technology. This society does not exist to serve its economy; the economy exists to serve society.
*Pub. April 14.*

The earth needs a number of organizations to fight the disease that now threatens the planet: "Cirrhosis" of the environment. There is only one environment that will sustain us and other living things we share the planet with. Man's diminishing of the earth is a crime, and the worst one of all is grand larceny against the future.
*News conference, San Francisco, Sept. 16.*

**George E. Brown, Jr.**
*United States Representative, D-Calif.*

The current quality of our air is a national disgrace. And America's automotive syndrome has been the major contributing factor to the steady decline of that quality. For years, Government attempted to use the carrot approach to entice auto manufacturers to do something about the problem, and, for years, the manufacturers procrastinated as they claimed that they were indeed doing all they could do . . . And so, if the carrot does not work, it is time to use the stick.
*Before the House, Washington, Sept. 3.*

**J. Phil Campbell**
*Under Secretary of Agriculture*
*of the United States*

That there is environmental pollution is a fact. That it stems primarily from agricultural use of pesticides and plant nutrients is not a fact. The danger is that too many of the American people will tie the fact and the non-fact together in one package.

*Pub. Oct. 13.*

**Barry Commoner**
*Chairman, Department of Botany,*
*Washington University, St. Louis*

The time has come, because of atomic fallout and the effects of insecticide poisoning, to forge a great alliance in this nation: among scientists, conservationists and the public at large. We all now know that, if we are to survive, the environment must be maintained as a balanced harmonious whole. We must all work together to preserve it. If we fail, we shall abandon the place where we live—the thin skin of air, water, soil and living things on the planet earth—to destruction.

*Before National Audubon Society,*
*St. Louis, April 26.*

The new technological man carries strontium 90 in his bones, iodine 131 in his thyroid, DDT in his fat and asbestos in his lungs. There is now simply not enough air, water and soil on earth to absorb man-made poisons without effect. If we continue in our reckless way, this planet before long will become an unsuitable place for human habitation.

*Pub. Aug. 15.*

**Rene Jules Dubos**
*Bacteriologist,*
*Rockefeller University*
*of New York*

The more a population is exposed to modern technology, the more it appears to be subject to certain forms of chronic and degenerative diseases, diseases called, for precisely that reason, the diseases of civilization. Men and women are working all the time in the midst of the infernal noise caused by machines and telephones, in an atmosphere polluted with chemical fumes and tobacco smoke.

*Before World Health Assembly,*
*Boston, pub. Aug. 9.*

Man can be adapted to anything—to the dirt and noise of New York City . . . and that is what is tragic. As we can accept worse and worse conditions, we don't realize that there is something worse than extinction—the progressive degradation of human life . . . Yes, we do become adapted, but we do (so) by sacrificing something at each step—and we don't know yet what we are sacrificing.

*At Argonne University Association*
*conference, Chicago, pub. Sept. 2.*

**Thomas F. Eagleton**
*United States Senator, D-Mo.*

Noise, crowding, pollution and the sheer rush of our complex, modern society are rapidly becoming as oppressive to many individuals as the worst kind of political dictatorship.

*Washington, pub. November.*

**Henry Ford II**
*Chairman, Ford Motor Company*

I cannot emphasize too strongly my own personal concern and that of Ford Motor Company with removing automobile-related pollutants as a threat to the environmental quality. This concern will be reflected not only in words, but in specific, concrete actions based upon all the scientific, engineering and manufacturing skills at our command. We are making this commitment because of our recognition that the quality of the environment warrants extraordinary effort on the part of all who may be in a position to improve our physical surroundings.

*News conference, Dearborn, Mich.,*
*Dec. 10.*

**Howard Frazier**
*President, Consumer Federation*
*of America*

Air is, literally, the breath of life. Yet we murder this precious body with 142 million tons of poison a year. Each of us has a corporate responsibility for contributing three-quarters of a ton per person, from motor vehicles, power plants, municipal dumps, incinerators. And the fact that you may not own a power plant has nothing to do with it. You own the air, and when you acquiese in its union with pollutants, you are giving the bride away.

*Los Angeles, pub. Nov. 27.*

**Ira N. Gabrielson**
*President, Wildlife Management Institute*

Never before, in my experience, has such strong concern been expressed about necessary efforts to restore and protect the quality of the environment. Those political leaders who apparently did not know or care before should know now that many people have a deep concern about their native land.

*At North American Wildlife and Natural Resources Conference, Washington, March 5.*

**David Gates**
*Director, Missouri Botanical Garden of St. Louis*

We're still in the Stone Age. This is pure speculation, but think about it: Influenza epidemics have followed very closely periods of great volcanic activity. Maybe the dust in the atmosphere from that activity reduces the sunlight and triggers a virus or our susceptibility to it. So what happens if man loads the atmosphere with dust from combustion and construction projects and *then* there is a major volcanic action—the worst flu epidemic in history? As I say, that's all speculation —but it's the kind of thing we should know, and we don't.

*Interview, St. Louis, pub. Oct. 5.*

**Bob Golden**
*Staff Member, Sierra Club*

There are moments when I expect to wake up next morning and find out the mountains have been repealed, the U.S. Park Service has become the U.S. Parking Service . . .

*Pub. April 14.*

**Aire J. Haagen-Smit**
*Chairman, Air Resources Board*

Our ancestors lived in the happy cer-

tainty that the earth was infinite, that there was enough soil, water and air to go around forever. But now, looking at the earth from an astronaut's vantage point, we have begun to realize that the earth isn't so big, and that the apparent stability applies only to our own time, an infinitely small thing in the time scale of geologic changes.

*At International Symposium on Man and Beasts, Washington, May 14.*

**Edward T. Hall**
*Professor of Anthropology, Northwestern University*

The quality of life has declined several hundred per cent since I was born. Take meat, for example. It has been all hormoned up, doesn't taste as good anymore. Chicken—the same thing. Or consider housing. Rooms get smaller, walls more transparent to sound, ceilings lower. Views are cut off by high buildings. This is exactly what people don't want. And what it is doing to them we don't even know for sure.

*Chicago, pub. Nov. 16.*

**Thor Heyerdahl**
*Author, Explorer*

Modern man seems to believe that he can get everything he needs from the corner drugstore. He doesn't understand that everything has a source in the land or sea, and that he must respect those sources. If the indiscriminate pollution continues, we will be sawing off the branch we are sitting on.

*Interview, pub. Aug. 15.*

**Walter J. Hickel**
*Secretary of the Interior of the United States*

They say that people will be watching us more closely than any other Cabinet member. Well, I'll be watching them, too. Watching when conservation legislation I want comes up—and there will be plenty of it; watching the conservationists when we consider development projects that are clearly in the public interest; watching the developers when they play games with our fish, wildlife, forests, parks and wilder-

(WALTER J. HICKEL)

ness areas; watching anybody who goes about polluting our environment.

*Denver, Feb. 12.*

When we emerged from an agricultural to an industrial society at the turn of the century, we literally busted out all over. There were no guidelines for development, there was desecration of the earth and abuse of raw materials. Nobody wants to go back to that. But we have to decide what we want. If we want open spaces, fresh water and clean air, we should be willing to sacrifice the concentration of industry. When you put ten massive industries side by side on one river, even if you scientifically eliminate the pollution problem, you still have the environmental problem of unsightliness.

*Pub. Aug. 1.*

**Alfred Hulstrunck**
*Assistant Director, Atmospheric*
*Sciences Research Center,*
*State University of New York*

If transportation continues to grow in the direction it's going, it's possible the next generation will never see the sun.

*Pub. July 7.*

**John E. Jacobs**
*Vice president for manufacturing,*
*Bethlehem Steel Corporation*

Industry is a prime target for the politicians because we are visible. But, until the public becomes educated to the seriousness of what is happening to its lakes and streams through municipal and agricultural wastes, the problem is going to get worse.

*Interview, Burns Harbor, Ind.,*
*pub. Nov. 7.*

**H. David Kerr**
*Research physician,*
*University of Maryland*

People believe what they want to believe. They believe that air pollution is harmful, and it probably is. But we can't prove it yet . . . I'm sure that air pollution codes are important. I just wish we had some hard knowledge to base them on. We're all interested in doing some-

thing about pollution, but no one knows what needs to be done. I'm all for clean air; but how clean is clean? We don't know. If we ask companies to reduce sulfur dioxide levels to some certain percentage, it seems like a license to pollute up to that percentage.

*Pub. Nov. 13.*

**Louis M. Kessler**
*President, American Institute of*
*Certified Public Accountants*

I am not so naive as to believe that a manufacturer of synthetic yarns or a refiner of petroleum products will voluntarily cease pouring chemical wastes into a river or odorous fumes into the air if that is the cheapest way to make his product. Nor can he be expected to be a nice fellow and increase his costs while his competitors are still polluting away.

*Interview, Los Angeles, Dec. 9.*

**Virginia H. Knauer**
*Adviser to the President of the*
*United States for Consumer Affairs*

We are surrounded by potential hazards to our health and life in the environment in which we live. Of what use is the financial and economic protection of the marketplace if we do not have the elementary and basic protection of clean air to breathe, pure water to drink and uncontaminated food to eat? If we cannot live and function in our environment, it becomes pretty academic as to how we spend our money or whether the right label is on the right can. Our over-all concern must be environmental health.

*Philadelphia, pub. May 26.*

**Vern O. Knudsen**
*Chancellor Emeritus,*
*University of California*

Noise, like smog, is a slow agent of death. If it continues for another 30 years, as it has done for the last 30, it could become lethal.

*Pub. July 20.*

**Joseph Wood Krutch**
*Author*

When I first came to live in Tucson (Arizona) 19 years ago, I had a sudden lifting of the heart, almost a feeling I had been here in some previous incarnation. I climbed a rock overlooking the valley. No work of man was visible. This is the way the world was, *before man was.* Now, the skies are less clear; the stars, less bright. Ugliness in the slums is the result of poverty. The ugliness in Tucson is the result of prosperity.

*Pub. Nov. 4.*

**L. W. Lane, Jr.**
*Publisher, "Sunset Magazine"*

. . . in the drain we are placing on nature's bounty that makes it possible to be the best-heeled nation and help others, we are becoming environmental paupers. The price in consumption and destruction has been great. Many basic resources are gone from within our own boundaries. The goose that has been laying the golden eggs is short of good air to breathe, has smarting eyes, wants a drink of good water, is sometimes hungry, is thinking of taking the pill and laying fewer eggs because she's beginning to feel the pond is a bit too crowded to swim in, and generally longs for a little peace and quiet to enjoy life.

*Before U.S. National Commission for UNESCO, San Francisco, Nov. 27.*

**Norman F. Lent**
*New York State Senator*

A few days ago, the Federal Government declared a ban on cyclamates on the basis of far less evidence of risk than that available on DDT. Yet it continues to hedge on the DDT issue . . . We continue to play a game of chemical roulette with man's biological future. We've got to stop this—if not on a Federal level, then by pressure from the states.

*Nov. 5.*

**Charles McC. Mathias**
*United States Senator, R-Md.*

Technology has compounded our problems. In this consumer-oriented age, every person and the industries and commerce which attend him, generate some 9.7 pounds of solid wastes per day—bottles, packages, papers, plastics which are often so intenuous that they are virtually impos-

sible to dispose of. Chemists used to joke about creating the perfect solvent, and having nothing to keep it in. Our problem now is that we have created almost perfect packaging—and have no proper place to throw it away. So the land must collect all of the refuse of our disposable culture. Along many of our roadsides we can't see the erosion for the trash. At the bottom of many of our streams, where once we found the geologic strata of the ages, we now find inches of muck and the typical fossils of our age, rusty beer cans. As Walt Kelly's character, Pogo, says, "we have met the enemy and they are us."

*Before Howard Soil Conservation District, Howard County, Md., Oct. 1.*

**Brooks McCormick**
*President, International
Harvester Company*

Any management today that does not understand its responsibility to society for degradation of the environment is derelict in its duty. But an even greater dereliction would be its failure to perceive and adopt a strategy of action that will provide the income for maintaining the profitability of the enterprise. Industry can spend nothing it does not first earn in profits.

*Before Water Pollution Control Administration, Washington, Oct. 23.*

**K. Mellanby**
*Director, Nature Conservancy's
Monks Wood Experimental Station*

. . . Modern synthetic insecticides, including DDT, have saved millions of lives from insect-born diseases, and have raised food production . . . The impression that . . . without chemicals (pesticides) mankind would be healthier and more prosperous is completely false.

*Before British Association for the Advancement of Science, Exeter, England, pub. Sept. 10.*

**H. Peter Metzger**
*Biochemist*

It took the AEC (Atomic Energy Commission) three years to acknowledge that strontium 90 appeared in milk and was a hazard to human health. The last time

(H. PETER METZGER)

they supervised anything in Colorado, they allowed uranium miners to leave radioactive tailings lying around that could be blown over homes, farms and grazing lands and carried hundreds of miles downstream by rivers. The AEC is always saying things are 95% safe. We worry about the other 5%.  *Pub. Aug. 29.*

**Rogers C. B. Morton**
*United States Representative, R-Md.*

I believe that the great commitment of the '70s and '80s is to be to the environment. We've gotten the interest of the user and the resource out of balance. This is becoming very fundamental. Everybody is beginning to recognize it. And if we fail to clean up the air, clean up the water and provide a healthful, esthetically beautiful environment, then I think civilization will fail. It's that simple.
*Interview, Washington, pub. December.*

**Maynard Munger, Jr.**
*Conservationist*

There are two kinds of conservationists. The first is the ironfisted type: "By God, there isn't going to be one inch more development." The second is my kind. I believe we can accomplish as much by friendly persuasion. I don't believe in total capitulation of the enemy or pounding your shoe on the table.  *Pub. April 14.*

**Gaylord Nelson**
*United States Senator, D-Wis.*

In a single generation, DDT has polluted our environment on a worldwide basis, infiltrating the atmosphere, the water and the tissues of most of the world's creatures, pushing some, like the peregrine falcon and the bald eagle, to the brink of extinction . . . The future of all the Great Lakes will be imperiled unless action is taken soon to stop this poisoning of our waters by these pesticides.
*Before the Senate, Washington, April 1.*

**Thomas F. Patton**
*Chairman, Republic Steel Corporation*

In recent years, the public and the gov-

ernment have become more cognizant of air and water control . . . Now this is a job that cannot be done by private industry alone or government alone. We are going to have to have the cooperation of the industries and people in the community and of the governmental agencies at local, state and national levels. I believe we will get it. But this can't be achieved overnight. Remember, this has been in the making for almost 200 years.
*Interview, pub. October.*

**Kenneth S. Pitzer**
*President, Stanford University*

A highly annoying sonic boom will necessarily accompany each plane in supersonic flight. But much of the earlier planning assumed that our people would acquiesce in this annoyance, and only economic and technical feasibility factors were considered. In my view, however, the top priority should be given to the desires of the majority of people, who do not want to be annoyed by sonic booms. The convenience of faster travel for a few people should be strictly secondary.
*Pub. June 12.*

**James M. Roche**
*Chairman, General Motors Corporation*

The great challenge in the '70s is to fulfill our responsibility to the American environment. Some day we (the auto industry) will achieve our goal. We are coming closer every day. We can be proud that we are now less a part of the problem and more a part of the solution.
*Detroit, Dec. 23.*

**Elvis J. Stahr, Jr.**
*President, National Audubon Society*

We are running out of places in this country—even on this planet—that are the way nature made them. It is tragically possible to foresee a time when nothing purely nature's would be left.
*New York, pub. March 2.*

**William S. Storey**
*Vice president, Institute of Scrap & Steel*

It is a profligate waste of our natural resources to permit old automobiles, refrigerators, stoves and the like to molder in our fields and clutter our streets while we mine increasing amounts of natural resources (and) iron ore, and rely heavily on imported iron ore to help meet our needs.

*Interview, New York, pub. Jan. 26.*

**John E. Swearingen**
*Chairman, Standard Oil Company of Indiana*

Public enthusiasm for pollution control is matched by reluctance to pay even a modest share of the cost. This attitude will have to change.

*Before Water Pollution Control Administration, Washington, Oct. 23.*

**Russell E. Train**
*Under Secretary of the Interior of the United States*

Is there any difference, really, between the right of the farmer and the rancher to go about their business secure from harm resulting from oil operations, and the right of the motel owner, the marine operator, the commercial fisherman to be secure from the same hazards? What of the right of the tourist to expect a clean beach; the right of the sports fisherman to expect fish where fish normally are to be found; the right of the marine biologist to make his observations in a habitat undisturbed by pollutants? Is there any difference, in principle, in responsibility for operations that, on one hand, leave a dead steer on the range and, on the other, a dead bird on a beach?

*Before American Petroleum Institute, pub. Dec. 3.*

**Richard D. Vaughan**
*Director, Bureau of Solid Waste Management, Department of Health, Education and Welfare of the United States*

I sometimes don't understand Americans. In Europe, you almost never see anyone discard anything in the street. In the United States, I've seen "Don't Litter" signs practically covered with litter. Americans are litterers. The problem is so bad that we have sociologists working on the problem, trying to find out why Americans have such an untidy streak.

*Pub. Aug. 18.*

**Lowell P. Weicker, Jr.**
*United States Representative, R.-Conn.*

Practically every important water resource in this country is polluted to some degree. No one can say just how much it will cost to clean up the nation's polluted waters and to keep the still-clean waters from becoming polluted. At today's prices, the bill could run as high as a hundred billion dollars. When we short-change water pollution control, we have agreed to give our children a toilet bowl, rather than the clear spring that was left to us.

*At Southwestern Connecticut Girl Scout Council Conference on Natural Resources, Hartford, pub. Sept. 2.*

**Lee C. White**
*Chairman, Federal Power Commission*

The American people are increasingly concerned . . . with environmental considerations—the destruction of scenic values, atmospheric pollution and thermal pollution . . . Too much of the (utility) industry still regards conservationists as the enemy, who must be run over.

*Interview, Washington, July 27.*

# Crime

---

**Joseph L. Alioto**
*Mayor of San Francisco*

A heavy percentage of . . . youthful offenders are black. Last year (in San Francisco), of seven young murder suspects arrested, six were black. Of 544 youths investigated for robbery, 439 were black . . . These figures are not a racial slur, nor are they intended to flame the fires of white racism against blacks. They are stated as an imperative for action to strike at the injustices and the despair that lie at the root of so much crime . . . the social evils of bad housing, sterile education, unemployment and ghettoized neighborhoods.

The (Black) Panthers may describe themselves as a political party, but they are not. They are a gang of hoodlums and gunmen, a small-time Murder, Inc. They have gained a certain notoriety for their writings and, I might add, their rantings, and I believe it undeserved. Their philosophy is narrow and paranoid, filled with hate and distrust, and they openly drill for murder and terror.

*Before House Select Committee on Crime, Washington, July 29.*

**George J. Beto**
*Director, Texas Department of Corrections*

Society has failed to recognize that the most stringent aspect of prison punishment is sexual deprivation, especially since 50% of the inmates in state prisons are under 25.

*Pub. April 17.*

**Thomas Bradley**
*Los Angeles City Councilman*

Most of the police trainees' time is taken up with learning how to catch crooks. But only 10 per cent of their time in the field is spent in that activity. Most of their time is spent dealing with people and people's problems, and they are not prepared for it.

*News conference, Los Angeles, Feb. 4.*

**McGeorge Bundy**
*President, Ford Foundation*

It would be a dangerous mistake for any of us to think that the actions of citizens groups can take the place of the massive reinforcement of every section of our public system of criminal justice, which will surely be required before we can expect to arrest, let alone to turn downward, the statistics of remorselessly increasing crime.

*San Francisco, Feb. 4.*

**Warren E. Burger**
*Chief Justice of the United States*

Without effective correctional systems, an increasing proportion of our population will become chronic criminals with no other way of life except the revolving door of crime, prison and more crime.

*At American Bar Association conference, Dallas, Aug. 11.*

**Robert C. Byrd**
*United States Senator, D-W.Va.*

Unless we have a safe society, we are not going to have a free society.

*Pub. Feb. 14.*

**Clifford P. Case**
*United States Senator, R-N.J.*

I am not opposed to education and this and that and the other thing, but it's seemed to me for a long time that the real problem was not enough men . . . to patrol the streets, not enough men to investigate crime and not enough men in the courts . . .

*Pub. December.*

**James Curran**
*Assistant Professor of Police Science,*
*State University of New York*
*at Farmingdale*

The (police) man who lives in the country is avoiding the city. He is a voyeur, a member of an occupying army. It will be impossible to get really good police work until a much larger part of the (police) department lives in the city and has its wives and children walking the streets.

*Pub. June 3.*

**Martin B. Danziger**
*Chief, Organized Crime Programs*
*Division, Law Enforcement Assistance*
*Administration of the United States*

Organized crime cannot exist without, among other things, the willing cooperation of the business community.

*Pub. August.*

**Everett McKinley Dirksen**
*United States Senator, R-Ill.*

You have criminals who are out on bail running around the place who probably have been put on bail two or three years ago. In that time they probably commit three or four or five more felonies. So, when they finally get to these congested courts, judges just don't have the time to try them any more. Obviously, this is no way to run a railroad.

*News conference, Washington, Jan. 28.*

**Thomas J. Dodd**
*United States Senator, D-Conn.*

As characterized by the top men in the field, the "correctional system" is fraught with problems of suicide, torture, sexual exploitation and outright murder. Our hearing record reads like an 18th-century horror story. The result is that of the 400,000 persons confined in our prisons today, over 90% will be released in a few years in worse shape than when they were committed, and with more hostility in their hearts and more violence in their minds.

*Washington, Sept. 16.*

**Howard Earle**
*Chief, Administration Division,*
*Los Angeles County Sheriff's Department*

We give our officer a club, gun and uniform, and an impossible task. The problems in our cities—under-education, under-employment, poor housing—are society's, but we get them.

*California State College,*
*Los Angeles, March 24.*

**Roger O. Egeberg**
*Assistant Secretary for Health and*
*Scientific Affairs, Department of*
*Health, Education and Welfare*
*of the United States*

Laws that threaten the user of marijuana . . . with lengthy prison terms are unjustified, unnecessary and very probably unenforceable.

*Washington, Oct. 14.*

**Thomas A. Flannery**
*United States Attorney for the*
*District of Columbia*

(Poverty itself is not) a root cause of crime. (Most criminals) commit crimes because they feel they can get away with it. The way to reduce crime is to convince the criminal that, upon the commission of a crime, he will be speedily apprehended, convicted and punished.

*Washington, June 5.*

**Abe Fortas**
*Former Associate Justice,*
*Supreme Court of the United States*

. . . the only thing you can say about . . . training and correctional institutions for juveniles is that they do provide training; but it's training in vice and crime. They do expand the circle of the juvenile's business associates; but the associates are in the business of vice and crime . . . the juveniles should not be and must not be put in those institutions if there is any alternative whatever.

*Before Juvenile Court Practice Institute,*
*Washington, pub. Dec. 1.*

**Sanford D. Garelik**
*Chief Inspector, Police Department,*
*City of New York*

. . . Prisons, for the most part, fail in at-

(SANFORD D. GARELIK)

tempts to rehabilitate criminals. One reason for this, of course, is that most penal institutions are crowded to the breaking point and there is no chance to accomplish much in the way of reforming prisoners. For many young offenders, prison becomes a post-graduate school in crime.
*Pub. March 10.*

**Ephraim R. Gomberg**
*Executive vice president,*
*Philadelphia Crime Commission*

Philadelphia spends $250 million of its tax money on law enforcement, but not 10 cents for research in this area. No corporation with a record like that could survive for a year.
*Pub. Feb. 18.*

**Charles E. Goodell**
*United States Senator, R-N.Y.*

. . . The choice before the American people on the issue of crime is to make either sound, reasoned judgments, or decisions based on emotion, misinformation and slogan. The first course is difficult and frustrating, but the second is dangerous and dishonest.
*Before the Senate, Washington, Sept. 18.*

**Kenneth Hahn**
*Member, Los Angeles County*
*Board of Supervisors*

One overwhelming fact is that the increase in crime is due to swift and sure justice not being applied in many criminal cases. By the time a trial gets to court, witnesses have moved, their memories are not as clear as when the incident happened and there is a constant turnover in judicial and prosecution personnel.
*Los Angeles, pub. Feb. 19.*

**Geoffrey C. Harzard, Jr.**
*Executive Director,*
*American Bar Foundation*

. . . What is happening, particularly in the black ghettos of the inner city, is that youth crime is becoming a self-conscious act of political rebellion. (The whole phenomenon) is a political problem and the sooner we recognize it to be such the more quickly we can deal with it in a useful way . . . In dealing with youth crime, we are talking about a problem of social policy, of which the kids are now very much aware, but we are dealing with it as though it were simply a police matter or a kind of exaggerated case of bad deportment.
*Before House Committee on Crime, Washington, July 30.*

**Roman L. Hruska**
*United States Senator, R-Neb.*

It is roughly estimated that the Mafia's profit is $30 billion a year; when measured in terms of profits, this makes the Mafia larger than United States Steel, Ford, American Telephone & Telegraph, General Motors, Standard Oil of New Jersey, General Electric, International Business Machines, Chrysler and Radio Corp. of America, combined. What a drain on our economy.
*Before the Senate, Washington, Sept. 3.*

**John E. Ingersoll**
*Director, Bureau of Narcotics and*
*Dangerous Drugs, Department of*
*Justice of the United States*

All too often, because of the present penalty structure, there is real hesitancy on the part of prosecutors and courts to handle possession cases because of the potentially high penalties involved. By allowing the court to prosecute the possessor who intends to sell, as a felon, and the possessor for one's own use, as a misdemeanant, I believe we will have better law enforcement and better respect for the law.
*Washington, Oct. 20.*

**Richard G. Kleindienst**
*Deputy Attorney General*
*of the United States*

Supporters of tougher police controls tend to link social protest and street crime as branches of the same tree, while many who articulate the grievances of the ghetto see police efforts to increase crime-fighting efficiency as efforts not to fight crime but to deal more harshly with protesting minority groups. (As a consequence,

America cannot) re-establish itself as a law-abiding society (unless there is) a recognition on the part of police and citizen alike that dramatic new moves must be made to develop cooperative relationships and mutual trust.

*At Police Community Relations Conference, St. Louis, May 4.*

**Frederick B. Lacey**
*United States Attorney*
*for New Jersey*

Organized crime, in the vernacular, is taking us over. For a few rotten dollars, mobsters have been able to corrupt officials in various governments. Organized crime will not even go into a community unless and until it has bought its protection against raids and arrests.

*Pub. Dec. 21.*

**Milton Luger**
*Director, Division of Youth,*
*State of New York*

It would probably be better for all concerned if young delinquents were not detected, apprehended or institutionalized. Too many of them get worse in our care.

*At Senate subcommittee hearings on juvenile delinquency, Washington, pub. March 17.*

**Lester G. Maddox**
*Governor of Georgia*

I'm disgusted with sorry, no-good, cowardly politicians. Mothers, wives, daughters and sisters, in an ever-increasing frightening number, are being molested, attacked, raped, and law enforcement officers and other citizens in increasing numbers are being attacked, beaten, stabbed, shot and killed. And public officials in Atlanta and elsewhere, who have restricted and are now restricting the courageous men in blue from doing a good job of law enforcement, must accept much of the blame.

*News conference, Atlanta, Oct. 2.*

**Norman Mailer**
*Author*

The causes of crime are more ugly than crime itself. The promise of a huge police force is a false solution. Historically, the worst governments are the ones with the largest numbers of police.

*New York, pub. June 8.*

**William Manchester**
*Author*

. . . We should go beyond registration of guns—go to confiscation.

*Pub. March 30.*

**John L. McClellan**
*United States Senator, D-Ark.*

The nature and extent of crime today transcend the crime we knew yesterday, and yesterday's criminal laws and procedures are not equal or adequate to the challenge that organized crime poses today.

*Washington, pub. March 17.*

With its infiltration of legitimate business, organized crime poses a new threat to the American economic system. The proper functioning of a free economy requires that economic decisions be made by persons free to exercise their own judgment. Force or fear limits choice, ultimately reduces quality and increases prices. When organized crime moves into a business, it usually brings to that venture all the techniques of violence and intimidation which it used in its illegal businesses. Competitors can be effectively eliminated and customers can be effectively confined to sponsored suppliers.

*Pub. August.*

**Gordon Misner**
*Professor of Criminology,*
*University of California*

Incompetency in higher echelons is the most serious problem facing the police today, much more serious than "subversive" Supreme Court decisions.

*Pub. Nov. 30.*

**John N. Mitchell**
*Attorney General of the United States*

Crime control is more than a matter of apprehending law violators. It reaches out to broad social problems of poor housing, poor schools and lack of employment.

*Pub. Feb. 16.*

(JOHN N. MITCHELL)

I will spare no effort to attack the nationwide organization of racketeers who corrupt our youths with illegal narcotics, who taint our public officials with bribes and corruption, who pervert the outstanding ideals of the labor union movement, who employ murder and torture to collect their debts.

*Before Fordham University Alumni Association, New York, March 8.*

It is a plain fact that those who have fled the inner cities have not escaped crime. The smug suburbanite who remains unwilling to help the core city solve its crime problem will soon find the problem on his own doorstep.

*Before Federal Bar Association, Washington, March 10.*

(Wire tapping is) one of our most useful tools in the investigation of organized crimes . . . I strongly believe in the right of privacy and I recognize the abuse to which wire tapping may be subjected. But we must balance the equities.

*Gatlinburg, Tenn., June 12.*

If you're monitoring the activities of the Mafia, it's hard to make that out as an invasion of privacy unless you regard privacy as a right that enables you to carry out a crime.

*Washington, pub. Sept. 8.*

I personally believe in sentences which are reasonably calculated to be deterrents to crime and which also will give judges sufficient flexibility to tailor the sentences to the requirements of the drug violator or narcotics addict. Prison is not the only logical alternative. In some cases, it may be advisable to use Federal rehabilitation programs, halfway houses, and private medical treatment while on probation or parole.

*Before the Senate, Washington, Sept. 16.*

. . . This Administration is sympathetic to law enforcement, and . . . in areas of doubt we tend to put our faith in the good intentions of police, rather than rely on the bad intentions of criminals.

There has been a tendency to ignore the law enforcement community in favor of social scientists. They, of course, can explain the motivations of the criminal but they can do little to protect the innocent against the mugger or robber . . . While I sympathize with physical conditions and emotional problems which may cause persons to commit crimes, I cannot sympathize with those who seek only to excuse criminals.

*Before International Association of Chiefs of Police, Miami Beach, Sept. 29.*

Every day that Congress delays passing anticrime legislation and appropriations only means that it will take longer to implement our anticrime program. And this delay, in turn, means that more innocent citizens will lose their lives and their property to street criminals, narcotics traffickers and organized gangsters. Effective anticrime programs are a moral, legal and economic necessity. This administration wants it and our citizens want it. But Congress is stalling the administration's efforts to implement a national anticrime campaign by its failure to act.

*At United Press International conference, Hamilton, Bermuda, Oct. 6.*

I believe that the pretrial release of potentially dangerous defendants constitutes one of the most serious factors in the present crime rate.

*Before House Judiciary Subcommittee, Washington, Oct. 21.*

Organized crime can only exist when it can do business with the government. I am very unhappy to report that most organized crime syndicates are protected by state and local governments at one level or another.

*Before International Bankers Association, Boca Raton, Fla., Dec. 10.*

Organized crime cannot exist without a measure of public corruption. I believe that such corruption among police and public officials could be routed out quickly if cities and police departments would begin cleaning house today. Find the corrupt officials, and then prosecute them and send them to prison.

> *At Republican Governors Conference,*
> *Hot Springs, Ark., Dec. 13.*

Even when we convict prominent members of organized crime syndicates, they can be replaced temporarily. When they finish what may be a short prison term, they return to control their business enterprises. However, if we can levy treble damages against their trucking firms, if we can seize their restaurants, if we can find their real estate operations, we can strike a critical blow at organized crime's business operations.

> *Pub. Dec. 16.*

## Richard M. Nixon
*President of the United States*

As far as this Administration is concerned, our attitude toward electronic surveillance is that it should be used very sparingly, very carefully—having in mind the rights of those who might be involved —but very effectively, to protect the internal and external security of the United States.

> *News conference, Washington, June 19.*

## Claude Pepper
*United States Representative, D-Fla.*

Our nation has no national or sensible program for corrections and rehabilitation. Our correctional programs are largely a relic of another age. They just do not correct. We have been told by many experts that youthful offenders would be better off—and so would society—if they were never caught. It is an abomination that a society that consecrates human values could permit the sordid and inhuman practices that take place in some of these institutions.

> *Pub. Sept. 4.*

## Peter J. Pitchess
*Sheriff, Los Angeles County*

I'm not about to warn you that organized crime may move in. They are already here. They have established a strong foothold, and, if that doesn't shock you, it should. We must recognize that a vehicle presently exists that is bringing big crime to our area and enabling these criminals to establish themselves. We must accept the fact that Los Angeles is the smut and pornography capital of the world, and that the right conditions exist for organized crime.

> *At meeting of Western Insurance*
> *Information Service, Los Angeles,*
> *Dec. 16.*

## Mario A. Procaccino
*Controller, and candidate for*
*Mayor of New York*

It is claimed there are about 5,000 members of the Mafia in these United States, 5,000 punks or bums or whatever you want to call them who have besmirched the reputations of millions of decent, honest, hard-working Italian-Americans. I will fight them, I will beat them and put them behind bars.

> *News conference, New York, Oct. 16.*

## Joseph E. Ragen
*Former Warden,*
*Illinois State Penitentiary*

Reform schools are not the place to raise good citizens. What a kid doesn't know about crime when he enters a reform school, he learns from others who are there. If you follow the records of prisoners at Joliet (Illinois State Penitentiary), you'll find that most of them started at the reform school.

> *Interview, pub. Aug. 11.*

## Ronald Reagan
*Governor of California*

In 1900, ninety per cent of the people in the United States lived in poverty, but today just over 11 per cent of the residents are poverty-stricken, while crime has risen out of all proportions.

> *Newport Beach, Calif., pub. Feb. 15.*

## Frank L. Rizzo
*Police Commissioner of Philadelphia*

I want a force of professionals. Real professionals. Law enforcement is no job for amateurs.

> *Pub. Feb. 18.*

**Charles H. Rogovin**
*Administrator, Law Enforcement
Assistance Administration of the
United States*

One of the best hopes of reducing crime is to reduce the number of crime repeaters. The first step toward that goal is to develop correctional procedures that really do correct.

*Before Correctional Council of
Delaware; Wilmington, pub. May 27.*

. . . We should look closely at the recent ambush slayings of policemen in Detroit and Cleveland by groups of heavily armed men. We should ask ourselves if that kind of thing is going to be common five years from now, as civil disorders and campus disorders are today. If we have even the slightest inkling that it may be, the time to plan prevention and control is now—not five years from now when a kind of guerilla war has exploded in our midst and scores, or hundreds, of persons have been killed.

*At Southern Regional Conference,
National Council on Crime and
Delinquency, New Orleans, June 4.*

The criminal-justice system is in serious trouble . . . the American people will not tolerate failure. If local law enforcement fails, then something else will replace it. A pattern has emerged that, when State and local governments do not respond, the Federal Government does. I do not raise the specter of a federal police force merely to frighten . . . Look at the organized-crime field. We now see a substantial federal effort there—and not simply because organized crime is interstate in nature. It is also because local enforcement has failed to do its job . . .

*Before International Association of
Chiefs of Police, Miami Beach, Oct. 1.*

The policeman can protect lives, save lives, help untwist twisted lives, help bring sanity out of chaos. His actions can permit the young to flower. He operates in most areas as the only around-the-clock service agency. He can help bring justice to the oppressed. Reforms occurring in police work are being triggered in large part by bright, capable men—most of them college graduates—now rising into middle and upper-command levels. They entered police work to change it, reform it, make it better. College students should flock to join their ranks.

*University of Arizona,
Tucson, pub. Dec. 22.*

**Stephen H. Sachs**
*United States Attorney for Maryland*

I'm afraid that corruption everywhere is more widespread than most people, including the news media, like to admit. Somebody once said that, if we could stop kickbacks and payoffs in this country, we could cure inflation. That may overstate the case to make the point, but I think there's more than a grain of truth to it.

*Pub. Dec. 7.*

**Allan Shivers**
*Former President, Chamber of
Commerce of the United States*

To ignore the danger of organized crime to legitimate business is to deny reality. Racketeers have exploited manufacturing, wholesaling, retailing, banking, trade associations and transportation enterprises, among others.

*Pub. August.*

**Sirhan Bishara Sirhan**
*Accused Assassin of
Senator Robert F. Kennedy*

I killed Robert F. Kennedy willfully, premeditatedly, and with 20 years of malice aforethought.

*Testimony at his trial, Los Angeles,
Feb. 28.*

**Johannes F. Spreen**
*Police Commissioner of Detroit*

The police in America are in trouble. Most people today just don't like them.

*Pub. March 24.*

**John Stennis**
*United States Senator, D-Miss.*

It is the certainty of punishment—*the*

*certainty of punishment*—which restrains people in a large degree from crime.
*Washington, June 9.*

**Charles S. Stenvig**
*Mayor of Minneapolis*

It's going to take public officials with backbone instead of weak spines to let the police do the job they were hired to do, and that's enforcing the law for everyone.
*Minneapolis, pub. Dec. 7.*

**Donald F. Taylor**
*Chairman, advisory panel on crime, Chamber of Commerce of the United States*

For too long, too many leaders of organized crime—identified as such by our law enforcement agencies—have been able to conduct their operations. The increasing use of legitimate businesses by such people . . . is a serious problem in the nation and to legitimate businessmen who cannot compete against businesses financed through the vast receipts from unlawful activities, such as illegal gambling and sale of narcotics.
*Pub. August.*

**Jesse M. Unruh**
*California State Assemblyman*

To close out the career of Robert Francis Kennedy (late United States Senator) by exacting the life of another human being (Sirhan Bishara Sirhan)—sane or insane, mad killer or demented exhibitionist—is not the last chapter that ought to be written in the brilliant public record of a gentle man who bore hate for no man, woman or child and who sought instead to eliminate violence and suffering from American society.
*Sacramento, April 24.*

**Robert F. Wagner**
*Former Mayor of New York*

Every experienced law enforcement officer, every knowledgeable social worker, every doctor and minister acknowledges that, after poverty, narcotics addiction is the second greatest source of crime. Students I've seen suggest that half the serious crimes stem from addicts' need

for money for a "fix." Any long-run attack on crime must deal with these aspects.
*New York, June 12.*

**Jerry V. Wilson**
*Chief of Police, Washington, D.C.*

The problem is we don't have swift justice. Chief Justice Burger has said that many people will be deterred from serious crime if they believe that justice is swift and sure. Nobody believes that now—and they are right . . . We need treating of the whole justice system.
*Washington, Oct. 9.*

**Joseph I. Wood**
*Sheriff, Cook County, Illinois*

You can't baby those who want to riot. They must know that you will face force with force. There is only one way to control a mob—through fear.
*Chicago, pub. March 31.*

**Stanley F. Yolles**
*Director, National Institute of Mental Health*

I know of no clearer instance in which the punishment for an infraction of the law (possession of marijuana) is more harmful than the crime.
*Before Senate Subcommittee on Juvenile Delinquency, Washington, pub. Oct. 19.*

**Samuel W. Yorty**
*Mayor of Los Angeles*

I think the proper answer (to the drug problem) is to hit the source and the distributor. If one is sincere about not giving youthful experimenters police records which might adversely affect their lives in later years, then, as a first priority, let's keep marijuana and drugs out of their hands to begin with . . .
*Before Senate Subcommittee on Juvenile Delinquency, Washington, Sept. 25.*

**Evelle J. Younger**
*District Attorney, Los Angeles County*

We've got to realize that the only difference between a student who assaults a professor or a group who burns a building

(EVELLE J. YOUNGER)

or a young man who assassinates a senator of the United States is a difference of degree.

*Los Angeles, Sept. 3.*

We must insist that everyone, whatever his color, whatever his religion, no matter that he may have been the victim of prejudice or discrimination, notwithstanding the fact that our great-great-great-great grandparents may have been cruel to their great-great-great-great grandparents, obey the law. We must say, "We are sorry, and we are going to try to solve some of our problems." But, while we do, everyone—man, woman and child, black, brown, yellow or white—is going to follow the rules. And, where there is a violation, we will move promptly and vigorously to apprehend and prosecute the persons who commit the violation.

*Los Angeles, Oct. 21.*

**Spiro T. Agnew**
*Vice President of the United States*

Education is being redefined at the demand of the uneducated to suit the ideas of the uneducated. The student now goes to college to proclaim rather than to learn. The lessons of the past are ignored and obliterated in a contemporary antagonism known as the generation gap.
*At Republican fund-raising dinner,
New Orleans, Oct. 19.*

If we are not going to have revolution within our educational community, we will be wise to take a revolutionary look at our institutions of education. We should not be reluctant to ask daring questions or consider bold solutions.
*Baltimore, Dec. 10.*

**Henry D. Aiken**
*Professor of Philosophy,
Brandeis University*

The various groups in a university are alienated because they don't know what the others are doing. Their "knowledge" is all bookish.

*Interview, Waltham, Mass., pub. Jan. 28.*

**James E. Allen, Jr.**
*Commissioner of Education of
the United States*

The states simply must play their part in the renaissance of education. They must release the power for innovation, an accomplishment that's bottled up in local communities . . . We have built a middle-class type of education taught by middle-class teachers and run by middle-class administrators for middle-class kids. But rarely have we provided the type of teaching that a deprived child really needs.
*Pub. Feb. 14.*

I think we ought to begin to think in terms of how we can help colleges and universities achieve changes in curricula; how they can handle legitimate student protests and legitimate requests from students for change. We should also seek to bring about those changes which are so long overdue . . . We could accomplish far more this way than we could through any kind of punitive, negative legislation.

The inner city public school, as it operates today, unfortunately succeeds in satisfying almost nobody. Teachers don't like it because it's a tough place to teach. Children don't like it because the environment is too regimented and the curriculum is largely irrelevant. Parents don't like it because their children don't learn.
*Interview, Washington, pub. May 28.*

A great part of our educational system . . . seems to give both young people and society a feeling that the schools are really preparing students for the world of the past more than for the world of the future. So I think we need changes in programs as well as in techniques in many school systems . . . It is important for all communities to experiment, to evaluate their schools in terms of the quality and the relevance of their efforts.
*Interview, Washington, pub. June 30.*

This (teaching Johnny to read) is education's "moon"—the target for the decade ahead. With the same zeal, dedication, perseverance and concentration that made possible man's giant step of last

(JAMES E. ALLEN, JR.)

July 20th, this moon, too, can be reached.
*Before National Association of State
Boards of Education,
Los Angeles, Sept. 23.*

The students ought to have a major role (in campus decisions). They ought to participate in making educational policy—after all, they are the consumers.
*News conference,
San Francisco, Sept. 24.*

**Richard Armour**
*Author, Humorist*

Trustees are men of trust, often heads of trust companies. They are wealthy, often tend to be men of affairs, sit on lots of boards and are much too busy to look into inconsequential matters such as the competence of teaching and relevance of the curriculum. A trustee's viewpoint is usually as different from a student's as possible, which some educators think makes for balance and others for trouble.
*Interview, pub. Dec. 21.*

**Samuel Fisher Babbitt**
*President, Kirkland College,
Clinton, N.Y.*

The . . . cry for consistency, which manifests itself in undergraduate complaints about the ways in which universities invest their funds and the direction in which faculty expend their research energies, has a strong and penetrating logic to it. Interestingly enough, our undergraduates would be satisfied with either of two actions on the part of the major universities. Either we should make our policies consistent with our ideals, or we should readjust our statement of ideals to be more in line with our policies.
*Kirkland College, pub. Sept. 5.*

**Stringfellow Barr**
*Educator*

The university professor has turned go-getter. His booty includes a fat salary from a business firm, eager to wear that professional look, or a juicy fee as consultant, or a federal grant big enough to support him and a staff of assistants. In the last case, our professor is in a position to squeeze the president for promotions and other favors by threatening to move himself and his staff to some other campus.
*Pub. July 21.*

**Jacques Barzun**
*Professor of History,
Columbia University*

If a student is, in fact, capable of framing curricula, he should be given a diploma, not a voice, because he will know everything necessary for earning that diploma.
*Before House Special Subcommittee
on Education, Washington, May 9.*

**Daniel Bell**
*Professor of Sociology,
Columbia University*

The husbanding of talent and the spread of educational and intellectual institutions will become a prime concern for the entire society; not only the best talents, but eventually the entire complex of social prestige and social status, will be rooted in the intellectual and scientific communities.
*Pub. July 21.*

**Bruno Bettelheim**
*Professor of Psychology and
Psychiatry, University of Chicago*

In my opinion, there are, today, far too many students in the colleges who essentially have no business to be there. Some are there to evade the (military) draft, many others out of a vague idea that it will help them to find better jobs, though they do not know what jobs they want. And again, many go to college because they do not know what better to do and because it is expected of them.
*Before House Special Subcommittee
on Education, Washington, May 9.*

**Hugo L. Black**
*Associate Justice, Supreme Court
of the United States*

I have always had the idea that the schools were to educate children and not children to educate teachers.
*Washington, Feb. 24.*

**Daniel J. Boorstin**
*Professor of American History,*
*University of Chicago*

In the university, all men are *not* equal. Those better endowed or better equipped intellectually must be preferred in admission and preferred in recognition . . . If we give in to the armed demands of militants to admit persons to university because of their race, their poverty, their illiteracy, or any other non-intellectual distinctions, our universities can no longer serve all of us—or any of us. If any ill-informed person can receive the imprimatur of the university because a bomb will explode if he does not, the university has begun to cease to be a university.
*University of Tulsa, June 1.*

**Kingman Brewster, Jr.**
*President, Yale University*

. . . it is . . . demonstratable that, to the average student, the purpose of university life is learning and living, not governing. The long and unimpressive history of "sandbox" student government is fair warning that student politics, like the politics of professional associations, cannot be counted on always to draw out the most talented members of the constituency or to capture the attention and concern, day in and day out, of the eligible voters.
*Yale University, Sept. 24.*

**Andrew F. Brimmer**
*Member, Federal Reserve Board*

. . . I think it would be a tragic mistake for Negro students to waste their college years languishing in "black studies" and similar sheltered workshops which do little or nothing to prepare them to meet the vigorous competition for employment opportunities in the post-college world. After all, it should be obvious to Negro students that, while some of them are gaining a measure of heightened pride through enrollment in "black studies," the vast majority of both black and white students are devoting themselves to the attainment of enough expertise in some area of specialization to allow them to compete at least for beginning professional jobs once they leave college. So, rather than supporting the rise of a new cult of incompetence—which "black studies" can only assure—the academic community (including faculty and students, both black and white) should get on with meeting the real challenge of education today: The preparation of disadvantaged young people to take their place in an open and integrated society.
*At convention of Phi Epsilon Pi Fraternity, Miami Beach, Aug. 28.*

**Jerome S. Bruner**
*Professor of Psychology,*
*Harvard University*

In case we forget, this generation is reacting to an enormous technological and social revolution. The best we can do is help them shape a new order. That takes experiment, not minority seizures and . . . local Ronald Reagans. Give the students and their teachers a chance.
*Interview, Cambridge, Mass., April 24.*

**Al Capp**
*Cartoonist*

Today, at Harvard, any student with the currently fashionable color of skin is given rights denied to students of the currently unfashionable color. Harvard, which educated the President who brought America into the war that defeated fascism, today honors and encourages and rewards its fascists. Harvard, which once turned out scholars and gentlemen, now turns out thugs and thieves—or let me put it this way: now, if you are a thug or a thief, Harvard won't turn you out.
*Franklin Pierce College, Rindge, N.H., April 27.*

**Malcolm Carron**
*President, University of Detroit*

I think we're going to see quite a change in the corporate nature of the university. Tradition has dictated that boards be external. It was an unwritten rule that faculty and students were excluded. Students are asking why they can't have representation on the controlling body, the one with the legal power. When you think about it, there aren't any good reasons why not.
*Pub. June 16.*

**James E. Cheek**
*President, Shaw University of
North Carolina; president-designate
of Howard University, Washington, D.C.*

There shouldn't be a distinction between students and faculty. They're senior scholars and junior scholars. I say here that our students don't come to Shaw to get an education—they come here to participate in an education.

*Television interview,
Washington, June 12.*

**Kenneth B. Clark**
*Professor of Psychology,
University of Rochester*

I think that the people who propose special education, special this, special that, for minority group children are violating the law of parsimony. When *equal* conditions are established and it is found that the children do not respond, then, and only then, are we justified in looking for special methods, special techniques.

*Interview, pub. Dec. 26.*

**Jeffery Cohelan**
*United States Representative, D-Calif.*

We are mightily concerned about losing the arms race but we are apparently contented to lose the education race. We won the moon race, but will we win the education race? We will not prevail as an independent, free and just society if we are ignorant and uneducated. Education costs money.

*Before the House,
Washington, pub. Aug. 3.*

**Dale R. Corson**
*President, Cornell University*

To destroy the universities is the surest and quickest way to destroy mankind.

*Before Constituent Assembly,
Cornell University, Sept. 14.*

**Thomas J. Cottle**
*Assistant Professor of Social Relations,
Harvard University*

I don't think universities survive in anywhere near a productive way if they don't realize the tremendous responsibilities of their activities or their inactivities, and I feel very grateful that students of any political predisposition would forcibly present these issues to the point of their being acted upon. I don't think that Harvard has reacted sufficiently to the content of the demands, and I hope that more than promises are being made and more than good faith is being offered.

*Interview, Cambridge, Mass., April 24.*

**Clarence H. Cramer**
*Dean, Adelbert College,
Case Western Reserve University*

The authority of the university is intellectual and moral, not physical. This is because a university's basic commitment is to truth and to the mind rather than the fist—and no exercise of force can extract an ounce of truth from a university.

*Cleveland, pub. Feb. 25.*

**Robert D. Cross**
*President, Hunter College
of New York*

The (college) president's job is getting a little impossible in most places, but I don't go much for the crocodile tears about it. College presidents are getting paid pretty good salaries on the whole, and nobody's forcing them to do it. I get a little tired of the weeping and gnashing of teeth.

*Pub. June 15.*

**Charles DeCarlo**
*President, Sarah Lawrence College*

When asked why, in an age of bureaucratic largeness, I come to a small college; why, in an age of increasing public assumption of responsibility, I come to a private college; why, in an age dominated by science and technology, I come to a liberal arts college—and why, in an age when the traditional role of women is changing, I come to a *woman's* college—I answer: "Because to be small, to be private, to be engaged in the liberal arts, and to be grown from women, is to be possessed by qualities dear and urgently needed."

*New York, Nov. 19.*

**Karl W. Deutsch**
*Professor of Political Science,
Harvard University*

I agree . . . that the grading system

should not be so restrictive as to be stifling. Students should be evaluated in more than one dimension. Some work better at a leisurely pace and might say, "I'm a fuddy-duddy like Einstein," and others seem to work better under pressure, like McGeorge Bundy. The system ought to recognize the value of both.

*New York, pub. Sept. 3.*

**John Doar**
*President, Board of Education,*
*City of New York*

The first principle of government is to maintain order. If you can't maintain order in the schools, then we're not going to have schools.

*Television interview, New York, March 9.*

**Dan W. Dodson**
*Professor of Education,*
*New York University*

Public education is perhaps the chief instrumentality through which a society seeks to perpetuate and extend its goals and objectives. Said another way, the public schools are a handmaiden of the established power arrangement of the society, whose responsibility is the socialization of the youth into the myths, rituals and ideologies of the dominant society.

*Teachers College, New York, July 8.*

**Roger O. Egeberg**
*Assistant Secretary for Health and*
*Scientific Affairs, Department of*
*Health, Education and Welfare*
*of the United States*

A dean is supposed to be to the faculty, students and administration what a fire hydrant is to a dog.

*Interview, Washington, pub. Dec. 14.*

**Paul Ehrlich**
*Professor of Biology,*
*Stanford University*

Universities, because they are relatively free, are also relatively fragile. Society, through the mindless right on the outside, and the defiant, know-nothing left on the inside, can easily destroy the university. If that occurs, homo sapiens will have blown his last slim chance of survival.

*Stanford University, April 22.*

**Lloyd H. Elliott**
*President, George Washington*
*University, Washington*

We are peddling academic snake oil . . . The implication is that exposure to the liberal arts will somehow transform a student into a contemporary Renaissance man. The plain fact is that universities change students very little.

*Before Middle Atlantic Association of*
*Colleges of Business Administration,*
*Washington, Oct. 16.*

**Alvin C. Eurich**
*President, Academy for*
*Educational Development*

The greatest gap in education has always been between theory and practice, between what we claim to be doing for young people and what we actually are doing. Educators tend to be bold in thought and timid in action. All too often educators have built grand theories while the schools and colleges stayed in their comfortable ruts.

*Pub. Sept. 1.*

**Robert H. Finch**
*Secretary of Health, Education and*
*Welfare of the United States*

They are still teaching children on the basis we were taught 30 years ago. And the child today who comes into kindergarten has had from 3,000 to 4,000 hours sitting in front of that television tube absorbing more unstructured data than we had when we came in. That takes the child clear past "Dick and Jan," and the system doesn't respond to that.

*Television interview, Washington, Feb. 2.*

As important as job training is, a job is simply not enough . . . We must be concerned with career education for the young and continuing education for those presently employed.

*Pub. November.*

**John H. Fischer**
*President, Teachers College, New York*

Much of the trouble that we're experiencing in schools today is because the "establishment," which I'd say is necessary, is too ingrown. The people who are

(JOHN H. FISCHER)

running the schools too often have nothing but schools. They haven't enough experience with other agencies to sense the kinds of relationships that have to be developed between schools and other agencies, because schools can no longer be isolated in the way that we once thought was proper.

*Pub. April 28.*

For the young person who would make the most of himself and of his place in society, no less than for the nation as a matter of public policy, higher education must be recognized as a universal necessity. The transition to such a view will be neither easy nor simple. It happens, however, to be imperative, and in one way or another we shall have to manage the changes in (the) personal attitude and institutional policy that it requires.

*New York, pub. June 20.*

### Houston I. Flournoy
*Controller of California*

How will a degree in black studies help the black man help his race? With all the needs . . . easily documented, for black doctors, lawyers, businessmen and so forth, does the production of black graduates with degrees in black studies rate a first priority?

*University of Southern California, April 15.*

One of the most critical aspects of the current challenge to quality higher education is the all-too-common notion among faculty members and students that the "public" as such should keep its nose out of their business. They too frequently ignore that we are talking about *public* quality higher education. By definition, the public *is* involved, and, furthermore, whether the public should interfere or not, they are involved if for no more than the prosaic reason that they are being asked to pay the bill.

*Stanislaus State College, pub. Oct. 24.*

### William T. R. Fox
*Professor of International Relations,*
*Columbia University*

I've always felt that ever since the time of Sputnik, and also when colleges began to get crowded, our undergraduates have been pressed to jump over higher and higher hurdles. A good deal of the discontent about so-called irrelevant teaching and meaningless requirements is a product of an emotional fatigue from continuous competition.

*Pub. June 16.*

### John Hope Franklin
*Professor of American History,*
*University of Chicago*

It takes a person of stout heart, great courage and uncompromising honesty to look the history of this country squarely in the face and tell it like it is . . . And when this approach prevails, the history of the United States and the history of the black man can be written and taught by any person, white, black, or otherwise. For there is nothing so irrelevant in telling the truth as the color of a man's skin.

*New School for Social Research,*
*New York, pub. Sept. 29.*

### Arthur W. Galston
*Professor of Biology, Yale University*

R.O.T.C. is like singing in the Whiffenpoofs—a perfectly fine activity, but one we don't think merits any academic standing.

*Pub. Feb. 2.*

### John W. Gardner
*Chairman, Urban Coalition*

The universities have not, on the whole, been receiving the loving care that they may need very much at this perilous moment in their history, and I count myself as guilty as others on that score. Faculty members have all too often regarded the universities as little more than convenient stepping-stones or bases in an active career. Students have too often treated the university as a scapegoat for the problems of society, as an available target for the anger that is in them. People such as myself, who are interested in solving social problems, have urged the universities to run in all directions at once to cope with the issues of the day.

*Stanford University,*
*Palo Alto, Calif., pub. July 6.*

**Edmund J. Gleazer, Jr.**
*Executive Director, American*
*Association of Junior Colleges*

The major assignment of the community junior college is to *extend* educational opportunity. We now have two million students in our system. You wonder what would have happened to them without community colleges . . . It's the aim of the community college to keep open the student's educational options as long as possible.

*Pub. May 5.*

**Armand Golang**
*Director of Social Studies,*
*Seattle School District*

We have to look at it qualitatively. What we need to do is incorporate black history into regular American history. To kids who demand separate Afro-American courses I say: "You are at 9 AM yesterday, when it is 4 PM today."

*Pub. Feb. 9.*

**Simeon Golar**
*Human Rights Commissioner,*
*City of New York*

We need to bring in more black teachers. But we can't bring them in at the expense of the white teachers. Happily, we don't have to. The truth is, we can't get enough teachers, white or black . . .

*Radio interview, New York, March 9.*

**Samuel B. Gould**
*Chancellor, State University of New York*

If our students regard as the truth that the university is intolerant, establishmentarian and even illegal in its forms of governance, there is just as much truth in realizing that, among all social institutions today, it allows more dissent, takes freedom of mind and spirit more seriously, and, under considerable sufferance, labors to create a more ideal environment for free expression and for the free interchange of ideas and emotions than does any other institution anywhere.

*Colgate University, pub. Sept. 23.*

**Clifford P. Hannum**
*Brig. Gen., United State Army;*
*Deputy Director, R.O.T.C.*

I think some of the professors who at-tack the Reserve Officers Training Corps in the name of academic freedom should stop to think that they are attacking an institution which is helping to preserve a general freedom within which academic freedom exists.

*Pub. July 6.*

**Billy James Hargis**
*Evangelist, The Christian Crusade*

I don't want any kids under 12 to hear about lesbians, homosexuals and sexual intercourse. They should be concerned with tops, yo-yos and hide-and-seek.

*Boston, pub. Sept. 14.*

**John D. Harper**
*President, Aluminum Company*
*of America*

A whole carload of urban problems has blown up in our faces, because most of us honestly didn't detect them in time. I am suggesting that the detached observers of the academic world might well develop some form of early-warning system that could alert us to such problems before they reached the point of crisis. It would seem to me that the academic community is the agency of our society best suited to develop a "social inventory" of America, getting into corners of our national life where the light is none too good and the housecleaning infrequent.

*Washington, pub. Sept. 8.*

**J. George Harrar**
*President, Rockefeller Foundation*

I'm bearish on the impact of big enrollments on the final quality of Americans intellectually. The big growth in education may make more people more tolerant, or even more respectful toward learning. But it won't necessarily make them better educated.

*Pub. July 21.*

**S. I. Hayakawa**
*Acting President,*
*San Francisco State College*

. . . literary intellectuals all take a big, big pride in being alienated from the culture. They pass on this sense of alienation to their students and therefore, if you want to spit in the eye of the establishment,

you are praised for it, you are encouraged for it, and you are told you're a bright boy.
*Television interview, Washington, Feb. 2.*

In all too many high schools, students believed to be low in academic talent are shunted into "vocation" courses, as if the brighter students were never going to have to work. Such a distinction is arbitrary and invidious. I sometimes suspect that schools exist not so much to educate the young as to keep them off the labor market.
*Columbia University, pub. Dec. 21.*

### Ray L. Heffner
*President, Brown University*

The university must not be aloof from the most pressing problems of our time. And yet the university cannot be so committed to transforming society along definite lines that it loses its function as objective analyst and critic of society.
*Pub. April 18.*

. . . if there is tension in society, it is going to be maximized in the university. If there is generation tension, it is going to be maximized in the university. If all this is true, then tension is going to be greatest in the office of the president.
*Resignation address, Providence, R.I., May 9.*

### James M. Hester
*President, New York University*

In our efforts to serve increasing numbers of students, we have in this country and abroad allowed the educational experience to suffer the same depersonalization that depresses the entire society. If universities seek to set standards for civilization, they should strive to rid themselves of practices that frustrate and discourage individuality.
*New York, June 11.*

### Roger W. Heyns
*Chancellor, University of California at Berkeley*

I believe one of the most important functions universities have today is to show that democratic institutions can change to meet legitimate social needs. It is crucial to the future of our nation that our young people know that they can work within the system to make it more responsive.
*Before Comstock Club, Sacramento, April 14.*

The greatest skepticism among young people today has to do with the ability of our institutions to change. We can't ask people, as we so often do, to work inside the system if the system doesn't change.
*Pub. June 23.*

### Charles J. Hitch
*President, University of California*

If a regent expresses concern about the appointment of an individual on the grounds that he believes the candidate will use his faculty position to indoctrinate and propagandize, the faculty reaction may be that a political test is being applied. The chancellors and I are firmly committed to the preservation of the university as a free institution open to the expression of all views, right or wrong, heretical and conformist, sensible and ridiculous. This commitment demands that we resist all efforts to interfere with the integrity of the process by which we select and promote members of the faculty.
*Pub. Oct. 9.*

### Sidney Hook
*Professor of Philosophy, New York University*

Recent events on American campuses have precipitated a genuine crisis in higher education. Because of events at Harvard, Cornell and other institutions, it is no exaggeration to say that American higher education is confronted with the most fundamental challenge to its basic principles in history. And by its basic principles, here, I mean the principles of academic freedom. After all, the demand on the part of students to determine not only the nature of the curriculum but who is to teach them, and who is to be hired and fired, implies an abandonment of the traditions of academic freedom.
*Interview, pub. May 19.*

**Ralph G. Hough**
*Director of Admissions,*
*Shimer College, Mt. Carroll, Ill.*

While colleges and universities provide extensive counseling and advisory facilities, it is up to the student to make use of them. Most colleges refuse to play the role of parent, and few, if any, schools will spend much time running after a student who needs advice.
*Mt. Carroll, pub. Feb. 9.*

**Roger Howell, Jr.**
*President, Bowling Green College*

College administrators are being boxed in—by students, by faculties, by governing boards and by public opinion—to the point at which they can no longer function effectively . . . There will come a time when the supply of able academics, willing to risk heartache and personal abuse for the sake of education at large, will diminish to the vanishing point.
*Brunswick, Me., May 15.*

**Hubert H. Humphrey**
*Former Vice President*
*of the United States*

I can remember when the academic life was a meadow of meditation in an island of tranquility. Now, the president and faculty get combat pay.
*University of Minnesota, Feb. 26.*

**Arthur R. Jensen**
*Professor of Educational Psychology,*
*University of California at Berkeley*

As long as people assume there are no differences between the races, then we are not going to understand them and give children the education they need. It's sort of like assuming everybody's digestive system is the same and will thrive on the same diet.
*Telephone interview, pub. March 30.*

**Howard W. Johnson**
*President, Massachusetts Institute*
*of Technology*

Of all the institutions in our society, the university is most nearly defenseless. It has to be. The university exists so that there may be somewhere a place for the courageous and direct confrontation of ideas. The free flow of ideas cannot take place in an atmosphere of physical confrontation. An open mind cannot long exist in the face of force or threat.
*Cambridge, Mass., Nov. 3.*

**Sanford H. Kadish**
*Professor of Law,*
*University of California at Berkeley*

Just as physicians don't want their standards set by patients, the faculty doesn't want its standards defined by students.
*Pub. Feb. 24.*

**Edgar F. Kaiser**
*Chairman, Kaiser Industries Corporation*

To combat the growing mood of anti-intellectualism, education needs the support of business. Business must be ready to give financial support to education; but giving money alone is not enough. Universities must understand that business backs them.
*New York, pub. Nov. 9.*

**William Loren Katz**
*Author, Editor, Consultant on Education*

If I were a high-school principal or college dean, and students came to me with a demand for any legitimate body of knowledge, I would find it hard to turn them down. After all, the biggest problem that teachers generally face is student apathy. If they're already fired up with a hunger for knowledge, I'd be inclined to give three cheers and to make it available.
*Interview, pub. July.*

**William Rea Keast**
*President, Wayne State University*

Many students would like to ask "Why?" of us, and I don't see why not. Students could probably question matters such as admissions policy, curriculum, academic tenure, academic freedom and "why a president and why a vice president?" If they got good answers, they would see the point. If the answers were bad, we would see the point.
*Pub. June 16.*

**Martin Kilson**
*Professor of Government,*
*Harvard University*

Quite frankly, I don't believe it is the proper or most useful function for a university to train ideological or political organizers of whatever persuasion. A university's primary function is to impart skills, techniques and special habits of learning to its students. The student must be free to decide himself on the ideological application of his training.

*At Convention of National Association*
*for the Advancement of Colored*
*People, Jackson, Miss., July 2.*

**John J. Kirvan**
*Former Chaplain,*
*Wayne State University*

. . . there is so much more awareness and experience outside the classroom that school is dull, dull, dull. Let's face it— the educational system is one big bore.
*Interview, Detroit, pub. Feb. 10.*

**Douglas M. Knight**
*President, Duke University*

The way things are today, a (university) president can't be liked by everybody. It is like sitting on top of an elephant. You can do nothing, and balance there. But if you want to go forward, you are going to run into irreconcilable forces that will eventually knock you off.
*Pub. April 7.*

**Warren P. Knowles**
*Governor of Wisconsin*

Education is the very cornerstone of all social and economic growth. It is the passport of each individual to his individual success. And it is the only hope we have for preserving and protecting our system of democracy.
*Interview, pub. March 3.*

**James D. Koerner**
*Educator*

The real trouble with teachers' salaries, when it comes to attracting talented individuals, is the single salary scale—the fact that most teachers, good or bad, are paid exactly alike, according to their time in the profession . . . When a really first-rate teacher can command whatever the market will pay for his talents, as in any other profession, teaching will attract many more of the able young persons graduating from college.
*Interview, pub. Sept. 15.*

**William Kornhauser**
*Professor of Sociology,*
*University of California at Berkeley*

The faculty operates as a guild; it is primarily interested in protecting its own interests. Soon, the students will have to wage their battles against the faculty rather than the administration.
*Pub. Feb. 24.*

**William Kramer**
*Rabbi, and Instructor in*
*Cultural History,*
*Hebrew Union College of Los Angeles*

Sex education is going on in the home— and it's all bad. Sex, the most personal thing in the world, may somehow have to be taught impersonally, and thank goodness it is taught in the schools.
*Pasadena, Calif., pub. May 8.*

**Robert N. Kreidler**
*Executive vice president,*
*Alfred P. Sloan Foundation*

The gap in education between the best and the worst is growing. And there is something else new and important: Those at the bottom know it.
*Pub. Sept. 1.*

**Dan Kuykendall**
*United States Representative,*
*R-Tenn.*

If the federal government had a contract with a private concern to manufacture an item necessary to our national survival, and that concern stopped producing the items, the funds would stop immediately. Our colleges are producing the most essential product of the age—young people with sharpened minds. To me, it's simply a question of stopping federal funds when the school administrations allow the educational process to stop.
*Washington, April 15.*

**Sam Levenson**
*Writer, Humorist*

Look, how long does it take to understand human plumbing? You draw maps of it on the wall. But I think there are areas that should remain secret, about which children in the post-potty group should remain innocent. They don't need long lectures about sperms and eggs holding clandestine meetings in cellars.

*New York, pub. Nov. 30.*

**Edward H. Levi**
*President, University of Chicago*

Most of the truly learned men I know became learned late in life, but not all of them. The (educational) system should be open. A man ought to be able to leave it with honor at any time, with or without a degree, and to come back into it at any time. Further, it might be terribly important for a man to be able to change careers in the middle of his life; many of the finest achievements have resulted from such changes. We shouldn't tie him down until he is past 20 before he can even try one career.

*Chicago, pub. July 6.*

Universities must respond and change. Their greatness, if they have it in any measure, is not to be found in their ability to express a popular will. They are very much of the society, but they are also separate from it. They are in themselves places of criticism, discovery and dissent. They must often go it alone, just as the individual scholar must find his own way. They may not be the most important institutions in the world (but) if they lost their character, they have no importance at all.

*Chicago, Nov. 4.*

**John V. Lindsay**
*Mayor of New York*

The university that refuses to listen to its students, that ignores the feelings and rights of its neighbors, or that is too inflexible or remote to respond positively to a troubled and inconsistent world, is a university headed for severe trouble.

*Pittsburgh, Jan. 14.*

**Lester G. Maddox**
*Governor of Georgia*

It's totally ridiculous for government to tell private institutions what to teach and how to teach. That is like Russia. There should be no state standards for private education.

*Trenton, N.J., Oct. 25*

**Lewis B. Mayhew**
*Professor of Higher Education,*
*Stanford University*

College faculty members have generally been resistant to educational change and innovation because change threatens a style of life and interests faculty members have found congenial.

*Western Washington State College,*
*Bellingham, June 13.*

**John U. Monro**
*Director of Freshman Studies,*
*Miles College, Birmingham, Ala.*

It is idiotic, or worse, to talk about depending on Harvard or the University of Alabama to educate black children. The black community is here to stay, and I'm persuaded that the black colleges are, too.

*Interview, New York, pub. March 2.*

**Richard M. Nixon**
*President of the United States*

As far as our colleges and universities are concerned, I think that young people, students, are correct in asking that they have a voice; a voice in determining what the courses should be, a voice in determining what the rules should be. But then I say that while they should have a voice, under no circumstances should they be given control of the colleges and universities.

*Before Chamber of Commerce*
*of the United States,*
*Washington, April 29.*

Our colleges have their weaknesses. Some have become too impersonal, or too ingrown, and curricula have lagged. But with all its faults, the fact remains that the American system of higher education is the best in this whole imperfect

(RICHARD M. NIXON)

world—and it provides in the United States today a better education for more students of all economic levels than ever before, anywhere, in the history of the world. This is no small achievement.

Instead of seeking to raise lagging students up to meet the college standards, the cry now is to lower the standards to meet the students. This is the old, familiar, self-indulgent cry for the easy way. It debases the integrity of the educational process. There is no easy way to excellence, no short-cut to the truth, no magic wand that can produce a trained and disciplined mind without the hard discipline of learning. To yield to these demands would weaken the institution; more importantly, it would cheat the student of what he comes to a college for: his education.

*General Beadle State College,*
*Madison, S.D., June 3.*

**Allan W. Ostar**
*Executive Director,*
*American Association of State Colleges*

Trying to get good people has become a serious problem. Almost 10 per cent of the schools in our group are looking for new presidents. This is quite unusual at this time of year, so close to the new term. The disturbing thing is that many good people are saying, "Why should I stick my neck in the meat grinder?" Unfortunately, all of this comes at a time when colleges need leadership most.

*Pub. July 28.*

**Robert Powell**
*President, National Student Association*

Almost everyone—students and faculty —really thinks the educational system we have is rotten. My own view is that it is not good for anything but job accreditation because it really has nothing to do with education or with the issues that the country must face—racism, technology, wealth and leisure.

*Interview, Washington, Feb. 22.*

**Roman C. Pucinski**
*United States Representative, D-Ill.*

. . . the time has come to liberate vocational education from its subservient role as handmaiden to the rest of American public education. Widespread student dissatisfaction with the present-day curriculum attests to the growing meaninglessness of traditional education for the modern working world. It also points to the need for making career development the central theme of education in the seventies.

*Before the House, Washington, Oct. 15.*

**Nathan M. Pusey**
*President, Harvard University*

Each time we thoughtlessly or emotionally allow ourselves to chip away at the painfully erected structure of academic freedom for which time and time again in our role as leaders we have had to man the barricades, we not only do ourselves but our country an irreparable disservice.

*Cambridge, Mass., Feb. 18.*

**Max Rafferty**
*Superintendent of Public Instruction,*
*State of California*

If there's one thing which is guaranteed to raise my hackles instantaneously to a 45-degree angle, it's a teacher who deliberately panders to the worst in his students instead of trying his hardest to bring out the best in them . . . these prostitutes of my profession deserve to be drummed conspicuously out of education . . .

*Before Los Angeles Lions*
*"Host" Club, Sept. 5.*

**Ronald Reagan**
*Governor of California*

There are political tests in certain departments at state colleges now. If a man is not far enough left, he doesn't get hired. This is true if you have a leftist clique in the department. You almost never have a rightist clique.

*Bakersfield, Calif., April 11.*

Research, a vital and essential part of the (university) process, must not be the standard by which the university rates itself. Its function is to teach and its record must be established on the quality of graduates

it offers to the world—not on the collection of scholary names in the catalogue.
*Before Commonwealth Club,*
*San Francisco, pub. Aug. 4.*

**George B. Redfern**
*Associate Secretary, American*
*Association of School Administrators*

Some (school) administrators are becoming militant, too. They see the rise of teacher power as an erosion of their own authority.
*Interview, Atlantic City,*
*N.J., pub. Feb. 19.*

**James A. Rhodes**
*Governor of Ohio*

I'm here to defend the high school dropouts. They are really throwouts or kickouts. We are following a bankrupt system that concentrates almost entirely on college preparation and does nothing to train youngsters for vocational and technical jobs they would like to fill.
*At Midwestern Governor Conference,*
*Wichita, Kans., June 30.*

**Hyman G. Rickover**
*Vice Admiral, United States Navy;*
*director, Division of Naval Reactors,*
*Atomic Energy Commission of*
*the United States*

Today, a good deal of teaching in our universities is done by young graduate students working for their final degrees. The professors are often off campus, traveling from one place to another under Government contract, attending panel meetings, consulting, doing research in foreign countries—all at Government expense. It is not so very surprising that the students feel they are being shortchanged by their professors.
*Before Senate Foreign Relations*
*Committee, Washington, pub. June 2.*

**David Riesman**
*Professor of Social Sciences,*
*Harvard University*

The administration and trustees are scapegoats for the real seat of power— the faculty. Any university president who loses the support of his faculty is finished.
*Interview, pub. May 12.*

**Nelson A. Rockefeller**
*Governor of New York*

I had thought, when I took office in 1959, that we'd reach a level in excellence in education that would stabilize—some plateau we could settle on. But I found, as I went along, that as the rates of state school aid went up, the demands kept increasing, too. Excellence was only relative, it was related to increased money. I have finally come to the conclusion that there is no plateau visible ahead.
*Albany, N.Y., pub. Jan. 19.*

**George W. Romney**
*Secretary of Housing and Urban*
*Development of the United States*

I suggest we seriously consider whether it would not be more desirable to leave secular education to the state, with churches—all the churches—concentrating on expanding religious and moral instruction . . . Once we start down the road of state aid to private and parochial schools, it would only be a matter of time before they were getting as much aid as public schools.
*Detroit, Jan. 6.*

**Samuel Rubin**
*President, American*
*Symphony Orchestra League*

Why can't we have a cultural center in every small community, to take the place of the poolhalls and the jukeboxes? The schools must direct emphasis toward the performing arts. There is no reason why interest in poetry, music, the theatre cannot be developed, if teachers and schools are given new perspectives.
*Interview, New York, pub. Oct. 19.*

**Arthur M. Schlesinger, Jr.**
*Professor of Humanities,*
*City University of New York*

If the contemporary university sustains and staffs the great organizations, it also incites and nourishes the mutiny against organization . . . If some of the graduates become contented technicians, satisfied by the grey flannel suit, the key to the executive washroom and the retirement plan, others become ardent critics of the

(ARTHUR M. SCHLESINGER, JR.)

consumer society. As a result, the American university today is simultaneously a center of collaboration and a center of resistance.

*Rhode Island College, Providence,*
*pub. June 9.*

## David Selden
*President,*
*American Federation of Teachers*

As long as teachers are underpaid and overworked, school systems cannot be selective. There is a nationwide teacher shortage. If we really want good schools, we have to make up our minds that we have to pay good money to attract and retain good people.

*Washington, April 1.*

## Thaddeus Seymour
*President, Wabash College, Indiana*

This year there are seven million students on American campuses; one study conservatively predicts 14 million by 1985. Sheer force of numbers has produced an educational process which is more process than educational. At the same time, too much professional concern, what I can only call the "graduate school mentality," has promoted the concept of "publish or perish." It has been effective, creative classroom teaching which has perished in the process.

*Inaugural address, pub. Nov. 14.*

## Charles E. Shain
*President, Connecticut College*

. . . this shift away from women's colleges represents not a temporary situation but a growing conviction that, in this age, a young American's education, when it is shared with the opposite sex, is superior in its basic learning conditions to an education in a single-sex environment.

*Pub. Jan. 27.*

## Karl Shapiro
*Poet; Professor of Literature and*
*Writing, University of California at Davis*

(Students today) can no longer read, can no longer construct a simple English sentence, much less a paragraph, and cannot speak. We have the most inarticulate

generation of college students in history . . . (The bestsellers they buy) are universally trashy. Students don't want to read; they want to "experience." They don't want to learn; they want to "feel." They have become almost impossible to teach.

*Pub. Dec. 20.*

## Charles E. Silberman
*Member, Board of Editors,*
*"Fortune" Magazine*

. . . The public schools are quite literally destructive of human beings. I think they are the most grim, joyless places on the face of the earth. They are needlessly authoritarian and repressive—not because teachers and principals are stupid or venal, but because nobody ever asks why—why the rules or why the curriculum.

*Interview, pub. Jan. 26.*

## Kinsley Smith
*Former Professor of Psychology,*
*Pennsylvania State University*

There's too great a tendency today to look at someone who is argumentative and say he's bright. I haven't found students today to be any brighter or more inquisitive than those I taught 20 or 30 years ago. And there is no reason to expect that they should be. After all, the evolutionary process hasn't changed that much in 30 years, and that controls mental development in man.

*Interview, pub. Oct. 19.*

## Charles W. Socarides
*Psychiatrist, Albert Einstein*
*College of Medicine*

No aspect of life is untouched by the rich benefits and rewards of fulfilled sexuality, or, conversely, by the impoverishment and disability which emerges from disturbed sexuality. In doing away with sex education we may be throwing away untold benefits that will probably come from the programs, including a decrease in crime, violence, and lives blighted by sexual maladjustments.

*Pub. June 2.*

## Edward J. Speno
*New York State Senator, R-N.Y.C.*

Higher education presumes to establish

the foundation for a continuous process of learning that extends into business and professional life. Yet, higher education lags so far behind the business and professional world in ability to adapt to a changing environment. If higher education were a business, it would long since have gone bankrupt. If higher education were a governmental administration, it would soon be out of office. If higher education were a play trying to please an audience and critics, it would have closed. But higher education has enjoyed the luxury of not having to be accountable for its actions . . . or inactions . . . until now.

*At Niagara University Seminar,*
*Niagara, N.Y.; pub. July 14.*

**Elvis J. Stahr**
*President, Indiana University*

It's not like running out of gas—it's more like burning out your bearings. I'm not a deserter or a quitter. I've done my share: 27 years of working like a dog. It's impossible to be the president of a university—and a useful member of a family.

*Upon resigning his post,*
*pub. July 28.*

**David Tyack**
*Professor of Education,*
*University of Illinois*

. . . Education shouldn't be a punitive enterprise involving punishment for failure in terms of bad grades. Where did we ever get the idea that everyone has to be right the first time?

*Urbana, Ill., pub. Jan. 24.*

**Durward B. Varner**
*Chancellor, Michigan State University*
*at Oakland*

There is an important area of concern that students have identified—how is university policy to be determined? I believe they have a genuine right to have their voices heard in the determination of that policy. It's their education we're talking about.

*Oakland, Mich., pub. June 16.*

**Irving Wallace**
*Author*

Our schools really have little to do with the world today. Schools teach a little math, a little of this and that, but the world has jumped ahead. History should be taught the way it is, politics the way it is . . . a writing course today would never prepare a student to be a writer.

*Interview, Los Angeles, pub. March 16.*

**Lionel Wiggam**
*Poet*

. . . To be cultivated is not to be educated. Many illiterates have college degrees; many cultivated people do not. Any fool with a photographic memory can get through college today . . .

*Los Angeles, pub. May 21.*

**Roy Wilkins**
*Executive Director,*
*National Association for the*
*Advancement of Colored People*

If students want to study about their ancestors, they should study them on the side and concentrate in school on algebra, calculus, jets and the great world of communications. If this is to be a black world, as the militants would like, black people better learn to run computers, how to levy tariffs and have a better knowledge of the world. It's not how a black man wears his hair, but what he has inside his head.

*At NAACP fund-raising dinner,*
*New York, May 12.*

**George Williams**
*Professor of English, Duke University*

I am old-fashioned and believe that requirements are good for the soul. Requirements are always talked of as hurdles to learning. They're not hurdles—they're challenges.

*Interview, Durham, N.C.,*
*pub. March 17.*

**Gerald S. Witherspoon**
*President, Goddard College,*
*Plainfield, Vt.*

What happens to a kid inside a college has a helluva a lot more importance than what happens in the state house or in the Congress. This is where the action is for them . . . An institution as important as a college should be run by everyone who is in it. Even the cooks and bottlewashers

(GERALD S. WITHERSPOON)

will have a vote, while the trustees will be more concerned with raising money for the school . . .

*Pub. Sept. 24.*

**John Womack**
*Assistant Professor of History,*
*Harvard University*

Students just simply refuse to learn what they don't want to learn. They are less willing to do the necessary groundwork to form their opinions. They rely more upon insight and a sort of induction that I haven't figured out. In my day, the professor would beg the students, "Don't just read the material; think about it." Today, the problem is almost the opposite.

*Pub. March 14.*

## STUDENT DISSENT

**Dean Acheson**
*Former Secretary of State*
*of the United States*

The necessary evil is that the young, who don't start wars, get into them by being young. The unnecessary evil is the impatience with restraint and discipline. If I were running the universe, I would act a little more harshly than this society does. If you say, "Don't do so and so," students will do what you've forbidden. But if your words remain flexible and your actions prove firm—you don't permit things to happen—that's more sensible.

*Interview, Washington, Oct. 9.*

**Spiro T. Agnew**
*Vice President of the United States*

This is not mere delinquency, not mere disruption. Both words dismiss too lightly the grave implications of campus disorders and the reaction to them that is reverberating across the country . . . When administrators and faculties capitulate before storm-trooper tactics, they are doing not only a grave disservice to academic freedom, but to all freedoms.

*Brigham Young University, May 8.*

**Joseph L. Alioto**
*Mayor of San Francisco*

Talk of bayonets on campus is symptomatic, but it offers no remedy. It merely widens discontent, fuels exhortations to violence and solidifies the ranks of protest.

*University of California at Riverside,*
*Jan. 31.*

Dissent should be encouraged, even fostered, at universities and colleges . . . But, when students block a doorway, take over a corridor or a building, all the police power necessary to remove them should be employed.

*Catholic University, Washington, May 3.*

**James E. Allen**
*Commissioner of Education*
*of the United States*

. . . disrupters and their sympathizers are usually the brightest of our students and the most socially concerned. Negative or punitive legislation or administrative action not only is unwelcome, but is likely to exacerbate the situation. The Government should emphasize the responsibility of the higher institutions to respond to change and to handle their own problems, except where outside help or law enforcement is clearly called for.

*Cornell University, May 31.*

**Walter H. Annenberg**
*United States Ambassador*
*to the United Kingdom*

(The time has come) to call an end to giving in to students, an end to making decisions out of expediency, an end to appeasement . . . (I condemn the) permissive and apathetic leadership which, while providing innumerable advantages for youth, has failed to inculcate in youth the understanding that there is a corresponding responsibility for each advantage enjoyed.

*London, May 28.*

**Joan Baez**
*Folk Singer*

You have to define what you mean by revolution, and it certainly isn't what's going on at San Francisco State (College). They're (students') demands are shortsighted; they're asking for a bigger slice of the American pie. I used to think the American pie was moldy; now, I think it's positively ptomained.

*Interview, San Francisco,*
*pub. Jan. 26.*

**Stephen K. Bailey**
*Member, New York State*
*Board of Regents*

We have so many advantages over them (student dissidents): the cops, the Army, the registrar's records, the keys to the library. We can beat them in a fight; but, my God, they have a life to live, and the best of them are trying to tell us something. Soon enough, many of them will subside and conform and enable us to sigh, "Well, now they have finally grown up." But the magic of dreams and beautiful claims of the irreverant and the restless will have died away as well.
*New York, Feb. 14.*

**Vernon L. Barkhurst**
*Director of Admissions,*
*University of Oregon*

It used to be that we talked with parents about dorms, activities and so on. Now it's, "Do you have an active S.D.S. here? Or a Black Students Union?"
*Pub. April 21.*

**Bruno Bettelheim**
*Professor of Psychiatry and Psychology,*
*University of Chicago*

The reason why the present brand of campus revolutionaries, who are of anarchist and nihilist persuasion, are so much more dangerous is that they can point to success after success of their disrupting tactics . . . these militants must want to destroy the universities, because they do not want to be students—because to be a student means to prepare oneself to do something more worthwhile in the future. The militant student's cry is for action now, not preparation for action later. In this real sense, he is no longer a student at all, since he clearly rejects knowledge as a pre-condition of any meaningful activity.

There are no militants among students of medicine, engineering, the natural sciences. They are busy with doing things that are important to them; they are working in the laboratory and at their studies. It is those students who do not quite know what they are preparing themselves for and why, the students who sit around waiting for examinations rather than doing

active work, who form the cadres of the student rebellion.
*Before House Special Subcommittee*
*on Education, Washington,*
*pub. March 23.*

**Hugo L. Black**
*Associate Justice, Supreme Court*
*of the United States*

If the time has come when pupils of state-supported schools—kindergarten, grammar school or high school—can defy or flout orders of school officials to keep their minds on their own school work, it is the beginning of a new revolutionary era of permissiveness in this country, fostered by the judiciary.
*Washington, pub. March 2.*

**Daniel J. Boorstin**
*Professor of American History,*
*University of Chicago*

If we give in to the armed demands of militants to admit persons to the university because of their race, their poverty, their illiteracy or any other non-intellectual distinctions, our universities can no longer serve all of us—or any of us . . . For all their talk of equality and the future, (student militants are the) most unashamed claimants of special privilege.
*University of Tulsa, pub. June 9.*

**Kingman Brewster, Jr.**
*President, Yale University*

The answer to the legitimate student demand to have protection against incompetent and unrealistic administration is not formal representation in all matters. It is administrative accountability.
*Yale University, pub. Sept. 26.*

**William F. Buckley, Jr.**
*Editor, "National Review"*

It seems to me that any college where order is maintained by the National Guard is at least on the brink of destruction. But by destruction I mean, of course, a situation in which the people one feels most about (key professors) leave.
*News conference, St. Louis, Aug. 29.*

**Robert C. Byrd**
*United States Senator, D-W.Va.*

The country has been treated to the

nauseous spectacle of campus rebels, from both student and faculty ranks, forcing weak-kneed, spineless administrations to kowtow to outrageous demands.

*Washington, April 22.*

**John Caffrey**
*Member, American Council on Education*

We in higher education have not been thinking strategically . . . Only one (college president, in a survey) . . . had a plan (for student unrest situations). All the rest said, "Oh, well, it won't happen here"—and they were so shocked, it was like talking to ministers about prostitutes among the deacons. But, when it happens, they start running around like chickens with their heads cut off.

*Pub. May 4.*

**Al Capp**
*Cartoonist*

They (student militants) are absolutely the most ill-educated bunch the world has ever seen. They have no sense of history; that's why we have to relive the age of the Brownshirts, when students marched into German universities and took them over.

*Pub. April 11.*

I've lived in Cambridge (Mass.) over 30 years. My children and grandchildren were born and raised in Cambridge. I help pay the taxes that support Harvard. I help provide Harvard with the police that it will increasingly need to protect it from the once-decent kids it has corrupted into thugs and thieves—and the worst kind of thugs and thieves: the sanctimonious kind. I ask, and my neighbors in the Cambridge community are asking: If a horde of howling, half-educated, half-grown and totally dependent half-humans can attack visitors in their cars and deans in their offices, and get away with it, how long before they'll widen their horizons a block or two and attack us in our homes? If they can use clubs and meat cleavers on the Harvard community today and get away with it, who stops them from using clubs and meat cleavers on the Cambridge community tomorrow?

*Franklin Pierce College,*
*Rindge, N.H., April 27.*

**Charles**
*Prince of Wales*

I am not the sort of person who might march or demonstrate. I do not agree with violence. I am very suspicious of mobs and mob influence. I can't help feeling that a lot of troubles at universities is because people don't have any responsibilities to anything in particular.

*London, pub. June 30.*

**Kenneth B. Clark**
*Professor of Psychology,*
*University of Rochester*

The campus is little more than a sensitive indicator of tension in the entire society. Campus issues cannot be treated as though they are special, or restricted to a particular age group. The college student, contrary to some reports, is not radicalized, is not irrational, is not just playing college games. He is one of the most concerned citizens of the times, and one of our greatest resources, if we are to resolve our worldwide problems. We need to understand the problem, and to respond in ways that make sense.

*Before American Psychological*
*Association, Washington, pub. Sept. 7.*

**Douglass Clarke**
*Acting Principal,*
*Sir George Williams University, Montreal*

The time for generosity (to student militants) is over . . . Painful as the task may be, the university has the duty to see that academic freedom is preserved and that no one is permitted to threaten or destroy its function.

*Pub. Feb. 21.*

**Joseph Copeland**
*Acting President,*
*City University of New York*

It must be recognized that criminal conspiracy and treason are not to be confused with or included within the area of academic freedom. It is recognized that campus unrest and disorder have been fomented and planned by groups of students . . . (and) by persons outside, or agents . . . With such revolutionary militants, there can be no compromise and no understanding.

*At Congressional hearing,*
*Washington, pub. July 27.*

**Andrew W. Cordier**
*Acting President, Columbia University*

I've found that (referring to student demands), if you listen to anyone long enough, they'll eventually say something you can agree with.
*Pub. March 7.*

The curtailment of funds to a university, or to its students, as a measure to bring an end to disruptions, strikes at the innocent more than it does the guilty. Few among the disrupters are the needy and serious students on the campus. The hard-core leadership of the disrupting group generally comes from affluent backgrounds and does not receive Federal aid. The curtailment of funds to an institution would affect admission policies by denying to needy students the possibility of pursuing their education.
*Before Senate Permanent Subcommittee on Investigations, Washington, Aug. 5.*

**Douglas Dowd**
*Professor of Economics,*
*Cornell University*

These kids are bored as hell and have very little respect for the faculty in general. They don't give a damn for authority. They consider the university's authority "illegitimate," since it supports a racist and corrupt society. Perkins (President of Cornell) says you'll be automatically suspended if you do something; to them, that's just a way of saying, go ahead! As for the faculty, it cannot take black students seriously. The first thing, they are young; the second, they are black. The faculty is afraid of the young. They've all got kids of their own. They don't like the kids' hair, the kids' culture. They don't like the kids who don't want to be like them. And they don't care about what the students want to learn. Students don't have any respect for these people. So, when an issue surfaces, all hell breaks loose.
*Interview, May 12.*

**Glenn S. Dumke**
*Chancellor,*
*California State College System*

There is nothing new about student nihil-ism, student revolution. It existed before the Russian Revolution, in the 19th century. Now, it is popping up all over the place, with certain organizations, such as the S.D.S., acting as communication centers . . . The most advisable way to bring it to an end would be to have the people in the academic profession realize that they (and) their service to society will be destroyed unless they bring it to a stop.
*News conference, Los Angeles, Feb. 18.*

**Fred Dutton**
*Member, Board of Regents,*
*University of California*

People should realize that the police may be winning the short-term battles (with student militants), but what we're really doing is radicalizing a whole generation of students. In the long run of history, flowers are always going to win against fences, and students are always going to win against old men.
*Berkeley, pub. June 2.*

**Edward D. Eddy**
*President, Chatham College, Pittsburgh*

I think there's an increasing feeling that you'd better choose the right time and the right place for being firm (with student militants). If you choose it too soon, you lose. If you choose it too late, you also lose.
*Pub. March 7.*

**Novice G. Fawcett**
*President, Ohio State University*

During their college years, the true activists rarely make headlines. They're far too occupied with assimilating knowledge, sharpening their analytical powers and building the kind of foundation which is necessary for wisdom.
*Columbus, Feb. 28.*

**Lewis Feuer**
*Professor of Sociology,*
*University of Toronto*

Student movements are the most sincerely selfless and altruistic the world has seen. But they are distorted and pulled toward extreme and amoral means because the driving energy comes from unconscious sources . . . Student movements commonly escalate to terrorism, and sometimes assassination, not because these tactics are politically wise, but because they satisfy the needs of generational hatred on the latent, unconscious level. This symbolic parricide runs through every student movement I studied.

*Interview, New York, pub. Feb. 14.*

**Robert H. Finch**
*Secretary of Health, Education and Welfare of the United States*

I think we need to have a long, hard look at what is behind this student unrest. It is not simply the Vietnam war. In my opinion, it is a failure of the governance of education, the governing bodies, the institutional apparatus, to respond. Probably, they've been more rigid than almost any other institution in our whole society . . . in the face of very fast-changing conditions.

*Interview, Washington, pub. May 11.*

**Frank E. Fitzsimmons**
*General vice president,*
*International Brotherhood of Teamsters*

I, for one, do not believe that the so-called generation gap is something which cannot be bridged. I believe that a constructive and meaningful dialogue can be established with the youngsters, if only we take the time to talk to them. Just standing back and shaking our heads when they storm a university or when they demonstrate is not enough.

*Washington, May 26.*

**Robert Fleming**
*Michigan State Senator*

The public is sick of being billygoated by these shaggy-haired idiots disrupting campuses.

*Lansing, Jan. 28.*

**J. William Fulbright**
*United States Senator, D-Ark.*

I don't like the (student) excesses, but, on the other hand, I do like their concern about the state of this country . . . Think of how much more depressed you would

be if all of your students were going about shouting the equivalent of "Heil Hitler!"

*May 6.*

**John Kenneth Galbraith**
*Professor of Economics,*
*Harvard University*

·I·am struck by the gloom that pervades the modern university community. It is a widely-held view that Harvard is tottering on the brink; one slight, further nudge and it will tumble into the Charles River, and the splash will be noted even here at M.I.T. . . . Let us not be too depressed. Universities are going to survive.

*Massachusetts Institute of Technology,*
*June 12.*

**Buell G. Gallagher**
*President, City College of New York*

The frustration spawned by a society which has inverted its values and reversed its priorities, putting war ahead of human well-being and preferring privilege to justice—these frustrations have pushed the on-coming college generation into an activism which overreaches immediately attainable goals . . . When the forces of angry rebellion and stern repression clash, the irrepressible conflict is joined. A man of peace, a reconciler, a man of compassion must stand aside, and await a moment when sanity returns and brotherhood based on justice becomes a possibility.

*Resignation speech, New York, May 9.*

**John W. Gardner**
*Chairman, Urban Coalition*

A year ago, a young acquaintance of mine confidently said, "The universities can be destroyed," and I laughed at him. I laugh no longer.

*Stanford University, June 14.*

**Ira Glasser**
*Associate Director,*
*New York City Civil Liberties Union*

It ill behooves educators as a class to suddenly sound the alarm about student disruption, when indeed they have done more violence to the students by trying to regiment them.

*New York, May 10.*

**Barry Goldwater, Jr.**
*United States Representative, R-Calif.*

. . . what must be done (to restore peace to the college campus) cannot be done from the federal level. It really can't be done from the governor's office. I think the real emphasis has to be placed in the area of control of those who have the responsibility—school boards, trustees, regents of universities and colleges and right down to the chancellors and presidents of schools. These are the people who can do something about it. That's what they're there for. In order to get them to do something, you have to have the people—the mothers and fathers, the voters—demand that they take action.
*Interview, pub. August.*

**Glenn C. Gooder**
*President, Los Angeles City College*

One of the greatest dangers is that too many people insist upon a simple definition of militancy and a single response to student unrest. Militancy is as varied as there are militants. Included in militancy are idealism, activism and gangsterism. These differences must be understood, and responses must be appropriate to each.
*Pub. May 5.*

**Ralph Guglielmi**
*Former All-American quarterback,*
*Notre Dame University*

I was kicked out of school a whole semester for coming in 25 minutes late one night. Nowadays, you bust up a school, and they beg you to come back.
*Pub. May 19.*

**Arthur G. Hansen**
*President, Georgia Institute of Technology*

My fear is that faculty, administration and students may lose sight of the good that has been achieved over the past centuries. Perspective must be kept. To yield to every demand for the sake of "keeping peace," and to forget the basic principles by which any society lives and works together in a state of harmony will destroy all that has been gained.
*Atlanta, Nov. 20.*

**William H. Harsha**
*United States Representative, R-Ohio*

. . . somebody has got to inject a spine in the spineless (college) administrators.
*Before House hearing on student unrest, Washington, May 7.*

**S. I. Hayakawa**
*Acting President,*
*San Francisco State College*

Student obstructors never had it so good. As soon as they create a little disturbance, the television cameras arrive, and they see themselves on the six o'clock news. They feel terribly inflated and important as a result of the fantastic attention they get. So successive numbers of people intoxicate themselves with appearances on television.
*Pub. Jan. 28.*

The bravest young people on our campus are the non-violent young black students who keep on attending classes at the risk of physical attack from black militants and in the face of distrust on the part of the majority of white students.
*Before House Education Subcommittee, Washington, Feb. 3.*

When President (Dwight D.) Eisenhower used Federal troops to open up schools in Little Rock, the liberals didn't raise a squawk at all. Whether to protect the liberty of white people or the liberty of black people, you ultimately have to use force; and I, for one, am not going to hesitate to use it.
*Pub. March 10.*

Professors, in a way, love their students, so they want earnestly to believe that whatever their students do is rationally motivated . . . They're willing to condone anything, because, after all, they've been devoting their lives to teaching students rational behavior. So, if the students violate the common courtesies and even resort to violence, they sit around agonizing and say there must be something terribly wrong with the world if the students feel that way.
*Interview, San Francisco, April 17.*

San Francisco State has remained open every day since I took over, damn it.
*Before California Police Officers Conference, Los Angeles, April 25.*

They (many college students) make a cult of hedonism, despise the useful citizen and find some of their greatest gratifications in shocking the middle and lower classes by outrageous speech, dress and behavior. They have a profound contempt for the democratic process through which the butcher, baker and candlestick maker have a voice equal to their own in the conduct of affairs.
*Before Senate Permanent Subcommittee on Investigations, Washington, May 13.*

## S. I. Hayakawa
*President, San Francisco State College*

Most student rebels are of the upper middle class. They are to be found largely in the Liberal Arts departments and the Social Sciences—disciplines in which verbal facility is highly prized, and (in) which it is not always necessary to check one's words against the stubborn facts of life (as you have to in Chemistry or Home Economics) in order to pull down an "A."
*Columbia University, pub. Dec. 21.*

## Morris J. Heldman
*President, West Los Angeles College*

I'm really not able to understand what it is that students caetegorically are looking for . . . Previous revolutions—mind you, I'm not calling it that yet—but previous revolutions have had a goal. I don't see what the goal is here.
*Interview, Los Angeles, pub. Feb. 9.*

## Theodore M. Hesburgh
*President, University of Notre Dame*

Most far-out students are trying to tell society something that may also be worth searching for today, if they would only lower the volume so we could hear the message.

*University of Notre Dame, pub. Feb. 28.*

You find many benefactors of private universities who are drawing back and taking universities out of their wills. You find a kind of revulsion in much of the large middle segment of the public that feels that, perhaps, they are being disillusioned about what was the fair child of other days, the institutions of higher learning.
*Pub. June 2.*

## Roger W. Heyns
*Chancellor, University of California at Berkeley*

Very definitely, there are people on the far right who want to use the fact of unrest on the campus to change the nature of the university. They're opposed to dissent, they're opposed to certain ideologies and they would like to use the occasion of disruption on the campus to influence the appointment process, to influence the admissions function, and a number of other vital functions.
*Pub. March 10.*

## Eric Hoffer
*Author*

You need chancellors of universities and mayors of cities who will get up in the morning and spit on their hands and say, "Who am I going to kill today?" These are the people who save you . . . If Grayson Kirk (former President of Columbia University) had got mad and got a gun and went out and gunned a couple of them (student militants) down, he might have saved Columbia.
*Before Senate Permanent Subcommittee on Investigations, Washington, May 9.*

San Francisco State (College) is being destroyed by a bunch of crummy punks. Who the hell would have dreamt that a thing like this was possible? Ignorant, bedraggled, illiterate punks! Our institutions are tremendously vulnerable. What are we afraid of? Of the government? Of the police? Of Congress? No, for God's sake, we're afraid of the individual, of the beast masquerading as man.
*Pub. December.*

## Sidney Hook
*Professor of Philosophy, New York University*

When you yield to violence anywhere,

(SIDNEY HOOK)

you weaken the resistance to violence everywhere.
*Interview, New York, May 10.*

. . . it is obvious—especially after what has happened at Cornell—that the faculties, by and large, have been trying to buy peace by capitulating to threats of violence and to the forces of unreason. They will discover that the logic of appeasement is the same in education as it is in politics: It only whets the appetite of the students to make more and more unreasonable demands. If Harvard is the "Munich" of American education, Cornell is its "Pearl Harbor."

. . . when students say that they want to determine the nature of the curriculum and have the right to hire and fire professors, we understand very well what they are saying. What they are saying is demonstrable nonsense, because to make such a demand is to equate experience and inexperience, maturity and immaturity, knowledge and ignorance.
*Interview, pub. May 19.*

They (the faculty) are afraid of violence, afraid of arson, afraid of confrontation. Some cannot believe that the extremist students are in earnest. They feel that, if they indulge the movement, it will go away. This combination of fear and appeasement has made the turmoil on campus possible. The administration is equally at fault, for, without faculty support, it quickly capitulates. If the administration and the faculty acted together, the revolutionary students could not win. Only courage tames fanatics.
*Pub. June 30.*

**J. Edgar Hoover**
*Director, Federal Bureau of Investigation*

Many of the school administrators appear unable to distinguish between legitimate protest and unlawful acts, and there are far too many bleeding hearts among them whose attitude has served only to magnify the problem by encouraging the escalation of demands and further disorders. What is needed is more guts on the

part of many presidents of the universities and colleges. They should expel the violent militants who take the law into their hands, rather than grant them amnesty for their criminal acts.
*Before House Appropriations Subcommittee, Washington, April 17.*

**Harold E. Hughes**
*United States Senator, D-Iowa*

I do not agree with those who would squelch all (student) dissent, apply excessive force and submerge rights and reason and freedom of expression to retain order. If university and civil officials are competent, this is not necessary. Nor is repressive legislation the answer. The educators should handle these matters, not the police—except where absolutely necessary —and certainly not the state legislature or the Congress.
*Before American Public Power Association, Washington, May 8.*

**Hubert H. Humphrey**
*Former Vice President of the United States*

You cannot afford to, and you cannot in the name of peace on the campus permit, a handful of young men and women—who are determined to have their will and their way—destroy property, destroy university records, disrupt classrooms, intimidate the professors or intimidate the student body . . . The discipline I'm asking for is suspension for those who are violating every rule of the university and, secondly, expulsion and, thirdly, not to grant amnesty when those things have taken place that are truly violating every standard of the university. (But) you have to understand the difference between a man who is determined to commit an act, a crime, and a person who is determined to change things on a university by a modest act of civil disobedience.
*Interview, St. Paul, Minn., May 25.*

**Mahalia Jackson**
*Gospel Singer*

Students do have a right to learn about themselves—what they are and where they come from—and they will find out, if they can keep calm long enough.
*Interview, Los Angeles, pub. March 13.*

**George Jessel**
*Entertainer*

My visit to Tyler Junior College made me feel deeply optimistic about our youth today—not a hippie or a yippie in the place.

*Tyler, Tex., Feb. 26.*

**Edward M. Kennedy**
*United States Senator, D-Mass.*

(The student uprisings and other dis-·orders come from) a disillusionment with the kind of war we fight, the kind of suffering we overlook, the kind of society we are. Its sources are legitimate, but its methods do damage to the foundations of our country.

*Before Atlanta Bar Association, May 9.*

**Clark Kerr**
*Former President,*
*University of California*

. . . Too many people on campuses today react to an arrest for violence or disruption as a boy scout badge of honor.

*At Southern Governors Conference,*
*Williamsburg, Va., Sept. 15.*

**J. W. Kilgore**
*Chairman, Department of Philosophy,*
*Baylor University*

The right to dissent includes the right to dissent from the dissenters. If they (the student militants) refuse to permit opposing views to be expressed, activitists are aping some of the worst features of fascism.

*McMurray College,*
*Abilene, Tex., Feb. 25.*

**Douglas M. Knight**
*President, Duke University*

Recently a black militant called me "a pig in a gray flannel suit." If I'd responded as some wanted, I would never have heard him say some very rational things later on. We could have got hung up right there. But, fortunately, I was made to realize this was something this fellow had to call me before we could sit down and talk together as men. But we must come to understand we are dealing with a truly cooperative venture. We'll never get at the

problem until we all realize it is a cooperative, and not some cold, vertically structured factory. The people can talk.

*Interview, pub. May 12.*

**John W. Lederle**
*President, University of Massachusetts*

None of us likes to admit that the tactic of student take-over has been successful; but it has. Students have succeeded in forcing decisions on issues that are usually debated long and hard. But we, as university presidents, can never say that violence is justified . . . We have to get students to communicate through the normal, regular channels; we have to, also, speed up the decision-making process to eliminate the need for violence.

*Interview, Amhert, Mass., pub. April 18.*

**Seymour M. Lipset**
*Professor of Government and*
*Social Relations, Harvard University*

The best way to deal with the (student) radicals is to give them dialogue, which they don't want, instead of police and prosecution, which they do.

*Before House Special Education*
*Subcommittee, Washington, May 9.*

**Vince Lombardi**
*Football coach,*
*Washington "Redskins"*

The college man today is more restless . . . but he is also more intelligent. You hear the expression that this is the "now" generation; but I don't think that's quite the right interpretation. I would call it the "why" generation. They don't want a yes or no. They're asking why. We can't have them defying authority on such places as campuses, but that's not the whole story. They're raising some questions that aren't being answered.

*Telephone interview,*
*Potomac, Md., pub. March 11.*

**Marvin Mandel**
*Governor of Maryland*

Students who attempt to revolutionize society by first destroying the university are like an army which begins a war by wrecking its own base. Without the uni-

(MARVIN MANDEL)

versity, there would be no students. The position of the students, even as agitators, depends on there being a university.
*Towson State College, Md., June 1.*

**Herbert Marcuse**
*Professor of Philosophy,*
*University of California at San Diego*

If the students occupy a building, is that violence? If they refuse to leave and police storm them, is that violence? The monopoly on violence rests with the established authorities; but that's legalized violence.
*Interview, San Diego, pub. Feb. 23.*

The practitioners and propagandists of truly murderous and suicidal violence on a global scale have neither the civil nor moral right to call for violent suppression of campus dissent.
*Before American Civil Liberties Union,*
*San Diego, May 17.*

**Tom McCall**
*Governor of Oregon*

Americans are fed up to their eardrums and eyeballs (with campus demonstrations).
*Pub. May 4.*

**Eugene J. McCarthy**
*United States Senator, D-Minn.*

I don't think any good is served by having the President and the Attorney General telling college presidents to crack down on student demonstrators. This is not a Presidential matter. It is much easier to be President of the United States today than to be president of a college.
*Radio interview, Washington, May 7.*

**John L. McClellan**
*United States Senator, D-Ark.*

The use of force (by student militants) to occupy college buildings, to destroy personal or community property and to make physical attacks upon faculty members and students cannot, by any standards, be considered a legitimate form of protest or dissent. Such acts are criminal and intolerable.
*Before the Senate, Washington, July 22.*

**Robert G. McCloskey**
*Professor of American History and*
*Government, Harvard University*

My chief disappointment (during the Harvard student disorders) was in the behavior of the moderate students, the kind I have been teaching and liking for more than 20 years. In the emotion of the moment, large numbers of them were duped by the S.D.S. into becoming the instruments of that organization's purposes. I had hoped that we had communicated to them a stronger commitment to rationality. It seems that we have not. If American education needs a new look, and it probably does, I think the first concern of all of us should be with that failure.
*Interview, Cambridge, Mass., April 24.*

**Margaret Mead**
*Anthropologist*

It is those who have never been to college, but who are sending or hope to send their children to college, who are most angry at what's been going on at university campuses. The news deprives them of the hope that there is a safe and socially-approved road to a kind of life they themselves have not had, but their children can.
*New York, pub. April 21.*

**John N. Mitchell**
*Attorney General of the United States*

. . . the time has come for an end to patience. The time has come for us to demand, in the strongest possible terms, that university officals, local law enforcement officers and local courts apply the law. If arrests must be made, then arrests there should be; if violators must be prosecuted, then prosecutions there should be. It is no admission of defeat, as some may claim, to use reasonable physical force to eliminate physical force. The price of civil tranquility cannot be paid by submission to violence and terror.

When a violent outbreak occurs, they (university officials) should not take it upon themselves to decide how long the violence should endure and what rights should be trampled upon until local government is called in . . . when people may be injured, when personal property may be destroyed and when chaos begins, the university official only aids lawlessness by procrastination and negotiation.

Apathetic students should stand up for the rights of those who wish to pursue civility and scholarship in the academic community. To the extent that they remain neutral or refuse to act, they are all accessories to the tyranny we are now witnessing.

*Before Detroit Bar Association, May 1.*

**Malcolm C. Moos**
*President, University of Minnesota*

It is time we accept the fact that the lion's share of the student body wants major changes. If we are not flexible in the face of these requests for change, we run the risk of radicalizing our moderate students.

*Pub. May 5.*

**Edmund S. Muskie**
*United States Senator, D-Maine*

Our representative institutions will have to accommodate to the steady onslaught of demands made on them in the name of justice; but, if their every failure to provide an immediate response is to be met with disruptive protest, it is equally clear those institutions cannot survive.

*George Washington University, Washington, June 8.*

**Richard M. Nixon**
*President of the United States*

No group, as a group, should be more zealous defenders of the integrity of academic standards and the rule of reason in academic life than the faculties of our great institutions. If they simply follow the loudest voices, parrot the latest slogan, yield to unreasonable demands, they will have won, not the respect, but the contempt of their students.

The student who invades an administration building, roughs up a dean, rifles the files and issues "non-negotiable demands" may have some of his demands met by a permissive university administration; but the greater his victory, the

more he will have undermined the security of his own rights.

*General Beadle State College, Madison, S.D., June 3.*

**Louie B. Nunn**
*Governor of Kentucky*

. . . I'm damn sick and tired of this kind of thing (campus disruptions) . . . any time, any type. Police or National Guard or anybody under my control (is) empowered to use whatever force or means are necessary (in dealing with these disorders) . . . (they can) fire, if fired upon . . . (they can) drag 'em out, if they want to be dragged out . . . (disruptors can) walk into bayonets, if they want to walk into bayonets.

*News conference, pub. May 4.*

**John F. O'Connor**
*Chief of Police, Syracuse, N.Y.*

When parents see their young children threatened, they act. I have never seen any reaction to crime and disorder to equal the reaction to violence in the schools. Parents talk of bringing baseball bats to school to protect their children. The radicals may be digging their own graves by reaching down to the high-school and junior-high level. That galvanizes people into action.

*Syracuse, pub. June 2.*

**Robert W. Packwood**
*United States Senator, R-Ore.*

I have a great tolerance for dissent, until it reaches the point of violence. Then my own (lawyer's) conservatism takes over, and I hold that change must be achieved by non-violent means within our political framework.

*News conference, Los Angeles, Feb. 14.*

**Charles Palmer**
*President, National Student Association*

If the political system in this country wants our support, then those who now control the system must prove that it, and they, can respond constructively to the American crisis. If the system cannot respond then we will do it our way ourselves. This is not a threat, it's a warning.

(CHARLES PALMER)

. . . We are going to show those in power that to brand students as radicals is a way of evading the issues we are raising. The problems we face are real.

*News conference, Washington, Sept. 10.*

**Paul VI**
*Pope*

We cannot deny that many problems which the young often denounce with so much violence and bitterness are true problems. We cannot consider illegitimate the condemnation of certain excessive and unreasonable forms of authoritarianism, the wish of the youths to be a more active element, with some responsibility in social life. It is not difficult to see, in the student protest, a reflection of the crisis of all authorities which troubles the modern world.

*Vatican City, Feb. 10.*

**James A Perkins**
*President, Cornell University*

Surely, within the last couple of years, the problem of maintenance of order and stability has become an increasingly important pre-occupation (on the campus). We're (college presidents) becoming experts on the judicial system, experts on confrontations and how not to deal with them. So I think we're becoming "campus strategists," in a sense never contemplated, instead of "education strategists" —and it's leading a number of my colleagues to say it's not any "fun" anymore to be a university president.

*Interview, May 29.*

**Robert S. Powell, Jr.**
*President, National Student Association*

(The responsibility for campus disorders rests) squarely on the shoulders of the university for creating some of the most undemocratic and authoritarian institutions through which young people must pass in order to achieve an educated adulthood.

*Before House Education Subcommittee, Washington, March 26.*

**Nathan M. Pusey**
*President, Harvard University*

Their (student revolutionaries) aim is, they would say, to *re*structure American society . . . It seems to me their aim can only be to *un*structure American society.

*Harvard University, April 24.*

**Michael Radock**
*Vice president,*
*University of Michigan*

Newspaper headlines and the intensive coverage of student demonstrations by the electronic media have resulted in an image of the contemporary university as a conglomerate of protest, pot, pills, long hair, beards, beads and un-patriotism. The great tragedy for both the institutions and for society dependent upon educated leadership is that the bizarre is being accepted as typical of college culture.

*Before American College Public Relations Association, Pittsburgh, pub. Feb. 2.*

**Ronald Reagan**
*Governor of California*

I believe in youthful dissent. I believe in young people wanting change. We all benefit from that. But it should be done in a manner that does not infringe on other people's rights . . . (In handling campus violence) you either fight or surrender; and, if you surrender, they have won a victory and have taken over . . . If you pay a blackmailer, he's back the next day with more demands.

*News conference, Sacramento, Jan. 8.*

Those who want to get an education, those who want to teach, should be protected in that at the point of a bayonet, if necessary. This confrontation has to be won.

*Pub. Jan. 20.*

Destruction is the goal of the anarchists. It is not ours. Rather, ours is the protection of true academic freedom. To achieve this, we must first insure that the universities and colleges are still standing.

*Sacramento, Jan. 26.*

By and large, the academic community has found itself confused with sympathy for some of the expressed views of the dissidents—some of what they construe as their demands—and they have failed to see in proper perspective the simple issue of whether you can submit to coercion, force and violence.

*News conference, Sacramento, Feb. 12.*

You have this (campus violence) on one side, and you can't point to even a single expulsion of a student on the other side. I think this is the kind of balance that shows that some place the reaction to the violence and the vandalism has not been swift enough, certain enough and firm enough.

*News conference, Sacramento, March 11.*

Any time that you have widespread opinion, as you do now on the part of the people, that not enough action was being taken at the campus level (against militants), you run the risk of government taking back into its hands the powers that formerly were given to the Regents, and I don't think this is good.

*News conference, March 19.*

The new subversives on our campuses will be a problem much easier to handle if the members of that so-called great silent majority (of students) have inner convictions, beliefs and confidence in our society, and in us as adults.

*Before Commonwealth Club,*
*San Francisco, pub. Aug. 4.*

It (student unrest) began the first time someone old enough to know better declared it was no crime to break the law in the name of social protest. It started with those who proclaimed, in the name of academic freedom, that the campus was a sanctuary immune to the laws and rules that govern the rest of us. It began with those who, in the name of change and progress, decided they could scrap all the time-tested wisdom man has accumulated in his climb from the swamp to the stars.

*Washington, Oct. 14.*

**Tom Reddin**
*Former Chief of Police, Los Angeles*

First, (student) dissidents find a cause; second, they find a triggering incident; third, they rally support and emotions; fourth, they cause confrontations; fifth,

they rally more support; sixth, they submit demands—some of which can be implemented, but many others that can't; and the confrontations go on.

*Pepperdine College, Nov. 7.*

**Abraham A. Ribicoff**
*United States Senator, D-Conn.*

There are a lot of innocents who get sucked into the S.D.S. They are suckers . . . they are being used by cynical leaders for their own ends . . . The days of S.D.S. are numbered. The day is not too far off when S.D.S. will disintegrate because of the internal split.

*Washington, June 17.*

**Hyman G. Rickover**
*Vice Admiral, United States Navy;*
*director, Division of Naval Reactors,*
*Atomic Energy Commission*
*of the United States*

It seems to be supremely important (that) we recognize that what goes euphemistically by the mild term of "student unrest" is violence of a kind that would nowhere else be tolerated. That they tolerate it makes the college and university authorities accessories to criminal conduct.

*Before House Special Subcommittee*
*on Education, Washington, May 22.*

**Clinton Rossiter**
*Professor of American Institutions,*
*Cornell University*

My feeling is that a man can't teach at a place that is in a condition of turmoil. I don't mean I want a place of constant serenity; I feel once in a while a crisis is good for us—it reminds people on the outside that we are a part of the real world. But we can't operate in this state of anomic behavior. I could have privatized myself over the last 96 hours and quietly walked my own way; but we cannot have a place where every change that is made is the result of confrontation.

*Interview, Cornell University, April 22.*

If the ship (Cornell) goes down, I'll go with it—as long as it represents reason and order. But, if it's converted to threats

(CLINTON ROSSITER)

and fear, I'll leave it and take a job as a
night watchman in a bakery . . . I can
live with ferment but not with violence.
*Pub. May 2.*

### Bayard Rustin
*Civil Rights Leader; executive director,*
*A. Philip Randolph Institute*

. . . stop capitulating to the stupid demands of Negro students, (and) see that
they get the remedial training they need.
What the hell are "soul" courses worth in
the real world? In the real world, no one
gives a damn if you've taken soul courses.
They want to know if you can do mathe-
matics and write a correct sentence . . .
A multiple society cannot exist where an
element in that society, out of its own
sense of guilt and masochism, permits
another segment cf that society to hold
guns to their heads in the name of justice.
*Before American Jewish Committee,*
*New York, April 27.*

### Ake Sandler
*Professor of Political Science,*
*California State College at Los Angeles*

This (Students for a Democratic Society) is not a bunch of philosophical
anarchists. They are hardened agitators
who have gone to school on Hitler and
Stalin and Mao and Castro. They are
small-time tyrants looking for excitement
and thriving on publicity.
*Pub. May 25.*

### Arthur M. Schlesinger, Jr.
*Professor of Humanities,*
*City University of New York*

There is nothing that the Columbia
University students did which was not
totally consistent with the American version of democracy. There is nothing—
and I will repeat it—in what they did
which is in the slightest degree extra-
democratic.
*Pub. Aug. 1.*

### Terry D. Schrunk
*Mayor, Portland, Ore.*

We should not tolerate, either through
city administrators or through our court

systems, the continued development of
the great permissive society. I feel that
we should also speak loudly and clearly
against the actions of fuzzy-thinking
professors and wrongly-motivated militants who would destroy our nation.
*Before United States Conference of*
*Mayors, Pittsburgh, pub. June 19.*

### Bernard G. Segal
*President-elect,*
*American Bar Association*

You can't curb dissent. We must cherish
the right of dissent. If it hadn't been for
the privilege of dissent, there wouldn't
be any America. It was how this country began. But those youngsters who engage in violence must be taught they are
violating the law, and they must pay the
penalty. But the penalty must fit the offense, and then they should be permitted
to continue with their educations. We
simply cannot meet excess with excess.
*Interview, Philadelphia, pub. May 18.*

### Edgar F. Shannon
*President, University of Virginia*

Reason . . . is the ultimate source of
authority in any university and in a democratic nation. If reason is lost in the academy, it is certain to be lost in the nation
and supplanted with raw power and repression.
*University of Virginia, June 8.*

### Edward Short
*Minister of Education and Science*
*of the United Kingdom*

It is monstrous to disrupt the life of a
college, university or school because of
Vietnam, Nigeria, or race, or because
you are opposed to capitalism . . . They
(student militants) are not socialists nor
even respectable Marxists. They are a
new brand of anarchist. Some are Maoists
and some of a new brand of revolutionaries for whom as yet there is no name.
They are wreckers. They are there to disrupt society. Their weapons are lies, mis-
representations, defamation, character
assassination, intimidation and, more recently, physical violence. In the short
term, they are causing harm to the educational chances of the vast majority of

students who are just as idealistic and decent as they ever were . . . This whole miserable episode is clouding the university system and fouling the good name of a whole generation of young people.

*Before Parliament, London, Jan. 29.*

**Allan F. Sindler**
*Chairman, Department of Government, Cornell University*

If the faculty yesterday had said that it acceded (to student militants) because we are a university and not a civil governmental entity capable of defending itself, and said to the students, in effect, "You win, but because we're under duress and not for any reasons of principle that anyone can accept," I might, I just might, have gone along with it. To acknowledge that it was a coerced decision would at least have been more manly. But many dedicated student groups, plus individual students and faculty, have no appreciation whatsoever of what academic freedom is about. I expected the faculty, as an aristocratic elite, to close ranks, as we did back in the McCarthy days—but it didn't. A university is not a collection of politicized groups. If "Fascist pig," "Commie something or other" or "racist" is the terminology to be used, I want none of it.

*Cornell University, April 24.*

When legitimate forms of student dissent shift to illegitimate varieties of coercion, force and resistance, a university should not condone these in the name of the goodness of the goals, the sincerity of the students, or the prideful impotence of an institution devoted to reason. To the maximum extent feasible, a university should endeavor to handle campus unrest by its own rules and with its own resources. If, however, a campus disturbance exceeds a university's capacity to handle, a reliance upon public authority is clearly legitimate.

*Before American Psychological Association, Washington, pub. Sept. 7.*

**Adlai Stevenson III**
*Treasurer of Illinois*

Force (on campus) cannot be part of the persuasion of a free society. It is self-destructive, for it opens the same option to all contenders—mounted deputies on the bridge at Selma and night riders in Mississippi.

*University of California, Berkeley, April 24.*

**Joseph L. Sutton**
*President, Indiana University*

With full appreciation for the enthusiasm, the ambitions and the overall knowledge possessed by our student population, I must say that I do not believe that politics of confrontation has a role in university life. In this respect, I must report that I will entertain no so-called non-negotiable demands; or, more precisely, I will not entertain demands of any kind. Neither I nor any member of the administration, local or regional, will yield to coercion. If force is used in any form, I give you my pledge that it will be met with an adequate response.

*Addressing the students, Bloomington, Ind., Sept. 30.*

**Herman E. Talmadge**
*United States Senator, D-Ga.*

If this movement (campus violence) were right-wing or politically conservative, I believe it would have been crushed a long time ago by the wrath of American citizens whipped up by the liberal establishment.

*Before the Senate, Washington, May 1.*

**William P. Tolley**
*Chancellor, Syracuse University*

Court injunctions put the lawless in conflict with the courts as distinguished from conflict with the university. For the first time, college students know that a jail sentence—not amnesty—is at the end of the violence rainbow.

*Syracuse, N.Y., June 6.*

**S. J. Tonsor**
*Professor of History, University of Michigan*

Student and professor activists inside the university, and certain ideological groups outside the university, no longer believe the truth must be essential to the

(S. J. TONSOR)

academy. Both the extreme right and the extreme left hold the same destructive view. Both Mark Rudd of Columbia and Governor Wallace of Alabama stand in the schoolroom door; and, seen from the vantage point of the academy, they both hold the same low view of reasoned discourse. These groups cannot be permitted to disrupt and destroy the institutions they so obviously do not understand.

*Before National Association of Manufacturers, Washington, April 1.*

**Mark Van Doren**
*Poet, Author*

I certainly do not agree with the ones who say, "To hell with the students." They (the students) are agitated about something real. Our society is insane, and they are trying to say so. Of course, sometimes *they* act insane, too.

*Interview, New York, pub. June 9.*

I am temperamentally not a revolutionary. I have a natural dislike for violence. It is very painful to me to see students charging through hallways, breaking things, yelling obscenities, pulling file drawers open. It seems so senseless, yet I understand the need.

*Interview, New York, pub. June 11.*

**George Wald**
*Professor of Biology, Harvard University*

People wonder why students rebel against the university. The answer is, because it's there. At Harvard, there is a small group who want to close the university. It may be necessary to get rid of them. But we have a whole spectrum of students, and those who want to close the place down are isolating themselves.

*Interview, pub. May 12.*

**Eric A. Walker**
*President, Pennsylvania State University*

If they (student militants) prevent any student from going to class, if any professor is prevented from teaching class, the axe will fall.

*Pub. March 7.*

**Theodore H. White**
*Author*

To me, there is an absolute difference between healthy dissent and the kind of thing I saw last year. I saw (Vice President) Hubert Humphrey heckled and booed wherever he went, to prevent him from giving his views. What the Constitution won't allow, the hecklers allowed themselves. The vigor of the student rebellion I appreciate; the meaning escapes me. In fact, nothing irritates me more than the students and their ideas. They have the "military-industrial complex" just as though we never had the "merchants of death." The kids bore me stiff because their ideas are old.

*Interview, New York, pub. July 27.*

**Roy Wilkins**
*Executive Director, National Association for the Advancement of Colored People*

Knuckling under to raucous demands for blanket amnesty for those detained for acts of trespass, violence and destruction is no contribution to the development of fiber, in white or black youths.

*C.W. Post College, Greenvale, N.Y., pub. June 9.*

**Logan Wilson**
*President, American Council on Education*

The inactivity of the faculties has really been a big part of the (campus unrest) problem. They're just not getting behind their administrations. Some of them are even a little gleeful when trouble comes.

*Pub. August.*

**Gerald Francis Yates**
*Professor of Government, Georgetown University*

There are hundreds of deanships and college presidencies going begging because no one wants to stand up in a shooting gallery.

*Washington, pub. July 28.*

**Charles E. Young**
*Chancellor, University of California at Los Angeles*

. . . we have difficulty teaching respect

for law and order in the universities. That's something society has to do, and I'd say society, up to now, has done a lousy job.

*Town Hall, Los Angeles, April 29.*

**Evelle J. Younger**
*District Attorney, Los Angeles County*
Some administrators seem to think the campus is a sanctuary, that police can't be called in when laws are broken. I feel that it is in the interest of the community, the school and the administrators themselves to inform them (the students) that assault and arson are no different on the campus than they are on Main Street.

*Los Angeles, pub. Aug. 26.*

# Foreign Affairs

**E. Ross Adair**
*United States Representative, D-Pa.*

. . . If there is a person in the Peace Corps who feels he cannot support U.S. foreign policy, then he ought not to be in the Peace Corps and should be promptly brought home.

*Before House Foreign Affairs Committee, Washington, July 24.*

**George D. Aiken**
*United States Senator, R-Vt.*

Vietnam has ended the illusion that our military power bestows on us an equal influence in world politics. It has taught us, or should have taught us, the vital importance of finding a halfway house between the innocence of isolationism and the arrogance which says we ought to play the world's policeman.

*Norwich University, Northfield, Vt., Oct. 11.*

**Babiker Awadalla**
*Prime Minister of Sudan*

It is ironic that the President of the United States should state, without qualification, that his country has not turned away from the world. Some of us cannot help but wish that it had. Some of us cannot but feel that the world would have been a better place if it were free of American orbiting spies in the sky, free of their intelligence ships, free of their military bases, their loaded aid, and the pervasive machinations of the CIA—free, in short, of all the devices and intrigues that United States imperialism has been employing to impose its will in the world in the name of freedom.

*Before the General Assembly, United Nations, N.Y., Sept. 23.*

**Chester Bowles**
*Former United States Ambassador to India*

Today we're not roaming around the world trying to be loved and fawned upon. We've learned that aid does not buy friends—or buy votes in the United Nations.
                    *New Delhi, pub. Feb. 9.*

**Willy Brandt**
*Chancellor of West Germany*

It is quite understandable that people in the United States ask themselves, "Why shouldn't our partners take over more responsibility?" It's quite understandable that people say, "We have so many problems at home." It's understandable that they ask themselves whether there have been elements of over-commitment in the developments of recent years. But I think, after asking all these questions, Americans will always return to a policy of responsible cooperation with friends and allies and partners.

*Interview, Bonn, pub. Dec. 29.*

**Edward W. Brooke**
*United States Senator, R-Mass.*

Those of us who have been most critical of recent governmental policies in foreign policy and defense matters are obliged to realize the significant truth contained in the old maxim that "politics stops at the water's edge." The truth of that ancient insight lies not in any suggestion that critical discussion of the nation's international problems is taboo. Rather, it consists of the understanding that a democratic government cannot operate effectively in an often hostile international environment if there is serious division on the home front regarding the wisdom and justice of the nation's foreign policies.

*Before the Senate, Washington, Sept. 18.*

**David Bruce**
*United States Ambassador*
*to the United Kingdom*

The cardinal rule for an ambassador to a foreign country is to cherish no anti-pathies or attachments for particular domestic political parties or programs. This, fortunately, does not forbid him to contract friendships, regardless of parties, or love the country of his residence dis-passionately.
*London, pub. March 21.*

**Zbigniew Brzezinski**
*Professor of Public Law and*
*Government, Columbia University*

In my view, we ought to be moving as rapidly as possible (toward talks with the Soviet Union) . . . because there is a particularly good opportunity today, given the kind of problems the Soviets have with China, given the kind of difficulties they are facing in Czechoslovakia, for us to take the initiative—not only to propose arms talks but to propose a general confer-ence on the European problems. Let not the other side always take the initiative . . .
*Television interview, New York, April 6.*

**Alastair Buchan**
*Director, British Institute*
*for Strategic Studies*

If the United States is a race-ridden, riot-ridden, poverty-ridden society, the dan-ger is not just that you get greater and greater anti-Americanism, but you get greater neutralism on the part of your allies. The American position, therefore, is weaker . . .
*Interview, London, pub. Feb. 17.*

**Frank Church**
*United States Senator, D-Idaho*

I suggest . . . that we abstain from mili-tary intervention in the internal affairs of other countries . . . short of a clear and certain danger to our national security, and that we adhere to this principle, whether others—including the Russians and Chinese—do or do not.
*Washington, March 5.*

Faith in the viability of freedom will not, in itself, guarantee our national secur-ity; but it can and should help allay our extravagant fear of Communism. It should enable us to compete with confidence in the market of ideas. It should free us from the fatal temptation to fight fire with fire by imitating the tactics of a rival who cannot be as sure of the viability of his ideas in an open contest. The Russians, when you come down to it, have a better reason to fear freedom in Czechoslovakia than we have to fear Communism in Vietnam.
*Before the Senate,*
*Washington, pub. Sept. 7.*

Our foreign policy has become so un-hinged from our historic ideals that American ambassadors are now regarded abroad as symbols of oppression, while our role in the world becomes increas-ingly meaningless to our own young people.
*Pub. Sept. 14.*

**Silvio O. Conte**
*United States Representative, R-Mass.*

I have long felt that the United States should not become the weapons arsenal for the so-called free world. It is bad enough when the recipient can afford our new and shiny weapons. It is even worse when the recipient cannot . . .
*Before the House, Washington, Dec. 9.*

**Alan Cranston**
*United States Senator, D-Calif.*

(The evidence of the last fifty years) is overwhelming that our present policy of withholding recognition from govern-ments of which we disapprove, and with whom our relations are particularly hostile, has failed totally to advance our values or to achieve any other of its intended pur-poses. There are few, if any, cases where our present policy of non-recognition has succeeded either in moving another gov-ernment to change its policies or in isolat-ing it from the world community . . . Recognition of a foreign government is done not to confer a compliment but to secure a convenience, and is intended not as an ineffective stamp of moral approval but as a step designed to serve our national interest.
*Washington, May 27.*

(ALAN CRANSTON)

I see no wave of isolationism sweeping America. What is sweeping America is a demand that we readjust our priorities and goals so that we tackle the immense problems we face at home and abroad with realism, and not with rhetoric.

*Washington, pub. June 16.*

**Carl T. Curtis**
*United States Senator, R-Neb.*

There's no question but what the United States is committed too heavily in too many places in the world. Candor and honesty require that notice be given that people will have to help themselves. Furthermore, United States efforts can only succeed when we are trying to help someone who is really trying to help themselves.

*Washington, pub. July 27.*

**Thomas J. Dodd**
*United States Senator, D-Conn.*

We are now heading into the most perilous period in the history of our republic . . . If we succumb to the neo-isolationalism and anti-militarism that have become so prevalent in our society, if we appear to lack the will to defend ourselves and our allies, then I truly fear for the future.

*Washington, pub. June 20.*

**Peter H. Dominick**
*United States Senator, R-Colo.*

I do not think there are any of us who want the United States to be a world policeman. Certainly I do not. I do not think this administration does, and I do not think anyone else in the country wants us to be a world policeman. Nevertheless, we have to assume the role of leadership in the free world, and we have to be able to provide support for our allies in the event that they are threatened or attacked.

*Before the Senate, Washington, Sept. 4.*

**Cyrus S. Eaton**
*Chairman, Chesapeake & Ohio Railway*

I think our opportunity is in world trade. First, the world needs food and the U.S. produces it in immense quantities—

we even have to hoard it. If we would sell these people (Communist nations) food on time—extend them credit—some of the credit would not be good, but a hell of a lot of it would do us more good than our armies.

*Interview, Cleveland, pub. July 27.*

**John S. D. Eisenhower**
*United States Ambassador to Belgium*

Being an ambassador is primarily a communications job. You have to get along with people, and understand them. It's a matter of sitting down and talking and finding out what the other side thinks or wants. You have to be a damn good listener. It's also making sure your own government understands the position of the country where you're stationed, without ifs, ands or buts. This is essential.

*Interview, Valley Forge, Pa.,*
*pub. April 20.*

**Allen J. Ellender**
*United States Senator, D-La.*

The most important thing for the United States and Russia to do is understand each other. We have our system. They have theirs. But we've got to work together. If we do, we can maintain the peace of the world. If we don't, there will be another war.

*Pub. June 10.*

**Paul Findley**
*United States Representative, R-Ill.*

. . . U.S. moves showing that we want to normalize relations with China and Eastern Europe will do more than anything else to make Soviet behavior more reasonable.

*Washington, pub. May 1.*

**Ed Foreman**
*United States Representative, R-N.M.*

Never before in the history of mankind has there been demonstrated such short-sighted generosity as our expensive, badly executed, unrealistic, uncontrolled and uncontrollable foreign aid giveaway program. This is the only Federal aid program I know of that does not exert Federal control along with the granting of Federal funds. Since its inception, we have dished out $182 billion, counting the interest we have paid on the money we have borrowed to give away, to over 100 of the 120 nations on the face of the earth, and we have less international respect and fewer friends than we did when we started this runaway boondoggle.

*Before the House, Washington, Nov. 20.*

**Donald M. Fraser**
*United States Representative, D-Minn.*

If the time ever comes when Peace Corps volunteers are not free to express their views, then I shall vote to kill (the Peace Corps) quickly, rather than let it die on the vine as it would.

*Before House Foreign Affairs Committee, Washington, July 24.*

**John Freeman**
*United Kingdom Ambassador to the United States*

Ambassadors, perhaps even more than others in public life, do best if they keep their mouths shut until they know what they are talking about . . .

*London, pub. Jan. 12.*

**J. William Fulbright**
*United States Senator, D-Ark.*

I have the impression that Mr. (William P.) Rogers (U.S. Secretary of State) is a broad-gauged man. He's not a doctrinaire. He isn't committed to the dogmas of the past. He's willing to adapt himself to changing conditions . . . He hasn't made up his mind that the United States has got to run the world, that we're the only good people in the world, or that we can't negotiate with communist countries.

*Before Senate Foreign Relations Committee, Washington, pub. Jan. 19.*

A democracy simply cannot allow foreign policy to become an end in itself, or anything more than an instrument toward the central, dominating goal of securing democratic values within our own society. I would indeed lay it down as a fairly confident prediction that, if American democracy is destroyed within the next generation, it will not be destroyed by the Russians or the Chinese, but by ourselves,

by the very means we use to defend it.

*National War College, Washington, May 19.*

The choice before the nation is whether the U.S. wants to set a humane example to the world, or wants the maintenance of a *Pax Americana*, with the imposition of peace by force of arms. We must stop being a busybody abroad and come back home to pay attention to domestic ills.

*Washington, pub. June 16.*

. . . neither Senate resolutions or any organizational or procedural devices are likely to restore Congressional authority in foreign affairs. The restoration of Constitutional balance will depend on decisions of a more fundamental nature, decisions as to the kind of country we want America to be and the kind of role we want it to play in the world.

*Washington, pub. June 20.*

Power is a narcotic, a potent intoxicant, and America has been on a trip.

*Washington University, St. Louis, Dec. 10.*

**James H. Giffen**
*Vice president, Satra Corporation*

We (the United States) discourage exports to the Soviet Union with restrictions, but complain about our balance of payments situation and preach free trade. We refuse to sell so-called strategic commodities to the Soviet Union but openly and unhesitatingly purchase such goods from them. We announced that we want to leave the period of confrontation and begin an era of negotiation but refuse to negotiate matters concerning trade.

*At Town Hall, Los Angeles, Aug. 26.*

**Barry M. Goldwater**
*United States Senator, R-Ariz.*

The history is clear. The language is clear. An implied provision has become attached to the (nuclear non-proliferation treaty) . . . that would bind the United States to guarantee the security of any non-nuclear-weapon party that is a victim of nuclear aggression or threat of such aggression . . . thus, the role of the United States as the policeman of the

(BARRY M. GOLDWATER)

world will truly be assured if the Senate approves this treaty.

*Before the Senate,*
*Washington, pub. March 9.*

**Albert Gore**
*United States Senator, D-Tenn.*

Never before have two great nations had such a mutuality of interests as now exists between the United States and the Soviet Union. It is the mutuality of self-preservation—the first law of nature and man.

*Before Senate Foreign Relations*
*Committee, Washington, March 21.*

**H. R. Haldeman**
*Assistant to the*
*President of the United States*

He (President Nixon) doesn't run out and say we're going to totally shift American foreign policy. He builds the groundwork for doing that. He builds the confidence, man by man, one by one, with the key leaders of the world. They'll deal with him in ways they wouldn't deal with others. And it's because of the confidence they have in him.

*Interview, Washington, pub. December.*

**Edward T. Hall**
*Professor of Anthropology,*
*Northwestern University*

We (Americans) insist that everyone else do things our way. Consequently, we manage to convey the impression that we simply regard foreign nationals as "underprivileged" Americans.

*Before Senate Foreign Relations*
*Committee, Washington, pub. June 12.*

**John A. Hannah**
*Chairman, United States*
*Commission on Civil Rights*

Certainly we have to solve the problems of the black people and of the cities. But when two-thirds of the people of the underdeveloped countries live in poverty, hunger and despair and we have to live in the same world, we are not likely to have peace in the world, or the United States either, unless we help these peo[ple] make some progress.

*Before House Foreign Affa[irs]*
*Committee, Washington, June*

**William H. Harsha**
*United States Representative, R-Ohio*

. . . I find it both ironic and shock[ing] that three countries which have receiv[ed] substantial U.S. aid—Korea, Thaila[nd] and Taiwan—are now loaning mo[ney] back to us at 6-per cent interest. It see[ms] rather ridiculous to debilitate our o[wn] economy in such a manner and then [to] these countries more money to keep [their] own economy solvent.

*Before the House, Washington, Nov.*

**U. Alexis Johnson**
*Under Secretary of State*
*for Political Affairs of the United State[s]*

While the United States interests rem[ain] essentially the same and our commitme[nt] firm, we must recognize that there[ is] undeniably a change in the mood of [the] American people. They will be cauti[ous] about undertaking new commitme[nt] They are becoming somewhat impati[ent] with carrying what many consider to [be] a disproportionate share of the bur[den] of security and economic assista[nce] abroad. They are asking more and m[ore] frequently what other countries are [do]ing to help themselves and each ot[her] to share these burdens. It is a good [and] proper question.

*San Francisco, pub. May*

**Henry A. Kissinger**
*Assistant to the President of the*
*United States for National*
*Security Affairs*

There are people in this country [to] whom talking to the Russians takes [on] aspects of psychotherapy. I do the [Rus]sians the honor of taking them seriou[sly] I think that 50 years of trouble betw[een] two countries suggests some fundame[ntal] reasons for that trouble. Do not misun[der]stand me, I am not against talking to [the] Russians; but I don't think that fu[nda]mental differences will be set aside [just] by having good personal relations [with] them. I think our approach is better fo[r] d on a cool assessment of the situation. eople who believe that talks would solve ıings *per se* should reflect on the fact ıat every summit visit has been fol- ›wed by worse relations.

*Washington, pub. Aug. 22.*

**lfred M. Landon**
*ormer Governor of Kansas*

We (the United States) are the most ›nerous people of the world, the most ›mmitted to the protection of freedom, e most altruistic, but, despite those qual- es, there are limits beyond which we ınnot reasonably exercise our will and solve to assume, alone, the role of world ›liceman and benefactor.

*Kansas State University, June 24.*

**ılter Lippmann**
*ıthor, Newspaper Columnist*

The overexpansion which President Nix- has used as a keynote of his foreign licy is now increasingly evident to all › young, middle-aged and old people. ıat overexpansion in the 1950's—begin- ıg before the Korean War, beginning lly with the Truman Doctrine—has ›n the cause of the distortion of our ›ole way of political life.

*Interview, Seal Harbor, Me., pub. Sept. 14.*

**ırman P. Lloyd**
*ited States Representative, R-Utah*

t is said we cannot be policeman for world, and I agree. Yet, there are edom-loving people who need encour- ›ment in being their own policeman ınst aggression; and in an age when men lk on the moon, we cannot, as a civiliz- ınation, be an island unto ourselves.

*Before the House, Washington, Dec. 1.*

**ıuel Lujan, Jr.**
*ited States Representative, R-N.M.*

merica's annual giveaway program for ›d and foe alike is before the House of ›resentatives for funding—and I hereby ›ster the loudest possible protest from poverty-stricken people of America vote "no." This is no time for America ›hrow her largesse to the rest of the ›ld. Rather, it is time for all those coun-

tries who have been on the receiving end of our patronage to realize that the goose that lays the golden eggs is in process of being cooked. It is time for them to say, "Save yourself, America, for without your strength we are lost."

*Before the House, Washington, Nov. 20.*

**John N. Mitchell**
*Attorney General of the United States*

The foreign policy of this Government canno†—and will not—be formulated in the streets of Washington or in any other street of this nation . . . The negative cyni- cism of demonstrators cannot be allowed to replace the affirmative program of those in government charged with con- ducting our foreign policy and carrying out our national security.

*Milwaukee, Nov. 11.*

**Edmund S. Muskie**
*United States Senator, D-Me.*

The United States is and will continue to be a world power. Our population, our resources and our economic strength give us a weight in world affairs we cannot avoid . . . To counsel retreat from involve- ment in international problems is to at- tempt the impossible. But to suggest a new look at the way we relate to other nations is the beginning of wisdom.

*University of Maryland, June 7.*

**Richard M. Nixon**
*President of the United States*

Let us help our friends who help them- selves, but let us not help any who help our enemies.

*Pub. Jan. 12.*

Let all nations know that during this administration our lines of communica- tions will be open. We seek an open world —open to ideas, open to the exchange of goods and people—a world in which no people, great or small, will live in angry isolation. We cannot expect to make every- one our friend, but we can try to make no one our enemy. Those who would be our adversaries we invite to a peaceful competition—not in conquering territory or extending dominion, but in enriching the life of man.

(RICHARD M. NIXON)

The peace we seek to win is not victory over any people but the peace that comes with healing in its wings, with compassion for those who have suffered, with understanding for those who have opposed us, with the opportunity for all the peoples of this earth to choose their own destiny.

*Inaugural address, Washington, Jan. 20.*

As I look at this trip (to Europe) and what it may accomplish, I want to make very clear that this is only a first step in achieving a purpose that I have long felt is vital to the future of peace for the United States and for the world. And that is the strengthening and revitalizing of the American-European community.

I think you could describe me best as not being a "half-worlder," with my eyes looking only to Europe or only to Asia, but one who sees the whole world. We live in one world and we must go forward together in this whole world.

*News conference, Washington, Feb. 6.*

. . . free-world leadership, in my view, does not mean dictatorship to the free world. It means consultation with the free world and developing from the leaders of the free world the best possible thinking that we can develop for attacking our common problems.

*Washington, Feb. 22.*

As we enter what I have described as a period of negotiations with those who have been our opponents, we recognize that, for those negotiations to succeed, it is essential that we maintain the strength that made the negotiations possible.

*Before West German Parliament, Bonn, Feb. 26.*

I believe all of us . . . have no illusions about the limits of personal diplomacy in settling great differences between nations. A smile or handshake or an exchange of toasts or gifts or visits will not, by themselves, have effects where vital interests are concerned and where there are great differences.

I believe that it is far more effective in international policy to use deeds, rather than words threatening deeds, in order to accomplish objectives.

. . . I think, as far as (world) commitments are concerned, the United States has a full plate.

I, first, do not believe that we should make new commitments around the world unless our national interests are very vitally involved. Secondly, I do not believe we should become involved in the quarrels of nations in other parts of the world unless we are asked to become involved and unless, also, we are vitally involved.

*News conference, Washington, March 4.*

Living in the real world of today means unfreezing our old concepts of East versus West, while never losing sight of great ideological differences.

*At conference of North Atlantic Treaty Organization, Washington, April 10.*

Imagine for a moment . . . what would happen to this world if . . . America were to become a dropout in assuming the responsibility for defending peace and freedom . . . If America would turn its back on the world, there would be peace that would settle over this planet, but it would be the kind of peace that suffocated freedom in Czechoslovakia. The danger to us has changed, but it has not vanished. We must revitalize our alliances, not abandon them; we must rule out unilateral disarmament, because in the real world it won't work.

*U.S. Air Force Academy, Colorado Springs, Colo., June 4.*

One of the legacies of Vietnam almost certainly will be a deep reluctance on the part of the United States to become involved once again in a similar intervention on a similar basis.

*Guam, pub. July 27.*

Our (U.S. and Romania's) differences are matters of substance. Indeed, no nation's range of interests are identical to any other nation's. But nations can have widely different internal orders and live in peace. Nations can have widely differing economic interests and live in peace.

*Bucharest, pub. Aug. 5.*

It is not my belief that the way to peace is by giving up our friends or letting down our allies.

*Before General Assembly,*
*United Nations, N.Y., Sept. 18.*

**Olaf Palme**
*Premier-elect of Sweden*

I don't think you can conclude that the United States, by not sending an ambassador (to Sweden), is saying that it does not approve of the Government of Sweden. To argue this is to argue that the United States does approve of the Governments in Greece, South Africa, Spain and Bulgaria, where it does have ambassadors.

*Stockholm, Oct. 1.*

**Otto E. Passman**
*United States Representative, D-La.*

As I understand it, we were an underdeveloped country 180 years ago, with a population of 3,000,000. While we were underdeveloped, some of the now underdeveloped countries were then developed. Now that they are underdeveloped, we are becoming underdeveloped helping those underdeveloped countries become developed again. When we finally become underdeveloped and the underdeveloped nations are developed, I wonder if they will come to our aid.

*Pub. Oct. 13.*

**Lester B. Pearson**
*Former Prime Minister of Canada*

The priorities in the United States are guns, butter, outer space and then foreign aid. And the danger is that, when the (budget) cuts come, the foreign aid gets hurt most.

*Ottawa, pub. Oct. 2.*

**Charles H. Percy**
*United States Senator, R-Ill.*

It's no longer necessary for us to subsidize the defense of Europe.

*News conference, Boston, April 7.*

Fresh, loud voices in America are calling for retaliation in kind against Japanese import controls. Ultimately, this trend, if allowed to go unchecked, will harm Japan, which will be the biggest loser, and it will harm the United States. Politically and economically, our two nations should enjoy the closest ties, if we are to live in peace and stability.

*Shimoda, Japan, Sept. 5.*

**Robert D. Price**
*United States Representative, R-Tex.*

. . . the main problem with our foreign aid program, as presently conceived and operated, is that we are using a shotgun instead of a rifle approach. We should trade our costly, expansive, and widebased foreign aid program for a limited and narrow-gaged program strictly designed to promote our national interest. We should give foreign aid only to promote the economic health and well-being of nations that are either firm allies or potential allies of the United States, and that are willing to help themselves.

*Before the House, Washington, Nov. 20.*

**Roman C. Pucinski**
*United States Representative, D-Ill.*

If the average American corporation had as many failures in the conduct of its business as the State Department has had in conducting our international affairs, we would all be bankrupt.

*Before the House, Washington, Oct. 6.*

**William J. Randall**
*United States Representative, D-Mo.*

I oppose military and supporting assistance to dictatorships in Spain, Greece, Haiti, and various less-developed countries. While we are fighting in Vietnam, ostensibly to defend the South Vietnamese right of free elections and self-determination, it seems anomalous to donate American treasure to the aid of governments systematically oppressing their citizens, and this is particularly wrong in the case of military aid.

*Before the House, Washington, Dec. 9.*

**Elliot L. Richardson**
*Under Secretary of State*
*of the United States*

We have learned at home that neglect of the poor and underprivileged can have explosive effects. It is only prudent to

(ELLIOT L. RICHARDSON)

apply 'that lesson to a world which is growing even smaller and more inter-dependent . . . The developed countries, including the United States, cannot allow themselves to become isolated islands of affluence in a sea of poverty and frustration.

*Before House Foreign Affairs Committee, Washington, June 9.*

Each (Russia and China) is highly sensitive about American efforts to improve relations with the other . . . We are not . . . going to let Communist Chinese invective deter us from seeking agreements with the Soviet Union, where those are in our interest. Conversely, we are not going to let Soviet apprehensions prevent us from attempting to bring China out of its angry, alienated shell.

*New York, Sept. 6.*

**David Rockefeller**
*Chairman, Chase Manhattan Bank of New York*

Even if hunger and birth control problems are solved . . . poor countries remain at a serious disadvantage technologically . . . We have every right to expect urgent trade representations from them in the months and years immediately ahead. They have a strong moral case, but the political and economic case for responding constructively to these representations is, in my judgment, just as strong.

*At International Industrial Conference, San Francisco, Sept. 15.*

**William P. Rogers**
*Secretary of State of the United States*

(In international affairs) the weak can be rash, the powerful must be more restrained. Complexity in world affairs should teach us the need to act responsibly, to substitute cooperation for coercion and to move from confrontation to negotiation on the issues that divide nations.

*Before American Society of Newspaper Editors, Washington, April 16.*

There will be no attempt or willingness on the part of the United States to resolve

any issue with the Soviet Union at t expense of our allies.

*At United States-Japanese Econon Conference, Tokyo, July*

I am convinced our general approach taking a fairly low tone—but being perfe ly frank and outspoken—is the way foreign policy should be conducted in future. That expresses our basic Ameri viewpoint. We must show that we are e to get along with, but that we are weak or soft-headed . . . There is no in the world who doesn't know we powerful. We have great strength ec omically, militarily, technologically. have landed two men on the moon. do not have to tell other countries t Our problem is to use that power wi in a manner which is not abrasive to convince people that the things say, we mean. This has been one of failures of the past; we have not persua others that we really meant what we s

*Interview, Auckland, New Zeal Aug.*

**Dean Rusk**
*Secretary of State of the United States*

One of the things that I may fin chance to comment on after I le office is the myth of the world's po man. There is just no truth in the gestion that, somehow, we look u ourselves as the country that is suppo to go around everywhere in the w tidying up all the disputes that occur intervening in them.

*News conference, Washington, Ja*

**Dean Rusk**
*Former Secretary of State of the United States*

I once had a count made when I wa the Department. Out of the 400 last c in the world involving the use of viole the United States had directly particip in only six of them.

*Television interview, New Y Marc*

I feel that diplomacy requires c Diplomacy has worked for hundred years to eliminate the accidents of sonality from the conduct of state af

That's why, for example, we sign a diplomatic note, "Accept, Excellency, the assurances of my highest consideration," when, in fact, you're telling him to go to hell.

*Television interview,*
*Washington, pub. April 7.*

**Walter F. Schlech, Jr.**
*Rear Admiral, United States Navy*

Let it be remembered, American flag ships are generally the most conspicuous American visitors to foreign ports. In some cases they are the only American visitors . . . The very presence of American seamen in American ships abroad is of considerable value today, because fear, distrust and suspicion of the United States have been deliberately fostered among certain peoples of the world. Our American flag ships with American crews, by their mere presence, are an overwhelming denial of these false impressions. Our American flag ships plying the trade routes of the Seven Seas, and putting into the ports of the world, are living positive proof of the vigor and stout character of our American system.

*Tulane University, New Orleans,*
*March 24.*

**Arthur M. Schlesinger, Jr.**
*Professor of Humanities,*
*City University of New York*

I think that one can't glide over the fact that he (Lyndon B. Johnson) was the last President, I hope, who is committed to the proposition . . . of American omnipotence . . . I think this was an avoidable and disastrous course.

*Pub. Jan. 19.*

**Robert L. F. Sikes**
*United States Representative, D-Fla.*

The power and prestige of the United States do not suggest a hat-in-hand approach or obeisance in our dealings abroad; nor do we need bluff and bluster. We have shown our good intentions time and again to nearly every country in the world; we should combine this background with strong implementation of U.S. policy in support of democratic ideals, and we should be sufficiently practical to limit our help abroad to those who help us.

*Before the House, Washington, Sept. 8.*

**John Stennis**
*United States Senator, D-Miss.*

. . . it is a fact of life that we have binding moral commitments with many nations that we cannot ignore or neglect. To do so would be to repudiate our word. solemnly given. I strongly favor re-negotiating many of the agreements, but I do not favor running out on our promises as to a single one.

*Before the Senate, Washington, Sept. 3.*

**Joseph D. Tydings**
*United States Senator, D-Md.*

(The United States should) cut off military assistance to reactionary regimes and discontinue our clandestine efforts to undermine revolutionary movements.

*Goucher College, Towson, Md.,*
*June 15.*

**Pierre Uri**
*French Economist*

It's not so much that LBJ (former President Lyndon B. Johnson) had a wrong approach toward Europe—he had no approach whatsoever.

*Pub. March 10.*

**Frances E. Willis**
*Former United States*
*Career Ambassador*

The United States is so powerful that we have seen some of the results in terms of limitations (of our power). In the world today, military and economic power cannot accomplish whatever a strong nation wants. We must follow policies to win voluntary cooperation from other nations.

*Interview, pub. May 11.*

# Government

## Dean Acheson
*Former United States
Secretary of State*

The world is very largely a struggle between stupidity and intelligence, between short-term views and long-term views, and what you find omnipresent is weak, minority government. In the U.S., a minority voted for the President. Congress is in the hands of a different party and our people are deeply divided. We have a middle class concerned more with tranquility than with anything else, and evangelical liberals who believe all governments ought to be governed by pure democracies.

I think we're going to have a major constitutional crisis if we make a habit of destroying Presidents. We'll have the situation we had after the Civil War, when the Presidency practically disappeared—from Andrew Johnson to McKinley.

*Interview, Washington, Oct. 9.*

## Spiro T. Agnew
*Vice President of the United States*

I fully feel that by the time a year has gone by and I'll have been functioning in this expanded Vice President's role that's been given me, and particularly in regard to intergovernmental relationships with the cities, that what I do and what I stand for is going to be so obvious that it's going to be very difficult for the people who are attempting to cast me in the role of the Neanderthal man to continue to think that way.

*Television interview, New York, Jan. 7.*

We shall attempt to bring the best minds in America to bear on our nation's problems. We shall call upon every citizen to make his maximum contribution to their

resolution. We recognize and shall proudly represent that preponderant majority of Americans who too long have been called the forgotten Americans and considered only as the silent center of our citizenry. Yet, these are the Americans who have defended our country in war; who built our economy back up from cataclysmic depression; who have never lost faith in our free and open system of government.

*New York, Jan. 25.*

Sometimes (in the office of vice president) you feel like a three-pound hen trying to lay a four-pound egg. No matter how it comes out, it hurts.

*Baltimore, pub. March 27.*

As Vice President, I know what minority employment is. This office isn't exactly the exercise of raw power.

*Before National Alliance of Businessmen,
Washington, April 8.*

This country is too big to be run from Washington.

*Sacramento, May 6.*

I believe in Constitutional dissent. I believe in the people registering their views with their elected representatives; and I commend those people who care enough about their country to involve themselves in its great issues. I believe in legal protest within the Constitutional limits of free speech, including peaceful assembly and the right of petition. But I do not believe that demonstrations, lawful or unlawful, merit my approval or even my silence where the purpose is fundamentally unsound.

*Harrisburg, Pa., Oct. 30.*

A little over a week ago, I took a rather unusual step for a Vice President. I said something.

*Harrisburg, Pa., pub. Nov. 7.*

**Svetlana Alliluyeva**
*Daughter of the late Josef Stalin,*
*Premier of the Union of*
*Soviet Socialist Republics*

I feel only one thing. This (the United States) is a free society, where everyone can do what he wants and express his own opinion. Probably the result is disorder, but it's much better than order based on oppression. I prefer to be free in disorder.
*Interview, Princeton, N.J.,*
*pub. Sept. 9.*

**Hannah Arendt**
*Professor, New School*
*For Social Research*

The country seems to have fallen under a spell and nothing seems to work any more . . . I'm very pessimistic. I believe all the large Western European governments suffer the same power loss. It is very characteristic for our time that only small governments still can rely on the support of their citizens, and still can solve problems because their problems are still manageable.
*New York, May 22.*

**Birch E. Bayh**
*United States Senator, D-Ind.*

I think that direct election is an idea whose time has arrived.
*Washington, Feb. 21.*

**Alexander M. Bickel**
*Professor of Law, Yale University*

I believe that, in its essential features, our present system for electing Presidents and Vice Presidents—the electoral college, with the vote of each state cast as a unit—works out better—more equitably, and with greater safety to other institutions that we value—than any alternative I have heard proposed.
*Before House Judiciary Committee,*
*Washington, pub. March 2.*

**Winton M. Blount**
*Postmaster General of the United States*

I didn't come to this office with my eyes closed—but the facts are far worse than I dreamed.
*Pub. March 3.*

. . . We have . . . to bring this Department (the Post Office)—kicking and screaming —into the last third of the twentieth century. If we can do that, we will have done something pretty dramatic.
*Interview, Washington, pub. March 31.*

I'm going to take time to turn this (postal) system around, and we think we've got to start and we think we'd better start pretty quick. Because if we don't, a few years from now this system could collapse of its own weight.
*Washington, June 1.*

I am the sixth Postmaster General in this decade, and with each new office holder has come new policies and politics. No organization could be expected to operate smoothly and efficiently under such a revolving door management.
*Before National Postal Forum,*
*Washington, Sept. 8.*

**Omar N. Bradley**
*General, United States Army (Ret.);*
*former chairman, Joint Chiefs of Staff*

Self government is not a luxury we may use to grow fat and indulgent. It is an instrument to safeguard individual freedom. Democratic self-government tries its people with a sterner challenge than any other system in the world.
*Los Angeles, Nov. 11.*

**Clifford P. Case**
*United States Senator, R-N.J.*

The only body, the only group of people in the world, who can challenge a decision by the President is Congress. The President is bound to get from people he seeks advice from, the advice they think he wants to hear. Only in this body, in Congress, particularly in the Senate, with its longer terms of office, with its overlapping terms, terms overlapping one administration, does there exist the political independence which can provide the real criticism in a constructive way . . .
*Before the Senate, Washington, Sept. 12.*

**Emanuel Celler**
*United States Representative, D-N.Y.*

Victor Hugo once said: "When the time for an idea has come, nothing can stop

(EMANUEL CELLER)

it." The time for the idea of changing our method of electing the President and the Vice President has indeed come, and nothing, I can assure Members (of the House), can stop it.

*Before the House, Washington, Sept. 9.*

## Shirley Chisholm
*United States Representative, D-N.Y.*

Apparently all they know here in Washington about Brooklyn is that a tree grew there . . . It is time for the House of Representatives to pay attention to other considerations than its petrified, sanctified system of seniority, which is apparently the only basis for making most of its decisions.

*Washington, Jan. 29.*

Congress is so traditional, so tied to the old ways. I really don't think we can rely on it to lead the way. The answer has to come from the people.

*St. Louis, pub. Sept. 18.*

## Frank Church
*United States Senator, D-Idaho*

Prospects seem to be improving for legislation which will one day require all high officials of the Federal Government, both elected and appointed, to make a periodic disclosure of their income and assets. I personally feel that the enactment of such a comprehensive disclosure statute, applicable to the executive, legislative, and judicial branches of the Government, is long overdue. It would go far toward restoring healthy public confidence in our political institutions and in the men who hold public office.

*Before the Senate, Washington, Sept. 12.*

## Ramsey Clark
*Former Attorney General of the United States*

Dissent is the principal catalyst in the alchemy of truth, and, without it, neither this society nor its Government can effectively change to meet rapidly changing needs of its people . . . Today's dissent is the means through which the powerless people of this country can be heard.

There is no security without it, and, f that matter, the best way to debilita security is to restrict the freedom dissenters.

*Before the Senate, Washington, Sept. I*

## Manuel F. Cohen
*Chairman, Securities and Exchange Commission of the United States*

. . . although I am a regulator, I wou feel more comfortable with less regul tion were I sure that the private secto would undertake the self-discipline whi is not only necessary to the continu growth of our financial communitie and public confidence in them, but is tru for the best interests of the industry. U fortunately, the time is not yet. Probabl it never will be. Only a Pollyanna like n can still cherish the hope.

*Before Economic Club of Detro Jan. 2*

. . . the exercise of political powe whether by government or business, ca not be legitimate unless it is non-autho tarian—that is, unless it is subject to fr and systematic analysis and criticism. some extent, federal regulatory agenci have provided this function.

*Detroit, Jan. 2*

## Wilbur J. Cohen
*Former Secretary of Health, Education and Welfare of the United States*

When anyone asks me to make a co ment critical of Mr. (Robert H.) Fin (present HEW Secretary), I don't do Why take potshots at a man whose dif culties I'm absolutely familiar with? The but for the grace of God go I.

*Pub. Oct.*

## John Conyers, Jr.
*United States Representative, D-Mich.*

Today, the American people are longer willing to stand by silently and ele a man President who has polled few votes than his opponent. This has ha pened three times before in the history our nation. The time has come to era cate the possibility of its ever happen again. I do not think that we should e

gain subject the American people to the
ossibility that, between election day
November and the meeting of the
lectoral college in December, they might
e forced to wait while two candidates
argain with a third for the Presidency.
*Before the House,Washington, Sept. 18.*

**listair Cooke**
*orrespondent, "Manchester Guardian"*

No matter what they say, I still sub-
ribe to H. L. Mencken's definition of
e Vice President as the man who is sit-
ng in the outer office of the President
aiting for him to sneeze.
*New York, Jan. 13.*

**ominick V. Daniels**
*nited States Representative, D-N.J.*

A major argument against the direct
ection plan seems to be that the small
ates are against it, thus dooming any
roposal which requires ratification of
ree quarters of all the states. I do not
gree. Polls taken as late as 1968 indicate
e preference of a majority of state legis-
tors, including those in small states, for
e direct election plan. These legislators,
d a substantial majority of the people
roughout the country, understand that
eir common interests are not regional;
t geography does not confine problems
a single area of the country; that prob-
ms in the South are shared by those in
e North and West; that the people of the
idwest express many of the same de-
ands as those living in the East. In a
deral election, it is these common prob-
ms which find expression in the vote for
President. I strongly believe that the
merican people are capable of choos-
g their President.
*Before the House, Washington, Sept. 18.*

**obert B. Docking**
*overnor of Kansas*

I have certain reservations about revenue
aring (by the Federal Government).
ou first have got to have the revenue to
are. And the Federal Government has as
ght a budget as the states. To be any
od, such a program must be taken over
long period of time consistent, from
ar to year, for 10 years.
*Pub. Sept. 19.*

**Robert Dole**
*United States Senator, R-Kan.*

They've got a bunch of jerks at the
White House at the staff level, and that's
where a lot of decisions are made.
*Pub. Sept. 21.*

**Peter F. Drucker**
*Professor of Management,*
*New York University*

There is mounting evidence that government is big rather than strong; that it is fat
and flabby rather than powerful; that it
costs a great deal but does not achieve
very much. Indeed, government is sick
—and just at the time we need a strong,
healthy and vigorous government.
*Pub. Sept. 15.*

**Bob Eckhardt**
*United States Representative, D-Tex.*

The important thing about the system
that exists today is that when a President
is elected, history has shown us he is
nearly always elected by a sweeping electoral vote. This may not appear important
to people today, but it has unified this nation for 180 years. For some reason—and
I think it is a reason closely akin to the
intelligent pragmatism of the common
law—the electoral vote magnifies the
popular vote majority . . . It is that fact
which gives the people a feeling of finality
in our presidential elections, a feeling that
the election was a valid determination by
and for the nation. It seems to me we
make a mistake if we argue over a number of different percentages and come
out with a conclusion that a man elected
by, say, 35 or 40 or 45 per cent, thus receives a mandate of the people to lead
the nation.
*Before the House, Sept. 18.*

**Dwight D. Eisenhower**
*Former President of the United States*

. . . The best thing is just good common
sense in government.
*Pub. Jan. 29.*

**Milton S. Eisenhower**
*Director, Freedom's Foundation*

There is a lot of good common sense
in the statement that those who are old
enough to carry out the foreign policy of

(MILTON S. EISENHOWER)

this country by offering their lives in war are also old enough to decide (through voting) if they are to have a war.

*News conference, Washington, Nov. 25.*

**Dorothy Elston**
*Treasurer of the United States*

There are so many women with responsible jobs in government, and treated with great respect, that I'm not so quick to say that women have been discriminated against, save at the cabinet level.

*Pub. June 10.*

**Sam J. Ervin, Jr.**
*United States Senator, D-N.C.*

Crusading bureaucrats are power hungry officers of the executive branch of the Government who steal a mile of authority for every inch given them by law.

*Before the Senate, Washington, Nov. 5.*

**Robert H. Finch**
*Secretary of Health, Education and Welfare of the United States*

. . . with all of our institutions under fire, it is going to be terribly exciting to head an agency that must deal simultaneously with both the attacked and the attackers. HEW is where the action is.

*Pub. May 2.*

**J. William Fulbright**
*United States Senator, D-Ark.*

(The United States) is already a long way toward becoming an elective dictatorship, more or less complete over foreign policy and over those vast and expanding areas of our domestic life which, in one way or another, are related to or independent upon the military establishment . . . (Thus) the future can hold nothing for us except endless foreign exertions, chronic warfare, burgeoning expense and the proliferation of an already formidable military-industrial-labor-academic complex— in short, the militarization of American life. If . . . America is to become an empire, there is very little chance that it can avoid becoming a virtual dictatorship as well.

*Washington, June 19.*

**Cornelius E. Gallagher**
*United States Representative, D-N.J.*

One of the great tragedies of the European democracies is that they too often succumbed to multiparty factionalism . . . If we now are to provide for a grab bag popular election, with no tempering forces, then we may actually encourage the formation of numerous splinter parties. In other words, in our current rush to prevent the election of a minority demogogue, we may in reality be paving the way for the election of such an individual.

*Before the House, Washington, Sept. 18.*

**John W. Gardner**
*Chairman, Urban Coalition*

The departments of the Federal Government are in grave need of renewal. State government in most places is a 19th century relic. In most cities, municipal government is a waxworks of stiffly preserved anachronisms. The courts are crippled by archaic organizational arrangements. The unions, the professions, the universities, the corporations, each has spun its own inpenetrable web of vested interests.

When people, for whatever reason— oppression or laziness or complacency— take no part in their institutions, the institutions themselves decay at an accelerating rate. But it is not essential that everyone participate. As a matter of fact, if everyone suddenly did, the society would fall apart. Participation should simply be an available option.

*Harvard University, pub. April 11.*

The Speaker of the House is 78. Thirteen Senate and House committee chairmen are over 70, six of them over 75, two over 80. They are full of years and honors. They can serve best by stepping aside. That would be patriotism at its highest.

*Before National Press Club, Washington, pub. Dec. 26.*

**Eric F. Goldman**
*Professor of History, Princeton University*

I would like to see a constitutional amendment which will end the position of vice presidency (of the United States), because it is demeaning and humiliating to any man of calibre.

*News conference, California Institute of Technology, Feb. 24.*

**Barry Goldwater, Jr.**
*United States Representative, R-Calif.*

If, under our present system, someone wanted to lower the voting age to 18, I'd say No . . . if they lower the voting age to 18, they should lower all ages: drinking, the age of consent and so forth. In other words, if a person is old enough and intelligent enough to assume the responsibility of voting, then he should be old enough to assume these other responsibilities.

*Interview, pub. August.*

**Edith Green**
*United States Representative, D-Ore.*

. . . in these restless years for a nation in search of new directions and workable methods for social progress, the clarion call has gone out: America must be realistic; America must submit to the admittedly fascinating, but rigidly doctrinaire and wholly uncompromising, politics of the "New Left." For that one I would like to quote the prominent philosopher Charlie Brown: "Rats."

*Before the House, Washington, Oct. 29.*

**John A. Gronouski**
*Former Postmaster General
of the United States*

When I can have a mailman pick up a letter at my door and another mailman hand-deliver it to the door of a friend in California, often the next day, at a cost of six cents, I am receiving a service very hard to duplicate this day and age.

*Before House Post Office and Civil Service Committee, Washington, pub. July 31.*

**Durward G. Hall**
*United States Representative, R-Mo.*

The Senate has never been known as a body that has done its homework.

*Washington, pub. May 12.*

**William H. Harsha**
*United States Representative, R-Ohio*

. . . Have we arrived at the place in our national history where the leaders of our nation should start to follow policies dictated by street demonstrations? Are we hereafter to have government by demonstration rather than by representation? The pathways of history are cluttered with the ruins of once great nations whose downfall can be traced to the point where legitimate representative government gave way to leaders who tried to accede to the mercurial whimsies of mob rule.

*Before the House, Washington, Oct. 15.*

**George B. Hartzog, Jr.**
*Director, National Park Service*

The cardinal principle in communications in a public agency, I believe, is complete candor. If you don't know the answer to a question—say so. It is much better for people to conclude that you are ignorant than for them to find out later that you are a liar.

*Washington, pub. Aug. 22.*

**Richard G. Hatcher**
*Mayor, Gary, Ind.*

Capitalism for the most part has been able to progress only by exploitation of the masses. There is something wrong with capitalism because we have such a wide disparity—70 to 80 per cent of all the wealth in this country is controlled by about 5 per cent of the people.

*Gary, Feb. 7*

**Philip M. Hauser**
*Professor of Sociology,
University of Chicago*

The Federal Government will be turning funds over to state governments which, by any standards, are more inept, more subject to special pressures, more incompetent to do the job and more corrupt than any other branch of government.

*Before National League of Cities, San Diego, pub. Dec. 7.*

**S. I. Hayakawa**
*Acting President,
San Francisco State College*

When enough people are disillusioned

(s. i. hayakawa)

about the ability of government to govern, the time is ripe for a dictator. There is no . . . dictator in the wings that I know of, but creation of doubt is an important goal for them.

*Washington, pub. Feb. 9.*

**Donald Herzberg**
*Executive Director,*
*Eagle Institute of Politics,*
*Rutgers University*

I used to teach that the states were the ideal laboratories of democracy. But now I just don't see many states breaking loose from the mold they've been forced into for so long. They're not flexible any more; their muscles have atrophied from disuse.

*At National Governors Conference,*
*Colorado Springs, Colo., Sept. 1.*

**David Hilliard**
*National Chief of Staff,*
*Black Panther Party*

We advocate the very direct overthrow of the government by way of force and violence—by picking up guns and moving against it; because we recognize it as being oppressive, and, in recognizing that, we know that the only solution to it is armed struggle.

*Pub. Dec. 14.*

**Chet Holifield**
*United States Representative, D-Calif.*

Although over 73 million Americans went to their polling places in November of 1968, only 538 of them—the members of the electoral college—really participated in the election of Richard M. Nixon as President of the United States. This dangerous gamble with the fate and legitimacy of our government occurred—as it has for almost 200 years—because of the outmoded electoral system under which we function. That the system has functioned at all for this amount of time can only be attributed to the kind of luck usually described only in legend. Any process which permits a man to become President without winning the popular vote is intol-

erable, and inconsistent with the ba aims of our country.

*Before the House, Washington, Sept. 1*

**Hubert H. Humphrey**
*Former Vice President*
*of the United States*

Why shouldn't the voting age be lower to 18? They have a helluva lot me upstairs than my generation did in the 3

*Interview, pub. Feb.*

Nixon is coasting. He is in trouble. is taking aspirin for relief when he shou be taking something stronger for a cu A President needs long-range vision, a daily balance sheet.

*Interview, pub. Aug.*

It's like being naked in the middle of blizzard with no one to even offer you match to keep you warm—that's the vi presidency. You are trapped, vulnerab and alone, and it does not matter w happens to be President. Anyone w thinks that the Vice President can take position independent of the President his Administration simply has no knov edge of politics or government. You his choice in a political marriage, and expects your absolute loyalty.

*Interview, pub. Nov.*

**Edward Hutchinson**
*United States Representative, R-Mich.*

I believe that desirable reforms can accomplished within our federal (ele toral) system and that it is not necessa to destroy the system. The committe proposal, House Joint Resolution 6 instead of strengthening our familiar s tem, destroys it . . . The committee p posal has been promoted on the groun that it provides for the direct election the President by the people. The truth that the people already elect our Preside directly but they do it through a fede system where their role as citizens of th states is also preserved. Though I am enamored with the committee approac I am no less dedicated to the propositi that the people shall elect their Preside They do that now.

*Before the House, Sept.*

**Andrew Jacobs, Jr.**
*United States Representative, D-Ind.*

The only things of nobility that get done around here are done by people who don't realize they can't be done.

*Before House Judiciary Committee,*
*Washington, March 13.*

**Lyndon B. Johnson**
*President of the United States*

Throughout this time (his political career), I have been sustained by my faith in representative democracy—a faith I had learned in the Capitol Building as a Congressman and a Senator. I believe in the ultimate purposes of our nation— described by the Constitution, tempered by history, embodied in progressive laws, given life by men and women elected to serve their fellow citizens.

*State of the Union Message,*
*Washington, Jan. 14.*

**Lyndon B. Johnson**
*Former President of the United States*

It is not difficult to do the right thing as President. What is difficult is knowing what is right.

*San Clemente, Calif., Aug. 27.*

My father told me one time, when I was little boy, that I'd never know what it meant to be a father until I was a father. And one never knows what it is to be a President until you are a President.

*Arcata, Calif., pub. Sept. 5.*

**Nicholas Johnson**
*Commissioner, Federal*
*Communications Commission*

(The U.S. has become a) government of the people, by the corporations and for the rich.

*Television interview, New York, Aug. 25.*

**Jenkin Lloyd Jones**
*President, Chamber of Commerce*
*of the United States*

. . . the government . . . whether we like it or not, is in our hair. It is going to bug us increasingly as time goes on. For the bigger business becomes, the smaller the consumer feels, and the smaller he feels the more he turns to government as his protector and guardian. Let's not try to buck this tide. Let us recognize that it is merely an extension of a very old and very powerful trend dating way back to steamboat boilers, air brakes and fire escapes.

*Washington, Feb. 17.*

**F. R. Kappel**
*Former Chairman,*
*American Telephone & Telegraph Co.*

The post office is a nineteenth century institution trying to do a twentieth century job when the twenty-first century is right upon it.

*Pub. May 19.*

**Henry A. Kissinger**
*Assistant to the President*
*of the United States*
*for National Security Affairs*

I'm not making policy in the White House basement. When policy comes to be seen as my policy, then I've failed. If Cabinet officers sense that I use this position to regulate the flow of information so that the outcome is in the direction of my proffered point of view, then I've lost my effectiveness.

*Pub. Feb. 14.*

**Herbert G. Klein**
*White House*
*Director of Communications*

. I don't think there's a value in trying to form policy for the United States Government, or any government, from crowds on the street. If you go to that belief, then you have to believe that the strong shall rule the weak, either vocal or silent.

*Television interview,*
*Washington, Nov. 16.*

**Melvin R. Laird**
*Secretary of Defense*
*of the United States*

I do not expect unanimous acceptance of the decisions we (the Nixon Administration) will make in the coming months and years, but neither do I expect to be held accountable for the decisions by others which have been made in the past.

*Before Senate Armed Services*
*Committee, Washington, March 19.*

**Alfred M. Landon**
*Former Governor of Kansas*

We've got the welfare state accepted now—we're over the period of whether to have it or not. But now, we've got to make it work. We've got this unique American combination of capitalism and socialism, and it has to be made to work.
*Topeka, Kan., pub. Oct. 1.*

**John V. Lindsay**
*Mayor of New York*

We must bring the remote powerful institutions of America under a measure of public supervision—so that the giant utilities, the giant corporations, as well as the governments of this nation, treat individual citizens fairly.
*Before National League of Cities, San Diego, Dec. 3.*

**Helen MacInnes**
*Author*

If I knew Nixon, I would suggest to him that he urge every member of his new cabinet to take up the game of chess. We need chess-sharpened minds in Washington . . . more than ever before. In chess, you learn to think of four or five future moves you might make, and three or four counter-moves your opponent could make. Counter-intelligence is pure chess work.
*Pub. Jan. 28.*

**Lester G. Maddox**
*Governor of Georgia*

We have to guard against the intellectuals, who have created havoc on the campus, from moving into higher positions in government and spreading havoc there.
*At Southern Governors Conference, Williamsburg, Va., Sept. 15.*

**Mike Mansfield**
*United States Senator, D-Mont.*

A Vice President should not interfere in Senate affairs, regardless of his party. He is not a member of the Senate. He's a half-creature of the Senate and a half-creature of the Executive.
*Pub. Nov. 14.*

Checks and balances make this democracy unique. And, while democracy is a risky business, perhaps it's the risk in it which makes it the democracy that it is: unique, strong, self-reliant—but, at the same time, allowing all elements within our population to be heard, and allowing for a great deal of flexibility and leeway within and among parties.
*Interview, Washington, pub. Dec. 1.*

**Gale W. McGee**
*United States Senator, D-Wyo.*

Government careers must be competitive and comparable with private industry in wages and salaries, otherwise government cannot hope to attract and retain the people needed to do the job that must be done.
*Washington, pub. Feb. 14.*

. . . I share a reluctance to scrap the electoral college simply because it threatens to be unworkable. To use a tired cliche, we would be throwing the baby out with the bathwater, for it is the electoral system of counting votes for the Presidency which has . . . given our politics a fundamental steadiness through the years. We do not have a multitude of political parties because they lack hope of achieving electoral votes. Thus, our two-party system survives. Decidedly, the time has come to improve the system, to guard against faithless electors, and to insure against a small group of men, acting on their individual opinions and motives, being able to select the President. But we need not scrap the electoral principle itself in order to perfect it.
*Before the Senate, Washington, Oct. 6.*

**Theodore R. McKeldin**
*Former Governor of Maryland*

The toughest job ever conceived by the mind of man has to be the presidency of the United States. Nowhere else is there the collection of responsibilities, demands, tensions, decisions and grueling hours. One often speaks of the loneliness of the presidency, for here is a job in which, more than in any other mortal job, the man who holds it is alone with the fate of his decisions and the responsibilities of his actions. As the sign on (former) President Truman's desk read: "The buck stops here."

*Before Rotary Club,*
*Laurel, Md., pub. Sept. 15.*

**Hans J. Morgenthau**
*Professor of Political Science and*
*Modern History, University of Chicago*

Majority rule, for which men have striven for centuries, has produced a situation in which men are more impotent, more powerless to influence their government than 150 years ago.

*New York, May 22.*

**Thruston B. Morton**
*Former United States Senator, R-Ky.*

The post office is the most outstanding example in this country of the way not to run a business. It is losing more than a billion dollars a year; most of its equipment is anywhere from 30 to 100 years old, without any meaningful plans or funds for modernization; there is absolutely no control over costs or selling prices; and management is not allowed to deal with the unions in any important matters. Some say it is mismanaged. I say under the present system it *can't* be managed.

*Washington, pub. Aug. 24.*

**Stanley Mosk**
*Associate Justice,*
*Supreme Court of California*

I reject the argument that only intellectuals can understand the philosophy of our system of government. The people can understand it, and they must understand it if our society is to endure.

While the history of the world reveals social orders, both good and bad, created through violent uprisings, no one can point to a single constructive society maintained by force. Useful social structures exalt the mind, not the biceps.

*Napa. Calif., pub. Jan. 20.*

**Daniel P. Moynihan**
*Assistant to the President*
*of the United States*
*for Urban Affairs*

The stability of a democracy depends very much on the people making a care-

ful distinction between what government can do and what it cannot do. To demand what can be done is altogether in order; some may wish such things accomplished, some may not, and the majority may decide. But to seek that which cannot be provided, especially to do so with the passionate but misinformed conviction that it *can* be, is to create the conditions of frustration and ruin.

*Notre Dame University, pub. June 20.*

**George Murphy**
*United States Senator, R-Calif.*

The federal government's performance record, insofar as the American Indian is concerned, should give pause to those who believe that solutions to our problems should be packaged in and dictated from Washington. The federal government must help, but, however good its intentions, without local cooperation, initiative and commitment, chances for success are slim.

*Before the Senate,*
*Washington, pub. Feb. 27.*

**Edmund S. Muskie**
*United States Senator, D-Me.*

. . . there's only one thing lower than a defeated candidate for Vice President, and that's a victorious one.

*Washington, pub. March 10.*

. . . democracy chokes on too many non-negotiable demands. If every wrong demands a holy crusade, we shall have many crusades, but little peace and less freedom.

*Boston University, May 18.*

If you asked me whether I was ready to accept the responsibility of the Presidency tomorrow, I suppose I'd probably say yes. That's the kind of challenge a man is in public life to accept. But that's not the reality. It's not that I'm afraid of the seat and the strain and the heartache, but the reality is that to become President you have to let the pursuit of the office consume your life.

*Washington, pub. Aug. 4.*

**Ralph Nader**
*Lawyer, Consumer Rights Advocate*

The early signs reveal (President) Nix-

(RALPH NADER)

on's style. He wants only reluctant regulators.

*Pub. Sept. 29.*

We hear a lot about law and order on the streets. I thought we ought to find out how law and order operates in the regulatory agencies. It doesn't.

*Pub. Dec. 12.*

## Richard M. Nixon
*President of the United States*

What has to be done has to be done by government and people together, or it will not be done. The lesson of past agony is that without the people we can do nothing. With the people we can do anything.

*Inauguration address,*
*Washington, Jan. 20.*

I don't believe that policy should be made, and particularly foreign policy should be made, by off-the-cuff responses in press conferences.

*News conference, Washington, Jan. 27.*

I hope that, by what we do in terms of dealing with the problems of all Americans, it will be made clear that the President of the United States . . . has no state constituency, he has no congressional constituency, he does not represent any special group. He represents all the people. He is a friend of all the people . . . I hope I can gain the respect, and I hope eventually the friendship, of black citizens and other Americans.

*News conference, Washington, Feb. 6.*

Practicality demands recognition that the electoral system is deeply rooted in American history and federalism . . . I doubt very much that any constitutional amendment proposing abolition or substantial modification of the electoral vote system could win the required approval of three-quarters of our 50 states by 1972.

*Pub. Feb. 28.*

. . . to challenge a particular policy is one thing; to challenge the government's right to set it is another—for this denies the process of freedom.

*General Beadle State College,*
*Madison, S.D., June 3.*

. . . the President of the United States, under the Constitution, makes nominations with the advice and the consent of the Senate. I have found in my short term of office that it's very easy to get advice and very hard to get consent.

*News conference, Washington, June 19.*

After a third of a century of power flowing from the people and the states to Washington, it is time for a new federalism in which power, funds and responsibility will flow from Washington to the states and to the people.

*Television address, Washington, Aug. 8.*

One of the key points I want to make is, in a sense, very similar to one that I made on my recent visits to our NATO partners and to our friends in Asia: Washington will no longer try to go it alone (in domestic affairs); Washington will no longer dictate without consulting. A new day has come in which we recognize that partnership is a two-way street, and, if the partnership is to thrive, that street has to be traveled—both ways.

*At Governors Conference,*
*Colorado Springs, Colo., pub. Sept. 4.*

In making decisions, I believe a President should listen not only to those who tell him what he wants to hear, but to those who tell him what he needs to hear. It is most important to get independent judgments from individuals who are expert on the factors to be considered, but who are not directly involved in the operations themselves.

*Television address, Washington, Dec. 15.*

## Lawrence F. O'Brien
*Former Postmaster General*
*of the United States*

When I became Postmaster General in 1965 I was confident that once I cleared out the deadwood and began to apply sound management principles, I could provide the kind of mail service that our citizens demand. I was in for a rude awakening. There was very little deadwood in personnel, but, whenever I tried to apply sound management principles, there was usually some antiquated law that prevented me from doing so.

*Pub. Sept. 9.*

**Charles H. Percy**
*United States Senator, R-Ill.*

Should we have a totally different code for judges and administrators than we have for legislators regarding their associations, their commitments and their obligations? Unfortunately, the zeal of Congress to disclose private holdings and thereby prevent a conflict of interest in the Executive and Judicial branches does not extend to itself.
*Before the Senate, Washington, Nov. 24.*

**William J. Randall**
*United States Representative, D-Mo.*

. . . I believe a majority of the American voters should be able to pick their President . . . without any constitutional bypass, detour or stoplight. Today is historic because, after years of apathy and false starts, the House is in a position to do something about changing a system which the Chairman of the Judiciary Committee and the Dean of the House described . . . as "horrendous, dangerous, unsportsmanlike, and unconscionable." What he meant was that in at least three cases in our history, in 1824, 1876, and in 1888, the winners became the losers and the losers became the winners.
*Before the House, Washington, Sept. 18.*

**Ronald Reagan**
*Governor of California*

There is too much centralization in our government. The Federal Government is taking action that should be left to the states. And state governments are taking action that should be left to the communities.
*News conference, Hong Kong, Sept. 7.*

Politics is too important to be left to the politicians. Businessmen must take a more active part in the affairs of state. To sit back hoping that some day, some way, someone will make things right is to go on feeding the crocodile, hoping he will eat you last; but eat you he will.
*London, pub. Nov. 7.*

**L. Mendel Rivers**
*United States Representative, D-S.C.*

Whenever we look for reductions, every-

body looks to the military. This Congress hasn't got the guts to get out here and stop some of the crazy programs *we've* got.
*Before the House, Washington, May 20.*

**George W. Romney**
*Secretary of Housing and
Urban Development
of the United States*

We should stop making big promises we cannot meet and leading people to false illusions and violence. It's easy to trot out great, big, grandiose programs, as has been done over the last several years. This causes frustration when those who are to receive the benefits have their expectations raised and you are left worse off than you were when you started.
*News conference, Washington, Feb. 4.*

As government involvement replaces personal involvement, individuals and voluntary associations lose their capacity for problem-solving . . . that's not just a theory—we've seen it start to happen. It must be reversed.
*Salt Lake City, Feb. 17.*

. . . the human and social problems we face today . . . more difficult than putting men on the moon . . . cannot be solved by government. The centralization of authority in Washington just hasn't worked, even though the revenues are here, (the reason being that) government can never bring the sensitivity necessary (to solutions of problems in local areas).
*Washington, Sept. 24.*

**Raymond P. Shafer**
*Governor of Pennsylvania*

The Nixon approach (to Federation) is excellent. It is a gigantic step forward in federal-state relations. It will add dynamism to the whole country.
*Pub. Sept. 19.*

**Frank J. Shakespeare, Jr.**
*Director, United States
Information Agency*

I think the most important role of Government today is to tell the story of the (American) people to other people We tend to get bogged down in the big blocks of Government, but what we need

(FRANK J. SHAKESPEARE, JR.)

to foster is a people-to-people relationship, to tell the world what Americans are like and what they stand for. It's a relatively new function of Government, but it must be done.

*Interview, pub. Jan. 14.*

### Henry P. Smith, III
*United States Representative, R-N.Y.*

. . . the people of this country are demanding this reform—that the election of the President and Vice President be under a system which guarantees that the winner wins and the loser loses; which eliminates any possibility that the Congress might choose the President or Vice President; and which guarantees that, in the election of the President and Vice President, the vote of the citizens of Nevada or Delaware or Alaska will count exactly the same as the vote of the citizens of New York or California or Illinois.

*Before the House, Washington, Sept. 30.*

### Theodore C. Sorensen
*Former Special Counsel to
President John F. Kennedy*

The Electoral College is a live bomb in the Constitution that must be de-fused before, not after, it explodes in our faces . . . Should it ever again produce a President who was defeated by rank-and-file voters, the potential for violent and bitter reactions would be truly tragic.

*Washington, pub. Jan. 26.*

### Robert O. Tiernan
*United States Representative, D-R.I.*

Today we exist with an electoral system that has, within its archaic mechanics, the ability to deny the rights of the majority. This amendment (to abolish the electoral college system) will help insure the fact that, regardless of in what city, State or section of the country a voter resides, his ballot will be counted on an equal basis with all others . . . With our present system we have seen how power brokers can be born, we have seen how sectionalism can arise, and how the intentions of the majority can be ignored by the electors of any given State. . . . the people,

and only the people, should be power brokers. The deadlocks and bargaining that could well become reality under our present system must be eliminated.

*Before the House, Sept. 18.*

### Jesse M. Unruh
*California State Assemblyman*

. . . millions upon millions of people have lost faith in those who govern them. These people have . . . come to the conclusion that a great many politicians are nothing but thieves. And if these people don't view politicians as thieves, they view them as hypocrites.

*News conference, Sacramento, Jan. 30.*

No modern politician who values his profession dares to argue that the American electorate is incompetent to elect the President of the United States. If this is so, all rational argument against popular presidential election disappears. The Electoral College is a useless and occasionally dangerous appendage on our body politic. It must be removed.

*Pub. September.*

### Joe D. Waggonner, Jr.
*United States Representative, D-La.*

. . . if you want your President and my President to have a mandate and be one who can unite the people—and we want a true democracy and not a raw democracy —then let us forget the idea of plurality Presidents; we are going to a direct vote, and let us elect majority Presidents who do have a mandate from the people. What is wrong with that? Not a thing in the world. Do not kid the people. If we are going to have a direct vote we should require a majority, not a plurality.

*Before the House, Sept. 18.*

### Earl Warren
*Former Chief Justice
of the United States*

I have no fear at all of our future as long as people are interested in government. No matter how they disagree, as long as they are interested in government, and will have the great debate in order to get things established, I have no concern about the future at all. American people, in the aggregate, are wise and they're good and they will decide things in the right way if we can get everybody interested in the affairs of government.

*Interview, Washington, June 23.*

**Arnold R. Weber**
*Assistant Secretary for Manpower,*
*Department of Labor of the*
*United States*

I have now held my present position for approximately nine months. In human biological terms, this time period is normally associated with one cycle of creativity. Whether or not this pattern applies with equal relevance to bureaucratic activities is still an open question. However, if prospective mothers had to fill out as many forms to achieve their objectives as we do to attain ours, there would be little concern about over-population. With some resignation, I have learned that the surest form of bureaucratic birth control when confronted by a fertile idea is to direct your colleague to put it in a memo.

*At Interstate Conference of*
*Employment Security Administrators,*
*Kiamesha Lake, N.Y., pub. Oct. 21.*

**Theodore H. White**
*Author*

I don't really think we need an academy for Presidential hopefuls. But some day it might be a good idea to have a board of examiners who would pass on candidates.

*New York, pub. Nov. 9.*

**John J. Williams**
*United States Senator, R-Del.*

Our Government today is spending an average of $50 million per year to subsidize the production and sale of tobacco products, both here and abroad, while at the same time other agencies of the Government are spending millions to point out to the American public the dangers of using such products. I strongly recommend that one of the first orders of business of the new Administration be to correct this absurdity.

*Before the Senate, Washington, Feb. 25.*

**James C. Wright**
*United States Representative, D-Tex.*

The Electoral College has long since outlived any useful purpose. It is a relic of a bygone day. It has no more relevance to the modern age than powdered wigs and snuffboxes and goose quill pens. At best, it is a quaint, clumsy appendage awkwardly interposed between the people and their chosen leaders. At its worst, it can be a positive menace to the free elective process.

*Before the House, Washington, Sept. 18.*

**Samuel W. Yorty**
*Mayor of Los Angeles*

I've had ten years as part of the legislative process, first in the State Legislature and then as a congressman. All they do is yak, yak, yak. You really can't get anything done.

*Interview, Los Angeles, pub. Sept. 16.*

**Stephen M. Young**
*United States Senator, D-Ohio*

The difference between the American way of life and the Communist dictatorships of Russia and Red China is the difference between government of law and government of men. In the Red Square in Moscow, what do they have on display under glass? The embalmed corpse of Lenin. In the beautiful Archives Building in Washington, what do we have on display? We proudly display under glass the Constitution of the United States and the Bill of Rights. This illustrates the difference between government of men and government of law. Our freedom and democracy rest entirely on our heritage of respect for the law.

*Before the Senate, Washington, Oct. 1.*

# Labor and the Economy

**I. W. Abel**
*President, United Steelworkers*
*of America*

. . . I would suggest that we strive for a work week of four days with work-free weekends of three days each. This is an objective that is not only reasonable and attainable, but one that is imperative if we hope to stave off economic disaster in the years ahead.

The next downturn in our economy will have a far greater impact on those we represent than ever before in history. This is because we will experience, during the next recession, the influence of a new force, capable of overturning almost every aspect of our modern way of life. I am referring to automation.

*At AFL-CIO convention,*
*Atlantic City, N.J., Sept. 25.*

**Joseph A. Beirne**
*President, Communications*
*Workers of America*

All those who suggest restraint on the part of unions in wage negotiations speak with little knowledge of the workingman or the economy of this nation. Union members want more, not less, money. This rat race of wages chasing prices is as old as history. Unions will have to consider the pattern of 7 per cent increases set in this year's industrial-union bargaining. Labor also will want more cost-of-living clauses—or we will have to go to one-year contracts in order to protect our members against rising prices.

*At AFL-CIO convention,*
*Atlantic City, N.J., pub. Oct. 13.*

**Chester Bowles**
*Former United States Ambassador*
*to India*

If you leave economic development to the economists you leave out the human factor.

*Pub. Aug. 28.*

**W. A. Boyle**
*President, United Mine Workers*
*of America*

If a doctor, a psychiatrist, a lawyer, an actor or other professional is worth $50 an hour or more, the men who risk their lives in the highly skilled work of the coal mines are worth far more than $50 a day.

*At Labor Day Rally,*
*Logan, W.Va., Sept. 1.*

Joseph Yablonski (Boyle's challenger for the UMW presidency) lies through his teeth. Because he is guilty of lies, defamation of John L. Lewis, conflict of interest and anti-union acts, Joseph Yablonski . . . will be rejected by the membership as a power-hungry opportunist and hypocrite.

*Pub. Dec. 15.*

**Andrew F. Brimmer**
*Member, Federal Reserve Board*

I realize that some further rise in the level of unemployment, which is currently in the neighborhood of 4 per cent, cannot be avoided if we are to restore a reasonable degree of price stability. Rather than pretend that it (increased unemployment) can be avoided, we should get on with the modifications in public policies that will be necessary to insure that the burden of restoring price stability does not fall excessively on those least able to bear it.

*Pittsburgh, Dec. 2.*

**Arthur F. Burns**
*Incoming Chairman,*
*Federal Reserve Board*

If interest rates remain at anything like their present level during the next few

years, I would consider myself and the Federal Reserve Board a failure.
*Before Senate Banking Committee, Washington, pub. Dec. 19.*

**Harry F. Byrd, Jr.**
*United States Senator, D-Va.*

I might say I have never understood exactly how one fights inflation by taking money out of the top pockets of the taxpayers so they cannot spend it and giving it to the Government so they can spend it.
*Before the Senate, Washington, Nov. 25.*

**Patrick J. Clifford**
*President, New York State
Bankers Association*

We must make it absolutely clear that it is the Federal monetary authorities who are attempting to control inflation by reducing availability of credit, and it is they, not the banking industry, that is responsible for today's credit crunch.
*Before New York State Bankers Association, Lake Placid, N.Y., June 13.*

**Peter H. Dominick**
*United States Senator, R-Colo.*

. . . When we try to talk to our constituents and the country about the need for controlling inflation, and someone comes back and says, "How can you do that when you have just voted yourself a 40% increase in salary," I'm going to find myself tongue-tied.
*Washington, pub. Feb. 9.*

**Otto Eckstein**
*Professor of Economics,
Harvard University*

If a drastic cure is imposed on inflation, it could well be far worse than the disease. There are far more important problems facing the nation, especially in the social sphere, which would not be improved by creating an economic downturn.
*New York, Feb. 5.*

**Francis E. Ferguson**
*President, Northwestern Mutual
Life Insurance Company*

Our society is being trapped into believing that there is a hedge against inflation—and that just isn't so. Maybe you and I can come out ahead, but, when great pools of capital start to turn their backs on fixed-income securities, then our whole capitalistic structure is in trouble. Inflation is an exceedingly serious national problem, one that, one way or another, we'll have to control.
*Interview, pub. Sept. 7.*

**Robert H. Finch**
*Secretary of Health, Education and
Welfare of the United States*

Unions . . . have probably done more in many areas to retard the disadvantaged and the Negro than our other institutions.
*Television interview, Washington, Feb. 2.*

**Gaylord A. Freeman, Jr.**
*Chairman, First National Bank
of Chicago*

. . . If, in the United States—the richest, safest, the best-educated nation in the world, in a time of relative ease—we are unwilling to assume the discipline necessary to maintain the value of our currency, we cannot escape the conclusion that, except for short periods of unplanned recession, no currency is very likely to maintain its value. Whether this means that, at least in this respect, democracy has failed or whether it demonstrates that mankind has not yet developed the moral strength to maintain the implied promise of its money, I do not know. I only know that we—not the President, for he will only be reading our minds—have failed the test of our integrity.
*Before New Mexico Oil & Gas Association, pub. Oct. 14.*

**John Kenneth Galbraith**
*Professor of Economics,
Harvard University*

The present Administration is about to come up with something new—a combination of an intolerable level of unemployment with an intolerable level of inflation.
*New York, Oct. 9.*

**Carl A. Gerstacker**
*Chairman, Dow Chemical Company*

I don't like them (wage and price con-

(CARL A. GERSTACKER)

trols). I don't think they work well. But, at this late date and with the (Vietnam) war on, I think they are the only way to quickly contain inflation.

*Pub. June 8.*

**Barry Goldwater, Jr.**
*United States Representative, R-Calif.*

I am utterly opposed to having the government attack inflation by attacking business. Inflation is basically caused by the irresponsibility of government spending and monetary practices. It's not all because business is spending money. It's not because the consumer is spending money.

*Interview, pub. August.*

**Roger W. Gunder**
*President, Stauffer Chemical Company*

I don't believe that this country is in a political or economic crisis of sufficient magnitude to seriously consider wage and price controls at this time. Such a remedy has been resorted to only in instances of dire national emergencies. Even then, such controls were not completely satisfactory.

*Pub. June 8.*

**George G. Hagedorn**
*Chief Economist, National Association of Manufacturers*

There is a widespread illusion that, through toleration of inflation, we can have lower levels of unemployment than would otherwise be possible. No one is quite willing to advocate that we buy full employment with acceptance of inflation. But the false belief that this option is always open to us is a dangerous bit of economic mythology . . .

*Before Joint Congressional Economic Committee, Washington, March 6.*

**H. Frederick Hagemann, Jr.**
*Chairman, State Street Bank & Trust Company, Boston*

We feel that high interest rates and inflation aren't caused by the banks but by the Federal Government spending more than it has and financing the deficit by printing-press money.

*Interview, Boston, pub. December.*

**Ronald Haughton**
*Professor of Labor Relations, Wayne State University*

. . . I am reluctantly prepared to advocate binding arbitration in the public sector as the only valid *quid pro quo* in exchange for the loss of the union's right to strike.

*Before Commonwealth Club, San Francisco, Sept. 19.*

**Alfred Hayes**
*President, Federal Reserve Bank of New York*

There will surely be a long and arduous way to go before we return to a satisfactory degree of price stability. Yet, such a return is essential, not only for the health of our economy at home, but for the preservation of confidence in the dollar abroad.

*Pub. Jan. 27.*

**Walter Heller**
*Economist*

Putting on (wage and price) controls would be giving up the game. That's about the last resort. The penalties in distortion are enormous. Any attempt to substitute human judgment (through controls) for the cybernetic market system is a self-defeating proposition.

*Pub. June 8.*

**James D. Hodgson**
*Under Secretary of Labor of the United States*

A (labor) union must be recognized for what it is—an organization granted special privileges by government statute with special public policy responsibilities, not an organization that can continue to be operated largely as a private association . . .

*Pub. February.*

**W. Sprague Holden**
*Chairman, Department of Journalism, Wayne State University*

I can't understand the total lack of excitement in the U.S. about labor courts. It's absolute madness not to have a place to take industrial disputes to be adjudicated. After all, we have courts for almost every other type of grievance.

*Interview, Detroit, pub. Feb. 10.*

**Sidney Homer**
*Investment Banker*

Wage-price controls do not control inflation; they merely postpone it. If they were impending, wages and prices would go through the roof while being debated. Wage-price controls only work with heavy patriotic commitment when huge savings are enforced. In peacetime, such a thing is inconceivable.

*Pub. June 8.*

**Hubert H. Humphrey**
*Former Vice President
of the United States*

What we have witnessed in the past eight months is a virtual abdication of the President's responsibility—yes, even his duty—to take the lead in fighting inflation, in both prices and wages . . . The President can, and he should, plead, request, argue, persuade and cajole. He does have jawbone power, especially if he adds a little backbone to the jawbone.

*Before AFL-CIO convention delegates,
Atlantic City, N.J., Oct. 6.*

. . . no White House advisor playing Monopoly games with the economy has the right to toy with the lives of millions of our citizens and accept rising unemployment as a trade-off for price stability. In the past 10 months, inflation has run wild; it is clearly one of the most dangerous developments on the national horizon. But unemployment is not and never will be an acceptable consequence of its control.

*Before Junior Chamber of Commerce,
Minneapolis, Nov. 20.*

**Conrad C. Jamison**
*Vice president, Security Pacific
National Bank of Los Angeles*

It would be a political mistake for the banks to raise (interest) rates again; but, to a considerable extent, blaming the banks for the high rates is like blaming the thermometer for heat waves.

*News conference, Los Angeles,
Aug. 12.*

**David M. Kennedy**
*Secretary of the Treasury
of the United States*

It will be my purpose to maintain a strong dollar both at home and abroad. We will not seek an answer to our problems by a change in the monetary price of gold. We see no need or reason for such action.

*Washington, Jan. 22.*

This Administration is absolutely resolved to keep the Federal Budget in surplus.

*Washington, March 14.*

The world monetary system functions —importantly—with the help of the International Monetary Fund. The IMF has worked very well. But no system will work if countries let inflation or their economies get out of kilter. There's nothing on earth that I know of that will take care of any international mechanisms if nations don't discipline themselves and live within their means.

*Interview, Washington,
pub. May 5.*

**Mary Keyserling**
*Director, Women's Bureau,
Department of Labor
of the United States*

As the nation faces increasing manpower needs today and in the years ahead, it will find a rich source of needed skills as it draws more fully on the as yet far from adequately-used talents and capabilities of its women . . . we need to encourage women to appreciate the diversity of occupation open to them and to prepare realistically for them.

*Interview, pub. Jan. 6.*

**J. Hugh Liedtke**
*Chairman, Pennzoil United*

Guidelines get at the effects rather than the cause of inflation. More progress can be made by closer central control of the money supply and the Federal budget.

*Pub. Feb. 10.*

**Herbert Marcuse**
*Professor of Philosophy,*
*University of California at San Diego*

The high standard of living in the United States depends on a constant elaboration of luxuries, on the immensity of the military arms industry and on aggressive expansion abroad, all of which are the stimuli for the American economy.
*Rome, pub. June 29.*

**William McChesney Martin, Jr.**
*Chairman, Federal Reserve Board*

I think we can disinflate without deflation. This has never been done before, but I hope we can achieve it.
*Before Joint Congressional Economic Committee, Washington, pub. Feb. 27.*

We have been told that the world has accepted inflation as a way of life. I don't believe it. There will be a good deal of pain and suffering before we resolve this thing. It won't be resolved with gadgets.

If we get inflation as a way of life, we may get government moves toward forced savings. I agree these are fighting words.
*At International Monetary Conference of American Bankers Association, Copenhagen, June 20.*

**Paul W. McCracken**
*Chairman, Council of Economic Advisers to the President of the United States*

We have been to some extent, I think, economic hypochondriacs. You get a wiggle in a statistic . . . and everyone runs out to get the thermometer.
*Interview, pub. Feb. 3.*

. . . A dollar less of Federal spending has a greater economic effect than a dollar more of taxes.
*Washington, pub. Feb. 21.*

No one is going to propose dealing with the problem of inflation by a deliberate policy of unemployment. But no one can honestly say that we can deal with this problem with no increase in unemployment.
*Television Interview, Washington, Feb. 23.*

(Price controls) would inevitably mean specific shortages, standing in line, items available only to those with pull, and a bureaucracy to administer the complex price controls and rationing that would inevitably have to develop . . . There is an essential morality in the impersonal market place, for all its imperfections, where performance is the route to success—rather than pull or influence, or skill in working an angle.
*University of Wisconsin, Aug. 18.*

In an ideal world, the immediate results of any policy of disinflation would be that the inflation itself, the rise in the price level, would roll over and play dead, and nothing else would happen; but the economic process doesn't work that way. You cannot approach this kind of policy of disinflation and say that it can be done without running the risk of some adverse effect on unemployment.
*News conference, Washington, Oct. 16.*

**Marshall McLuhan**
*Professor of English,*
*University of Toronto*

In this age of circuity the consequences of any action occur at the same time as the action. Thus, we now experience a growing need to build the very consequences of our programs into the original design and to put the consumer into the production process.
*Pub. September.*

**George Meany**
*President, American Federation of Labor-Congress of Industrial Organizations*

We believe that free trade unions are a guarantee of a free society and that free societies are in the interests of the United States, especially in the Western Hemisphere. When the Communists want to take over a country they don't bother with the banks or big business and industry. They try to infiltrate and take over the free trade unions. That's the way they worked in Prague in 1948. It's the way they tried to work it in Italy and France. We fought them then without a dime of help from this Government. And if the Government of the United States withdraws all of its assistance to us we'll still carry on the work in Latin America and wherever we have programs.

*Testimony before Senate Foreign Relations Committee, Washington, Aug. 1.*

We have people who are constantly worrying about the lack of militancy on the part of labor. Labor, to some extent, has become middle class. When you have no property, you don't have anything, you have nothing to lose by these radical actions. But when you become a person who has a home and has property, to some extent you become conservative. And, I would say to that extent, labor has become conservative. I don't think there is any question of that. But, at the same time, the programs of the trade union movement—the things we lived for—there is nothing conservative about that. We still want to break through with new ideas.

*Interview, Washington, Aug. 28.*

The cost of living continues to rise month after month, and it is now up 5.5 per cent from just one year ago. Well, what is the economic theory behind all this when you strip away the pious platitudes and blatant baloney? You drive the cost of living down, you beat inflation and you increase unemployment . . . You cool off, you slow down the entire economy, you increase interest rates, discourage expansion, but keep prices up. The consumer clams up, sales go down, more unemployment . . . Keep this up and finally . . . you have a serious unemployment problem.

*At AFL-CIO convention, Atlantic City, N.J., Oct. 2.*

There are some of these do-gooders with official hats, or without official hats, who feel that the so-called minority groups should be provided a short cut to attaining the skills necessary to become skilled building-trades mechanics. Well, you and I know there is no short cut . . . Handing out journeymen's cards without proper qualifications is no answer to the minority problem . . . No matter what happens, don't lower your standards.

*Before construction union leaders, Atlantic City, N.J., pub. Oct. 6.*

**Patsy T. Mink**
*United States Representative, D-Hawaii*

It is perfectly clear that the Administration wants to increase unemployment. It apparently feels that, when people are out of work and can no longer buy food, clothing, housing and other necessities of life, the demand for these things will be reduced and prices will therefore go down. This is an extremely heartless and inhumane way of cooling down the economy. I protest this policy and urge its condemnation.

*Before the House, Washington, Nov. 13.*

**George W. Mitchell**
*Member, Federal Reserve Board*

You can give everyone a job—trained and untrained—if you work the economy at forced draft, as we did in World War II. The trouble is that you also get serious inflation. The answer to today's unemployment problem is training to prepare the teen-agers and the Negro jobless for work they can handle. The answer is not an inflationary boom to try to keep unemployment at rock bottom.

*Interview, Washington, pub. Jan. 20.*

It is possible that if banks began to ration credit earlier in a period of monetary restraint, rather than waiting until liquidity and liability positions forced them to do so, the degree and duration of monetary restraint required to do the job might well be moderated.

*San Juan, P.R., Oct. 26.*

**David A. Morse**
*Director-General, International Labor Organization*

. . . back in 1919, in the period when ILO was just beginning . . . people in the electrical industry (in New York) were working for five dollars a week, and without any restrictions on hours . . . Today, in the same industry, you have a 25-hour week, and something like $7 or $8 an hour . . . This is a tremendous revolutionary change, the like of which the world has never known. This didn't happen by itself—in this and other trades —but through the whole process of collective bargaining, development of the

(DAVID A. MORSE)

trade union movement in this country, which is a phenomenon of the last 25 to 30 years, since the period of the big depression.

*Interview, United Nations, N.Y., pub. Oct. 23.*

## John A. Morsell
*Assistant Executive Director, National Association for the Advancement of Colored People*

Negroes pretty generally agree that the one desperate need now is jobs. If private business can provide them, fine. But the Government must become the employer of last resort . . .

*Interview, pub. Feb. 24.*

## John E. Moss
*United States Representative, D-Calif.*

I cannot . . . understand the rationale behind the idea that for some reason railroad workers are different from any other industrial employees. We have denied them the right to fully explore the power of collective bargaining by mandating settlements, and we are doing further violence to free collective-bargaining processes if we adopt . . . legislation which would impose a mandatory retirement at 65.

*Before the House, Washington, Sept. 30.*

## Daniel P. Moynihan
*Assistant to the President of the United States for Urban Affairs*

It (inflation) has to be dealt with. There is no liberal or conservative position on it. Only a damned fool would ignore the problem.

*Pub. April 11.*

## Richard M. Nixon
*President of the United States*

. . . the primary responsibility for controlling inflation rests with the national administration and its handling of fiscal and monetary affairs. That is why we will have some new approaches in this area. We assume that responsibility. We think we can meet it, that we can control inflation without an increase in unemployment.

Unless we do control inflation, we eventually will be confronted with massive unemployment, because the history of economic affairs, in this and other countries, indicates that, if inflation is allowed to get out of hand, eventually there has to be a bust.

*News Conference, Washington, Jan. 27.*

Anybody who bets on a continuing inflation will lose that bet, because our Government policies are beginning to work, and we are going to stick to those policies until we cut the rise in the cost of living.

*News conference, Washington, Sept. 26.*

We have undertaken a policy that is slowing down the rise in prices. Unfortunately, some industries and some individuals will feel this necessary adjustment more directly than others. But, difficult though it may be and unpopular though it may become when the water gets a bit choppier, by curbing inflation we do what is best for all the American people.

Let's face it: Holding down government spending and holding up the tax rate and making it harder for people to get credit is not the kind of policy that makes friends for people in politics. We have asked the American people to take bitter medicine. We believe that the American people are mature enough to understand the need for it.

Wage and price controls are bad for business, bad for the workingman, bad for the consumer. Rationing, black markets, regimentation—that's the wrong road for America, and I will not take the nation down that road.

Today, in a prosperity endangered by a speedup of prices, the only thing we have to fear is fatalism—that destructive habit of shrugging our shoulders and resigning ourselves to a hopeless future on a wage-price treadmill. I say to my fellow Americans: The runaway cost of living is no cross we are obliged to bear. It can be brought under control. It is being slowed by firm and steady action that deals with its root causes.

The dollar you earn should be worth a

dollar. The dollar you save should stay worth a dollar. This is no impossible dream; this is something you are entitled to. The cost of living affects the quality of life. Together, we are going to improve the quality of life; and, together, we are going to succeed in slowing down the rise in your cost of living.

*Radio address, Washington, Oct. 17.*

**Arthur M. Okun**
*Former Chairman,*
*Council of Economic Advisers*
*to the President of the United States*

We have to hope that our economy is not brittle—that it can bend without breaking. So far, the formula has not yet been found for bending our economy in times of inflation without breaking it.

*Pub. April 7.*

. . . if you look at the anatomy of inflation over the last few years, it just has not been driven by shortages, bottlenecks or acute excess demand situations. Basically, my diagnosis is that markets have just been so strong that the usual disciplinary factors over wage and price increases haven't exercised enough influence. It's that little extra froth on the boom, or head on the beer, that has made the difference.

*Interview, pub. May 25.*

No economist enjoys conveying the message that there is a tradeoff between employment and price stability. But surely the Congress and the American public should be told the facts of life. President Nixon has had to face and accept this unpleasant reality, which he did not recognize a year ago when he declared that the only extra unemployment necessary to cure inflation was the unemployment of (President Lyndon) Johnson's economic advisers.

*Before the Senate-House Economic Committee, Washington, Oct. 13.*

**Leif Olsen**
*Senior Economist*
*First National City Bank of New York*

I am definitely not in favor of wage and price controls. They won't be a solution to inflation. They never have been. When a boiler has a full head of steam,

you're not going to tie down the safety valve. You've got to bank the fire underneath. That can only be done by monetary policy.

*Pub. June 8.*

**Wright Patman**
*United States Representative, D-Tex.*

You (William McChesney Martin, Jr., Chairman, Federal Reserve Board) have been the most costly public official in the history of the world. You have a terrible record.

*Before Joint Congressional Economic Committee, Washington, pub. Feb. 27.*

This committee is certainly willing to listen to the explanation of . . . bankers, but in all honesty I must say that I find it incredulous that so many bankers woke up on Monday morning, June 9, with the identical thought in mind (to raise the prime rate). We have always heard that bankers think alike, but this coincidence seems too much, even for the monolithic banking industry.

*Before House Banking and Currency Committee, Washington, pub. June 22.*

**Walter P. Reuther**
*President, United Auto Workers*

If you are making $4,000 a year as a wage earner and you are working your heart out with the wife to stretch that $4,000 to cover your family budget and you go to the bargaining table to get another $1,000, the hue and cry goes up in America that that must be stopped because it is highly inflationary and it will undermine the stability of the economy. But, when one of these corporation executives is getting $400,000 a year and he goes to $500,000, that suddenly is non-inflationary and the expression of the highest kind of motivation in our free enterprise system. Well, I think that kind of economics is for the birds, and we don't buy it.

(Government leaders) have the mistaken notion that the way to fight inflation is to increase the level of unemployment (and to) put the economic burden of fighting inflation upon workers and their families—the very economic group least able

(WALTER P. REUTHER)

to carry that burden. The source of the problem is not the fact that American workers are fighting for their legitimate wage claims; (it is) the giant corporations of America who control the marketplace and have been going after higher and higher profits through higher and higher prices.

*Detroit, Nov. 8.*

### Pierre A. Rinfret
*Economist*

This is a galloping economy—and if we don't restrain it, we won't contain it.
*New York, pub. March 2.*

The greatest miscalculation in the last 20 years by economists is the great underestimation of the United States economy.
*Before American Iron and Steel Institute, New York, May 21.*

There ain't gonna be no recession in 1970, period. Not only will there be no recession, but I think we will smash every economic record that has been established in the history of the world.
*At Business Week Conference on Money and the Corporation, New York, Dec. 9.*

### J. L. Robertson
*Vice chairman, Federal Reserve Board*

Inflationary psychology has already become so deep-seated that painful measures seem to be necessary to moderate it. We hope that the measures will be no more painful than necessary and be continued no longer than need be. But we must not temporize with the problem. It often happens that gradualism, based on the hope of easing the pain of a difficult problem, only prolongs the agony.
*Pub. Dec. 22.*

### Nelson A. Rockefeller
*Governor of New York*

We used to think strikes were a weapon of last resort, but some of your powerful unions here seem to be making them a weapon of first resort.
*Before Central Labor Council, pub. Feb. 9.*

### Hans Scharer
*Banker, Union Bank of Switzerland*

A devaluation of the dollar? You just have to laugh about it when you see the financial strength of this country (the United States) and the economy that's behind it. It's impossible!
*New York, April 3.*

### George P. Shultz
*Secretary of Labor of the United States*

I believe that a boycott directed against an employer's merchandise designed to force that employer to sign a union contract is antithetical to this purpose. It has no necessary relationship to what the worker wants and may have consequences far beyond those directly concerned. It is not a satisfactory way to settle labor conflicts, especially those involving issues of representation.
*Before Senate Labor Committee, Washington, May 6.*

Just as it is possible to price goods out of the market, it is also possible to price labor out of the market.
*News conference, Washington, July 25.*

The railroads, and (the) unions in that industry, seem to feel that an emergency board is a God-given right and that, to a great extent, it's perfectly appropriate not to bargain until after the emergency board has made its recommendations. Then they try to use the recommendations as the basis of bargaining. That's the theory they have. It's a cockeyed theory.
*Interview, Washington, pub. Dec. 1.*

That's what wrong with inflation—people get hurt right and left. The problem in dealing with it is that you can't shift policies too abruptly, or you will make the burden too heavy for some to bear. Suppose the unemployment rate were to go up to 6 per cent—and I don't mean it will get up to that figure—you still would have 94 per cent of the labor force at work. So who gets hurt? Well, it's the unskilled, the unschooled, the Negroes, people from city slums. They are the first to be hit by too-restrictive measures to control inflation. That just isn't right. We have to work out something better.

*Washington.*

**Albert T. Sommers**
*Economist, National Industrial*
*Conference Board*

The basic problem is that the Government is committed to full employment, and everybody knows it. This reduces the power of statements designed to halt inflationary psychology. There does not seem to be any riskless, costless, comfortable escape from the psychology of inflation.

*Pub. June 20.*

**George Spatta**
*Honorary Chairman,*
*Clark Equipment Company*

. . . labor unions are getting too powerful. There is going to have to be some restraint on their part about wages. If a part costs 10 cents to make, and labor wants 15 cents to make it, prices are going to have to go up. It's a never-ending thing. Sure, I know the guy on the line will say, "But my last raise is used up." Of course, every raise will be used up. But you have to keep some profitability for your stockholders if you're going to stay in business.

*Interview, pub. December.*

**Maurice H. Stans**
*Secretary of Commerce*
*of the United States*

I don't want the Labor Department to think everything that comes out of Commerce is bad for labor, just as I don't want us to think everything that comes out of the Labor Department is bad for business. I want us to think in terms of the American economy as a whole.

*Pub. September.*

**Louis Stone**
*Economist*

It is plain nonsense to talk about controlling inflation through monetary restraint. If the Administration thinks that it can break the unions' demands by cutting down the employers' ability to pay, it is heading straight for a recession and

unemployment on a scale that will be politically unacceptable . . . The only way that the vicious spiral of labor costs and prices can be broken is through a change (in such fundamentals as present labor laws).

*Pub. Aug. 11.*

**John Vaughn**
*President,*
*Los Angeles Chamber of Commerce*

The present structure of the National Labor Relations Act was not written for agriculture's special needs or for the nation's need for an assured food supply. A strike at harvest time could ruin a grower and would give no immediate help to farm workers. Ripe food doesn't wait for arbitration. Legislation must protect both the grower and the worker, but should not force workers to join a union if they don't want to.

*Washington, May 26.*

**Paul A. Volcker**
*Under Secretary of the Treasury*
*for Monetary Affairs*
*of the United States*

To put low interest rates and better availability of money first on our list of priorities would be self-defeating. For the attempt could add only more fuel to the fire of inflation, and, thus, to the distortions and strains in financial markets.

*Before Joint Congressional Economic*
*Committee, Washington, Feb. 19.*

**DeWitt Wallace**
*Co-chairman,*
*The Reader's Digest Association*

The (four-day work week experiment) has been a conspicuous success. I have never known greater enthusiasm for a project among employees. I've received many dozens of letters and oral comments and they have all been deeply gratifying in reinforcing our conviction that a four-day week can be both beneficial and workable.

*Pub. Sept. 28.*

**W. Willard Wirtz**
*Former Secretary of Labor*
*of the United States*

I have real concern about all this talk

of cooling off the economy . . . with all that there is to be done, if we decide to slow up, it's a confession that we don't know how to use our strength . . . We'd better recognize that the higher unemployment, or most of it, would come in the slums and ghettos. I think the slums would explode.

*Interview, Washington, Jan. 10.*

I wish somebody would say plainly that cooling off the economy will mean 250,-000 or 500,000 people out of work.

*Before Equal Employment Institute of American Bar Association, Washington, March 28.*

### Joseph A. Yablonski
*Member, executive board,*
*United Mine Workers of America*

The United Mine Workers used to be trailblazers in the labor movement. Lo and behold, we've become the trailers. Other unions have better pay, benefits, safety conditions and pensions than coal miners. And, by God, I don't like it!

*Oakwood, Va., pub. Nov. 24.*

### A. W. Zelomed
*Professor, Graduate School of Business,*
*University of Virginia*

The longer hemline always has preceded a less dynamic economic trend in the United States. Lengthening of skirts preceded the 1929 crash. Dior's New Look in 1947 preceded the first post-World War II recession. The hemlines are flashing the signal again. The long-awaited slowdown is nearing.

*Pub. Aug. 28.*

### Ronald Zeigler
*White House Press Secretary*

The President is not for wage and price controls. In the past, he has consistently taken this position. This Administration is pursuing a course of action to cool the economy and the strategy which this Administration is following does not include wage and price controls.

*News conference, Washington, July 16.*

## I. W. Abel
*President, United Steelworkers*
*of America*

Nominations to the nation's highest court should be the climax of a distinguished legal career during which the nominee has served justice by protecting and advancing the rights of those seeking justice. However, in the present case (President Nixon's nomination of Judge Clement F. Haynsworth), we believe the nomination is designed more to the plowing of domestic political fields than to the sowing of the seeds of hope, and more to the placating of a particular power body than to the consideration of economic and social justice.

*Washington, Aug. 26.*

## David L. Bazelon
*Chief Judge,*
*United States Court of Appeals*
*for the District of Columbia*

If we agree to confine—by civil commitment or criminal process—only those drug users who are dangerous to others, we are left with the vast numbers of drug users who harm only themselves. For these people, the criminal laws against drug use interfere with essentially private conduct. Like laws against suicide, or laws against riding a motorcycle without a helmet, they limit one man's liberty without protecting anyone else. Putting a man in jail is a rather primitive way of protecting him.

*At Anglo-American Conference on*
*Drug-taking in the Younger Generation,*
*Oxfordshire, England, pub. Dec. 22.*

## Alexander M. Bickel
*Professor of Law, Yale University*

You shoot an arrow into the far distant future when you appoint a (U.S. Supreme Court) Justice. And not the man himself can tell you what he will think about some of the problems that he will face.

*Pub. May 23.*

The most important extra-judicial assignments (taken by Federal judges) distract from judicial tasks, and lesser ones may bring involvement in controversies detracting from judicial impartiality and aloofness.

(It is) unrealistic to say a Justice should never talk to a President, but if he's worthy of his robes . . . he ought to have a sixth sense of what is proper . . .

*Before Senate subcommittee,*
*Washington, July 16.*

It (wire-tapping) is the most breathtaking claim for untrammeled executive authority since Lincoln—and he had a Civil War on his hands.

*Pub. Sept. 8.*

## Hugo L. Black
*Associate Justice,*
*Supreme Court of the United States*

It is high time this Court, in the interest of the administration of criminal justice, made a new appraisal of the language and history of the Fourth Amendment, and cut it down to its intended size. Such a judicial action would, I believe, make our cities a safer place for men, women and children to live in.

*Washington, pub. May 5.*

## Warren E. Burger
*Circuit Judge,*
*United States Court of Appeals,*
*District of Columbia*

Guilt or innocence become irrelevant in the criminal trial as we flounder in a

(WARREN E. BURGER)

morass of artificial rules, poorly conceived and often impossible of application . . . Like the hapless centipede on the fly-paper, our efforts to extricate ourselves from this self-imposed dilemma will, if we keep it up, soon have all of us immobilized.

*Pub. May 26.*

The seeming anxiety of judges to protect every accused person from every consequence of his voluntary utterances is giving rise to myriad rules, subrules, variations and exceptions which even the most alert and sophisticated lawyers and judges are taxed to follow. Each time judges add nuances to these "rules," we make it less likely that any police officer will be able to follow the guidelines we lay down.

*Pub. June 2.*

**Warren E. Burger**
*Chief Justice of the United States*

All over America—indeed all over the world where the daily events of Americans are followed avidly—people are asking this same question: "Why should it (justice) take so long?" . . . and I must provide an answer. Part of that answer is that the legal profession must condemn —and I repeat that—must condemn as unprofessional conduct every tactic, whether by the prosecution or the defense counsel, in which delay is used as a tactical weapon for selfish purposes. I must also add that when we find a judge who contributes to delay, he, too, must be called to account.

Talk of outside activities of judges is totally irrelevant to the matter of improving the administration of justice. This is our business. Far from withdrawing from such outside activities, I intend to intensify them.

*At National Judicial Conference,*
*Jackson Lake, Wyo., July 1.*

The problem of what we should do with those who are found to be guilty of criminal acts . . . is one of mankind's large unsolved and largely neglected problems . . . There must be some way to make our correctional system better than the revolving-door process which has made "recidivist" almost a household word in America.

Increasingly over the past 30 years, with a sharp acceleration in recent years, we have afforded the accused offender the most elaborate procedures and the most comprehensive system of trials, retrials, appeals and post-conviction reviews and remedies of any society in the world. None can match us in these manifestations of concern for the accused. If I were sure—and I am not sure either way —that all this was good for the accused in the long run sense that it helps him, I would be enthusiastically in favor of all of it.

A friend of mine expressed some surprise 8 or 10 years ago that I had become so deeply concerned with the administration of criminal justice and asked "Why?" I answered with a question, in the common fashion of lawyers. "If we do not solve what you call the problems of criminal justice, will anything else matter very much?"

*Before American Bar Association,*
*Dallas, Aug. 11.*

**Robert C. Byrd**
*United States Senator, D-W.Va.*

The real reasons for the high pressure campaign to defeat the (Judge Clement) Haynsworth nomination are his judicial philosophy and the fact that he is a white, conservative Southerner. To be brutally frank, President Nixon was elected because his political position appeared to be less liberal than that of the candidate of my own party. Now Mr. Nixon is criticized because he does not adopt the politics of the losers in appointing Supreme Court judges. Haynsworth has a conservative image but that, after all, is what our nation voted for.

*Washington, Nov. 17.*

**Ramsey Clark**
*Former Attorney General*
*of the United States*

You have to have respect for the law. But you can't respect the law when the

law is not respectable.
*Before Senate Judiciary Committee,*
*Washington, pub. Nov. 5.*

Law must become the principal instrument of social change, but it must move faster and in a more responsive way to social needs. In the question of racial integration, for example, if we were to move at the same rate as the first nine years since the Supreme Court decision, it would take us another nine centuries to do the job effectively.
*New York, pub. Dec. 14.*

**Lynn D. Compton**
*Chief Deputy District Attorney,*
*Los Angeles County*

Charles Dickens once wrote in a book, "The law is an ass." I think that's true. I think the law became an ass the day it let the psychiatrists get their hands on the law . . . I say reject them.
*Summation at Sirhan B. Sirhan*
*murder trial,*
*Los Angeles, April 14.*

The great majority of psychiatrists are opposed to capital punishment. This causes them to say to themselves, "This man shouldn't be executed," and they proceed to diagnose the case in such a way that the diagnosis will support their views on capital punishment . . . The average non-psychiatrist doctor wouldn't do things that way. But psychiatrists start with the bias that there is something wrong.
*Los Angeles, pub. June 22.*

**John Conyers, Jr.**
*United States Representative, D-Mich.*

Judge (Clement F.) Haynsworth's confirmation (as Associate Justice of the U.S. Supreme Court) would serve notice that our Government intends to block off the few avenues that are now available for legal attack on the bastions of racism in our country.
*Before Senate Judiciary Committee,*
*Washington, Sept. 25.*

**Grant B. Cooper**
*Lawyer*

It is a lawyer's duty to represent a guilty man, but not to free him.
*Los Angeles, pub. April 13.*

**William O. Douglas**
*Associate Justice,*
*Supreme Court of the United States*

The Bill of Rights of 1792 was designed to make it difficult for the government to do anything to the individual. That's why this country is such a great and exciting experiment . . . Our purpose is to make it difficult for government to do something to someone. Once it becomes easy for the government to do something to one individual, then it becomes easy to do it to you, to everyone.
*Interview, Los Angeles, Aug. 11.*

I have consistently dissented (in obscenity cases) not because, as frequently charged, I relish obscenity. I have dissented before and now because I think the First Amendment bars all kinds of censorship.
*Washington, Dec. 15.*

**Gerald R. Ford**
*United States Representative, R-Mich.*

There is a strong feeling, not only in Congress but in the country, that if the United States Senate does establish new ethical standards for (U.S.) Supreme Court nominees, then these same standards ought to be applicable to sitting members.
*Television interview, Washington, Nov. 7.*

**Percy Forman**
*Lawyer*

The classic adversary system in the United States not only encourages, it demands, that each lawyer attempt to empanel the jury most likely to understand his argument, or least likely to understand that of his opponent. You don't approach a case with the philosophy of applying abstract justice. You go in to win.
*Pub. Feb. 3.*

**Jacob D. Fuchsberg**
*Former President,*
*American Trial Lawyers Association*

Juries are not stupid. I think the average juror does not try to act out of prejudice.

(JACOB D. FUCHSBERG)

He wraps himself in civic virtue. He's a judge now. He tries to act the part and do the right thing.
*Interview, New York, pub. June 6.*

**Arthur J. Goldberg**
*Former Associate Justice,*
*Supreme Court of the United States*

If law is not made more than a policeman's nightstick, American society will be destroyed.
*Pub. June 22.*

**Jay Goldberg**
*Lawyer*

I am a mercenary. A person who is accused of something comes into my office and he wants me to be his sword, he wants me to protect his rights. I must, if I accept his case, close my eyes to the needs of society, and I do what I can to protect him within legal ethics, without any regard to society's needs or anyone else's needs. The fact is that society gains most of all by seeing to it that the rule of law applies to all. It is not tested with the law-abiding middle class, but with the people who need it most.
*Interview, New York, pub. May 24.*

**William T. Gossett**
*President, American Bar Association*

It may well be that the rule of law faces graver and more pervasive danger in this country than it has since the tragedy of the Civil War . . . I put it to you bluntly—the rule of law can be wiped out in one misguided, however well-intentioned, generation. And if that should happen, it could take a century of striving and ordeal to restore it, and then only at the cost of the lives of many good men and women.
*Before American Bar Association,*
*Dallas, Aug. 11.*

**William T. Gossett**
*Former President,*
*American Bar Association*

If respect for the courts and for their judicial process is gone or steadily weakened, no law can save us as a society. Yet today we are going through an ugly and hazardous period, when wide and some-times thoughtless resentment of court decisions has motivated vituperative and violent attacks upon the courts themselves. Lawyers, whatever their views on controversial decisions, must inspire respect for the judiciary.
*Before Canadian Bar Association,*
*Ottawa, Sept. 3.*

**Edward V. Hanrahan**
*State attorney, Cook County, Illinois*

There has been abroad in the land a trend toward much more leniency toward defendants, leading to a very large number of sentences of probation, both in State and U.S. courts. I think this trend is very harmful. Criminal prosecutions and indictments have lost a large part of their deterrence impact because offenders realize the likelihood of probation.
*Published Aug. 11.*

**Robert M. Hutchins**
*President, Center for the*
*Study of Democratic Institutions*

I have no objection to nine aging gentlemen, appointed for life, interpreting the law; but I would deprive them of the last word, of the necessity for making these decisions. The people ought to be able to say, with some ease: "This is not the way we want the Constitution to be." The amending clause should be simplified so that it would be possible for the people, in some rational, serious way, to reconsider the Constitution in whole or in part.
*Interview, Santa Barbara, Calif.,*
*pub. June 17.*

**Sir Eric St. Johnston**
*Chief Inspector of*
*Constabulary, London*

The real trouble (in the United States) is that the police are not backed by the judges. The courts are far too ready to listen to defense lawyers and let people out on bail . . . I cannot help but feel that 200 well-trained British policemen, unarmed, would soon restore peace and tranquillity to Berkeley (Calif.). But this would only work if they were supported by the British judicial system and procedures, and not the American system.
*Interview, London, pub. June 15.*

**Sanford H. Kadish**
*Professor of Law,*
*University of California at Berkeley*

It seems as if the Department (of Justice) sees the values of the Bill of Rights as no more than obstacles to be overcome. There seems to be a single-minded effort to cut the crime rate, with little sense of the constraints of the Constitution.

*Interview, pub. July 25.*

**Irving R. Kaufman**
*Judge, United States Court of Appeals*
*for the Second Circuit*

Edmund Burke is supposed to have said, "Law sharpens the mind by narrowing it." It seems to me that the words were meant less in praise of the profession than in warning to it. We run the risk of becoming oracles who speak of lectures delivered 10, 20, or 30 years ago, adequate for their time but not for ours. To the extent that the judicial profession becomes the daily routine of deciding cases on the most secure precedents and the narrowest grounds available, the judicial mind atrophies, and its perspective shrinks. What most impresses us about great jurists is not their tenacious grasp of a fine point, honed almost to invisibility; it is the moment when we are suddenly made aware of the sweep and direction of the law, and its place in the lives of men.

*At Institute of Judicial Administration,*
*pub. Aug. 26.*

**Joseph P. Kimble**
*Chief of Police, Beverly Hills, Calif.*

I don't like to see any convicted person get out of jail. But I also don't like to see the abridgment of constitutional rights as a way of getting a conviction. The Supreme Court has reflected social change and not deliberately created it, in my opinion; but I don't think many of my colleagues would agree.

*Interview, San Carlos, Calif.,*
*pub. April 14.*

**Richard H. Kuh**
*Lawyer; former Chief,*
*Criminal Courts Bureau,*
*City of New York*

There are a number of judges, of course,

who take their responsibilities seriously. The trouble is that these men stand alone and that both the Supreme Court and the criminal courts are leaderless. The panacea of just making more judges, more courts and more court clerks is not a panacea if you don't soundly administer the men and resources available to you.

*New York, pub. Feb. 10.*

**Ellis C. MacDougall**
*Commissioner of Corrections*
*of Connecticut*

Probably about half of all crimes are committed by people who have spent time in correctional institutions. Thus, it is pretty clear that corrections aren't correcting. If judges are turning to probation increasingly, an important reason is the conditions that exist in our prisons—along with indications that many more types of offenders can be helped by probation than once was thought possible.

*Pub. Aug. 11.*

**Archibald MacLeish**
*Poet, Playwright*

A Supreme Court without a vision of America to pursue, to attempt to realize, would be a mechanism—a computer like (any) other . . . the vision of America held and defined and implemented by the Warren Court was the noblest and most honorable of them all—a vision of justice in its ultimate form, the form of freedom. It may not have been perfect. No vision ever was—including Lincoln's. But it dared to turn from darkness and to face the sun.

*New York, Oct. 14.*

**Thurgood Marshall**
*Associate Justice,*
*Supreme Court of the United States*

A state has no business telling a man, sitting alone in his own house, what books he may read or what films he may watch . . . Whatever may be the justifications for other statutes regulating obscenity, we do not think they reach into the privacy of one's own home.

*Court decision, Washington, Apr. 7.*

Chief Justice (Earl) Warren became the image that allowed the poor Negro share-

(THURGOOD MARSHALL)

cropper to say, "Kick me around, Mr. Sheriff; kick me around, Mr. County Judge; kick me around, Supreme Court of my state. But there's one person I can rely on; there's one court that'll bring you to book." I don't know how much it meant to these people, but I know it meant a whole lot. And I know it spread all over the world. I have yet to go to Africa that I don't find a good word for the U.S. Supreme Court. I have yet to go in any country in this world but that I don't find somebody, usually a judge or a chief judge, who will say, "Send my best to your Chief Justice."

*New York, Oct. 14.*

**Charles Morgan**
*Southern Director,*
*American Civil Liberties Union*

There are some kinds of cases—like those of Lee Harvey Oswald, Sirhan Sirhan and, now, Songmy—where it may be impossible to get an unbiased jury, whether military or civilian; cases involving deeds so national in scope and so political in nature that there's no way to avoid having the First Amendment conflict with the Fifth and Sixth Amendment guarantees of due process and a fair trial. In cases of this kind there may be irreconcilable conflicts between constitutional guarantees, and we must recognize these inevitable conflicts.

*Pub. Dec. 15.*

**Robert M. Morgenthau**
*United States Attorney for the*
*Southern District of New York*

If the affluent flagrantly disregard the law, the poor and the deprived will follow the leadership. If the indigent who is brought into the precinct station rightly believes that the affluent are going unpunished for their crimes, then we have not only failed to achieve our goal of equal justice, but we have also created the conditions that will breed further disrespect for the law.

*New York, June 26.*

I leave this office with regret, because I believe that all citizens, and especially the poor and the young, respect the law only when they are confident that law enforcement is above politics. It appears to me that the White House, for all its statements about law and order, has failed to recognize that in law enforcement, as elsewhere, the customs and principles of the old politics are no longer relevant. I hope my fight for independence will make it easier for my successor to withstand the harsh, narrow, partisan views on law enforcement currently in favor at the Department of Justice in Washington.

*News conference, New York, Dec. 22.*

**Stanley Mosk**
*Associate Justice,*
*Supreme Court of California*

People obey the law not only out of fear of punishment, but because of what it does for them; the durability of continuity it gives to basic institutions and the expectation, conceived in experience, that the just process of the law will right wrongs and grievances.

*Napa, Calif., pub. April 20.*

**Ralph Nader**
*Lawyer, Consumer Rights Advocate*

These big Washington law firms are a powerful institution in the United States. Together they constitute a national power center . . . The corporation lawyer is the chief power broker between the special interests and the Government. He is also the most irresponsible factor in this equation because he hides behind the client-lawyer relationship to pursue all kinds of anti-social policies.

*Interview, Washington, pub. Feb. 9.*

The most important thing a lawyer can do is become an advocate of powerless citizens. I am in favor of lawyers without clients. Lawyers should represent systems of justice. I want to create a new dimension to the legal profession. What we have now is a democracy without citizens. No one is on the public's side. All the lawyers are on the corporations' side. And the bureaucrats in the Administration don't think the government belongs to the people.

*Pub. Oct. 3.*

**Richard M. Nixon**
*President of the United States*

. . . when we consider what a Chief Justice has in the way of influence on his age and the ages after him, I think it could fairly be said that our history tells us that our Chief Justices have probably had more profound and lasting influence on their times and on the direction of the nation than most Presidents have had.
*Television broadcast, Washington, May 21.*

I hold in my hands the fate of the man (Judge Clement Haynsworth). I will not be a party to destroying the man. Unless some new fact comes in, I will stick by Haynsworth, even if he gets only one vote. Will I withdraw him? I will not!
*Washington, pub. Oct. 29.*

**Francis T. P. Plimpton**
*President, Association of the Bar of the City of New York*

We hear much these days of strict construction and strict constructionists . . . Strict construction of the Constitution? That yellow document of erratic spelling and uncertain punctuation, miraculously hammered out by 39 perspiring men in the hot Philadelphia summer of 1787 as a compromise between 13 quarreling little Eastern seaboard states, would not today be the world's oldest living written constitution, governing a complex continent, if it had been constricted by the strict construction for which some now seem to yearn. The reason that document is still living is that it has been kept living by a Supreme Court alive to the challenge of change and unafraid to infuse new interpretations into the time-tested fabric of its fundamental structure.
*New York, Oct. 14.*

**Adam Clayton Powell**
*United States Representative, D-N.Y.*

The main thing (about the Supreme Court decision restoring his seat in Congress) which we have established is that the principle of three branches of government has been reaffirmed. It affects not only me, but 220 million people. You can't have a Government in the United States that believes in law and order if the Congress of the United States does not believe in law and order.
*News conference, Bimini Island, June 17.*

**Hyman G. Rickover**
*Vice-Admiral, United States Navy; director, Division of Naval Reactors, Atomic Energy Commission of the United States*

As industry becomes more sophisticated in finding and exploiting loopholes in the law, Congress must become more diligent in closing them.
*Washington, Jan. 16.*

**Bernard G. Segal**
*President-elect, American Bar Association*

When we put our judges in an ivory tower, you put justice in an ivory tower.
*Pub. Aug. 15.*

**Potter Stewart**
*Associate Justice, Supreme Court of the United States*

I shall not today attempt to further define the kinds of material I understand to be embraced within that shorthand description (hard core pornography); and perhaps I could never succeed in intelligibly doing so. But, I know it when I see it.
*Washington, pub. Nov. 5.*

**Strom Thurmond**
*United States Senator, R-S.C.*

(Retiring Chief Justice Earl Warren's decisions) are milestones on the retreat from civilized order. (His) overdue retirement as Chief Justice of the U.S. Supreme Court brings to a close a period marked by growing social disintegration and chaos . . . The Warren Court's decisions on criminal practice have unleashed a reign of terror upon law-abiding citizens of all races.
*Washington, June 29.*

**John N. Turner**
*Minister of Justice and Attorney General of Canada*

Substantive and procedural law benefits

(JOHN N. TURNER)

and protects landlords over tenants, creditors over debtors, lenders over borrowers, and the poor are seldom among the favored parties.

*Pub. Dec. 7.*

## Joseph D. Tydings
*United States Senator, D-Md.*

. . . any off-the-bench activity that a judge performs for compensation, unless subject to scrutiny and criticism by reason of public disclosure, is fraught with potential for undermining the appearance of rectitude that the judiciary must maintain.

*Washington, Nov. 7.*

## Theodore Voorhees
*Chairman, judicial selection committee, American Bar Association*

The public appears willing to accept a judiciary that contains a distressingly high percentage of the second rate.

*Pub. Sept. 3.*

## Earl Warren
*Chief Justice of the United States*

The F.B.I. budget is infinitely higher than the whole Federal court system . . . Other branches of Government proliferate without end—but not the courts.

*Washington, pub. March 24.*

I have heard a great many people say to me, "Well, I agree with your opinions on these civil rights, all right, but don't you think you are going too fast?" Of course, the answer to that is, "We haven't anything to say about how fast we go." We go with the cases that come to us; and when they come to us with a question of human liberties involved in them, we either hear them and decide them, or we let them go and sweep them under the rug, only to leave them for future generations.

*At Judicial Conference of the District of Columbia, Washington, June 2.*

It is not likely ever, with human nature as it is, for nine men to agree always on the most important and controversial things of life. If it ever comes to such a pass, I would say that the Court will have lost its strength and will no longer be a real force in the affairs of our country.

*Washington, June 23.*

I think the reapportionment, not only of state legislatures, but of representative government in this country, is perhaps the most important issue we have had before the Supreme Court. If everyone in this country has an opportunity to participate in his government on equal terms . . . most of these problems that we are now confronted with would be solved through the political process rather than through the courts.

*Sacramento, pub. June 27.*

A man, whether he is a Communist or a Fascist or a Ku Klux Klanner, or whatever he might be, is entitled to have his rights protected in the courtroom, and, if his rights cannot be protected in the courtroom, the rights of no one can be secure.

*Interview, pub. June 27.*

Someone always must be a scapegoat when there is a crime. Police can take their case to the public. Prosecutors can take their case to the public. The only people who cannot talk back, but must do their job day by day, are the courts.

*Interview, London, pub. Oct. 19.*

## Earl Warren, Jr.
*Municipal judge, Sacramento, Calif.*

Most people think . . . that trial judges can make law, and they think they should rule whatever way they think is appropriate, and nothing could be farther from the truth. Trial judges have to follow the law as it exists. We can't insert our personal opinions, our personal morals or standards or our likes and dislikes. We have to follow guidelines set by the law. The same thing is true of the jurors.

*Interview, Sacramento, pub. Oct. 19.*

## Jack Webb
*Actor, Television Producer*

Police methods have changed so drastically through court decisions to protect the rights of suspects that we can't use any of the old scripts (for TV's "Dragnet" series). They would have to be completely

redone, and it isn't worth it. Personally, I go along with what Truman Capote said: "You take away a policeman's right to interrogate and you cut off his hands."
*Interview, Los Angeles, pub. Jan. 27.*

**Robert Welch**
*President, John Birch Society*

You'll have to stretch your imagination to call (U.S. Chief Justice) Warren Burger a conservative.
*News conference, Los Angeles, Nov. 10.*

**Charles E. Wyzanski, Jr.**
*Chief Judge, United States
District Court for Massachusetts*

. . . if you don't get reversed (by the U.S. Supreme Court) one-third of the time, it shows you are not courageous. The guy with the perfect record is entitled to be buried.
*Interview, pub. March 17.*

**Whitney M. Young, Jr.**
*Executive Director,
National Urban League*

To ask a judge to determine whether an accused man might commit a crime if released on bail is to replace law and reason with crystal-ball gazing . . . black people are rightly fearful that preventive detention proposals are a first step that could lead to a system of racial containment at some future, crisis-ridden time.
*Before American Bar Association,
Dallas, Aug. 13.*

# Law and Order

**Hugh Addonizio**
*Mayor, Newark, N.J.*

. . . the potential for violence remains a fact of everyday life in American cities, and anyone with the nerve to praise himself or anbody else for maintaining harmony is a fool. No single man, group or issue can cause and then sustain a major riot, and no single man, group or issue can ensure a continued absence of violence. It is all rooted in deeper matters, which I hope the rest of the nation is finally beginning to understand and come to grips with.

*Pub. Sept. 15.*

**Muhammed Ali (Cassius Clay)**
*Former World Heavyweight*
*Boxing Champion*

Violence is the worst thing we can think of. It's like a bull running into a locomotive. You can admire the bull for his courage, but he'll still end up splattered all over the track.

*Before National Council of*
*Black Students,*
*Minneapolis, pub. Feb. 21.*

**Allen H. Andrews, Jr**
*Superintendent of Police, Peoria, Ill.*

The public is not so much interested any more in what causes crime and violence and disorder. They just say: "Stop it!" It is said that Americans don't act until they get worked up or until there is a crisis. Now there is a crisis, and American people are worked up.

*Peoria, pub. June 2.*

**William Banowsky**
*Executive vice president,*
*Pepperdine College*

The time has come to put the defiers of order on the defensive; for the only hope of achieving a better world for all is to work within the bounds of law and order. Ours is not a negative "freedom from," but a dynamic "freedom to." We seek freedom as a means to seek a newer world. Our forefathers had to pay a price to achieve freedom. We must pay the price to preserve it.

*Before Pacific Coast Electrical*
*Association, Los Angeles, May 22.*

**David Brothers**
*Deputy chairman,*
*New York State Chapter,*
*Black Panther Party*

You can wait-in or sing-in all you want, but power comes from the barrel of a gun . . . Violence is as American as cherry pie. You put a .38 on your hip and you get respect.

*New York, June 25.*

**H. Rap Brown**
*Chairman,*
*Student Coordinating Committee*

We do not accept unconditional nonviolence as a tactic. All tactics must be considered. Violence must be considered. We live in a world of violence.

*Interview, New York, July 22.*

**Lynn D. Compton**
*Chief Deputy District Attorney,*
*Los Angeles County*

Because of the nature of what the police represent, they are the first target of attack by subversives. They are the one arm of government on the front lines protecting society and institutions against violent attack from those disposed to bring down the government. They are the soldiers in the trenches. It is only natural, when they realize they are under attack, that they would resist or react.

*Los Angeles, pub. Sept. 7.*

**William C. Cramer**
*United States Representative, R-Fla.*

How ironic that rioters against the fair trial of the "Hate 8"—"Hate America 8"— should be publicized, glorified and given . . . prime TV time to mouth even their hatred for our trial system and the trial underway in a court of justice. This performance is proof positive that no institution in America is safe from their physical attack, their verbal abuse and their organized hatred. As the author of the Antiriot Act, I believe this performance fully justifies the wisdom of enacting this law and of fully prosecuting under it.
*Before the House, Washington, Sept. 30.*

**Charles R. Gain**
*Chief of Police, Oakland, Calif.*

Many people deify individuals in the Black Panther Party. Many whites identify with the plight of the poor Negro. Because of a deep guilt complex, they feel they must pour their hearts and money out to anyone who presumes to speak for the Negro. These people denigrate the police, and this goes on and on.
*Oakland, pub. Sept. 7.*

**John W. Gardner**
*Chairman, Urban Coalition*

I do not blame the ghetto residents for being angry, but they must not let their anger lead them into self-destructive moods. They must seek—as the college activist must seek, as we all must seek— a world in which man's destructive impulses are brought within a framework of law and rationality. Anyone who unleashes man's destructive impulses had better stand a long way back.
*Harvard University, pub. April 11.*

There is no doubt that today's revolutionary is pursuing that goal with all the energy at his command; and, in that pursuit, he is wholly cynical in his manipulation of others. The rights of the majority are irrelevant to him . . . He will devise traps to demean those in authority, destroying their dignity, if possible. He will exploit the mass media, feeding their hunger for excitement and conflict . . .
*Godkin Lectures, Harvard University, pub. April 25.*

There are the extremists, right wing and left wing, with their promises of salvation through violence and coercion. They disguise themselves as saviors, but there is a satanic gleam in their eyes. They believe that hatred will cure and that violence will pave the way to a better world. They do not understand that, in her hour of agony, America needs physicians, not executioners . . . The student with an inclination toward violent and coercive action, and the patrolman with a taste for brutality, are waiting for each other. The politician with a fondness for repressive measures, and the ghetto leader with a leaning toward violence, are waiting for each other—and eventually they will find each other.
*Stanford University, pub. July 6.*

**Erving Goffman**
*Professor of Anthropology,*
*University of Pennsylvania*

What are the minimal demands for the preservation of public order? Thanks to hippies, we've learned in the last five or ten years that we can get along with a lot less order than we thought. The trumpet blows, but the wall doesn't come down or even levitate.
*Interview, Philadelphia, pub. Feb. 12.*

**John J. Harrington**
*National President,*
*Fraternal Order of Police*

I personally believe that looters should be shot. Under the court systems today, it is impossible for a policeman to stop a riot. You arrest a rioter. Then you have to tell him of his rights, get him a lawyer, make him comfortable and all this sort of stuff before you can question him. Why, you don't have enough policemen to handle 100 rioters this way—and you're likely to have thousands of rioters out there. The only sensible way to stop a riot is to forget that you may lose votes on Election Day—on the other hand, you might gain a lot of votes—and declare martial law. Under martial law, it's automatic: Looters would be shot. You'd have one riot, and that would be the last riot.
*Interview, Washington, pub. Dec. 22.*

**Theodore Hesburgh**
*President, Notre Dame University*

Law and order is no good if it is meant only to defend the status quo. Law and order can't be an end in itself. It's got to function as a matrix for human development, for opportunity and justice for all. If it doesn't, then we don't deserve law and order.

*Pub. Nov. 18.*

**Eric Hoffer**
*Author*

You better watch out. The common man is standing up and someday he's going to elect a policeman as President of the United States.

*Pub. Oct. 6.*

**Edward M. Kennedy**
*United States Senator, D-Mass.*

If rage replaces reason, if confrontation replaces argument and compromise, if every passionate interest must get what it wants, we will be a land where no one will be sure, where no one will be safe, where the majesty of the law is deposed by the passion of the moment.

*New York, May 15.*

Discontent can be met, or it can be repressed. We can keep faith with those who seek improvement, or we can ignore them. If the vigilante spirit grows in the United States, if we believe that our most difficult problems can be smashed rather than solved, there is no doubt that violence will continue, repression will grow and the liberties of us all will be endangered.

*University of Massachusetts, May 31.*

**Ralph Lazarus**
*Chairman,*
*Federated Department Stores*

The great challenge to leadership in our age is the challenge of violence—the violence that follows a head-on collision between the forces of change and inflexible, de-humanized organizations in too many areas of American life, including business. This violence is weakening our institutions. It is opening the doors to repression and shifting the odds that freedom can survive

the conflicts and complexities of tomorrow.

*University of Southern California, April 2.*

**Jerris Leonard**
*Assistant Attorney General,*
*Civil Rights Division, Department of*
*Justice of the United States*

Of all violence, police violence in excess of authority is the most dangerous. For who will protect the public when police violate the law?

*Before President's Commission on*
*Violence, Washington, pub. Feb. 20.*

**Thurgood Marshall**
*Associate Justice,*
*Supreme Court of the United States*

Anarchy is anarchy, and it makes no difference who practices it. It is bad; it is punishable; and it should be punished.

. . . nothing will be settled with guns, firebombs or rocks. The country can't survive it if the perpetrators go unpunished. It's that simple.

*Dillard University, New Orleans, May 4.*

**Richard M. Nixon**
*President of the United States*

What I feel is this: I do not believe the great majority of the American people in our cities are anti-Negro. I do not believe they're anti-poor or anti-welfare or reactionary or members of hate groups. I do believe, however, this—and this is the message that comes through rather loud and clear: The American people in our cities, in our small towns and in this country are fed up to here with violence and lawlessness, and they want candidates who take a strong stand against it. And I think that's the message for the candidates in the future.

*News conference, Washington, June 19.*

**Sargent Pitcher, Jr.**
*District Attorney,*
*East Baton Rouge Parish, La.*

Unless the Federal Government . . . stops interfering with law enforcement on the local level, police morale, already low, will vanish, and, when that happens, I am . . . certain . . . that the people of this country will rise up to protect themselves. They are sick and tired of seeing looters and rioters getting away with murder, arson and property damage, and if the Government will not protect them, they will be forced to take the law into their own hands to protect themselves. When this happens, we'll have a full scale shooting race war in this country.

*Before Sons of Confederate Veterans, New Orleans, Aug. 14.*

**Adam Clayton Powell**
*United States Representative, D-N.Y.*

I don't think there is any place for violence until you come to the breaking point when all reason does not succeed and by some act of violence something can be done to bring those who will not reason to a point of reasonability.

*Notre Dame University, March 17.*

**William H. Rehnquist**
*Assistant Attorney General,*
*Office of Legal Counsel,*
*Department of Justice*
*of the United States*

To deplore violence without likewise deploring disobedience to law, whether violent or nonviolent, misses a large part of the point. Disobedience cannot be tolerated, whether it be violent or nonviolent disobedience.

*Newark, Del., May 1.*

**Fritz Riwotzki**
*Commissioner of Police,*
*Dortmund, West Germany*

The right to demonstrate is the first right—it stands before all others. On the other hand, the police must not be used as a doormat for everyone to wipe his feet on or as a vacuum cleaner to clean up the mess of society.

*Interview, Dortmund, pub. Jan. 25.*

**John P. Spiegel**
*Director, Lemberg Center for the Study of Violence, Brandeis University*

There is still the possibility of violent response to injustice, but no longer is it a mass protest against mass injustice. Now we are getting down to specific and local issues: What's to happen in schools, welfare, hospitals, labor, etc. If there is to be a major disturbance, it is likely to grow out of these localized issues—and probably because a local issue has been mishandled. However, we also have improved official responses now. Officials are aware that these local situations need sophisticated handling in ways that will reduce tensions, confine the situation to the issues involved and keep it from exploding into a big conflagration.

*Pub. June 2.*

It is not clear whether he (President Nixon) is going to take action that will relieve the problems of the cities, whether he's going to take no action, or take action that will make those problems worse. At some point, this "wait and see" attitude will come to an end, and if there has been really no improvement, then things may begin to get worse. We know that young people in black communities are heavily armed. I don't regard that as reassuring.

*Rockport, Mass., Sept. 5.*

**Carl B. Stokes**
*Mayor of Cleveland*

Only those of us dealing with these problems every day realize the life and death struggle of the cities. We are losing control of our cities. We can't stop the black violence—and the white violence will surely come next.

*Washington, pub. May 5.*

**Whitney M. Young, Jr.**
*Executive Director,*
*National Urban League*

Whites seem to be able to distinguish their own crackpots from the rest; but, when there is a riot of blacks, it's all just blacks.

*Pub. April 4.*

# National Defense and the Military

**Dean Acheson**
*Former Secretary of State
of the United States*

One of our failings as a people . . . is a preoccupation with witches . . . The witch has changed and is now the "military-industrial complex . . . ." I see no basis for the notion that we tend to overdo the military aspects. To the contrary, the nation has repeatedly neglected to provide the military basis to match its policy or to cope with aggressive forces. We tried unilateral arms reduction in the interwar period—we got Pearl Harbor. We reverted to habit after World War II—we got the Korean War. With respect to military power, I do not share the worries of those who discern and deplore dangers of too much . . .

Every time we relax our efforts in the defense field, we regret it. The present argument is we are spending too much. I say we are spending too little. The power of the United States alone blocks the Sino-Soviet ambitions.
*Before Joint Congressional Economics Subcommittee, Washington, June 11.*

**Spiro T. Agnew**
*Vice President of the United States*

No domestic program can be placed on an equal footing with a program to help us exist as a country. We can spend billions on our cities, but if they go up in a cloud of nuclear dust, all would be lost. It (the proposed Safeguard ABM System) both strengthens our deterrent to nuclear aggression and increases our leverage for disarmament negotiations. Its protection of our retaliation forces against direct attack stops any enemy from launching a first strike war.

The (anti-ballistic missile) system will

work. I can convinced it will work. *I am convinced it will work.*
*Before Commonwealth Club, San Francisco, May 7.*

I do not want to see this nation spend one dollar more on defense than is absolutely necessary, but I would hate to see this nation spend one dollar less on defense than is absolutely necessary.
*At Republican fund-raising dinner, New Orleans, Oct. 19.*

**George D. Aiken**
*United States Senator, R-Vt.*

In a day wnen we can determine the denomination of a postage stamp from 50 miles up, I doubt that there are many secrets left.
*Washington, April 9.*

**Charles A. Anderson**
*President, Stanford Research Institute*

The results (of decreasing university defense research) aren't yet catastrophic. But if this trend continues over the long run, it will dry up the resources of research and will have a significant effect on our national defense position.
*Interview, San Francisco, pub. June 8.*

**George W. Anderson, Jr.**
*Admiral, United States Navy (Ret.); former Chief of Naval Operations*

Where there has been developing a very great deficiency in United States total sea power is in the deterioration of our merchant marine . . . I actually believe that, if we allow our Navy and other seagoing assets to fall into disrepair, we are allowing our nation to become second or third-rate. I think we have to remember that the decline and fall of almost every great nation was heralded by the decline of their sea power.

*Interview, Washington, pub. Jan. 20.*

## Leslie C. Arends
*United States Representative, R-Ill.*

. . . it is argued that the Soviets have no intention of developing a first strike force. But we cannot develop our forces according to what their intentions might be. We cannot predict what their intentions will be in the mid-seventies—we cannot even predict who their leaders will be at that time. But we must develop our forces in such a way as to be able to meet their capabilities regardless of how sanguine some might feel about their intentions.

*Before the House, Washington, Oct. 2.*

## Helen Delich Bentley
*Chairman,*
*Federal Maritime Commission*

. . . it is most unfortunate that we have not convinced more Americans that it is a bona fide Soviet intention to "bury us at sea." Make no mistake about it. The oceans of this globe are, in fact, the maritime springboard for launching the worldwide aggression of Soviet imperialistic ambitions.

*Before Navy League, Phoenix, Dec. 13.*

## Adolph A. Berle, Jr.
*President, 20th Century Fund;*
*former adviser to the President*
*of the United States*
*on Inter-American affairs*

. . . I am against ABM (anti-ballistic missiles) deployment because I do not think it will be effective; I do not agree with some critics of ABM who say that, economically, the country cannot afford it. That is nonsense. The maximum estimate is that ABM would cost $50 billion. The United States can afford that. and more.

*At Center for the Study*
*of Democratic Institutions,*
*Santa Barbara, Calif., pub. Feb. 10.*

## Leonard Bernstein
*Former Musical Director,*
*New York Philharmonic Orchestra*

MIC (Military-Industrial Complex) is a monster that is eating up America alive. It is a chimera that invades our dreams, that has almost succeeded in displacing our traditional dream, what we have always called the American dream. This monster feeds on selfishness; it is nourished by greed; and it operates mostly in secrecy. Now and then we catch a glimpse of it, bellowing fire, smoke, pollution and corruption into our lives.

*New York, Oct. 23.*

## Jonathan B. Bingham
*United States Representative, D-N.Y.*

American prisoners (of war) are forced by the name and rank and service number limitation . . . to suffer and often die for nothing.

*Washington, Jan. 29.*

## Omar N. Bradley
*General, United States Army (Ret.);*
*former chairman,*
*Joint Chiefs of Staff*

The military has to have organization. I am a very strong believer in the proper organizational structure because it keeps too much power from getting into the wrong hands. Everybody knows what they are supposed to do, what their colleague is supposed to do and they know their responsibilities. We couldn't function in the Army without good organization.

*Interview, Beverly Hills, Calif.,*
*pub. April.*

The Armed Forces, which have been called upon when diplomacy failed, seem to be under attack from those whose servants they are. They have kept faith with their country and with those of us who follow. It is now our turn to keep the faith.

*Los Angeles, Nov. 11.*

## Clarence J. Brown
*United States Representative,*
*R-Ohio*

The doves who had been cooing for military spending reductions are squawking like wounded eagles now that their chickens are coming home to roost.

*Before the House, Washington, Oct. 28.*

**Harold Brown**
*Former Secretary of the Air Force
of the United States; president,
California Institute of Technology*

(Of) those who have served as civilian officials in the Defense Department at the level of Presidential appointment, whether their professional training and experience was in science or technology, economics, law, business or whatever, the overwhelming majority have recognized the severely limited utility of military power and the frightening dangers in its exercise, as well as the sad necessity of its possession.

*California Institute of Technology,
June 13.*

**Alastair Buchan**
*Director, British Institute
for Strategic Studies*

. . . if President Nixon insists on strategic superiority as a principle, then you are in the most appalling rat race—with uncertainties not only about numbers but also about what the numbers mean.

*Interview, London, pub. Feb. 17.*

**Harry F. Byrd**
*United States Senator, D-Va.*

In my judgment, the American people are becoming more and more concerned at both the cost of government and the competence of those who are handling their tax monies, and much concern applies to the Department of Defense as well as to the Office of Economic Opportunity and other welfare programs. I, for one, expect to view with skepticism the entire military budget.

*Washington, May 1.*

**Howard W. Cannon**
*United States Senator, D-Nev.*

I believe it is essential to maintain a strategic deterrence posture with a mixture of all three elements of strategic force—bombers, land-based missiles, and sea-based missiles. This has been our official policy as stated by the Department of Defense for several years and I thoroughly agree with it.

*Before the Senate, Washington, Sept. 15.*

**Clifford P. Case**
*United States Senator, R-N.J.*

The greatest reason for concern about the ABM (anti-ballistic missile system), in connection with disarmament, is not its possible effect (in) deterring the Russians from coming to the conference table. I think they want to come. It isn't even a question of the cost, although the waste of money is outrageous. A bigger effect is in its effect on the escalation of the arms race itself . . . We will be much less able to negotiate effective arms reduction, among other reasons, because, at a higher and more sophisticated level of armaments on both sides, we will be unable to be sure, without the kind of inspection the Russians will never permit, that they are abiding by their agreement.

*Before Senate Foreign Relations
Committee, Washington, pub. April 7.*

**John H. Chafee**
*Secretary of the Navy
of the United States*

Any time you reduce the Navy's readiness, you are reducing the Navy's ability to respond to national emergencies or to handle national commitments. The thing that disturbs me is the belief that we can have the same kind of defense establishment after making . . . very sizeable cuts.

*Washington, Aug. 22.*

We believe it is wiser for the future of our country to have a smaller, less capable Navy now, and to take the savings and invest them in research and development and production of the types of weapons, ships and planes we might need to fight an enemy in the 1970's or 1980's.

*Before Chicago Executive Club, Sept. 12.*

**Abram Chayes**
*Professor of Law, Harvard University*

You simply can't launch a test nuclear attack on the United States across Canada just to see how *Sentinel-Safeguard* (anti-missile system) can respond. The fact is that the first time anyone will know for sure whether the system will work is when it is called upon to meet an actual attack. In buying this system, the United States will be paying $6.6 billion for a package marked "Do Not Open Until Doomsday." Then it will be too late to send it back to the manufacturer for a better model.

*Washington, May 5.*

**Don H. Clausen**
*United States Representative, R-Calif.*

The knowledge, competence and expertise we develop in the aerospace-aviation technological field will ultimately determine our strength as a nation. We cannot relinquish our lead in the aviation field. If we are to avoid getting bogged down in future Vietnams, I admonish America and this Congress to stay first in both civil and military aviation. They are totally interdependent and will serve to benefit future American generations and the peoples of developing free nations looking to us for hope and leadership.

*Before the House, Washington, Oct. 3.*

**William Clay**
*United States Representative, D-Mo.*

At present, not the Congress nor the American public has any working knowledge or control over the determination of the strength of our armed forces. It is determined by the generals who flout their trumped-up notions of security and war over the heads of the public interest and welfare. With the present military establishment to protect us, we do not need foreign enemies. They will, given the authority they presently wield, protect us right into holocaust.

*Before the House, Washington, Oct. 3.*

**Clark M. Clifford**
*Former Secretary of Defense
of the United States*

The hard fact is that we may never again expect to be in as favorable a position as we now enjoy for entry into talks about a freeze in strategic nuclear armaments. The Soviet Union continues to produce and perfect its nuclear missiles. Technological developments may well make any arms limitation agreement more difficult to develop and enforce a year from now or six months from now than it is today.

*Feb. 17.*

**Benjamin V. Cohen**
*Lawyer; former diplomat*

When we rightly condemn some of the younger generation's irrational and self-defeating conduct—their extravagant demands, violence and obscenities—in opposition to our defense programs, let us remember that some of our actions appear equally irrational and self-defeating to them.

*Washington, Nov. 9.*

**J. B. Colwell**
*Vice Admiral, United States Navy;
deputy chief of naval operations*

If there were such a thing as a highly polished, smoothly functioning military-industrial complex working for the mutual benefit of both parties, would our shipbuilding industry be in the shape it is in today? Would 58% of U.S. naval combatant ships be 20 years old or older? Would our aging, overworked fleet be on the verge of obsolescence?

*Before New York Chapter,
American Ordnance Association,
pub. July 20.*

**Albert O. Connor**
*Lt. Gen., United States Army;
deputy chief of staff for personnel*

We are getting more kooks into the Army . . . We are getting more young men who are coming in undisciplined, the product of a society that trains them to resist authority.

*Before House Appropriations
Subcommittee, Washington, March 11.*

**Silvio O. Conte**
*United States Representative, R-Mass.*

It certainly seems to me that our national security is not in danger at this time. It looks like we have plenty of time and plenty of elbow room to continue further research on the ABM before we deploy it. We are talking about a huge investment, specifically $345.5 million for procurement, and I for one want to be sure we really need this before we dump all this money into it.

*Before the House, Washington, Oct. 2.*

**John Sherman Cooper**
*United States Senator, R-Ky.*

The United States and the Soviet Union continue to maintain a capability of destroying each other no matter which country makes the first strike. If one deploys an ABM (anti-ballistic missile) system, the other will do so, and will develop concurrently more effective and powerful offensive nuclear weapons . . . These delicate balances—including the nuclear deterrent—should not be upset by the commencement of another kind of nuclear arms race.

*Before the Senate, Washington, Feb. 4.*

The pursuit of security through nuclear power alone will never end. It will waste the fruits of the earth and make the labor of men empty. It will increase the sense of futility, particularly among the young. For we and the Soviets, with all our technology, can be reduced to dust at any moment. The green earth and millions who live on it can be burned to gray ashes. This spector is the essence of the nuclear arms race. This is our present security.

*Before the Senate, Washington, Aug. 6.*

**W. C. Daniel**
*United States Representative, D-Va.*

There are . . . those who argue that to deploy the (anti-ballistic missile) system will dim our prospects for disarmament. Wise old Patrick Henry once said that the only lamp by which his feet were guided was the light of experience. Mr. Henry said: "I know of no better way to judge the future than the past." Those who harbor such thoughts ignore the lessons of history. What little success we have experienced in our international negotiations has been when we have negotiated from a position of strength.

*Before the House, Washington, Oct. 2.*

**Everett M. Dirksen**
*United States Senator, R-Ill.*

I have no position (on the anti-ballistic missile program) . . . I'm afraid to lean; it's too easy to get pushed.

*News conference, Washington, March 10.*

There is a point where review (of the proposed Safeguard anti-missile system)

has to stop and hard action begin. Do we leave the country defenseless against a direct strike or against an accidental strike?

*Washington, March 24.*

**Thomas J. Dodd**
*United States Senator, D-Conn.*

If ABM did nothing more than protect the United States from an accidental missile firing, it would still be the cheapest life insurance that money could buy.

*Before the Senate, Washington, Aug. 1.*

**Peter H. Dominick**
*United States Senator, R-Colo.*

If you are going to have a military at all that is going to provide a defense, you had better give them the equipment with which they can do it. If you do not do that, you cannot ask them to provide the defense. It seems very simple to me to analyze the issue on that basis. This does not mean we have to do everything they want, or do it all at once. But it does mean we ought to go forward with the production of usable weaponry and modern technology, and do it, rather than simply study it for the next 5 years before we get going on any production models.

*Before the Senate, Washington, Sept. 4.*

**Allen J. Ellender**
*United States Senator, D-La.*

We must not overlook the fact that we are living in a nuclear missile age and if ever a war breaks out between us and our chief adversary, Russia, (aircraft) carriers will be of no use to us. As I see the picture, we are merely preparing for conventional brush fire wars. We are still pursuing our old policy of supporting, militarily, all of the free world countries so as to protect ourselves from the Russians. I am quite certain that the so-called free world countries will continue to rely upon us and do little or nothing for their own defense.

*Before the Senate, Washington, Sept. 12.*

**John Erskine**
*Physicist, Argonne National Laboratory*

The Army has never convinced us— the scientists—that this (the Sentinel anti-missile system) is a safe device. The stu-

pidity can be summed up in three words: costly, useless and dangerous.
*Pub. Feb. 17.*

**Jules Feiffer**
*Writer, Cartoonist*

My first 20 years, until I was drafted into the Army, I lived underground. The Army was very valuable because it taught me how to hate. In school, at home, I couldn't express my hostility very well: there were always too many reasons why THEY were right. But in the Army, in this perfect atmosphere of fascism, I knew immediately who the enemy was. It was the United States Army. They were the bad guys, I was the good guy.
*Interview, New York, pub. Jan. 26.*

**O. C. Fisher**
*United States Representative, D-Tex.*

. . . the lives of millions and millions of people could be involved in the outcome of this issue (the proposed anti-ballistic missile system). But time is running out. We are playing for keeps. The hour is late. If we make any mistake, let us make it in favor of trying to save 20 million to 50 million lives . . .
*Before the House, Washington, Oct. 2.*

**A. Ernest Fitzgerald**
*Deputy for Management Systems, United States Air Force*

I want to assure this subcommittee, the Congress and the American people that all of the officials and employes of the Department of Defense—and particularly those who play a part in managing its affairs—are dedicated to rooting out waste and inefficiency wherever and whenever they appear.
*Before Joint Congressional Economy-in-Government Subcommittee, Washington, June 11.*

**Gerald R. Ford**
*United States Representative, R-Mich.*

If you have to gamble and err (on the anti-ballistic missile system), it is better to gamble and err on the side of strength and not weakness.
*Washington, pub. March 12.*

**John S. Foster, Jr.**
*Director of Research and Engineering, Department of Defense of the United States*

. . . let there be no question on this point: we cannot now design an ABM (anti-ballistic missile) system that would be fully effective against the known and growing Soviet force. Nevertheless, the Safeguard deployment represents an important "balancing" of our overall strategic posture. It will fulfill its designed goals, and, in my judgment, it will not destabilize the strategic situation.
*Before House Armed Services Committee, Washington, April 30.*

There are some eminent scientists who, for one reason or other, claim it (the ABM system) won't work . . . They have offered no problem which we have not long since addressed and resolved . . . I want to point out that one does not obtain a meaningful technical judgment by taking a vote of the scientific community, or even of Nobel laureates.
*Before Aviation-Space Writers' Association, Dayton, Ohio, May 12.*

Intentions of a potential enemy are a secret he can easily keep. We do not have a crystal ball; yet, in order to deter nuclear war in the future, we must decide on future weapons now.
*Pub. June 6.*

The hard truth is this: our past and present methods of acquiring weapons have lost us the confidence of the public and are threatening our country's future security . . . We are losing our historic superiority in defense research and development because the Soviet Union has been increasing its research and development in defense, in atomic energy and space, while the total American effort in those areas has been roughly constant. And now, the critical attitude toward the Defense Department may result in an actual reduction of the American effort.
*Before Armed Forces Management Association, Washington, Aug. 19.*

Since secrecy usually hides much of the capability of the Soviet Union, we in fact rely heavily on technology to ensure us

(JOHN S. FOSTER, JR.)

against disastrous surprises. We must have broad technological superiority over any potential enemy. Not parity—superiority.

*Washington, pub. Aug. 29.*

It is the policy of the United States to develop and maintain a defensive chemical-biological capability so that our military forces could operate for some period of time in a toxic environment if necessary; to develop and maintain a limited offensive capability in order to deter all use of chemical and biological weapons by the threat of retaliation in kind.

*Pub. Oct. 18.*

**William C. Foster**
*Former Director,*
*Arms Control and Disarmament Agency*
*of the United States*

Few worthwhile enterprises are devoid of all risks, and arms control is no exception . . . What matters is not that there are risks associated with a particular measure, but rather how do these risks compare with the risks of not having the measure.

*At Strategy for Peace Conference,*
*Warrenton, Va., pub. Oct. 16.*

**J. William Fulbright**
*United States Senator, D-Ark.*

Non-nuclear states signing this (nonproliferation) treaty are signing away the option to manufacture or acquire nuclear weapons for their defense. We can do nothing less than show our good faith by being responsive to the desire of the smaller powers to halt. the nuclear arms race and to reduce existing nuclear arms arsenals.

*Washington, March 10.*

With military expenditures providing the livelihood of some 10% of our work force; with 22,000 major corporate defense contractors and another 100,000 subcontractors; with defense plants or installations located in 363 of the 435 congressional districts; with the Department of Defense spending $7.5 billion on research and development this year, making it the largest consumer of research output in the nation—millions of Americans whose only interest is in making a decent living have acquired a vested interest in an economy geared to war.

*Pub. Sept. 8.*

**James M. Gavin**
*Lt. Gen., United States Army (Ret.);*
*former United States*
*Ambassador to France*

The military drive you crazy. Nixon says he wants two ABM (anti-ballistic missile) test sites, and . . . he's right. But go across the Potomac River (to the Pentagon) and *they* are talking about twelve. Then they say it will cost $6 billion to $12 billion, which is absolutely wrong—it's $13 billion to $20 billion for certain. They drive you crazy and they wonder why they're under fire.

*Pub. June 9.*

**Barry M. Goldwater**
*United States Senator, R-Ariz.*

(Robert) McNamara put too much faith in missiles. I haven't changed my mind since I said in New Hampshire in 1964 that our missiles are not dependable.

*Interview, Washington, Jan. 13.*

. . . the real danger, the mortal threat to the United States and the Free World, does not really rest in existing weapons. It is the danger of a major breakthrough in the huge Russian research and development establishment.

*Atlanta, Jan. 27.*

I wish to be very blunt. I believe it is nothing short of a disgrace that such a defense (of the U.S. military) has to be made. (But if it is not), we will soon develop a national frame of mind against anything that smacks of defense. We will be permitting an erroneous public attitude to develop, which can spell nothing but trouble for the defense of the United States and the security of the free world.

*Before American Fighter Pilots*
*Association, pub. March 31.*

What would the critics of the military-industrial complex have us do? Would they have us ignore the fact that progress occurs in the field of national defense as well as in the field of social sciences? Do they want us to turn back the clock, disband our military establishment and do away with our defense-related industrial capacity . . . ? Rather than deploring the existence of a military industrial complex, I say we should thank heavens for it. That complex gives us our protective shield. It is the bubble under which our nation thrives and prospers. It is the armor which is unfortunately required in a world divided.

Its (the military-industrial complex's) ultimate aim is peace in our time, regardless of the aggressive, militaristic image which the left wing is attempting to give it. (Many) Pentagon problems stem not so much from a military-industrial complex as they do from the mistakes and miscalculations of . . . a civilian-computer complex . . . the Pentagon hierarchy of young civilians, often referred to as the "Whiz Kids," which was erected during the McNamara era in the questionable name of cost effectiveness.

. . . in World War II, we were forced to come from far behind in the production of munitions and in the building of military strength. Fortunately, we had the time to do the job before the Axis powers overwhelmed the civilized world. We have no such guarantee that, in new circumstances, we would enjoy a sufficient period of grace.

*National War College,*
*Washington, May 21.*

Opposition to the ABM did not reach anything like its present crescendo when the program was being called Sentinel and was being propelled by a Democratic Administration and a liberal-oriented Secretary of Defense.

*Before the Senate, Washington, July 22.*

The primary purpose of our strategic forces is to prevent nuclear war. Let us be very clear just what this means. If we are attacked, it is likely that over half of our people will be killed and most of our cities will be destroyed. We will not have to worry about the unemployed—they will no longer be with us. Those who feel that we can adopt a minimal level of defense and still avoid attack should look

at history. Weakness has always invited aggression. In fact, aggressors have often used an imagined inferiority on the part of an opponent as a reason for going to war.

I think we all know that the shock troops in the war against defense are coming from the ranks of those "Whiz Kids" whose former boss, Robert McNamara, was dedicated to the concept of downgrading American military strength. They have lost their old master to the World Bank, but their ardor is undiminished, as we can plainly see.

*Before the Senate, Washington, Sept. 12.*

**Mike Gravel**
*United States Senator, D-Alaska*

Our own arms efforts only stimulate and encourage Soviet efforts. There is no solution but to stop the Soviet weapon program, and this can be done only by negotiating to stop our own.

*Pub. Aug. 11.*

**Charles S. Gubser**
*United States Representative, R-Calif.*

This military-industrial complex isn't as dangerous as people make it out to be. I thank God we have a military-industrial complex, because I'd be scared to death without it.

*Washington, Sept. 18.*

How can a defensive weapon start a new arms race? In our military history we had H-bomb superiority, and Russia met it and surpassed it; we had the B-52 superiority, and she met that. With respect to every one of our deterrents, she has met them. We have the ICBM, and she is fast meeting that. We have the Polaris deterrent, and surely she will meet that . . . my point is that this (the proposed ABM system) will not set up an arms race because . . . there is one in progress right now and Russia is winning it. It is just that simple . . . Do we need an ABM? The answer lies in another question: Will Russia or China launch a first strike against us? The answer to that question only lies in the minds and the hearts of the men in the Kremlin and in Peking.

*Before the House, Washington, Oct. 2.*

**G. Elliott Hagan**
*United States Representative, D-Ga.*

As we stand on the threshold of the 1970s, we face this disquieting situation: The United States is ahead of the world in flags on the moon . . . but Soviet Russia is ahead, and moving faster every day, with flags on the high seas.
*Before U.S. Propeller Club,*
*Savannah, Oct. 17.*

**Seymour Halpern**
*United States Representative, R-N.Y.*

. . . while national wealth has increased, the lion's share of it has gone into fueling America's military machine, a staggering monolith that has come to have its own life—free of public approval or congressional review . . . Criticizing military spending does not mean the United States should compromise its defenses. The fact is, our military superiority over the Soviet Union has reached the stage of overkill, and alleged stories of Russian buildups are pure fantasy which, if believed, could only lead us to escalating the arms race to doomsday proportions.
*Before the House, Washington, Oct. 3.*

**Clifford P. Hannum**
*Brig. Gen., United States Army;*
*deputy director, R.O.T.C.*

I think some of the professors who attack R.O.T.C. in the name of academic freedom should stop to think that they are attacking an institution helping to preserve a general freedom within which academic freedom exists. If we were to lose our civilian-military character, we might become the kind of inbred army that takes over countries.
*Interview, Washington, pub. June 8.*

**Clifford P. Hansen**
*United States Senator, R-Wyo.*

It is surprising, in the light of recent events, that there should be an attempt to disapprove funds for the continuation of a weapons system (aircraft carriers) which history has proven as one of our most effective instruments in support of national policy. Since its inception, the carrier and its aircraft have been an unequaled success

as a weapon of war . . . To doubt the value of the carrier is to doubt the value of airpower itself . . .
*Before the Senate, Washington, Sept. 12.*

**Mark O. Hatfield**
*United States Senator, R-Ore.*

I feel strongly that a volunteer military manpower system will work. But, for such a system to be given a chance to prove its merit, we must dispel the myth that the draft, however undesirable, is inevitable.
*Washington, Jan. 22.*

Congress—not the Pentagon—must decide what are the fundamental threats to our national security. Congress—not the Pentagon—must judge the condition in our world and determine defense policies that are an appropriate response. Congress —not the Pentagon—must determine the size of our militia and where they should be placed throughout the world. And Congress—not the Pentagon—must determine the need for new weapons.
*Before the Senate, Washington, Sept. 3.*

**Wayne L. Hays**
*United States Representative, D-Ohio*

I think they ought to change the name of it (the ABM system): from the Sentinel to the Civil Servant, because it would not work and you cannot fire it.
*Pub. April 8.*

**Lewis B. Hershey**
*Lt.-Gen., United States Army;*
*director, Selective Service System*

The military needs status. The service should be considered a profession, on a par with any other. It can be developed that way, and it will then have enough volunteers—until there is an emergency. Then we'll have to resort to compulsion.
*Anaheim, Calif., Feb. 7.*

This world is not showing any indications of passing into the millenium. We have a lot of defense problems we didn't have 50 years ago. Then, we could figure any danger could only develop at a limited speed. Now, with transportation so nearly instantaneous, we are vulnerable to sudden danger in the world. We are a very big

nation, and I think a large nation has got to have large forces. I do not believe you can have large forces without compulsion.
*Interview, Washington, pub. April 21.*

I'm the operator. I didn't make the gasoline or provide the service station; but, if the armed services say they need 10 gallons of gas, we pump it in.
*Before Association of Student Governments, Washington, pub. Sept. 24.*

**Chet Holifield**
*United States Representative, D-Calif.*

We must at all costs maintain the factor of deterrance, in order to buy time to achieve mutual disarmament.
*Before the House, Washington, Oct. 1.*

**Ernest F. Hollings**
*United States Senator, D-S.C.*

Although we reach for the stars today, we continue to be pressed on all sides here on earth by the Communists. Today, as the world watches Apollo, the Russian people were not given a chance to see it. The leaders of the Communist world are the ones we must fear.
*Before the Senate, Washington, July 17.*

**Jeanne M. Holm**
*Colonel, United States Air Force; director, Women in the Air Force*

Women's draft would not be accepted in this country, except in the case of a major emergency when there would be conscription of all of our natural resources. But we must face up to a basic question: Whether or not women have the same obligation of citizenship as their contemporaries.
*Before Women's Division, Los Angeles Chamber of Commerce, May 22.*

**Harold E. Hughes**
*United States Senator, D-Iowa*

In the simplest language, the priorities for our military are to spend and keep spending. The priorities for our cancerous domestic problems are neglect, postponement and tokenism.
*News conference, Washington, June 16.*

**Hubert H. Humphrey**
*Former Vice President of the United States*

. . . I don't believe it (the proposed ABM system) would help one bit.
*Cincinnati, March 30.*

I do not believe the Soviets could seriously delude themselves into thinking a first-strike (nuclear attack) was possible (for them).
*Washington, April 3.*

**Richard H. Ichord**
*United States Representative, D-Mo.*

Continuing the policy of college (draft) deferments in time of a shooting war is one of our biggest mistakes.
*Washington, Oct. 16.*

**Daniel K. Inouye**
*United States Senator, D-Hawaii*

I believe we must make a decision now as to whether our security and our future lies in the direction of ever increasing levels of armed might and another great step in the arms race, or whether we will finally also take some risks in the name of peace.
*Before the Senate, Washington, July 22.*

**Henry M. Jackson**
*United States Senator, D-Wash.*

It would be tragic for the United States of America to remain naked while the Soviets have even a limited ABM system.
*Television interview, March 16.*

. . . three danger spots in the world show no signs of quieting down: the threatening situation on the Sino-Soviet border, where both sides have piled up vast arsenals; the potentially explosive conditions in Central Europe, where the Kremlin is using force to turn back the clock in Czechoslovakia; and the Middle East, where no agreements are in sight, and where the bitter conflict goes on. Crises in any one of these areas— and in other areas—could get out of hand; the trouble and violence could spill over and involve us directly. Hence, there is everything to be said for the United States maintaining a strong and prudent defense posture.

(HENRY M. JACKSON)

We don't settle an issue like ABM by claiming it won't work. Distinguished scientists will be found on both sides of this sort of issue. Trying to make one's case by the method of scientific authority won't wash . . . we Senators have to use our own heads and exercise our own judgment in evaluating the conflicting points of view and in weighing all the relevant considerations. Some critics . . . have tried to give the impression that the whole scientific community is up in arms against the Safeguard ABM. This is a wild distortion of the facts. Even the scientists who appeared before the Senate Armed Services Committee as opponents and critics of the Safeguard system did not go out on the limb of saying Safeguard would not work.

*Before the Senate, Washington, Aug. 6.*

### Jacob K. Javits
*United States Senator, R-N.Y.*

There is a real determination in Congress that the military budget is never again going to be treated as a sacred cow.

*Pub. Feb. 24.*

### Clarence L. Johnson
*Vice president,*
*Lockheed Aircraft Corporation*

I think we need a new fighter for air superiority, beyond the F-15, that can go at least Mach 3 and be able to operate up to 80,000 or 90,000 feet. I'm sure the other side will have a plane that can operate up this high, and I don't think we should let the enemy have this airspace all to himself.

*New York, Feb. 19.*

### Charles R. Jonas
*United States Representative, R-N.C.*

. . . since 1956, while the budget for national defense was going up 100 per cent, the budget for the social welfare programs has gone up 700 per cent. So I do not think the argument can be sustained that we are increasing funds for national defense and decreasing funds for social programs. However, there will not be any social programs to support if we fail in the national defense of our country.

*Before the House, Washington, Oct. 3.*

### Joseph E. Karth
*United States Representative, D-Minn.*

I am one who disagrees strongly with those who insist that our nation is the lone culprit; that, if our country refrained from providing for a national defense, all other nations would do likewise; that *our* leaders are the rascals and the Hos and Maos, and others, are nice guys. Please be assured, that is hogwash, pure and simple.

*Before the House, Washington, Oct. 3.*

### Edward M. Kennedy
*United States Senator, D-Mass.*

I firmly believe that deploying Sentinel (ABM) would be a major national error. I shall do what I can to see that it is not deployed.

*Before the Senate, Washington, Feb. 19.*

Today's draft law produces some gross inequities, creating unfairness for some of our young men and uncertainty in the lives of others. It was a law designed in other times for other situations and is an outdated patchwork.

*Pub. March 2.*

We know our country is troubled. We know part of the problem is that our domestic programs are starved for funds. Yet, when we ask for justification for our defense programs, we get slogans, not logic; we get scare, not reason. Unless we adjust our policies, our cities will continue to suffer, not because of a nuclear attack, but because of poison in the air and warfare in the streets.

*Fordham University, New York, June 7.*

Respect for the military service can hardly be enhanced if those who protest the system are the first people chosen to fight for our country.

*Washington, Nov. 2.*

### Carleton J. King
*United States Representative, R-N.Y.*

No one wants a Military Establishment simply for the glory of having one, least of all those who serve in it, either willingly or unwillingly. But the hard military facts of life today regarding the number of military threats around the world prove that it is hardly the time to cut military expendi-

tures or impair our defense readiness. While some may disagree, I have been unable to find any mellowing on the part of Communist aggressive aims. It is not evident in Vietnam, nor at the Paris Peace Conference, nor in Czechoslovakia, nor in Korea.
*Before the House, Washington, Oct. 1.*

**Henry A. Kissinger**
*Assistant to the President*
*of the United States*
*for National Security Affairs*

If the only thing wrong with an ABM (system) is that it will not work, the worst thing it does is to waste relatively little money, while if those who argue that it will not work happen to be wrong, the error might really jeopardize tens of millions of lives.
*Interview, Washington, pub. Aug. 12.*

**Herbert G. Klein**
*White House Director*
*of Communications*

The Government has a right not to comment in situations involving national security. But I have long felt that the Government has no right to lie.
*Before Sigma Delta Chi,*
*Washington, Feb. 18.*

**Melvin R. Laird**
*Secretary of Defense*
*of the United States*

. . . I am more concerned with defense (against the Chinese) than I am about any other kind of defense at the present time.
*Television interview, New York, Feb. 13.*

The (draft) law as currently written . . . must be changed, and one of the first pieces of legislation which will be sent to the Congress by the new Administration will be in this area—to do away with the inequities that presently exist in our Selective Service Act.
*News conference, Washington, Feb. 18.*

My responsibility as Secretary of Defense is to maintain the strength of the United States of America and to maintain the security and safety of the people . . .

When it gets into the matter of our strategic strength, our conventional strength, I will speak out to maintain a strong posture for the United States.
*Pub. March 3.*

The potential threat from the Soviet Union lies in the growing missile force which could destroy a portion of our deterrent, or destroy a portion of our retaliatory force. We cannot stop a massive Soviet attack on our cities. Technically, we just don't know how. We must rely on our deterrents to insure that a nuclear attack doesn't start in the first place.
*Before Senate Armed Services*
*Committee, Washington, March 20.*

We have sufficient strength today—in combination with our strategic forces, our missiles, our bombers, our Polaris capability—to respond to any attack that might be launched against (us). As Secretary of Defense, it is my obligation, it is my intention, to keep it that way beyond any reasonable doubt.

With the large tonnage the Soviets have, they are going for our missiles and they are going for a first-strike capability. There is no question about that . . . If they were going to go just at our cities and not knock out our forts . . . it would not require weapons which have such large mega-tonnage.

If the Soviet threat turns out to be, as the evidence now strongly indicates, an attempt to erode our deterrent capability, we must be in a position to convince them that a first strike would always involve unacceptable risks.
*Before Senate Foreign Relations*
*Committee, Washington, March 21.*

It is important for everyone to understand that, at the time of the Cuban missile crisis in 1962, the United States was in a position of vast strategic nuclear superiority. We are not in that same position today. The Soviet Union is now in a position where it has more ICBM's on launch pads and under construction than the United States does. It has the capability in the next few years of going ahead of us in submarine-launched missiles. It has a tre-

(MELVIN R. LAIRD)

mendous capability in intermediate-range missiles, which are targeted against our allies in Europe. We must have a credible deterrent so that the Soviet Union knows that, if they use these weapons, if they make that kind of mistake . . . then they will surely suffer the consequences.

*Interview, Washington, pub. April 7.*

If a mistake in assessing the potential threat (from an enemy in the future) is to be made, it would be far safer to err on the side of overestimating the threat. Nobody predicted the Russians were going to move missiles into Cuba . . . Nobody predicted the Russians were going to move into Czechoslovakia.

I know it's much more popular to talk like a Secretary of State, but I feel—and the President feels—that I should talk like a Secretary of Defense.

*Interview, pub. May 9.*

Much of the harsh criticism now being leveled at the military . . . is totally misplaced. Civilians decide our national security policy; civilians decide the strategies we shall follow; civilians decide our forces' structure; and civilians run the Department of Defense . . . then men and women of our armed services execute these policies, with courage and determination and loyalty.

*Before Military Order of the World Wars, Chicago, May 16.*

As much as we deplore this kind of weapon (chemical and biological), if we want to make sure this weapon is never used, we must have the capability to use it.

*Washington, July 28.*

I shall strive to insure that the (defense budget) cuts have the least possible impact on our readiness, but I want the American people to know that there will be an inevitable weakening of our worldwide military posture.

*News conference, Washington, Aug. 21.*

In determining the level of military strength appropriate for the United States, we cannot ignore what is going on in the Soviet Union . . . Our over-all military capability today, together with the effort we have programmed in our defense planning, provides sufficient protection to the nation for the immediate future. But if we project the trends which I have pointed out beyond the next few years, doubts about our future security do arise. It would be folly to disarm unilaterally or to permit a general weakening of our military strength.

Without adequate research and development, the American military in the future will find itself outmaneuvered, outgunned and overmatched.

*Before American Legion, Atlanta, Aug. 26.*

Nothing would delight me more than to live in a world in which the international climate would permit drastic reduction in defense spending. But the time has not yet come when we can drastically slash the military budget without exposing the American people to inordinate risks.

*Before National Security Industrial Association, Washington, Sept. 18.*

**Lyman L. Lemnitzer**
*General, United States Army;*
*Supreme Allied Commander, Europe*

The Communist ideology, pronounced by every head of the Soviet Union for the past 50 years, aims at ultimate world domination. As long as this threat exists, I don't believe that the United States, or any NATO nation, has any alternative . . . but to maintain a reasonable military posture in order to defend themselves as long as this threat of international Communism exists.

*Interview, Supreme Headquarters, Allied Powers, Mons, Belgium, pub. May 12.*

**Roger Lewis**
*Chairman,*
*General Dynamics Corporation*

. . . I place my confidence in America's history and tradition of concern that the military not be dominant in our political life, that our Founding Fathers were right when they separated the powers of the Government, provided for civilian control of the military and insured freedom of speech and freedom of the press. It is in this climate that the free-enterprise system can operate so effectively to contribute greatly to the preservation of the kind of government we have. And it is this climate that should quiet fears that companies like ours have a vested interest in preserving the cold war. The executive branch determines policy, the Defense Department devises the strategy, Congress provides the money, and industry does its job in a tough, competitive atmosphere. All of this public interest is healthy, however, and is to be welcomed.

I don't see anything improper in the relationship between the military and industry. We don't have a government like those of prewar Germany and Japan. Further, there are tens of thousands of companies doing defense work, and numerous echelons of authority both within the executive branch and within the Congress that must study and approve procurement policies and actions. And it is all done through the free-enterprise system: The competition is severe, the risks great, the profits generally lower than in commercial practice.

*Interview, pub. Aug. 26.*

### John V. Lindsay
*Mayor of New York*

Now, at the very time that big cities across the country are facing their worst financial crisis . . . we hear new calls to spend $6 billion on an anti-ballistic missile system . . . But where is the outcry over the billions of dollars in unfinished or abandoned exercises of defense? Where was the outcry when a former budget bureau official disclosed that in the last decade $25 billion worth of contracts had either been cancelled, phased out or found to be 75 per cent unreliable?

*Polytechnic Institute, Brooklyn, March 5.*

### Clarence D. Long
*United States Representative, D-Md.*

We've long been aware that much of the Navy equipment is old and obsolete. I'm asking the Defense Department to inquire whether this might also be true of the Navy

top command.

*Before House Appropriations Subcommittee, Washington, June 4.*

### Allard K. Lowenstein
*United States Representative, D-N.Y.*

. . . weapons that do not work do not afford anyone much protection against anything, even against stray missiles fired by madmen, whether they be Russian colonels, Chinese dictators, or anyone else. That is why money for ABM research makes sense, and why money for ABM deployment at this time does not.

*Before the House, Washington, Oct. 2.*

### Mike Mansfield
*United States Senator, D-Mont.*

I see no safety for this nation in bristling and burnished missiles, whether they stand tall around deteriorating cities or rise in the empty fields of an impoverished rural society. I see, rather, the beginnings of deep trouble if we ever permit a driven pursuit of an elusive security against threats abroad to distract us from the rising tide of insecurity at home.

*Pub. March 17.*

The day the Pentagon just had to ask in order to receive is over. We're really going to scrutinize that Defense budget in depth . . . If we keep on spending for all the things the military wants and do not achieve a solution to our internal problems, what have we profited? What has the nation gained?

*Interview, Washington, pub. March 31.*

The ABM proposal is not just another public works project. It is not some trivial boondoggle, a minor item out of the military pork barrel. It touches questions which go to the structure of a free society and to the civilized survival of this nation, the Soviet Union, and, perhaps, of all nations.

*Before the Senate, Washington, April 1.*

I don't question the patriotism of anyone. But I do question the judgment of creating a military-industrial-labor complex which exercises such great power. You have to control the money—control the

(MIKE MANSFIELD)

spigot—and then you can get into philosophy.
*Pub. Aug. 26.*

The performing of research to meet the needs of defense is honorable work. Scientists and universities who receive defense funds for a valid defense need should be proud, never ashamed. It is only when the sponsorship of a project is questionable, or the subject matter of the mission is questionable, does any element of shame enter the relationship.
*Before the Senate, Washington, Dec. 6.*

**Eugene J. McCarthy**
*United States Senator, D-Minn.*

The military-industrial-academic establishment in America is rapidly becoming a kind of republic within the republic.
*Pub. April 21.*

**J. P. McConnell**
*General, and Chief of Staff,*
*United States Air Force*

I am quite certain the accelerating pace of technology will result in advances during the next decades that will revolutionize the art and techniques of warfare even more dramatically than have the nuclear bomb and ICBM. For the sake of this nation's security, I hope and pray that our science and industry will succeed in always keeping us ahead in the technological race with the Communist world, as they have to this day.
*Before Air Force Association,*
*Houston, March 19.*

**John W. McCormack**
*United States Representative, D-Mass.*

I wonder how many of you realize how close we came to losing World War II. I don't want to take a chance again.
*Before the House,*
*Washington, pub. Oct. 5.*

**George S. McGovern**
*United States Senator, D-S.D.*

We have been told that the Sentinel (ABM) is oriented against China and has virtually no value against the Soviet because of the relative simplicity of overpowering or decoying it. If bargaining power is what we are looking for, I suggest that all we prove by deployment is that we're willing to waste $5-to-$10 billion, or more, on a useless system.
*Washington, Feb. 4.*

. . . the debate over military budgets will not end when the ABM issue is settled. It's just the beginning.
*Washington, pub. March 10.*

Since World War II, we have come to accept this outrageous military expenditure as somehow necessary and unquestionable; we have been conditioned to accept it in the name of defense, when in fact its real name is war.
*At National Rural Housing Conference,*
*Warrenton. Va., June 10.*

Like Vietnam, missile defense is a bottomless pit. It will swallow as much as we pour into it without a dependable increase in our security . . . And President Nixon will have to face the people with this millstone around his neck in 1972, just as my (Democratic) party had to face the people encumbered by Vietnam in 1968.
*Washington, Aug. 4.*

I don't think there's any conspiracy between the military and industry, but it does develop a momentum. Even the clergymen know their congregations are swollen by defense installations. There's a subtle influence on labor unions, business and community groups.
*Pub. Aug. 26.*

. . . perhaps what we really need is a new definition of what constitutes national defense. It should go beyond military spending alone, and put all of the needs of the country into the balance. I think we can reach much more profound judgments as to what it is that really contributes to the strength of a great country such as the United States . . . We simply cannot afford to build systems which are unnecessary or unworkable. Before we decide to "err on the side of strength," we must determine whether it is necessary to err at all.
*Before the Senate, Washington, Sept. 12.*

**Robert S. McNamara**
*Former Secretary of Defense*
*of the United States*

The mood has certainly changed since my day. Now the Congress is protesting military spending. I spent too much of my time fighting a Congress that wanted to spend too much on useless military projects . . . The Congress, you see, has bought defense the way women buy perfume. If it costs more, they conclude it must be better. Anything that's shinier, brighter, prettier they think the generals and "our boys" ought to have. The mood has certainly changed now.
*Interview, pub. June 14.*

I get charged with the TFX (fighter plane). It's nothing compared to the Bay of Pigs or my failure for four years to integrate off-base military housing. I don't want you to misunderstand me when I say this, but the TFX was only money. We're talking about blood, the moral foundation of our future, the life of the nation, when we talk about these other things.
*Pub. June 15.*

**Matthew S. Meselson**
*Professor of Biology,*
*Harvard University; consultant,*
*Arms Control and Disarmament*
*Agency of the United States*

I myself do not see any sense for the United States in stockpiling biological weapons. I think we do ourselves far more harm than good by stimulating interest in these weapons, by breaking down the barriers against them. I think we are adequately safeguarded, insofar as deterrance is functional at all, by nuclear weapons which are reliable.
*Before Senate Foreign Relations*
*Committee, Washington, April 30.*

**Jack Miller**
*United States Senator, R-Iowa*

(Opponents of the ABM system show) a naivete toward the Soviet leaders, an inexplicable tendency to overlook their words, and especially their deeds, and to proceed on the basis of hope rather than on the basis of realism . . .
*Washington, Aug. 4.*

**Walter F. Mondale**
*United States Senator, D-Minn.*

I think Mr. (Lewis B.) Hershey should no longer be head of the Selective Service System. Indeed, I favor the feature (of pending legislation) that would limit the term of any Selective Service director to six years.
*Washington, June 1.*

(Those pushing for an increased carrier fleet), like their predecessors who defended the horse cavalry and the battleship, are following a path of tradition rather than reason.
*Before the Senate, Washington, Sept. 10.*

We have no quarrel with the U.S. Navy. Now, as in the past, it can do splendidly the jobs required of it by the nation. We say only that the time has come for Congress to reexamine those jobs to see not only whether there may be better ways to do them, but whether they need doing at all. As a perceptive admiral once put it: "There is nothing more useless than doing something with great efficiency that should not be done at all."
*Before the Senate, Washington, Sept. 12.*

**Thomas H. Moorer**
*Admiral, United States Navy;*
*Chief of Naval Operations*

I believe our aircraft carriers are the key to our present superiority. With too few, or none, the Soviets would probably be the leading naval power.
*Before Veterans of Foreign Wars,*
*Philadelphia, Aug. 19.*

Up until the time of Pearl Harbor there was little apparent unity in this country, and we passed the draft law by only one vote. The Japanese once told me that this was one of the overriding factors that made them decide to attack Pearl Harbor. Because of that vote, they didn't think we had the heart and will to do anything about it. And I think that's one of the causes of concern here today over public demonstrations in some quarters. I think it would be unfortunate if we gave the idea abroad that the United States doesn't have the will and the heart to protect its own interests.
*Interview, Washington, pub. Dec. 1.*

**Karl E. Mundt**
*United States Senator, R-S.D.*

We may have beaten the Russians to the moon, but they have beaten us in the construction of a defense system which can destroy missiles in flight.

*Washington, July 22.*

**Edmund S. Muskie**
*United States Senator, D-Me.*

Secretary (of Defense) Laird refers to the Safeguard (ABM) as a "building block for peace," painting the system as not being provocative—a judgment that strikes me as illusory.

*Before the Senate, Washington, April 3.*

In today's world of rapidly advancing technology, available to our political enemies as well as to ourselves, adequate provision for national defense necessarily entails a large military budget. But our domestic needs are also urgent. An excessively large military budget, coupled with polluted air and water, congested cities, falling educational standards and racial discontent, is not the hallmark of a strong and secure nation. Our problem is not to choose up sides for or against military spending in general, but to take a selective approach to the military budget, approving those programs whose contributions to our national security are sufficient to justify their heavy costs, and turning down those which fail to pass this test.

*Before the Senate,*
*Washington, Sept. 18.*

A moratorium on testing our multiple re-entry missiles would not involve any appreciable risk to our security. It (the moratorium) is proposed as a meaningful step to stimulate efforts by the United States and the Soviet Union to control the escalation of nuclear weapons systems before it is too late.

*New York, Oct. 21.*

**Lucien N. Nedzi**
*United States Representative, D-Mich.*

. . . we are no more willing to place the destiny of our country in the hands of the Soviets or the Chinese hawks than in the hands of any other hawks, and, so long as any nation retains military might capable of inflicting harm on us, we have to have a military defense against it . . . We are not naive enough to believe that unilateral disarmament will necessarily cause others to disarm. Unilateral disarmament, as a matter of fact, may well create irresistable temptations which would be totally counterproductive as far as peace in the world is concerned . . .

*Before the House, Washington, Oct. 2.*

**Richard M. Nixon**
*President of the United States*

. . . I think "sufficiency" (in defense) is a better term, actually, than either "superiority" or "parity."

*News Conference, Washington, Jan. 27.*

I have always supported the goal of halting the spread of nuclear weapons. I opposed ratification of the (Nuclear Nonproliferation) Treaty last fall in the immediate aftermath of the Soviet invasion of Czechoslovakia. My request (for passage) at this time in no sense alters my condemnation of that Soviet action . . . I believe that the Treaty can be an important step in our endeavor to curb the spread of nuclear weapons and that it advances the purposes of our Atoms for Peace program.

*Washington, Feb. 5.*

Although every instinct motivates me to provide the American people with complete protection against a major nuclear attack, it is not now within our power to do so.

Our (ABM) system is truly a safeguard system, a defensive system only. It safeguards our deterrent and under those circumstances can in no way, in my opinion, delay the program which I hope will continue to be made towards arms talks.

*News conference, Washington, March 14.*

That gap (the U.S. nuclear superiority over the Soviet Union) has been closed. We shall never have it again because it will not be necessary for us. Sufficiency, as I have indicated, is all that is necessary. But I do say this: I do not want to see an American President in the future, in the event of any crisis, have his diplomatic credibility be so impaired because the United States was in a second-class or inferior position. We saw what it meant to the Soviets when they were second. I don't want that position to be the United States's in the event of a future diplomatic crisis.

. . . I want to make it crystal-clear that my decision on ABM was not made on the basis of Republican versus Democrat. It was made on the basis of what I thought best for the country . . . I am going to fight as hard as I can for it because I believe it is absolutely essential to the security of the country.

When planes of the United States or ships of the United States are in international air space, they are not fair game. They will not be in the future. I state that as a matter of fact.

*News conference, Washington, April 18.*

I believe that the basis for decisions on defense spending must be "What do we need for our security?", and not "What will this mean for business and employment?" The Defense Department must never be considered a modern-day WPA; there are far better ways for Government to help insure a sound prosperity and high employment.

The American defense establishment should never be a sacred cow. But, on the other hand, the American military should never be anybody's scapegoat.

If I have made a mistake (in the decision to deploy the Safeguard ABM system), I pray that it is on the side of too much and not too little. If we do too much, it will cost us some money; if we do too little, it may cost us our lives.

I believe that every man in uniform is a citizen first and a serviceman second and that we must resist any attempt to isolate or separate the defenders from the defended.

*U.S. Air Force Academy,*
*Colorado Springs, Colo., June 4.*

It remains my firm conviction that the military draft should be abolished and the armed services of the United States be manned entirely by volunteers.

*Washington, June 6.*

I hereby reaffirm that the United States will never be the first country to use chemical weapons to kill. And I have also extended this renunciation to chemical weapons that incapacitate.

*Washington, Nov. 25.*

**Richard L. Ottinger**
*United States Representative, D-N.Y.*

We are told that if we do not give the military everything it wants, there are not going to be any cities left for us to rebuild and there are not going to be any children left for us to educate. I believe that statement can just as well be turned around to say that if we do not do something for the cities of this country and if we do not do something for the impoverished who suffer amidst plenty in this country, there are not going to be any cities left for the military to defend.

*Before the House, Washington, Oct. 3.*

**David Packard**
*Deputy Secretary of Defense*
*of the United States*

I could not recommend any (anti-ballistic missile) system which would rely on the decision of a computer.

*Washington, March 16.*

. . . the Soviet Union has the capability of being able to destroy substantially all of our land-based Minuteman (missile) capacity in hardened silos, if they chose to do so.

*Before Senate Armed Services*
*Committee, Washington, March 20.*

**John O. Pastore**
*United States Senator, D-R.I.*

. . . sometimes we are a little too critical of the Defense Department and its requests without considering the fact that the Defense Department has to follow the commitments made by the State Department. If the State Department is going to commit us all over the world and is going to involve us in treaties of every kind and character and place these commitments on the desks of the Joint Chiefs of Staff, they have to begin to calculate what our military posture should be.

*Before the Senate, Washington, Sept. 18.*

**James B. Pearson**
*United States Senator, R-Kan.*

The Military-Industrial Complex is a fact of modern American life. No amount of wishing will make it go away . . . We must have it, but we must control it. We must be vigorous in our efforts to see to it that it is a servant of peace and prosperity rather than the servant of war and destruction.
*Before the Senate, Washington, Aug. 11.*

**Charles H. Percy**
*United States Senator, R-Ill.*

I am not today convinced that deployment of the modified . . . ABM system at this time adds one iota to our national security.
*Washington, March 21.*

**Stefan T. Possony**
*Director of International Political
Studies, Hoover Institution,
Stanford University*

. . . the position of ABM critics is totally unjustified. Their arguments are often quite misleading because they are based upon a partial understanding of the problems of strategic planning and the intentions of our foreign policy . . .
*News conference, Los Angeles, April 1.*

**Richardson Preyer**
*United States Representative, D-N.C.*

Defensive weapons systems . . . are a stabilizing influence; they do not constitute a threat of immediate destruction, and so improve the chances for a negotiated arms agreement with the Soviet Union . . . Defensive weapons systems are in the humane American tradition. Their purpose is to save lives, not destroy lives. An emphasis on defense, rather than solely on offensive weapons, can help destroy the false image of America as an aggressive "imperialistic" nation and make clear the true America that seeks peace—to all the world and to ourselves.
*Before the House, Washington, Oct. 3.*

**Winston L. Prouty**
*United States Senator, R-Vt.*

I envisioned a President faced with the knowledge that enemy missiles were heading toward the United States. I inquired as to what options are now available to him in response to such attack. I discovered that there are now two grim alternatives—do nothing, or push the button that unleashes our devastating nuclear fury . . . But if there was another button available, a button to trigger our missiles designed to intercept and destroy these incoming weapons, the President could push it and halt the attack without immense loss of lives at home or the catastrophic consequences of full retaliation . . . Safeguard provides an additional alternative, an extra button . . .
*Before the Senate,
Washington, pub. July 28.*

**William Proxmire**
*United States Senator, D-Wis.*

The result (of defense spending) is a system not unlike the medieval knight who was so encased in armor that he was unable to move . . . we could get more security for the country by spending smaller amounts more efficiently.
*Washington, March 10.*

If the weapons of secrecy and classification are used without warrant to cover the tracks of embarrassing or wasteful or inefficient decision making . . . this nation places in serious jeopardy its reputation as a free and open society. It is my hope that we can knock down the paper curtain which the Pentagon has for years raised between it and the Congress and between it and the citizens of the United States.
*Washington, June 13.*

Defense spending is out of control. The system is top-heavy. The military-industrial complex writes its own budgetary ticket . . . after World War II, we overreacted with respect to contracts for weapons systems. Nothing was too good for the military . . . the military has had a blank check. It could be said that we have had over two decades of *carte blanche* for defense.
*Published Aug. 3.*

Not too long ago it was commonplace to hear that this nation could afford both guns and butter—that we could provide for our defense, meet our world commitments and take care of pressing national problems. Now it has become fashionable to take the opposite view—we can have either guns or butter, but not both.

*Before the Senate, Washington, Sept. 3.*

. . . the Russians are not 10 feet tall. In fact, based on our military outlays and economic strength, if we are six feet tall, the Russians by comparison are three feet tall, and the Chinese are six inches tall.

*Washington, Dec. 27.*

**Roman C. Pucinski**
*United States Representative, D-Ill.*

There is one thing that is certain around here. Our friends say, "We want more research (on the proposed ABM system), but we do not want deployment; we do not want procurement." We know the rule around Congress is that the best way to kill a project is to study it to death. This (ABM) has been studied, researched, and experimented. They have found that it works. Now is the time for action.

*Before the House, Washington, Oct. 2.*

**William J. Randall**
*United States Representative, D-Mo.*

. . . the opponents of the ABM (system) have either forgotten their history or have not read enough of our own history about how between wars we have allowed ourselves to become unprepared. In every instance we have reasoned that it was inconceivable that there could be a First World War, or a Pearl Harbor, or a Korea. But they all happened. We live in a day now that it takes a long leadtime to build sophisticated weapons. We must deploy the Safeguard now while there is still time available.

*Before the House, Washington, Oct. 2.*

**John R. Rarick**
*United States Representative, D-La.*

. . . once again the peaceniks raise the cry that all would be well with the world if only the United States would totally disarm. We have seen attacks on the entirely defensive ABM, on the imperative MIRV, on CBW, and on everything connected with our armed forces. Most Americans do not believe that throwing away your weapons and demonstrating your helplessness is the best method of protecting yourself against an armed assailant . . . our Communist enemy has repeatedly promised to both hang us and bury us . . .

*Before the House, Washington, Nov. 5.*

**George W. Rathjens**
*Member, Weapons Systems*
*Evaluation Group,*
*Massachusetts Institute of Technology*

The sad fact is that while we can have almost no confidence in an ABM system working, an adversary can have almost no confidence that it will not work. Thus, we must expect the Soviet Union to react to even a "light" or "thin" deployment . . . not because an ABM system will be effective and not because it will be expanded, but simply as a     ervative hedge against those possibilitie

*Before Senate Arme. Services Committee, Washington, pub. May 11.*

I see absolutely no urgency for the Safeguard program. This country easily could wait a year or two. During this time, hopefully, we could negotiate with Russia to halt the arms race. This would indeed increase our security much more than a costly and ineffective ABM program.

*News conference, San Francisco, May 12.*

**Stanley R. Resor**
*Secretary of the Army*
*of the United States*

None of us prefers to see the world this way. But it is the world we live in. In the absence of another way to offset the Soviet threat and to provide the nation a means to ensure its survival, reliance on retaliation as our deterrent has been affirmed by every President since General Eisenhower. And in all likelihood we will have to continue to rely on . . . assured destruction as our deterrent until, either by agreement or by parallel action, we and the Soviets move to some other basis for our security.

*Before Union League Club, New York, April 28.*

**Walter P. Reuther**
*President,*
*United Auto Workers of America*

It seems to us in the UAW that the time has come for the American people and the Congress to blow the whistle on war-game strategists, and their swollen budgets and sweetheart deals with defense contractors, and to demand a mobilization of our great resources in behalf of strategies for world and domestic peace.

*Before Joint Congressional Economic Subcommittee, Washington, June 10.*

**Hyman G. Rickover**
*Vice-Admiral, United States Navy;*
*director, Division of Naval Reactors,*
*Atomic Energy Commission*
*of the United States*

We have now reached the stage in the Defense Department where there are more and more "managers" and fewer people left to do the work . . . (We need to) go back to basic principles and realize that people, not systems, will solve our problems . . . I'm deeply concerned that, if something is not done, the U.S. defense effort will be overmanaged into impotency.

*Before Joint Congressional Committee on Atomic Energy, Washington, April 23.*

I would rather have . . . the (Soviet submarine) force, as it exists and is programmed, than ours, as it exists and is programmed.

*Before Senate Armed Services Committee, Washington, pub. August.*

**L. Mendel Rivers**
*United States Representative, D-S.C.*

I'm not at all sure I'd favor a volunteer Army. Even if I were for it, I don't know if we'd be able to raise a volunteer Army if we let the draft expire. It's a known fact that the existence of a draft law helps in getting volunteers.

*Interview, pub. March 30.*

We have all manner of experts in this country telling us that we should be stopping our own national security developments, that the Russian threat will go away. Who believes this? You have not forgotten what happened in Czechoslovakia, have you? They are just plainly not kidding. You do not think that they are in the Mediterranean just for the purpose of a leisurely Mediterranean cruise. If you think so, just go down and look at them. They are loaded for bear. Take that from me. You can get all kinds of brilliant analyses from people who have never smelled gunpowder.

*Before the House, Washington, Oct. 1.*

**Howard W. Robison**
*United States Representative, R-N.Y.*

When one considers the massive retaliatory strength we now have—with its tremendous "overkill" capacity—in our vast and diversified deterrent force . . . plus such tactical weapons as we may have here and there in Europe and elsewhere, it would clearly seem that we remain immune from any possible first-strike reach by Russia, if that is even contemplated, for some time to come.

*Before the House, Washington, Oct. 2.*

**Leonard Rodberg**
*Professor of Physics,*
*University of Maryland*

We're being presented with a third or fourth version of the missile gap as a pretext for going ahead with the ABM. The new missile gap looks as unreal as the ones that preceded it. As a response, the (proposed) ABM is premature and inappropriate.

*Before Federal Employes for a Democratic Society, Washington, May 4.*

**William P. Rogers**
*United States Secretary of State*

The quicker we can have successful negotiations (with the Soviet Union) on mutual disarmament, the better it will be for the peace of the world and the foreign policy of the United States generally.

*Before Senate Foreign Relations Committee, Washington, Feb. 18.*

Suppose we start our (disarmament) talks in a few months, and the first thing that's said by the Soviet Union is, "Let's do away with our defensive missiles." We'd have no problem. We'd be delighted.

*Before Senate Foreign Relations Committee, Washington, March 7.*

## Walt W. Rostow
*Former Adviser to President Lyndon B. Johnson on Foreign Affairs*

. . . it was Nikita Khrushchev's belief that the threat of nuclear weapons, and the threat of their use, in Berlin and in the Cuban missile crisis, would lead the United States to back away without running the risk of standing in the face of nuclear blackmail . . . President Kennedy, at Berlin and at the Cuban missile crisis, made it clear that ours was a society that could stand up against that threat, and hopefully it will not be mounted again; but men can never count on that.

*Radio interview, Jan. 5.*

## Jerry Rubin
*Organizer, Youth International Party*

The old order is protected by its military power; but our military is overextended throughout the world. While it is overextended, defending American influence overseas, we are chipping away here. Yippies are chipping away, blacks are chipping away, the enemy overseas is chipping away. If you keep on hitting the man from every side, punching him, laughing at him, ridiculing him, he will eventually collapse. That's what is going to happen in America.

*Pub. May 19.*

## Dean Rusk
*Former Secretary of State of the United States*

If we were to abandon the ABM system and they (the Russians) go ahead, they just might get a technical breakthrough that would make an enormous difference in the strategic relationship between the two sides . . . The real question is . . . do we have, from a scientific point of view, a good horse to bet on? Do we have first-class workable ABM's? If we don't have those, then let's put (in) more research

and development until we have something that we think is worth deploying.

*New York, March 24.*

## Richard B. Russell
*United States Senator, D-Ga.*

We have already opened up our atomic installations to the Russians and the East Germans and everybody else . . . I am getting scared. I frankly don't see where we are achieving any stability (with the proposed nuclear non-proliferation treaty) when the only nation really bound down by this treaty to inspection is the United States.

*Pub. March 17.*

(The) Russians have been working on a first strike capability for years. In the SS-9 they have a missile with many, many times the destructive capability that we have. I don't think the Russians are going to hit us tomorrow, next week or next year. But if we continue our trust-the-Russians euphoria, some day we may be in a position where they will not have to fire a missile but simply say, "This is it."

. . . if we ever hope to get a meaningful treaty in this dread field of nuclear armaments, we will have to have at least military equality with the Russians. I am waiting for the critics of the Safeguard system to offer an alternative to a militarily strong America.

*Interview, Washington, April 6.*

## John D. Ryan
*Chief of Staff-designate, United States Air Force*

Whether biological weapons should be used or not is a decision beyond the military.

*Before Senate Armed Services Committee, Washington, July 24.*

## Alvin Saperstein
*Professor of Physics, Wayne State University*

It is not a question of trusting the Russians or the Chinese. You can't trust them. But I don't trust our own military not to lead us to disaster either. If I felt the

(ALVIN SAPERSTEIN)

ABM system were effective, I'd live with the damn thing in my back yard. But it isn't.

*Pub. March 14.*

### David E. Satterfield
*United States Representative, D-Va.*

The best assurance we have against war, particularly general war, lies in maintaining that high degree of strength which will deter our potential enemies from attacking us. If we fail to maintain, as an integral part of that strength, an effective modern attack carrier force, then all of our other efforts in this direction will no longer be credible.

*Before the House, Washington, Oct. 3.*

### Henry C. Schadeberg
*United States Representative, R-Wis.*

Until such time when despotic governments determined to rule the world are no longer a threat to the freedom of the world, we do not have a choice but a moral responsibility to leave no stone unturned in the defense of this nation. The ABM system will not give us peace. Perhaps it will not even prevent war. But, with it, we will have a chance to pursue peace and freedom. Without it, we may not even have a future.

*Before the House, Washington, Oct. 2.*

### Charles L. Schultze
*Former Director,*
*Bureau of the Budget*
*of the United States*

I do not believe that the problem of military budgets is primarily attributable to the so-called military-industrial complex. If defense contractors were all as disinterested in enlarging sales as local transit magnates; if retired military officers all went into selling soap and TV sets instead of missiles; if the Washington offices of defense contractors all were moved to the West Coast—if all this happened and nothing else, then I do not believe the military budget would be sharply lower than it now is.

*Pub. Sept. 8.*

### Fred Schwengel
*United States Representative, R-Iowa*

It is my conviction that we must have a system of defense; that it must be both military and spiritual and moral. We, of all nations, need to have an adequate defense. The principal reason for this admonition is that we have more to defend than any other nation in all history.

*Before the House, Washington, Oct. 3.*

### Robert C. Seamans, Jr.
*Secretary of the Air Force*
*of the United States*

We cannot provide the necessary weapons for defense without the help of university research laboratories . . . (The Pentagon-university relationship) prevents the defense establishment from becoming isolated in its knowledge, and it provides our scientists with continuous access to new ideas which originate on the campuses.

*Before New Orleans*
*Chamber of Commerce, May 15.*

### Abram Shayes
*Professor of Law, Harvard University*

From the standpoint of achieving strategic arms-limitation agreements, we are much better off in the position we are now in—with no ABM system on our side and an obsolete one, difficult to upgrade, on theirs (the Russians')—than if each side were engaged in competitive deployment.

*Before Senate Armed Services*
*Committee, Washington, pub. May 11.*

### David M. Shoup
*General (Ret.); former Commandant,*
*United States Marine Corps.*

. . . he (former U.S. Secretary of Defense Robert S. McNamara) was the best damned thing that ever happened to the Pentagon. I know they're all coming along now and giving him the debits for the F-111 and all that. But, when I was there, I was impressed by the new blood and the new outlook and his extreme capability for grasping all the problems facing us.

*Pub. June 15.*

**Robert L. F. Sikes**
*United States Representative, D-Fla.*

It is estimated, by those who are experts and who have possession of the facts— and I stress fact rather than rumor—that Russia has ten times the capability in this field (chemical and biological warfare) than we have.

*Pub. June 29.*

**Joe Skubitz**
*United States Representative, R-Kan.*

If an ABM system is built and it deters any nation from attacking us, it is worth every cent we spend on it. If we build a system and we are attacked and it does not work, we have lost everything anyway: money, property and lives—but at least we tried. But if we do nothing in order to save money and, by our failure to act, are attacked and are destroyed, then we have failed those who relied upon our wisdom and judgment.

*Before the House, Washington, Oct. 3.*

**Margaret Chase Smith**
*United States Senator, R-Me.*

I do believe in America, but I don't believe in the ABM. I am for our American way of life, but I don't believe in the ABM. I am for free enterprise, but I don't believe in the ABM. The ABM is not an acid test of patriotism.

*Washington, pub. Aug. 7.*

**John Stennis**
*United States Senator, D-Miss.*

When I came on this (Senate Armed Services) committee, submarines cost $30 million. Now they cost $180-$200 million. But you've got to have modern weapons.

*Interview, Washington, May 5.*

. . . when you consider the international situation, you come back to the same man—the President of the United States. He is the one who is going to have to carry on negotiations with the Soviets. He is the spokesman for the country. His judgment as to whether he'll be better off, or worse off, with this weapon (ABM) . . . should carry great weight. He is the man who is trying to keep our carriage of Government on the tracks. Negatively, if this or any

other major weapon is voted down by the Congress, Russia will think they know where the President is—and that is, in the middle of a bad fix.

There's always an argument about whether to defend your weapons or defend your people. But I believe there's great logic and force in the idea that we should start by defending our offensive power . . . It's like keeping your powder dry. In the old days, when you had the barricades, perhaps you were more careful to keep the powder dry than you were to keep the baby dry. You had to have those arms ready to use if you were attacked.

*Interview, Washington, pub. July 14.*

Take out the tanks; take out the carriers; take out this, take out that. I just do not believe that it is the way to proceed (in trimming the Pentagon's military budget).

*Washington, pub. Aug. 22.*

Certain well-intentioned people have stated there will be no conventional war with the Soviet Union. I also earnestly hope there will be no conventional war with the Soviet Union, or any other nation, for that matter. However, my earnest belief and hope does not provide me with the luxury of eliminating or substantially reducing our Military Establishment. The world that we live in today confronts us with far more hard-hitting realities. We cannot base our national security on well-intentioned and earnest beliefs or opinions. Well-intentioned people have been proven wrong in the past, and in some things we cannot afford to take chances.

*Before the Senate, Washington, Sept. 3.*

I think that (aircraft) carriers are the greatest deterrent we have, so far as keeping down trouble, being available, patrolling the seas, and going into troubled spots. That is my opinion. It has versatility. It is instantly available, day and night. It is a floating air field.

*Before the Senate, Washington, Sept. 12.*

**Jeremy J. Stone**
*Associate, Institute for*
*Strategic Studies, London*

The (U.S.) Department of Defense has

(JEREMY J. STONE)

become an inventor and merchandiser of exaggerated fears. It has become an unscrupulous lobbyist for the weapons to answer those fears. Worst of all, through the action-and-reaction phenomenon, its aggressive pursuit of the arms race has greatly undermined the security of the nation by stimulating, unnecessarily, Soviet efforts to keep up.

*At Congressional Conference on Military Budgets and National Priorities, Washington, pub. May 25.*

**William H. Stoneman**
*Former special adviser to*
*United Nations*
*Secretary-General Trygve Lie*

What I find difficult to understand is the manner in which . . . opposition to the action in Vietnam has developed into a widespread opposition to military action or even to military preparedness. This could have fatal consequences to NATO, and the end result to democratic Europe could be disastrous. Of one thing we can be deadly sure. The faceless men who run the Soviet Union, many of them holdovers from the Stalin days, and all of them accomplices in the Czech affair, are watching our every move. We can only hope that what they see will not be encouraging.

*Before Rotary Club, Ann Arbor, Mich., Nov. 5.*

**Samuel S. Stratton**
*United States Representative, D-N.Y.*

I remember the strong words of Franklin D. Roosevelt which he sent to Winston Churchill in those days when England was fighting with her back against the wall. We should remember those words . . . when the question is whether we are going to keep the U.S. Navy supreme. Roosevelt sent to Churchill those famous lines from Longfellow:

Sail on, oh Ship of State.
Sail on, oh Union strong and great.
Humanity, with all her fears,
And all her hopes and future years,
Is hanging breathless on thy fate.

The free world today is literally hanging breathless on the future of a strong and modern American Navy.

*Before the House, Washington, Oct. 2.*

I do not imagine that anybody likes chemical warfare. But I do not think anybody likes this other kind of warfare either. And I do not think it is worse to be killed by a chemical agent than it is to be killed by a bit of shrapnel or by a bomb. The fact of the matter is, we do have a chemical and bacteriological warfare capability for exactly the same reason that we have long-range missiles. We have them because we hope that capacity will deter the enemy from using his capability, and that we will never have to use them.

*Before the House, Washington, Oct. 3.*

**Stuart Symington**
*United States Senator, D-Mo.*

I am quite surprised that after voting for what will be, after this year, over a trillion dollars, I am criticized for believing this (the ABM system) will not work, because I have studied it carefully. I came out of the electronics industry. I opposed it during the Johnson Administration, and I think it is even more absurd, the new application of it in this Administration.

*Television interview, Washington, June 1.*

Today we are spread all over the world, and it's terribly expensive. We still have some 80,000 Americans in Japan, counting dependents, and that is a country we are supposed to have left. Twenty-five years after the end of the war, we still have five divisions in Germany. It was once emphasized they would only be there for a maximum of 18 months. They've been there for over a quarter of a century. When we went into Korea, we were only going to be there a short time. We've been there for 19 years . . . Yes, there is a very great desire to start rethinking about our priorities and our values. We are overcommitted. Things cannot go on this way indefinitely, if we are to remain a strong and viable nation.

If we get the idea we can dig a lot of holes in the ground (referring to the proposed ABM system) to guarantee the security of the United States, then we'd

better look out. Such a philosophy smacks of a modern Maginot Line—or that very expensive defense line south of the DMZ in Vietnam, which turned out to be a bust.
*Interview, Washington, pub. July 14.*

Under our form of government, no matter what the nature of the enemy, without public support no administration should wage a foreign war.
*Washington, pub. Oct. 26.*

**Albert Szent-Gyorgyi**
*Professor of Biology, Brandeis University*

Armies always tend to grow and become more powerful. In the end, they serve their own interest more than that of their country, swallowing up half the national income and creating incidents which make them needed.
*New York Academy of Sciences,*
*pub. Sept. 11.*

**Edward Teller**
*Nuclear Physicist*

It is safe to assume that most of our essential secrets are known to Moscow. Indeed, I fear that Russian military research has already found many of the secrets which we are yet to discover.
*Before Senate Disarmament*
*Subcommittee,*
*Washington, pub. May 14.*

. . . have you heard of any war where you knew ahead of time that your weapons really would work? There is always an uncertainty, and, in today's rapid developments, these uncertainties are greater than ever. I think it (the ABM) will work. They (the Russians) will be deterred by the very fact that it might work.
*Interview, pub. May 26.*

**Strom Thurmond**
*United States Senator, R-S.C.*

The question has been asked—why do we need a Navy? I will tell you why. It is simply a matter of geographical fact. One needs only to look at a map of the United States to realize that we have international borders with only two nations: Canada and Mexico. The rest of the world, including one of our states, lies overseas. Three-fourths of the world is covered by water

. . . If we in this country are to maintain and improve our present way of life, we must assure ourselves of the free passage of the seas, and of the air space over the seas.
*Before the Senate, Washington, Sept. 12.*

All available evidence suggests that the present Soviet leaders recognize clearly they may have to fight a nuclear war with the United States and that, if they do, they plan to have forces in being which will achieve their military objectives and support their postwar political aims. Their policies, programs, training and doctrine are based on the thought that a nuclear war may be unavoidable and, indeed, at some point in time, may be advantageous to them. Therefore, I totally reject the suggestion that the danger is that we may have more, rather than less, military might than we need.

. . . we know that modern weapons systems are not cheap, but we have also learned, by bitter experience, that adequate preparedness, even at today's prices, is a bargain if it accomplishes the purpose of deterring aggression and preventing war. I hope our memories are not so short that we ignore the lessons of history. They have taught us that the price of freedom is both high and recurring.
*Before the Senate,*
*Washington, Sept. 18.*

**Michael van Horn**
*Chairman, United Republicans*
*of California*

We are constantly told Communism can only take root in oppressed societies. That is simply not true. It can happen here. It is happening here. Unless all of us stand up and speak our minds, our freedom is in very real danger. Freedom is slipping away here just as it did in my birthland (Czechoslovakia) 20 years ago, and we're all too busy to notice, or we think it isn't as serious as it is.
*Before the Rotary Club, Fresno, May 1.*

**Charles A. Vanik**
*United States Representative, D-Ohio*

The days of a blank check for defense are over—and that is to the credit of this

(CHARLES A. VANIK)

Congress . . . Since World War II, we have spent about $1 trillion for defense. We must stop offering blank checks to the military, for they have shown little inclination to go sparingly on the taxpayers' money.

*Before the House, Washington, Oct. 3.*

## W. Allen Wallis
*President, University of Rochester*

. . . abolish the draft; abolish it completely, lock stock and barrel; abolish it immediately, with no ifs, ands or buts.

*Before American Legion of Monroe County, N.Y., pub. April 28.*

## Lewis W. Walt
*Lt. Gen.; assistant Commandant, United States Marine Corps*

I know this: If I were a private first class, or the parent or brother or sweetheart of one, and we were going into battle, I'd like to know that the men behind me were not only self-disciplined people, but self-disciplined members of a team. If they are, we might survive. If they are not, if they place dissent above duty, then I think the chances are pretty good we will all die. Isn't that more of a price than the majority should pay for the dissent of a few?

*Interview, pub. May 30.*

## Earle G. Wheeler
*General, United States Army; chairman, Joint Chiefs of Staff*

What the military has tried to do for nearly two centuries of American history —and I hope will go on trying to do—is, if possible, to prevent wars, minimize the pain of peacetime defense as much as possible, and yet protect the American people so that they can live in peace and freedom as they wish.

An ICBM (intercontinental ballistic missile) is at least a million dollars a throw; a nuclear carrier, half a billion; an ABM (anti-ballistic missile) system, seven billion. And it is all blamed on the military, because, at first glance, our weapons and our uniforms are easily identified.

*Interview, pub. April 11.*

I have argued, am arguing and will argue for an American military posture which is (1) strong, but not belligerent; (2) too determined to be frightened and too strong to be defeated; and (3) unwavering, despite setbacks, disappointments and opposition, in following that course which we know is the right path to organize a stable and durable peace.

*Pub. May 5.*

The technology which makes possible our growing mastery of space does not stop at the water's edge. And it is this same technology, in the hands of others, that creates the weapons which menace us. The Soviet Union today, and Communist China in the near future, have large and expanding national technologies which have produced, and are producing, weapons at an increasing rate which pose a direct threat to us . . . We know full well that the technology which created the threat can also move us—by means of the Safeguard system—away from the growing peril. To accept heightened risk and a less stable deterrent as a national posture would confuse unthinking personal preference for real-world policy alternative. The choice demanded by the new technology is still between the quick and the dead.

If I'm in a conspiracy (the "military-industrial complex"), I have yet to meet my fellow conspirators . . .

*McDill Air Force Base, May 17.*

I think there are very few indeed who try to take advantage of their former positions in the military to sell us defense products. During my five years in this job, and my two years as Chief of Staff of the Army, only on one occasion have I had a retired officer come in and talk to me about anything to do with business. He told me he was having trouble getting a yes or no response from the Army and asked me to give him the name of somebody to contact. I gave him a name, and that was that. Most officers are not salesmen. A friend of mine who retired and went into industry told me, "The idea of going back and trying to peddle products on the basis of my military friendships

is so repulsive to me that I would rather starve to death." And so would I.
*Interview, pub. Aug. 26.*

**E. B. White**
*Writer*

I'll say this . . . Every country is entitled to a few mistakes. The Vietnam war is a mistake. The Selective Service is inequitable. Yet, even a country that is in the midst of a mistake must have an armed force loyal to its basic beliefs and prepared to defend its general principles. If that were to go, all would go.
*Interview, North Brooklin, Me.,*
*pub. July 11.*

**Jerome B. Wiesner**
*Provost, Massachusetts*
*Institute of Technology*

I believe one should try to assess Russian capabilities, but not intentions. The security of the United States should not be dependent on another man's intentions.
*Interview, pub. May 26.*

Anti-Communism has been so virulent in the United States that it will almost certainly one day be viewed as a mental disease which led the United States to many self-destructive acts. And many false images of the United States have guided Soviet policy. In any event, these pressures have made it very easy to motivate the United States to carry out its part in the (arms) race, and apparently it has not been difficult to arouse similar reactions in the Soviet Union.
*Interview, pub. Dec. 30.*

**Bob Wilson**
*United States Representative, R-Calif.*

Very simply stated, in the light of the overall strategic balance between the United States and the Soviet Union— a balance that is much too close for comfort these days—this country needs to have a triple-threat capability. It needs its Polaris missile submarine; it needs its Minute Man missile force; and it needs a modern and effective bomber force—and that is

the whole thing in a nutshell.
*Before the House, Washington, Oct. 1.*

**Albert Wohlstetter**
*Professor of Political Science,*
*University of Chicago*

There is a striking inconsistency in the way ABM opponents treat the Chinese and the Russians. They assume that the Russians cannot, by 1976 or 1977—twenty years after Sputnik—do what we know how to do now. When considering the ability of the Chinese to penetrate an ABM defense, they attribute to them penetration systems that cost us many billions of dollars, a dozen years of trials and many failures to develop. These are rather backward Russians and very advanced Chinese.
*Pub. July 11.*

**Louis C. Wyman**
*United States Representative, R-N.H.*

History is proof of the senselessness of relying on treaties with Communist nations. The road that led to war in Korea and Vietnam is littered with broken Communist commitments. Those who urge that a treaty on the subject of nuclear nonproliferation should take the place of U.S. military power in reserve are like those who would patch the hull of a battleship with paper and sealing wax . . . We should have treaties, of course, but let us not take them too seriously when they are with Communist nations. Let us always firmly resolve that we will back them up with the necessary military hardware, just in case.
*Before the House, Washington, Sept. 3.*

**Herbert F. York**
*Professor of Physics,*
*University of California at San Diego*

The direction we are going in is not toward the ultimate weapon but toward ultimate absurdity. We are getting to the point in complexity and in the time scale where there is no time for humans, and decisions are made by computers.
*Before Senate subcommittee,*
*Washington, March 11.*

# Patriotism

**Spiro T. Agnew**
*Vice President of the United States*

We cannot honor our ideals or our veterans unless we honor our obligations to secure peace and freedom in America and throughout the world. While our soldiers secure the frontiers of world freedom, let us expand to new horizons in America . . . Let us not shirk our responsibilities, but stand resolute that free men and free governments shall not perish from this earth. Let us respond to the sacrifices of our servicemen by assuring that the principles they fight for abroad are vigorously practiced at home.
*Arlington National Cemetery,*
*Washington, May 30.*

The man who believes in God and country, hard work and honest opportunity, is denounced for his archaic views. The nation which has provided more justice, equality, freedom and opportunity than any nation in world history is told to feel guilty for its failures. The time has come to call a halt to this spiritual Theatre of the Absurd, to examine the motivation of the authors of the absurdity and challenge the star players in the cast.
*Montpelier, Vt., Oct. 11.*

**J. Glenn Beall, Jr.**
*United States Representative, R-Md.*

Certainly there are those today who sneer at patriotism, who speak derogatorily of superpatriots and flag wavers, who downgrade pride in country and any talk of national honor . . . but . . . the kind of leadership the free world needs comes only from patriots and men with a sense of national destiny.
*Before the House, Washington, Nov. 4.*

**Hugo L. Black**
*Associate Justice,*
*Supreme Court of the United States*

If there's anybody in the world who despairs less about this Government than I do, I'd like to see the color of his eyes or his hide or something about him so I can identify him.
*News conference, pub. March 10.*

**Omar N. Bradley**
*General, United States Army (Ret.);*
*former chairman, Joint Chiefs of Staff*

I doubt that there has been any time in history that there has been a greater need to give thought to what we owe our country . . . Too many have not learned that freedom is not free, that democracy can expect stern repayment from those who share its bounty.
*Torrance, Calif., May 17.*

**Al Capp**
*Cartoonist*

It has become unfashionable to say this; it may be embarrassing to hear it; but I believe that America is the most lovely and livable of all nations. I believe that Americans are the kindest and most generous of all people. I believe there are no underprivileged Americans; that even the humblest of us are born with a privilege that places us ahead of anyone else, anywhere else: the privilege of living and working in America, of repairing and renewing America—and one more privilege that no one seems to get much fun out of lately: the privilege of loving America.
*Franklin Pierce College,*
*Rindge, N.H., April 27.*

**Robert Dole**
*United States Senator, R-Kan.*

Today's America sees the right of free speech being exercised to an unprecedented extent through protest marches, rallies, seminars, sit-ins and demonstrations. That such activities are taking place is largely due to our veterans—their time, their blood and their lives. White crosses around the world in Verdun, Iwo Jima, Seoul and Arlington mark the resting places of those whose lives assured that the October (anti-Vietnam) moratorium could take place.

*Before the Senate, Washington, Nov. 11.*

**Mark Doran**
*Assistant Clinical Professor of Psychiatry, University of California at Los Angeles*

. . . flag-waving is a reaction on the part of the good guys who like their children and their wives, and get real mad when anybody rocks their barbecue pits.

*Pub. July 11.*

**Ira Glasser**
*Associate Director, American Civil Liberties Union*

Patriotism is a word monopolized by the right, and, in the rightist view, it involves a sort of mindless allegiance based on accident of birth. It's transplanted into a belief that unpopular views must be suppressed. And it has little to do with values underlying the Bill of Rights . . . It's frightening that good people can end up subscribing to totalitarianism through misuse of patriotic symbols, but that is exactly what's happening.

*New York, pub. Nov. 23.*

**Roosevelt Grier**
*Entertainer; former football player*

I never saw poverty like the poverty there (Mexico). It made me think how better off we are in the United States and what a wonderful country this really is. I know it's far from perfect but, if people would search deeply enough within themselves, we could live in harmony.

*Interview, New York, pub. Jan. 17.*

**John A. Howard**
*President, Rockford College*

Patriotism is not just blind love for a piece of property. Nor is it simply a mutual defense pact that remains in force only as long as there is an external threat. Patriotism, true patriotism, is an eternal and legitimate love affair with a set of principles, with a common vision of the good life.

*Rockford, Ill., pub. Oct. 9.*

**Mills B. Lane**
*President, Citizens & Southern National Bank of Atlanta*

There's an innate Americanism in everybody. All you have to do is water the damn plant.

*Pub. June 30.*

**William L. Lindholm**
*President, Chesapeake & Potomac Telephone Company*

There is, indeed, a great absence of misery in this country today . . . These non-miserable millions . . . populate this land we love and call America—a country that, in 50 years, has ended two world wars and started none; fought, and is fighting, to prevent Communist take-over in two other wars; a country that has beaten off a savage depression, played the major role in rebuilding a shattered world and, almost as an afterthought, created the most healthy, wealthy and learned a nation the world has ever seen at any time or at any place. And, as Eric Hoffer has pointed out, all these good things have happened in the "only nation founded by the ordinary people, by the masses. All other societies have been shaped by exclusive kings, nobles or priests."

*Pub. Dec. 21.*

**John V. Lindsay**
*Mayor of New York*

I know that today some people think the N.A.A.C.P. is out of date, that lawful change is too difficult, that the problems of poverty and injustice are too urgent for us to insist on the political process. And I know, too, that some people have given up on America, that they have turned

(JOHN V. LINDSAY)

their backs in fury and despair and determined not to share the destiny of the majority. I want to say that I understand that kind of anger, that kind of frustration —and I share it, because none of us is equal until all of us are equal. And none of us is free until all of us are free. But I am like the N.A.A.C.P.: I have not given up on America.

*New York, Oct. 3.*

**Russell B. Long**
*United States Senator, D-La.*

Do you know of a group called S.D.S. (Students for a Democratic Society)? They are the most sorry, contemptible, over-privileged people in the world. These people ought to be put in the penitentiary at hard labor. I'd put them on a rock pile— if you don't work, you get shot . . . I guess I'm an old, outdated war veteran, but old-fashioned patriotism appeals to the Senator from Louisiana.

*Before the Senate, Washington, June 5.*

**Shirley MacLaine**
*Actress*

(John Wayne is) a marvelously patriotic man—whose ideas are full of crap.

*Interview, Washington, June 25.*

**Lester G. Maddox**
*Governor of Georgia*

Unless we are willing to rededicate ourselves . . . to God and to the principles for which this nation stands, then in another 10 years we won't have to worry about preserving freedom and democracy and constitutional government, because these things won't be around to worry us.

*Trenton, N.J., pub. Nov. 23.*

**Edgar F. Magnin**
*Rabbi, Wilshire Boulevard Temple,*
*Los Angeles*

To use the word "patriotic" today is almost a dirty gesture.

*Los Angeles, Jan. 7.*

**Clarence E. Miller**
*United States Representative, R-Ohio*

It is a remarkable fact that great num-

bers of very ordinary people in distant lands understand the American dream better than some Americans. If, by some magic, all barriers to emigration and immigration around the world were lifted tomorrow, by far the single biggest human caravan would start moving in one direction—our way, toward the United States. This is living testimony, not abstract argument, from men who know the meaning of America in their bones and marrow. The dream lives on, and we are the keepers of the dream. That is what is right with America.

*Before the House, Washington, Nov. 25.*

**Richard M. Nixon**
*President of the United States*

Patriotism is considered by some to be a backward fetish of the uneducated and the unsophisticated. Nationalism is hailed and applauded as a panacea for the ills of every nation—except the United States of America.

*U.S. Air Force Academy,*
*Colorado Springs, Colo., June 4.*

When we consider where we would like to be and where we would like to live, and we look at the other nations and at the United States, this is the time and this is the place I would want to live.

*Pub. Nov. 30.*

**Bertram L. Podell**
*United States Representative, D-N.Y.*

Patriotism is sacrificed for by many, yet understood by few. It is often a protective robe for reactionaries who, in the process, degrade both the nation and its priceless heritage. Slogans and marble statues are cold parents of such a warm word as patriotism. We must look elsewhere for its progenitors. We find it in a poor man raising his eyes to the heights of new opportunity. In an underpaid, exploited person daring to join a union. In a minority's desperate clutch for rights under our Constitution. In an outcry against that which pollutes our land, poisons our dream, and degrades our brothers. It is a belief in America causing people to seek redress of grievances within our system rather than trying to destroy it from without. Peaceful protest, then, can be patriot-

ism, for it is also an affirmation of belief in our values.
*Before the House, Washington, Nov. 12.*

**Thomas Reddin**
*Chief of Police, Los Angeles*

I think it's time apologists in our society wake up and stop excusing the wrong-doer and placing the blame on law enforcement for all the ills of our society. I'm an unashamed patriot. I'm disgusted with the "down with America" speakers . . . The final answer is going to come when the good guys finally rise up and say, "That's not going to happen anymore."

*Palm Springs, Calif., April 16.*

**Jackie Robinson**
*Former Baseball Player*

I wouldn't fly the flag on the Fourth of July or any other day. When I see a car with a flag pasted on it, I figure the guy behind the wheel isn't my friend.
*New York, Sept. 7.*

**William L. Shirer**
*Author*

I'm not saying all flag-wavers are fascists, but are the flag-wavers thinking about patriotism or are they really expressing opinions against war dissenters, blacks, the long-haired young? Many of the flag-wavers have been so brainwashed by the government they think anyone who holds a differing view is un-American.
*Interview, Lenox, Mass., pub. Dec. 29.*

**Red Skelton**
*Actor, Comedian*

I don't think I have to explain why I love my country. If I could, I would pick it up and cradle it in my arms.
*Pub. March 24.*

**Susan Sontag**
*Author*

Probably no serious radical movement has any future until it can revalidate the tarnished idea of patriotism. Flag-waving has become too associated with the right wing, something the American Legion does.

*Pub. Nov. 16.*

**John G. Tower**
*United States Senator, R-Tex.*

. . . this generation of Americans . . . still knows that freedom is our greatest gift and that we would rather die as free men than live as slaves.
*Washington, Nov. 11.*

**George Wald**
*Professor of Biology, Harvard University*

A few months ago, Senator Richard Russell of Georgia ended a speech in the Senate with the words: "If we have to start over again with another Adam and Eve, I want them to be Americans and I want them on this continent and not in Europe." That was a United States Senator making a patriotic speech. Well, here is a Nobel Laureate who thinks that those words are criminally insane.
*Massachusetts Institute of Technology, March 4.*

**DeWitt Wallace**
*Co-chairman,*
*The Reader's Digest Association*

The display of the flag is one way to show that we know what a privilege it is to be an American. Don't you get a thrill when you see the flag flying outside a post office, a factory, or an office building? I do.

*Pub. Sept. 8.*

**Jonathan Winters**
*Actor, Comedian*

Perhaps this is going to sound very corny, but I'm at a stage when I don't care. The (American) flag represents what I still believe: freedom of speech, freedom of religion, *freedom*. It's the Constitution. It's the Declaration of Independence . . . This country is still the greatest place on earth to live, to exist, to work together, to die together. I believe in this country. If it doesn't work here, it won't work anywhere. It's got to work here.
*Interview, Los Angeles, pub. March 8.*

# Politics

**Giovanni Agnelli**
*Chairman, Fiat Company of Italy*

He (Richard Nixon) seems like a man who is selling a new approach to ideas. He is reserved and modest, but forceful at the same time. But, if he were a used-car dealer, I would certainly buy one from him.

*Pub. March 7.*

**Spiro T. Agnew**
*Vice President of the United States*

I just want to be the best Vice President the country ever had. That's the limit of my aspirations. I don't foresee myself as a candidate for President. I haven't attempted to stake out any independent position from those of the Administration, and I don't intend to.

*Interview, Seattle, July 28.*

Political participation remains the citizen's most effective lever. All too often, citizens are reluctant to involve themselves in partisan politics. Entrepreneurs, who have never carried a precinct, have a condescending attitude toward politicians who have never met a payroll. Some think of politics as messy and believe that the best people should be above it. To say that politics is beneath us is to say that democracy is beneath us. A failure to participate in politics is a sign of ignorance, not innocence.

*Before National Muncipal League, Philadelphia, Nov. 10.*

**George D. Aiken**
*United States Senator, R-Vt.*

Until there is a responsible political bureaucracy, charged with the primary duty of helping the President to define our real national interests overseas and to fashion policies to implement those interests, we will not have really learned the lessons of the New Deal years—the innocence that led to Yalta, the arrogance that led to Viet Nam.

*Before the Senate, Washington, Oct. 15.*

**Carl Albert**
*United States Representative, D-Okla.*

Republicans are still far more interested in Wall Street than Main Street, far more concerned about financial centers than poverty centers.

*Pub. Nov. 2.*

**Saul Bellow**
*Author*

If they (politicians) haven't acquired an education before they take office, there's no time for them to do it afterward. How could Mayor Daley (of Chicago) or L.B.J. read the poems of Wallace Stevens, even if they were inclined to do it? The people who are inclined, like Eugene McCarthy, make torpid politicians.

*Interview, Chicago, pub. Dec. 1.*

**Shirley Temple Black**
*United States delegate
to the United Nations*

Everybody has the impression that I am such a right-wing conservative. That's what my opponents in the 1967 Congressional race (in California) tried to make people think, and I guess they succeeded. I refuse to be put in a box politically. I am conservative in one way—when it comes to fiscal planning and the use of taxpayers' money. But I'm very liberal on international affairs.

*Interview, New York, pub. Dec. 12.*

**Bruce Bliven**
*Lecturer in Communication
and Journalism, Stanford University*

Liberals are complaining terribly right now, but, in the last 60 years, it seems that people have told me liberalism is dead about 20 times, and it has always come back. Liberalism cannot die. It's like the United Nations: If it did not exist, it would have to be invented.
*Interview, Palo Alto, Calif., July 26.*

**Winton M. Blount**
*Postmaster General of the United States*

A lot of people will get mad (at the elimination of patronage in the Post Office Department), but they'll get their mail delivered on time.
*Pub. Feb. 17.*

**Kingman Brewster, Jr.**
*President, Yale University*

It is hard not to be cynical when so much of politics seems dominated by string-pulling interest groups.
*Pub. Sept. 21*

**William F. Buckley, Jr.**
*Editor, "National Review"*

New York has become a conservative city. It may, accordingly, survive.
*After New York mayoral primary,
June 18.*

**Hugh Burns**
*California State Senator*

We're going to reward our friends and punish our enemies. That's been the axiom of politics from the year one.
*Sacramento, pub. Jan. 12.*

**Maxine Cheshire**
*Society Columnist, "Washington Post"*

The Nixon era will be an Emily Post society. All will be perfectly done but their parties won't differ much from those given by a president of a bank in Des Moines, Iowa. Entertaining is a responsibility, and the Nixons will always fill their obligations. They won't enjoy it, though. It won't be fun.
*Interview, pub. Feb. 28.*

**Harry S. Dent**
*Deputy Counsel to the
President of the United States*

Basically, people in the South have had the feeling for a good long while that Washington has been anti-South. Today, there's a feeling that the Administration, while it may not be pro-South, is not anti-South. There's a feeling that the President and the Administration are trying to treat them as they would any other section of the country. This is a big, important change. When the President stopped in Mississippi after Hurricane Camille, it was a real uplift to the people of the state. They hadn't seen a President there in years. When he went to Arkansas to see the Texas-Arkansas football game, you'd be surprised at how good it made the people of Arkansas feel.
*Pub. Dec. 15.*

**Everett M. Dirksen**
*United States Senator, R-Ill.*

The President of the United States lives essentially an isolated life. He has people around him. He has to depend on them to give advice, to see that he makes no untimely mistakes, to shield him from many things. I'd be an awfully poor Republican leader if I were not willing to shield the President of the United States from people I feel do him no good and could do him harm . . . The President knows all the time what I'm up to. He knows that, if there is anyone on this hilltop he can count on, it's the fellow from Illinois.
*Interview, pub. May 9.*

**Robert Dole**
*United States Senator, R-Kan.*

President Nixon would be a great President. The trouble is that the people around him are stupid.
*Washington, pub. July 29.*

**Robert H. Finch**
*Secretary of Health, Education and
Welfare of the United States*

The hard fact of the matter is, once you start down that route . . . even go in for being a candidate for the second spot, you're making a commitment you want

(ROBERT H. FINCH)

to run for the Presidency—not an avowed commitment, but it's there. Take Muskie, Humphrey, F.D.R.—if you're propelled into national candidacy, at some point, (you) can be considered for President. I've been close to it, enough to see it isn't anything I want to do. I don't pretend to know global problems (adequately).

*Interview, Washington, pub. Sept. 21.*

**Gerald R. Ford**
*United States Representative, R-Mich.*

The Republican Party is not a party of promises, not a party of idle conversation, but a party of action. Ours is not only a party of action, but a party of ideas. It is good for America that the Republican Party is alive and well because the Democratic Party has failed America—and we are now approaching the Seventies, a decade of decision.

*Before National Federation of Republican Women, Washington, Sept. 27.*

**J. William Fulbright**
*United States Senator, D-Ark.*

Mr. (Lyndon B.) Johnson was formerly a very great and very successful majority leader of the Senate and, as such, tended to take the Senate for granted once he entered the White House. He seemed to think the Senate would do his bidding, no matter what he asked.

*News conference, Washington, Feb. 4.*

**John Kenneth Galbraith**
*Professor of Economics,*
*Harvard University*

Let me plead for a little more well-considered malice in our political life. We have become far too charitable and forgiving.

*At Americans for Democratic Action testimonial dinner, pub. December.*

**Sanford D. Garelik**
*President-elect, New York City Council*

I'm a realist (in politics). Very much so. While I'm sentimental, even emotional, I'm a political realist. I understand there are times when you have to compromise.

Life is a compromise. But you do not compromise your integrity. The key is: What do you compromise? With whom do you compromise? Who do you go to bed with?

*Interview, New York, Nov. 6.*

**Barry M. Goldwater**
*United States Senator, R-Ariz.*

Too many Republicans are complaining when they should be applauding. Taking over the Government is not an easy or a quick thing. He (President Nixon) is a Republican and will start to put in a Republican program as soon as he can clean up the godawful mess he inherited from President (Lyndon B.) Johnson.

*Washington, March 13.*

**Mike Gravel**
*United States Senator, D-Alaska*

I'm going to spend my time learning. It probably will take a year to learn enough to start being of service . . . I'm going to be a good senator. When you're ranked 100th, there's no place to go but up.

*Interview, Anchorage, pub. Jan. 5.*

**Edith Green**
*United States Representative, D-Ore.*

I considered myself a liberal by any standard that was applied then (when she entered Congress 15 years ago) and, if anything, I would be more liberal now by those same standards. But the ultra-liberals have moved so far to the left that they have distorted the position of all other liberals.

*Washington, pub. Dec. 3.*

**Harold E. Hughes**
*United States Senator, D-Iowa*

The people of America, as well as the Democratic Party, need to know that the Democratic Party is in damn bad shape; not only organizationally, but financially.

*New Orleans, July 19.*

**Hubert H. Humphrey**
*Vice President of the United States*

We (the Democrats) are a national party. Let us not fall into the weakness of being a regional party.

*Washington, Jan. 14.*

. . . I don't rule out a thing. I'm the youngest 57 that you ever met. I feel good. And I intend to stay active. And we're going to rebuild this political (Democratic) party, modernize it and strengthen it. We have good leadership for it and I'm going to be in there pitching.

*Interview, Washington, Jan. 25.*

If the whole crowd of young, militant, non-educated Negroes can't find a home within my party, they will not vote Republican—they will start a new party.

*Pub. Feb. 10.*

I think we ought to remember one thing: The Republicans did not win this (1968) election. We (the Democrats) defeated ourselves.

*Chicago, Feb. 11.*

I'm glad to see the Humphrey program moving ahead under President Nixon.

*News conference, Denver, April 11.*

Inflation, interest rates, civil rights, education, conservation, consumer protection, anti-trust—you name it and the Nixon-Agnew Administration has remembered its friends and forgotten the rest of us.

The great problems of this country are not being dealt with . . . We see an administration that has a couple of policies for everything . . . We see an administration with a different policy every week on the issue of school desegregation . . . You see an administration where civil servants rise up in open revolt . . . You see an administration which has its own priorities, and here they are: Mars, that is one; SST, supersonic transport, that is two; and ABM (anti-ballistic missiles), that is three . . . As worried as I am as to whether there is any life on Mars, I am a lot more concerned about the quality of life on this good earth.

*At AFL-CIO convention, Atlantic City, N.J., Oct. 6.*

## Manuel Frago Iribarne
*Information Minister of Spain*

The political enemy is the worst of all. Precisely because he does not aspire to rob a purse or break a law, but to break everything. Therefore he is the most dangerous and the one who must be treated with the greatest rigor. This is an imminent truth of politics.

*Interview, Madrid, pub. Sept. 28.*

## Lyndon B. Johnson
*President of the United States*

I hope it may be said a hundred years from now that together we helped to make our country more just for all its people, as well as to insure the blessings of liberty for our posterity. I believe it will be said that we tried.

*State of the Union Message, Washington, Jan. 14.*

As President, we've had lots of debates on the war and fiscal matters, but I don't have an enemy in the Senate as far as I'm concerned . . . I've been treated fairly. I'm mighty grateful.

*Washington, Jan. 16.*

## Herbert Kaplow
*White House Correspondent, National Broadcasting Company*

To me, he (Richard M. Nixon) is the greatest comeback story in political history . . . For a man who's essentially introverted, he's an amazing natural politician, and the way he threw himself into working for local Republican candidates in '64 and again in '66 . . . I knew a miracle might be in the making.

*Interview, pub. Feb. 10.*

## Edward M. Kennedy
*United States Senator, D-Mass.*

. . . there is a challenge in politics. You say to yourself, "Wonder if I can do it," and then, later, you might say, "I think I can do it," and you try, and you succeed, and it's a wonderful thing.

Some say that 1972 is the year I must make a move for the Presidency, or 1976 or 1980. But how do I know that some young fellow—say, Jay Rockefeller— won't suddenly come on the scene and make everybody forget that anybody ever considered Ted Kennedy for the Presidency? And so I just try to work in the areas and on the problems that were my

(EDWARD M. KENNEDY)

brothers' concern and let the future take care of itself.

*Interview, McLean, Va., pub. March 4.*

**Herbert G. Klein**
*White House*
*Director of Communications*

There are many ways to capture the imagination of the people at this time. A lot of gimmicks is not what the American people want, and, besides, that doesn't fit into Nixon's style.

*News conference, Washington, Jan. 29.*

**Russell B. Long**
*United States Senator, D-La.*

I don't think I could have been defeated (for Senate majority whip) by anybody else in the United States Senate, and my guess is I would have taken any other opponent by about a two-to-one margin . . . This happens to be a race where it was a nationwide proposition, and, while I had Senator (Edward M.) Kennedy outgunned in the United States Senate, he had me outgunned in the United States.

*Interview, Washington, Jan. 3.*

**Allard K. Lowenstein**
*United States Representative, D-N.Y.*

If the country hasn't stopped (Vietnam) deaths; if we haven't cut the tremendous over-expenditures for the military . . . if the middle class hasn't begun to feel relief from the burdens of inflation; if the poor people haven't begun to find ways they can eat and get housing and job opportunities; if, in fact, his (Nixon's) program is where it is now, he is politically dead no matter what kind of speeches people make now about middle-of-the-road or swings to the right, and I think he knows that.

*Television interview, Aug. 3.*

**Norman Mailer**
*Author*

I'm the only one on the left who can talk to the right. I'm telling both the left and the right to regain control of their lives from the psychopathological center. I'm asking everyone, from Black Panthers

to Goldwaterites, to blow just half their minds. It's the only way to head off the class war between left and right that they both seem to want.

*Pub. May 5.*

**Frank F. Mankiewicz**
*Journalist; former press secretary for Senator Robert F. Kennedy*

The appeal of a Robert Kennedy, just as the appeal of John Lindsay, George Wallace, Eugene McCarthy or Ronald Reagan, lies not in the fact that they are Democrats or Republicans, liberals or conservatives, hawks or doves—many of their followers don't even know—but they appear as enemies of the established order, as non- or even anti-politicians who care deeply about the way things are and want to change them.

*Before Western States Advertising*
*Agencies Association,*
*Beverly Hills, Calif., Dec. 9.*

**Mike Mansfield**
*United States Senator, D-Mont.*

As far as the people are concerned, it appears to me that they're becoming less Democratic and less Republican-minded, and that more and more they are going into the middle. That is a good thing, in my opinion, because it gives them the chance to shift from side to side; and, instead of voting on the basis of party, they vote on the basis of an individual: what he stands for, what his record is and what they think he will do.

*Interview, Washington, pub. Dec. 1.*

**Eugene J. McCarthy**
*United States Senator, D-Minn.*

I was asked whom I would have preferred to face if I had won the Democratic nomination (for the Presidency)—(Richard M.) Nixon or (Nelson A.) Rockefeller. I replied that Rockefeller had his good and bad days, but I could depend on Nixon to give up six or seven runs every time I faced him. There was a lot of baseball talk during the campaign, and I said that Nixon was pretty good at throwing curves and that he was throwing a spit ball before it was outlawed.

*Washington, May 28.*

I know what I want to do. Whether I'll do what I want to do is another question.
*Pub. Aug. 1.*

**George S. McGovern**
*United States Senator, D-S.D.*

I can't fault the man (Richard Nixon). I like both the deliberate pace and the prudent, thoughtful approach he has been giving to difficult questions. I fully expect a rather constructive and satisfactory relationship between the White House and Congress.
*Washington, pub. Feb. 10.*

**Robert E. McNair**
*Governor of South Carolina*

Extremism breeds extremists . . . To yield our (Democratic) Party now to either extreme would most certainly touch off a chain reaction which could reshape the entire political structure of our nation and damage permanently the traditional concept of our party's broad ideology. Unless I misread all the political signs in our nation today, I do not think our people are ready for a political party of extremism. I think the people of America today are looking for the politics of moderation . . .

*Before Democratic National Committee, Sept. 18.*

**George Meany**
*President, American Federation of Labor-Congress of Industrial Organizations*

I think he (Senator Edward M. Kennedy) is too young. I think he needs a good deal more experience. I was certainly a great admirer of John Kennedy but I don't think being the brother of a President is, in itself, any qualification at any time. I think Teddy works harder as Senator. I think he has done a good job for the people of Massachusetts. But I feel that he needs a whole lot more experience before he could convince me that he has the qualifications of President of the United States.
*Interview, Washington, Aug. 28.*

**Charles Morgan, Jr.**
*Southern Director, American Civil Liberties Union*

The Democratic Party in the Deep South now consists of local officeholders intent on maintaining their own fiefs, educating no voters, avoiding all national party affiliations . . . They are intent on living out what is to them a generation of Negro and national idiocy. "Survive, survive," is their creed. To sneak by the voters "just one more time" is their challenge.
*Interview, pub. Nov. 29.*

**Wayne L. Morse**
*Former United States Senator, D-Ore.*

The greatest disillusionment in my Senate career has been seeing liberals decide that principles are not as important as getting elected again six years later . . . Let me emphasize, what is important is not the next election, but the next century.
*Princeton University, pub. Feb. 26.*

**Rogers C. B. Morton**
*United States Representative, R-Md.*

The question is are we (the Republicans) a political party capable of attracting new generations, capable of establishing government in our own right, capable of winning elections because of what we are and how we perform? Or are we a standby for the majority of Americans to use only as a substitute for failure? I, for one, will not accept for the Republican Party the role of spare tire in American politics.

. . . much of the vote we (the Republicans) have gotten in recent elections has been motivated by reaction. It has been cast by the dissatisfied, not by the Republican enthusiast.
*Before Republican National Committee, Washington, April 14.*

**Karl E. Mundt**
*United States Senator, R-S.D.*

Under (President Lyndon B.) Johnson, the Federal Government said, "Do thus and so, and you will get Government money." Now we are to have, under (President Richard M.) Nixon, political partnerships, not political pressures.
*Interview, pub. March 10.*

## Edmund S. Muskie
*United States Senator, D-Me.*

I have decided to postpone, for the moment at least, strengthening my position in the Senate. In time, I may regret that I put aside an opportunity to advance in the Senate. But, if that is true, I may even regret having run for Vice President; but I don't think so. I think that, in this business, you have to go where the fates take you—as long as you make progress.
*Washington, Jan. 22.*

I am not certain I consider the Presidency a possibility now, but if it became one, I would certainly not shrink from it. It's the kind of challenge I would feel is the ultimate experience in political life.
*News conference, Washington, Aug. 6.*

## Robert Nisbet
*Professor of Sociology,*
*University of California at Riverside*

(President) Nixon is tremendously reassuring to middle-class Americans. If you started out to design a human being who would be an answer for this kind of person in this kind of time, you couldn't design a better one than Nixon. His kind of corny, square, ketchup-on-cottage-cheese image is very reassuring to these people.
*Pub. Oct. 6.*

## Richard M. Nixon
*President of the United States*

Looking at the future and looking at the time when I leave office, I would appreciate it if you would keep my seat warm.
*Before the Senate, Washington, Jan. 29.*

Reform of the postal system is long overdue. I consider it essential, as a first step, that the Congress remove the last vestiges of political patronage in the Post Office Department.
*Washington, published Feb. 28.*

I think we should all say, by reason of the role women have played in politics in America, a woman can and should be able to do any political job that a man can do.
*Washington, April 17.*

Everett Dirksen was a politician in the finest sense of that much-abused word. If he were here, I think he might put it this way . . . A politician knows that, more important than the bill that is proposed, is the law that is passed. A politician knows that his friends are not always his allies, and that his adversaries are not his enemies. A politician knows how to make the process of democracy work and loves the intricate workings of the democratic system. A politician knows not only how to count votes, but how to make his vote count. A politician knows that his words are his weapons, but that his word is his bond. A politician knows that, only if he leaves room for discussion and room for concession, can he gain room for maneuver. A politician knows that the best way to be a winner is to make the other side feel it does not have to be a loser. And a politician—in the Dirksen tradition—knows both the name of the game and the rules of the game, and he seeks his ends through the time-honored democratic means.
*At memorial services for*
*Senator Dirksen,*
*Washington, pub. Sept. 12.*

. . . when the security of America is involved, when peace for America and for the world is involved, when the lives of our young men are involved, we are not Democrats, we are not Republicans, we are Americans.
*Before the House, Washington, Nov. 13.*

I have always derived a great deal of benefit from criticism, and I have never known when I was short of it.
*News conference, Washington, Dec. 8.*

## Wright Patman
*United States Representative, D-Tex.*

I have no fear of the outcome of either the congressional elections of next year or the next presidential election. With policies of the Nixon Administration, such as that which led to a 4-per cent unemployment rate and which I predict will go higher, the Democratic Party has no problems.
*Before the House, Washington, Oct. 7.*

**Bertram L. Podell**
*United States Representative, D-N.Y.*

Heartlessly, dispassionately, uncomprehendingly, this administration pulverizes the working people of this country into powder under its fist. They talk peace and make war. They prattle of balanced budgets and cut essential programs. They bellow of prosperity and create an economic desert. They whine about jobs and create unemployment. They howl about work and the unemployment lines lengthen. Has there ever been such a gap between promise and performance? Never. We have the reincarnation of the Republican Party of the 1920's and 1930's in control. They are crippling the economy, and the worst has not yet arrived.
*Before the House, Washington, Oct. 7.*

**Adam Clayton Powell**
*United States Representative, D-N.Y.*

I've fought too long for many things. I told my attorneys, "Let's fight this thing (restoration of his seniority and $55,000 in pay denied him during nearly two years of exclusion from the House) right down to the wire." Then we'll find out if this land is a democracy or if it's a fake.
*Washington, Sept. 29.*

**George W. Romney**
*Secretary of Housing and
Urban Development
of the United States*

I've been very accommodating with the people of the press, radio and television of this state. I've been direct and forthright—and that's been one of my problems all along . . . I've answered questions as I've got off planes; I've gone for radio interviews when I didn't have time to gather my thoughts. I just went too far in that respect . . . Mr. Nixon's in the White House because he didn't.
*News conference,
Lansing, Mich., Jan. 15.*

**John J. Rooney**
*United States Representative, D-N.Y.*

I am the first known member of Congress to be forced to campaign for reelection against the awesome financial resources of a tax-exempt foundation (Frederick W. Richmond Foundation). This time it happened in my district. It can—and probably will—happen in your districts. In the appeal of this political gimmick is a threat to every officeholder, in Congress or elsewhere, who does not have access to a fat bankroll or to a business or to a tax-exempt foundation.
*Before House Ways and Means
Committee, Washington, pub. March 3.*

**Clinton Rossiter**
*Professor of American Institutions,
Cornell University*

I thought I knew him (Richard Nixon) in 1962; I thought I knew him during the last campaign. But now, I'm not so sure I know him. I don't think anyone has a clear idea of what Nixon's going to do on any issue.
*Pub. March 28.*

**Hugh Scott**
*United States Senator, R-Pa.*

The Democratic-controlled Congress has been relaxed in action and rather laxative in political reaction.
*Washington, pub. Oct. 8.*

**Raymond P. Shafer**
*Governor of Pennsylvania*

Our Party (Republican) has gained its recent strength because it has been broad enough to take in the attitudes and politics of all sections of our country. Our history shows that a party which chooses to base its appeal on sectionalism cannot remain strong for long.
*Boston, Dec. 2.*

**William K. Shearer**
*Chairman, American
Independent Party-California*

A candidate springs from the party and not the party from the candidate. The party should not be candidate-directed. While we have great respect for Mr. (George C.) Wallace (A.I.P. Presidential candidate in 1968), we do not think there should be a candidate-directed situation. We want our party to survive regardless of what Wallace does.
*Interview, Louisville, Ky., Feb. 21.*

**Theodore C. Sorensen**
*Former Special Counsel to
President John F. Kennedy*

(Senator Edward M. Kennedy) certainly
is not going to be elected President of the
United States in 1972. And, to be very
frank . . . I don't think he should be.

*Television interview, New York, Aug. 21.*

**Jack Spaulding**
*Editor, Atlanta "Journal"*

Lester Maddox has successfully demonstrated that Georgia does not need a
governor. I expected a good deal of damage when Maddox got in, and we haven't
seen it. Atlanta sails on with unexcelled
prosperity.

*Pub. Dec. 22.*

**Strom Thurmond**
*United States Senator, R-S.C.*

A man in public office has got to *appear*
to be right as well as be right.
*Before the Senate, Washington, June 9.*

**Morris K. Udall**
*United States Representative, D-Ariz.*

After 1964, a lot of people complained
that they had elected (Lyndon B.) Johnson and gotten (Barry M.) Goldwater's
foreign policy. Now, we've elected (Richard M.) Nixon and, to a large extent,
we're getting Johnson's domestic policies.
*Pub. Feb. 21.*

**George C. Wallace**
*Former Governor of Alabama;
1968 Presidential candidate*

I've got one eye on him (President
Richard M. Nixon), and he's got one eye
on me, and we two are watching each
other, and he knows that if he don't do
what he told everybody he was gonna'
do, that I'm gonna catch him, just as sure
as shootin', and this time he knows we'll
be a lot more ready for him than we were
before . . . All he saw in the final returns
was the tip of the iceberg. People went to
the polls to vote for me, and they said,
"No, I'm afeared a (Hubert) Humphrey,
so I gotta vote for Nixon." Now, if Nixon
don't bring about an honorable peace, and
if he don't cure inflation, and if he don't
bring about law and order, and if he don't
do a lot of other things, he's gonna' see
the whole iceberg. I hope and pray he does
a good job, but I'm a-waitin'.
*Richmond, Va., pub. July 24.*

I wish I had copyrighted or patented
my speeches. I would (now) be drawing
immense royalties from Mr. Nixon and
especially Mr. Agnew.
*Television interview, Nov. 30.*

I think I represent the majority viewpoint in this country. And if I don't now,
I will by 1972.
*Interview, Montgomery, Ala.,
pub. December.*

**Theodore H. White**
*Author*

The power of TV is incredible. A smart
politician like Nixon realizes that a minute or a minute-and-a-half on Cronkite
and Huntley-Brinkley is worth 10,000 rallies and speeches and hand-shaking and
news releases. The thrust of the modern
politician is strictly for that minute on the
national news and forget the rest. It can
be frightening because a flamboyant stunt
will get more time on the air than the most
carefully considered statement of policy.
*Hollywood, pub. Sept. 7.*

**Ralph D. Abernathy**
*Chairman, Southern Christian*
*Leadership Conference*

The prior Administration ignored us. The present Administration has finally come up with a hunger program which asks the poor and hungry to wait still another two years, until 1971, before being fed and, even then, to be content with half a loaf. We do not and cannot accept this. We are hungry now, and we expect to be fed now.

> *Before Senate Select Committee*
> *on Nutrition and Human Needs,*
> *Washington, May 14.*

**Spiro T. Agnew**
*Vice President of the United States*

We do not need a transfer of dollars from the space program to other programs. We need a transfer of its spirit—an infusion of American dedication to purpose and hard work.

> *At Western Governors Conference,*
> *Seattle, July 28.*

**Ivan Allen**
*Mayor of Atlanta*

The significance of President Nixon's welfare reforms is that they are the first real attempt to view the needs of the poor in light of current problems, not circumstances which existed in the depression. They represent a change from an outmoded public assistance program to a flexible system for a rapidly changing society.

> *Pub. Aug. 17.*

**Julian Bond**
*Georgia State Legislator*

Small farmers who can't compete with big farmers, housewives dissatisfied with rising food prices, tenant farmers who refuse to pay rents, high school students who want to wear their hair more than one inch long . . . They are caught up for very good reasons—that no one cares for them. What is true for them is that this nation is not for them. This nation, for these people, is likely to fail as long as Saigon holds priority over Selma and men on the moon hold priority over men on earth.

> *At conference of Black Elected*
> *Officials, Virginia State College,*
> *Petersburg, Va., Oct. 3.*

**Stan Brooks**
*News Correspondent,*
*Westinghouse Broadcasting Company*

One out of every ten Americans is old—over 65 . . . One third are poor—living below the poverty level. They live alone, most of these old people, tucked away on the edges of our cities and towns or buried deep in the decaying center . . . Many of these old people are victims of the "retirement revolution" that has been sweeping America. As a Senate committee has pointed out: "Most of the aged did not become poor until they became old." Ironically, these men and women helped to build the country earlier this century. They ran the machines and worked the farms and contributed to the great wealth other Americans now enjoy. But these older people struggled through two world wars and a major depression, and so their life savings are skimpy at best. They lived too soon—before they could reap the full benefits of social security and the more generous pension programs industry now provides today's workers. And what little these people did put away for a rainy day has been wiped out by inflation. The high cost of food and housing and medical care has been too

(STAN BROOKS)

much for fixed incomes, and the old people are suffering from an income gap. And now, in their so-called golden years, they find they are broke as well as forgotten.

*Radio broadcast, pub. Dec. 19.*

**Arthur F. Burns**
*Counsellor to the*
*President of the United States*

We concentrate too much on the total amount of money that is spent (to combat poverty). Far more important is how that money is spent. Why, the sums being spent are so staggering, I hesitate to cite them . . . All this has created a Governmental maze that is costly, inefficient and difficult to grasp intellectually.

*Television interview, Washington,*
*April 13.*

A strict work requirement will reduce the welfare rolls, bring many now on welfare into the mainstream of productive activity, relieve the burden on taxpayers and redress the sense of bitterness on the part of millions of people who work hard and honestly to earn the little they have. If we were to make money available to able-bodied people, whether they work or not, our economic and social system would disintegrate.

*Interview, Washington, pub. July 14.*

**Al Capp**
*Cartoonist*

Anyone who can get to the welfare office can get to work.

*Pub. April 11.*

**Wendell Chino**
*President, National Congress*
*of American Indians*

There isn't an Indian problem today that money wouldn't cure.

*At NCAI convention,*
*Albuquerque, N.M., Oct. 6.*

**William Clay**
*United States Representative, D-Mo.*

The simple truth is that a hungry child cannot learn and a hungry adult cannot work. Until poor people are properly fed, we cannot expect to educate them, to train them, or to free them of the devastating effects of the poverty cycle. We must remove hunger from the stage of reports, recommendations and rhetoric. Hunger in America is a real problem—that it exists is shameful, but the lack of a national commitment to eliminate it is disgraceful. As one mother put it—if you want to beautify America, fatten up a child. Trees would not fill his stomach or put a smile on his mother's face.

*Before the House, Washington, Dec. 9.*

**Wilbur J. Cohen**
*Former Secretary of Health,*
*Education and Welfare*
*of the United States*

Eligibility for welfare payments should be uniform and determined by Congress. The present hodge-podge of 50 different systems should be scuttled. It's a morass of contradictions that penalizes many of the states.

*News conference, Los Angeles, April 29.*

**John Conyers, Jr.**
*United States Representative, D-Mich.*

Some of our better political cartoonists have taken to depicting our cities as dilapidated, vermin-infested shantytowns squatting in the shadows of glistening, gigantic anti-ballistic missiles. In my view, this is a dead accurate representation of the situation. We do not need augmented military protection for our country; our existing nuclear deterrent is more than sufficient to do this many times over. We need to take this money and use it to improve the society we are so concerned about protecting.

*Before the House, Washington, Oct. 2.*

**Alan Cranston**
*United States Senator, D-Calif.*

I oppose it (a guaranteed income). I think you tend to make people serfs or slaves by giving them something without expecting anything in return.

*Interview, Washington, pub. March 2.*

**Kingsley Davis**
*Professor of Sociology,*
*University of California at Berkeley*

What kind of population do we want in the United States? Until we get that straightened out, we cannot talk about means (to control population). I happen to think this country would be better off with half the population. With present technology and the population of the 1930's, the country would be a paradise. As it is, it's getting to be like hell—too many places getting like New York City.
*Interview, Berkeley, pub. Oct. 5.*

**Paul Rand Dixon**
*Chairman, Federal Trade Commission*

Let me say categorically that it is time to stop kidding ourselves and the American public by passing consumer protection laws without also providing enough money to enforce them in a meaningful way.
*Before Senate executive reorganization subcommittee, Washington, April 24.*

**William H. Draper, Jr.**
*Chairman, Population Crisis Committee*

. . . over the next decade, I believe that at least 5 to 10 per cent of our foreign assistance funds should regularly be allocated for population limitation . . . I believe that at least 10 per cent of all foundation grants and private contributions should also be directed toward curbing population growth. So critical is the population explosion that, unless present growth rates are checked, it is not likely that any of the other objectives of many developing countries can be achieved.
*Before House Foreign Affairs Committee, Washington, July 30.*

**Lee A. DuBridge**
*Science Adviser to the President*
*of the United States*

If the rate of population growth is not reduced, we will get to the point where we will have to run very hard to stay in the same place . . . But the urges of evolution and traditions of history are not so easily suppressed. Men have always been proud of large families. Nations have always been proud of—and have fostered —growing populations. "Growth" is a hallowed word. "Motherhood" is a sacred one. Can we reverse the urges of a billion years of evolving life? Can we reverse the cultural traditions of thousands of years of human civilization? We can.
*Interview, Washington, pub. Dec. 21.*

**Thomas F. Eagleton**
*United States Senator, D-Mo.*

Our priorities surely need re-evaluation when twice as much money is spent every year on ammunition for Vietnam as on the entire elementary and secondary educational programs; when we spend as much to build a costly, unneeded, unworkable and escalatory anti-ballistic system as we spend on programs to feed the hungry in this land of plenty.
*Pub. July 5.*

**Paul Ehrlich**
*Professor of Biology,*
*Stanford University*

More people mean a frantic effort to grow more food. Those people who go around saying that we can feed 7 billion people in the year 2000 ought to go back to high school for elementary biology, meteorology, economics and anthropology.
*At Sierra Club Wilderness Conference, San Francisco, March 14.*

Some biologists feel that compulsory family regulation will be necessary to retard population growth. It is a dismal prospect—except when viewed as an alternative to Armageddon.
*Before United States Commission for UNESCO, San Francisco, Nov. 24.*

**James Charles Evers**
*Mayor, Fayette, Miss.*

I don't agree with George Wallace, but I admire him. He's a big man. He's no fool. Look what he could do with the poor whites. I represent the poor blacks. What a coalition we could make.
*Fayette, pub. Nov. 9.*

**James L. Farmer**
*Assistant Secretary for Administration,*
*Department of Health, Education and*
*Welfare of the United States*

In the past, no black leader would have advocated more facilities in the ghettos and barrios. It was thought that they would disappear. Now, it is quite clear that those areas called ghettos and barrios will continue to exist in the foreseeable future. This is not separatism; it is a cultural pluralism, in which groups love and honor and respect other groups. This concept is not as American as apple pie. It is as American as pizza pie and gelfilte fish.

*Before National Recreation and Park*
*Association, Chicago, pub. Sept. 22.*

**Robert H. Finch**
*Secretary of Health, Education and*
*Welfare of the United States*

. . . Federal involvement in the areas of health, education and welfare is an established fact—and rightly so. But it is also an established fact that too much of what is now being done, with all the best of good intentions, and too many of the dollars being spent, are simply not hitting their targets.

*Washington, pub. Feb. 3.*

How do you rationalize the fact that unemployment is way down, and the relief roles are way up?

*Pub. March 17.*

Sure, there are always those who are going to say, "Well, given any amount of money, a guy is going to prefer to lay on his duff and drink beer." But we are betting that most guys, just in terms of self respect . . . want a job. If you can't bet on that, I don't know what you can bet on.

*Interview, Aug. 13.*

**Thomas S. Foley**
*United States Representative, D-Wash.*

Who's for consumers? Everybody and nobody. The consumers don't have the kind of attention span or organization to really push, while industry has a long memory, a big war-chest and political clout. There's very little political value in consumer protection. Consumers don't

give massive contributions to campaigns.

*Washington, pub. Sept. 21.*

**Gerald R. Ford**
*United States Representative, R-Mich.*

President Nixon has adopted a responsible common-sense approach to our urban problems. His answer is jobs and job training. The accent is on the solid American ethic of working for a living. The President's approach is based on the idea that a man never stands so tall as when he stands on his own two feet. Workfare instead of welfare. That is the American way. That is Dick Nixon's way. A hand up instead of a handout. That's the only way to bridge the gap between the Haves and the Have-Nots in America.

*Before National Federation of*
*Republican Women,*
*Washington, Sept. 27.*

**Milton Friedman**
*Professor of Economics,*
*University of Chicago*

It (public housing) was instituted in the 1930s to improve the housing of the poor, give the poor a sense of pride, and reduce juvenile delinquency. The effect in each case has been exactly the opposite. Public housing is a total failure. The major beneficiaries are the people who sell their property for housing projects. Some of the poor benefit, but at the expense of other poor people who are forced to vacate bad housing and occupy worse.

*Pub. Dec. 19.*

**Betty Furness**
*Former Adviser for Consumer Affairs*
*to the President of the United States*

If you're mad enough to stop buying Aunt Gladys' raisin cookies because they don't have enough raisins, you must tell the manufacturer, or he'll think his advertising hasn't gotten to your area, and he'll put more money into ads instead of raisins.

*Before National Association of Bank*
*Women, San Francisco, Sept. 23.*

**John W. Gardner**
*Chairman, Urban Coalition*

When someone asks whether anything can happen without violence, they are usually implying that nothing much happens under peaceable circumstances. But it is wrong to say that nothing has happened. At least 12 million people have been lifted out of poverty in the past 10 years. That means a major difference in the lives of a lot of people. Nobody remembers that kind of statistic, but there it is. And a substantial number of those were black people.

*Interview, pub. Sept. 30.*

**Sydney S. Gellis**
*Chairman, Department of Pediatrics,*
*Tufts Medical School*

There is no doubt that a balanced diet can be developed and purchased with the money provided (by welfare). But it requires a level of sophistication and motivation not present in many of these (welfare) families.

*Pub. April 28.*

**Mitchell I. Ginsberg**
*Human Resources Administrator,*
*City of New York*

There are very few able-bodied men on welfare . . . Anybody who has been on it, or close to it, knows it's a miserable way of life.

*New York, March 13.*

Despite major limitations, the welfare proposal (of President Nixon's) can represent the beginning of a turnabout in national welfare policy. The establishment of national minimum standards, even though woefully inadequate; the provision of assistance to the working poor; the setting up of national criteria for eligibility; and the involvement of the Social Security Administration in administering the income program are of major importance. I believe these steps will inevitably and appropriately lead to the assumption by the national Government of the entire income maintenance program, thus allowing the local community to concentrate on services.

*Pub. Aug. 16.*

Personally, I favor mothers on welfare working, and we encourage it. But I'm against making work compulsory. They should have the same right as anyone else to decide what's best for the family.

*New York, pub. Sept. 18.*

**Harry Golden**
*Author*

There's hope for this country because we've witnessed two miracles in the last decade. The first: a changing of an entire social order in the South. Fifteen years ago, they said "Never." Fifteen years ago, Dr. Ralph Bunche couldn't get a room in the Hotel Charlotte. Two years ago, the same hotel had a sign up that read: "Welcome, delegates from the NAACP." I just stood there and laughed. The second miracle is the move to eradicate poverty, and they're forcing the government to do something about it. It will take time, and President Nixon's new welfare program isn't all that great. But you've got to admit it's a step in the right direction.

*Interview, Beverly Hills, Calif.,*
*pub. Aug. 16.*

**Sanford R. Goodkin**
*Real estate management and*
*marketing consultant*

The name of tomorrow is density. The forces of inflation will still be haunting anyone who wants to build or buy a normal single detached dwelling. The apartment will become the fort, the bastion, the refuge, the country club, the melting pot and, finally, the home to most of the people moving from one place to another.

*Pub. Dec. 8.*

**Bess Myerson Grant**
*Commissioner of Consumer Affairs,*
*City of New York*

The great faith which innocent consumers and trusting readers place in the seals awarded by *Good Housekeeping* and *Parents'* magazines to the products of their advertisers is quite without justification.

*Before National Commission*
*on Product Safety,*
*Washington, Sept. 30.*

**Fred R. Harris**
*United States Senator, D-Okla.*

We always hear the farthest rumble of a distant drum, but not the voice of a hungry child.

*Washington, March 11.*

(FRED R. HARRIS)

Before you criticize a welfare mother, I suggest you go and visit one.

*Interview, pub. March 18.*

**Philip A. Hart**
*United States Senator, D-Mich.*

Students are upset because they live in a society that talks peace but drops napalm. Their youthful and inexperienced eyes seem to see an inconsistency in that. I've met young people who are irritated because our system can build luxury apartment buildings so high that they can be seen from slums miles away. And there are even some students who wondered how our system could send men to the moon on Christmas Day while on earth thousands of homes went unvisited by a kindlier aeronaut, Santa Claus.

*University of Michigan, pub. Feb. 23.*

**Walter J. Hickel**
*Secretary of the Interior
of the United States*

A great national park is a glorious thing, but the boy sitting on the steps of a ghetto tenement deserves a place where he can discover that the sky is larger than the little hole he can see between the buildings.

*Pub. March 24.*

**Ernest F. Hollings**
*United States Senator, D-S.C.*

Many is the time that friends have pointed a finger and said, "Look at that dumb nigger." The charge is all too often accurate—but not because of the color of his skin. He is dumb because we denied him food. Dumb in infancy, he has been blighted for life.

*Before Senate Select Committee
on Nutrition and Human Needs,
Washington, pub. Feb. 28.*

**Jacob K. Javits**
*United States Senator, R-N.Y.*

What we have experienced in the '60s is not so much the conscious neglect of the Middle Americans, but the determined effort of the Federal Government to begin providing the civil rights, welfare programs and manpower education and housing opportunities to the poor and the non-whites who came to demand a larger share—and, I might say, a deservedly larger share—of the American dream.

*Harvard University, pub. Dec. 2.*

**Jenkin Lloyd Jones**
*President, Chamber of Commerce
of the United States*

The argument for this idea (guaranteed annual income) is that it would stop the snooping by the welfare case worker and give everybody a solid base he could count on. It would do away with a great deal of bureaucracy, which has a stake in maintaining welfare recipients' dependency. But what I want to know is, if you give a man $3,500 or $4,000 a year just for being the head of the family, what do you do if he spends it all on women, liquor or horse races? Where is the guarantee that people will not continue to act irresponsibly, neglect their families and throw them back on public relief? All you have then done is richly subsidize one bum. I think that question has to be answered first.

*Interview, pub. May.*

**Edward M. Kennedy**
*United States Senator, D-Mass.*

In the United States today—the wealthiest nation in the history of man—millions of our citizens are sick. And they are sick because they are poor. Their sickness is the shame of America. Of all the faces of poverty, the sickness of the poor is the ugliest. Of all the effects of poverty, it is the sickness of the poor that we could attack most easily, had we the will.

*Portsmouth, N.H., pub. July 6.*

**Coretta Scott King**
*Widow of Rev. Martin Luther King, Jr.*

There is no middle ground between right and wrong. There is no middle ground between integration and segregation . . . We must continue to define the issues . . . We have done it through massive demonstrations. I think we must continue our picketing, we must continue our sit-ins, we must continue all forms of pressure, nonviolent pressure, in trying to bring about real, meaningful gains in terms of creating life, new life, for people, the poor people of this nation.

*Television interview, Sept. 28.*

**Herbert G. Klein**
*White House Director
of Communications*

I think one disgrace of the moment is for Senator (George S.) McGovern and others to make hunger a political cause.

*Washington, March 15.*

**Virginia Knauer**
*Adviser for Consumer Affairs to the
President of the United States*

We know one of the consumer's major problems. When he gets illegally taken at the marketplace, the loss is generally lower than a lawyer's fees.

*Washington, pub. Aug. 24.*

Consumer fraud is an insidious economic cancer which eats at the vitals of our society. The fact that it continues to the extent it does erodes the respect of the individual, especially the poor, for law enforcement. It rots their faith in the equal application of the law to the white collar fraud-robber and to the family who cannot pay for shoddy merchandise they were tricked into buying by that self-same operator. It withers our moral fiber. It misdirects our economic resources. It saps the strength of our free enterprise system.

*Before Senate Commerce Committee,
Washington, Dec. 16.*

**Franklin I. Kral**
*Judge, City of Chicago;
specialist in urban housing*

Just about all public housing is a series of zoos. It makes animals out of people.

*Pub. Dec. 16.*

**L. S. B. Leakey**
*Archaeologist*

Feed the poor people's children; give them adequate health care. Don't worry about schools . . . if they have intelligence, they can catch up later. Don't worry about housing; just so it's warm. Feed them.

*Interview, Los Angeles, pub. March 16.*

**Claude Levi-Strauss**
*Anthropologist*

Most of the phenomena we encounter in mankind today and can expect in the coming decade are phenomena of a change of scale, linked, to put it simply, to the population explosion . . . What worries me is that the time may be coming when humanity will have such a feeling of getting in its own way that we will enter an era of massacre beside which these colonial wars would be absolutely nothing.

*Interview, Paris, pub. Dec. 31.*

**John V. Lindsay**
*Mayor of New York*

The same Congressmen who would laugh a rat-control bill off the floor, or who could spend hours debating the spending of $100,000 for a hunger study, would pass a $70 billion defense appropriation without a murmur, without debate, almost without a quorum—as I often saw on the floor of the House of Representatives . . . Indeed, I sometimes have thought that the fastest way to get funds for the cities is to introduce a national defense middle- and low-income housing bill.

*Polytechnic Institute of Brooklyn,
March 5.*

Welfare is damned by the left and the right, the liberals and conservatives alike. Welfare is resented by those who receive it. Welfare is derided by those who administer it. Welfare is hated by those who pay for it.

*New York, May 2.*

**Walter Lippmann**
*Author, Newspaper Columnist*

I don't take the view of those who say that the $25 billion, or whatever we spent on getting to the moon, should have been spent at home in clearing up the slums and so on, because I don't believe it would have been spent on that. I think under no conceivable circumstances would the Congress of the United States or the American taxpayer have voted all that money for any form of social improvement, because they couldn't have agreed on what improvement to spend it on. They'd have spent it,

(WALTER LIPPMANN)

instead, on liquor, cosmetics, television sets and whatnot.

*Interview, Seal Harbor, Me.,*
*pub. Sept. 14.*

### Carl M. Loeb
*President, National Council*
*on Crime and Delinquency*

I think the Government should operate gambling the way they do in six other countries and shortly will in Canada . . . When you do that, organized gambling can't compete . . . It would be nice for the Government to take that (money) in and then use it for the poor people who are losing it to the mobsters . . .

*Before Rotary Club, Boston, Oct. 1.*

### Charles Upton Lowe
*Chairman, Committee on Nutrition,*
*American Academy of Pediatrics*

Poverty is much more than a lack of cash. It is a way of life, all-pervading, crushing, immobilizing and destructive. It is self-perpetuating and infectious, spreading through regions like an infectious illness. And it is cruel, enervating and dehumanizing.

*Pub. Feb. 20.*

### Lester G. Maddox
*Governor of Georgia*

If President Nixon is able to get his new welfare program through Congress, he will go down in history as a crowning king.

*Aug. 9.*

I am opposed to the Federal Government taking over all the cost of welfare. This indicates a desire on the part of the States to abdicate their responsibility. It will bring about more centralization in the Federal Government.

*Pub. Sept. 15.*

Liberalism is wanting to do things for people that they can do on their own. Doing things for the underprivileged is my duty as a man who believes in God— and I do them only for the underprivileged, not the bums and parasites.

*Pub. Dec. 22.*

### Marya Mannes
*Author, Journalist*

With the condition the world is in today, to have a large family is a public disservice. It is monstrous self-indulgence and an anti-social act.

*Interview, Washington, pub. Nov. 10.*

### Catherine May
*United States Representative, R-Wash.*

The information gap between business and Congress must be closed or there may be one-sided decisions made in the name of consumer protection. It is no more fair for the housewife to put her thumb under the scale than it is for the butcher to put his on the scale.

*Before Los Angeles*
*Chamber of Commerce,*
*pub. June 3.*

### Jean Mayer
*Special Consultant on*
*Food, Nutrition and Health to the*
*President of the United States*

If we can give an overfed businessman a dinner in a plane flying at 600 miles an hour, 10 miles up, we ought to be able to feed poor children in a classroom.

*News conference, Washington, Sept. 10.*

I am concerned about the areas of the globe where people are rapidly becoming richer. For rich people occupy much more space, consume more of each resource, disturb the ecology more and create more land, air, water, chemical, thermal and radioactive pollution than poor people. So it can be argued that, from many viewpoints, it is even more urgent to control the numbers of the rich than it is to control the numbers of the poor.

*Washington, pub. Nov. 27.*

### George S. McGovern
*United States Senator, D-S.D.*

If we can get the concept established that the poorest people ought to get fed for free, we're well on the way to eliminating malnutrition in the United States.

*News conference, Washington, Feb. 20.*

I am at a loss to understand a sense of

priorities which places a highly questionable anti-ballistic missile system above the needs of our poorest children for food which can turn them from anemic, often brain-damaged victims of malnutrition into productive American citizens.

*Washington, March 22.*

I believe the Nixon Administration's efforts in food assistance constitute its most important domestic achievement in 1969. It has been a year of progress for which the present Administration deserves a major share of the credit.

*Pub. Dec. 29.*

**Floyd B. McKissick**
*Former Director,*
*Congress of Racial Equality*

People talk about a guaranteed income. I favor a guaranteed job.

*Interview, New York,*
*pub. Feb. 24.*

**Robert S. McNamara**
*President, International Bank for*
*Reconstruction and Development*

We are now on the brink of an agricultural revolution as significant as any development since the Industrial Revolution. The chances are probably 3 to 1 that, even with modest improvements between now and 1975, there won't be large-scale famine.

*Pub. Feb. 3.*

The threat of unmanageable population pressures is very much like the threat of nuclear war. Both threats are undervalued. Both threats can—and will—have catastrophic consequences unless they are dealt with rapidly and rationally.

*University of Notre Dame, May 1.*

We have shortages of food for the hungry, shortages of housing for the ill-housed, shortages of schools for the ill-educated, and we have surpluses of many, many goods in our society. Until we learn that there is nothing ethically wrong or politically unsound or economically disastrous in increasing procurement of goods in short supply, and reducing procurement of goods in surplus, we'll never solve the problems of hunger and poverty, either

domestically or internationally.

*Interview, Washington, pub. Nov. 9.*

**John N. Mitchell**
*Attorney General of the United States*

The prior Administration attempted to solve problems through the illusion of words—through the projection of succeeding images of impossible dreams, which were replaced by more impossible dreams when previous commitments could not be met. (As a result) the poor and the black who had relied on Utopian promises . . . now distrust the government's ability to act on their behalf.

*Milwaukee, Nov. 11.*

**Rogers C. B. Morton**
*United States Representative, R-Md.*

How can we expect people who live with rats and filth and squalor to embrace the American dream?

*Pub. Feb. 27.*

**Daniel P. Moynihan**
*Assistant to the President*
*of the United States for Urban Affairs*

. . . many of the problems we now associate with black Americans are simply problems of poor Americans and Americans who don't have a stable place in the employment market . . . The problem of the poor people is they don't have enough money, and I would put my faith in any effort that put more resources into the hands of those that don't now have them. Cold cash—it's a surprisingly good cure for a lot of social ills.

*Television interview,*
*Washington, Feb. 2.*

Efforts to improve the conditions of life in the present caste-created slums must never take precedence over efforts to enable the slum population to disperse throughout the metropolitan areas involved.

*Syracuse University, May 8.*

**George Murphy**
*United States Senator, R-Calif.*

In outlawing minimum residency requirements for potential welfare recip-

(GEORGE MURPHY)

ients, the Supreme Court has once again blatantly exercised its self-induced disposition to meddle and muddle, and, in so doing, has prepared a financial load for California's already overburdened taxpayers. We Californians are tired of having our State used as a test laboratory for sociological experiments. We are fed up with being treated as guinea pigs.

*Washington, April 22.*

## Ralph Nader
*Lawyer, Consumer Rights Advocate*

The socialization, the fraternization, the comradeship, the first-name familiarity between (Interstate Commerce) commissioners and the (travel) industry people is one of the most important underminers of the public interest.

*Interview, Washington, pub. Aug. 24.*

## Richard M. Nixon
*President of the United States*

In the final analysis, we cannot talk our way out of poverty; we cannot legislate our way out of poverty; but this nation can work its way out of poverty. What America needs now is not more welfare, but more "workfare." The task of this Government, the task of our people, is to provide the training for work, the incentive to work, the opportunity to work and the reward for work.

To put it bluntly and simply—any (welfare) system which makes it more profitable for a man not to work than to work, and which encourages a man to desert his family rather than stay with his family, is wrong and indefensible.

*Television address,*
*Washington, Aug. 8.*

Dreams of unlimited billions of dollars being released once the war in Vietnam ends are just that—dreams. True, there will be additional money—but the claims on it already are enormous. There should be no illusion that what some call the "peace and growth dividend" will automatically solve our national problems.

*At National Governors Conference,*
*Colorado Springs, Colo., Sept. 1.*

## Otis G. Pike
*United States Representative, D-N.Y.*

Old ships (in the U.S. Navy, and the need to replace them)? Yes, and we have old schools and old hospitals and old highways, too. Our air smells old, our water tastes old and there are people who are old and not being adequately cared for . . .

*Washington, pub. Oct. 5.*

## Bertram L. Podell
*United States Representative, D-N.Y.*

Instead of (tax) reform, what will we receive? In the name of peace and defense, we shall genuflect ever deeper before Mars. More shiny toys for the military. More preference for oil companies which rob the public. More cross-Brooklyn expressways which threaten neighborhoods. More rich subsidized farmers. More auto pollution. More riots. More traffic jams. New aircraft carriers of the "sitting duck" class. More millionaires who pay no taxes. Higher supermarket prices. More fat and rotten chicken in hot dogs . . . While buildings rot. And paint peels. And potholes grow deeper. And rats scurry. And waters darken. And air thickens. And lakes die. And rivers foul. And sirens wail. And trains run slower and collide more often. And taxpayers flee. And poverty spreads. And the elderly sink into deep despair. And drugs cost more. And hatred deepens. And violence gets bloodier. And tear gas plops. And sewers and drains smell worse. And airports clog up further. And the administration watches.

*Before the House,*
*Washington, Sept. 4.*

Prosperity deteriorates before our eyes. Men are losing their jobs. Homes and other necessities are increasingly out of the reach of millions. All the while, the administration is worrying about how to better help out the rich. Heaven help us if this is the logic governing the reasoning of our elected leaders. They are carrying on a holy war against working people and horsesense.

*Before the House,*
*Washington, Sept. 9.*

**Carl Rachlin**
*General Counsel,*
*National Welfare Rights Organization*

The Nixon (welfare) proposal clearly calls into question the Administration's credibility in the eyes of poor people. First, it sets an income maintenance standard they cannot survive on—indeed, no one can survive on. Second, the present welfare system is an atrocity created by the states, and the new one would only seem to give the states greater freedom to act oppressively with job mandates and so forth. The states will be able to operate without any constraint by the Federal Government. The proposal, as I read it, will end all the basic rights presently insured by the Social Security Act . . .

*Pub. Aug. 16.*

**Merrill S. Read**
*Program Director,*
*Growth and Development Branch,*
*National Institute of Child Health*
*and Human Development*

Providing food is not enough to solve malnutrition. Malnutrition is part of a constellation of social problems. We can cure hunger by feeding people. Malnutrition takes a long time.

*University of California at Irvine,*
*June 6.*

**Joseph Reid**
*Executive Director,*
*Child Welfare League of America*

We need a complete and radical re-examination of our whole philosophy on parental rights. We need a hard evaluation of judicial decisions and interpretations of statutes. Perhaps, most of all, we need an educational campaign to establish the rights of the child as paramount, even above the rights of parents—certainly equal to the rights of parents. Parenthood means more than fathering or giving birth to a child. If a parent abandons, neglects or abuses a child, his rights to the child should be terminated.

*Pub. July 27.*

**James A. Rhodes**
*Governor of Ohio*

All of our social ills among the able-bodied on welfare come from lack of education and training. The present welfare system as we know it is bankrupt. The National Guard and crime control acts are not the answer. We are reaping the results of 35 years on the dole instead of educating people for jobs.

*At Midwestern Governors Conference,*
*Wichita, Kans., June 30.*

Welfare is a national disgrace. All the social ills among able-bodied people in Ohio come from unemployment . . . We've been giving doles and handouts instead of job training and education. The way to break through the cycle is through vocational education. Unless we do this, we just compound the misery of the poor.

*News Conference, Washington, July 17.*

**George W. Romney**
*Secretary of Housing and*
*Urban Development of the United States*

. . . the people of this country would respond in overwhelming numbers if their leaders asked them to give "a tithe of time" in constructive volunteer effort. Four hours—10 per cent of a 40-hour week—spent in well-conceived volunteer effort at the local level could reshape America faster than Federal programs ever will.

*Pub. Jan. 25.*

There is even a higher goal than reaching for the stars of the physical universe which lies beyond our planet. The higher goal is to reach for other stars in the universe of human potential . . . How much more meaningful our accomplishment would be if we were to carry to completion in the '70s our 20-year goal of a decent home and a suitable living environment for all Americans, rather than content ourselves with setting another priority goal in space on the heels of our landing on the moon.

*Washington, July 22.*

I think it is time we recognized that we do not really promote our welfare or that of our country by creating isolated enclaves composed of people of the same economic and social and racial back-

(GEORGE W. ROMNEY)

grounds.

*Interview, Washington, pub. July 28.*

It is only the minority of Americans, desperate for decent housing, who feel the impact of our housing shortage and high costs. In recent opinion surveys of the public problems most on people's minds, housing is not at the top or near the top of the domestic list. It should be.

*Before Mortgage Bankers Association of America, New York, Oct. 20.*

**Benjamin S. Rosenthal**
*United States Representative, D-N.Y.*

Today's typical consumer is tempted into the marketplace by promises of product perfection. But the system that produces, promotes, sells and services that product can more accurately be characterized by the reality of planned obsolescence and poor quality control.

*Before New York State Council of Retail Merchants, Ellenville, N.Y., Oct. 5.*

**Hilary J. Sandoval**
*Administrator,*
*Small Business Administration*
*of the United States*

I believe in selling free enterprise instead of welfare.

*Washington, pub. Feb. 21.*

**Richard Sanville**
*Executive Director,*
*Regional Family Planning Council*
*of Los Angeles*

Most of the problems of our times— smog, water pollution, poverty, violence, crime, congestion—are all caused by the fact that we're practicing death control (improved medical care for the elderly, longer life spans) without birth control. We need some important world figure, like Mr. Nixon, to get up and say again and again, "Listen, world, this beautiful island in space we live on is no longer to be beautiful because we can no longer support the number of people who are

here and who are going to be here, and we've got to do something about it."

*Los Angeles, pub. July 23.*

**Glenn T. Seaborg**
*Chairman, Atomic Energy Commission*
*of the United States*

In years ahead, today's outcries about the environment will be nothing compared to cries of angry citizens who find power failures, due to lack of sufficient generating capacity, have plunged them into prolonged blackouts—not mere minutes, but hours, perhaps days—when their health and well-being and that of their families may be seriously endangered. The environment of a city whose life energy has been cut, whose transportation and communications are dead, in which medical and police help cannot be had and where food spoils and people ·stifle or shiver while imprisoned in stalled subways or darkened skyscrapers—all this also represents a dangerous environment.

*Before Joint Congressional Committee on Atomic Energy, Washington, Oct. 29.*

**Betty Shapiro**
*International President,*
*B'nai B'rith Women*

We are non-political, but I cannot help (but) feel some frustration with President Nixon's Family Welfare Program, which is not slated to go into effect until 1971. What happens between now and then? Are people going to starve and die in ghettos because Government projects won't get going for a couple of years? Time is precious.

*Montreal, pub. Sept. 4.*

**George P. Shultz**
*Secretary of Labor of the United States*

A welfare job is no substitute for a welfare check.

*Before House Ways and Means Committee, Washington, Oct. 16.*

**Charles B. Shuman**
*President, American*
*Farm Bureau Federation*

Like all its predecessor national emergency programs, the hunger program will probably result in a huge federal bureaucracy busily soliciting clients to put on the free food list. By making it easy to get food without work, many people will be encouraged to reduce their efforts to help themselves and thus become eligible for food stamps. The hunger situation may actually worsen rather than improve under this kind of approach.

*Before American Farm Bureau Federation, Washington, Dec. 9.*

**Edward V. Sparer**
*Professor of Law,*
*University of Pennsylvania*

On balance, even though some important principles are advanced by the (Nixon welfare) plan, I consider it a step backwards. Our single greatest need in welfare today is to define and guarantee an adequate money grant to the poor. No state welfare system does that today. This Nixon plan does not help, and may hurt, that issue.

*Pub. Aug. 16.*

We guarantee income to farmers for not producing crops. We guarantee subsidies to railroads and to oil companies. It seems to me only reasonable that we should guarantee the subsidy of life to those who are starving and to those without shelter or medicine—reasonable not only on humanitarian grounds, but because there is a 14th Amendment, which guarantees equal protection of the laws.

*Interview, pub. Sept. 28.*

**Herbert Stein**
*Member, Council of Economic*
*Advisers to the President*
*of the United States*

There will be no Santa Claus when the Vietnam war ends. It is unrealistic to think that, if resources were released from defense programs, they will automatically become available for social programs.

*Pub. Oct. 19.*

**Dirk U. Stikker**
*Former Secretary-General,*
*North Atlantic Treaty Organization*

We cannot continue to live in an uncommitted, impenetrable castle of affluence in the midst of a global slum.

*San Francisco, pub. Sept. 21.*

**James L. Sundquist**
*Senior Fellow, Brookings Institution*

. . . the historic significance of the Nixon (welfare) program is simply that the war on poverty goes on. What was conceived in the Great Society days in an atmosphere of partisanship is now confirmed by the country's conservative party as a bipartisan national objective.

*Pub. Aug. 16.*

**Richard Turner**
*Attorney General of Iowa*

I think the Iowa (welfare) law requiring a one-year residence is completely justified. I think these people (welfare recipients) ought to have to wait a reasonable time before dipping their hands into our pockets.

*Pub. May 5.*

**John Veneman**
*Under Secretary of Health,*
*Education and Welfare*
*of the United States*

The only way to break the cycle of welfare is to direct our efforts to the children. We must do something for the child *before* the school gets him. By then, it's too late.

*Pub. March 17.*

**Kenneth E. F. Watt**
*Professor of Zoology,*
*University of California at Davis*

If we can't lick the population problem, we'll have to increase the size of the planet or put people in eight-by-eight-foot cells and feed them algae. I'm not proposing these things, but people have to face up to the necessity of birth control if they want freedom to move around, to be healthy, to have a balanced diet, to live like humans.

*Pub. Aug. 15.*

**George A. Wiley**
*Director, National*
*Welfare Rights Organization*

. . . there is no such thing as an illegiti-

(GEORGE A. WILEY)

mate child. We say every child is a legitimate child. We say every child who draws breath in this country is something to be loved, something to be wanted, something to have the opportunity to grow and to develop.

*Washington, April 25.*

**Harrison A. Williams, Jr.**
*United States Senator, D-N.J.*

None of us likes to admit there are starving people in the nation, but we know there are—and many of them are old. We know that they' exist, and yet we do not know to what extent, nor do we know where they are. Looking away will not make the problem disappear.

*Before Senate hearing on nutrition of the elderly poor, Washington, Sept. 9.*

**Harry A. Wilmer**
*University of California*
*School of Medicine*

Most of our runaway children are pushaway children.

*Pub. March 18.*

**Marshall Windmiller**
*Professor of International Relations,*
*San Francisco State College*

Rather than send scholars to developing countries to investigate how the skills and resources of the United States might be utilized to help their development, we might send scholars, bureaucrats and community leaders to the developed countries to study these governmental functions which they do better than we do. It would serve truth (as well as health) for Americans to be better informed about the social security and Medicare systems of Western Europe, which by some accounts are decades in advance of our own.

*Before American Psychological Association, Washington, pub. Sept. 7.*

**Lester L. Wolff**
*United States Representative, D-N.Y.*

It has been clearly demonstrated that trading stamps add 2 per cent to the cost of food for the average family. Since the annual cost of food is $50 billion, this means the annual cost of trading stamps is $1 billion . . . Without the cost of trading stamps, every American family could have the equivalent of one week's groceries free every year.

*Before Federal Trade Commission, Washington, Feb. 24.*

**Wendell Wyatt**
*United States Representative, R-Ore.*

For the first 1,600 years since Christ, the earth's population doubled from 250 million to 500 million. It took 100 years for the earth's population to double from one billion to two billion, and our world's population will be four billion in a period of just fifteen years, by 1975. At this rate, in thirty more years, by the year 2000, the earth's population will be *seven* billion persons. After that, it is predicted that one billion people will be added to our population at least every five years. We are literally turning our planet into a human ant hill.

*Before State convention, AFL-CIO, Portland, Ore., Sept. 26.*

**Whitney M. Young, Jr.**
*Executive Director,*
*National Urban League*

We have asked for a domestic Marshall Plan; instead, we get a domestic missile plan.
*Television interview, New York, April 7.*

By its own spending actions, the government makes a mockery of its claim that it can't afford vital and long overdue social programs. If war-inspired inflation is a problem, let's have wage and price controls such as all countries have when they are at war. Let's have meaningful tax reforms that close the loop-holes available to the rich, instead of a surtax that affects all . . . But let's not ask the poor, who have waited so long and so patiently, to wait still further—for the war's end, or for completion of costly and questionable military hardware purchases before they get their fair share of America.

*Before National Urban League, Washington, July 28.*

**Joseph M. Barr**
*Mayor of Pittsburgh*

The key problem is that the city depends mainly upon real estate taxes for revenue. And that is a losing game. You cannot build a modern city on a real estate tax base. We have raised real estate taxes to the point where they cannot be raised much more, homeowners cannot take it any more. If we tried to raise real estate taxes now, our bridges would not be wide enough to accommodate all the people fleeing, bag and baggage, to outlying areas. We are killing the goose that laid the golden egg.
*Interview, Pittsburgh, pub. April 21.*

**Joseph W. Barr**
*Former Under Secretary of the Treasury of the United States*

. . . the middle classes are likely to revolt against income taxes not because of the level or the amount of taxes they must pay, but because certain provisions of the tax laws unfairly lighten the burdens of others who can afford to pay . . . Our income tax system needs major reforms now, as a matter of importance and urgency.
*Washington, pub. Jan. 19.*

**John W. Byrnes**
*United States Representative, R-Wis.*

. . . why couldn't the taxpayers submit certain data to the Government? Then the Government would run it through a computer and send the taxpayer a form, all filled out, except for his signature. If he agreed with the total, he would sign the form and pay his bill. If he didn't, he could argue with the Internal Revenue Service.
*Pub. Feb. 10.*

**Mortimer M. Caplin**
*Former Commissioner,*
*Internal Revenue Service*
*of the United States*

It soon becomes apparent (regarding tax inequities) that the definitions of "reform" and "loopholes" vary greatly among us, depending on our individual economic and social circumstances. A loophole to one is frequently a life line of economic survival to another; and often the reform program we favor most vigorously is the one that takes away from someone else the tax benefits on which he has relied for many years.
*Pub. Feb. 24.*

**Sheldon S. Cohen**
*Former Commissioner,*
*Internal Revenue Service*
*of the United States*

The ideal revenue commissioner is not necessarily an accountant or a technician, although I believe he ought to have some technical skill. But, most importantly, he must be a business manager, capable of running an organization that affects 115 million taxpayers, with 65,000 employees and a budget of 750 million dollars a year. Beyond that, I would tell my successor the job is all right, provided he wears asbestos pants and doesn't pay much attention to what people say about him.
*Interview, Washington, pub. Feb. 3.*

**Wilbur J. Cohen**
*Former Secretary of Health,*
*Education and Welfare*
*of the United States*

There are many moderate-income retired people who are now paying tax, and

(WILBUR J. COHEN)

many high-income people who are paying
no tax. Is this a fair burden? I don't think
it is.

> *Before House Ways and Means
> Committee, Washington, March 3.*

**Vance O. Hartke**
*United States Senator, D-Ind.*

Apparently President Nixon believes that
his Forgotten American is a president of a
corporation.

> *Before the Senate, Washington,
> pub. Oct. 3.*

**Michael J. Howlett**
*Auditor, State of Illinois*

I am for revenue-sharing. The states and
local governments need more money from
the federal government. But I question
the proposal to award bonuses to the
states and local governments with a record of "tax effort," meaning those that
take the biggest bite from the personal
income tax dollar of their residents.

> *Before National Association of
> State Auditors, Comptrollers and
> Treasurers, Jackson Hole, Wyo., Sept. 1.*

**Charles S. Joelson**
*United States Representative, D-N.J.*

The hot issue today is tax reform. It's the
middle class—the people who earn from
$8000 to $20,000 a year—who are saying,
"You have helped the poor and the wealthy, but not us." The middle class has now
found its voice and is articulating. Congress will not be able to ignore demands of
the middle class for correction of unfair
tax laws.

> *Pub. April 28.*

**Vivien Kellems**
*Industrialist*

Income tax is like a pregnancy. They
both start small but soon swell to alarm-
ing proportions. Eventually they both
must terminate.

> *Interview, pub. Dec. 14.*

**David M. Kennedy**
*Secretary of the Treasury
of the United States*

If you stopped the war in Vietnam today

or tomorrow, which would be the best
thing on earth, it wouldn't change my
recommendation on the need for the surtax one iota.

> *Interview, Washington, pub. June 19.*

Everyone welcomes lower taxes; but
there is a point at which too deep a slash
in federal revenues could perhaps force
retrenchment in important domestic programs and even increase the already severe
inflationary pressures, which, in the long
run, would cost all of us much more than
any temporary gain we might get through
tax reductions.

> *At dedication of new Philadelphia Mint,
> Aug. 14.*

**Thomas J. McIntyre**
*United States Senator, D-N.H.*

To many people, and with good justification, the tax treatment of the oil industry is the most notorious of the many
loopholes now in our tax laws . . . Elimination of the oil depletion allowance is
synonymous with tax reform.

> *Before the Senate, Washington, Sept. 12.*

**George Meany**
*President, American Federation of
Labor-Congress of
Industrial Organizations*

The single most costly loophole, and the
one that is the prime culprit of unfairness,
is the capital-gains loophole (under which
long-term income gains are subject to only
a 50 per cent tax). We see no justice to a
tax provision which says that a married
taxpayer with $8,000 in capital gains should
pay a tax of $354, while a married tax-
payer with the same amount of wage
income should pay $1,000.

> *Before Senate Finance Committee,
> Washington, Sept. 22.*

**Wilbur D. Mills**
*United States Senator, D-Ark.*

Anybody who enjoys some preferential
(tax) treatment should be required to come
to the Congress periodically and make
his case before the public . . .

> *Pub. Feb. 21.*

**Joseph G. Minish**
*United States Representative, D-N.J.*

At least on a par with Vietnam is the

question of taxes and tax reform. People are more alert now to inequities in the tax laws—the loopholes. The people want a fair shake. They are willing to pay their share, but don't like it when they see that Joe Jones earns a million dollars and pays almost no tax. People wonder what is going on when this is allowed to happen.

*Pub. April 28.*

**Walter F. Mondale**
*United States Senator, D-Minn.*

Although (tax) reform is needed, I believe the record of the private foundations in this country is such that we ought to support them and stand behind them in their magnificent work. All of us know that many of the creative ideas with which we deal here in Government, which we see in our country, are derived from the splendid work of these worthy foundations. I think anybody who wants to cut off that dynamic and creative and competitive area of life threatens to diminish and reduce the vitality of our nation.

*Before the Senate, Washington, Dec. 5.*

**Frank E. Moss**
*United States Senator, D-Utah*

If we don't succeed in achieving genuine tax reform, if we don't require rich people to pay their share of the tax burden, and if we don't relieve the middle income citizen who has had his backbone bent by taxes for far too long, I think we may have a tax mutiny on our hands in this country.

*Before Senate Finance Committee, Washington, Sept. 29.*

**Richard M. Nixon**
*President of the United States*

Eight months ago, I submitted a sweeping set of proposals to the Congress for the first major tax reform in 15 years, one which would make our tax system more fair. My proposals were carefully balanced to avoid increasing the pressure on prices that were already rising too fast. Congress has passed an unbalanced bill that is both good and bad. The tax reforms, on the whole, are good; the effect on the budget and on the cost of living is bad . . . Seldom is any piece of major legislation fully satisfactory to a President. This bill is surely no exception. But I sign it because I believe that, on balance, it is a necessary beginning in the process of making our tax system fair to the taxpayer.

*Washington, Dec. 30.*

**Wright Patman**
*United States Representative, D-Tex.*

. . . most bluntly, philanthropy—one of mankind's more noble instincts—has been perverted into a vehicle for institutionalized, deliberate evasion of fiscal (taxes) and moral responsibility to the nation . . .

*Before House Ways and Means Committee, Washington, Feb. 18.*

**Jeno Paulucci**
*Founder, Chun King Corporation*

I've paid close to $25 million in taxes in my life and have been glad to do it. Where else but in America can a man with the name Jeno Paulucci go into the Chinese food business in a Scandinavian state (Minnesota) within the shadow of iron ore dumps and end up worth close to $100 million? The small working guy is paying too much in taxes, and the money just has to come from corporations and rich people.

*Pub. Sept. 29.*

**William Proxmire**
*United States Senator, D-Wis.*

The 10% surtax has been a complete failure. It was passed to slow inflation, to reduce interest rates and to improve our international trade business. It has not only failed to achieve any of these objectives . . . the inflationary outlook is actually worse now then it was last July, when the surtax went into effect.

*Before the Senate, Washington, March 17.*

Any tax system which requires 2,200,000 people under the poverty level to pay federal income taxes, yet allows Atlantic Richfield (Oil Company) to earn over $464,000,000 between 1964 and 1967 without paying one red cent in federal income taxes clearly requires revision . . . Imagine, gigantic Richfield paid less in federal income taxes than the janitor who cleaned this room last night.

*Before Senate Finance Committee, Washington, Sept. 30.*

**John D. Rockefeller, III**
*Philanthropist*

I believe that all individuals who are able should pay some reasonable tax, including those who have become entitled to the unlimited deduction privilege. A figure of 10 to 15 per cent of adjusted gross income occurs to me as a reasonable tax for such individuals.

> *Before House Ways and Means Committee, Washington, Feb. 27.*

**Mitchell Rogovin**
*Former Assistant Attorney General of the United States*

. . . achieving tax reform is like chasing the bluebird of happiness. You never catch it.

> *Pub. Feb. 24.*

**Charles L. Schultze**
*Former Director, Bureau of the Budget of the United States*

When the chips are down on tax cuts, those who talked about priorities for pollution control and education and an end to hunger voted for beer and cosmetics and whitewall tires.

> *Pub. Dec. 26.*

**Dan Throop Smith**
*Professor of Finance, Harvard University*

I don't think any tax is good. I am inclined to say the least bad is the best. But income taxes, at rates anything like we have now, must inevitably produce many distortions. I know we must have very high federal revenues for a long time to come, and it would seem better to have a variety of taxes with not very high rates rather than a single tax with very high rates . . .

> *Interview, pub. April.*

**Stanley S. Surrey**
*Assistant Secretary of the Treasury of the United States*

There is no one so pessimistic about the future of his country or his industry as a taxpayer who is about to lose a tax preference.

> *Before Senate Finance Committee, Washington, Sept. 25.*

**Joseph D. Tydings**
*United States Senator, D-Md.*

The surtax is a regressive levy. It falls most heavily on those who can least afford it. Extending it can only be justified if steps are taken to offset this regression by closing the loopholes that riddle our Federal tax structure.

> *Pub. June 2.*

**Robert C. Tyson**
*Chairman, Finance Committee, U.S. Steel Corporation*

. . . tax reform represents to many a citizen the opportunity to practice tax-manship—that is, that "a good tax is a tax that the other fellow pays and a bad tax is a tax that I pay." Consider, for example, the proposal to plug the so-called loophole of tax exemption of municipal bond interest. To be sure, the purchaser of such a bond saves some taxes—but at the price of a smaller yield than he could have gotten on, say, a taxable corporate bond of comparable risk. If municipal bonds were no longer in the tax-exempt category, their yields would naturally have to rise, forcing municipalities to increase local tax rates unless otherwise relieved. As now proposed in the House Tax Reform Bill, a Federal subsidy would provide at least partial relief . . . So I believe that far and away the most important long-range tax reform for economic development, and for the general wellbeing of both the public and private sectors, is tax reduction. Let me hurriedly add that tax reduction presupposes expenditure control. At any rate . . . a tax cut is the kindest cut of all.

> *Before Governor's State Economic Development Conference, Salt Lake City, pub. Aug. 26.*

**Charles E. Walker**
*Under Secretary of the Treasury of the United States*

In February, following the January disclosures relating to the now famous taxless millionaires, the Treasury Department gripe mail on taxes exceeded the total for all of 1968. You can be sure that these same taxpayers also wrote their congressmen. Following income tax payments in April —with the 7½ per cent for the surcharge added—the volume of mail rose even higher . . . The message that came through in both letters and personal contacts was loud and clear: close the loopholes and make the tax system fair. Polls have indicated that this feeling was so deeply held by so many people that the foundations of our voluntary system for payment of federal income taxes might well have been threatened.

*Before American Bankers Association,*
*Honolulu, Sept. 30.*

# Transportation

**Willis C. Armstrong**
*Associate Dean, School of*
*International Affairs, Columbia University*

If a man wants to go to Cuba by commercial aircraft, he has to go to Mexico and take a plane to Cuba. It is a long way; it costs a great deal of money. It is cheaper to buy a gun.
*Before Canadian Senate Committee,*
*Ottawa, Canada, Sept. 3.*

**James G. Brown**
*Pilot, National Airlines*

. . . this (airplane hijacking) is no joke. It is a tragedy waiting for someplace to happen.
*Washington, pub. Feb. 17.*

**Virginia Mae Brown**
*Chairman, Interstate Commerce*
*Commission of the United States*

We now have 100 less trains providing service to the public than we had in mid-1968. We have about 60 others involved in discontinuance proceedings. If this trend continues, it seems clear that we are approaching the end of the tracks for the passenger train. It does not have to be that way.
*Washington, pub. Sept. 28.*

**Gordon A. Christenson**
*Professor of Law,*
*University of Oklahoma*

Why is it that we can become nationally aroused by a single murder, but be completely passive about 55,000 horrible deaths on the highways each year?
*Washington, pub. Feb. 23.*

**W. Graham Claytor, Jr.**
*President, Southern Railway System*

In spite of our admitted problems, in spite of strong competition from other modes, and in spite of all the pot shots taken at us from various governmental and financial quarters, the railroads of this country are on the move, are working together as they never have before to solve their common problems and not merely complain about them, and . . . as a result, the railroads are going to be a greater, not a lesser, factor in transportation in the great decade of the 1970s.
*Pub. Dec. 21.*

**Edward N. Cole**
*President, General Motors Corporation*

Charges by our critics which imply that we, as an industry, are purposely short-changing the public are not only unrealistic —but from a business point of view are ridiculous. We pay a high penalty for defects in terms of costs for recall campaigns and warranty expenses—but we pay even more dearly in customer satisfaction and less in owner loyalty which have detrimental effects on repeat sales and public reputations.
*Martinsburg, W. Va., June 13.*

**Thomas F. Eagleton**
*United States Senator, D-Mo.*

If Malthus were alive today, he might well be calculating the rapid increase in automobiles and commuters, while noting with great alarm the failure of roadways, despite the addition of many new limited-access highways, to meet their transportation needs. It takes no Malthusian scholar to predict the cataclysmic consequences of these trends.
*St. Louis, pub. April 6.*

**James D. Edgett**
*Chairman, North American Van Lines*

I think I am safe in saying that our economy, as we know it today, wouldn't exist without the truck . . . We just couldn't possibly get along without them . . . Speaking of our own company, I think that we need government and need it badly. I think that the trucking industry would be chaotic without Interstate Commerce Commission controls . . .

*Interview, pub. February.*

**Henry Ford, II**
*Chairman, Ford Motor Company*

We can build a tank, if you want to ride around in a tank; you won't get hurt. You won't be able to afford one, though. Neither will I.

*Interview, Dearborn, Mich., pub. Oct. 19.*

**J. William Fulbright**
*United States Senator, D-Ark.*

The administration talks about saving money, and then decides to allocate huge sums of money for this plane (the supersonic transport). And to make it a matter of prestige represents the worst form of vanity.

*Washington, Sept. 23.*

**Thomas M. Goodfellow**
*President, Association of American Railroads*

We often hear the argument that the railroads have to keep passenger trains running because the highways and airways are over-crowded, and these services are subject to interruptions when the weather is bad . . . we can, and do, disagree with the implication that a private industry should pick up the tab for what amounts to rainy-day, stand-by services.

*Washington, pub. Sept. 28.*

**William Haddon, Jr.**
*President, Insurance Institute for Highway Safety*

Highway crashes and their consequences represent a national problem area, one which accounts for death, human misery and impairment, and economic loss on a scale that the average person does not comprehend. It is one of the tragedies of our time that we so long have permitted this

situation to evolve without committing resources to the development of countermeasures at a level at all commensurate with the problem.

*Before Senate Commerce Subcommittee, Washington, pub. April 21.*

**Philip A. Hart**
*United States Senator, D-Mich.*

More than 53,000 Americans are killed on the highways each year, and more than 10,000 are injured each day. Those injured exceed the aggregate of all crimes of violence by nearly 10 to 1. I think it is about time we recognized that all this is not caused by "pilot error," but that maintenance—and the bad luck we have with (auto) repairs—has more than a casual relationship to the totals.

*Washington, June 1.*

**Vance O. Hartke**
*United States Senator, D-Ind.*

For years the general public and people in government have assumed, incorrectly, that railroad safety is primarily a problem to be dealt with by the railroads themselves. This myopia has allowed an extremely dangerous situation to develop. The sad truth is that Federal laws pertaining to railroad safety are grossly inadequate.

*Washington, pub. June 2.*

We're on our way to Mars. We're going to spend $1 billion in taxpayers' money to build this high-speed airplane (supersonic transport), and I can't get from Indianapolis to Chicago on a decent train.

*Washington, Sept. 23.*

**Semon E. Knudsen**
*President, Ford Motor Company*

It is worth remembering that in the first two decades of this century streetcar congestion was widely regarded as the curse of the cities. To say that the automobile is the cause of urban congestion is like saying the sniffle causes the cold. By making it possible for the city to spread out its residential areas and to decentralize its commercial, cultural and recreational areas, the automobile actually has been

(SEMON E. KNUDSEN)

the greatest single contributor toward relieving urban congestion.

*Before Society of Automotive Engineers, Detroit, Jan. 15.*

**William P. Lear**
*President, Lear Jet Corporation*

I foresee the auto companies putting out steam cars within five years.

*Interview, New York, pub. April 7.*

I don't see any possibility of adoption of a steam car. It is so utterly ridiculous. No one is going to do it. It is just too complicated. You couldn't find a garage mechanic who could fix one. It is practically unserviceable by the average gas station. I told the Federal Government this, much to their chagrin. They thought the steam car was the answer to the pollution problem, and I was the savior. But I let them down.

*Detroit, pub. Nov. 13.*

**Charles A. Lindbergh**
*Aviator*

We've reached the point (in aviation) where it's very difficult to look into the future—maybe more difficult than it has been since the early days. For many years we've been able to see the improvements coming—in speed, in lower fares and increased ranges and more comfort and safety. It's now awfully hard to project this forward in the same way. It looks as though we have reached the point where the future of aviation depends on things outside of aviation—on economy, on politics, on war, on the unforeseen. Therefore, to look into our future, we have to look outside of our industry more than ever in the past.

*Before Air Line Pilots Association, pub. May 24.*

**Robert Monagan**
*California State Assemblyman*

Cars kill cities just as surely as they kill people. It could be that we are building the world's biggest freeway system to serve the world's biggest ghost town.

*Pub. Nov. 7.*

**Ralph Nader**
*Lawyer, Consumer Rights Advocate*

(Railroading) is the only industry I know of where a company has made toilet maintenance part of its cost-cutting program. The railroads have tried to make toilets so dirty that people just won't use them. This is just part of the total effort to drive passengers away.

*Pub. December.*

**Joseph O'Connell**
*Chairman, National Transportation Safety Board*

With the railroads hauling more hazardous materials, the potential for catastrophic accidents bothers the hell out of me.

*Pub. March 7.*

**Charles H. Percy**
*United States Senator, R-Ill.*

Development of the SST (supersonic transport) is essential to preserve the primacy of the United States in world civilian aircraft markets, and to prevent an even more serious erosion of the balance of payments deficit.

*Washington, Sept. 23.*

**Bertram L. Podell**
*United States Representative, D-N.Y.*

After torpedoing the urban mass-transit fund, and preventing significant Justice Department action on automobile pollution, the Government now turns around and subsidizes a plan (the SST) that will allow us to cross the ocean in two hours so we may be stuck in traffic jams for three.

*Pub. Sept. 29.*

**William Proxmire**
*United States Senator, D-Wis.*

(The proposed supersonic transport plane is) a frill, a plaything for the jet set.

*Washington, Sept. 23.*

... there is actually only one justification for the U.S. decision to develop an SST: national prestige and competition ... The United States already demonstrated its technological superiority by winning the race to land a man on the moon. It should be obvious ... that the United States cannot hope to be first in everything; it should be enough that in achieving an escape from the earth's gravity, it was the United States that had the capability, and developed the technological know-how, to succeed in this effort. This was an achievement that some have said was the greatest since the Creation . . . How many times must we prove ourselves?

*Before the Senate, Washington, Sept. 26.*

There are just two extremely strong arguments for the (Boeing) SST—one is the senior Senator from Washington, and the other is the junior Senator from Washington.

*Pub. Dec. 30.*

**Ogden R. Reid**
*United States Representative, R-N.Y.*

As our highways become increasingly crowded, our air increasingly polluted, and our green spaces diminished as a result of the American citizenry's reliance on automobile transportation, it becomes more and more clear that the railroads could play a very important role in public transportation in this country—a role on which they have defaulted in recent years. I am hopeful that as a result of (proposed legislation) rail service will be upgraded to the point where travelers in this country will once again find it safe, economical, reliable and efficient. Only when that happens will we begin to solve the problems of traffic jams on the highways and ease the air pollution caused by automobiles.

*Before the House, Washington, Sept. 18.*

**Henry S. Reuss**
*United States Representative, D-Wis.*

We simply cannot allow Concordes and SST's to assault the peace and quiet of millions of Americans just so a few jetsetters can get where they're going a few hours faster.

*Washington, Nov. 11.*

**Michael Rock**
*Chairman, Professional Air Traffic Controllers Organization*

Too many of our airports today are accidents waiting to happen. It's a credit to our men that more accidents haven't hap-

pened. They've patched this system and patched this system, but now we've run out of band-aids.

*Pub. Aug. 18.*

**Benjamin S. Rosenthal**
*United States Representative, D-N.Y.*

Something is wrong with a system which permits a private pilot with only 38 hours of experience to be in the same air space where an airliner is descending for a landing.

*News conference, Overseas Press Club, New York, Sept. 12.*

**Stuart Saunders**
*Chairman, Penn-Central Railroad*

The obsolescence of present railroad passenger service is a by-product of a lop-sided and haphazard transportation system, which has paid little attention to a balanced utilization of all modes of transport.

*Washington, pub. Sept. 28.*

**David D. Thomas**
*Deputy Administrator,*
*Federal Aviation Administration*

I am frequently asked why, if we know enough to land a man on a moon, we can't land a man in New York at 5 p.m. on a Friday afternoon. The answer is that we know enough, but we have invested $24 billion getting to the moon and only $1.5 billion in air traffic and navigation facilities since the Wright Brothers' flight.

*Pub. August.*

**Clifton F. von Kann**
*Vice president, Air Transport Association*

The FAA's proposed airport capacity limitations are about as responsive to the true problem we face today as a band-aid is to a broken leg.

*New York, pub. Feb. 9.*

**John A. Volpe**
*Secretary of Transportation*
*of the United States*

It will be the policy of the Department of Transportation during this Administration that any mode of transportation that commandeers or violates large sections of

(JOHN A. VOLPE)

the landscape is going to be subject to a brutal analysis. Land is too precious a resource to be squandered.

It is the President's determination, as it is mine, to confront the crisis of the cities boldly, to provide leadership that rocks the boat; leadership that acts upon the premise that transportation is totally related to welfare, education, recreation and all other aspects of urban life.

*At International Conference on Urban Transportation, Pittsburgh, March 10.*

Highways alone are not going to do the job. You can build twelve lanes, fifteen lanes—I don't care. Unless you tear down half the city for parking lots, you won't solve the problem.

*Pub. March 17.*

If you get down to a point where automobiles have to travel five miles an hour, well, you know how long people are going to use them . . . Either we make a great deal more progress in mass transportation than we've made in the last five years, or, within the next year or two, you're going to have to come to some type of restriction on certain areas within . . . the core city on the utilization of the automobile.

*Interview, Washington, pub. March 27.*

We ought to get rid of the idea, once and for all, that public transportation must make a profit at the fare box. I wish it could . . . My position is that public transit is so important that we must look at its financing much like most any other public service. We don't expect the Army to make a profit. We don't expect user charges for police protection . . . These services are considered so important that the entire community must agree to share the burden of supporting them.

*Washington, April 17.*

Industry leaders should insist that their cars be designed from road to rooftop as mobile safety systems. If we cannot halt accidents entirely, then we must be sure that all accidents at least become the kind you can walk away from.

*Interview, New York, June 3.*

**Tom Atkins**
*Boston City Councilman*

You talk of megatons. We are interested in snow removal. You talk of penetration aids. What we want is housing. You talk of nuclear sufficiency. I say there is massive insufficiency as far as our domestic sanity is concerned.
*Lexington, Mass., pub. March 14.*

**Joseph M. Barr**
*Mayor of Pittsburgh*

A mayor must be a sack of concrete. They come in all day, every day, and beat at you with baseball bats.
*Pub. April 21.*

Any mayor who's not frustrated is not thinking. The problems are almost insurmountable . . . The main problem of any mayor of any city of any size is money . . . The legislatures are dominated by suburban and rural constituencies, and until that changes there's no hope for mayors who are trying to run their cities and run them properly. If the mayors don't get relief from the legislatures, God help them!
*Interview, pub. June 29.*

**Vito P. Battista**
*New York State Assemblyman*

Mayor (John V.) Lindsay entered the city scene (New York) on the basis of a great political drama, with him as its dramatic star. It soon became a comedy—filled with errors—and today rivals the saddest Shakespearean tragedy. Lindsay lost his script and forgot his lines. Today we have a complete shambles in our city.
*News conference, New York, Jan. 30.*

**Thomas G. Currigan**
*Former Mayor of Denver*

I hope to heaven cities are not ungovern-

able, but I'll admit there are some frightening aspects that would lead one at least to think along these lines . . . Our cities were structured financially when we were a rural nation, and our structures of government are such that the mayor lacks not only the financial resources but the authority to do the job.
*Interview, pub. June 29.*

**Rene Jules Dubos**
*Bacteriologist, Rockefeller University of New York*

Man can be adapted to anything—to the dirt and noise of New York City—and that is what is tragic. As we can accept worse and worse conditions, we don't realize that there is something worse than extinction—the progressive degradation of human life.
*Pub. July 30.*

**John W. Gardner**
*Chairman, Urban Coalition*

The typical American city is in fragments—a variety of worlds wholly out of touch with each other.
*Pub. Oct. 5.*

We get richer and richer in filthier and filthier communities until we reach a final state of affluent misery—Croesus on a garbage heap.
*Washington, Oct. 8.*

One cannot blame racial tensions for our monumental traffic jams, for the inexorable advance of air and water pollution, for the breakdown in administration of the courts, for the shocking inefficiency and often corruption of municipal government. It is true that when urban systems malfunction, minorities and the poor are hit first and hardest, but the problem

(JOHN W. GARDNER)

is deeper and broader and ultimately affects us all.

*Before National Press Club,*
*Washington, Dec. 9.*

**Charles S. Joelson**
*United States Representative, D-N.J.*

Most of the people in this country, except the poor, just want to be left alone; they don't want to be called to greatness. And we can't afford that kind of attitude. I ride through the rotting cities of the Northeast and I realize that the people of suburbia are living in a dream world. They don't want to know the slums exist.

*Interview, Washington, pub. May 31.*

**J. Bracken Lee**
*Mayor of Salt Lake City*

I don't know of any qualifications (to be mayor). You just run for office. If you get enough votes, you could be elected if you couldn't read or write.

*Salt Lake City, pub. Nov. 9.*

**John V. Lindsay**
*Mayor of New York*

If I could write the epitaph for my administration, I would say, "It takes courage and toughness to change institutions which operated under a business-as-usual philosophy and which no longer work well for people." I would like to be remembered as the Mayor who had the courage to begin to reshape and rebuild our institutions.

*Interview, New York, pub. May 16.*

The mayor has to be an activist, and I think that he's got to be willing to use the power of his office in order to lead, to innovate, to bring about changes, and to try new things.

*News conference, New York, Oct. 10.*

**Richard G. Lugar**
*Mayor of Indianapolis*

The problems of the cities are considerable; but they are unlikely to be worked out satisfactorily by indulging in an excess amount of self-pity and merely indicating that we are charitable wards that must be picked up by somebody else.

*Indianapolis, Dec. 6.*

**Norman Mailer**
*Author*

New York cannot begin to solve its budgetary problems until it becomes the 51st state . . .

*Interview, New York, pub. May 12.*

**Gordon J. McDonald**
*Vice chancellor for Research,*
*University of California at*
*Santa Barbara*

The feelings of alienation and discouragement which we find so prevalent today are not independent from the problems of suffocating smog, agitating noise, urban sprawl, endless concrete and the heat of the cities.

*Pub. Dec. 11.*

**Daniel P. Moynihan**
*Assistant to the President*
*of the United States for Urban Affairs*

The plain fact is that architects are, with respect to the quality of public building, much in the position of stockholders. Whether the market rises or falls, you still get your commissions. And the present American city is the result. This is something to be ashamed of.

*At joint convention of American*
*Institute of Architects and*
*Royal Architectural Institute of Canada,*
*Chicago, June 23.*

The simple fact is that most American cities are broke. Their fiscal basis has simply given out. They are dependent to an extraordinary degree on a tax structure that is not flexible, that is increasingly retrograde, and, at certain points, becomes counter-productive.

*Birmingham, Ala., pub. June 30.*

**Arthur Naftalin**
*Mayor of Minneapolis*

Experience to date demonstrates that the involvement of the states weakens rather than strengthens Federal assistance for the larger cities in the field of law enforcement . . . The states inevitably dilute attention to the needs of the larger cities because they regard their primary responsibility as statewide and thus place on the same level the needs and demands of urban, suburban and rural communities, regardless of the degree of need.

> *At United States Conference of Mayors, Pittsburgh, pub. June 21.*

**Arthur Naftalin**
*Professor of Public Affairs,*
*University of Minnesota;*
*former Mayor of Minneapolis*

The plain and simple and unchallengeable fact is that our state governments are in default as regards their responsibilities to the urban centers, and there is no evidence to suggest that this historic pattern of indifference will be reversed. To round out the dismal picture, while the national Government retreats and the state governments remain in default, the local governments are in a state of paralysis.

> *Before American Psychological Association, Washington, pub. Sept. 7.*

**Richard M. Nixon**
*President of the United States*

There are 200 million Americans now. By the end of the century there will be 300 million. Where are those 100 million going to be? You can't pour them into New York, into Los Angeles, into Chicago and choke those cities to death . . . it is necessary for America to grow toward its heartland, toward the center.

> *Before American Farm Bureau Federation, Washington, pub. Dec. 16.*

**Mario A. Procaccino**
*Controller, and candidate for*
*Mayor of New York*

In my opinion, the job of a mayor is like that of a judge; and that is to stand in the middle of an opposing conflict, to act as mediator first.

> *News conference, New York, Oct. 10.*

**Nelson A. Rockefeller**
*Governor of New York*

We don't need Band-aids on the problems (of Federal aid to cities and states) . . . We need a blood transfusion.

> *Buffalo, Feb. 7.*

**David H. Rogers**
*Mayor of Spokane*

It's time to recognize that the mayors

are not the village idiots, but probably have more knowledge and ability on urban affairs than any other group.

> *Interview, pub. February.*

**Carl B. Stokes**
*Mayor of Cleveland*

You've got to rely on community good will. You've got to rely on hope that people are basically good. I'm an inveterate optimist . . . Despite the litany of the sorrows of the city, we must believe in the ability of man to respond to the problems of his environment.

> *Yale University, April 2.*

You have got to accept the fact that you're not going to accomplish any overnight miracles. It (being mayor) is long, hard, grinding, laborious work, and there isn't any book on this business. Those looking for glory just don't understand it. The only satisfactions you get are personal—the satisfactions of fulfilling your own sense of commitment.

> *Pub. May 26.*

**Kenneth O. Tompkins**
*Mayor, Johnstown, Pa.*

The suburbanite should realize he is dependent on the city for a livelihood and should help to defray city expenses and not run to the woods every evening and leave the city to fend for itself.

> *Interview, pub. February.*

**Earl Warren**
*Former Chief Justice*
*of the United States*

No rational person can look at our cities and say they're not deteriorating. What can we expect of our children and grandchildren unless we give very high priority to conditions in the cities, to the environment of our children, to their education—all of which are worsening day by day?

> *Interview, San Francisco, July 30.*

**C. V. Wood**
*President, McCulloch Oil Company*

. . . there are going to be another 140 million more Americans in the next 30 years, and they're going to need a place

(C. V. WOOD)

to live. There are only three ways to grow: There's urban redevelopment. That's where you tear down the homes of a thousand people and put in high rise apartments for 10,000, destroying a city's balance. There's urban sprawl, just miles of patchwork growth that's ruined every city in America. Developments spring up where they weren't meant to be, and the city is always 10 years behind in roads, schools and public services . . . Or, you can build an entirely new city.

*Interview, Los Angeles, pub. July 30.*

PART TWO

# The World

**Mahmoud Soliman al-Maghreby**
*Premier of Libya*

The revolution of September 1 will mark the opening of a glorious page in the history of Libya and will bring a better and prosperous life to the people . . . Our policy will be based on the broad lines traced by the Revolutionary Council and will realize the hopes of the people for the building of a democratic, popular and modern regime, which will lead the country toward economic, social and cultural development. Our government will strengthen ties of friendship and cooperation with all the Arab countries and support, morally and materially, the people of Palestine in their long struggle for liberation until final victory.

*Tunis, Sept. 8.*

**Okoi Arikpo**
*Commissioner for*
*External Affairs of Nigeria*

When the Ibos come back in (after the Nigeria-Biafra war), they will be surprised when they sit down to talk with us about the political future. They will find a lot of people speaking their language.

*Lagos, pub. Feb. 9.*

**Obafemi Awolowo**
*Vice chairman,*
*Federal Nigerian Executive Council*

All is fair in war, and starvation is one of the weapons of war. I don't see why we should feed our enemies (Biafrans) fat, only to fight us harder.

*Pub. July 11.*

**Allison A. Ayida**
*Permanent Secretary,*
*Ministry for Economic*
*Development of Nigeria*

As far as we are concerned, foreign capital is foreign capital, whether it comes from traditional sources or from our newer friends . . . This war (with Biafra) might be over right now if we had given the Russians a free hand. They were quite willing to re-equip our whole army if we wanted. But we want to decide our own destiny, without ties to any ideology, so we keep them at arm's length.

*News conference, Lagos, pub. March 9.*

Until the other side (Biafra) is willing to give up its basic political goals, secession —or until we are willing to give up our basic objective, one Nigeria—no one is going to be able to find a solution to this war.

*News conference,*
*Monrovia, Liberia, April 20.*

**V. C. R. A. C. Crabbe**
*High Court Justice of Ghana*

You can't borrow too much from other countries. The American constitution, after all, was largely an attempt to get away from George III . . . taxation without representation and all that. We didn't have a Boston tea party. But we did have (Kwame) Nkrumah.

*Accra, Ghana, pub. Aug. 28.*

**Mohammed el Khazafy**
*Chairman, Revolutionary*
*Council of Libya*

We cannot accept foreign bases. We shall use all sensible methods to liberate our land, but, if fighting is a must, we shall fight.

*Pub. Oct. 17.*

**Anthony Enahoro**
*Commissioner for Information*
*and Labor of Nigeria*

We are determined to keep Nigeria one.

(ANTHONY ENAHORO)

You might say that in a sense we are fighting for the soul of Nigeria. But it is not true to say that the Biafrans are fighting for the survival of the Ibos.
*London, Jan. 13.*

**Yakubu Gowon**
*Maj. Gen.; head, Military*
*Council of Nigeria*

This is a war (with Biafra) with a difference. We do not take the Ibos as our enemies; they are our brothers. As far as I am concerned, I'm fighting a war to keep the country one and united. I therefore cannot afford to be callous in the way I prosecute this war. I have got to think of the problems of reconstruction, reconciliation and winning the heart, if we are to have a happy country in the end.

Our friends' doors have been shut to us and opened to Ojukwu (leader of Biafra), even though we offer to pay cash for help, and he doesn't have an economy. Where is the morality of this world? We remove the word hate; we remove the word victory; we remove the word enemy; what we get back is poison.
*Interview, Lagos, pub. July 4.*

**Chukuemeka Ifeagwu**
*Biafran Diplomat*

We want security for our people, our lives and our property. From experience, we have found that these objectives are best secured by being an independent sovereign state. To us, One Nigeria means 1966, when more than 30,000 Biafrans were slaughtered. If Nigeria has any new idea of what One Nigeria means, it will come to the conference table.
*Los Angeles, pub. Oct. 26.*

**Ejike Ikeji**
*Brigade Commander, Biafran Army*

We're young and we're crazy. We long ago forgot the difference between life and death.
*Pub. March 24.*

**Abeid Amani Karume**
*President of Zanzibar*

There will be no elections in Zanzibar for the next 60 years.
*Pub. May 19.*

**Julius L. Katz**
*Deputy Assistant Secretary of State*
*for International Resources and*
*Food Policy of the United States*

(Despite) abhorrence of the South African policy of racial discrimination . . . we believe it is important to permit lawful trade with South Africa and to keep open our lines of communication with South Africans. We do not believe that economic quarantine or isolation would lead the South African government to abandon apartheid.
*Before House African Affairs*
*Subcommittee, Washington, April 15.*

**Jomo Kenyatta**
*President of Kenya*

Anyone who does not wish to accept that we are masters in our own country should pack up and go now.
*Nairobi, Nov. 16.*

**Mwai Kibaki**
*Minister of Commerce and*
*Industry of Kenya*

People have gotten used to the idea of independence. It is no longer possible to cash in on history. A chap can't parade anymore about what he did in the thirties. He has to talk about what to do with the present issues. That is what a voter is interested in now. It is one of the most healthy changes in the attitude of the Kenya voter.
*News conference, Nairobi, Dec. 8.*

**Sir Louis Mbanefo**
*Chief Justice of Biafra*

We are especially resentful of the ambivalent pretenses the United States makes that it is trying to help us. If we are condemned to die, all right, we will die. But at least let the world, and the United States, be honest about it.
*Interview, Owerri, Biafra, pub. Nov. 8.*

**Marcel Naville**
*President, International*
*Red Cross Committee*

Within the next few days, hundreds of thousands of children in Biafra may die of starvation. If the use of famine as an instrument of war is accepted, it would be the start of a worldwide slide into barbarism.
*Pub. July 14.*

**Julius K. Nyerere**
*President of Tanzania*

Africa is learning the wrong lesson from the Nigeria tragedy. We are saying, if Biafra is allowed to secede, every country in Africa will have its own Biafra. That is nonsense. The only thing the people of Nigeria have in common is that they are all Africans and have all been under the same British rule for a few decades, and Britain governed them virtually separately. It would be infinitely easier for the peoples of Scandinavia to form one nation than for the peoples of Nigeria. Those who do not see this do not understand Nigeria's problem.

*Addis Ababa, Ethiopia, Sept. 7.*

**Odumegwu Ojukwu**
*Chief of State of Biafra*

The young will fight; the children unborn will fight; and their children will fight, until they (Nigeria) leave us alone . . . Since to give up for us is a fate worse than death, there remain only two alternatives. Either Nigeria and her collaborators call off their mad ambition to deny 14 million people their rights and their lives or we both prepare for a war of attrition.

*Umuahia, Biafra (Nigeria), Feb. 10.*

The key to Africa falls upon the United States. Whichever way she jumps—and until she jumps—we won't really know where Africa will jump.

*Interview, Umuahia, Feb. 19.*

We believe their (Nigeria's) intention is genocide. But I'd like to clarify that. Genocide, though it means wiping out a people individually, does not restrict itself to that meaning. To destroy a people— to remove or destroy that which makes a people—that is genocide. The Nigerian attitude toward us aims directly at destroying those things that make of us a people—our institutions, our organizations and our ability to resuscitate those institutions.

*Interview, Umuahia, March 24.*

We remain prepared to reach an accommodation with Nigeria, provided our internal and external security are guaranteed along with an international pres-

ence. We cannot ever again entrust our security into the hands of other people and cannot accept a situation . . . where we shall not be able to reach direct to the world for a hearing.

*Owerri, Biafra, May 1.*

We in Biafra are convinced that the Negro can never be his own until he is able to build modern states based on a compelling African ideology. This is Biafra—the plight of the black struggling to be man.

*Owerri, Sept. 8.*

Nigeria insists that Biafra is part of Nigeria. Let Nigeria go to the conference table with that thought in mind. We say we are separate. Allow us to go to the conference table thinking we are separate. Then, in the give-and-take of discussion, whatever emerges might present a solution.

*News conference, Owerri, Nov. 4.*

**Harry F. Oppenheimer**
*Industrialist*

I'm sick and tired of hearing how sound South Africa's economy is. I don't think that the economy of a country which deliberately sets out not to trade and not to make proper use of 80 per cent of its potential working population can be described as sound.

*Pub. Dec. 7.*

**Alan Paton**
*Author*

I cannot think of another country where you can live such a rich life of personal relationships (as in South Africa). And the challenges are so great that they must eventually lead to change. This is a land of fear, but it is a land of courage as well. The two go together.

*Interview, Durban, South Africa, pub. Dec. 23.*

**Paul VI**
*Pope*

Your experience will have taught you that independence does not imply either opposition or isolation between African peoples and non-African peoples; on the contrary, the new African states will be truly independent to the extent that they are capable of collaborating freely with

(PAUL VI)

other states and with the entire, orderly, international family of the world.

*Before African heads of state,*
*Kampala, Uganda, Aug. 1.*

**Peter Randall**
*Former assistant director,*
*South African Institute*
*of Race Relations*

Public debate on the morality of apartheid is never far below the surface, and the indications are it is now beginning to resume with more vigor. A great many South Africans are perplexed and confused and would welcome new leads based firmly on morally justifiable principles.

*Johannesburg, July 26.*

**Elliot L. Richardson**
*Under Secretary of State*
*of the United States*

Recognition (of Biafra) would have no tangible effect on the hostilities (between Nigeria and Biafra). To the contrary, it would only harden the positions of both sides, at the risk of rising Soviet influence in federal Nigeria. This Administration, therefore, does not contemplate either support for or recognition of the secessionist authorities.

*Before Senate subcommittee,*
*Washington, July 20.*

**Mohammed Siyad**
*Commander-in-Chief,*
*Army of the Somali Republic*

The officers and the men of the armed forces were always closely following the developments taking place in our country. The discontent of the people was shared by the armed forces. We were only waiting for the time when it was necessary to take over . . . and that occurred now.

*News conference, Mogadishu,*
*Somali Republic, Oct. 25.*

**Ian Smith**
*Prime Minister of Rhodesia*

Why is America persecuting us? The United States is one of the most active countries in enforcing sanctions against

us. Yet we are holding the line here against Communist encroachment in Africa through Zambia and Tanzania . . . We've fought alongside Americans in World War II. Now we've found the same weapons on Communist armed guerrillas here as are killing American boys in Vietnam. We aren't asking for a single dollar or a single American life or a single gun to help us. All we ask is that you leave us alone.

*Interview, Salisbury, pub. Sept. 11.*

**Michael Stewart**
*Foreign Secretary of*
*the United Kingdom*

I believe that an attempt to solve the Rhodesian question by force would have resulted in such a destruction of life and wealth, and such bitterness throughout Africa, that the end we all want in Rhodesia of a just regime for men of all colors would have been definitely postponed.

*Before House of Commons,*
*London, March 19.*

**Balthazar J. Vorster**
*Prime Minister of South Africa*

On the one side, we shall have a white nation of Afrikaans-speaking and English-speaking people; on the other side, we shall have a colored nation. They will be in one land. That is the dilemma of South Africa, in respect of which our children will have to find a solution.

*Before Parliament, July 20.*

Outsiders think we fear independence for our blacks. To us it is perfectly natural that they will have their independence, in their own states. South Africa is not a multiracial state. It is a multi-national state. It is our task to lead the various nations within our borders to full independence.

*Pretoria, pub. Oct. 8.*

**Emile Derlin Zinsou**
*President of Dahomey*

I have chosen a hard course (against striking students and teachers). I know that. I'm asking for sacrifices. I know that. But we are not a rich industrial nation like France or America, and we cannot afford to have our schools disrupted. The road I have decided to travel is the only road to international dignity, the only road to true national independence and the only road to economic independence.

If the people decide that they don't want my policies, I will say goodbye. I'm not interested in power for motorcycles and sirens. I'm interested in it for what I can accomplish.

*Interview, Cotonou, Dahomey, May 14.*

# The Americas

### Juan Velasco Alvarado
*President of Peru*

No person with a conscience, no people, no government, not even a court of law, can any longer support the despoilation of the natural resources of a generous people, who have always offered, and continue to offer generously, guarantees of law to foreign investors who came, are coming and will come to live and work here honestly.
*Address after seizing
International Petroleum Company,
Lima, Feb. 6.*

Peru, today, is the Latin American country which has decided to reconstruct its destiny and, at last, to exercise its sovereignty . . . Peru expects and demands the solidarity of brother Latin American countries. If Peru falls today, no national future will be secure in this part of the world.
*Before United Nations Economic
Commission for Latin America,
Lima, April 14.*

This Government is not Marxist—it is nationalistic, it is revolutionary. We will not maintain the status quo. We will modify it, and we are modifying it profoundly.
*Lima, July 28.*

### Rene Barrientos
*President of Bolivia*

Every citizens must be a participant in the building of this country. Otherwise, the common man will continue to be managed.
*Pub. Feb. 7.*

### Adolf A. Berle, Jr.
*President, 20th Century Fund;
former adviser to the
President of the United States
on Inter-American Affairs*

The social structure of every Latin American country is its own affair . . . If the people of a country decides to be Communist, that is their business.
*New York, Jan. 15.*

### Jean-Jacques Bertrand
*Premier of Quebec*

The important thing for Quebec citizens is not to be able to speak French, as individuals, in all parts of the country—it is to be able to live collectively in French; it is to be able to base their community life on their culture. Without Quebec, you can have French-speaking minorities, but there would no longer be a French Canada.
*Richelieu, Quebec, Aug. 31.*

### Hans Blumenfeld
*Professor, University of Toronto*

What disturbs me about the guaranteed annual income is that we would go from capitalism to communism without any intervening period of socialism.
*Kingston, Ont., Aug. 24.*

### Leo Cadieux
*Defense Minister of Canada*

It's wrong to say we are withdrawing from Europe. We do not intend to reduce our military expenditures for the next few years, and we are not trying to pass the buck.
*News conference, Brussels, May 28.*

### Dom Helder Camara
*Bishop of Recife, Brazil*

For the next ten or fifteen years, armed movements will be impossible in Latin America. A violent establishment exists in a country which causes misery for millions of people. Material underdevelopment has, as a consequence, moral underdevelopment, and, as a consequence, absence of courage. There is no reason for living, so it is difficult to find a reason for fighting.

*Pub. Feb. 17.*

## Alfredo Ovando Candia
*President of Bolivia*

Our political line is economic nationalism, and our objective is the recapture of the natural resources of the country which are in the hands of foreign business—when they should belong to the state.

*Interview, La Paz, pub. Dec. 1.*

## Fidel Castro
*Prime Minister of Cuba*

The Cuban revolution will consistently and decisively support any revolutionary process carried out by any Latin American country.

*Havana, July 14.*

It is worth pointing out that there is another Latin American country in which the armed forces are playing a revolutionary role. That country . . . is Peru. This fact, too, is very important, as the armed forces are the instruments which the imperialists use in those countries to maintain their privileges and hegemony. This is why we are watching with great interest the development of the political process in Peru, where, without the slightest doubt, a new phenomenon has developed.

*Before Cuban armed forces, Nov. 4.*

From now on, we will assassinate, without a single thought of any kind, everybody who tries to sabotage the (sugar) harvest . . . To him who jokes about this, I say that it is a joke that he won't have the chance to repeat.

*Radio broadcast, Cuba, Dec. 21.*

## Frank Church
*United States Senator, D-Ida.*

(These grants-in-aid) are used against us by increasing numbers of Latin Americans who see it as a prop for armies that stand guard over the status quo, while diverting themselves occasionally with Gilbert-and-Sullivanesque border escapades. It is time to stop our military grant-in-aid programs throughout Latin America. It is time to bring our military missions home.

*Before the Senate, Washington, July 30.*

The precipitous slide toward militarism in Latin America certainly underscores the failures of the political objectives of the Alliance (for Progress) of promoting democratic governments.

*Mexico City, Sept. 11.*

## Anastasio Somoza Debayle
*President of Nicaragua*

It may sound funny coming from a capitalist, but I have to think about the needs of the people for education and social services. That is my responsibility as head of the government; and the only way the differences in living standards can be reduced is by government action.

*Managua, pub. Dec. 10.*

## Thomas J. Dodd
*United States Senator, D-Conn.*

As one American, I salute the efforts of those Cubans who, despite our indifference, seek to call the attention of the free world to the massive crimes against human rights which are being perpetrated in their country; and I bow my head in shame that this outrage against humanity which is taking place almost within sight of our shores should call forth so little protest and indignation in our own country.

*Before the Senate, Washington, Sept. 30.*

## Ralph Dungan
*Former Ambassador to Chile from the United States*

U.S. military policies and programs in Latin America have been disastrous, from a political point of view. There is no shaking the prevailing Latin conception of the U.S. as a society dominated, to a very large measure, by the Pentagon.

*Before Senate Foreign Relations Committee, Washington, June 24.*

## Francois Duvalier
*President of Haiti*

I know the Haitian people because I *am* the Haitian people . . . The people of Haiti have always called me "Papa Doc."

(FRANCOIS DUVALIER)

I was their first doctor. Now I am also their President for life . . . The people of Haiti are happy with their Papa Doc.
*Interview, Port au Prince, pub. Jan. 19.*

My successor is still in high school.
*Interview, Port au Prince, April 24.*

Trust in my destiny as you trust in my arm of iron.
*Radio address,*
*Port au Prince, pub. June 23.*

**Cyrus S. Eaton**
*Chairman, Chesapeake & Ohio Railway*

(Fidel) Castro is dedicated to the country (Cuba) and the people. You can condemn him for other things, but not for that. He has set an example of hard work and thrift; and he has made the people work and develop thrift. He works fifteen hours a day, seven days a week.
*Interview, Cleveland, pub. Jan. 12.*

**Ludwig Erhard**
*Former Chancellor of West Germany*

I cannot understand the drastic (trade) protection given to incipient national industries as practiced in Latin American countries. These nations need to become integrated to the world's economy.
*Interview, Buenos Aires, pub. April 27.*

**Gordon Fairweather**
*Member of Canadian Parliament*

One nation's deserter may be another's hero; one nation's humanity must not be turned off to suit another nation's draft law.
*Pub. March 16.*

**Dante B. Fascell**
*United States Representative, D-Fla.*

. . . I admit that the initial record of the Alliance for Progress inspires more gloom than satisfaction. This is not to say that the Alliance has failed in its undertakings. Rather, the undertakings of the Alliance have been too narrow and too timid in scope to contend with the pressure of a rapidly increasing population.
*Washington, Feb. 23.*

**Luis A. Ferre**
*Governor of Puerto Rico*

People are getting tired of (Fidel) Castro. He has built up a system that is oppressive, and the people resent it. I know that from hearing from those who come out. How long Castro remains in power depends on how soon somebody there can offer the Cubans an alternative.
*Interview, Washington, pub. March 17.*

**Andrei A. Gromyko**
*Foreign Minister of the*
*Union of Soviet Socialist Republics*

Cuba, a far-off and, at the same time, a close country, belongs to the community of Socialist countries. The Soviet Union does everything to help the republic of Cuba, its people, to withstand . . . pressure and provocations. We attach great significance to further strengthening of friendship and cooperation with Cuba. And our people always remember that a flag of freedom and independence hoisted by the courageous people assuredly flutters in the area of the Caribbean Sea.
*Before the Supreme Soviet,*
*Moscow, July 10.*

**Ernst Halperin**
*Authority on Latin America,*
*Massachusetts Institute of Technology*

The Russians are not much interested in delivering economic assistance to countries they cannot control. But arms are a completely different question. They are the Russians' main instrument of expansion into an area, as they showed in Guatemala in 1954 and, a year later, in Egypt.
*Pub. Feb. 28.*

**George Hees**
*Member of Canadian Parliament*

The trouble with this government is that they want to operate Parliament like a computer. They want to decide what's best for Canada, process the legislation through Parliament, and have it come out on a prescribed schedule.
*Ottawa, pub. Sept. 25.*

**Felipe Herrera**
*President, Inter-American*
*Development Bank*

This may be a dream, but I am convinced that the solution for Latin America could be a type of political confederation of the states. Whatever I can do I will do to work for this, but I think the moment is not right.

*Pub. Dec. 14.*

## Yu Chi Hsueh
*Ambassador to Canada from*
*Nationalist China*

By adding prestige and power to the Maoist regime (in Communist China), Canada's recognition could make the prospect of peace in Asia and the Pacific dimmer and more remote . . . what lever or influence could Canada . . . hope to wield with which to persuade the Maoist regime to be less war-like and more peaceful? . . . The hour may be late, but perhaps not too late, for Canada to decide, for the sake of peace in Asia and friendship with the Chinese people, to abandon the policy of recognizing the Communist regime in China.

*Before Richelieu Club,*
*Quebec, Sept. 10.*

## Karl Hudson-Phillips
*Attorney General-designate of Trinidad*

How come they (the British) let a bandit like Ian Smith put 4 million black people in his pocket and run away with the country (Rhodesia)? They (the British) sent a whole regiment into Anguilla, an island of 16 square miles.

*Pub. Nov. 16.*

## Edgardo M. Jarrin
*Foreign Minister of Peru*

The future of Latin America must not continue to be tied in an economic knot with powerful industralized countries whose interests are not in accord with those of the third world and whose attitude toward it many times flares up in the form of paternalism, threats, and pressures. The economic assistance given to an underdeveloped country in a spirit of solidarity and humanity should not later be used as a sledgehammer to weaken our economic structures and, consequently, cause them to collapse. Nor should it be used to impair our national sovereignty.

. . . the objectives which Latin American nations must follow are: to reach the stage of development and economic aid, political independence, and to establish a continental development program which will benefit both individual nations and the continent as a whole. These elements can thus serve to establish the basic lines of a doctrine for the development of Latin America.

*Interview, Lima, pub. Sept. 18.*

## Sol M. Linowitz
*Ambassador to the Organization*
*of American States*
*from the United States*

One of my greatest disappointments in the time I've been in office has been our failure to make clear to the people in the U.S. the depth of U.S. interest in Latin America and what it means to our whole future. We must recognize that the Latin Americans are sensitive, intelligent people of high cultural and educational traditions, people of dignity, who want to be treated with respect and encouraged in their aspirations. We have got to develop in this country a greater awareness of Latin America and a greater feeling for our common stake in what happens in this hemisphere.

*Interview, pub. April 14.*

Our policy in Latin America can succeed only to the extent that it supports change—for that matter, encourages change.

*Interview, Washington, April 27.*

This is the critical moment in our relations in the hemisphere. We really are at the moment of decision between peaceful revolution and violent revolution. Eight years ago, there was launched this peaceful revolution called the Alliance for Progress. It started, deliberately, a revolution of rising expectations. Now, a number of the most important goals have not been achieved. The point is, though, that we can't afford to lose heart at this point. This is no time for disappointment; this is no time for turning our backs. The worst thing you can do for people, and we have found this in our own country, is to raise their expectations and then dash them.

(SOL M. LINOWITZ)

One Latin American president told me recently he had two loans from the United States during his administration, and he managed to survive both of them. They have not found it easy to be at the other end of munificence, and I think we ought to understand that . . . We can't exist as an island of wealth in a sea of poverty. We are not going to have a secure world up here if there is an insecure world below us. It's a matter of self-preservation. It is of critical significance to us that we focus on it and not wait for a Dominican Republic or a Cuba to remind us.

*Interview, pub. April 28.*

**George C. Lodge**
*Former Assistant Secretary of Labor
for International Affairs
of the United States*

We have failed to acknowledge that in fact, today, the Communist Party apparatus-general in Latin America is neither a revolutionary force nor a major threat to U.S. interests.

*Before Senate Foreign Relations
Latin American Subcommittee,
Washington, June 24.*

**Bryce Mackasey**
*Minister of Labor of Canada*

We look below the border at the U.S. slums and ghettos somewhat smugly because we believe we have no discrimination in Canada; but we *do* have it. Canadians have no right to be smug. Canadians should not be satisfied with a standard of living that permits one person to go to bed hungry, or prevents one person from working because that person is an Indian, a Negro or a Jew.

*Ottawa, Sept. 18.*

**Emilio G. Medici**
*President-designate of Brazil*

The technology of this century makes it possible to anticipate the irresistable realization of Brazil's destiny of greatness because she is a country that has, within her frontiers, all the resources necessary to the promotion of her humanized development.

*Rio de Janeiro, pub. Oct. 8.*

**Emilio G. Medici**
*President of Brazil*

I believe it is necessary to consolidate and dignify the system of representation, based on several parties and a guarantee of the fundamental rights of man.

*Inauguration speech, Rio de Janeiro,
Oct. 30.*

**Lee Moore**
*Official spokesman for Robert Bradshaw,
Premier of the
St. Kitts-Nevis-Anguilla Federation*

Every member of the (St. Kitts Trades and Labor) union is addressed by fellow members as comrade. I detect an interest in the word. No, we are not Communists. We are a leftish movement, Socialist oriented, but not Communists.

*Interview, Basseterre,
St. Kitts, pub. March 24.*

**Wayne L. Morse**
*Former United States Senator, D-Ore.*

If we can sit with Cuba in the United Nations, maybe we should sit with her in the O.A.S. . . . If Canada to the North of us can survive with an Ambassador in Havana, maybe we should risk it if Cuba would agree to the re-establishment of diplomatic relations. At least she permits the return of our hijacked planes. It would seem that the time has come for the O.A.S. to give some thought to a reappraisal of its relations with Cuba.

*Mexico City, Sept. 9.*

**Pablo Neruda**
*Chilean Poet*

The United States will remain a threat to Latin America as long as its foreign policy is tied to its industrial interests.

*Isla Negra, Chile, pub. April 8.*

**Antonio Delfim Netto**
*Prime Minister of Brazil*

While we do not incline to the belief that business profit has divine origin or is the businessman's sacred right, that does not mean we view business profits with aversion.

*Pub. March 10.*

**Richard M. Nixon**
*President of the United States*

The difficulty in the past, a well-intentioned difficulty, has been that we have been putting too much emphasis on what we are going to do *for* Latin America and not enough . . . on what we are going to do *with* our Latin American friends.
*News conference, Washington, Feb. 6.*

**John N. Plank**
*Member, Senior Staff,*
*Brookings Institution*

Independence in Latin America has only one referent today, and that is independence from the United States.
*Pub. July 11.*

**Don Galo Plaza**
*Secretary-General,*
*Organization of American States*

Unfortunately, throughout Latin America today, there is a profound disenchantment with the United States. There is a fear that recent cutbacks in United States aid to the Alliance for Progress are symptomatic of a general downgrading of interest in Latin America. This will be a difficult impression to correct.
*Pub. Feb. 23.*

The commitments of the Alliance (for Progress) continue to be valid. What we must determine now is what must be done in the coming decade to fulfill the goals which were too ambitious for just one decade.
*Port of Spain, Trinidad, June 2.*

**Carlos Quijano**
*Magazine publisher, Uruguay*

The President is ruling by decree, with no effective checks by Congress. There is a highly repressive censorship of the press. Union activity is suppressed by the Army. Political figures and strikers have been arrested by the hundreds, with no trial or civil guarantees. The right of free assembly no longer exists, and legal opposition to the Government is hard pressed to survive. Democracy in Uruguay is no longer more than a label.
*Montevideo, Pub. Aug. 14.*

**Carlos Lleras Restrepo**
*President of Colombia*

. . . I have more patience now than I used to have, but I do believe that there are moments when it is necessary to fight or see one's program go down the drain. After all, I am not here in the Presidency to be liked, but to push programs through and get things done.
*Interview, Bogota, pub. March 3.*

It is not true that Latin Americans are incapable of organized, disciplined behavior. The fault is to be found with international rules of the game, which take from the poor and give to the rich.
*Before National Press Club,*
*Washington, June 13.*

**Nelson A. Rockefeller**
*Governor of New York*

The fact of the matter is that we (the United States) have neglected Latin American relations, and our neighbors feel it. Our alliances are in disarray because we too often confuse consultation with elaborating on American blueprints.
*Pub. March 17.*

**Carlos Raphael Rodriguez**
*Member, Central Committee of Cuba*

Cuba is not interested in any agreement or contract with the United States, in any case as long as Washington persists in its aggressive imperialist policies . . . Actually, we have demonstrated that we don't need contact with the United States. Speaking purely personally, I feel the way Lenin did when he said, "May the capitalist countries just leave us alone . . ." It is more important for other Latin nations to have relations with us than it is to Cuba. I repeat, we have made our way alone and can continue to do so. When they begin to follow independent policies, no longer under the heel of the Yankees, then they may be interested in having normal relations with us.
*Interview, Lima, April 26.*

**William P. Rogers**
*Secretary of State of the United States*

There is no part of the world more important to us (than Latin America). It

(WILLIAM P. ROGERS)

would be tragic if our relations deteriorated in Latin America, and this Administration has no intention of letting that happen.

*News conference, Washington, June 5.*

### Claude Ryan
*Publisher, "Le Devoir"*

Quebec at the moment has a climate of intellectual, spiritual, moral and social anarchy. Authority has never been so weak in Quebec, and the minds of the people have never been so much in search of new values.

*Pub. Sept. 18.*

### Mitchell Sharp
*Secretary of State for*
*External Affairs of Canada*

If the Government does recognize the People's Republic of China (Communist China), relations between Formosa (Nationalist China) and Canada will, of course, be affected, since the Government of the "National" Republic of China does claim jurisdiction over the whole of China, and we cannot have two conflicting authorities.

*Ottawa, pub. Feb. 11.*

We don't expect that our trade relations with (Communist) China will be notably improved (by formal diplomatic recognition). We believe that, looking at ourselves as a Pacific nation, our chances of achieving our objectives in that area, of promoting peace as we try to promote it in the Atlantic area by membership in NATO and otherwise, will be better if we can bring about an exchange of diplomats between Peking and Canada. At least, it will be one contribution.

*Before Foreign Correspondents Club,*
*Tokyo, April 15.*

### Luis Adolfo Siles Salinas
*President of Bolivia*

I am a weak man before the armed forces . . . and I am a weak man before any determined group of five persons who wants to overthrow me. But, in Bolivia, I now represent the Constitution, and I think the people understand that. I believe that, in Bolivia, we have finally reached an understanding that in the law rests the best protection of all.

*News conference, La Paz, May 8.*

### Sebastian Soler
*Argentine Jurist*

The definitions of what is the security of the State are wide and vague in Brazil today. Vague laws are bad laws because they are open to any interpretation. This is the traditional system of oppression by any kind of dictatorship.

*Pub. Nov. 27.*

### Michael Stewart
*Foreign Secretary of the*
*United Kingdom*

If people insist on regarding it (British invasion of Anguilla) as comic or tragic, I should much prefer they regard it as comic . . . there was, at the time, no lawful police on the island, and there was a group, whom I have moderately described as disreputable characters, some from outside Anguilla, who wanted to treat it not as a place in which 6,000 human beings have a right to a proper life, but simply as a sort of estate for their private convenience.

*Before House of Commons,*
*London, March 24.*

### Stuart Symington
*United States Senator, D-Mo.*

The contribution of Canada to NATO has . . . become more and more a symbolic gesture of solidarity with its allies, no longer an operation which could be justified in military terms. But Canada is morally bound to assist, in one way or another, with the defense of the Western world and to the same proportional extent as its friends.

*Washington, pub. Sept. 16.*

### Edward Teller
*Nuclear Physicist*

There is nothing to prevent Cuba from developing a nuclear capability in the next few years if they are helped to do so by the Russians, (and) such a development would certainly pose a serious danger to our (United States') security.

*Pub. March 27.*

## Pierre Elliott Trudeau
*Prime Minister of Canada*

Canada is in the extraordinarily fortunate position of not having to defend itself, because we know darn well the United States will defend us. So, in a sense, we are much freer than other nations, and I believe we should use this freedom to explore ways in which middle-size nations can move the world towards peace in a way which many European countries cannot.

*Interview, Ottawa, Jan. 1.*

The fact that Canada has lived and flourished for more than a century as the closest neighbor to what is now the greatest economic and military power in the history of the world is evidence to all countries of the basic decency of United States foreign policy.

Living next to you (the United States) is, in some ways, like sleeping with an elephant. No matter how friendly or even-tempered is the beast, if I can call it that, one is affected by every twitch and grunt.

*News conference, Washington, March 25.*

. . . we cannot be neutralists; we must be aligned.

*News conference, Ottawa, April 3.*

We are not only a one-ocean country; we are a three-ocean country. We have got the Arctic and we have got the Pacific and the great population centers of Asia and South America . . . We are a natural for trading with that world in terms not only of economics, but of culture, of travel. This is why we have put such great emphasis on recognition of Red China, of increasing trade and exchange with Japan, which, in the year 2000, will be one of the four or five great nations of the world.

*Interview, Ottawa, pub. April 27.*

We are not enthusiastic about the (anti-ballistic missile) system, but this is a defense system being built in another country. It will not help if a Prime Minister of Canada says to the United States what he thinks they should be doing.

*Pub. June 1.*

I have always resisted security measures (for personal protection) which seem to me unnecessary or too elaborate. I hope it will be possible to continue this policy. I believe it is a risk worth taking in order that public officials will not be isolated from the individual Canadian citizen, from the realities of his life and his feelings toward his government.

*Ottawa, pub. Aug. 26.*

## Gabriel Valdes
*Foreign Minister of Chile*

Private investments have meant, and mean today, for Latin America that the amounts that leave our continent are many times as high as those invested in it. In a word, we hold the conviction that Latin America gives more than it receives.

*Pub. July 11.*

# Asia and the Pacific

**Charles H. Bonesteel, III**
*Commanding General,*
*United States Eighth Army in Korea*

It has been openly and many times reiterated by North Korea's dictator, Kim Il Sung, that his aim is to reunify the country under Communism, by force if necessary, and the sooner the better. Having failed once to achieve this end, and scornful of the legitimate means of free choice, North Korea has rebuilt its conventional war machine and developed a large unconventional warfare capability. It steadily prepares for possible new aggression.
*Pub. April 28.*

The confrontation with . . . North (Korea) does not present an inevitable war situation. If . . . South (Korea) can continue to develop at the present rate for a slightly longer period, it will be so far ahead of the North that something like what we see in Eastern Europe can develop, where the people on the Communist side will want contact with the other side in order to improve their wellbeing and sense of individuality.
*Seoul, pub. Sept. 8.*

**Willy Brandt**
*Foreign Minister of West Germany*

China, the great Chinese people, will play a role, not only in Asia, during the coming years, but elsewhere in the world. And we begin from the basic assumption that not too much time should pass before the Chinese republic finds its place in the organized community of nations.
*Radio interview, Bonn, March 9.*

**Zbigniew K. Brzezinski**
*Professor of Public Law and*
*Government, Columbia University*

The Soviets see their relations with Hanoi in terms of their rivalry with the Chinese. The Soviets want to prevent the formation of an Asian Communist bloc under Peking's domination, a trend back to the situation in 1963 and 1964. The Soviets want to reconstruct the world Communist movement and to isolate the Chinese as extreme left-wing deviationists.
*Saigon, Sept. 5.*

**Lord Caradon**
*Ambassador to the United Nations*
*from the United Kingdom*

All our efforts should be directed not toward keeping them (Communist China) out (of the United Nations), but toward persuading them to come in . . . It is important to the people of China; it is important to this assembly.
*United Nations, N.Y., Nov. 5.*

**Liu Chieh**
*Ambassador to the United Nations*
*from Nationalist China*

I do not presume to suggest what the United States should or should not do in regard to Peking . . . But I wish to point out that Peking's hostility toward the United States cannot be removed by American gestures of goodwill.
*News conference, Los Angeles, Aug. 5.*

**Dalai Lama**
*Former Chief of State of Tibet*

Tibet can even be a Communist state, if that's what the majority of the people want. It doesn't matter what they choose, as long as it is what the Tibetans themselves want . . . our main hope remains with the young Tibetans. They have a strong sense of resistance, including the young Tibetan Communists.
*Interview, Dharamasala, India,*
*pub. Sept. 25.*

**Chou En-lai**
*Premier of Communist China*

The peace we anticipate is based on five principles: mutual respect of territorial integrity and sovereignty, mutual nonaggression, mutual noninterference in internal affairs, equality and reciprocal advantages and peaceful co-existence.
*On eve of 20th anniversary of founding of Communist China; Peking, Sept. 30.*

Ostensibly it was (President) Nixon who agreed to return to Japan the United States base for aggression in Okinawa, but in fact it was Eisaku Sato who agreed to turn the whole of Japan into an Okinawa.
*Peking, Nov. 29.*

**Gordon Freeth**
*Minister of External Affairs of Australia*

Australia is primarily concerned with her own security. But any threat to peace in this region (Asia) is a threat to Australia.
*Before Foreign Correspondents Club, Hong Kong, June 14.*

**Aiichiro Fujiyama**
*Former Foreign Minister of Japan*

I think the security of Japan is guaranteed now by the treaty with the United States; but the peace of Japan in the future cannot be guaranteed without peace in Asia. Tension between China and her neighbors must be relaxed, and to do so we must change the American attitude toward China.
*Television broadcast, Tokyo, Dec. 16.*

**Indira Gandhi**
*Prime Minister of India*

Ours is such a huge mass, so poor and backward, that we can't afford just to let events take their course. The state must manage many things, rather than leaving them to private enterprise, which seeks a profit. We are pragmatic. We use the word socialism as the nearest equivalent, but have no particular prophet. We seek a new and middle path.
*Interview, New Delhi, pub. March 16.*

I think that, in this changing world, the one thing that has remained valid is non-alignment. It is no specific policy; it just means that we do not align ourselves with anyone. We judge each thing on its merit, and if it's right, we support it.
*News conference, Tokyo, June 25:*

I personally think that we will not exist for long if we do not convert into a real socialist party.
*Before the Congress Party, Bangalore, India, pub. July 28.*

There has been a campaign against me calling me a Communist, saying that I have ties with some countries outside India. There is no basis for these allegations.
*Pub. Nov. 9.*

**Minoru Genda**
*Member of Japanese Diet*

No nation can stand alone today in a world of superpowers. Even the United States and Russia feel the need for allies. Fortunately, Japan is surrounded by sea. Even with our present forces, we could repel almost any aggressor by ourselves. But we would be no match for a super power. We need the U.S. as an ally.
*Interview, Tokyo, pub. Oct. 27.*

**John A. Gronouski**
*Former Postmaster General of the United States*

The United States can do little to sweeten the pot (for Communist China). When Peking is ready to talk seriously, it will—it is as simple and as frustrating as that.
*Pub. June 6.*

**Venkatagiri Varaha Giri**
*President of India*

I am not a Leftist—I am a trade unionist and a Gandhian, and you know the difference.
*New Delhi, pub. Aug. 21.*

**John Grey Gorton**
*Prime Minister of Australia*

... for our part, speaking for Australians, wherever the United States is resisting aggression; wherever the United States or the United Kingdom or any other

(JOHN GREY GORTON)

country is seeking to insure that there will be a chance for the free expression of the spirit; wherever there is a joint attempt to improve not only the material but the spiritual standards of life of the peoples of the world, then, sir, we will go waltzing, Matilda, with you.

*Washington, May 6.*

We will adhere to our decision to maintain in the region of Malaysia-Singapore forces of all arms—and will maintain in Australia a capacity for swift additional assistance. We will continue to support the concept of a regional security pact in that region in which we will participate. But we will exert all the influence at our command to prevent participation by Russia in such an agreement. We believe that our security would be threatened by the establishment of any Russian naval or military base in that area.

*Sydney, pub. Oct. 19.*

**J. Edgar Hoover**
*Director, Federal Bureau of Investigation of the United States*

The potent threat to our national security posed by Red China still exists. In fact, the blatant, belligerent and illogical statements made by Red China's spokesmen during the past year leave no doubt that the United States is Communist China's Number One enemy.

*Before House Appropriations Subcommittee, Washington, April 17.*

**Hubert H. Humphrey**
*Former Vice President of the United States*

The United States needs more than might for an Asia policy—it needs a feeling for the area. That Japan can give us. They have a feeling for these cultures as we do not. We jumped into this area without knowing what we were jumping into.

*Interview, Tokyo, Oct. 22.*

We have friends and partners in Asia, and we will not desert those friends. All we ask is that the free countries of Asia do what must be done in the way of get-ting together and standing together for their own security.

*Seoul, Oct. 30.*

**Walter H. Judd**
*Former United States Representative, R-Minn.*

Re-evaluating our policy (on Communist China) means weakening it.

*Pub. June 6.*

**Herman Kahn**
*Director, Hudson Institute*

The driving force in Japan today is prestige. They will insist on a status equal to the United States and the Soviet Union, or just below, and this includes getting a permanent seat in the United Nations Security Council.

*Pub. Dec. 14.*

**Chiang Kai-shek**
*President of Nationalist China*

The day of national recovery is drawing near. We should strengthen solidarity and strive toward the goal of national salvation. We shall continue and intensify this struggle. Whatever else may happen in the world, our determined confidence in mainland recovery and the liberation of our compatriots can never be shaken.

*Taiwan, Oct. 10.*

**Nicholas deB. Katzenbach**
*Former Under Secretary of State of the United States*

It is (Communist) China's position that is inflexible, not ours. Our relations are not bad because of something we are not doing.

*Pub. June 6.*

**Ichiro Kawasaki**
*Former Ambassador to Argentina from Japan*

The Japanese people tend to act collectively, and this group-psychology can be dangerous. There is no goal for the Japanese people to work for today. We are living from day to day, enjoying only our unprecedented economic prosperity. If you couple this absence of a goal with

Japanese group-psychology, it is hard to be optimistic about this country.

*Before Foreign Correspondents Club, Tokyo, May 29.*

## Kenneth B. Keating
*Ambassador to India*
*from the United States*

(The economic policies of Prime Minister Indira Gandhi are) the only way to preserve free government in India and prevent a Communist takeover or, at the other extreme, a right-wing takeover by the military . . . In my judgment, she is not a Communist, she is not working for the Communists and she is a firm believer in free government and free elections. I see a great distinction between Socialism and Communism. You must recognize that if democracy is to be preserved in a country with such great poverty, such a fantastic number of under-privileged people, which is the breeding ground where Communism makes its strides, the government must achieve a middle ground that is going to be left of what we call middle ground. And I believe this is what she (Mrs. Gandhi) is trying to do.

*Sprinagar, India, Sept. 23.*

## Edward M. Kennedy
*United States Senator, D-Mass.*

Surely, in the entire history of American foreign policy, there has been no fiction more palpably absurd than our official position that Communist China does not exist . . . We should make it clear that we regard (Communist) China as a legitimate power in control of the mainland, entitled to full participation as an equal member of the world community . . .

*New York, March 20.*

## Yahiya Khan
*President of Pakistan*

I wish to make it absolutely clear that I have no ambition other than the creation of conditions conducive to the establishment of a constitutional government.

*Rawalpindi, March 26.*

## Thanat Khoman
*Foreign Minister of Thailand*

The presence of foreign troops is always corruptive of a country.

*Pub. Feb. 16.*

We told President Nixon that Thailand is not going to be another Vietnam. We told him that we never asked for American soldiers to come and fight in defense of Thailand. We pledged that we will not ask for American soldiers to come and fight in defense of Thailand in an insurgent war . . . As far as it is a people's war, a revolutionary war, a war of national liberation, we shall deal with the problem ourselves, because we are better able to deal with it than outsiders are. We believe sincerely that foreign personnel are not well suited to dealing with this kind of situation.

*At foreign correspondents dinner, Bangkok, Aug. 19.*

(Thailand has) been urging for years that the (South) Vietnamese must defend themselves. We have been fighting the Communists in our own country for years without asking for a single soldier from outside. What more evidence could anyone require that we are sincere in this approach?

*Bangkok, Aug. 19.*

If the non-Communist nations in this part of the world cannot meet the challenge (of defending themselves with a reduced U.S. presence) successfully, then they don't deserve to be independent and sovereign nations. They deserve to go down, and likewise those who want to be great and who have actually great military power, military might, economic might—if they don't face up to their responsibilities as great powers, they themselves will not deserve to be a great power.

*Interview, Bangkok, Sept. 8.*

## Han Ju Kiong
*Secretary to the Korean*
*Armistice Commission*
*from North Korea*

The new American Government has sent various envoys to Korea to take a

(HAN JU KIONG)

look at the preparations being taken in the South in the event of another war. Provocations against us have multiplied. We do not have any faith in the peaceful policies that President Nixon brags about. They are just a trick to hide his real aims . . . After all, we are not the occupying army. We did not capture the (U.S.S.) *Pueblo* off the American coast or shoot down the spy plane in the American sky. We have not even thrown a single pebble on American soil. If the United States pulled its troops out of South Korea, there would be no problems between us.

*Interview, Kaesong, North Korea,*
*pub. Aug. 19.*

**Henry A. Kissinger**
*Assistant to the President*
*of the United States*
*for National Security Affairs*

The turbulence in Asia is a matter of imbalance rather than ideology alone—it is the result of the size of China, 700 million people. It is not a matter of what government they have but the fact that they are all united behind one government.

*Washington, pub. Aug. 22.*

**Thanom Kittikachorn**
*Premier of Thailand*

. . . the United States will not desert us and let us fight against the Communists on our own.

*Bangkok, July 19.*

**Nguyen Cao Ky**
*Vice President of South Vietnam*

I don't know but what it might be better for the United States to face the (Communist) Chinese now than later. Some day (the U.S.) will have to fight China. It might be better if it happened now instead of ten years from now.

*Interview, Paris, pub. March 4.*

**Melvin R. Laird**
*Secretary of Defense*
*of the United States*

Communist China . . . still constitutes the most dangerous potential for threatening the peace in Asia. Its vast army and

relatively large air and naval forces are **now** on the verge of being supplemented by an operational nuclear capability, giving Communist China the possibility of being one of our gravest national security problems in the 1970's.

*Before Senate Armed Services*
*Committee, Washington, March 19.*

**Mike Mansfield**
*United States Senator, D-Mont.*

Okinawa is Japanese; we have never claimed otherwise. I see no just or rational alternative other than to try to arrive at a fixed time schedule for the progressive and prompt return of administrative control over the Ryukyu Islands to Japan.

*Kansas State University, March 10.*

**Ferdinand E. Marcos**
*President of the Philippines*

There is not a single country in Asia—whether Japan, India, Indonesia or any other—capable of balancing the military power of Communist China, either alone or together. There is a need still for a U.S. defense umbrella over all of Asia. So it would be ridiculous for any Asian leader to say that he wants the United States to get out of Asia.

The new Philippine position on relations with the Communists is that there should be trade on an experimental, country-to-country basis with certain socialist countries in Eastern Europe. But not with Red China or Russia.

*Interview, Manila, pub. March 31.*

If there should ever be any attempt to subvert our free institutions and our republic . . . the Philippines can stand alone, can fight alone and win alone.

*Manila, July 27.*

If the Asian countries cannot get together under the nuclear umbrella of the United States to protect themselves, I have a feeling that Russia may just about be the counterfoil to Red China in Asia. This is something that Asian leaders have been talking about for some time, quietly.

*Interview, Manila, July 28.*

Japan, being the most economically advanced in this region, should now persuade herself to be more active than she has been so far in helping other Asian nations to develop . . . Instead of merely engaging in trade, Japan should now assume some of the burdens of the United States in the improvement of Asian living standards.

*Manila, pub. Sept. 14.*

Our relationship with the United States is not about to terminate in anger. It is just that we have matured . . . We will defend ourselves, if necessary, alone. A regional arrangement will be imperative, first with the help of allies, but later, in 10 or 20 years, among Asian nations alone.

*Before Overseas Press Club, Manila, Oct. 26.*

The two principal problems in Asia right now are economic development and security. On the economic side, we ask for trade, not outright aid . . . Regarding internal security, subversion should be a matter attended to by each country individually alone. External aggression is something else.

*Interview, Manila, pub. Dec. 28.*

## V. K. Krishna Menon
*Former Minister of Defense of India*

You cannot stay nonaligned in the sense that you take no sides. But we are nonaligned in the sense of not getting involved in a war block. I don't think either the United States or the Soviet Union think we are in their camp.

*Interview, New Delhi, pub. June 1.*

## Kiichi Miiyazawa
*Japanese economist*

For years, our people learned to cope with poverty. We do not yet know how to cope with plentifulness.

*Tokyo, pub. Aug. 1.*

## Wayne L. Morse
*Former United States Senator, D-Ore.*

We are the outlaws in Southeast Asia. We have violated article after article of the U.N. and Geneva agreements . . . We've got to get out of Asia, militaristically, and stay out of Asia . . . The Asian nations don't want a Western power on their soil. We're the only Western nation that hasn't learned this yet. The French learned it. The British learned it, the Dutch did, too.

*Television interview, New York, Aug. 26.*

## Edmund S. Muskie
*United States Senator, D-Me.*

The national consensus is clear. While we may cooperate with others as we have in the past, we will not attempt to play policeman of the world any longer. All options in the reduction of American commitments are open, including withdrawal from the Western Pacific. And if the Japanese don't want us here, we will get out even if it hurts the best interests of our two countries.

*Tokyo, Feb. 11.*

## Richard M. Nixon
*President of the United States*

Taking the long view, we simply cannot afford to leave China forever outside the family of nations, there to nurture its fantasies, cherish its hates and threaten its neighbors. There is no place on this small planet for a billion of its potentially most able people to live in angry isolation. But we could go disastrously wrong if, in pursuing this long-range goal, we failed in the short range to read the lessons of history . . . The world cannot be safe until China changes.

*Pub. Jan. 29.*

We see the world as they (the Australians) see it. They are among those who understand, as I think most of us . . . understand, how much rides on what happens in the Pacific. They are a Pacific power, as we are; and at a time when most of the world, whatever they may think privately, will not speak up publicly with regard to what the United States is doing in the Pacific. And, as indicated in the very difficult war in Vietnam, our friends in Australia know why we are there, and we know that they are there with us.

*Washington, May 6.*

I realize . . . that if war is to come, it is most likely to come again from the Pacific and from Asia in the last third of this century. But the other side of that

(RICHARD M. NIXON)

rather pessimistic outlook is that, if peace is to come, it must come primarily from the initiatives of those who live in Asia, and from the United States. Because we who live on the rim of the Pacific have within our hands the power to avoid another war in Asia, to bring peace; and, if we have that peace, then we can see the exciting possibilities for progress in the last third of (this) century.

*Manila, July 26.*

If peace is to come to Asia . . . And I emphasize this point—the United States will play its part, and provide its fair share. But peace in Asia cannot come from the United States. It must come from Asia. The people of Asia, the governments of Asia—they are the ones who must lead the way to peace in Asia.

*Manila, July 27.*

The treaty that we have with Thailand means that it is not just another treaty, not just another piece of paper, but that it is one that has a significance far beyond that . . . We will honor our obligations under the treaty. We will honor them not simply because we have to, because of the words that we have signed, but because we believe in those words . . . We have been together in the past; we are together at the present; and the United States will stand proudly with Thailand against those who might threaten it from abroad or from within.

*Bangkok, July 28.*

Having won the peace together, we (and South Korea) have worked together to maintain that peace. Together we have stood guard along the Korean border for 16 years. Together we have resisted harassment from the North during the last two years. Together we have discovered that the danger from the North has only stiffened our resolve. And we know that we cannot be shaken, that we will not be intimidated should there ever be any renewal of such activity.

*San Francisco, Aug. 22.*

Whenever the leaders of Communist China choose to abandon their self-impos-ed isolation, we are ready to talk with them in the same frank and serious spirit.

*United Nations, N.Y., Sept. 18.*

**U Nu**
*Former Premier of Burma*

It is a sin to kill, to be violent, to resort to violence. But it is a greater sin to look on with folded arms when I see many of my countrymen are suffering under tyranny. So, in my case, I choose the lesser evil.

*Interview, Washington, pub. Sept. 21.*

**Chung Hee Park**
*President of South Korea*

(If the Korean war is ever resumed, it would be) a long war this time, another Vietnam, and in due course of time the U.S. might want to get out of this trouble, as it does now in Vietnam. That is what the North Korean Communists want to achieve, and, knowing this, we have exercised our policy of self-restraint. We should not succumb to their tricks or fall into their trap. The only reason we are able to limit the tension in this area is that the Republic of Korea and the United States are maintaining their policy of self-re-straint.

It would be wrong for the United States to return Okinawa (to Japan) without any conditions. Japan should be prepared to promise to contribute to the defense of free Asia, including the Republic of Korea. The bases there are not only to help in the defense of Japan, but for the security of other Asian countries as well.

*Interview, Seoul, May 31.*

The increase in Japanese strength does not necessarily mean Japan can or will replace the United States (in Asia). To qualify for leadership, a country must accept the responsibilities of power and contribute to the betterment of all Asia. Japan shows few signs of doing so, and the Japanese record contrasts sharply with the generous U.S. contributions on a wide front.

Many nations are unwilling to harbor nuclear arms because of the horrifying implications of thermonuclear warfare. However, our people are intimately familiar with the Communist threat. We have already experienced one brutal war started by them. Therefore, we value the power of deterrence and would tolerate the introduction of nuclear weapons into our territory (by the United States).

*Interview, Seoul, pub. Aug. 25.*

The reason they (the North Koreans) are not executing their invasion plans is because the U.S. forces are in Korea. A withdrawal of U.S. forces is not foreseeable until the threat has been eliminated. And, until then, the continued presence of U.S. forces will be required.

*Seoul, Aug. 28.*

**Charles H. Percy**
*United States Senator, R-Ill.*

It's not a question of the government being rightist or leftist in India. The question here is who responds to the needs of the people.

*New Delhi, Aug. 25.*

**Prince Souvanna Phouma**
*Premier of Laos*

International relations would be much better today if one of our neighbors (North Vietnam), expansionist and totalitarian, wanted to let the Laotians settle their own affairs themselves.

*Vientiane, March 23.*

The bombing carried on by American planes in Laos in the frontier region is a fact that springs from the 1962 Geneva accords. At Geneva, the signatory countries guaranteed the independence, neutrality and territorial integrity of Laos. From the moment that one signatory does not respect the accords, it is the duty of all the other signatories to intervene to enforce respect for them. If North Vietnam wants the bombing to stop, it is necessary that they withdraw their troops from Laos.

*Interview, Vientiane, pub. June 14.*

Too much attention is paid to the Vietnam war. Everyone forgets that *Laos* has been invaded by North Vietnam.

*Interview, Vientiane, Aug. 14.*

Hanoi intensifies its policy of aggression, multiplies its acts of war throughout the territory of Laos, daily violates our frontiers, foments rebellion and, in a word, reneges every day more and more on the obligations solemnly undertaken at Geneva in 1962. It is high time that many of the signatory powers of the 1962 (Geneva) accords, trustees of peace in the Kingdom of Laos, became aware of the dangers that the expansionist policy of the Democratic Republic of Vietnam poses, not only for our nation, but also for Southeast Asia and, perhaps, for the peace of the world.

*Washington, Oct. 8.*

**Lin Piao**
*Defense Minister of Communist China*

The nature of U.S. imperialism as a paper tiger has long since been laid bare by the people throughout the world. U.S. imperialism, the most ferocious enemy of the people of the world, is going downhill more and more . . . They have made so many airplanes and guns, so many nuclear bombs and guided missiles. What is all this for? To frighten, suppress and slaughter the people and dominate the world.

Our aim is to smash revisionism, seize back that portion of power usurped by the bourgeoisie, exercise all-around dictatorship of the proletariat in the superstructure, including all spheres of culture, and strengthen and consolidate the economic base of socialism so as to insure that our country continues to advance in giant strides along the road of socialism.

The general trend of the world today is still as Chairman Mao (Tse-tung) described it: "The enemy rots with every passing day, while for us things are getting better daily."

*Before Chinese Communist Party,*
*Peking, pub. April 29.*

We are determined to liberate Taiwan (Nationalist China). We warn United States imperialism: the heroic Chinese people and the Chinese People's Liberation Army, armed with Mao Tse-tung's thought, are invincible. Should you (the United States) insist on imposing war on the Chinese people, we will keep you

(LIN PIAO)

company and resolutely fight to the finish. On the vast land of China, wherever you go, there will be your burial ground.

*At annual National Day mass meeting,
Peking, Oct. 1.*

**Nikolai V. Podgorny**
*President of the Union of
Soviet Socialist Republics*

The United States must realize that the discontinuation of flights of military planes and of concentration of naval forces near the territories of the Democratic Republic of (North) Korea and the Soviet Union accords with the interests of peace in the Far East and, in the long run, accords with the interests of the United States people themselves.

*Pyongyang, North Korea, May 18.*

**Tunku Abdul Rahman**
*Prime Minister of Malaysia*

I will only go if I am kicked out.

*Kuala Lumpur, May 13.*

**Sinnathamby Rajaratnam**
*Foreign Minister of Singapore*

I do not think that, in this vastly shrunken world, America can shake off Asia and its problems by retreating to the other side of the Pacific and into Europe. Sooner or later, it is bound to bump into Asia . . . therefore . . . a more rational approach is for Asians and Americans to accept the fact that we are deeply involved in one another's affairs and try to make the best of what some Americans and Asians might consider an intolerable situation.

*Singapore, pub. Jan. 19.*

Our ultimate goal is to make every citizen a soldier.

*Singapore, pub. July 2.*

For the first time in 200 years, Southeast Asia will be on its own. The West has withdrawn one by one. First the Dutch, then the French, then the British. The United States will withdraw militarily, too . . . For the first time, the Soviet Union is taking a positive interest in this area. Before, it was interested only in diverting Western countries from Moscow's main area of interest, Europe—in pinning down their resources in Southeast Asia. But now, it has an interest for its own sake.

*United Nations, N.Y., pub. Oct. 16.*

**Jagjivan Ram**
*Minister of Food and
Agriculture of India*

The overpowering influence of the caste system has not been eradicated but has become inherent in the entire Indian society.

*Pub. Feb. 1.*

**Edwin O. Reischauer**
*Former Ambassador to Japan
from the United States*

There is no need to complicate matters further, as we do now, by pretending that Taiwan (Nationalist China) is the real China. This it most assuredly is not; but what it actually is remains to be defined —a second China, an independent Taiwan or a part of China that, in practice, enjoys full autonomy.

*At Center for the Study of
Democratic Institutions,
Santa Barbara, Calif., Jan. 26.*

We have been transfixed with China and our problems in Vietnam for so long that we often forget about Japan. Japan is *the* great power in Asia, and what happens between us and the Japanese is sure to be more important in the long run than what happens in Vietnam or even our relations with China.

*Harvard University, pub. April 23.*

In the long run, the chief problem that China presents may not be the danger that it will be so rich and strong, as well as hostile, that it menaces our basic interests; but, rather, that it may fall so short of meeting the economic needs and aspirations of its people that it remains an unstable and sick fifth of humanity.

*Pub. Oct. 3.*

**William P. Rogers**
*Secretary of State
of the United States*

. . . we are willing to do what we can do to have more friendly relations with Red China, but we are not going to do it in the spirit of exploiting it because we think it will give us some advantage against the Soviet Union.

*News conference, Washington, April 7.*

. . . we are willing to talk to Communist China. We are willing to take steps such as we've taken to show we are very serious in our attempts to try to relieve tensions in the world, and one way of relieving tensions is to talk to the people who are causing tensions.

*News conference, Hong Kong, Aug. 4.*

We recognize, of course, that the Republic of China on Taiwan and Communist China on the mainland are facts of life.

*Canberra, Australia, Aug. 8.*

We would like discussions with them (Communist China). We want to make clear that their isolation is of their own choosing, and if they have a belligerent attitude toward the world it is their belligerence and not ours.

*News conference, Washington, Aug. 20.*

I think what Congress probably is concerned about is the prospect that somehow we could be dragged into another land war in Thailand . . . And I have said to the Senate Foreign Relations Committee and the House Foreign Affairs Committee that we fully understand the necessity for support of any military venture, both by Congress and the public. If there is one thing that Vietnam has made clear, it's that.

*Washington, Aug. 20.*

We are not going to fight any major wars on the mainland of Asia again . . . unless we have the American public and the Congress behind us.

*Television interview, pub. Nov. 29.*

## Carlos P. Romulo
*Foreign Secretary of the Philippines*

After Vietnam, I do not think the American people will ever again consent to involving their troops in Asia. Thus, an American defense of the Philippines in the future is highly dubious. The Americans must now think of themselves—and I don't blame them.

*Manila, pub. Jan. 20.*

In its defense function, SEATO—like NATO—has never been tested. But, unlike NATO, SEATO is incapable of immediate response. It is, in fact, an ineffective instrument for collective security . . . mainly because of a basic lack of unity and consensus among member countries.

*At SEATO conference, Bangkok, May 20.*

Let us not confuse American intention to withdraw troops from Vietnam with American intention to withdraw from Asia. I believe that America can never withdraw from Asia. When Hawaii and Alaska were made part of the union, America proclaimed to the world that she intends to remain a Pacific power.

*News conference, Ito, Japan, pub. June 12.*

Go into the (Philippine) countryside and tell any farmer that you are an American. You can be sure that the farmer will kill his best chicken and cook it for you.

*Manila, pub. Dec. 11.*

## Richard B. Russell
*United States Senator, D-Ga.*

. . . I hope that we will find some way to have some kind of relations with (Communist) China . . . it's seldom that you cause wars by talking to people, and you sometimes avoid it.

*Interview, Washington, pub. Jan. 29.*

## Harrison E. Salisbury
*Associate Managing Editor, "The New York Times"*

(Communist) China is at the center of a very grave crisis. It is in a state of extreme aggression toward its neighbors and is also at the heart of the biggest problem facing the world—the Niagara of population.

*Los Angeles, Jan. 28.*

## Eisaku Sato
*Prime Minister of Japan*

We would welcome any development in which Communist China would be widely received as a member of the international community. However, although the Cultural Revolution is beginning to taper off, Communist China is still beset by a num-

(EISAKU SATO)

ber of problems, both domestic and external, and has not yet taken any initiatives in external relations based on international understanding and cooperation with all countries of the world.

*Tokyo, Jan. 27.*

Regarding the problem of Asian security, it is Japan that is going to play the leading role, while the United States will be cooperating from the sidelines.

*Pub. Oct. 19.*

The Japanese people should have the spirit to defend their own country by their own efforts. But it is no shame to depend on a collective security formula; it is no shame to be under the American nuclear umbrella.

*News conference, Tokyo, Nov. 7.*

**Hugh Scott**
*United States Senator, R-Pa.*

(Communist) China is a closed society, and you cannot get at the pearl until you find a means of opening the oyster.

*News conference, Tokyo, Feb. 15.*

I've held the position, since the Korean War, that no nation at war with the United Nations should be a member. The Panmunjom agreement was only an armistice and not a peace, so Red China is technically still at war with the U.N.

*News conference, Washington, Mar. 21.*

**Franz Seda**
*Minister of Communications*
*of Indonesia*

The traditional flow of economic aid from the West to (the) East is changing. We look to Japan as the great new industrial nation.

*At Ministerial Conference for*
*Economic Development of Southeast*
*Asia, Bangkok, April 3.*

**Mitchell Sharp**
*Secretary of State for*
*External Affairs of Canada*

We have reached the stage when none of the big questions—detente, arms control, narrowing the gap between rich and poor, building a stable world society and insuring world peace—can be solved without having regard for the (Communist) Chinese quarter of mankind. My government believes that a solution must involve broadening the scope and direction of China's contacts with the other nations of the world.

*Before North Atlantic Treaty*
*Organization, Washington, April 10.*

**David M. Shoup**
*General (Ret.) and former Commandant,*
*United States Marine Corps*

. . . I don't think the whole of Southeast Asia is related to the present and future safety and freedom of the people of this country (or) is worth the life or limb of a single American . . . I believe that if we had and would keep our dirty, bloody, dollar-crooked fingers out of the business of these nations so full of depressed, exploited people, they will arrive at a solution of their own.

*Pub. Oct. 15.*

**Prince Norodom Sihanouk**
*Chief of State of Cambodia*

I used to be the most anti-American in the world. But the Communists . . . wanted Cambodia and the United States to remain enemies. This is not in our interest while we have a war on our land and Red foreigners burn our schools.

*News conference, Phnom Penh, April 16.*

It was with great sorrow that I had decided to reject the American overtures (to resume diplomatic relations). I always react harshly when Cambodia's frontiers are being questioned . . . Everybody is against us; everybody is killing us.

*News Conference,*
*Phnom Penh, May 3.*

I want only one thing: the survival of my country, even if it has to become Communist or Maoist.

*Pub. May.*

Despite assurances that they would always recognize our present frontiers, and, although they swear by all the Communists gods that they would never intervene in our affairs, our Vietnamese socialist

friends are communizing our people and overtly Vietnamizing our territory . . .
*Phnom Penh, pub. Sept. 10.*

**Ram Subhag Singh**
*Leader, Syndicate bloc of*
*Indian Parliament*

We will resist with all force Mrs. (Indira) Gandhi's attempt to establish personal rule. We shall never allow Hitlers and Mussolinis to come to power.
*At Syndicate convention,*
*Gujerat State, India, Dec. 21.*

**Theodore C. Sorensen**
*Former Special Counsel to*
*President John F. Kennedy*

If the American people are willing to have our Government offer an exchange of diplomats, businessmen, tourists and artists to Moscow, despite Soviet action in Europe and the Middle East, they should be willing to have a similar offer made to Peking.
*New York, March 20.*

**T. N. J. Suharto**
*President of Indonesia*

The encouraging situation in Indonesia —stability in politics, economics and the military—is ironic now that the American people are tending to withdraw their assistance. It is unfortunate that now Indonesia has the opportunities to grow, and the American people want to decrease their overseas aid.
*Interview, Jakarta, July 22.*

What we have done is to heal the deep economic wounds that for years had wrecked the body of our nation, like someone who had been bleeding seriously and whose wounds are now healing. We have again begun to walk and to work.

We reject any form of military alliance. Military pacts, evidently, are not an effective form of defense (and) will only provoke other sides to strengthen their armaments and form counter military pacts.
*Independence Day Address,*
*Jakarta, Aug. 10.*

**Nguyen Van Thieu**
*President of South Vietnam*

Asians could never live in peace if the Communists in this part of the world are not destroyed.
*Taipei, Taiwan, May 30.*

**Haki Toska**
*Vice Premier of Albania*

The People's Republic of China has become a great world power. She now executes an exceedingly important function, affecting practical developments and safeguarding world peace and security. Without the direct participation of the People's Republic of China, no significant international political problems can be resolved in a manner that benefits the people of all countries and serves the cause of world peace.
*Peking, pub. Oct. 9.*

**John G. Tower**
*United States Senator, R-Tex*

. . . there is growing Communist terrorist activity in Thailand and increasing infiltration into that country. It is apparent that Mao Tse-tung was not kidding when he earmarked Thailand as the next target for a so-called "war of national liberation."
*News conference, Washington, April 14.*

**Arnold Toynbee**
*Historian*

I don't think there is any evidence that the Chinese want to overrun Southeast Asia; or, indeed, that they could permanently, because, after all, Vietnam did successfully resist absorption for many, many centuries; and, if she were united, she certainly would spend all her energies resisting being absorbed by China.
*Interview, London, pub. March 18.*

**Yumzhagin Tsedenbal**
*Premier of Mongolia*

As is known, Communists have the fairest approach to the solution of the national problem. They are guided by the principles of equality, mutual respect, friendship and cooperation of different peoples and national minorities. These principles are fully realized in Mongolia as in the

(YUMZHAGIN TSEDENBAL)

Soviet Union. We have always supported the idea that all nationalities in all states, whether in China, the U.S.A. or another country, live in friendship and complete equality without humiliation, discrimination or exploitation.

*Interview, Ulan Bator, Mongolia, May 19.*

**John V. Tunney**
*United States Representative, D-Calif.*

It is time for the United States to stop assuming the entire burden of maintaining peace in Asia. It is time for Japan to pick up its fair share . . . Japan no longer has a wartorn economy, and she should begin acting like a great nation.

*Pub. Sept. 21.*

**Robert Welch**
*President, John Birch Society*

. . . There is no more reality of a rift between Russia and China than the moon being made of green cheese.

*News conference, Los Angeles, Mar. 7.*

**Theodore H. White**
*Author*

We think of Japan as docile, but they're our biggest foreign problem of the 1970's. We ravaged their industry, and last year they outbuilt us in ships 19 to 1. They'll make their own deal with China, and we haven't begun to think about the consequences of that yet.

*Interview, New York, pub. July 27.*

**Hobyo Yara**
*Chief Executive of the Ryukyu Islands*

Being ruled by someone of a different race simply is not right. I'm sure that, however good or bad American rule might have been, we would always have had a movement for reunification with Japan.

*Interview, Naha, Okinawa, Feb. 7.*

**Lee Kuan Yew**
*Prime Minister of Singapore*

When, instead of dams and power stations, irrigation works, roads and railways, we have Rolls Royces, executive mansions —not to mention golden bedsteads—then I suggest we of the less developed countries must look at ourselves.

*Pub. Jan. 25.*

By 1972, we must demonstrate that we have the wherewithall to make it extremely unpleasant for anybody contemplating taking liberties with us . . . Foreign observers trained to discern and assess the fighting qualities and military skills of others must be left in no doubt that Singapore is a community that cannot be subjugated and turned to economic serfs for the well-being of others.

*Singapore, pub. July 2.*

If South Vietnam is lost, the chances are that whoever forms the Communist Government will want to be the successor of French Indo-China, which includes Laos and Cambodia. Whether they will be able to go on and create an insurrection in Thailand is quite another matter. I feel that if the Thais do not let their will melt away at the thought of being on their own—with American aid in arms and resources, but not men—then Thailand will manage to stay non-Communist. If Thailand sticks, then Malaysia has a better chance, and so Singapore will stick.

*Interview, Singapore, pub. July 25.*

**Chung Ku Young**
*Former President of North Korea*

. . . we do not have freedom of speech in our country (North Korea) at this time as you know it in the United States. How many members of the Assembly can speak out as I am speaking? There are many who agree with me, but they live in the valley of fear.

*Seoul, Sept. 13.*

**Paul Yu-pin**
*President, Fu-jen University, Taiwan*

. . . if Lin Piao (Defense Minister of Communist China) takes charge after Mao Tse-tung passes, China will be in the hands of an even less intelligent man. It will be a case of going from bad to worse.

*Before Overseas Press Club,*
*New York, pub. May 17.*

## THE PUEBLO INCIDENT

**Don E. Bailey**
*Crew member, U.S.S. "Pueblo"*

All the beatings we took (while captive in North Korea) didn't hurt half as much as the fact that, when we were pleading for help, we got no assistance from the largest navy in the world. This hurt me more than any beating I took.

> *Before Naval Court of Inquiry,*
> *Coronado, Calif., Feb. 28.*

**Lloyd M. Bucher**
*Commander, United States Navy;*
*Captain, U.S.S. "Pueblo"*

I did not feel at that time (during the seizure) there was any point in going to war with those ships surrounding me. I was completely, hopelessly outgunned.

> *Before Naval Court of Inquiry,*
> *Coronado, Calif., pub. Feb. 3.*

I was flattened out with a good blow across the kisser. They (the North Koreans) kicked me and pulled me to my feet and beat me into semi-consciousness . . . they reverted to the idea I was a Central Intelligence Agency agent, and now they were sure of it; and CIA agents don't live to tell about it when they are caught in Korea. I was prepared for the fact that they were going to do me in.

> *Before Naval Court of Inquiry,*
> *Coronado, Calif., March 11.*

I hereby state unequivocally that, at the time of that seizure, we did not have the power to resist.

> *Before Naval Court of Inquiry,*
> *Coronado, Calif., pub. March 17.*

Suppose they (North Korea) sent a couple of subs into San Diego harbor and attacked two of our carriers—I wonder what we'd do about that. I mean, I wonder just how far we are going to permit them to go without doing something about it.

> *Pub. April 28.*

I have tried for months to point out that the North Koreans are a cruel, fanatical, almost incorrigible people, without any regard for law, life, reason or the rights of others. To the North Korean government, international law is a joke and a mockery; they simply don't recognize it . . . We simply cannot treat North Korea under its present government as a member of the civilized family of nations—it is not; it is a renegade, outlaw nation of marauders.

> *Interview, pub. May 18.*

**Stephen R. Harris**
*Lieutenant, United States Navy;*
*crew member, U.S.S. "Pueblo"*

The code of conduct kept going round and round in my mind, and it emerged (that) we were not involved in any war with these people. We were not prisoners of war, and it was therefore difficult to know if the code of conduct applied.

> *Before Naval Court of Inquiry,*
> *Coronado, Calif., Feb. 19.*

**Timothy Harris**
*Lieutenant, United States Navy;*
*crew member, U.S.S. "Pueblo"*

. . . I wanted to kill myself, but I couldn't . . . I kept waiting for our bombers to come . . . the North Koreans gave me a plant for my room, but I hated them so much I urinated on it and killed it . . .

> *Before Naval Court of Inquiry,*
> *Coronado, Calif., Feb. 19.*

**E. Miles Harvey**
*Attorney for Commander*
*Lloyd M. Bucher*

A court of inquiry such as this is a cruel business because it cannot bring back Duane Hodges (killed in seizure of the ship), because it cannot return the U.S.S. *Pueblo*, or completely heal the scars that

(E. MILES HARVEY)

many of the crew will carry for the rest of their lives, or eliminate the nightmares that will continue for most of the crew.
*Before Naval Court of Inquiry, Coronado, Calif., March 13.*

**Lee Roy Hayes**
*Crew member, U.S.S. "Pueblo"*

I would rather be killed by my own people than by the Communists.
*Before Naval Court of Inquiry, Coronado, Calif., pub. Feb. 21.*

**Frank L. Johnson**
*Rear Admiral, United States Navy;*
*Chief, U.S. Naval Forces-Japan*
*at time of "Pueblo" capture*

I was not in favor of arming (the *Pueblo*). I did consider that they (guns) might well be provocative.
*Before Naval Court of Inquiry, Coronado, Calif., Jan. 29.*

I would suggest that a bookmaker would give you such fantastic odds (against the possibility of capture of the *Pueblo*) that someone as rich as Howard Hughes could not pay it off.
*Before Naval Court of Inquiry, Coronado, Calif., pub. Feb. 7.*

**Charles Law**
*Crew member, U.S.S. "Pueblo"*

If they (North Korea) were fanatical enough to take us off the high seas, there wasn't any doubt in my mind they would kill us. We waited for the United States to come in and annihilate this bunch of barbarians.
*Before Naval Court of Inquiry, Coronado, Calif., Feb. 21.*

**Alton A. Lennon**
*United States Representative, D-N.C.*

If this nation (the United States) can capitulate and get on its knees and admit things it's not guilty of, what do you expect of a human being?
*Before Special House Investigating Committee, Washington, April 28.*

**Richard B. Russell**
*United States Senator, D-Ga.*

They (crew of the *Pueblo*) are heroes in the sense that they survived . . . but they did sign a great many statements that did not reflect any great heroism in my mind.
*Pub. Jan. 13.*

**Ulysses S. Grant Sharp**
*Admiral, United States Navy;*
*commander, U.S. Naval Forces-Pacific*
*at time of "Pueblo" capture*

I had to consider everything in my area and what I could expect from the United States to back it up; and I didn't think that was enough to wage two wars (in Vietnam and Korea).
*Before House Armed Services Subcommittee, Washington, pub. July 29.*

**J. Victor Smith**
*Vice Admiral, United States Navy;*
*commander, U.S. Pacific Fleet,*
*Amphibious Forces*

The North Koreans, as well as the South Koreans, are of Mongolian descent . . . a hardy but cruel race, and, the further North, the more cruel.

These people (the North Koreans) just don't have any regard for the things we think are important. They are one step above animals—that is, the low-level people. The top level are intelligent, but completely without scruples or conscience.
*At U.S.S. Pueblo hearings, Coronado, Calif., March 10.*

# VIETNAM

**Creighton Abrams**
*General, United States Army;*
*commander, U.S. Forces in Vietnam*

. . . before I came here this last time, I was in Boston and saw Leinsdorf conduct Beethoven's *Fifth.* Now, that's the way the war should be run. He calls on his strings —and he gets a little bit of strings. He calls on his drums—and he gets a little bit of drums. That's the way we should do it— a little bit of air support just when it's needed, not a goddamned hour of air support; a little bit of artillery, not a goddamned hour of artillery.
*Interview, Saigon, pub. Oct. 5.*

**Dean Acheson**
*Former Secretary of State*
*of the United States*

. . . once people are convinced, as I am convinced, that the President (Nixon) wants to bring this thing (the war) to a close as much as anybody in the country does, and that he is doing his very best to that end, they will support him as they should support him, and not criticize every step as not being enough.
*Television interview, New York, Sept. 28.*

**Spiro T. Agnew**
*Vice President of the United States*

We have invested more than 35,000 American lives to prove confrontation is costly. The Viet Cong remains intransigent because of the slender hope that the voices of dissent at home will force us to alter— perhaps even abdicate—this policy. This Administration wants peace, but not at that price.
*At Midwestern Governors Conference,*
*Wichita, Kans., July 1.*

Certainly the citizens have a right to protest this war. But they have picked the wrong target. They should protest the policies of the North Vietnamese who have rejected every move at the conference table; they should protest the Viet Cong's slaughter by the thousands of South Vietnamese; they should protest the inhuman treatment of prisoners of war . . .
*Dallas, Oct. 8.*

A spirit of national masochism prevails, encouraged by an effete corps of impudent snobs who characterize themselves as intellectuals. It is in this setting of dangerous oversimplification that the war in Vietnam achieves its greatest distortion.
*At Republican fund-raising dinner,*
*New Orleans, Oct. 19.*

. . . (the) arrogant ones and their admirers in the Congress of the United States are bringing this nation to the most important decision it will ever have to make. They are asking us to repudiate principles that have made this country great. This course is one of applause for our enemies and condemnation for our leaders. Their course is a course that will ultimately weaken and erode the fiber of America. They have a masochistic compulsion to destroy their country's strength, whether or not it is constructive. And they rouse themselves to a continual emotional crescendo—substituting disruptive demonstration for reason and precipitate action for persuasion.
*Jackson, Miss., pub. Oct. 26.*

In the case of the Vietnam Moratorium, the objective announced by the leaders, immediate unilateral withdrawal of all our forces from Vietnam, was not only unsound but idiotic. The tragedy was that thousands who participated wanted only to show a fervent desire for peace, but were used by the political hustlers who ran the event.

This is not Richard Nixon's war . . . but it will be Richard Nixon's peace, if we only let him make it.
*Harrisburg, Pa., Oct. 30.*

## George D. Aiken
*United States Senator, R-Vt.*

The North Vietnamese are just as sick of the war as we are.

*Pub. April 12.*

. . . we have now accomplished our purpose as far as South Vietnam is concerned. So it is my belief that the United States would do well to advise the South Vietnamese government immediately of our intentions and then start an orderly withdrawal of our military personnel, turning that country and that war back to its rightful owners. It may take some time to complete this operation, but it should be started without delay.

*Before the Senate, Washington, May 1.*

## George Andrews
*United States Representative, D-Ala.*

There is but one way to get out of South Vietnam honorably, and that is to win the war and defeat the enemy. I have said for years the greatest way to fight this war is just to pick up the telephone and call them in Hanoi and say, "If you are not out of there within 30 days, we are going to bring you to your knees. We think we can do it with conventional weapons." Now, let us act like men. Let us act like Americans. Let us fight this war to win, or, as was said in the Navy when I was in the Navy, "Get the hell out of there."

*Before the House, Washington, Oct. 1.*

## Leslie C. Arends
*United States Representative, R-Ill.*

Those who persist in criticizing our President's efforts and who persist in a specific plan for our withdrawal are simply saying, unwittingly or not, to Hanoi that there is no need to negotiate—in due course the United States will capitulate. This we must never do. At no time in our history has this great country of ours, set upon an honorable course, hauled down its flag and surrendered.

*Before the House, Washington, Oct. 3.*

## John M. Ashbrook
*United States Representative, R-Ohio*

If the good, honorable, and sincere people who oppose the war were not so naive they would not tie up with the worst revolutionary elements in the country. This is one thing I have never been able to understand about the American left. Why did not the good liberals say, "You nuts go ahead and have your demonstrations on October 15 and November 15. Thanks, but we will have our protest on November 1 or some other time."

*Before the House, Washington, Oct. 16.*

## Thomas L. Ashley
*United States Representative, D-Ohio*

I am sympathetic to the purposes of the moratorium, but I think it is important that we refrain from making the administration's quest for peace more difficult than it already is. To the extent that the moratorium and other demonstrations indicate a deep-seated desire for peace, a useful purpose may be served. But to the extent that these and other activities result in reducing options available to the administration, we jeopardize the very cause we seek to serve.

*Before the House, Washington, Oct. 15.*

## Truong Van Nguyen Be
*Lt. Col., Army of South Vietnam; head of National Training Center*

It's like a friend of mind who became addicted to opium and sleeping pills. He could do nothing for himself. I tried to help him, but there was not much I could do. The opium and sleeping pills— they are strangely like (the U.S.) B-52s. Much of the fighting is done for us and it affects our self-reliance. We must do this job ourselves, and I think we can.

*Vungtau, South Vietnam, pub. Aug. 17.*

## Jonathan B. Bingham
*United States Representative, D-N.Y.*

. . . if, after all this time and effort, after all the lives lost and bodies mangled, after the extensive training to Vietnamese forces and after the enormous amounts of materiel that we have given them and will give them, the Republic of South Vietnam would collapse upon the departure of American troops, then I say we have been engaged in propping up a shell of a regime with no strength of its own and should recognize the task as not only hopeless but useless.

*Before the House, Washington, Oct. 14.*

### Madame Nguyen Thi Binh
*Foreign Minister, National Liberation*
*Front of South Vietnam-Viet Cong*

The (National Liberation) Front practices a policy of scrupulous clemency and generosity toward captured American soldiers.

*Interview, Paris, pub. May 14.*

The withdrawal of the 25,000 American troops from South Vietnam is a U.S. trick to deceive public opinion. Therefore, the so-called peace measures lauded by the American delegates (to the Paris peace talks) are but perfidious U.S. maneuvers to stick to South Vietnam and realize U.S. neo-colonialism.

*Paris, July 10.*

It is obvious that the so-called "solution for free elections" of (President) Nguyen Van Thieu is but a maneuver of the United States aimed at opposing the formation of (a) coalition government in South Vietnam, deceiving and appeasing public opinion which strongly demands that the United States withdraw its troops, that the Thieu-Ky-Huong regime be replaced and a peace cabinet set up so as to provide favorable conditions for the correct settlement of the South Vietnamese problem.

*Paris, July 17.*

Monsieur Nixon declared during the Presidential campaign that, if he were elected President, he would end the war in Vietnam in six months. Now eight months have elapsed, and Monsieur Nixon has spared no effort to violate the security and sovereignty of the Democratic Republic of Vietnam (North Vietnam).

*Interview, Paris, Oct. 12.*

### Benjamin B. Blackburn
*United States Representative, R-Ga.*

If ever a time existed when the citizens of a democracy should stand as one behind their duly elected leader, then that time is now. Over 38,700 of America's finest young men can never share in the bounties of our nation because they have

given the final commitment in support of their nation's policy. Our President has reassured us that those who have died shall not have died in vain . . . Let us reassure our President that, while the mouths which cry out for American surrender are being heard, the hearts, hands and minds of the great majority of American people are pledged to the support of their country.

*Before the House, Washington, Sept. 29.*

### George Brown
*Deputy Leader, British Labor Party;*
*former Foreign Secretary*
*of the United Kingdom*

I wish Americans would stop weeping (over Vietnam). They have taken over a role that Britain has played so long, and we played it tough and strong. Why don't the Americans get on and finish the job?

*Radio interview, London, pub. Dec. 8.*

### David Bruce
*United States Ambassador*
*to the United Kingdom*

. . . the resumption of bombing of the North would start British demonstrations against us all over again. The British, and Europeans in general, feel that the resumption of bombing would reopen a case they consider had been closed when the truce talks started in Paris.

*London, pub. March 14.*

### Ellsworth Bunker
*United States Ambassador*
*to South Vietnam*

It is true that there are large segments of the American people who are extremely articulate in opposition to our role in Vietnam. But there are even more substantial numbers of Americans who recognize that the responsibilities of a great world power like our nation are not easy or cheap to carry out and, at times, require sacrifices by the people. A great power must have patience to carry out a successful foreign policy. I feel these people realize that the prospects for peace in the world would not be improved if we desert an ally who has made enormous sacrifices partly in reliance on our promise to stand by him.

(ELLSWORTH BUNKER)

Our objective has never been a military victory in the conventional sense. We have been fighting a limited war, with limited objectives and with limited resources. We have sought to prevent the North Vietnamese from taking over the South by force, and, to the extent that we have been able to frustrate these efforts, we have been successful. This may not be a victory in the usual sense of the word, but it is, nevertheless, success.

*Interview, Saigon, pub. Nov. 17.*

**Henry A. Byroade**
*United States Ambassador*
*to the Philippines*

Many bitter things have . . . been said about the arrangements for the support of PHILCAG (Philippines civil action group) in Vietnam. I do not know why or how things can get so much out of perspective. In every war (it has fought) . . . the U.S. has shared its resources with its allies. The Russians, the French, the Poles, the English and the Filipinos that fought with us in World War II did not consider themselves mercenaries; nor do other allies that are still fighting with us to help Vietnam. Why should this ugly word be used now?

*Before Rotary Club, Manila, Dec. 4.*

**Kyu Han Choi**
*Foreign Minister of South Korea*

Both military and diplomatic efforts of the allies should be continued in Vietnam until a genuine and just peace shall have been attained . . . in the absence of a corresponding action on the part of the Communists, unilateral withdrawal of even a part of the allied troops will hardly be a wise move.

*Bangkok, May 22.*

**Frank Church**
*United States Senator, D-Ida.*

For years we've heard the repetition of this same old fallow argument, (that) you must not speak up, even though you are a free people, because somehow this will not set well somewhere else and upset the President's plans. But if we hadn't spoken up . . . I don't think that the policy of accelerating the war would ever have been reversed. It was under the pressures of the dissent that President Johnson finally reversed the policy of acceleration.

If we remove all of our troops, it is hardly a move that would leave the Saigon Government naked before its enemies. There are 1,500,000 South Vietnamese troops in the field against 135,000 Viet Cong and 90,000 North Vietnamese. Now, if that vast army, supplied and equipped by the United States, can be inspired to defend the Saigon Government, it will survive, but if it cannot be inspired, then it does not deserve to survive.

(President Nixon's open-end approach to the Vietnam war) fails to really put the pressure on Saigon. Our biggest problem there is Hanoi, but Saigon is almost as big a problem . . . We fought and lost 45,000 men. Now, how much longer do we stay and fight for them and protect them from their own population?

*Television interview, Washington,*
*Oct. 12.*

**Don H. Clausen**
*United States Representative, R-Calif.*

. . . I question any demonstration against the war that criticizes *only* the President of the U.S.—that calls for the withdrawal of *only* U.S. troops—that calls on *only* the U.S. government to work harder for peace —or that condemns *only* one party to the conflict for the slow progress being made in negotiations at Paris. I also believe the American people are getting as tired of one-sided demonstrations in this country as they are of the war in Vietnam. . . . isn't it about time these demonstrations start "telling it to Hanoi?"

*Before the House, Washington, Nov. 13.*

**William Sloane Coffin**
*Chaplain, Yale University*

When the fighting stops in Vietnam, President Nixon must either grant amnesty to the thousands of young men who fled the country to avoid the draft, or he will create a band of permanent political exiles. If Mr. Nixon wants to be a peacemaker, and to bring the country together, he needs this act of reconciliation and generosity.

*Yale University, pub. March 17.*

**Benjamin V. Cohen**
*Lawyer; former diplomat*

Our retreat from Vietnam is not a retreat to isolationism. It is a retreat from what, with the wisdom of hindsight, if not foresight, we should recognize as an unfortunate mis-adventure in the internal affairs of another country.
*Washington, Nov. 9.*

**William M. Colmer**
*United States Representative, D-Miss.*

I have been a hawk (I would prefer the term "eagle"). But I have come reluctantly to the conclusion that we have to get out of Vietnam . . . I have come to it simply because we have made the mistake, under all the administrations that have been in power since this war started, of following the old appeasement policy. We have been permitting the other side to call the signals, and we have been running the defensive play. We cannot win a war that way. We cannot win a diplomatic peace that way any more than a football team can win under such rules of the game.
*Before the House, Washington, Dec. 1.*

**Thomas F. Connolly**
*Vice Admiral, United States Navy; deputy Chief of Naval Operations-Air*

The lack of success in the war is charged directly to the military, even though the war has been managed, directed and controlled by persons out of uniform.
*Washington, pub. Sept. 1.*

**Alan Cranston**
*United States Senator, D-Calif.*

Before it is too late, we must come to grips with the false god of "military victory." We must stop thinking of military escalation as an alternative to diplomatic frustration. No matter what happens in Paris (at the peace talks), we must not reverse what should be an irrevocable commitment to extricate ourselves militarily from Vietnam.
*Before the Senate, Washington, July 23.*

I believe we should pull all our troops out as fast as we can, considering only their own security and safety as they move out, without waiting any longer for Communists and Hanoi to make peace, or corrupt generals in Saigon to shape up.
*Los Angeles, pub. Nov. 2.*

**Raymond Davis**
*Maj. Gen., United States Marine Corps*

It makes no sense to watch 400 (North Vietnamese) trucks a day moving through Laos with ammunition to kill Americans. The quickest way to shorten this war is to destroy these sanctuaries. I'm not trying to raise the ante; but we came here to assure the freedom of South Vietnam, and I don't think that can be accomplished with anything less than the defeat of the North Vietnamese Army.
*Interview, Dong Ha, South Vietnam, April 1.*

**Michel Debre**
*Foreign Minister of France*

There will certainly still be procedural difficulties (in the Paris peace talks), and there will be yet other, greater, difficulties ahead; but the two sides, the four sides, are sharing a common sentiment—to make peace.
*Paris, Jan. 14.*

**Samuel L. Devine**
*United States Representative, R-Ohio*

Sometimes it looks like an auction—seeing who can outbid the President on (U.S. troop) withdrawals. And it is so obvious these vocal hucksters are completely lacking in qualifications to formulate an intelligent judgment. When President Nixon announces a proposed withdrawal of 50,000 troops, an eager politician bids 100,000; then, not to be outdone, a colleague goes for 200,000, and another starry-eyed hero, wearing an ensemble of dove-feathers, cries out for immediate withdrawal of everybody, yesterday . . . I do not know what solutions are offered by the instant withdrawal crowd, other than to appeal to the emotional responses of families who have loved ones involved. However, I do know it is not a traditional American posture to run up the white flag of surrender, to turn tail and run, to abdicate the honor of our commitments.
*Before the House, Washington, Oct. 1.*

**Everett M. Dirksen**
*United States Senator, R-Ill.*

What could be the impact on troop morale and discipline when a Senator (Edward M. Kennedy) 12,000 miles removed from Hamburger Hill (South Vietnam), calls that 10-day action "senseless and irresponsible"? Can it be interpreted in any other way than a direct reflection on the judgment and competence of our field commanders in Vietnam?

*Washington, pub. June 6.*

**William Jennings Bryan Dorn**
*United States Representative, D-S.C.*

This (Vietnam Moratorium) demonstration is not the way to legislate, promote peace or change foreign policy. It is a blatant attempt to force, by sheer weight of numbers and demonstrations, a change in national policy. It is pressure. It is a form of force which is a dangerous precedent—dangerous to the legislative processes and representative government. It is a threat to the President's Constitutional power, duties and responsibilities. It is an attempt to reduce the President of the United States to a cringing vassal, a stooge of mobs and demonstrators. If the President and the Congress can be pressured by mobs and demonstrations, then freedom and orderly legislative processes will become a mockery and a fraud.

*Before the House,*
*Washington, Nov. 13.*

**Paul J. Fannin**
*United States Senator, R-Ariz.*

I have followed some of the statements of recent days made by those who say that we must have peace in Vietnam, and that we must have it almost, apparently, at any price. The words have a ring about them that is reminiscent of Munich and the British Prime Minister's proclamation of "peace in our time." No one needs to be reminded that his call for peace came upon the eve of the most destructive war the world has ever known.

*Before the Senate,*
*Washington, Sept. 30.*

**Duane L. Faw**
*Brig. Gen. and Staff Judge Advocate*
*to the Commandant,*
*United States Marine Corps*

When you put hundreds of thousands of young men together in a combat environment, you're bound to have a certain number of bad eggs. But the vast, vast majority of men who've been in the field are completely dedicated individuals who take no joy in killing and will do anything possible to keep destruction to a minimum. Go to Vietnam, and 95 per cent of the guys you meet will be the kind you'd be proud to have as a brother.

*Pub. Dec. 15.*

**Gerald R. Ford**
*United States Representative, R-Mich.*

. . . if the United Nations is to be more than a debating society and a propaganda forum, the members of that organization must respond meaningfully to President Nixon's urging that they persuade Hanoi to engage in productive peace negotiations at Paris . . . If only a fraction of the U.N. members, but a sizable number, were to raise their voices in protest against the unyielding position of North Vietnam at Paris, the result might be to move the other side to some degree.

*Before the House, Washington, Sept. 18.*

**Ed Foreman**
*United States Representative, R-N.M.*

So long as hostilities in Vietnam continue, so long as Americans are fighting and dying in a foreign land, it is immoral, it is unconscionable, and it is un-American not to use every available means to stop vital supplies from reaching the enemy and flowing through channels provided by countries receiving American tax dollars in aid and grants and/or trade or exports.

*Before the House, Washington, Oct. 16.*

**Robert Frishman**
*Lieutenant, United States Navy;*
*former prisoner of war in North Vietnam*

I don't think solitary confinement, forced statements, living in a cage for three years, being put in straps, not being allowed to sleep or eat, removal of finger nails, being hung from the ceiling, having an infected arm almost lost without medical care, being dragged along the ground with a broken leg and not allowing exchange of mail for prisoners are humane.

*News conference, Washington, Sept. 2.*

## J. William Fulbright
*United States Senator, D-Ark.*

. . . it is not in our national interest to determine that there must be an independent, non-Communist South Vietnam.

*Washington, May 6.*

The courage and endurance of our fighting men (in Vietnam) command the respect of all Americans. The fault in our war policy lies not with them but with the political decisions which committed them to an impossible task.

*National War College, Washington, May 19.*

. . . in terms of flaunting by Government officials of the people's right to know the facts, there has been no period in American history comparable to that of our involvement in Vietnam. From the shoddy disregard of the Geneva accords, through the misrepresentation surrounding passage of the Tonkin Gulf resolution, down to the present-day attempt to pass off the dictatorial Thieu regime as a government which shares our values, the executive branch of the Government has failed— and continues to fail—to come clean with the American public.

*Before the Senate, Washington, Sept. 12.*

I think by liquidating this war at the earliest possible opportunity we show the greatest consideration for the people of Vietnam. We're not admitting a defeat. We're not bugging out on a war. We're liquidating a tragic mistake.

*Washington, Oct. 1.*

The U.S. has no vital interest in whether South Vietnam is governed by Communists, non-Communists or a coalition; nor is it a matter of vital interest to the U.S. whether North or South Vietnam are united or divided. Our interest is in the prevalence, whatever its form, of indigenous Vietnamese nationalism. Beyond that,

strategic interest gives way to ideological preference—if not, indeed, to ideological obsession.

This war is not now and never has been essential to our interests, essential, that is, to the freedom and safety of the American people. The exact terms of peace do not, therefore, matter very much from the standpoint of American interests. But the early restoration of peace matters enormously, because every day that this war goes on the sickness of American society worsens.

*Washington University, St. Louis, Dec. 10.*

## Cornelius E. Gallagher
*United States Representative, D-N.J.*

. . . to set a firm date for withdrawal from Vietnam—an action which is as unrealistic to us as it would be incredible to the other side—may be seen more as an ultimatum by the other side than as a peaceful gesture. Such a resolution might, indeed, force the hand of our President— leaving him with the alternatives in the field of a Dunkirk or a Dienbienphu. He could choose neither of these alternatives.

*Before the House, Washington, Sept. 30.*

## Minoru Genda
*Member of Japanese Diet*

War should be short. Force should be used swiftly, like an arrow shot from a strong bow. I do not approve of Russia's attack on Czechoslovakia, but, militarily, they did well. It was all over in a few days, just like the Israeli-Arab war. But the Vietnam war has dragged on for so long it is now very hard to end.

*Interview, Tokyo, pub. Oct. 27.*

## Vo Nguyen Giap
*Minister of Defense of North Vietnam*

We won a military victory over the French, and we'll win it over the Americans, too. Yes . . . their Dienbienphu is still to come; and it will come. The Americans will lose the war on the day when their military might is at its maximum and the great machine they've put together can't move any more. That is, we'll beat them at the moment when they have the

(VO NGUYEN GIAP)

most men, the most arms and the greatest. hope of winning. Because all that money and strength will be a stone around their neck. It's inevitable.

We're not in a hurry (at the Paris peace talks); we have patience. While the delegates talk, we fight. We want peace, but not peace at any price, not a compromise peace. For us, peace must mean total victory; the Americans must get out. A compromise would be a threat of enslavement; and we'd rather die than be slaves.
*Interview, Hanoi, pub. April 6.*

Vietnamization will become a tragedy not only for the puppet army (of South Vietnam) but also for the American troops. The U.S. and puppet troops, which have both taken severe beatings, will get yet harder ones.
*Pub. Dec. 21.*

### Arthur J. Goldberg
*Former United States Ambassador
to the United Nations*

The first step for us to break the logjam in Paris would be (to) stop all offensive action. This would include terminating the B-52 (bombing) raids and the seize-and-destroy missions. We should engage only in defensive operations. I believe if we did that, the logjam would be broken.
*Interview, Washington, Sept. 30.*

### Barry M. Goldwater
*United States Senator, R-Ariz.*

When you go to war, you make up your mind to win, or you do not go to war . . . I am convinced that we could have won that war six years ago, had we fought the war as wars should be fought. But, when we try to fight a war halfway, and have an enemy that wants to fight it all the way, we cannot win.
*July 11.*

If we pull out of Vietnam without either a victory on the field of battle or one achieved in Paris, we're going to watch our allies fall away from us and they're going to look around for somebody else to hitch their star to. They will know for certain the United States will not honor one of the 54 treaties we have made and the United States will become in that respect a dishonorable nation. If we renege this leadership, there's only one country that has the power and the political strength to move in and that would be Russia. I say to my friends in Congress, governors and mayors who have yielded to this political temptation of trying to appear dovish, that they're selling their country down the road. They're not going to achieve anything. The President has said that he will not pay any attention to them and I know he won't.
*New Orleans, Oct. 10.*

No amount of shouting or banner waving or street clogging or mass assemblies is going to help the cause of peace in Paris or Hanoi. The Communist press will take full note of the (October 15) moratorium demonstrations, add their own brand of exaggeration and misinterpretation and present the leaders of our enemies with more phony evidence that the people of the United States are opposed to the war in Vietnam.
*Anaheim, Calif., Oct. 15.*

On the subject of Vietnam, I willingly admit to the status of a hawk. In fact, I am indeed proud to be counted among those Americans who believe that, when our nation is committed to war in the name of human freedom, every effort should be made to win that war.
*Before Association of Old Crows,
Washington, Oct. 21.*

Unless we resume the bombing in the North, I can see no way that we can win this war. I even question whether we could, without such action, extricate ourselves from the involvement with any degree of honor and any assurance that South Vietnam will not be treated to the kind of bloodbath which overtook the unfortunate city of Hue when the Communists gained control.
*Washington, Dec. 18.*

### Barry Goldwater, Jr.
*United States Representative, R-Calif.*

Whether we should have gone in (to Vietnam) in the first place, I don't know; but we have a right and a duty to be there.

Whether to our present full commitment, I don't know. But there is an inherent danger in too many people looking on Vietnam as an isolated thing. We're fighting communism all over the world, and Vietnam is just another open wound. You have all these countries in Southeast Asia that are directly in line of the communist drive. We have to decide whether it's important for us to help maintain the freedom of millions of people over there.

*Interview, pub. August.*

**Charles E. Goodell**
*United States Senator, R-N.Y.*

The war in Vietnam was a mistake in the very beginning. But, now that we are there, we cannot let 33,000 American men (to) have died in vain. In other words, we cannot simply turn our backs and walk out. But there is another reason, too: Our credibility in the world in the future would be zero.

*Clarkson College, Potsdam, N.Y., pub. May.*

We have not won a victory in Vietnam. Victory is impossible through any military means acceptable to the American people. We have engaged in the wrong war, in the wrong place, at the wrong time, and we have embraced a wrong-headed concept of American power and responsibility in the world. At inordinate sacrifice, we have for six years given the people of South Vietnam their option of freedom from North Vietnam. It is now for them alone to exercise that option. Now, it is for them alone to rally their people for war or peace. It is time for the South Vietnamese to make hard and realistic decisions without the protective mantle of American troops. It is time we told the South Vietnamese leaders that, one year from now, they will be on their own.

*Before the Senate, Washington, Sept. 25.*

This slaughter (in Vietnam) must cease. The prosecution of the war with American troops must be ended, not merely reduced. The only way of halting the loss of our young men's lives is to establish a clear timetable for terminating all American combat operations and troop commitments in Vietnam within the near future.

*News conference, Washington, Sept. 26.*

**Robert P. Griffin**
*United States Senator, R-Mich.*

It is ironic and rather tragic that . . . demonstrations are to be directed at the U.S. Government and our institutions rather than at the Hanoi government and the Communists. For the record is clear that it is Hanoi and the Communists who have not budged, who have not given one inch, who have not negotiated realistically, and who have ignored the proposals for peace made by this administration and the previous administration over and over again.

*Before the Senate, Washington, Sept. 30.*

**Andrei A. Gromyko**
*Foreign Minister of the*
*Union of Soviet Socialist Republics*

The United States has been fighting the Vietnamese people longer than anyone else in its entire history since it became an independent nation, longer than it fought Nazi Germany and militarist Japan. It has not attained its goal in Vietnam—nor can it, for its cause there is unjust.

To think that the United States can obtain at the conference table what it has failed to achieve with a half-million-strong army on the battlefield . . . would mean to be obviously at variance with reality.

*United Nations, N.Y., Sept. 19.*

**Ernest Gruening**
*Former United States Senator, D-Alaska*

I want to see thousands of young men refuse to go (to fight in Vietnam)—until they have so many of them, they've filled all the jails.

*Seattle, Feb. 22.*

. . . our young men are asked to fight in a war they consider immoral, to kill people against whom they feel no grievance, maybe get killed or maimed in the process—with the alternative, if they follow their conscience and refuse—to go to jail for five years at hard labor, thereby probably ruining their future careers in civilian life. This is an infamous

(ERNEST GRUENING)

dilemma to which no American, or, indeed, no member of a society that calls itself free, should be subject.

*Nov. 13.*

**Philip C. Habib**
*Deputy Assistant Secretary of State*
*for East Asia and Pacific Affairs*
*of the United States*

Your voice is that of the propagandist, not the negotiator. Your words and your actions are inconsistent with peaceful intentions. They underline your continued reliance on violence and terror . . . We will not agree to unilateral allied withdrawal. The withdrawal of our forces must be lined to the withdrawal of North Vietnamese forces.

*Speaking to North Vietnamese*
*delegation at peace talks;*
*Paris, Aug. 22.*

**Clifford P. Hansen**
*United States Senator, R-Wyo.*

A sudden abandonment of our effort in Vietnam, no matter how sought after by so many, would greatly enlarge the possibilities of future involvement in other places. That is so because it would give encouragement to a number of ruthless leaders throughout the world who could take comfort from Hanoi's success and would be more than willing to risk a reckless confrontation with the United States.

*Before the Senate, Washington, Oct. 16.*

**W. Averell Harriman**
*Former United States Ambassador*
*to Paris peace talks*

The North Vietnamese . . . are fiercely nationalist . . . They want to be independent of Peking. They don't want to be beholden to Moscow . . . They want contacts with the West . . . We have got to work some sort of arrangements with them which will be to their interest to live with their neighbors in peace.

*Washington, Feb. 5.*

I don't see any progress going on in Paris. Maybe I'm wrong; I hope to hell

I am. How can we expect the enemy to end their fighting if we don't?

*Washington, June 10.*

Hanoi made it very plain that they didn't think much progress could be made as long as there was violence and as long as we were trying to spar to improve the position of the (Saigon) government a little bit. If we are going to talk peace, we've got to draw the line and say this is where we stand (militarily) today.

*Radio interview, Washington, June 17.*

I'm very much concerned that little or no progress has been made in Paris . . . they (the Nixon Administration) are going about it in the wrong way. We are still trying to win the war.

*Radio broadcast, New York, Aug. 19.*

I still say that the North Vietnamese and the VietCong want a reasonable settlement and do not want a military takeover (of South Vietnam). If anyone disagrees with that, they're wrong.

*Washington, Nov. 14.*

**Fred R. Harris**
*United States Senator, D-Okla.*

It is time to take the gloves off on Vietnam. I'm afraid that Mr. Nixon is rapidly losing the advantage he had by virtue of the fact that he could say, "I didn't start this war." I'm very alarmed that he really doesn't have a plan. His plan is a kind of Micawberism that maybe something will turn up.

*Pub. Oct. 3.*

**S. I. Hayakawa**
*President,*
*San Francisco State College*

I am tremendously proud of what the United States has done in the conquest of nazism and totalitarianism and in the defense for freedom. This sense of responsibility toward the world must be perpetuated. It marks us as a nation not interested solely in itself, but also in the fate of the rest of the world. The (Vietnam) moratorium movement calls for abandoning Southeast Asia and turning our backs on our tradition of international concern. I'm not at all sure that the moratorium movement is wise.

*San Francisco, pub. Oct. 19.*

**Wayne L. Hays**
*United States Representative, D-Ohio*

I heard a Member of the House of Representatives on television . . . say that the American people were not going to any further support the corrupt regime in South Vietnam. I am sure there is some corruption in the South Vietnamese Government, but at least it was elected by somebody. I cannot understand . . . these people who go around supporting Hanoi and never once admit that it is a dictatorship that nobody ever voted for.
*Before the House, Washington, Nov. 4.*

**Lee Sae Ho**
*Commander, South Korean
armed forces in Vietnam*

To gain an honorable end to the war, we have to be determined to fight the Communists down to the last minute, with no concessions.
*News conference, Saigon, pub. Aug. 11.*

**Harold E. Hughes**
*United States Senator, D-Iowa*

Those who disagree with the conduct of the Vietnam war include persons who are not iconoclasts, fuzzy theorists or summer patriots, but men of talent, who want to change our national policies in order to preserve our country's future.
*Westport, Conn., Oct. 15.*

**Hubert H. Humphrey**
*Former Vice President
of the United States*

My own view is that President (Lyndon B.) Johnson set in motion the processes of peace (in Vietnam) and Mr. Nixon is going to reap the harvest.
*News conference, Washington, Feb. 20.*

This is a war that no one can afford to say they lost and everyone will have to claim they won.
*New York, Sept. 7.*

Nixon is riding the bandwagon of Vietnam disengagement, but he's not driving recklessly, he's not drag-racing. He's going around tortuous curves and corners, and he's saying, "Please don't grab the wheel and please stop fighting in the back seat." On that, I support him . . . He not only

intends to withdraw our forces faster than anyone thinks, he is compelling the South Vietnamese to accept responsibility for their own defense—and *I want to help him.*
*Interview, Washington, pub. Dec. 15.*

**Samuel P. Huntington**
*Professor of Government,
Harvard University*

The (October 15 Vietnam) moratorium has reduced virtually to zero the possibility of a negotiated political settlement. Hanoi obviously will not accept compromise if it thinks the American people will give it victory. Perhaps it was to be expected, but I find it also ironic and sad that those who enthusiastically promoted negotiations in 1968 are busily undermining them in 1969. If the moratorium organizers make peace synonymous with defeat, they will delay the former and ensure the latter.
*Interview, pub. Oct. 17.*

**Tran Van Huong**
*Premier of South Vietnam*

The nearsighted and highly gullible are prone to be deceived into thinking that this is an internecine conflict, a sort of civil war involving people of the same blood . . . But you and I know it for what it really is, that is naked aggression by the Communist imperialists who seek to impose their dream of subjugating not only 14 million South Vietnamese, but also Asia and the whole world.
*Saigon, pub. Jan. 11.*

The Americans are too anxious to get peace. The North Vietnamese, the Red Chinese, consider this a sign of weakness, a sign of flagging will; so they exploit it. They ask their people to go the extra mile in order to achieve victory, because, they say, the Americans are already tired.
*Pub. June 2.*

**Jacob K. Javits**
*United States Senator, R-N.Y.*

. . . if support for Vietnam erodes in this country in 1970, and (withdrawal of troops) becomes some kind of pullout which is precipitous, it would be very much worse in terms of the peace negotiations.
*Interview, New York, June 29.*

**Herman Kahn**
*Director, Hudson Institute*

I don't think there's going to be a settlement in Paris. All the compromise settlements people are talking about are based on the assumption that the U.S. has lost the war. But that is a delusion. Nixon has a better chance of winning than Johnson did.

*Pub. Feb. 10.*

**Harold Kaplan**
*Spokesman for the American Delegation to Paris peace talks*

What they (the North Vietnamese) are saying is that the so-called Provisional Revolutionary Government will meet with other Vietnamese who believe in peace and independence to form a provisional government. Since they determine who believes in peace and independence, it's quite clear that they are going to be meeting with themselves.

*News conference, Paris, July 31.*

**James W. Kelly**
*Rear Admiral and Chief of Chaplains, United States Navy*

I have not the slightest doubt that history will just as surely vindicate America's involvement in Vietnam as it will vindicate South Vietnam's resistance to national and personal enslavement. But I see not the slightest need to await the verdict of history before we draw strength and inspiration from the moral correctness of our involvement . . .

*Pub. Sept. 2.*

**George F. Kennan**
*Historian; former diplomat*

It is improper and impractical to have the resources of this country committed to a war between competitive internal forces in a foreign nation. Even though one of these factions may appeal to us more than others, it's up to them to settle their differences—not up to us.

*Interview, pub. Nov. 10.*

**Edward M. Kennedy**
*United States Senator, D-Mass.*

President Nixon has told us, without question, that we seek no military victory, that we seek only peace. How, then, can we justify sending our boys against a hill a dozen times or more, until soldiers themselves question the madness of the action? The assault on "Hamburger Hill" is only symptomatic of a mentality and a policy that requires immediate attention. American boys are too valuable to be sacrificed for a false sense of military pride.

*Washington, May 20.*

No talk of concessions, no hints of compromise can cover up the fact that we have not been willing to consider the continued control of the Thieu regime as a negotiable question; and, as long as we remain unmoved on this issue there can be no peaceful solution (to the Vietnam war).

(. . . President Nixon's policy) is the road to war, and war, and more war. And as we follow this incredible path it will continue to erode the health, the economy and the moral and spiritual strength of the United States of America.

*Boston, Sept. 18.*

As a candidate, Richard Nixon promised us a plan for peace, once elected. As Chief Executive, President Nixon (has) promised us a plan for peace for the last 10 months. Last night he spoke again of a plan—a secret plan for peace sometime. There now must be doubt whether there is in existence any plan to extricate America from this war in the best interests of America—for it is no plan to say that what we do depends on what Hanoi does.

*Before the Senate, Washington, Nov. 4.*

**Tran Buu Kiem**
*Foreign Minister of the National Liberation Front of South Vietnam-Viet Cong*

Although he (President Nixon) has hidden his policy behind kind words of peace, the inauguration statement and the press conference of Mr. Nixon have clearly shown the dark and vile designs of his government.

*Paris, Feb. 27.*

**Henry A. Kissinger**
*Assistant to the President of the United States for National Security Affairs*

I can understand the anguish of the

younger generation. They lack models; they have no heroes; they see no great purposes in the world. But conscientious objection is destructive of a society. The imperatives of the individual are always in conflict with the organization of society. Conscientious objections must be reserved for only the greatest moral issues, and Vietnam is not of this magnitude.

*Washington, pub. Aug. 12.*

**Semon E. Knudsen**
*President, Ford Motor Company*

Anyone who believes American business wants the Vietnamese war to continue in order to keep sales and profits high just doesn't understand the way our economy operates.

*Atlanta, June 3.*

**Edward I. Koch**
*United States Representative, D-N.Y.*

Whatever we may think of him (Ho Chi Minh) . . . and knowing he was a dedicated Communist, we must recognize he was, above all, a patriot, regarded by his countrymen as the George Washington of Vietnam.

*Before the House,*
*Washington, pub. Sept. 14.*

**Alexei Kosygin**
*Premier of the Union of*
*Soviet Socialist Republics*

We are doing everything possible to see that the people of Vietnam triumph over the United States.

*News conference, New Delhi, May 7.*

**Dan Kuykendall**
*United States Representative, R-Tenn.*

We are not warmongers. We simply want to get out by a route that will preclude the necessity of getting back in.

*Before the House, Washington, Nov. 4.*

**Nguyen Cao Ky**
*Vice President of South Vietnam*

The Vietnamese people fervently hope for peace, but they are absolutely opposed to Communist domination.

*News conference, Paris, Jan. 24.*

For months and years they (the Viet Cong) always claimed they were the real majority in South Vietnam, and we were the puppets; that, without the Americans, we would be nothing. Now we challenge them to permit foreign forces to withdraw on both sides and let us meet face to face. If what they have claimed is true, what are they afraid of?

As I have said for months, we made many, many concessions, and are ready to make more. I am not asking concessions from the other side, but better understanding, and we tell them that directly.

*News conference, Paris, Feb. 3.*

There is no question why we cannot bomb Hanoi. Maybe you (the Americans) are afraid of them, but not me.

*News conference, Saigon, Feb. 24.*

It is impossible to expect Communists and Nationalists who have been fighting and killing one another for 20 years to sit down and harmonize things. How could you expect such a cabinet to work in harmony? Such a government would last two weeks, and the whole war would start again.

I am confident the Communists would not get a majority (in South Vietnamese elections). But, if the people vote Communist, I'll step down . . . I'll go into the jungle.

*Interview, Paris, pub. March 5.*

As a soldier, I know (and) appreciate how big a sacrifice you (American soldiers) made for my country. I have no words to say about your dedication and sacrifice . . . Believe me, we'll remember you . . . Some have the wrong belief that you fight for a bunch of Vietnamese military dictators . . . that we fight for American imperialism . . . we know that is not true. I am not a puppet . . . you are not come protecting profiteers . . . we are fighting a common enemy of humans . . . Communism. Be sure, if we have to go to (the) North again, I will lead a Vietnamese formation . . . be sure the fight will continue . . . Please, if you want, come to my country . . . I'm sure my children and grandchildren—when they grow up in a free South Vietnam—

(NGUYEN CAO KY)

will remember your names and faces and sacrifices.

*At Walter Reed Hospital,*
*Washington, April 3.*

Even the enemy is convinced they cannot win on the battlefield, militarily or politically. But there is still one thing the enemy are counting on, and that is the impatience of the American public opinion. So long as the enemy still think that with the impatience and opposition in America they can get something better, so long will they keep their present attitude and language unchanged.

*Pub. April 9.*

We cannot give any more concessions. There is no reason to. To retreat one more inch would amount to unconditional surrender. If we take one more step, we will fall into an abyss.

*Saigon, pub. July 28.*

I am satisfied that the maximum effort is being made now to equip our armed forces. On the other hand, I think this policy could have been applied at an earlier date. In 1965, as prime minister, I proposed a plan for a general mobilization, and requested U.S. assistance in training and equipment. But my plan met with opposition from the American government—in particular, Ambassador Maxwell Taylor . . . An earlier start of this plan would have allowed a much lesser U.S. troop commitment in the first place. And, naturally, it would have permitted an earlier withdrawal of whatever U.S. troops were here.

If the Paris talks continue to produce nothing but an exchange of meaningless words, I would favor stopping the talks and concentrating on a military solution. Nevertheless, if the Communists show a sign of willingness to negotiate seriously, I would be willing to go to Paris tomorrow.

*Interview, Saigon, pub. Oct. 13.*

At the end of 1970, we will replace all American combat troops . . . We don't want people to misunderstand that this is an American war. We don't want people

to believe that we are puppets of the Americans.

*News conference, Dalat,*
*South Vietnam, Nov. 5.*

## Melvin R. Laird
*Secretary of Defense*
*of the United States*

I believe it is essential that the American people . . . understand what Vietnamization is all about. They should know why Vietnamization, in the absence of progress in Paris, offers the best prospect for minimizing American casualties while resolving the war as quickly as possible without abandoning our basic objective.

*Washington, Oct. 9.*

## Pham Dang Lam
*Delegate to Paris peace talks*
*from South Vietnam*

. . . they (the Viet Cong) have succeeded in putting up a few so-called committees; but the day we organize free elections, believe me, all their committees will crumble.

There seems to be a lot of confusion over the difference between a government of national union and a coalition government. We are opposed to all coalitions.

*News conference, Paris, Jan. 7.*

The Vietnamese problem cannot be settled without settling the problem of Laos and that of Cambodia's frontiers, which means these frontiers must be controlled so as not to have these countries be sanctuaries for the Communists.

*News conference, Paris, Jan. 8.*

The Communists are wrong to act as though, juridically, South Vietnam were a vacuum and the people had not yet expressed their will. Similarly, it is unreasonable and anti-democratic, and therefore unacceptable, to demand a coalition government in advance, without concern for the outcome of elections. These and other provisions of the Communists' plan in fact seek nothing but to take over South Vietnam and subject its population to a Communist regime.

I think there is little practical interest in knowing if, yes or no, there will be elections before 1971. The constitution is not a thing for the government to decide, since the government is tied to it. Ultimately, it is for the entire South Vietnamese population to decide . . . If between now and 1971 we have succeeded in re-establishing peace and normal conditions to allow really democratic elections, that already would be a good thing.

*Before Anglo-American Press Club,*
*Paris, May 27.*

**Tran Van Lam**
*Member of the Senate of*
*South Vietnam*

Democracy with peace is not so hard. Dictatorship with war is not so hard, either. But democracy with war is practically impossible. Still, that's what the Americans want, so that's what we try to give.

*Saigon, pub. Aug. 20.*

**Nguyen Lau**
*Publisher, "Saigon Daily News"*

Although I oppose Communism because of its inhumanity and because it contradicts the traditional values of Asian and Vietnamese people, even today . . . I wonder if our people should continue to kill one another for an alien doctrine.

*News conference, Saigon, April 17.*

**Nguyen Thanh Le**
*Deputy delegate to Paris*
*peace talks from North Vietnam*

. . . I would like to speak about the so-called withdrawal of American troops. In this last session, both the delegates of the DRV (North Vietnam) and the PRG (VietCong) brought to light the farce which consists of the so-called withdrawal of American troops from South Vietnam. The Americans are now playing a game of magic. In other words, they are acting in such a way as to withdraw contingents on several occasions, but in the end there are more troops left in Vietnam than before they started withdrawing.

*Press conference, Paris, pub. Aug. 22.*

**Walter Lippmann**
*Author, Newspaper Columnist*

The kind of war we are fighting in Vietnam should never have been fought by conscripted troops. The draft should never be applied to a war that's far from the homeland; and Vietnam is as far as you can get from the homeland.

*Interview, Seal Harbor, Me.,*
*pub. Sept. 21.*

**Henry Cabot Lodge**
*Ambassador to Paris peace talks*
*from the United States*

No purpose is served by repeating the list of familiar charges or to recite once more the chronology which brought us here. Our responsibility is to the future, not the past.

*Paris, Jan. 18.*

I've always said that a military victory was not possible in Vietnam, and I don't see how anyone can say that is a hard line. I'm not a hard-liner or a soft-liner. I'm a realist.

*Before Senate Foreign Relations*
*Committee, Washington, pub. Jan. 23.*

The fact that we all sit together in a room for six-and-a-half hours and talk in a correct, courteous tone is in itself a gain—that is good. It is a very good sign, when you are through for the day, and everyone agrees unanimously to the next meeting at a certain time.

*Interview, Paris, Jan. 25.*

The United States believes that the essential elements of the 1954 (Geneva) accords, which we have all said we support as the basis for a future settlement, provide common ground on which to build the structure of peace in Vietnam.

*Paris, Feb. 20.*

We are ready to stay here until the chairs are worn out.

*Paris, June 27.*

To hold such a position (of unilateral American withdrawal) is to demand capitulation by our side. This is unreasonable. We shall not capitulate. No negotiated settlement of the war is possible until you (Vietnam Communists) modify that demand.

*At Peace talks, Paris, July 10.*

There is obviously not much sense sitting there (at the Paris peace talks) trying

(HENRY CABOT LODGE)

to respond when they (the North Vietnamese) are saying the same old intransigent and vituperative things. I hope our action today (walking out) may call attention generally to the completely negative attitude which has consistently characterized the other side . . .

*Paris, Oct. 23.*

### Allard K. Lowenstein
*United States Representative, D-N.Y.*

In a free society, the President does not have the unilateral authority to wage a war against the will of the majority, and the President better understand that.
*At political reception, MGM studios, Culver City, Calif., Oct. 19.*

### Mike Mansfield
*United States Senator, D-Mont.*

I would like to see him (the President) pull out our troops faster, I would like to see the war brought to an end sooner. And when we do (get out, we should) not maintain a residual number of troops in Vietnam, or in any other part of the Southeast Asian mainland.
*Washington, Oct. 20.*

Vietnam is a war unclaimed by this administration or its predecessors. It is a war unclaimed by this Congress or the ones before. Yet, this war belongs to us all. We cannot evade it—not this administration nor its predecessors, not this Congress nor its predecessors. We are all its possessors and we are all possessed by it. We are—all of us—the makers of the veterans of Vietnam. The relentless clicking which computes the casualties is our responsibility.
*Before the Senate, Washington, Nov. 11.*

### Ferdinand E. Marcos
*President of the Philippines*

We Asians don't understand pulling punches in a war.
*Interview, Manila, pub. July 30.*

### Kevin McCann
*Former aid to*
*President Dwight D. Eisenhower*

In alliance with the South Vietnamese

and their neighbors, we have invested too much gallantry and blood and human sacrifices now blithely to say: "We goofed; let's go home; this is not our ball game."
*Defiance College, Ohio, May 18.*

### Eugene J. McCarthy
*United States Senator, D-Minn.*

I think history would see nothing wrong if Nixon does preside over the first military defeat of this country, but would regard it, instead, as a measure of great statesmanship.
*New Brunswick, N.J., Oct. 15.*

### George S. McGovern
*United States Senator, D-S.D.*

The new Commander-in-Chief (President Nixon) must grasp what his predecessor (President Johnson) learned to his sorrow—that in any continuance of the war in Vietnam lies the seed of national tragedy and the certainty of personal policial disaster.
*Before the Senate, Washington, March 17.*

I'm glad for the withdrawal (of some U.S. troops), but I think we ought to begin taking them all out, and the faster, the better.
*Washington, pub. June 16.*

So long as we cling to our military policy of maximum pressure and our political embrace of General Thieu, the negotiations in Paris are a sham and a deception.
*Before the Senate, Washington, July 2.*

This (the first withdrawal of American troops) is the best chance we have had to achieve a breakthrough toward peace in Vietnam since the bombing halt last December. I think this is the moment to try . . . (an) experiment with a 30-day ceasefire—and see what happens. Of course, should Hanoi respond with a major military buildup and attack on our forces, then we would have to respond with everything we have.
*Interview, Boston, July 3.*

President Nixon should make an offer of asylum to provide for the safety of

South Vietnamese who would feel threatened by our withdrawal . . . Once that offer is made, and some reasonable time is provided to carry out the transfer of those Vietnamese who wish to take advantage of it, we should immediately withdraw all American forces . . .

*At Ford Hall Forum, Boston, Sept. 28.*

There is every indication the administration is more sensitive to the wishes of General Thieu than to the cry of our own citizens that the war be ended. Now. Their maneuvers will not work. The longer we linger, the longer we refuse to break with the policies of the past, the longer we shall be enmeshed in the futile waste of our blood and treasure in Southeast Asia—perhaps next in Thailand.

*At annual meeting of Associated Press Managing Editors, Hartford, Conn., Oct. 1.*

To me, the highest act of patriotism is not silence and a blind faith in the wisdom of our policymakers. The highest patriotism is to express one's own best judgments on policies that affect the national interest. I think that those people who are against the moratorium (on President Nixon's handling of the Vietnam war) really pay a great compliment to our political process in that they are saying: "It (the American political process) is still responsible to public concern." If you ever convince young people in America that Washington was not listening to anyone, then we really would be in deep trouble.

*Pub. Oct. 9.*

I regret that the President has said he will pay no attention to this effort (the October 15 Vietnam Moratorium demonstrations). If he holds to that course, he will learn, as his predecessor learned, that American foreign policy cannot be formed in defiance of the conscience and the common sense of the American people.

*Washington, pub. Oct. 17.*

### Thomas J. McIntyre
*United States Senator, D-N.H.*

We have learned some hard lessons in Vietnam. We have learned about a new kind of war. Perhaps we have learned that

wars which threaten national unity, indeed threaten national sanity, never should be fought at all. But this war has been fought, fought by men as brave as any we have ever sent into battle, men who were, in one sense, braver, for they fought without the comforting support of a nation united behind them.

*National Academy of Sciences, Hanover, N.H., Oct. 13.*

### George Meany
*President, American Federation of Labor-Congress of Industrial Organizations*

I haven't changed my mind on Vietnam. I think that we made a commitment there. I think it is unfortunate the way we got into it. I don't see how we can get out of it unless we can, in some way, insure that this area is not going to fall over, one country after another, to the Communists. I can't see anything that changed my theory that, if they take Vietnam, they will keep going. They will take Laos, Cambodia, and they will be knocking at the doors. I wasn't a critic of (President) Johnson on this war and I certainly am not going to be a critic of what (President) Nixon inherited . . . I know Johnson would have done almost anything within his power to get out of this war except surrender and withdraw unilaterally. And I don't think Nixon will do that.

*Interview, Washington, Aug. 28.*

### Thomas J. Meskill
*United States Representative, R-Conn.*

The U.S. Constitution provides that only Congress can make a declaration of war. And yet we find ourselves fighting a full-scale nonwar in Southeast Asia. Is it any wonder that some of our youths question the legitimacy of this operation? Is it any wonder that some refuse to fight in this conflict which Congress has never given its formal consent to? I have agonized with this problem of how to prevent a President from usurping Congress' power to commit drafted American boys to wars similar to Vietnam without their consent. I have concluded that we should not expect a draftee, a man who is serving involuntarily, to serve without his consent in a

(THOMAS J. MESKILL)

struggle when Congress has not declared that a state of war exists.

*Before the House, Washington, Sept. 30.*

## Robert B. Meyner
*Former Governor of New Jersey*

I say that we cannot continue to sink billions into the rice paddies of Asia, when there is trouble in the streets of America. The Republican candidate (for President) told us last year he had a plan to stop the killing and all the other tragic waste in Vietnam. America believed him. The people of America agreed and said to the Republican Party, "End the war, and pay attention to us at home"; but the plan has proved to be mere campaign talk. The Americans—all of us—are still forgotten.

*Moorestown, N.J., Oct. 4.*

## Abner J. Mikva
*United States Representative, D-Ill.*

We are running out of time in Vietnam. The light at the end of the tunnel has gone out. The corner around which victory was supposed to appear has turned into an abyss. The secret solutions and the 60-day solutions have all turned out to be no solutions at all. The only way to get out is to get out.

*Before the House, Washington, Oct. 14.*

The crisis in this country is too serious to give either North or South Vietnam a veto power which will preclude us from ending the crisis. Our extrication from the quagmire of Vietnam should be based on factors solely within *our* control, and neither the hot air of Paris nor the cold water of General Thieu should be allowed to swerve us from the path of withdrawing all American forces from Vietnam as quickly as the safety of our own personnel and our prisoners of war and the protection of those South Vietnamese desirous of asylum will permit. To give the power over the survival of this country to either a fast-talking diplomat from North Vietnam or a slow-training general from South Vietnam is untenable.

*Before the House, Washington, Nov. 5.*

## Ho Chi Minh
*President of North Vietnam*

After the total withdrawal of the U.S. and allied troops, and the complete liberation of South Vietnam from foreign invasion, the Provisional Coalition Government, provided for in the 10-point overall solution, will organize free and democratic general elections to enable the South Vietnamese people to determine themselves their own political regime, elect a constituent assembly, work out a constitution and set up the official coalition government of South Vietnam.

*Radio broadcast, Hanoi, July 19.*

## Wilmer Mizell
*United States Representative, R-N.C.*

. . . the people who take part in (the) moratorium must be prepared to shoulder the responsibility for the consequences which may result. These consequences might be severe. Encouraging the enemy to continue to fight rather than engage in meaningful negotiations would be a tremendous price to pay for a few headlines.

*Before the House, Washington, Oct. 14.*

## Walter F. Mondale
*United States Senator, D-Minn.*

I cannot express how deeply I believe that the war in Vietnam has wounded the capacity and the spirit of the nation. It is, as it should be, at the heart of student unrest . . . And, while the war takes wealth from all of us, it costs the young their bodies, lives and souls. For it is they who must finally serve or disobey.

*St. Olaf College,*
*Northfield, Minn., pub. June 9.*

## Thomas H. Moorer
*Admiral, United States Navy;*
*Chief of Naval Operations*

You've got to remember that the North Vietnamese, to this date, have never directly admitted that they have any forces in South Vietnam. So, when you talk about withdrawing their forces, they say, "What forces?" There's no clear-cut battle line, either, as we had in Europe. And you don't have a situation such as we had in Japan, where we had the enemy practically surrounded and were preparing to make an invasion of his homeland. So it is entirely possible that historians will not be able to say that on such-and-such a day in such-and-such a year the war in Vietnam ended.

*Interview, Washington, pub. Dec. 1.*

**Wayne L. Morse**
*Former United States Senator, D-Ore.*

No Western power will be allowed to stay in Asia. Forget peace in Vietnam from Paris. You may get a truce, but no peace.

*Cleveland, Feb. 17.*

**Edmund S. Muskie**
*United States Senator, D-Me.*

One of the most dangerous assumptions in a democratic society is to conclude that only the President, the Cabinet and the generals are competent to make judgments in the national interest. I regret the President has not seen (the October 15 Vietnam Moratorium demonstrations) as an opportunity to unite rather than divide the country. His participation, in a form of his own choosing, could have added a constructive dimension to this national dialogue.

*Lewiston, Me., pub. Oct. 17.*

In a sense, this tragic incident (alleged massacre by Americans at Songmy, South Vietnam) puts all of us on trial. All Americans see in it the questions that bother us about all involvement in South Vietnam. It shows the impact we have on Vietnamese society—and what the war may have done to our own people, in the sense of brutalizing our young men. Something has happened to our sense of values.

*News conference, London, Nov. 29.*

**Allan Nevins**
*Author, Historian*

There are great possibilities for both good and evil in the (Vietnam) demonstrations. Good, in that public opinion in the United States must make sure we have a clear set of goals and values in mind, that we are going to stand behind those goals and values. However, we cannot submit to violence, internal or external.

Demonstrations and public meetings in the streets and crossroads are of no value whatever in helping men determine and fix upon a policy. It is too rudimentary, elementary, to do that.

*Pub. Oct. 19.*

**Richard M. Nixon**
*President of the United States*

We have a new team in Paris, with some old faces; but a new team. We have new direction from the United States. We have a new sense of urgency with regard to the negotiations. There will be new tactics. We believe that those tactics may be more successful than the tactics of the past.

. . . this Administration believes that the better approach (to ending the war) is the one that Ambassador Lodge, under our direction, set forth in Paris—mutual withdrawal of forces on a guaranteed basis by both sides from South Vietnam.

*News conference, Washington, Jan. 27.*

. . . I believe that the Soviet Union shares the concern of many other nations in the world about the extension of the war . . . I believe the Soviet Union would like to use what influence it could, appropriately, to help bring the war to a conclusion.

The fact that we have shown patience and forebearance should not be considered as a sign of weakness . . . we will not tolerate attacks which result in heavier casualties to our men at a time that we are honestly trying to seek peace at the conference table in Paris.

Our objective is to get this war over as soon as we can on a basis that will not leave the seeds of another war there to plague us in the future. We have made, we think, some progress. We think that we are going to make some more.

*News conference, Washington, March 4.*

We have issued a warning. I will not warn again. And if we conclude the level of casualties is higher than we should tolerate, action will take place.

*News conference, Washington, March 14.*

(RICHARD M. NIXON)

If we are to have a negotiating position at the Paris peace talks, it must be a position in which we can negotiate from strength. And discussion about unilateral withdrawal does not help that position. I will not engage in it, although I realize it might be rather popular to do so. It is the aim of this Administration to bring men home just as soon as our security will allow us to do so. And, as I have indicated previously, there are three factors that we are going to take into consideration: the training of the South Vietnamese —their ability to handle their own defense; the level of fighting in South Vietnam— whether or not the offensive action of the enemy recedes; and progress in the Paris peace talks.
*News conference, Washington, April 18.*

We have . . . ruled out either a one-sided withdrawal from Vietnam or the acceptance in Paris of terms that would amount to a disguised American defeat . . . When we assumed the burden of helping to defend South Vietnam, millions of South Vietnamese men, women and children placed their trust in us. To abandon them now would risk a massacre that would shock and dismay everyone in the world who values human life. Abandoning the South Vietnamese people, however, would jeopardize more than lives in South Vietnam. It would threaten our long-term hopes for peace in the world. A great nation cannot renege on its pledges. A great nation must be worthy of trust . . . If we simply abandoned our effort in Vietnam, the cause of peace might not survive the damage that would be done to other nations' confidence in our reliability.

What the United States wants for South Vietnam is not the important thing; what North Vietnam wants for South Vietnam is not the important thing. What is important is what the people of South Vietnam want for themselves . . . Let me be quite blunt. Our fighting men are not going to be worn down; our negotiators are not going to be talked down; our allies are not going to be let down . . . In my campaign for the Presidency, I pledged to end this war in a way that would increase our chances to win true and lasting peace in Vietnam, in the Pacific and in the world. I am determined to keep that pledge. If I fail to do so, I expect the American people to hold me accountable for that failure.
*Television address, Washington, May 14.*

. . . I do not want to leave any doubt on this score—President Thieu is the elected President of South Vietnam; he is cooperating with the United States in attempting to bring this war to a conclusion . . . under those circumstances, there is no question about our standing with President Thieu. I would also say further that, insofar as our efforts are concerned, we are not going to accede to the demands of the enemy that we have to dispose of President Thieu before they will talk.

. . . the idea of a cease-fire . . . does commend itself to me. But I do not want us to cease and have the other side continue to fire. Because, basically . . . where we have a conventional war, a cease-fire is very relevant; then we know that the guns have stopped firing. In the case of the guerilla war, unless you have an international force or some outside force to regulate it, a cease-fire is a grave disadvantage to those forces that are in place.
*News conference, Washington, June 19.*

We have gone as far as we can or should go in opening the door to negotiations which would bring peace. It is now time for the other side to sit down with us and talk seriously about ways to stop the killing, to put an end to this tragic war which has brought so great destruction to friend and foe alike. I believe the record is clear as to which side has gone the extra mile on behalf of peace. We have stopped the bombing of North Vietnam; we have withdrawn 25,880 troops; they have been replaced by South Vietnamese; we have made . . . a peace offer as generous as any ever made in the history of warfare. It is a peace of reconciliation that is offered; a peace in which the people will decide; a peace that is just for both sides; a peace which is fair for both sides; a peace which

offers an equal chance to both sides.
*Saigon, July 30.*

I have been to North Vietnam—to Hanoi in 1953—and all over South Vietnam. I have seen the people of the North and the people of the South. The people of Vietnam, North and South, have endured an unspeakable weight of suffering for a generation and they deserve a better future. When the war ends, the United States will stand ready to help the people of Vietnam, all of them, in their tasks of renewal and reconstruction. And when peace comes at last to Vietnam, it can truly come with healing in its wings.
*United Nations, N.Y., Sept. 18.*

We and the South Vietnamese Government have announced we are prepared to accept any political outcome which is arrived at through free elections.
*Pub. Sept. 18.*

It is my conclusion that, if the Administration were to impose a cutoff time—say the end of 1970 or the middle of 1971—for the complete withdrawal of American forces in Vietnam, that inevitably leads to perpetuating and continuing the war until that time and destroys any chance to reach the objective that I am trying to achieve of ending the war before the end of 1970 or before the middle of 1971.

. . . I understand that there has been, and continues to be, opposition to the war in Vietnam on the campuses and also in the nation. As far as this kind of activity is concerned, we expect it. However, under no circumstances will I be affected whatever by it.
*News conference, Washington, Sept. 26.*

We can bring peace, we will bring peace (to Vietnam). And that peace will be due to the fact that Americans, when it really counted, did not buckle, did not run away, but stood fast—so that the enemy . . . had no hope but to negotiate a fair peace, which is all that we require from them.
*Washington, Sept. 30.*

If the critics know any way to get Hanoi to listen, I would appreciate their suggestions. Every time we have hopes that Hanoi will make a reciprocal proposal, the Hanoi negotiator quotes some senator as evidence that the President doesn't have the U.S. behind him.
*Washington, pub. Oct. 6.*

I will say confidently that, looking ahead just three years, the war will be over . . . It will be over on a basis which will promote lasting peace in the Pacific.
*Washington, Oct. 12.*

The other side (North Vietnam) doesn't seem to realize it, but I'm in here (the presidency) for another three years and three months. I'm not going to be the first American President who loses a war.
*Pub. Oct. 13.*

(The Vietnam debate) is not about any desire of the American people for war. The debate is about peace—how to achieve it. Honest men and honest women can disagree about those means. But let the world understand: The American people want peace. We believe in peace. We have fought four wars in this century because we wanted peace.
*Washington, Oct. 14.*

There are powerful personal reasons why I want to end this war. This week I will have to sign 83 letters to mothers, fathers, wives and loved ones of men who had given their lives for America in Vietnam. It is very little satisfaction to me that this was only one-third as many as I signed during my first week in office. There is nothing I want more than to see the day come when I no longer must write any of these letters.

It has become clear that the obstacle in negotiating an end to the war is not the President of the United States; and it is not the South Vietnamese Government. The obstacle is the other side's absolute refusal to show the least willingness to join us in seeking a just peace. It will not do so while it is convinced that all it has to do is wait for our next concession and the next, until it gets everything it wants.

Hanoi could make no greater mistake than to assume that an increase in violence will be to its own advantage. If I conclude

(RICHARD M. NIXON)

that increased enemy action jeopardizes our remaining forces in Vietnam, I shall not hestitate to take strong and effective measures to deal with that situation.

Let us be united for peace. Let us also be united against defeat. Because let us understand: North Vietnam cannot defeat or humiliate the United States. Only Americans can do that.

*Television address, Washington, Nov. 3.*

As our program for Vietnamization continues to work . . . I think the pressures for the enemy to negotiate a settlement will greatly increase because, once we're out and the South Vietnamese are there, they will have a much harder individual to negotiate with than they had when we were there.

*News conference, Washington, Dec. 8.*

After five years of increasing the number of Americans in Vietnam, we are bringing American men home. Our casualties continue to be at the lowest rate in three years. But I want you to know that, despite this progress, I shall not be satisfied until we achieve the goal we all want— an end to the war on a just and lasting basis.

There are some who believe that to continue our (troop) withdrawals at a time when enemy infiltration is increasing is a risk we should not take. However, I have consistently said that we must take risks for peace.

*Television address, Washington, Dec. 15.*

### Richard L. Ottinger
*United States Representative, D-N.Y.*

We simply have to learn, starting with Vietnam, that we cannot determine the future of other nations. It is not our proper role to intervene in the internal struggles of other countries around the globe, nor are we capable of doing so. If the South Vietnamese Government is not strong enough to command the support of its people, to cause them to wage an effective battle against the North, then the South Vietnamese Government does not merit our support. It will lose despite our efforts. It may be replaced by a government we

like less, but it is not for us to try to determine that result.

*Before the House, Washington, Oct. 14.*

### Kenneth S. Pitzer
*President, Stanford University*

It is a horrible shock to the Nation to realize that a war was a mistake, but that shock is less horrible than a continuation of the war. It wasn't easy for President Johnson to make an abrupt change (which implied that his former Vietnam policy was wrong) and to withdraw as a candidate for re-election. It isn't easy for President Nixon and his associates to bring the war—or at least his participation in it—to a close. But it seldom helps to delay unpleasant actions.

*Stanford University, Sept. 24.*

### Bertram L. Podell
*United States Representative, D-N.Y.*

. . . I say it is enough. Absolutely enough. We have not carved out this Republic, complete with ideals and promise, to send the flower of our youth to Vietnam any longer to perish for an Asian despotism whose jails bulge with non-Communist opponents of its autocratic rule. Calling them a freely elected government is like accusing Walter Ulbricht of being the prima ballerina of the Bolshoi Ballet.

*Before the House, Washington, Oct. 14.*

### Roman C. Pucinski
*United States Representative, D-Ill.*

It is no wonder our negotiators cannot budge a foot forward in Paris, when some of the most outstanding leaders in this country, in the other body (the Senate) and in various other places, are making great big speeches undermining every single effort of this country and its war effort. This is the first time in (our) history that we have seen supposedly responsible leaders of Government openly waging warfare with our own leaders as to how to conduct the war. It is no wonder the Communists think that, somehow or other, the spirit of America is going to collapse and they are going to be able to win this war in Washington . . .

*Before the House, Washington, Sept. 29.*

**John R. Rarick**
*United States Representative, D-La.*

If we lose the will to win, we also lose the morale to defend our country, our civilization. If we destroy the trust of American young men in their country, we will never again be able to restore any patriotism. We expect them to perform their duty to their country. It is our responsibility to see that their country performs its duty to them.
*Before the House, Washington, Sept. 29.*

Most Americans recognize the (Vietnam) Moratorium mob as the enemy's fifth column. Without these "dear American friends," Hanoi would have jumped at peace offers two years ago. Reliance on subversion in the United States has always been a key element in the enemy's war plans. The Moratorium leaders must be held personally responsible for having prolonged the war. The blood of every man killed in the past two years is on their hands, and the nation's leaders know this well.
*Before the House, Washington, Nov. 13.*

**Harry Reasoner**
*News Commentator,*
*Columbia Broadcasting System*

The (American people) have no idea of what the country (Vietnam) or its people are like. Yet, every month, thousands of young male Americans surrender themselves passively to the custody of a military machine that may send them to Vietnam to die . . . They seem to have accepted Vietnam the symbol, whether it's a true or false one. Vietnam, the symbol of U.S. commitment, must be maintained or, in some mysterious way, our national and personal probity is impugned.
*Radio broadcast,*
*pub. April 7.*

**Elliot L. Richardson**
*Under Secretary of State*
*of the United States*

We cannot, it now seems clear, do the job of fighting insurgency for someone else. We cannot provide the indigenous will and resolution, or the toughness and durability that are needed, if this kind of warfare is to be waged successfully . . . The job of countering insurgency in the field is one which must be conducted by the government concerned, making use of its popular support, its resources and its men.
*New York, Sept. 5.*

**William P. Rogers**
*Secretary of State of the United States*

On the political structure of South Vietnam, we believe that the issue must be resolved among the South Vietnamese themselves. We shall respect whatever choice they make about their political future, in a context free of compulsion and coercion by anyone.
*Before Senate Foreign Relations*
*Committee, Washington, March 27.*

We are obviously concerned about civil liberties in South Vietnam. You have to keep in mind, though, their country is at war, and they are under more pressure than we are in the United States. If you remember, the United States has done some things in wartime that we're not particularly proud of.
*News conference, Washington, April 7.*

When our forces are no longer needed in Vietnam, we shall not abandon in peace what we have fought for in war—the peaceful evolution of Southeast Asia.
*Before Southeast Asia Treaty*
*Organization, Bangkok, May 20.*

We are not wedded to any government in Saigon. The only principle to which the Administration is wedded is that the people of South Vietnam should have the right by free choice to decide their future, so that any government which represents the will of the people in South Vietnam is acceptable to the United States.
*Washington, June 5.*

The only reaction we get from the other side is totally negative. They call us names and use phrases like "swindle" and "fraud," which doesn't help the situation at all . . . I don't see any willingness on (their) side at the moment to be reasonable . . . I would hope that Congress and the public would focus more on their intransigence and their unreasonable tactics.
*Before House Foreign Affairs*
*Committee, Washington, July 17.*

(WILLIAM P. ROGERS)

The North Vietnamese so far continue to insist that the South Vietnamese government be replaced by what they call a coalition, without any expression of public views on this question. In effect, they want to impose a government and (have) an election to ratify it.

*At U.S.-Japanese Economic Conference, Tokyo, July 29*

**Dean Rusk**
*Former Secretary of State of the United States*

I have always felt myself that the chances were about 50-50 as between a negotiated settlement and a simple withering away of the violence.

*Television Interview, July 27.*

**Earl B. Ruth**
*United States Representative, R-N.C.*

The cost of continuing to support the Saigon generals is too high. The cost of repeating past mistakes is too high. The cost of perpetuating past policy is too high. In short, the cost of maintaining a client state in Southeast Asia is too high. The American people who gave the President a mandate to end the war recognize that the cost of continuing it is too high—that is what the moratorium is all about.

*Before the House, Washington, Oct. 14.*

**William J. Scherle**
*United States Representative, R-Iowa*

. . . Sweden, the European haven for American deserters and draft dodgers, has just announced plans to support Hanoi to the tune of $40 million in loans and grants over a 3-year period . . . In other words, "Sweden will roll the spit balls while Hanoi throws them . . ." The United States has always considered Sweden a friend . . . Apparently this friendship is a one-way street.

*Before the House, Washington, Oct. 3.*

**Hugh Scott**
*United States Senator, R-Pa.*

The enemy, of course, can end a cease-fire by shooting at us. But, if we proclaim a cease-fire, invite the enemy to join, and observe it ourselves, we have taken the first step. It might be a small step for us but a giant step for lasting peace.

*Before Overseas Writers Club, Washington, Oct. 22.*

**George P. Shultz**
*Secretary of Labor of the United States*

We believe deeply that, once the Hanoi regime is convinced we mean business in our search for an honorable peace, they will negotiate. With stronger, more articulate support for the President's course, the enemy will get the message, and we will be well on the way toward ending this war.

*Before AFL-CIO convention, Atlantic City, N.J., Oct. 2.*

**J. Edward Snyder**
*Captain, United States Navy; commanding officer, U.S.S. "New Jersey"*

If the President decides to retaliate against North Vietnam, there's nothing we'd like better. I'd be happy to oblige him on 10 minutes notice.

*Interview, aboard U.S.S. "New Jersey," March 8.*

**Benjamin Spock**
*Physician, Author*

(The military) does have to maintain discipline, (but men) should have the right not to serve in a particular war—and this . . . is a rotten war.

*News conference, Washington, June 17.*

The war in Vietnam is not just slightly illegal or slightly immoral. It is a total abomination.

*Washington, Oct. 15.*

**Sam Steiger**
*United States Representative, R-Ariz.*

There is a genuinely tragic misconception abroad in our land. It is spawned by the politically ambitious, nurtured by the posture of the media, consumed by a confused American public and used by our enemies as its most effective weapon. The misconception I refer to is the establishment of a time certain to abandon South Vietnam to violent destruction. Those elected officials who espouse this position recognize that they doom the Paris peace talks to certain failure. Their every public utterance strengthens the Communist conviction that delay must bring victory . . . What criminal nonsense to announce that we are willing to spend thousands of American lives for another 18 months and still accept certain defeat!

*Before the House, Washington, Sept. 29.*

### Herman E. Talmadge
*United States Senator, D-Ga.*

It grieves me when I see some of my colleagues in the Senate stand on the Senate floor and make speeches that will be used by the very enemies we are supposed to be negotiating with . . . The least any man can do in public life is to keep his mouth shut to the extent (that) what he says won't be used by the enemies of this government to spill more American blood.

*Forest Park, Ga., Nov. 29.*

### Olin E. Teague
*United States Representative, D-Tex.*

The issue is not war or peace—the issue is whether our leaders can, by pressures from a vocal minority who know how to perform for TV cameras, be forced to hasty decisions. I do not believe they can . . . Peace is not the issue. We all want peace. No thinking American wants American men to die in foreign lands needlessly. But lessons of history, the known intent of the monsters in Hanoi, and the total stability of the world are the basis for our commitment. And until the policy of this Government is changed by changed conditions, then I feel that to undermine and weaken those brave Americans who represent this nation in Vietnam is not only misguided but nearing on treason.

*Before the House, Washington, Nov. 13.*

### Duong Ding Thao
*Spokesman for*
*National Liberation Front of*
*South Vietnam-Viet Cong*

We see Nixon as a drowning man, trying to cling to a straw to save his life. Wherever he is, Nixon tries to present deceitful allegations justifying his aggressive war; but we are sure that, even at the (United Nations) General Assembly, there are countries approving our struggle and which will raise their voices to condemn the U.S. policy of aggression.

*Paris, Sept. 18.*

### Nguyen Van Thieu
*President of South Vietnam*

The Government (of South Vietnam) will never walk away from the conference table (in Paris). The Government knows how to be patient in peace talks. We will go step by step until the end.

*News conference, Saigon, Feb. 6.*

Monks and priests are free to go to their pagodas and churches to conduct ceremonies and to pray. But, if they deliver political sermons to stir up the people, the province chiefs should arrest them and then report to me.

*Mekong Delta, Feb. 6.*

I am sure that our people could not accept the betrayal of our country by ceding land to the Communists, by accepting a coalition government, or by permitting the open communization of South Vietnam. I will not accept this, and our soldiers will never let anyone accept such a condition.

*Radio address, Saigon, Feb. 17.*

I can tell you quite clearly these two things: There will be no coalition government with the NLF, and no Communist Party as such in South Vietnam. Some people ask me why not accept the Communists in South Vietnam, and I say we already have them and look what they have done.

*Saigon, March 25.*

If the forces of the free world wish to continue helping South Vietnam, they are welcome to do so. But if they wish to withdraw, the South Vietnamese people this year are able to shoulder their own responsibilities.

*Kienphong Province, April 16.*

. . . In the future, the only assistance we will need from our allies and the free world is money and weapons. We will

(NGUYEN VAN THIEU)

maintain the resistance with our own blood.

*Saigon, May 25.*

Today, in the struggle against Communist aggression, the most difficult battlefield for us is not the military battlefield in South Vietnam, where we have inflicted very severe losses on the enemy. Paradoxically, the free world is facing its gravest dangers in its own home front, where criticisms by a vocal minority are leveled, not at Communist aggressions, but at the defenders of freedom. While the Communist aggressors enjoy the full backing of the local Communist parties in every country, supported by various leftist and so-called liberal organizations, the allied countries which are opposing aggression have to wage the hardest battles in the rear against misunderstandings, impatience, weariness and illusions, because the farther the home front and the battlefield, the most vocal are the segments of public opinion misled by an inadequate understanding of the vital issues involved in this struggle.

*Taipei, Taiwan, June 2.*

. . . if the Communists are willing to lay down their weapons, abandon their ideology and abandon their atrocities, then they could participate in elections.

*Pub. June 6.*

I wish to declare to my compatriots that there will never be a coalition government (in South Vietnam), there will be no new cabinet, there will not be a transition government, nor will there be a reconciliation government . . . As for the questions, "When should the elections be held? Whom should we elect?", that can only be decided by the Vietnamese people.

*News conference, Saigon, June 9.*

Allied troops came to Vietnam after Communist aggression started, and are being reduced before the Communist aggressors agree to leave the scene. These are facts, and show clearly who, in this country, are genuinely for peace.

*Saigon, July 8.*

There must be an overall solution to the war. Only then can we talk about a cease-fire. There should not be a sudden cease-fire without knowing of what may follow, a cease-fire which might last for three or four years, during which the Communists could expand their forces, infiltrate more men and step up terrorism.

*Television interview, Saigon, Sept. 19.*

Why should I observe the Communists' cease-fire (following the death of Ho Chi Minh)? Would Hanoi lay down its guns for 72 hours if I died?

*Saigon, pub. Sept. 22.*

I will never leave the United States . . . but, if some day the United States says, "You must accept a coalition government with the Communists, or we will abandon you," then I will say, "Thank you. We'll continue the fight (without U.S. aid)."

*News conference, Saigon, Sept. 27.*

I hope, I request, that American public opinion will understand. I hope it will understand that we are not the invaders. We are the defenders. We have not invaded North Vietnam. We have not asked them to replace Ho Chi Minh. Why should we change the government of Thieu-Ky, the legal government? They won't stop making demands after the overthrow of Thieu and Ky. You can put Mr. A or Mr. B or Mr. C in this government, and this won't stop the demands. They are not trying to overthrow the man. They are trying to overthrow the legal government, because the legality is our strength. Since the beginning of the war, the Communists have told their people: "We have two goals to achieve—to repulse the foreign aggressors, who are the Americans, and to overthrow the legal government elected by the people of South Viet Nam." If we permit them to do that, then they have reached the ultimate goal. They won a war in *Paris* in 1954, not at Dienbienphu; and, this time, they are trying to win the war in Washington, while they are losing it in Vietnam. We must not let them continue to play this game.

We must continue to promote democracy, promote social reform, strengthen our nation in all fields. We will permit the men who are fighting against us to become full citizens under a liberal, democratic regime. What happens? They reject that. They continue the war. We want to stop the bloodshed. I don't believe in wars, ancient or modern. Nobody could be more generous in offering solutions than we are toward people who have been killing the people of South Vietnam for many years. We are ready to become friends from today, from tomorrow . . .

*Interview, Saigon, pub. Oct. 3.*

. . . In order to help the United States government in its internal problems and minimize the sufferings borne by the people of the United States, we, the Vietnamese people, are determined to replace the bulk of U.S. fighting units in 1970.

*Saigon, Oct. 6.*

I do not ask the U.S. troops to remain here 100 years, but I only ask the Americans to have the courage and the clear sight to remain here until we nationalists have enough military, economic and political strength. Those defeatists advocating unconditional United States troop withdrawals . . . are the dishonor of the free world because they accept capitulation. People who do not help us defend ourselves against the Communists may one day see thousands of people in their countries massacred, like these in Hue.

*At mass funeral, Hue, Oct. 14.*

The day when I feel I must do something because it is the right thing for the country, but the people oppose it, then I will leave this office, because I want to save this country, not merely hold on to the office of President.

*Television address, Saigon, Oct. 31.*

I have the courage to say this: This is a broad-based, popularly-elected administration. You can insult the President. You can vote against the President. They say I should more broaden my government . . . If all political parties were represented, there would be, frankly, disorder in Vietnam . . . We have to have a strong government—effective, efficient, not dictatorial —to conduct the war, pacification, social revolution. For a war, there is, perhaps, too much democracy, too much popular government.

*Interview, Saigon, pub. December.*

## Le Duc Tho
*Spokesman for North Vietnam at Paris peace talks*

The general election is an internal affair of the South Vietnamese people. There can be no international supervision under whatever form . . . because such supervision would constitute interference in the internal affairs of the South Vietnamese people and . . . would not respect self-determination.

*Interview, Paris, pub. June 24.*

## Strom Thurmond
*United States Senator, R-S.C.*

A "no-win" policy is disastrous and unknown in American history. I am confident that we could have won the Vietnam war a long time ago if our efforts had not been throttled by civilians.

*Before the Senate, Washington, July 10.*

## Xuan Thuy
*Chief Delegate to Paris peace talks from North Vietnam*

The total withdrawal of American troops is a legitimate demand of the Vietnamese people . . . It is evident that if they (the Americans) go on with troop withdrawals at the present drop-by-drop level, the situation cannot be truly changed. But if Mr. Nixon starts withdrawing troops in considerable numbers, and rapidly . . . well, then we will take this into account.

*Paris, Sept. 2.*

## John G. Tower
*United States Senator, R-Tex.*

Unless we get reasonable indications from Hanoi over the next few days, we must seriously consider the military options open to us. I think the time is fast approaching when, in the light of North Vietnamese intransigence, we must consider the exercise of additional military options available to us, such as the resumption of bombing in the North, interdiction of their lines of communication and supply on a saturation basis, and closing the port at Haiphong.

*News conference, Washington, Oct. 1.*

The intensification of military pressure on our enemies is the only thing that will

(JOHN G. TOWER)

bring them to terms. I don't believe that we should regard victory as either an evil word or an unattainable goal.

*Washington, Oct. 1.*

**Arnold Toynbee**
*Historian*

I think that, if the Vietnamese had a free choice between being divided and having foreign powers, which are Western powers, present in their country, or being united under a Communist Vietnamese regime and being independent, they'd have chosen union, even at the price of Communism.

*Interview, London, pub. March 18.*

**Joseph D. Tydings**
*United States Senator, D-Md.*

Whatever the terms of the peace settlement in Paris, there is no avoiding the harsh fact that the United States has lost the war . . .

*Goucher College, Towson, Md., June 15.*

**Joe D. Waggonner**
*United States Representative, D-La.*

I want some national and international honor left for this nation when it is over. I do not want it written across the pages of history that America pledged its word and copped out. I want some semblance of security for the entire world and there can certainly be none if the United States is driven out and humiliated.

*Before the House, Washington, Oct. 15.*

**George Wald**
*Professor of Biology,*
*Harvard University*

Most students want us to get out of Vietnam, and many, many of the older generation. I share their dismay; and, when skeptics ask me to be practical, I tell them how to get us out of Vietnam—we can get out in ships. And I'd offer one of those ships to the South Vietnamese government; but I wouldn't bring them here —I'd take them to Paris and give them to DeGaulle.

*Portland, Ore., April 16.*

**George C. Wallace**
*Former Governor of Alabama;*
*1968 United States Presidential candidate*

I'm no expert, but evidently there are no experts in the (U.S.) Government, either, or else the war would be finished. Unless we are going to win, we ought to get out.

*Hong Kong, Nov. 7.*

. . . those few (in the U.S.) who fly the Communist flag and call for Communist victory are not engaged in an academic freedom, but are engaged in an activity that I consider treasonable . . . I think the Justice Department ought to put a stop to those who raise money, blood and clothes for the North Vietnamese. I am not talking about humanitarian groups like the Red Cross, but I'm talking about those who say, "I want the Communists to win and defeat the American servicemen . . ." I am happy to say they represent a very few people.

*Saigon, Nov. 8.*

**Lewis W. Walt**
*Lt.-Gen., assistant Commandant,*
*United States Marine Corps*

In the past year, over 10,000 Americans have been killed in Vietnam. Those (in the U.S.) who dissent may not have fired a rifle or thrown a grenade, but they must bear a part of the responsibility for the losses of those gallant Americans.

*Oct. 10.*

The day the enemy firmly believes we are going to pull out, that is the day he will start talking in Paris, and not before. I have felt for a long time that, if we could have had the entire public back of us, this war would have been history a year ago.

*News conference, Danang, Nov. 22.*

**Albert W. Watson**
*United States Representative, R-S.C.*

. . . anyone who would even intimate praise of this ruthless dictator (Ho Chi Minh) does a disservice to America, a dishonor to the memory of the 40,000 young Americans who gave their lives in behalf of this country.

*Before the House,*
*Washington, pub. Sept. 7.*

**Theodore H. White**
*Author*

Everyone wants to get out of Vietnam, and the question is: will they let us get out short of surrender? The latest Nixon proposal goes beyond anything that was proposed by the most docile dove in 1968. The most amazing thing is how this Nixon plan—phased withdrawal, coalition government, local autonomy—so closely resembles Dick Goodwin's prose. Whether they will give us minimal satisfaction on these terms, neither I nor Nixon can possibly guess. It depends on how Hanoi reads the American mind. The enemy also has its madnesses and its self-intoxication and its delusions.

Lyndon Johnson was a figure of enormous tragedy. He made one mistake—and that's all you need. You elect a President, and his great decision is war and peace. Johnson took the best advice from the best brains—Professor Bundy of Harvard, Professor Rostow of M.I.T.—and the advice blew on him. Everything he did was flawed by the blunder of Vietnam, and he was trapped by that blunder.

*Interview, New York, pub. July 27.*

**Charles E. Wiggins**
*United States Representative, R-Calif.*

The issue is not just Vietnam. It is all Southeast Asia. And the question is—and always has been—will world peace be jeopardized if North Vietnam is permitted to pursue policies ranging from subversion and terror to open warfare against neighboring republics? The answer has been plain to every American President for the past 20 years, as it is now to most Americans. Pay no attention to Hanoi or their domestic cheerleaders, Mr. President. Do what you must—because it is right and in the long-range interest of world peace—and the American people will back you up.

*Before the House, Washington, Sept. 29.*

**Harold Winer**
*Assistant Director for Education-South Vietnam, Agency for International Development of the United States*

I have never seen a people of any country . . . respond so willingly and so unselfishly to the needs of education. They will do anything; they will give their last piaster to get a school going in their community . . . I know of nothing that has aroused the hatred of the people toward VC activity as the destruction of a classroom or the killing of a teacher. The people will sometimes gloss over other disruptive activity, but not when it comes to education and the opportunities it offers for a better life for their children.

*Interview, Saigon, pub. June 28.*

**Chalmers P. Wylie**
*United States Representative,*
*R-Ohio*

Weighing the cost of resistance and the price of capitulation, even a patriot might say we are better off to quit before more blood is spilled. Weak nations throughout history have capitulated to a strong aggressor rather than suffer loss of lives and devestation of their land . . . But we are not a weak nation. We do not need to suffer the indignities of a surrender so that communism can continue its march to complete our destruction. Are we ready to say, better Red than dead? Are we ready to say, at the least, to South Vietnam, better for you to be Red than dead? . . . I do not think the people of this great nation are ready to surrender to communism. Yet, a total surrender in Vietnam could only be interpreted as such, and a timetable withdrawal of all forces announced in advance is precisely that.

*Before the House, Washington, Oct. 1.*

**Chia-kan Yen**
*Vice President of Nationalist China*

We have pointed out that the Vietnam war, like the Korean war, is a prolongation of the Chinese mainland tragedy and an integral part of the Communist conspiracy of world domination. A solution of the Vietnam war can be found only in the eradication of the Peiping regime (which is at the root of all turmoil) from the Chinese mainland.

*Before Legislative Yuan,*
*Taipei, pub. December.*

**Lee Kuan Yew**
*Prime Minister of Singapore*

Politically, the South Vietnamese have got to create a government that commands the loyalty and support of the bulk of the population and galvanizes it into self-help. I hope that American troop withdrawals will be at such a rate as not to generate a sense of insecurity in the government of South Vietnam. There must be sufficient time for the South Vietnamese to be trained to stand up and fight for themselves. If they can't, well . . . that's that.

*Interview, Singapore, pub. July 25.*

**Stephen M. Young**
*United States Senator, D-Ohio*

Of course, the Saigon militarist regime headed by Thieu and Ky will strenuously object to any extension of the cease-fire or to any change in our policy, just as they originally refused to accept a three-day cease-fire. The fact is that these tinhorn dictators could not remain in power for more than three days without the support of our armed forces. They are well aware of the fact that, once there is peace in Vietnam, they will be forced to flee and to join their unlisted bank accounts in Hong Kong and Switzerland.

*Before the Senate, Washington, Sept. 9.*

To me it seems that our waging a ground war in a little Asiatic country torn by internal insurrection could be termed madness. Vietnam is of no importance whatever to the defense of the United States. It is an act of international insanity that the Johnson administration involved us on a huge scale in this immoral, undeclared war which is the most unpopular foreign war in the history of this Republic.

*Before the Senate, Washington, Sept. 30.*

**Whitney M. Young, Jr.**
*Executive Director,*
*National Urban League*

·I am totally convinced that this war has an extra dimension for black people that it does not have for many whites. We are suffering doubly. We are dying for something abroad that we do not have at home. At the same time, we are victims of backlash among the white majority— a backlash greatly sharpened by the tensions of the war. By a strange twist of human folly, the groups that are most at odds in our country today—whites and blacks from working class and poor families—are those whose young men are dying in disproportionate numbers in Vietnam.

*News conference, New York, Oct. 13.*

**Clement J. Zablocki**
*United States Representative, D-Wis.*

The recurring chant of "Peace Now" echoed across the nation last Wednesday, (Vietnam) Moratorium day. The Moratorium was intended to demonstrate, in the words of Nicholas von Hoffman of *The Washington Post*, that the American people do not care whether we "bug out, run out, march out, stumble out, crawl out or fade out of South Vietnam." There are, undoubtedly, some Americans who do indeed feel this way. However, I would seriously contest any assertion that they are anywhere near a majority, even though they shout the loudest. And the shouting is what I fear, what we—the representatives of all the American people—must fear. We must not let those who shout the loudest become a pseudo majority. We must beware of the tyranny of the loudest voice.

*Before the House, Washington, Oct. 23.*

**Melvin Zais**
*Maj. Gen, United States Army;*
*commander, 101st Airborne, Vietnam*

The country (the United States) is looking for a scapegoat (in Vietnam). First it was the draft, then recruiters, then Dow Chemical—and now it's the bloody generals.

*Interview, pub. April 11.*

. . . it is a myth that if we don't do anything to the enemy, he won't do anything to us. If we sit still, he will kill us. He will come in under our wire with satchel charges and weapons and kill and maim my men.

*Pub. June 2.*

**Andrei A. Amalrik**
*Russian Author*

I am against the (Soviet) regime not because it is dishonest, but from organic repulsion. For example, I cannot listen to the Soviet radio. I cannot read *Pravda*. It is crude, stupid and full of lies.
*Interview, Moscow, pub. Dec. 24.*

**George W. Anderson, Jr.**
*Admiral, United States Navy (Ret.); former Chief of Naval Operations*

I think there is a general recognition that the Soviet objective is world domination. Does that mean putting troops in New York or Washington or any other specific place around the world? I don't think so. Does it mean the destruction of our cities with atomic weapons? No, because they know they would get severe, immediate and certain retaliation on their own. What it does mean is Russia's having the principal nations of the world either accommodate or be subservient to the Soviet Union in matters that they consider of importance to them.

The Soviets want to avoid getting involved with their own military forces, unless it is absolutely necessary. In other words, they want to operate by proxy. They like to either create or exploit situations to their own advantage, which pose to us only courses of action characterized by disadvantages, risks and expense. This is their typical strategy. This is what they did in the Berlin situation; they did it in Korea and in Cuba. They have done it again in South Vietnam.

They (the members of the North Atlantic Treaty Organization) must realize that the United States is indeed providing the real deterrent forces, the mobile forces, the hard-hitting forces which they are not capable of providing; and they, in turn, must do more of which they are capable.
*Interview, Washington, pub. Jan. 20.*

**Raymond Aron**
*Professor of Faculty Letters, Paris University*

You must understand the natural irresponsibility of the French Presidency. I do not mean that de Gaulle is irresponsible; but he need not consult so broadly as . . . (the United States) President must; and he knows that, whatever he says, it will not change the face of the world, as an American statement might. If de Gaulle were President of the United States, he would operate in quite a different way.

Young people in France are not taken in by the Gaullist rhetoric of greatness. They sense that the resources necessary to play a great role in the world are not available to the French . . . They demonstrate against the United States, for Castro and Mao, and so forth; but it's all an alibi. They have no political dream that means anything.
*Interview, Ithaca, N.Y., March 7.*

**Vladimir Ashkenazy**
*Russian Pianist*

When an official Soviet spokesman says I move freely between Russia and the West, as I only wish I could, it is a gross and unfair distortion of the truth.
*Palea Edpidaurus, Greece, pub. Aug. 29.*

**George W. Ball**
*Former Under Secretary of State of the United States*

It would be monstrously imprudent to assume that NATO is no longer essential . . . We created the Western Alliance because the Soviet Union threatened to ex-

(GEORGE W. BALL)

pand its power and influence westward, unless organized force were systematically opposed to that expansion. Today, that threat persists. A dam is not redundant because there has been no flood since it was built.

*Pub. April 21.*

The Germans have pursued a nonassertive policy. This isn't going to last. In five or six years a new generation will be in control of (West) Germany, and we will have a whole new ball game.

*Pub. June 2.*

**Anthony Barber**
*Chairman, Conservative Party*
*of the United Kingdom*

If we can win the next election with a really substantial majority we shall have within our grasp a prize even greater than the return of a Conservative government —a chance to change, for all time, the very nature of the alternative government, to smash the doctrine and dogma of socialism. We mean to work for a return to real and effective freedom of choice and to the maximum freedom of individual decision . . . If national achievement could be measured by his (Prime Minister Harold Wilson's) promises, Britain would now be in the superpower class. If his pledges could magically be transmitted into reality, our standard of living would be the envy of the world . . . The straitjacket of socialism is not compatible with the kind of society which the majority of our people want to see.

*At Conservative Party convention,*
*Brighton, England, Oct. 8.*

**Enrico Berlinguer**
*Vice secretary,*
*Communist Party of Italy*

We have expressed our serious dissent towards the military intervention (by the Soviet Union in Czechslovakia in 1967), and we reaffirm this. We do not intend to interfere in the internal affairs of Czechoslovakia, but this affair involved questions of principle, like independence and sovereignty, socialist democracy and the freedom of culture . . . There cannot exist a single guiding center for Communism, nor a party guide, nor a state guide.

*Moscow, June 11.*

**Nigel Birch**
*Member of British Parliament*

I do not think many people are very interested in titles these days. Inflation has caught up with them. In the old days, when you said that someone was drunk as a lord, it really meant something; but to say as drunk as a life peer means nothing.

*Pub. March 2.*

**Prince Juan Carlos De Borbon y Borbon**
*King-designate of Spain*

I am close to the young. I admire them and I share their desire to find a better and more genuine world. I know that in the rebelliousness that worries so many there lives the best generosity of those who want an open future—often with impossible dreams, but always with a noble desire for the good of the people.

I want to serve my nation publicly, and for our people I want progress, development, unity, justice, liberty and grandeur. The monarchy can, and must be, an efficient instrument as a political system, so long as it knows how to maintain a just and real balance of power, and bases itself in the will of the people.

*At his investiture as future*
*King of Spain, Madrid, July 23.*

**Willy Brandt**
*Foreign Minister of West Germany*

Already at the time of the Khrushchev ultimatum, I knew that one dare not give up Berlin if one desired not to endanger the security of the West. Today, I am more convinced of that than ever.

*Interview, Bonn, pub. Feb. 22.*

Anything which seems to weaken the links between Berlin and West Germany— which encourages the feeling of being cut off, left alone—would be the same as weakening the economy. That is why we have been so insistent on holding our electoral assembly in Berlin, just as we have in '54, in '59 and in '64.

*Interview, pub. March 7.*

**Willy Brandt**
*Chancellor of West Germany*

I want . . . to make it clear that Hitler has been conquered, not only by foreign military power, but by his own people.
*Bonn, pub. Oct. 26.*

In the past years, many in this country feared that the second German democracy would go the way of the first . . . I have never believed this. I believe it still less today. We are not at the end of our democracy. We are at its beginning.

We have as little need for blind approval as our people have for strained dignity and pompous reserve. We're not looking for admirers; we need people who think critically. This Government will characterize itself as tolerant. It will appreciate solidarity that expresses itself in criticism.
*Bonn, Oct. 28.*

. . . recognition of the German Democratic Republic (East Germany) by the Federal Republic (West Germany) is out of the question.
*Before the Bundestag (Parliament), Bonn, Oct. 28.*

For us, there is no divided East and West policy. Our Eastern policy is imbedded in our policy in the West. We are not floating between East and West.
*Interview, pub. December.*

**Leonid I. Brezhnev**
*General Secretary, Communist Party of the Union of Soviet Socialist Republics*

It is easy to see how important it would be if the West German Government officially recognized the existing European frontiers, including the frontier between the Federal Republic of Germany and the German Democratic Republic; if it declares the Munich agreement null and void from the very start; and discards the unjustified claim to speak on behalf of the entire German people that was advanced by the government of the Christian Democratic Union.
*Moscow, Oct. 27.*

**Manlio Brosio**
*Secretary-General, North Atlantic Treaty Organization*

Defense, political solidarity and possible detente will remain its (NATO's) basic aims. Social cooperation may help but certainly not overtake them.
*NATO Defense College, Brussels, pub. Sept. 14.*

**George Brown**
*Deputy Leader, British Labor Party; former Foreign Secretary of the United Kingdom*

Withdrawal (by the United States) for bad reasons from Asia could easily be followed by an American withdrawal from here, from our continent. And then let us consider what the situation in Europe would be.
*Pub. December.*

**Alastair Buchan**
*Director, British Institute for Strategic Studies*

. . . the United States must retain a substantial degree of force in Europe to make the American nuclear commitment credible. That's very well understood on both sides of the Atlantic . . . I suspect that we will worry less and less about the threat of a general Russian attack on Western Europe, and we will be more and more concerned with local conflicts . . . If Yugoslavia were attacked, and the leading NATO powers decided that they must back that country, you might have to get forces into the Mediterranean and the Adriatic fast. But there's very little mobility in the European set-up today.

Being an ally of a country as powerful as the United States is a double-edged bargain: You gain a great deal in terms of security, but you have to give up quite a lot in terms of autonomy.
*Interview, London, pub. Feb. 17.*

**Nicolae Ceausescu**
*President of Romania*

I would like to stress that in the future we will continue to work for multilateral developments of our relations, friendships and cooperation with the Soviet Union and its Communist party, which has been one of the foundations of the foreign policy of our country.
*Before Romanian Communist Party, Bucharest, Aug. 6.*

(NICOLAE CEAUSESCU)

In our society, the whole press, be it daily or periodical, socio-political or cultural, must consistently and firmly promote the political line of the (Communist) party. All reviews and publications must mirror the concept and views of the political, social and cultural institutions to which they belong. It cannot be admitted for any reason that works of opinions be published . . . which run contrary to the ideology of our society.

*Prague, Sept. 26.*

### Jacques Chaban-Delmas
*President of the*
*French National Assembly*

Historians in the future will doubtless write that nothing was missing in the grand destiny of Charles de Gaulle, not even being paid with ingratitude.

*Paris, April 29.*

### Jacques Chaban-Delmas
*Premier of France*

Frenchmen too often prefer to fight for words, even if they cover dramatic failures, rather than for realities. This is why we do not succeed in accomplishing reforms otherwise than by pretending to make a revolution. French society has not yet managed to evolve in any way other than through major crises.

*Before Parliament, Paris, Sept. 16.*

### Charles
*Prince of Wales*

It is with a certain sense of pride and emotion that I have received these symbols of office, here in this magnificent fortress, where no one could fail to be stirred by its atmosphere of time-worn grandeur, nor where I myself could be unaware of the long history of Wales in its determination to remain individual and to guard its own particular heritage—a heritage that dates back into the mists of ancient British history, that has produced many brave men, princes, poets, bards, scholars and, more recently, great singers, a very memorable goon (comedian Harry Secombe) and eminent film stars.

*At his investiture, Caernarvon Castle,*
*Caernarvon, Wales, July 1.*

### Harlan Cleveland
*Ambassador to the*
*North Atlantic Treaty Organization*
*from the United States*

For as far ahead as the eye can see, we will need a Western solidarity organization, with sufficiency of defense military strength responsive to its political consensus. Whether, in time, people call it NATO will be a matter of taste. Whether they call it necessary will be a matter of survival.

*Interview, Brussels, pub. June 5.*

### James C. Cleveland
*United States Representative, R-N.H.*

. . . the young people of Hungáry yearn for freedom, for a land and circumstances they never knew. It is amazing that the young, born since World War II and brought up all their lives under communism, should yet yearn to be free. That is great evidence and a great tribute to the human spirit.

*Before the House, Washington, Oct. 29.*

### Learie Constantine
*First black member,*
*British House of Lords*

It is one of the great things in this country that a colored man has been taken into the Lords.

*London, pub. April 7.*

### Terence Cardinal Cooke
*Archbishop of New York*

Years ago, I was in Ireland as a young priest, and I found I had dozens of cousins. Then, when I was a Bishop, I found I had hundreds of cousins. And, when I went as a Cardinal, I found I had thousands. That's how it is in Ireland.

*New York, May 7.*

### Josef Cyrankiewicz
*Prime Minister of Poland*

The starting point for the beginning of the process of normalization between the Federal Republic of Germany and Poland is the recognition of Poland's western border on the Oder and Neisse (Rivers). There is not and there cannot be any other basis for the creation of the conditions for the further normalization between the two states.

*Before Parliament, Warsaw, Dec. 22.*

**Michel Debre**
*Foreign Minister of France*

If the French do not think first of their country, who will do it for them?

*Television address, Paris, Jan. 9.*

France considers that the British, who are always inclined to align themselves behind American positions, are not yet ready to join the European community, whose vocation is independence.

*Published Feb. 28.*

Has the Atlantic Alliance lost its *raison d'etre* in our eyes? My presence in Washington, for the twentieth anniversary of the signing of the treaty, is proof to the contrary.

*Before National Press Club,*
*Washington, April 9.*

How could a majority of Frenchmen reject he (President Charles de Gaulle) who was the artisan of their liberation, he who restored their independence? The strong ideas of our century, the freedom of men, the freedom of nations, detente, international cooperation, lose their most illustrious champion with the withdrawal of the General. Rarely has a leader left power dragging in his wake, such sorrow (felt by) men of all ages, all conditions, all religions and on all continents.

*Before the Cabinet, Paris, May 2.*

. . . we know we are a Western European nation, that the United States is the first power in the West, the reservoir of its strength and technical progress. It is our tradition, in our interest and our innermost feeling, to show the United States our constant concern for friendly and sincere relations.

*At Gaullist Party Congress,*
*Amboise, France, Sept. 11.*

**Charles de Gaulle**
*President of France*

There are certain things that do not change, and one thing is precisely our Franco-American friendship. We have found—and I have always found—that the Americans and French are capable of dealing with their problems, not only in a frank and cordial atmosphere, but in a true spirit of confidence with each other.

*Paris, pub. March 7.*

Here I am, submitting a solemn proposal of reform to our country. If the French people, by chance—for that is the word—were to oppose this reform, what kind of man would I be if I failed to draw the consequences of such a profound rupture at once and ridiculously tried to maintain myself in my present functions?

One day, one will measure the depths of the falls (and) the chasms that were spared the fatherland because the (French) people gave me its confidence whenever I turned to it.

*Television interview, Paris, April 10.*

**Suleyman Demirel**
*Premier of Turkey*

Military bases in Turkey are common Turkish-American bases intended for Turkey's defense. Turkey would not permit use of these bases for purposes that are irrelevant to Turkey's defense and that would be interpreted as interference in other countries' domestic affairs.

*Interview, Istanbul, pub. Nov. 1.*

**Maurice Couve de Murville**
*Former Foreign Minister of France*

I was beaten (for a seat in the National Assembly) by a coalition that was clearly composed by revolutionary socialism, the moderates of the center and the ultras of the rightwing . . . everyone will understand that this is not where the future of France lies.

*Paris, Oct. 26.*

**Konstantin Derevlyev**
*Architect, Moscow City Council*

This is not a fantasy. In this century, we will have in Moscow houses of 500 to 600 stories.

*Moscow, pub. June 1.*

**Luisa Isabel Alvarez de Toledo**
*Duchess of Medina-Sidonia, Spain*

Someday there has to be a democracy

(LUISA ISABEL ALVAREZ DE TOLEDO)

here, but it is taking a long time. If they don't hurry, they're going to miss it altogether.

*Madrid, March 27.*

## Eamon de Valera
*President of Ireland*

It will be a great shame for this generation if we let the Irish language die. We should strive as earnestly now to revive the language as we strove in the past to win our freedom . . . Those who fought for the freedom we enjoy today desired that the Irish nation should live. But, without the language, the Irish nation they had in mind will not live.

*Dublin, pub. Jan. 19.*

## Bernadette Devlin
*Member of British Parliament*
*from Northern Ireland*

If there (were) less bigoted religion in Ulster and more Christianity, there would be far less problems. Christianity is "love thy neighbor," but half the population of Ulster hates the other half in the name of Jesus Christ.

*Cookstown, Northern Ireland, April 19.*

The people of Northern Ireland are being oppressed, not only by a Tory Government, but by a corrupt, bigoted and self-interested Tory Government, with whom the Tories in this house should be ashamed to associate themselves.

There was never born an Englishman who understands the Irish people.

*Before House of Commons,*
*London, April 22.*

The one common point among all Ulstermen is that they don't like Englishmen telling them what to do.

*Pub. May 5.*

. . . (the House of Commons is) all so hidebound and stuffy. I feel like tearing down some of the barriers of bureaucracy. The other day, when I asked Harold (Wilson) something about the emergency in Ireland, he didn't give me a straight answer. I felt like saying, "Now, come along, Harold, let's quit the double talk." But the rules didn't allow me.

I don't expect to grow very old. There's a tradition of explosive violence in our country. We have a lot to do and many changes to make. In the civil rights movement we are very peaceful, but our enemies are not. A stick of dynamite . . . a bullet in the night . . . who knows?

*Interview, London, pub. June 12.*

The barricades will stay up in Northern Ireland until the government comes down.

*New York, Aug. 21.*

. . . the Catholics are not fighting the Protestants (in Northern Ireland) because they're Protestants. Nor vice-versa. It's the poor against the government. It's the oppressed Irish against the racist government. It's Irish freedom against British control.

My parliamentary salary has been used to buy petrol (gasoline)—and barbed wire.

*New York, Aug. 22.*

A very simplistic attitude of our struggle has reached America . . . (a view) of Irish Catholics and Irish Protestants at each others' throats. The reason Catholics and Protestants struggle is not because they disagree on how God should be worshipped. It is because of the shortage of work and the shortage of wages which have to be shared between them.

*Aug. 27.*

The Protestants created the division (in Northern Ireland). Fifty years ago, the prime minister of the time said, "We'll build a Protestant state for Protestant people." They have been actively discriminating against Catholics and they are terrified that they themselves might become the minority.

*Los Angeles, Aug. 28.*

I was in on the making of Molotov cocktails (during riots in Northern Ireland) and the organized throwing of them, so that none would be wasted. I believe it's not the justness of the cause that makes the politician, but when he is prepared to do something about it.

*Interview, pub. Sept. 5.*

I am a socialist because I think those who have little should get a little more from those who have a lot. But my kind of socialism isn't doctrinaire. I've never read Karl Marx, and that annoys the doctrinaires.

*New York, pub. Sept. 8.*

It has been as much as I can do to put up with the games they play in the House of Commons.

*Pub. December.*

**Milovan Djilas**
*Author; former Vice President of Yugoslavia*

Western Europe now borders on an empire (the U.S.S.R.) that is all the more unbridled, all the more terrible, because its only advantage is military force.

*Pub. Feb. 2.*

**Alexander Dubcek**
*Secretary, Czechoslovak Communist Party*

Either we manage to establish public order and prevent anti-Socialist, anti-Soviet manifestations . . . or we shall find ourselves back where we were at the end of August (1968).

*Television address, Prague, April 3.*

**Alexander Dubcek**
*Chairman, Federal Assembly of Czechoslovakia*

. . . if it were necessary for me to fight the enemies of Socialism, I would fight. They pretended that I was practicing anti-Sovietism. On the contrary, I have never thought that my policy could be developed outside our alliances and friendship with our Socialist friends. These are not merely words. I have always been tied to the Socialist parties and to the Soviet Union. I have always been, and will be, against manifestations of anti-Sovietism.

*Interview, Prague, pub. July 29.*

**Obi Egbuna**
*Biafran Novelist*

Where the American will tell you straight out he does not like you (a black man), an Englishman is very polite and makes a lot of excuses. It's the difference between a bad and a good slavemaster. I prefer the bad, since you know it is an evil; but, here, the (black) people actually enjoy their slavery.

*London, pub. May 26.*

**Francisco Franco (Bahamonde)**
*Chief of State of Spain*

Today it cannot be said that the monarchies represent the conservative sector of the people, and as we contemplate the different monarchies of northern Europe we must recognize the progress and social efficiency that have given them stability and a guarantee of continuity. But we need not look abroad to seek examples to prove that what is transcendental in institutions is not their name but their content. The monarchy of the Catholic kings, which has given the nation years of glory, is a perennial example of popularity and the constant defense of the social rights of our people.

*Before the Cortes (Parliament), Madrid, July 22.*

**Samuel N. Friedel**
*United States Representative, D-Md.*

. . . In the Czech experiment, the Soviets (came) face to face with the phenomenon of the idea of freedom asserting itself within the Communist environment. The Soviets could not tolerate this because it presented an irreconcilable contradiction: namely, the spirit of freedom in conflict with the principle of political tyranny. If extended throughout the East European bloc, it would threaten the foundations of their totalitarian system . . . What the Soviets could not accept was the basic right of nations to determine for themselves their own destiny; they could not accept the most elementary of human rights, the right of the individual to exist according to his own preferences. And so they invaded Czechoslovakia; they violated these basic human rights; they violated, too, the United Nations Charter, which had held the promise of all mankind that the rights of all would be preserved.

*Before the House, Washington, Sept. 3.*

**Joseph Fromm**
*Senior European Editor, "U.S. News & World Report"*

The political atmosphere in Bonn has

(JOSEPH FROMM)

been transformed since (Willy) Brandt took over in October. There's a new feeling of confidence. That, together with the country's enormous economic strength, insures that West Germany's voice will be heard increasingly in the 1970s—and will have to be listened to.

*Interview, Washington, December.*

**Barry M. Goldwater**
*United States Senator, R-Ariz.*

There is reason to believe that ratification at this time (of the Nuclear Non-proliferation Treaty) would, in effect, place the U.S. stamp of approval on an aggressive and militant move made by Russia to stamp out human freedom . . . A thousand non-proliferation treaties with the Soviet Union will not wipe out actions such as the invasion of Czechoslovakia.

*Washington, Jan. 14.*

**Sergei G. Gorshkov**
*Admiral, and Commander-in-Chief
of the Soviet Navy*

The flag of the Soviet Navy now flies proudly over the oceans of the world. Sooner or later, the U.S. will have to understand that it no longer has mastery of the seas.

*Pub. May 4.*

**Andrei A. Gromyko**
*Foreign Minister of the
Union of Soviet Socialist Republics*

We paid attention to the statement of President Nixon that he believes the period of confrontation is being replaced by the era of negotiation. The Soviet Union is all for negotiation, and, if the United States actually conducts this line, then our side, as before, is ready to come to an agreement, both on the question of bilateral relations with the United States and on outstanding international problems.

*Before the Supreme Soviet,
Moscow, July 10.*

**Denis W. Healey**
*Minister of Defense of the
United Kingdom*

We can withdraw our forces from the

Far East, but we cannot tow the British Isles away from Europe.

*Published Feb. 23.*

It is most important for the President (of the United States) to maintain European confidence in the American commitment to defend Europe. If confidence in the U.S. guarantee is maintained, Europe will be much more enthusiastic over U.S. talks with the Russians.

*Pub. Feb. 28.*

If the Canadians go along with their planned (NATO) troop reductions, and, even more, if this leads to a chain reaction among the other countries, the nuclear threshold will fall, and the point at which nuclear weapons would be used would arise very much earlier.

*News conference, London, May 30.*

The purpose of NATO is not to produce heaven on earth. It is to prevent hell on earth.

*London, pub. Oct. 17.*

**Edward Heath**
*Leader, Conservative Party
of the United Kingdom*

Our resources are slender. Some around the world even begin to doubt the strength of our character. We do not doubt your (United States') will—do not doubt ours. Do not write Britain off.

*Before National Press Club,
Washington, May 26.*

**Gustav Heinemann**
*President-elect of West Germany*

I am no opponent of the Bundeswehr, but an opponent of all hurrah patriotism. I respect the consciousness of duty with which soldiers of all ranks perform their duty. But I think that we should stick to that concept of the soldier's profession which is expressed in the formula, "citizens in uniform."

*Interview, Bonn, March 10.*

**Gustav Heinemann**
*President of West Germany*

A good German cannot be a nationalist. Today, a national-minded German can only be a European.

*West Berlin, July 19.*

The last consequence of the National Socialist adventure still cannot be sighted. How long will we remain a divided nation? How long will Berlin remain a sliced-up city? When will Europe attain a settlement of peace and an individual function in the world? There is still no answer to these and other questions 30 years after the beginning of World War II. But one thing is clear: None of the questions will be solved if we do not attain reconciliation with all our neighbors and gain new trust in each other.

*Television address, Bonn, Sept. 1.*

**Patrick Hillery**
*Minister for External*
*Affairs of Ireland*

We regard the whole of Ireland as our territory. My government has always wanted the reunification of Ireland, and we believe that there should now be negotiations and the constitutional position . . . Ordinary civil rights are still denied the (Catholic) minority in the six counties of Ulster. They are discriminated against in jobs; they have armed police at their back. It is a situation that would not be tolerated in any civilized country. You can't expect a man to raise a family in that situation.

*London, pub. Aug. 16.*

**Hubert H. Humphrey**
*Former Vice President*
*of the United States*

(Soviet Premier) Kosygin gave me a message to take back to the United States. He wanted me to tell the President and the American people that the Soviet Union wants to work with the United States for peace. I think there is a basic Soviet desire to negotiate in good faith on matters of substance.

*News conference, Moscow, July 21.*

**Gustav Husak**
*First Secretary,*
*Communist Party of Czechoslovakia*

I may be called the executioner of freedom, but one does not get ahead with a popular policy, being nice to everyone. We have to struggle without mercy for

(answers to) questions we have agreed to solve.

*Before Central Committee of*
*Czechoslovak Communist Party,*
*Prague, pub. April 25.*

I personally believe that if the old leadership had fought the antisocial forces, if it had put the mass media in order, and if it had maintained normal relations with fraternal parties, there would have been no August (1968) events and no introduction of (Soviet) troops.

*Pub. Aug. 22.*

Czechoslovakia is a fully sovereign, independent state, politically, economically and militarily.

*On first anniversary of Soviet*
*occupation, Prague, pub. Aug. 24.*

It is necessary to say clearly—and this is my opinion—that in no case was (the Soviet invasion) an unfriendly act against the Czechoslovak people and state . . . its motive was to bring help to our people and workers.

*Banska Bystrica, Czechoslovakia,*
*Aug. 29.*

We are not butchers, and our party is not a slaughterhouse. Our work is with living people. Reason and feelings play a big role here. The policy of the Communist Party cannot be made with sabers.

*At Czechoslovak Communist Party*
*Central Committee meeting,*
*Prague, pub. Oct. 12.*

The friendship and alliance with the Soviet Union are the main condition of our national and state existence.

*Moscow, Oct. 27.*

**Henry M. Jackson**
*United States Senator, D-Wash.*

Once the Kremlin is confident of possessing an equality or a preponderance of over-all nuclear capability, I believe it will be tempted to accept a far wider range of risks to pursue its purposes, especially in areas like Central Europe, where it has local superiority of conventional forces.

*Television broadcast,*
*Washington, March 17.*

(HENRY M. JACKSON)

What we see going on at this time (in the Soviet Union) is that the move is to the right. It is back toward Stalinism. We also see that the men who are in power are not exactly competent leaders. There is a real point of unpredictability about these people that is dangerous . . .

*Television interview, Washington, May 4.*

(The Soviet Union is) a dangerous, unpredictable opponent on the verge of a leadership crisis, the outcome of which we cannot forecast. In this perspective, the fast-growing military capabilities of the Soviet Union take on added significance . . . we do not know who will have the finger on the Soviet trigger in the months and years ahead. The enormous Russian arsenal will be at the disposal of whatever "strong man" or ascendant faction of tough, ambitious figures comes to the fore in the Soviet power struggle.

*Before the Senate, Washington, July 9.*

**Pyotr L. Kapitsa**
*Russian Physicist*

One can state with full objectivity that, in material and cultural development, in education, in science and defense capacity, both countries (the United States and the Soviet Union) have reached about the same level. We only lag behind in the field of technological development, and, because of this, our labor productivity has not reached the level of the United States.

*Before Presidium of Academy of Sciences, Moscow, pub. May 28.*

**Urho K. Kekkonen**
*President of Finland*

A guiding principle of our foreign policy is that, parallel with arranging our security-policy issues by pursuing a policy of neutrality we can best serve the interests of the international community. We are glad when this neutral policy of ours was recognized both by the East and the West.

*Interview, Helsinki, pub. Sept. 18.*

**Eric Kierans**
*Minister of Communications of Canada*

Instead of a genuine deterrent against a genuine threat, NATO has become a self-justifying deterrent against a non-existant military threat.

*Pub. Feb. 2.*

**Kurt Georg Kiesinger**
*Chancellor of West Germany*

As Germans, we cannot take it upon our conscience to . . . hinder further prosecutions of Nazi crimes.

*Pub. May 5.*

It would be folly for any of us to preach a new nationalism.

*Munich, June 14.*

It is a shame that 200 million Americans have to defend 300 million Europeans.

*Pub. June 22.*

. . . Europe must not think of being independent of America, and America must not think of withdrawing into isolationism. We both need one another, perhaps more in the future than ever before.

*Interview, Bonn, pub. Nov. 5.*

**Henry A. Kissinger**
*Assistant to the President of the United States for National Security Affairs*

In some respects, it was easier to deal with Stalin than with this timid, mediocre leadership (in the Soviet Union) that lets crises develop and has missiles.

*Pub. Feb. 14.*

Germany cannot have a nuclear capability because, if it did, the Russians would go to war.

*Washington, pub. Aug. 22.*

**Anatoly V. Kuznetsov**
*Russian Author*

It is no light matter to leave your country . . . I have read that the American writer, William Styron, thinks that I should not have left. Well, I have this offer for him. My rooms in Tula are vacant. Let him take them and live in the Soviet Union for a year and then see what he thinks. Please, he is welcome.

They (the present leaders of the Soviet Union) are all hawks.

The mood of the intelligentsia (in the Soviet Union) goes down, down, down. It has been that way since the trial of Sinyavsky and Daniel. Then came Czechoslovakia. That was the big turning point. Now what can anyone do? What can anyone write? When two writers meet, they say to each other, "What are you doing? What is your mood?" But the answer is the same. The mood is bad. There is nothing one can do. Everyone is in the same boat. No one can publish anything worthwhile. It is a very gloomy outlook. People feel they must save themselves if they can.

. . . Every day the Russian man-in-the-street is told, in his newspapers and over the radio, at lectures and meetings—everywhere—that what his government has done (in China and Czechoslovia) is a guarantee of peace. And (that) the farther our troops move into Europe and Asia, the greater the assurance that there will not be a war. That's all the ordinary man wants.

I am afraid that 90% of the people in Russia no longer believe in any kind of communism. It is a long time since there was any revolution or revolutionary spirit in Russia. It is a firmly established imperialist state of a special kind unknown in history.

*Interview, London, pub. Aug. 24.*

**Melvin R. Laird**
*Secretary of Defense*
*of the United States*

The Soviets are going for a first strike capability, and there is no question about it.

*Before Senate Foreign Relations Committee, Washington, March 21.*

I've always made it clear that I do not believe the Soviet Union would be foolish enough . . . to go ahead with a first strike (in a nuclear war).

*Washington, April 7.*

**Reidar T. Larsen**
*Chairman, Norwegian Delegation*
*to World Communist Conference*

There is an especially strong impulse, particularly in the Western European (Communist) parties, to orient themselves toward national conditions and to believe their own strength. They are more independent of Moscow, and this trend will continue.

*Moscow, pub. June 18.*

**Arthur J. Lelyveld**
*President, American Jewish Congress*

American Jews who travel to France, purchase French goods and use French services can take encouragement from the French people's strong opposition to the peculiar definition of neutrality which President (Charles) de Gaulle has sought to impose on the Middle East.

*Paris, Jan. 11.*

**John M. Lynch**
*Prime Minister of Ireland*

The united Ireland we desire is one in which there will be a scrupulously fair deal for all. The Protestants of the North need have no fear of any interference with their religious freedom or civil liberties and rights.

*Tralee, Ireland, pub. Sept. 21.*

**Malcolm Mackintosh**
*British specialist on Soviet affairs*

No Soviet Government will ever let a single bloc of 80 to 90 million industrious, technologically advanced Germans come together under one political roof—even a Communist one.

*Pub. June 16.*

**Nicholas Makarezoz**
*Minister for Economic*
*Coordination of Greece*

The post-revolutionary drachmes is one of the hardest currencies in the world. One does not commit suicide when one is healthy and rich, and the Greek government will not commit suicide by devaluating its currency.

*News conference, Athens, Oct. 4.*

**Mike Mansfield**
*United States Senator, D-Mont.*

I am not now advocating, and I have not in the past advocated, that all U.S. troops be removed from Europe. Our vital interest in what transpires in Eur-

(MIKE MANSFIELD)

ope remains, and a U.S. presence should remain. In this day and age, an armed attack on Western Europe will certainly involve us almost from the outset. It is to our interest, therefore, that we are present before the outset. That need can be met, in my judgment, and should be met, with a much smaller military force.

*Before the Senate, Washington, Dec. 1.*

**Laurence Martin**
*Professor of War Studies,*
*University of London*

Having achieved the best strategic balance they have ever enjoyed with their richer adversary, it would clearly be to Russian advantage to freeze the existing relationship. If the Russians could win an explicit acknowledgement of this position from the United States, they will move closer to establishing a parallel impression of parity in political status and influence.

*Pub. Nov. 10.*

**Golda Meir**
*Prime Minister of Israel*

(The Soviet Government is) the most realistic regime in the world—no ideals.

*Interview, New York, pub. Oct. 7.*

**W. Stratton Mills**
*Member of British Parliament*

She (Bernadette Devlin) is a Fidel Castro in a miniskirt.

*New York, Aug. 29.*

**Riccardo Misasi**
*Minister of Foreign Trade of Italy*

Italy is bound to the philosophy of freer trade. This is something that we have learned from America, and we have been faithful to it even during unfavorable periods, like those in 1963 and 1964 when the country suffered a recession.

*Interview, pub. Oct. 27.*

**Jean Monnet**
*Founder, European Common Market*

Some people have said that they fear that, when Britain joins the Common Market, it (the Market) will be radically changed, loosened, dissolved or subject to external influence. If we do our job properly, I believe we shall dispel these fears and demonstrate that, by including Britain, the European community will not only be enlarged, but will become stronger.

*At meeting of Action Committee for the United States of Europe, London, March 11.*

**Malcolm Muggeridge**
*Author, Editor*

Despite all its appalling disadvantages, I suppose that, by an accident of history, England does provide the freest environment there is.

*Pub. Sept. 11.*

**Richard M. Nixon**
*President of the United States*

I see for (NATO) an opportunity to be much more than it ever has been before: a bulwark of peace, the architect of new means of partnership, and an invigorated forum for new ideas and new technologies to reach the lives of our peoples.

The United States is determined to listen with a new attentiveness to its NATO partners, not only because they have a right to be heard, but because we want their ideas; and I believe we have a right to expect that consultation shall be a two-way street.

I have come (to Europe) for work, not for ceremony; to inquire, not to insist; to consult, not convince; to listen and learn and to begin what I hope will be a continuing interchange of ideas and insights.

*Brussels, Feb. 24.*

It's time we (the United States) began lecturing our European partners less and listening to them more.

*Brussels, pub. Feb. 26.*

One thing that has not changed is our devotion and dedication to the goal that the German people will again be united.

*At Cologne-Bonn Airport, Feb. 26.*

Bravery in a crisis is expected of those who cherish freedom. What is much more difficult, much more rare, is bravery day-by-day—the steady fortitude that resists subtle pressures and refuses to permit the slow erosion of liberties. That is the remarkable bravery of the Berliner . . .

Let there be no miscalculation. No unilateral move, no illegal act, no form of pressure from any source will shake the resolve of the Western nations to defend their rightful status as protectors of the people of free Berlin.

In the sense that the people of Berlin stand for freedom and peace, all the people of the world who want freedom are truly Berliners.

*West Berlin, Feb. 27.*

Sometimes we become rather disillusioned with our aid programs around the world, and we look back on our relations with Europe, particularly, and wonder if it was really worth all that we did immediately after World War II . . . Anyone who saw Europe as I did in that period of devastation after World War II . . . and saw it today, would realize that it was worth doing, because today a strong, prosperous, free Europe stands there, partly a result of our aid.

We now realize that this Atlantic Alliance deserves our attention, should be the center of our concern, should not be taken for granted. It will not be.

*News conference, Washington, March 4.*

Our allies do recognize the necessity to maintain NATO's conventional forces. They do recognize that they must carry their share or that the United States . . . (will) have much less incentive to carry our share. I believe they will do their share.

I would . . . point this out—an interesting thing about Soviet military and diplomatic history: They have always thought in defensive terms . . . (their) emphasis is on defense.

*News conference, Washington, March 14.*

Addressing the North Atlantic Council 10 years ago . . . President Eisenhower spoke of the need for unity. There is not much strength in one finger of a hand, he said; but, when five fingers are balled to a fist, you have a very considerable instrument of defense. We need such an instru-

ment of defense; the United States will bear its fair share of keeping NATO strong . . . We in America continue to consider Europe's security as our own.

*Before North Atlantic Treaty Organization, Washington, April 10.*

Those of us who have traveled in the Soviet Union know the Russian people and the American people are not natural enemies. The Russian people and the Americans are natural friends. The time will come when the Soviet people and the American nation will come to be rivals and compete as friends . . . competing to enrich and improve the quality of life.

*Washington, May 23.*

### G. Warren Nutter
*Assistant Secretary of Defense for International Security Affairs of the United States*

I have reasonable confidence in saying that (the Russians) don't give up anything for nothing, and they don't understand anybody who does. If you confront them with an overly generous concession, they figure you're a pushover or a weakling, or they're suspicious of your motives. They have a very healthy respect for someone at the other side of the table who plays it tough. They expect this.

We view warfare as a tragic extension of political activity—when all other means of achieving legitimate and vital national interests have been exhausted. (The Soviets) turn that upside down, on its head. Warfare to them is the normal state of affairs, and diplomacy is an extension of warfare.

*Pub. June 1.*

### Terence O'Neill
*Prime Minister of Northern Ireland*

No solution based on the ascendancy of any section of our community can hope to endure. Either we live in peace, or we have no life worth living.

*Farewell address, Belfast, April 29.*

### Lawrence Orr
*Member of British Parliament from Northern Ireland*

Here we know Bernadette Devlin to be just a silly, lightheaded girl whom no one

(LAWRENCE ORR)

takes seriously. But she becomes dangerous when she goes abroad and works on the prejudices of the American-Irish.

*Belfast, Aug. 26.*

**Ian Paisley**
*Protestant leader
of Northern Ireland*

The fight is on! This is not a garden party—it is a battle! We will show these compromising, pussy-footing Unionists there are still Protestants in this country not prepared to compromise.

*Pub. Sept. 21.*

**Olaf Palme**
*Prime Minister-elect of Sweden*

Although we are a neighbor of the Soviet Union, we have spoken some very hard words—about Hungary, the Berlin Wall, Czechoslovakia. Nobody then questioned our neutrality. But when, out of the same fundamental values, we criticize the war in Vietnam, there is talk that we are non-neutral and anti-American.

*Stockholm, pub. Oct. 5.*

We shall not overestimate our role and believe that we are wiser than others, but neither shall we underestimate the importance when a country not aligned to any great power and without conflicts with other states clearly and honestly expresses its opinions on international disputes. This will be seen, for example, by the reaction in the United States to our position on the Vietnam question and the reaction in the Soviet Union to our attitude on the Czechoslovakian problem. We shall continue to repeat simple but important truths: That the longing of peoples for freedom cannot be beaten by violence; that the aim of democracy can never be reached by means of oppression; that people have the right to decide their own destiny. We ourselves decide, and only we ourselves, what attitude we shall adopt to events in the world which have a bearing on war and peace and now concern all humanity. We ourselves determine the Swedish policy of neutrality. This is the basis of our foreign policy.

*Before Social Democratic Party
congress, Stockholm, pub. Oct. 8.*

**George Papadopoulos**
*Premier of Greece*

(If the Soviet Mediterranean naval threat is not met by the West) it may decide the social system under which the destinies of the world will be determined in the next 20 years.

*News conference, Athens, Feb. 6.*

We are all now facing the future with self-confidence and optimism. The revolution of April 21 (1967) represents the greatest and most serious effort of rehabilitation, reorganization and cleansing made since the beginning of national independence. Our friends have convinced themselves that a great task of a broader nature is being accomplished here, and our enemies must come to realize that they labor against us, but, sadly, in vain.

*Radio address, Athens, April 19.*

The patient (Greece) is no longer in the plaster cast. The patient is now in small splints. Let's hope he won't break his limbs again.

*News conference, Athens, Oct. 3.*

. . . We, and only we, shall decide when elections will be held in Greece.

*Athens, pub. Oct. 27.*

**Andreas Papandreou**
*Former Premier of Greece
now in exile*

Only on the basis of the background can one attempt to figure out what the U.S. position on Greece will be in the near future. At present, both the State Department and the CIA are convinced that the (Greek) colonels constitute a liability. They were only supposed to execute a technically perfect coup d'etat; but they insisted on keeping power, and have proved to be the worst of rulers. Five years of this kind of dictatorship would be the best way to lay the groundwork for the future success of the Communists in Greece. But the Pentagon is not yet ready to abandon (George) Papadopoulos. And, since American foreign policy decisions are being made more and more by the (U.S.) Joint Chiefs of Staff, nothing will change without their approval.

*Interview, pub. Oct. 5.*

**Stylianos Patakos**
*Deputy Premier of Greece*

Of course, there is a program (for return to an elected government) which fulfills the aims of the nation and the revolution, but the time required in connection with this program is such that it is impossible to be determined or announced.
*Interview, Athens, April 25.*

We do not look closely at those who like us abroad. But we look at those inside who love us, which is 92% of the population . . . This support is backed up by 72 bishops, 250 mayors and 6,500 community leaders who have at least 1,500 persons to hear from and then tell me.
*Athens, pub. Oct. 27.*

Better that the press should die so Greece may live. We preach the unity of the Greeks, while the newspapers preach division.
*News conference, Athens, Nov. 3.*

**Rolf F. Pauls**
*West German Ambassador
to the United States*

(West and East Germans) want to end the divided nation . . . but we are not dreamers. We see it in the framework of the unification of Europe, not in the restoration of a mighty German Reich.
*Before World Affairs Council,
Los Angeles, Dec. 3.*

**Prince Philip**
*Husband of Queen Elizabeth II*

If at any stage people feel that the monarchy (in Britain) has no further part to play, then, for goodness sake, let's end the thing on amicable terms without having a row.
*Pub. Oct. 26.*

**Nikolai Podgorny**
*President of the Union of
Soviet Socialist Republics*

We will never allow anyone to talk to us from a position of strength.
*Moscow, Nov. 6.*

**Alain Poher**
*Interim President of France*

I cannot pretend overnight to be the man who succeeds General de Gaulle. One does not succeed General de Gaulle.
*Paris, pub. May 4.*

France is not called upon to play a role of dominantion. For 10 years, we have disconcerted our traditional friends without convincing new ones. If I insist on the need to create a living Europe, it is to give our country the economic power indespensable to a great modern nation, a power which is the only means of insuring our independence. Isolated, we cannot have influence; jointly responsible within a community, our country can play a decisive role.
*Television address, Paris, pub. May 27.*

**Georges Pompidou**
*Former Premier of France*

I have always been conscious of the ties of Franco-American friendship, which are as much a matter of the heart as they are of sense. Perhaps we should pay more attention to the good sense.
*Pub. May 9.*

**Georges Pompidou**
*President of France*

. . . in the absence of happiness, he (Napoleon Bonaparte) reached the peaks of glory and covered France with it, to the point that, since then, our nation has never resigned itself to mediocrity and has always answered the call of honor. The history of our last years has shown this strikingly, thanks once again to the action of an exceptional man (former French President Charles de Gaulle).
*Ajaccie, Corsica, Aug. 15.*

. . . Every time a (French) housewife argues over a price and refuses to pay an unjustified price, she is defending the franc. Each time she puts off an unimportant purchase, she is defending the franc. Each time she puts a little money in the bank she is working for the country.
*News conference, Paris, pub. Sept. 25.*

**William Proxmire**
*United States Senator, D-Wis.*

. . . the notion that the Soviet Union is going to develop an overpowering military juggernaut far greater than she now

(WILLIAM PROXMIRE)

has is plainly unrealistic. To argue this is not to look at the facts. This is not to say that the Soviet Union would not like to overrun this country and the world. I will not dispute that for a moment. But the Soviet Union cannot do it. It does not have the economic power and force to do it.
*Before the Senate, Washington, Sept. 15.*

When you look at the overall situation and recognize that Western Europe has in fact, in the aggregate, more manpower than the Soviet Union, more skilled personnel, far greater production and economic resources and far greater military resources, there is no reason why, a generation after World War II . . . we should have to have our troops stationed there.
*Before the Senate, Washington, Dec. 1.*

**Pietro Quroni**
*Former Italian Ambassador*
*to the United Kingdom*

(Italians see France) as a dear old aunt, which we love dearly, but know she is a little crazy and would not trust with the management of our own house.
*London, March 27.*

**I. I. Rabi**
*Professor of Physics,*
*Columbia University*

When Russia invaded Czechoslovakia last summer, there was no violent resistance by the Czechs. You might ask whether this was wise or not. In one view, the Czech people were "chicken" for not standing up, even though the odds were hopeless. But is the survival of a people and their culture not more important than an "heroic" gesture?
*At Center for the Study of Democratic*
*Institutions, Santa Barbara, Calif.,*
*pub. Feb. 10.*

**John R. Rarick**
*United States Representative, D-La.*

(Swedish Prime Minister) Palme's babbling that he is not anti-American is the joke of the century. His party has announced their gift of $40 million to the Communist dictatorship of North Viet-

nam, and Palme's latest announcement is that the hard-working, tax-paying decent Swedish men and women will be called on to bear the additional burden of increased aid to Communist Cuba . . . Americans who have always had great affection for the people of Sweden watch with concern as Sweden's destiny falls into the hands of a potential Scandinavian Castro.
*Before the House, Washington, Oct. 3.*

**Jean Rey**
*President, Executive Commission,*
*European Common Market*

When we set up the community, there was no doubt that we wanted to do so with other countries, and with Britain as well. Now the French say that British membership would change the community. Certainly it would, but we knew that.
*Interview, pub. Feb. 24.*

**David C. Richardson**
*Commander, United States Sixth Fleet*

The thing that worries me most about the Russians is the determination they have shown in building their new navy in the face of Allied strength. It has been a steep, uphill, expensive effort, but they identify what is important to their national interest and pursue their long-range plans.
*Aboard U.S.S. Little Rock,*
*in the Mediterranean; pub. July 6.*

**William P. Rogers**
*Secretary of State of the United States*

I have difficulty in believing that the Soviet Union would initiate a first strike (in a nuclear war) . . . But certainly it is difficult to understand why the Soviet Union is deploying SS-9 (missiles).
*News conference, Washington, April 7.*

**Klaus Schutz**
*Mayor of West Berlin*

From my own experience, I can only warn against one thing—that anyone in Berlin bask in the illusion that the Soviets are more closely allied with the dear Federal Republic (West Germany) than with their friends in East Berlin. That is complete twaddle. He who tries to construct a policy thereon is running wild.

*Bonn, Feb. 26.*

Until the (Berlin) Wall, most of us thought German unity is still a possibility in a fairly short time. Now, people are much more realistic and see there is no easy Berlin solution or even any isolated German solution. There has to be a European rapprochement.

I always like to be in Bonn making a few jokes. Here (in Berlin), there are no jokes.

*Interview, West Berlin, pub. March 4.*

**Vladimir S. Semyonov**
*Soviet Delegate to the*
*Strategic Arms Limitation Talks*

. . . the Soviet Union has always been a proponent of the implementation of the principles of peaceful coexistence, of effective measures to end the arms race and of general and complete disarmament . . .

*Helsinki, Finland, Nov. 17.*

**Jean-Jacques Servan-Schreiber**
*Publisher of "L'Express," Paris*

For the first time in the life of a man of my generation, one may be proud of one's country. What France has just done (defeat President de Gaulle's reform initiative), no country, ever, had done before her. To reply "No" to a plebiscite is without historical precedent. And this victory over itself . . . which óur country has just won, should, at last, efface from our consciences the memory of so many defeats, collapses, renunciations which had not ceased to leave their mark on us since 1939.

*Paris, April 29.*

**Alexander N. Shelepin**
*Member, Politburo of the*
*Union of Soviet Socialist Republics*

Despite the wide scale of housing construction, the housing problem is still acute. We do not fully satisfy people's demands for consumer goods of high quality. There is an objective reason for that: Primarily, a complicated international situation that forces us to allot much money for defense.

*Before World Federation of Trade Unions, Budapest, Hungary, Oct. 22.*

**R. Sargent Shriver**
*United States Ambassador to France*

The French are a reserved people by American standards. At Arlington Park, outside Chicago, there's pandemonium when the horses make the run down the homestretch. At Paris' Longchamps track you could read a book.

*Paris, pub. Sept. 7.*

**Paul-Henri Spaak**
*Former Premier of Belgium*

I don't think that at the moment the Soviet Union is thinking of starting a war. But I certainly think that, if the Western European countries retreat behind their own frontiers and each tries to solve its own problems alone, the outlook is not very cheerful.

It's up to Europe to build its own future, and, if it is not capable of doing so, nothing the United States could do would solve the problem. The United States has already done, during the last 25 years, all it could do for a united Europe.

*Interview, Paris, pub. Nov. 2.*

**Alex Springer**
*West German Publisher*

Young people again follow a few leaders in an uncontrolled and unconsidered way. Our present democracy (West Germany) may not be perfect, but it gives 59 million people more freedom and prosperity than this country has ever known. I cannot understand why German students should want to destroy this, while their fellows across the wall are crying out for freedom.

*West Berlin, pub. Nov. 25.*

**Michael Stewart**
*Foreign Secretary of the United Kingdom*

It is tragic that Britain and France, two great nations who have done so much and who can do so much for Europe and the world, should be at variance. We ought to be working together to build up the splendid structure of Europe as part of the human alliance for freedom. But, where there are serious differences, it is necessary to state plainly what they are.

*Before the Labor Party,*
*London, pub. Feb. 28.*

**Franz-Josef Strauss**
*Minister of Finance
of West Germany*

A few days ago, I read a statement attributed to Mr. Nixon which I find most interesting. It was to the effect that he sees the most important value of the nuclear deterrent, not as a weapon, but as a factor in preventing—and I emphasize "preventing"—war. Now, I have never doubted that the Americans would defend Europe and Germany if the Russians attacked. But the problem is when, how, to what extent, where and with what means? We are much more interested in a full-scale American engagement to deter the Russians than in a calendar of war plans on how to defend Europe, right up to the moment of its total destruction.

*Interview, Bonn, pub. Jan. 13.*

I have only one regret (that Charles de Gaulle resigned as President of France)—and it is a personal confession that I would have liked to have seen him as first President of a United States of Europe.

*Bonn, April 29.*

**Stuart Symington**
*United States Senator, D-Mo.*

I am confident every American would agree that, when (Soviet Premier Josef) Stalin was alive, the cold-war aspect of our foreign relations was far more serious than today. Then there was a monolithic structure behind the Iron Curtain and a man running things whom we all knew was interested in taking over the world. That is far from true today.

*Washington, pub. June 20.*

The "remote presence" which is now made possible by rapid, heavy airlift can permit a sizable force to draw down in Europe with no loss in NATO response credibility . . . and it could be the one way to handle our security and well-being without having the cost of our defenses creating even more serious problems for our already endangered economy.

*Before the Senate,
Washington, Sept. 8.*

**Michel Tatu**
*French Correspondent*

It can never be repeated too often that the political structure and ideology of the U.S.S.R. are sick with conservatism and sclerosis . . . The average age, not only of its Politburo but of its entire leadership elite, is almost 60—older than in any other country of the world.

*Pub. Feb. 2.*

**Strom Thurmond**
*United States Senator, R-S.C.*

. . . It conclusively appears that the Soviets have regarded the U.S. unilateral initiative in holding down expenditures for strategic forces as presenting them with a unique and historic opportunity to achieve strategic superiority. Can we now close our eyes to the possible consequences? Even in the face of its strategic inferiority to the United States, the Soviet Union's ambitious policy of expanding Communism was well illustrated by the Berlin and Cuban crises, by its strong support of the militant Arabs in the Mid-Eastern crisis of 1967, and by last year's military occupation of Czechoslovakia. In view of its often declared long-range ambition to shape the world according to its own dogma, it would be the height of folly for us to assume that the Soviets will not follow an even more aggressive policy and undertake even more extensive and dangerous adventures if they attain demonstrable and clear military superiority over us.

*Before the Senate,
Washington, Sept. 18.*

**Enrique Tierno-Galvan**
*Spanish Socialist Philosopher*

Because of its cultural paralysis, Spain today is the country in Europe with the greatest hunger and thirst for ideals. We have a deficit of religious credulity and an increase of revolutionary credulity.

*Interview, Madrid, Sept. 28.*

**Josip Broz Tito**
*President of Yugoslavia*

Our society has a real democracy, where people speak freely and freely give vent to their initiatives. But it is clear that there must be no democracy for those who act from an anti-socialist position . . . We carry a tremendous responsibility, because the revolution has not yet been concluded.

*Aug. 27.*

In the West, some constantly are talking that Yugoslavia slowly moves toward the Western system. They do wish that. However, they are wrong if they think that Yugoslavia will move from her socialist position.

*Zadar, Yugoslovia, Aug. 28.*

**Walter Ulbricht**
*First Secretary,*
*Communist Party of East Germany*

If the government of the West German Federal Republic wants negotiations between the two German states about the settlement of their relations on the basis of equal rights and nondescrimination, then such negotiations can be initiated. We, on our part, consider it necessary for an internationally valid treaty between the German Democratic Republic and the West German Federal Republic to be based on unlimited mutual recognition of state borders, complete equality of rights and nondiscrimination.

*Before Central Committee of*
*East German Communist Party,*
*Berlin, Dec. 12.*

**Adolf von Thadden**
*Leader, National Democratic Party*
*of West Germany*

Why is the economic miracle our only source of pride? Behind that glittering facade, law and order are disintegrating . . . Our national consciousness has been shattered. The main pillars of our society have been destroyed . . . We (the National Democratic Party) are not against democracy. We are not neo-Nazis. How could we be? We know that would fail. And that's the truth.

*Idar Oberstein, West Germany, Sept. 14.*

For 14 days there will be headlines in the world. Then things will quiet down. A year later, not a single fellow is going to get excited that there is a fourth party in the Bundestag . . . and the question of whether one can work with our party will no longer exist. We want to be in a position, at the latest by 1973, to undertake, with others, the responsibility for government.

*Interview, Hanau, West Germany,*
*pub. Sept. 21.*

**Harold Wilson**
*Prime Minister of the United Kingdom*

Your (West Berlin's) security is guaranteed. We shall continue—you can count on this—to do all that is in our power to insure that your freedom is preserved.

*West Berlin, Feb. 14.*

May I say, for the benefit of those who have been carried away by the gossip of the last few days, that I *know* what is going on. *I* am going on. Your *Government* is going on. Your Government is going to build on the achievements of which you are proud and I am proud. *And your Government is going to win.*

*Before the Labor Party,*
*London, May 4.*

Europe needs us just as much, and many would say more, than we need Europe. It is the common interest of us all to achieve economic unity, but if this cannot be achieved, we can stand on our own feet . . . We can stand on our own feet at a heavy price for Britain, no doubt, but a heavier price for Europe and at a devastating price for Europe's influence on the world.

When the economic indices in any month give comfort to Britain's critics and enemies abroad, you can see all (the Conservatives') top people looking like Victorian undertakers welcoming a wet winter and the promise of a full churchyard.

*At Labor Party Convention,*
*Brighton, England, Sept. 30.*

# The Middle East

**Dani Afik**
*Israeli Agronomist*

If someone says we have taken land that does not belong to us, he is wrong. No one ever worked this land. No one ever lived here. We are not throwing anyone out. It does not belong to anybody, except to God. The earth is lifeless— smell it. It has no odor. We will put life back in it.

*Interview, Kallia (Occupied Jordan), pub. Feb. 28.*

**Yigal Allon**
*Deputy Prime Minister of Israel*

The trouble is that Nasser is the victim of Soviet policy in the Middle East, which has led him into an even more rotten situation than the one King Farouk faced before him under British influence. If Nasser had not followed his militaristic policy, and if he had tried to solve his country's economic and social problems, he could have become the Ataturk of the Arab world, and Egypt would have set out resolutely on the road to liberation and socialism.

In a war, there is always a winner and a loser. In an equitable peace treaty, both sides are victorious. Three times in twenty years the Arab states have put Israel to the test of *war*. I hope that, one day, they will put our good intentions to the test of *peace*.

*Interview, pub. June 11.*

Whenever the Arabs go to war, they know that someone is going to come to their rescue and they will recover their lost territories. They are becoming the spoiled nations of the world. They can permit themselves to do anything they want, thanks to oil interests and big-power politics.

*Interview, Jerusalem, December.*

**Abdullah Salum al-Samarrai**
*Minister of Information of Iraq*

Let everyone prick up his ears and listen. The Government of the Revolution is absolutely determined to punish spies—all spies—and fears nothing in this respect. If Israel is now beating her breast about the spies who were executed, let her be advised that we are going to have no mercy on any spy operating on her behalf, be he Jewish, Christian or Moslem.

*Baghdad, Jan. 31.*

**Mohammed Hassan al-Zayat**
*Official spokesman of the*
*United Arab Republic*

This country has decided not to accept any invitation to surrender or commit suicide by leaving any part of its land occupied forever. How can you expect an occupied country, wounded, to stay bleeding without doing anything about it?

It is not our understanding that the cease-fire is going to last 99 years.

*News conference, Cairo, March 12.*

**Yasir Arafat**
*Chairman, Executive Committee,*
*Palestine Liberation Organization*

Am I supposed to refuse Saudi money just because Saudi Arabia is rightist? I am using Saudi money to buy weapons from China. How do you describe this action—rightist or leftist?

*Interview, pub. Feb. 14.*

Let the big powers decide what they like. We have already made our decision —a decision based on the gun.

*Pub. Feb. 17.*

We have only one motto—namely, victory or death.

*News conference, Damascus, Oct. 28.*

**Uri Avnery**
*Member of the Israeli Knesset*
*(Parliament)*

Israel does not influence the Arabs in the occupied territories. We have nothing to say to them. This is now sinking in, and the Arabs are beginning to realize this is not a transitional thing. It is a permanent occupation, and they are reacting to occupation as any other people would.

I believe that we should give the West Bank back to the Palestinians—but no one in our Government is willing to settle for anything that any Arab can accept.
*Pub. March 25.*

**Babiker Awadalla**
*Prime Minister of Sudan*

We are Arabs and fanatics, as far as the Palestine question is concerned. We shall not allow any abandonment of one inch of Palestinian land to Israel. We advocate nonalignment in foreign policy, but we will stand fast against any country which supports Israel, be it Western or Eastern.
*Khartoum, May 26.*

**Chaim Bar-Lev**
*General, and Chief of Staff*
*of the armed forces of Israel*

I think we shall win, not only the next war, but all the next wars.
*Before Foreign Press Association,*
*Tel Aviv, March 4.*

Logically, their's (Arab terrorists') is a hopeless cause; but, for the individual, it's kind of a national service, an alternative to do nothing in a refugee camp.
*Jerusalem, pub. March 19.*

**David Ben-Dov**
*Consul General of Israel*
*at San Francisco*

The whole idea of the big powers' imposing a solution upon the small powers in the Middle East conflict is repugnant. We have outlived colonialism. The issue is not between the United States and the Soviet Union, but between Israel and Egypt.
*Before the Rotary Club,*
*Seattle, May 21.*

**Houari Boumedienne**
*President of Algeria*

Palestine is for the Palestinians, and no country has the right to bargain on Palestine.
*Algiers, Feb. 5.*

**Habib Bourguiba**
*President of Tunisia*

We are not in (a) position to denounce Israel's aggressiveness before world opinion so long as we proclaim our refusal to recognize, engage in negotiations and conclude peace with it. The Arab world is too behind technologically to beat Israel. A war with Israel is lost in advance. Our obstinate attitude has alienated international sympathy. Our all-or-nothing line has won international support for Israel.
*Pub. Aug. 10.*

**Al Capp**
*Cartoonist*

It's criminal for two million bloodthirsty Israelis to terrify 76 million helpless Arabs.
*At Young Americans for Freedom*
*convention, St. Louis, Aug. 31.*

**Lord Caradon**
*Ambassador to the United Nations*
*from the United Kingdom*

To prejudice the future of Jerusalem (by Israel's occupation of the Arab sector) would be to deny the hope, the possibility of any peaceful settlement at all (of the Middle East situation) . . . It would bar the door to peace.
*United Nations, N.Y., July 1.*

**Moshe Dayan**
*Minister of Defense of Israel*

All this talk of justice and peaceful aims coming from France is hypocrisy. It is being used to deny arms to a nation under seige (Israel) . . .
*Tel Aviv, Jan. 29.*

The war on terrorism has taken a new dimension—the dealing of blows (by Israel) even across the cease-fire lines, without waiting for an attack. We are not ready to allow them (Arab terrorists) to

(MOSHE DAYAN)

prepare themselves. We must hit everywhere, all the time, even if this arouses unsympathetic reactions within the (United Nations) Security Council.

*Afula, Israel, March 29.*

The Arabs have a patron—the Soviet Union; with France standing close by. On the other hand, I do not know whether our "consultant," the United States, can be considered our patron.

*Radio interview, Jerusalem, April 16.*

We want to sit down with the Arabs face to face, neighbor to neighbor, and we don't want any bullying.

*Pub. April 20.*

The state goes on living just as France did when it fought in Indochina and afterward in Algeria, and as the United States does in Vietnam today. But for us, every aspect of our lives will be affected, not only if we are defeated, but if there should be a collapse of the lines at Suez, on the Jordan, on the Golan Heights or in the war against terrorism.

*Tel Aviv, July 18.*

**Charles de Gaulle**
*President of France*

The Israelis think I am an enemy. This is untrue. I carry their hopes for peace and security in my heart.

*Paris, pub. April 11.*

**Suleyman Demirel**
*Prime Minister of Turkey*

I think the people in the United States should understand that this is a free country, just like the United States. They should understand the (anti-U.S.) demonstrations in Istanbul, so far away, for they are doing it themselves in front of the White House.

*Interview, Ankara, Feb. 23.*

**Simcha Dinitz**
*Minister, Israeli Embassy, Washington*

In Israel, there are people who disagree with her (Prime Minister Golda Meir), but nobody criticizes her for being a woman. When (Prime Minister David)

Ben-Gurion named her to his Cabinet, he said, "She's the best man I have."

*Interview, Washington, pub. March 18.*

**Abba Eban**
*Foreign Minister of Israel*

An imposed (peace) settlement (in the Middle East) is like a warm-cold wave; the contradiction is built in . . . If it is imposed, it isn't a settlement, because the parties against whom it is imposed would, at the first possibility, feel themselves free to disengage themselves from it.

*News conference, Tel Aviv,
pub. Jan. 18.*

The Iraqi Government has perpetrated an act of barbarity (by executing 9 alleged Israeli spies) which exceeds even what the world has come to expect from a country in which violence and murder have become almost a commonplace.

*United Nations, N.Y., Jan. 27.*

Nasser's policy is no peace, no recognition, no negotiation, no establishment of secure and recognized boundaries, no acknowledgement of Israeli sovereignty, no freedom of Israeli navigation in the Suez Canal, no agreement on arms limitation . . . His encouragement of those who murder people in supermarkets and passengers in civil aircraft is a true index of his character.

*Jerusalem, March 2.*

The members of these (Arab terrorist) organizations are not fighting for freedom. The image that world opinion should have of them is not the image of Maquis or resistance fighters, but the image of the S.S., the image of the guards at Auschwitz and at Bergen-Belsen. It is important that the world information media ponder very carefully, not on the picturesque actions of these groups, nor on the question of their individual valor, but on their ideology, their aims and the purposes to which they direct their efforts.

*News conference, Jerusalem,
pub. March 9.*

We don't have a policy for retaliation —we have a policy for survival.

*London, March 10.*

Of all the leaders of the time (of the 1967 Arab-Israeli war), President Johnson made the most serious effort to achieve an equitable peace. It was a formidable and lonely attempt. On the international scene, neither the United Nations nor most of the other Western powers were being very helpful.
*Interview, New York, March 24.*

Peace will not come to the Near (Middle) East as a consequence of Soviet plans. The Russians are not a neutral factor in this region; they are a spark for inflammable material. They share a large part of the responsibility for the outbreak of the (1967 Arab-Israeli war). Now they want to prevent peace.

Generally speaking, nations don't slide into war because one nation makes this or that mistake. They start a war because they decide to.
*Interview, pub. March.*

He (President Nasser) is too weak for war or for peace—too weak militarily at the moment for war, and he's not strong enough politically to take the audacious and statesmanship step of exploring peace. (He) is one of the deeper reasons for the continuing deadlock.
*Interview, Jerusalem, May 8.*

Settlement (in the Middle East) will begin when Egypt agrees to negotiate directly with us. If they don't sit down, we'll never move. Four (other) nations can't negotiate for involved parties who aren't there. Israel can't negotiate a Vietnam settlement. The effect of the four-power talks has been to encourage the Egyptians in the belief that they don't have to meet us face to face. What's happening in New York (at the U.N.) is an attempt to find a substitute for negotiations.

Victory is no proof of aggression, defeat no proof of virtue.
*Interview, Tel Aviv, June 13.*

We will not reconstruct a map symbolic of our vulnerability . . . There will not be a Middle East without a sovereign Israel at its heart.
*Before Board of Deputies of British Jews, London, Dec. 21.*

**Muhammad H. el-Farra**
*Ambassador to the*
*United Nations from Jordan*

What Israel, in effect, tells the Big Four in advance is: "Don't work for peace. Leave everything to us. We want either complete surrender, according to our terms or conditions, or continued war" . . . any accommodation of this Israeli arrogance will not bring peace.
*United Nations, N.Y., March 27.*

**Levi Eshkol**
*Prime Minister of Israel*

Between the design of genocide and its perpetration there stands the state of Israel—Israel and its strength.
*Jerusalem, Jan. 27.*

We have fought three wars in our brief lifetime of 20 years. If the Arab governments had accepted, as the whole world did, the establishment of the state of Israel, this would not have happened. In fact, there would have been no need to change our borders one jot. But, after the Six Day War (of 1967), it is a miracle that we are still here. So why should we now crawl on our hands and knees to the Arabs and say, "Please do us a favor and take it all back"? . . . I am still ready to fly to Cairo tomorrow. I don't want to talk to him (President Nasser) as a conqueror. I want to rid his mind of the ridiculous notion of a greater Israel . . . I can pledge my word to Nasser that greater Israel never has been and never will be our policy. I am ready to meet him anywhere, anytime, and I won't quarrel about procedure, agenda or the shape of the table.

The value of Israel to the West in this part of the world will, I predict, be out of all proportion to its size. We will be a real bridge between three continents, and the free world will be very thankful, not only if we survive, but if we continue to thrive in secure and guaranteed borders.
*Interview, pub. Feb. 17.*

**Pierre Gemayel**
*Leader, Tripartite Alliance*

To make the Lebanese people believe that conscription and its heavy financial

(PIERRE GEMAYEL)

burdens would protect the country against external danger would be to deceive them . . . Lebanon's strength was never, and will never be, in military ability or war equipment, but in its very weakness.

*Beirut, pub. Jan. 14.*

### Arthur J. Goldberg
*Former Ambassador to the*
*United Nations from the United States*

No good can come from any attempt to impose a settlement (on the Middle East). On the contrary, much mischief may result from such an enterprise. The clear lesson of the past is that the parties to the conflict should be parties to the peace and its making.

*At Institute of Jewish Affairs,*
*London, March 11.*

### Andrei A. Gromyko
*Foreign Minister of the*
*Union of Soviet Socialist Republics*

It would be short-sighted policy to repose hopes, as they do in Israel, in military superiority. The surest way would be to solve the problem on the basis of withdrawal of Israeli troops from occupied areas and simultaneous recognition of the right of all Middle Eastern states, including Israel, to independent national existence and the establishment of a lasting peace in this important area.

*Before the Supreme Soviet,*
*Moscow, July 10.*

Israel is the aggressor, occupying Arab territories which do not belong to it. Israel, as well as other Middle East countries, has a right to existence. But this is no reason for a crisis. The reason is that the Israeli government wants a reward for its aggression. We reject categorically such a concept.

*Belgrade, Sept. 6.*

### George Habash
*Commander, Popular Front for the*
*Liberation of Palestine*

Our men will continue operations, undeterred by either threats or actual Israeli retaliation. We, as Palestinians, have nothing to lose. We have lost everything already and, at present, have neither land, nor homes, nor a future.

*Interview, Amman, pub. Feb. 24.*

The world has forgotten Palestine. Now it must pay attention to our struggle. No matter what happens to the Arab world, we will keep fighting to leave our tents and go home (to Palestine). Whoever opposes our fight will have to fight us. If the world thinks the commando movement is superficial, it is much mistaken. It is the only way open to us to go home.

*Interview, Amman, pub. June 13.*

### Assad Hafez
*Defense Minister of Syria*

Our policy is based on positive neutrality. After all, we have relations with nations outside the Soviet bloc. We would welcome it if there were no obstacles between us and the West.

*Interview, Damascus, pub. June 15.*

### Muhammed Heikal
*Editor, "Al Ahram," Cairo*

All the experts say that, if the Arabs are able to make their war with Israel last from six to eight weeks, Israel would lose the war, whatever the area she occupies on the battlefield.

*Pub. March 24.*

### Mordecai Hod
*Commander, Israeli Air Force*

Since the balance is delicate and narrow, we have to react immediately and vigorously (to Arab attacks), whether on the Suez Canal or elsewhere. If Israel were a big country, that might not be true. But whereas the United States can afford to overlook something like the *Pueblo* incident, it would be fatal if we did so.

*Jerusalem, pub. Aug. 29.*

### Hussein I
*King of Jordan*

He (President Nasser) does not want war for the sake of war. He, like us, wants nothing more than the restoration of our rights and the establishment of a just and lasting peace in the area.

. . . the issue of peace in the Middle East is too important to be left to the parties, particularly when failure to find a peace could bring on World War III.

. . . Israel may have either peace or territory—but she can never have both.
*Before National Press Club, Washington, April 10.*

President Nixon appears to be determined to exert more pressure on the Israelis than was perhaps true of previous (U.S.) administrations. He wants peace in the Middle East that is just for all sides, and you cannot get it if you blindly support one nation over the others . . . I continue to be opposed to direct talks with the Israelis.
*Interview, Washington, pub. April 18.*

**Sasson Khdouri**
*Chief Rabbi of Iraq*

Iraqi Jews are proud of their patriotism and loyalty to Iraq. The verdicts of the revolutionary court were applied to all faiths. The campaign against Iraq is unfair. In my capacity as a man of religion and spiritual leader of my community, I proclaim that Iraqi Jews, like the Christians and Moslems, enjoy absolute freedom and exercise their worship in full freedom.
*Radio interview, Baghdad, pub. Jan. 31.*

**Teddy Kollek**
*Mayor of Jerusalem*

We have no intention of mixing or unifying (Arab and Israeli Jerusalem). We do not want to create a melting pot or a monoculture. There will be two cultures, but we will live better together.
*Jerusalem, pub. May 12.*

If we don't have brotherly love at the moment (between Arabs and Israelis in Jerusalem), we at least have a large measure of mutual tolerance. After all, in Montreal they have been one city for 150 years, and they still throw bombs at each other. It's all a slow process. We can't expect miracles, and maybe, finally, we can't really solve the problem with-

out a political settlement in the Middle East. But we can make progress—and we are making it.
*Jerusalem, pub. June 16.*

Certainly we have learned, in the last two years, that being an occupying power is an ugly, distasteful business. But it is better to be an occupier than to be occupied. And we have no other choice.
*Jerusalem, pub. Aug. 29.*

**Shlomo Lahat**
*Brig. Gen., Israeli Army*

We do not like losses, and if you strike you must lose men. So we like the (Suez) canal to be quiet. But if you ask me how long we can go on like this, the answer is simple. We can go on like this as long as need be, as long as we have to—one year, five years, 10 years, 20 years. Let Nasser or his successors make the choice.
*El Kantara, Sinai, pub. Aug. 26.*

**Mike Mansfield**
*United States Senator, D-Mont.*

No, I don't think we have any hard and fast commitment to go to the aid of Israel or any other country in that area, outside those which are members of the North Atlantic Treaty Organization. As far as what the United States can do, it is hard to say, except that I believe we ought to, whenever possible, work in concord with the Soviet Union so that, through our joint efforts, we may be able in some fashion or other to bring about peace to that unstable area.
*Television interview, Jan. 5.*

**Golda Meir**
*Prime Minister of Israel*

We probably sound obstructionist when we say that there must be direct negotiations (between Israel and the Arabs), but it's not a gimmick, not just a technique. It's the essence; it's fundamental. As long as the Arabs won't sit down with us, that means they don't accept our existence. I don't want to appear so naive or so demagogic as to say that, if Nasser sat down with us, there would be no problems; there are plenty of problems. But I sincerely and honestly believe that, if he

(GOLDA MEIR)

did—not in the first half-hour, not in the first few days, but finally—we can come to agreement.

*Interview, Jerusalem, pub. March 9.*

Our bitter experience makes it absolutely essential that, in signing a peace settlement, we must see to it that our borders are such that, if at any time the Arabs want to attack, they will not be able to do it from a point of natural superiority of borders.

*News conference, Jerusalem, March 18.*

When we are asked again to depend upon others . . . I think it is proper to say . . . that we refuse, absolutely, that we should be the one people in the world who should consent that its fate should be decided by others.

*Jerusalem, March 26.*

We are not in Czarist Russia. We are not in Auschwitz, either, or Bergen-Belsen. We do not have to choose: hide or be killed. Those things will never, never, never happen here.

*Interview, Jerusalem, pub. April 14.*

(The United States) is the greatest friend we have.

*Television interview, Tel Aviv, April 27.*

We cannot be an important factor in solving the refugee problem, if by that you mean taking them back . . . we should not be asked to do it. They should be free to hate us not from without but from within? I do not think so.

*Interview, Jerusalem, pub. May 1.*

If we lose a war, for us that is the last war. Then we are not here any more. If one doesn't understand this, then one doesn't understand our obstinacy.

*Interview, pub. May 23.*

There are some people (in Israel) who say that we should stand on the post-Six Days War (of 1967) boundaries. Others say we want peace, and we are prepared to compromise . . . There is no use having a Jewish squabble about Israel's future boundaries before there is an Arab ready to discuss this future with us. Speaking for myself, and not for my

Government, I am not one of those who say, "Not one inch of soil must be yielded up."

. . . if I have to choose between a lot of sympathy in the world toward Israel destroyed, and less understanding of Israel with Israel alive, I am sorry that we are not understood, but I think I would rather be alive.

*Interview, London, pub. June 16.*

If our plea (for peace) is ignored (by the Arabs), we can reach only one conclusion . . . If there is no quiet on our side, there will be no quiet on the other.

*July 24.*

. . . what concerns us is that our boys are being shot at, our settlements shelled and our children forced to spend the nights in shelters. It is shocking how little people write or worry about that. And the idea is shocking that everyone looks at us through a miscroscope, making us justify every act we take in our defense, but considers perfectly natural and unexceptional what the Arabs do. What are we expected to do? Go to the wailing wall and pray, first asking King Hussein's permission? The idea, after all that has happened to us in the Six Day War and since, that we should have to cross ourselves three times a day to prove that we're decent people!

*Interview, Tel Aviv, Aug. 6.*

. . . we do not want wars, even when we win.

*Tel Aviv, Aug. 14.*

We would be full of joy if we could just step across the border, not with tanks and not with planes, but with tractors, with our know-how.

*New York, Sept. 21.*

The Soviet Union is the enemy of Israel. The Soviet Union is the friend of the Arabs . . . and the lawyer of the Arabs. The Soviet Union carries at least as much responsibility for the war of 1967 as the Arabs. Their weapons were Russian weapons. The incitement to the war came out of Moscow.

*News conference,*
*Beverly Hills, Calif., Oct. 2.*

We have always said that in our wars with the Arabs we had a secret weapon: *no alternative*. The Egyptians could run to Egypt, the Syrians into Syria. The only place we could run was into the sea—and, before we did that, we might as well fight.

*Interview, Tel Aviv,*
*pub. Oct. 3.*

The non-Jewish world has been in two groups—those that killed us and those that pitied us. Before the (1967) war, the decent non-Jewish people were with us. Now we're alive, and we're certainly not pitied . . . Before '67, we were in danger, and I don't think that there was anybody who wasn't an anti-Semite who wasn't concerned. All of a sudden, all of the Arabs became poor Arabs. All of a sudden, people are concerned about our morale. Are we turning into militarists, into a Spartan state? . . . We haven't sinned in any way. What do you expect us to do when we have Fatah and terror?

*Interview, pub. Oct. 7.*

## Gamal Abdel Nasser
*President of the*
*United Arab Republic*

We will not give up one inch of Arab territory. We will not sit with the enemy around one table while our land is occupied . . . The Egyptian people know that the sound of guns is the only thing they want to hear. People do not want words—they want the sound of battle.

*Before National Assembly,*
*Cairo, Jan. 20.*

Obviously, you (the United States) would not sit down with a foreign power occupying part of the United States until it withdrew. But I can tell you we sat down with the Israelis after the 1948 war under the armistice agreement until the 1956 war, and that we are prepared to do so again.

*Interview, Cairo, pub. Feb. 3.*

The U.A.R. welcomes the participation of all Arab states in the battle of destiny . . . Those who think Israel is merely interested in safeguarding its borders and living securely inside them are mistaken. The truth is, Israel wants to build a Jewish state extending from the Nile to the Euphrates.

*Cairo, Feb. 4.*

You must believe me when I tell you that the Soviet Union wants a peaceful settlement. I am convinced that their motives are sincere. As for us, we do not want to go on mobilizing everything for war. We crave peace. We desperately need peace for economic development. But we must defend ourselves.

The Soviets have never asked me for anything. In Moscow, last July, I told Brezhnev, Kosygin and Podgorny, "All *I* do is ask, ask and ask, but you never ask *me* for anything. What can I do for *you* for a change?" They replied, "Nothing. We support your cause because it is a just one."

*Interview, Cairo, pub. Feb. 10.*

To be conquered is not a determined issue, but to surrender is. I am not going to surrender.

*Interview, Cairo, pub. March 10.*

I never said we will throw Israel into the sea. They can't find my ever saying that, because I did not say it.

*Interview, Cairo, pub. April 24.*

We wish to tell the world that, if the Israelis do not withdraw (from occupied Arab territory), we will fight them to *their* last man or to *our* last man.

*Cairo, May 1.*

It has been almost two years since the occupation of Sinai, and there is continuing occupation. We have agreed to a peaceful solution, implementing the 1967 (United Nations) Security Council resolution. Until now, Israel has not accepted it. She says she will not leave the occupied areas until we sit down with her and talk peace. But we refuse to sit—it is not called for in the Security Council resolution. If we sit now, we sit as defeated people, sitting only to capitulate. This we cannot do . . . I accept the reality of Israel, and so will my people, if there is a humanitarian solution. Call it Israel, or whatever they want to call it, and I will recognize it.

*Interview, Cairo, pub. May 16.*

(GAMAL ABDEL NASSER)

We have to fight for the restoration of our lands—and we shall fight. When I say the restoration of our lands, I do not mean Egypt alone; I don't mean just Sinai alone; but all Arab lands, and, above all, Jerusalem. We shall recover the West Bank, the Golan Heights. We shall recover all lands. It is our duty.

Today, we can be proud of our armed forces. The Six Day War (of 1967) has not ended. It will be the two-year war, the three-year war and the four-year war . . . We are ready for a long battle to drain the enemy's strength.

*Before Arab Socialist Union, Cairo, July 23.*

. . . there is no longer a way out of our present situation except by forging a road toward our objective, violently and by force, over a sea of blood and under a horizon blazing with fire.

*Before Parliament, Cairo, Nov. 6.*

**Kamel Nasser**
*Member, Executive Committee, Palestine Liberation Organization*

We expect to have a democratic state in Palestine, where the Jews and the Arabs can live in peace and love. We refuse to recognize the political entity of Israel, because it is a racial state, based on injustice and created at the expense of the Palestinians—human beings who now must live in the worst and most wretched conditions you can imagine . . . The Zionist movement is a twisted, sick movement; and our movement is an operation to liberate everyone in Israel, the Jews included.

*Amman, pub. March 10.*

**Jaafar Numeiri**
*President of Sudan*

Israel has closed all roads leading to peace, supported and encouraged by the United States, which supplies Israel with money, arms and equipment of all kinds and offers *Phantoms* to kill the Arabs. It goes as far as allowing the recruitment of its nationals to serve in the Israeli army. It must know that it places

itself in open confrontation with the Arab nations and unveils its face disguised behind its puppet Israel.

*At Arab summit meeting, Rabat, Morocco, Dec. 21.*

**Mohammed Reza Pahlevi**
*Shah of Iran*

In principle, how can any of us accept the idea of the acquisition of territory by force? If Israel can keep some other country's land and get away with it, then someone can do the same to us. But the other side of the coin is that Israel—for those who like it and for those who don't—is there. It must be recognized and accepted. It must be guaranteed secure borders.

*Interview, Teheran, pub. June 7.*

**Lea Rabin**
*Wife of Israeli Ambassador to the United States*

Unless you knew, you would never get the impression that a war was going on. We are building constantly and without interruption. Our art and music is flourishing, and our cities are filled with neon lights at night. If you do not live on the border, life takes a very normal course from day to day. We are concerned, naturally, but we do not let the war put fear in our hearts.

*Before Los Angeles Council of Pioneer Women, pub. Aug. 26.*

**Gideon Rafael**
*Director-General, Ministry of Foreign Affairs of Israel*

We can't cooperate with the Arab doctrine of cease-fire when it means we cease and they fire.

*Los Angeles, June 18.*

**Shaul Ramati**
*Assistant Director, Information Division, Foreign Ministry of Israel*

People used to see us as a plucky little nation whose neighbors wanted to destroy her. You get a lot of sympathy under those circumstances. You get much more sympathy, in fact, than when you overcome this threat, are occupying large areas and ruling a million people who don't want you. People feel as if we put one over on them in winning the (1967) war so easily. It's almost as if someone had cheated them into sympathizing under false pretenses.

*Radio interview, Jerusalem, pub. Feb. 4.*

**Mahmoud Riad**
*Foreign Minister of the United Arab Republic*

We are under no pressure at all to come to terms with them (Israel). Yes, they have the Sinai Desert—a lot of sand. Yes, they are on the (Suez) Canal—we used to get 85 million pounds a year in canal fees, and now, instead, we get 100 million pounds from our allies. No, the pressure is all the other way.

*Cairo, pub. April 7.*

It is within our right to ask the United States to follow in the Middle East a policy of justice compatible with the (United Nations) Charter and in its own commitments, and to proceed from the principle that the right of an Arab man to peace, his land and his home should not be sacrificed to satisfy Israel's dreams of territorial expansion.

*United Nations, N.Y., Sept. 23.*

**Abdul Monem Rifai**
*Foreign Minister of Jordan*

. . . The recent delivery by the United States to Israel of the heaviest destructive weapons, the F-4 *Phantom* jets after the *Skyhawk* fighter-bombers, at a time when Israel occupies vast regions of the Arab countries, at a time when Israel enjoys superiority in the air, and at a time when its air raids have become the order of the day, I must say that this measure on the part of the United States can in no way be justified.

*United Nations, N.Y., pub. Sept. 25.*

**William P. Rogers**
*Secretary of State of the United States*

The most important factor in the Middle East, the one factor that would guarantee a successful result, would be a willingness on the part of all nations to say we want to live in peace and that Israel is a nation and has a right to exist and

will continue to exist and we recognize it.
*News conference, Washington, April 7.*

Our policy is and will continue to be a balanced one. We have friendly ties with both Arabs and Israelis. To call for Israeli withdrawal without achieving agreement on peace would be partisan to the Arabs. To call for the Arabs to accept peace without Israeli withdrawal would be partisan toward Israel. Therefore, our policy is to encourage the Arabs to accept a permanent peace based on a binding agreement and to urge the Israelis to withdraw from occupied territory when their territorial integrity is assured.

*Washington, Dec. 9.*

**Dean Rusk**
*Secretary of State of the United States*

We call upon the Arab governments to recognize that they must do their utmost to restrain terrorist activity. We call upon Israel to recognize that a policy of excessive retaliation will not produce the peace that Israel surely desires.

*News conference, Washington, Jan. 3.*

**Hugh Scott**
*United States Senator, R-Pa.*

While I hope that mutual disarmament and permanent peace in the Middle East can eventually be achieved, it cannot be done by keeping Israel weak while the Russians continue to stock the Arab arsenal . . . It is only Israel's strength which prevents the outbreak of war in the area . . .

*Before the Senate, Washington, Sept. 12.*

**Ariel Sharon**
*Maj. Gen., and Chief of Israeli Training Command*

Nobody burns any draft cards here. I don't know of any other country where it is considered a real tragedy for a boy to be rejected by the army.

*Pub. Feb. 17.*

**U Thant**
*Secretary-General of the United Nations*

We may be witnessing in the Middle

(U THANT)

East something like the early stages of a new Hundred Years War.

*Pub. Dec. 7.*

## Jacques Torczyner
*President, Zionist Organization of America*

The new isolationism of the New Left is at least as dangerous as the isolationism of the far right before the Second World War. It has been our opinion for a long time that the problems of Vietnam and the Middle East are connected, and that Communist victory in Far Asia will encourage the enemies of Israel and the Arab terrorists in their vicious attacks against our fellow Jews.

*New York, Nov. 8.*

## Arnold Toynbee
*Historian*

The Arabs have got to accept as a fact what the Russians already publicly said: that Israel is on the map, and it's come to stay. And Israel has got to accept the fact that, even if she can actually defeat militarily anything the Arabs can put against her, the Arab world is like Russia or China—it's endless.

*Interview, London, pub. March 18.*

## Zorah Warhaftig
*Minister of Religious Affairs of Israel*

It is to the advantage of all faiths who deem Jerusalem as the holy city to recognize Israel's right to govern that city, because only then can they be assured of complete freedom and unhampered access to the sites that are sacred to them.

*Before Rabbinical Council of America, Fallsburg, N.Y., June 23.*

## Ezer Weizmann
*Chief of Operations, Israeli defense forces*

Yes, we are using them (rockets filled with nails) to kill the enemy—the enemy that has a nasty habit of shooting at us. Why is knifing somebody more humane than knocking him off with a piece of nail? We use napalm, and we will use anything to save (the) lives of our soldiers.

*News conference, Los Angeles, Dec. 10.*

## Charles W. Yost
*Ambassador to the United Nations from the United States*

Sooner or later, the violence in the Middle East may become so shocking and intolerable that compromise will be politically out of the question.

*Pub. Feb. 17.*

The Israeli Government has just called once again for "the advancement of negotiations between the Arab states and Israel for the establishment of a true peace in the Middle East." We do not believe that it is itself "advancing" such negotiations by a policy of "active defense," that is, of necessarily indiscriminate air attacks on the people with whom it wishes to negotiate.

*United Nations, N.Y., pub. April 7.*

# PART THREE

# General

**Jerome Alexander**
*Hair Stylist*

The mature woman doesn't want to look younger. She doesn't want to try to appear younger than her age, but simply more attractive. She's likely to be too concerned about what "the grandchildren would say" to have any desire to look kookie or kittenish.

*Dallas, pub. Feb. 28.*

**Cecil Beaton**
*Photographer, Fashion Designer*

Never in the history of fashion has so little material (in mini-skirts) been raised so high to reveal so much that needs to be covered so badly.

*Los Angeles, pub. Jan. 17.*

**Geoffrey Beene**
*Fashion Designer*

Some of my designs are really a put-on, but that's the way fashion should be viewed these days—with a sense of humor.

*New York, May 12.*

**Mr. Blackwell**
*Fashion Designer*

You can't tell women what to wear any more. They should feel free to reject what they don't like. Fashion should be every designer interpreting for his kind of woman, and no one designer should decide what all women should wear . . . I design for a woman who's made a decision to be a woman, who feels secure in herself. Her wardrobe isn't her security. She isn't one of those women who are so dependent on their clothes that they're nothing without them.

It (bralessness) is unclean and unpleasant. It's also impossible for women over 35. Nature didn't intend for things to be in the same place at 35 that they were at 12. Going without a bra is for age 12 and under . . . If you have to resort to exhibitionism, you're in bad shape. The women who inspired history and launched a thousand ships didn't have to run around naked.

*San Francisco, pub. Aug. 26.*

Fashion magazines? They're a hundred pages of illness. You might call them comic strips for adults . . . Fashion has become a pail of trash, and it will hit a still lower level before things can improve . . . Women have gotten tired of being bumped back and forth—the mini, the midi, the maxi . . . I'm sick, bored and disgusted with designers. They've killed their own thing. Geniuses are ignored; freaks are praised.

*Interview, Los Angeles, pub. Dec. 17.*

**Bill Blass**
*Fashion Designer*

Jackie Onassis is the greatest pacesetter of our time—without doing anything highly original. But fashion today is the whim of the moment and her whims have become everybody's whims. It isn't any longer a question of cuts and seams—it's a look.

*Interview, pub. June 13.*

**Marc Bohan**
*Fashion Designer*

If you're 18, unisex sportswear and evening wear can be amusing. There also can be inspirations borrowed from one fashion to another, just as the safari is a male look adapted to women. Otherwise, it is not a good idea and it can't work, because it makes people look ridiculous.

*Pub. Dec. 15.*

**Pierre Cardin**
*Fashion Designer*

I don't believe it (unisex) has a future. Men's fashion and women's fashion will both change greatly but in a parallel way. Man will not want to give up his look, which is distinctively virile.

*Pub. Dec. 15.*

**Antonio Cerruti**
*Fashion Designer*

The only reason why men and women are justified in wearing the same fashion is because they are having more and more similar lives. We are trying to make a fashion which is modern, and in doing this we realized there was a need to make men and women more similar, but women remain feminine and men remain masculine.

*Interview, London, pub. May 27.*

**Hubert De Givenchy**
*Fashion Designer*

The European woman uses her clothes either as a background for herself or sometimes as a foil for one perfect jewel —but never the whole bit at one time. Her statement is, in fact, understatement.

*Interview, Beverly Hill, Calif.,*
*pub. Sept. 22.*

**Howard Elliott**
*Designer-Decorator*

. . . Never do anything for status. Your home should be an extension of yourself.

*Interview, Los Angeles,*
*pub. March 3.*

**Halston Frowick**
*Fashion Designer*

Over-designed, over-fabricated, over-priced clothes no longer appeal, even to the rich.

*New York, pub. Feb. 24.*

**Valentino Garavani**
*Fashion Designer*

If a design is too radical, then it is not chic. If it is funny, amusing, then it belongs in boutique, not couture.

*Interview, New York, pub. March 13.*

**Rudi Gernreich**
*Fashion Designer*

Haute Couture is almost totally out. It isn't right for our way of life and our time. We have greater and greater freedom now. A woman walks down the street and we can see her breasts bouncing. It's very young, very free and very beautiful. But you wouldn't have seen it five years ago . . .

The skirt, as we know it, is on the way out. The whole concept of masculinity and femininity is being destroyed. More and more girls will wear pants, men will continue to wear long hair, enormous sleeves and see-through shirts. I definitely see something called unisex coming, and it has nothing to do with masculinity or femininity.

*Pub. April 14.*

Fashion has always reverted and borrowed from other periods, adapting along the way, but there has always been a progression. I feel very uncomfortable about the literal borrowing that is happening today. To me, that's not fashion. It is disturbing because that means there is nothing new being done.

*Interview, New York, pub. July 8.*

The true statement of our time is the emancipation of women. Unisex is a very important facet. It's the final emancipation.

*Pub. Dec. 15.*

**Rupert Lycett Green**
*Fashion Designer*

Flamboyant affectations are nothing more than the male emerging from his drab camouflage into the bright plumage which is the birthright of his sex.

*Pub. March 17.*

**Robert B. Haas**
*Head of Arts and Humanities*
*Extension Department,*
*University of California at Los Angeles*

The whole business for interior design has changed a lot, because, at one time, people used to ask for a Washington Room or a Victorian Room. But people today don't want these museum settings.

They want a home that doesn't look exactly like someone else's.

*Interview, Los Angeles, pub. March 14.*

## Deborah Kerr
*Actress*

The sophisticated set is now striving to wear clothes that were not designed for them. It's ludicrous the way some women get themselves up with minis, curls and bows. If you feel young inside, it projects, and you don't have to be preoccupied with exteriors.

*Interview, Malibu, Calif., pub. Feb. 2.*

## Gayle Kirkpatrick
*Fashion Designer*

There's nothing more awful than those designer scarves where a woman wears somebody's name all over her chest. If I had a wife and she wore one, I think I'd wring her neck with it. She might as well wear the words, "Mickey Mouse."

*Interview, New York, May 13.*

## James Mason
*Actor*

Few women can really carry it off (not wearing bras)—I mean psychologically, not physically. Very few can apply themselves to no-bra-ness unselfconsciously. It is an act of defiance that always proves a bit annoying. It is, however, attractive on ladies who are both formful and secure.

*Los Angeles, pub. Aug. 28.*

## Olga
*Fashion Designer*

A designer has as much social responsibility as an educator, a writer or any other artist. The pursuit of the sensational is not new in the history of fashion, but today's attempt to capitalize on tasteless nudity is no more good design than pornography is fine art . . . Fashion belongs within America's basic philosophy of individual self-respect.

*Interview, Los Angeles, pub. May 13.*

## Emilio Pucci
*Fashion Designer*

We are entering a neo-romantic era. It will be an era of masculine men and feminine women, away from this nonsense of unisex, which is a fad, or gimmick.

*Rome, pub. June 5.*

## Marc Sinclaire
*Hair Stylist*

Long hair (on women) has to continue. It's a feminine balance for the mannish clothes—*all those pants!*

*Interview, New York, Jan. 26.*

## Ruben Torres
*Fashion Designer*

Looking at a man's suit, as we know it, it is a leftover from the clothing worn 150 years ago when man was on horseback. And this is the spatial age. We have been using buttons that are simply decorations, though everything else has changed—transportation, communications, even women's wear, but not men's. So, to me, the tie belonged to the museum with the 19th Century clothes, and clothes that will be worn in 1980 are being developed today.

*Interview, New York, Jan. 28.*

## Mae West
*Actress*

It (bralessness) is not a very uplifting subject. I would have to categorize it with false teeth—those who need them wear them and those who don't, don't. Personally, I'm a firm believer in not tipping one's hand, or, in this case, other portions of one's anatomy. I've been getting by for years on what I didn't show the boys . . .

*Los Angeles, pub. Aug. 28.*

## Joanne Woodward
*Actress*

It (personal glamour) takes time to develop. You can't rush it. It is something you create out of yourself. It goes beyond a sense of clothes. There are a lot of models who know a great deal about fashion and make-up, but they fail to be glamorous because they do not project the inner glow of personality and integration.

*Interview, Los Angeles, pub. April 12.*

# Journalism

---

**Martin S. Ackerman**
*President, Curtis Publishing Company*

. . . The problem with publishing (i.e., *The Saturday Evening Post*) is that too many people get emotionally involved. Whether it's a magazine or a drugstore, it must be viable. Right? It must make a profit. You just can't go on running something at a loss. If I let my emotions tell me what to do, I would never have succeeded in business.

*Interview, Manhasset, N.Y., pub. Feb. 10.*

**Spiro T. Agnew**
*Vice President of the United States*

Gresham's law seems to be operating in the network news. The irrational is more controversial than the rational. Concurrence can no longer compete with dissent. One minute of Eldridge Cleaver is worth ten minutes of Roy Wilkins. The labor crisis settled at the negotiating table is nothing compared to the confrontation that results in a strike—or, better yet, violence along the picket line. Normality has become the nemesis of the evening news.

I am not asking for government censorship or any other kind of censorship. I am asking whether a form of censorship already exists when the news that 40 million Americans receive each night is determined by a handful of men responsible only to their corporate employers and filtered through a handful of commentators who admit to their own set of biases.

*Des Moines, Nov. 14.*

I don't seek to intimidate the press or the networks or anyone else from speaking out. But the time for blind acceptance of their opinions is past. And the time for naive belief in their neutrality is gone.

*Montgomery, Ala., Nov. 20.*

No person can be totally objective. The only answer (to TV news bias) is to have a diversity of partisans . . . two or three people who can balance each other out . . . The networks should recruit into their ranks people who don't think the way they do.

*Interview, Washington, pub. Dec. 7.*

**Russell Baker**
*Newspaper Columnist*

I never know what I'm going to . . . (write about) from one day to the next. But there are only six subjects: Sex, God, marriage, children, politics and baseball.

*Pub. March 3.*

**Rona Barrett**
*Television Commentator*

. . . I hate the word "gossip." I give *fact*—why call it gossip? I give news about Hollywood, and just because I raise my eyebrows and play it camp doesn't mean it isn't news. I camp it up because —well, in today's market to have an affair with somebody is not as disastrous as it was 30 years ago, so I try to make it funny, to make people laugh. And I think people do—except, I guess, the people involved; and that's because the truth always hurts. I mean, what husband likes to be the last to know?

*Interview, pub. March 21.*

**Betty Beale**
*Society Columnist,*
*"The Washington Star"*

No hostess with a grain of sense invites a reporter to a party who will sabotage her or her guests in her column the next day. To use someone's hospitality to hurt is self-destructive to a columnist. It closes doors. I think there are certain private things about everyone that shouldn't appear. I do not believe that is withholding news.

*Interview, Washington, pub. March.*

**Joseph Benti**
*News Commentator,*
*Columbia Broadcasting System*

We spend so much time on angry blacks, angry youth. But what about that vast forgotten army out there? How many hard-working, law-abiding whites are mad as hell because their story isn't being told?

*Interview, pub. Sept. 27.*

**Rudolf Bing**
*General Manager,*
*Metropolitan Opera Company*

What is the press? Six or eight people, with their own opinions, to which they have a right, of course.

*Interview, New York, pub. Jan. 15.*

**Jimmy Breslin**
*Author, Newspaper Columnist*

I worked for Newhouse, Scripps-Howard and Hearst—The Sing Sing, Leavenworth and Folsom of American journalism. People who are working for Newhouse shouldn't have the Guild as their bargaining agent. They should have the Mafia. And they should get the Pulitzer Prize for malnutrition.

*Pub. Feb. 28.*

**David Brinkley**
*News Commentator,*
*National Broadcasting Company*

There's an increasing displeasure with the state of affairs in this country. The people hear about it, tend not to like it and want me to shut up. If you're dissatisfied, the first thing you do is turn against the media that bring it to you.

*Pub. Sept. 5.*

**Otis Chandler**
*Publisher, "Los Angeles Times"*

Our role as a major mass circulation newspaper is a difficult one to fulfill. For this nation is in the midst of a revolution . . . A mass newspaper—like the *Los Angeles Times*—must remember that the preponderance of its subscribers have a basic interest in preserving the status quo—or they think they have. A mass newspaper . . . once it has begun to grasp the dimensions of the problems of its society, can begin slowly to document them—to fulfill one of its primary purposes, which is to educate.

*At stockholders' meeting,*
*Los Angeles, May 28.*

**Maxine Cheshire**
*Society Columnist,*
*"The Washington Post"*

My loyalty is to my column, and I have no loyalty to anyone else. My mother says she knows that if I found out about something, I'd even write about her.

*Pub. Jan. 27.*

Most of my reporting is done over the phone. People will tell you on the phone things they wouldn't dare tell their analyst.

*Interview, Washington, March.*

**William C. Cramer**
*United States Representative, R-Fla.*

The time is long overdue for the national TV networks to exercise responsibility, to report the news, and to stop giving millions of dollars worth of free, prime TV time to any rabble-rousing kook, any self-proclaimed leader of a hate-America-and-its-institutions group who is dedicated to destroying this country as we know it today. The more rabid and hate-mongering their utterances, the more likely the TV is to carry it . . .

*Before the House, Washington, Sept. 30.*

**Walter Cronkite**
*News Commentator,*
*Columbia Broadcasting System*

There are some who seem to believe that a little government control of broadcast news might be a good idea. Can they really believe that we can exist as a major communication medium half-free?

*University of Kansas, March 24.*

(WALTER CRONKITE)

We can't achieve total objectivity because we all have our prejudices, bias and position. But we are professional journalists, and we have been taught integrity, truth and honesty, and we practice it.

*St. Joseph, Mo., Nov. 21.*

**Robert J. Donovan**
*Washington Bureau Chief,*
*"Los Angeles Times"*

Even when the press is wrong or sensational or biased, its function is essential to a democracy. There is no conceivable substitute. Despite our errors, our abuses, occasional bias—despite many of the allegations against us—we are, I submit, much more likely to serve the interest of the public, and with much less bias, than any other form of communication that has ever been suggested. A government-controlled press would be the worst of all solutions, because it would establish a bias that could not be offset.

*University of Minnesota, Dec. 20.*

**Alex Dreier**
*News Commentator,*
*American Broadcasting Company*

Broadcasting news is really a job of acting. You can't stand up there and say there were 271 men killed yesterday in Vietnam. No, you must think of that one mother whose one son was killed and he was all the world to her. You must feel compassion for that one. You say: That bloody, awful war took the lives of 271 of our young men yesterday.

*Interview, Los Angeles, pub. May 23.*

**Milton S. Eisenhower**
*Director, Freedoms Foundation*

My one criticism of the mass news media is that for a long, long time it has given greater news value to conflict than it has to the fundamental knowledge that the people need in order to make wise, democratic decisions.

*Interview, pub. Dec. 16.*

**Abe Fortas**
*Former Associate Justice,*
*Supreme Court of the United States*

Holders of high political office must be exceptionally careful when they assail newscasters and the press for engaging in political criticism. They should realize that those who hold positions at the summit of government do not have the same freedom to criticize (as) an ordinary citizen has. Their words, however well intentioned, necessarily are intimidating in those regrettable circumstances where freedom of the press is dependent on short-term government licenses.

*Washington, Dec. 15.*

**Fred W. Friendly**
*Former President,*
*Columbia Broadcasting System-News*

The broadcast journalist knows how little news analysis appears on the air. Five or eight minutes after a major Presidential address is not interpretive journalism as much as it is time to be filled to the nearest half-hour or to the nearest commercial. He also knows that a half-hour, minus six commercials, is just not enough air time to present and analyze the news properly.

*California Institute of Technology,*
*pub. Nov. 23.*

**Philip Geyelin**
*Editorial-page Editor,*
*"The Washington Post"*

Editorials ought to inform and educate. They are necessary because most things that go on in government need to be interpreted.

*Pub. June 16.*

**Walter Gieber**
*Professor of Journalism,*
*San Francisco State College*

I refuse to take the underground press seriously. It'll do anything for a buck . . . (they) pander to sick people, contribute to psychopathic behavior . . . and some of the writers seem to do their work while stoned.

*Before Association for Education*
*in Journalism, University of*
*California at Berkeley, Aug. 26.*

**Julian Goodman**
*President,*
*National Broadcasting Company*

It is dangerous for any of us to conclude that the serious problems our nation faces would recede if television stopped showing and talking about them. The public, not the broadcaster, would be poorer as a result of federal censorship. The suggestion is that curbs on television news are in order, which can be translated to say that suppression of information is somehow desirable.

*Omaha, Neb., Jan. 27.*

If television is restricted in any of its abilities—especially in the area of news and information—its usefulness is basically impaired. If it is manipulated by and for special interests it stops being a public servant and may become a dangerous master. Our obligation to operate in the public interest should be absolute and this has a relevance for all of us, as citizens as well as viewers. We have no hesitation in showing our faults along with our virtues . . . We live in a troubled world, but it would be no less difficult if we refused to look trouble in the face. Yet there are some who would like to put a cover on the lens of the camera.

*Before Confederation of British Industry, London, April 22.*

Vice President Agnew's attack on television news is an appeal to prejudice. More importantly, Mr. Agnew uses the influence of his high office to criticize the way a government-licensed news medium covers the activities of the government itself . . . Evidently, he would prefer a different kind of television reporting—one that would be subservient to whatever political group happens to be in authority at the time.

*Pub. Nov. 24.*

**Charles L. Gould**
*Publisher, "San Francisco Examiner"*

. . . the real heart-beat of a great newspaper . . . the real thrust and drive and power comes not from the throbbing roar of the mammoth presses . . . it comes from the product. It comes from the words, the hopes, the dreams, the prayers, the criticisms and the inspiration woven into the fabric of the stories and editorials and features and

pictures that are the warp and woof of a newspaper.

*Before California Newspaper Advertising Executive Association, pub. Nov. 25.*

**Katherine Graham**
*Publisher, "The Washington Post"*

. . . the job of news media is to be tough-minded, fair-minded, weigh it all and play it as you see it . . . That old bromide about the mythical king who beheaded the messenger who brought him the bad news is true. People don't like to read about something that is happening that they wish weren't happening. But unless we do our job of interpreting very carefully and very well, they will not understand—and this would frighten them all the more.

*Los Angeles, pub. Nov. 10.*

**Philip A. Hart**
*United States Senator, D-Mich.*

Sure, there are a few who carp about papers being full of bad news; but, if they thought about it, they might find reasons to be grateful that bad news is still unusual enough to make Page 1.

*Pub. Dec. 18.*

**F. Edward Hebert**
*United States Representative, D-La.*

The record shows that today the news media, particularly television, finds news only in riots, disorders, obscenity, minority group protests, and antimilitary and antiGovernment demonstrations. Defiance of country, burning of draft cards, trampling of the American flag—now *that* is news!

*Before the House, Washington, Sept. 25.*

**Warren Hinckle III**
*Former Editor, "Ramparts Magazine"*

You have madness in publishing now. There is no relationship between the publisher and the reader. It's all between the publisher and the advertising agencies. The readers are there as consumer figures to be marketed and put together for the ad agencies. The readers don't

(WARREN HINCKLE III)

even get to say if they want a magazine to go out of business.

*Pub. Feb. 7.*

### Chester (Chet) R. Huntley
*News Commentator,*
*National Broadcasting Company*

Maybe we have been remiss in not finding enough positive things to report. But news, by its very nature, is usually not a happy thing—it deals with social and political irregularities. It is the exciting, the violent, the flagrant, the unusual that is news.

*Interview, New York,*
*pub. Nov. 24.*

### Norman Isaacs
*President, American Society*
*of Newspaper Editors*

The newspaper and broadcast arms of communications are rivals. For years they have been openly contemptuous of each other. Yet, whatever their differences, they are now driven together as the co-targets of what can only be described as an open campaign by the national Administration to discredit them —and, more importantly, to seek to bring them under some form of covert control.

*University of Michigan,*
*Nov. 19.*

### Jenkin Lloyd Jones
*President, Chamber of Commerce*
*of the United States*

Let 10,000 people march down Broadway in a patriotic parade and let 100,000 cheer them from the sidewalks. And then let 100 militants attempt to block the march somewhere uptown—and NBC, CBS and ABC will drop all else and rush to the spot. And on the evening news on videotape one gets the impression that New York erupted in fury that anyone should dare wave the flag. Let a distinguished American be invited to a campus. And let a dozen bathless, bearded revolutionaries storm the platform. The reporters all rush to interview the shouters and the speaker is forgotten.

*Skiatook, Okla., pub. Oct. 15.*

### Herbert Kaplow
*White House Correspondent,*
*National Broadcasting Company*

As far as I'm concerned, the White House itself is basically a dull assignment. News which would excite journalistic instincts is rarely made there, and a good part of the job is digesting handouts.

*Interview, pub. Feb. 10.*

### James Keogh
*Special Assistant to the*
*President of the United States*

This is my concern: I fear that journalism is becoming more and more a destructive force—a negative force—in our society at a time when the need for positive forces is as great as it has been at anytime in the history of this country. Now I recognize that news is essentially negative—that bad news is news—and it has always been so. All the way back in the first century, Plutarch referred to "That old proverb, 'Bad news travels fast and far.'" What bothers me is that in our revved-up era, bad news is travelling so fast and so far that the essentially-and-largely positive side of life is almost totally ignored.

*Before Omaha Press Club, Oct. 24.*

### John S. Knight
*Editorial Chairman,*
*Knight Newspapers, Inc.*

It is the press which audits government, exposes wrongdoing and prods the sluggards and papsuckers into action . . . (the press) and the press alone (had the) resources and determination to uproot crime and corruption . . . The loudest cries of "foul" come from bureaucrats who have been singed in the journalistic fires.

*Colby College, Waterville, Me.,*
*Nov. 14.*

### Bill Leonard
*Vice president in charge*
*of programming,*
*Columbia Broadcasting System-News*

Most reporting is *lousy.* It's lousy because people are lazy, because people don't think ahead, because they approach things in rote ways. We have these kinds of reporters here, unfortunately. The worst problem of all is the reporter who doesn't ask the next question—the *cheap, lousy* reporter who'll quote an attack but doesn't go to the other side because the answer might kill his story . . . And these producers who develop and edit a broadcast from the point of view of the way *they* want it to turn out—with their own prejudices showing. That happens quite often . . . If we could get rid of those people we'd be a lot closer to our goal of objectivity.

*Interview, pub. Sept. 27.*

**John Leonard**
*Critic, "New York Times Book Review"*

Aren't we faced with the peculiarity that dissent in this country has to seek, in petitioning redress of grievances, the media and not the government?

*Panel discussion, New York, pub. Dec. 30.*

**Peter Lisagor**
*White House Correspondent, "Chicago Daily News"*

A certain arm's-length position is a wholesome one on the part of press and President. If we're too close, we lose our detachment; and if he's too close, we keep seeing all the warts.

*Pub. May 2.*

**Elmer Lower**
*President, American Broadcasting Company-News*

There are those who question whether freedom of the press actually applies to electronic journalism. Well, I am not one of those who think the First Amendment (to the Constitution) was written to mean that only presses, machines—hardware, if you will—were to be free. I believe freedom of the press means untrammeled journalism. Perhaps if these same founding fathers were writing that same document in the midst of a technological boom like today's, they would have said Congress shall make no law abridging the freedom of the media.

*Before Montana Association of Broadcasters, Glacier Park, Mont., June 12.*

**John O. Marsh**
*United States Representative, D-Va.*

All news media must . . . differentiate between those happenings which are spontaneous and those which would not have happened if not for the presence of news media representatives . . . The important thing is that news and comment be insulated from show business—that a story not be oversold by the medium merely because it happens to be spectacular and exclusive, whereas its true impact on the course of events might be small.

*Waynesboro, Va., May 24.*

**Gale McGee**
*United States Senator, D-Wyo.*

(Today, the news media is) caught up in the very shaping of society. People's attitudes and ideas are given birth, after all, in the things they hear and read . . . your profession has, for too long, dodged responsibility for what it reports—and still does. How often have you said those words: "I don't make the news, I just report it"? Too often have I seen untruthful statements reported simply because someone—even a U.S. senator, perhaps—said them. No judgment exercised. No comment appended to state that there was contrary evidence available. No responsibility exercised to see that balance was maintained in presenting issues of public interest.

*Before National Newspaper Association, Denver, Oct. 17.*

**David Merrick**
*Stage Producer*

Television critics are totally incompetent. Anyone apparently can be a radio critic. I don't really think they get any salary, just two free seats to impress their girl friends. There's not a single one worth a dime. Worst of all is Edwin Newman. He's the poorest excuse for a critic that ever breathed air.

*Interview, New York, pub. May 25.*

**Richard M. Nixon**
*President of the United States*

. . . television stations might well follow the practice of newspapers, of sep-

(RICHARD M. NIXON)

arating news from opinion. When opinion is expressed, label is so, but don't mix the opinion in with reporting of the news.
*News conference, Washington, Dec. 8.*

### John B. Oakes
*Editor, Editorial Pages,*
*"The New York Times"*

We have an obligation to talk about every issue. We try to take a point of view that we think is beneficial to the country—broadly called liberal and generally internationalist—and then we go ahead and argue it as vigorously as possible. I rule the expression, "on the other hand," off the page.
*Pub. Jan. 16.*

### Charles H. Percy
*United States Senator, R-Ill.*

We have the best, the freest and the most uninhibited press in the world, and I don't believe anyone is going to shackle it by criticism. I'm not as concerned about the manipulation by the Fourth Estate as I am about the government's manipulation of the news.
*Washington, pub. Nov. 23.*

### Charles Roberts
*Correspondent, "Newsweek Magazine"*

In fourteen years, pursuing three Presidents, I have traveled a million miles in 35 countries by plane, train, car, bus, jeep, helicopter, submarine, aircraft carrier and small boat. I once traveled the last 10 miles to the site of a Presidential speech in the hopper of a garbage truck when Lyndon Johnson left his Boswells behind near Princeton, N.J., and I once had to hitchhike—after the murder of President (John F.) Kennedy in Dallas. I have been clobbered by Pakistani policemen, splattered with Australian eggs and felled by Montezuma's Revenge in Mexico. But, as a journalist, I wouldn't trade those fourteen years for equal time in Elysium.
*Pub. Jan. 20.*

### Hugh Scott
*United States Senator, R-Pa.*

I think the networks (in reporting the news) deserve a thorough goosing.
*Washington, Nov. 14.*

### Frank J. Shakespeare, Jr.
*Director, United States*
*Information Agency*

TV news, as it exists in the country today, is rather clearly liberally oriented . . . You sweat blood trying to be decent, objective and fair . . . the difficulty is that, when you have 8 or 10 people of the same ideological persuasion in a room, it is, in my judgment, psychologically impossible to be fair to the other position, even if you try.
*Before Radio and Television News*
*Directors Association,*
*Detroit, Sept. 26.*

### Merriman Smith
*White House Correspondent,*
*United Press International*

I have a front-row seat at history.
*Pub. Jan. 28.*

### Frank Stanton
*President, Columbia*
*Broadcasting System*

Today, many of our critics feel that the times now demand some type of formal restrictions or guidelines, either on the overall news media or at least on broadcast journalism, if only to insulate the public from what these critics consider to be the unwholesome and unhealthy quality of today's increasingly violent news . . . We at CBS categorically reject any such idea. If the agency (to administer such restrictions) were related to the government . . . honest journalism simply could not long survive. Broadcast journalism would be particularly vulnerable, since the renewal of broadcast licenses, in the United States, is at the discretion of government officials every three years, and these officials would now be armed with a set of rules that, at the very least, would act as a Damocles sword.
*International Press Institute,*
*Ottawa, Canada, pub. June 12.*

In my judgment, the whole tone, the whole content and the whole pattern of this government intrusion into the substance and methods of the broadcast press, and indeed of all journalism, have the gravest implications. Because a federally-licensed medium is involved, no more serious episode has occurred in government-press relationships since the Alien and Sedition Acts.

*News conference,*
*New York, Nov. 25.*

No healthy society and no governing authorities worth their salt have to fear the reporting of dissenting, or even hostile, voices. What a healthy society and a self-respecting government do have to fear—at the price of their vitality, if not

their life—is the suppression of such reporting.

*Pub. Nov. 30.*

**Avram (Av) R. Westin**
*Executive Producer, American*
*Broadcasting System-Evening News*

My politics are more conservative than Vice President Agnew would have people believe, but that doesn't matter. My job is to keep my politics and those of others off the air. You can't always be objective because you bring your experiences to things—so you try to be fair. We are on guard. We're not infallible. We try.

*Pub. Nov. 21.*

# Literature

## Conrad Aiken
*Author, Critic*

I think we're going through a very depressing decline in taste, which is on all levels everywhere. I don't think there is any first-rate fiction, and I mean to include everbody in that—Nabokov, Bellow and so on. I think neither is first rate, nor are any of the current novelists as good as they think they are.

*Interview, Brewster, Mass.,*
*pub. Aug. 5.*

## Woody Allen
*Actor-Writer-Comedian*

I am a voracious reader. You have to read to survive. People who read for pleasure are wasting their time. Reading isn't fun; it's indispensable.

*Interview, New York, pub. Feb. 14.*

. . . I have an absolutely Prussian self-discipline when it comes to my writing. Too many writers are premature; they should organize their ideas better before writing a piece. I do tremendous organizational layouts of my pieces before I actually write them; I take notes on matchbook covers, napkins, anything. Then, when the whole thing is pretty well worked out, I write the actual piece.

*Interview, Boston, pub. Feb. 16.*

There are no funny novelists. Because true humor in prose comes from style, not content. Benchley can write about not being able to pick up change from the table, and it's a scream. But it's also short. Obviously, he couldn't sustain that subject through a novel; it's his particular writing style that makes it hilarious. But a novel has other demands: a deep, realistic plunge into characters, moods and events. That doesn't sound very funny, does it?

*Interview, pub. June 29.*

## Richard Armour
*Author, Humorist*

Poetry is excellent for the writer because it makes him conscious of the individual word. John Updike is a good novelist, because he also writes poetry. John Milton and William Shakespeare both wrote poetry. The poet works word by word, and he's more exacting.

*Interview, pub. Dec. 21.*

## Aaron Asher
*Director of General Books,*
*Holt, Rinehart & Winston*

What we see going out now are the kinds of fiction—light fiction, adventure, that sort of thing—that television and movies can do better. What book publishers must recognize is that they have a large elite audience to serve, but not a mass audience. The number of book readers is not going up and up and up with no ceiling in sight . . .

*New York, pub. Sept. 22.*

## Clive Barnes
*Drama Critic,*
*"The New York Times"*

This may be the last generation of writers; in the future, everything may be taped . . . The young people talk better than they write.

*Albany, N.Y., pub. May 21.*

## Art Buchwald
*Newspaper Columnist*

Writers are funny about reviews: when they get a good one they ignore it—but when they get a bad review they never forget it. Every writer I know is the same way: you get a hundred good reviews, and one bad, and you remember only the bad. For years, you go on and fanta-

size about the reviewer who didn't like your book; you imagine him as a jerk, a wife-beater, a real ogre. And, in the meantime, the reviewer has forgotten all about the whole thing. But, twenty years later, the writer still remembers that one bad review. It's particularly true if the reviewer got close to the truth!
*Interview, pub. Oct. 5.*

**Pearl S. Buck**
*Author*

I write quite fast, but all my books take a long time in thinking—years, really . . . When my mind is set on a book, it works like a magnet, gathering iron filings. Everywhere you are, everything you do, the mind magnet pulls in thoughts. Over the years, my mind, my magnet so to speak, stores away things I want to use. I don't take notes. I have a good memory, and so gradually the book is built in my mind. Then I sit down and write.
*Interview, Philadelphia, pub. July 28.*

**Babette Deutsch**
*Poet, Author*

As long as I can remember, from the time I was a little girl, I have occupied myself with poetry. It has added a whole new dimension to my life, for a poet uses words as a composer uses a melody or a painter uses objects in space. To create a poem, using head, heart and language, is a privilege of a very special kind.
*Interview, pub. Sept. 14.*

**Daphne du Maurier**
*Author*

Perhaps it may sound like sour grapes in a woman of my age, but I do get bored with all this sleeping around they (women writers today) seem to write about all the time. I think there are far more interesting things in the world.
*Par, England, pub. March 20.*

**Will Durant**
*Author, Historian*

The authors in the libraries are more than friends because they can be silent when you wish to think. They are all waiting for you. Read, think well of mankind,

go to our libraries and rejoice.
*Before Los Angeles Library Association, Beverly Hills, Calif., pub. Feb. 5.*

**Clifton Fadiman**
*Author, Editor*

Traditionally, intelligent men tended to be interested in ideas, but today it doesn't matter. The new sensual novel has taken over the techniques of advertising. Dickens and Tolstoy knew all about sex, but you had to guess at it in their novels. They never put it on the line.
*Interview, New York, pub. May 5.*

**John Fowles**
*Author*

I get much more pleasure from writing books than from having them published. I like the creation of another world. That is very beautiful and satisfying for me. As soon as a book leaves this room, this house, there's always a diminution of pleasure.
*Interview, Dorset, England, pub. Nov. 9.*

All this advice from senior writers to establish a discipline—always to get down a thousand words a day whatever one's mood—I find an absurdly puritanical and impractical approach. Write, if you must, because you feel like writing, never because you feel you *ought* to write.
*Interview, Los Angeles, pub. Dec. 19.*

**Eliot Fremont-Smith**
*Chief Editor,*
*Little, Brown & Company*

We live in a most exciting time for books and for publishing. Real quality and commercial success are no longer, as perhaps they once were and were anyway assumed to be, mutually exclusive.
*Interview, pub. Feb. 25.*

**Joseph Heller**
*Author*

I have the feeling that if no more poetry were ever written, if no more paintings were ever done, that civilization would really not be much poorer

(JOSEPH HELLER)

than it is today. Fiction is more important because it says more—it's something for mentality to grapple with.

*Interview, pub. July 20.*

### Evan Hunter
*Author*

The trouble with writing is that the publishers tell you you have to go on radio and television to sell your books. It's usually degrading. The interviewer has hardly ever read your book and isn't the slightest bit embarrassed. Two years ago, when *A Horse's Head* was published, a guy with a radio show in Philadelphia said, "Evan, I haven't had a chance to read your book. What is it about?" I said, "Look, it took me over a year to write this book. If you didn't have the courtesy to read it, I'm not going to discuss it with you." He was absolutely furious, since apparently he *never* reads books. He's too busy interviewing authors.

*Interview, pub. Aug. 31.*

### Norman Mailer
*Author*

As we go whirling and twisting into the future, which by God we could swear we did not make, how sweet, how charming, how comic and nice that on a given year, to a given man, there came an award which was a measure of the plasticity of taste, the volatility of status and the essential good spirit of the literary world . . .

*Acceptance speech, National Book Award for Arts and Letters, New York, March 12.*

### William Manchester
*Author*

Writing is pure pain . . . Someone made a study, discovered most writers had been lonely youngsters. With no one to talk to, they learned to communicate in the written language. Believe me, if there were any other way to get rid of my thoughts, I'd do it.

*Pub. March 30.*

### Henry Miller
*Author*

What is my definition of pornography? I would say that it is that when it touches on sex in a slimy way—to tickle you—whereas I make a distinction between it and obscenity. Obscenity is direct and has a purity about it.

*Interview, Paris, pub. Aug. 18.*

### Malcolm Muggeridge
*Author, Editor*

There is no need to be mesmerized by the motley procession of writers, critics, crazed clerics and other miscellaneous intelligentsia prepared at the drop of a hat to pronounce the latest outpouring of substandard smut an essential contribution to contemporary letters.

*At International Festival of the Arts, Edinburgh, Scotland, Aug. 24.*

### Francoise Sagan
*Author, Playwright*

I have never written an erotic book, and I never will. I believe people should enjoy making love a lot, but not talk about it. Obviously, the old taboos had to be swept away, but why this sudden frenzy of talking about it as though making love were a brand new invention? I prefer to express everything in a single elegant phrase which allows the reader to conjure up his own sexual image.

*Pub. December.*

### Georges Simenon
*Author*

The great drama of writers is that we always die without knowing whether we are a success or not. After death, there's always a period of purgatory for a writer's reputation when it's uncertain what the final judgment will be. Maybe I'm a writer who counts, maybe not.

*Interview, Epalinges, Switzerland, pub. March 14.*

### Anatol Sofronov
*Editor, "Ogonyok," Soviet Literary Weekly*

I believe the poet's vocation is to help strengthen peace. I don't think you can find in the history of world poetry any poet who propagated hate and war. It's incompatible. Poets build bridges between nations.

*At World Congress of Poets, Manila, Aug. 28.*

**Theodore C. Sorensen**
*Former Special Counsel to President John F. Kennedy*

The book business is very nearly unique among the great industries of the world. Some industries cannot survive a depression, some cannot survive a war, some flourish only in wartime, some depend on a climate or on the availability of mineral resources. Some are unsuited to different economic systems. But the book industry needs only one assurance in order to flourish anywhere in the world —and that is the assurance of intellectual freedom. Books can be successfully written, published and sold wherever they can be freely purchased and read—but nowhere else.

*Before American Booksellers Association, Washington, pub. Aug. 4.*

**Rex Stout**
*Author*

Writers are forever saying what a lonely life it is. What bull. I feel, while I'm writing and when I've finished, not elation, but a sense of satisfaction. And I've had fun.

*Interview, Fairfield County, Conn., pub. Oct. 5.*

**Jacqueline Susann**
*Author*

Reviews can close a Broadway show, but not a book. A good review can help a book, but a bad review can't hurt it. The proof is that Leon Uris has never gotten good reviews. Harold Robbins never has. Irving Wallace hasn't. And I haven't. And I'd say we're the biggest sellers.

*Interview, New York, pub. June 16.*

There is no room for literature in the novel today. The competition is too great. People want to read a novel in bed at night, and there's Johnny Car-son and great old movies on *"The Late Show."*

*Interview, pub. June 20.*

People who read *The New York Times* aren't going to buy my books. Those people are going to buy coffee-table books or a book to impress a friend in the hospital. They go out and choose Nabokov to take to the hospital, but the friend would rather have Uris or Robbins any day.

*Interview, Hollywood, pub. June 29.*

A book that's written just for the sake of being dirty can't be successful. You have to get yourself involved with the characters and feel a certain empathy for them. Men like Robin Stone, in (her book) *The Love Machine*, do exist, and there's a Maggie in every cottage on Malibu Beach.

*Interview, New York, pub. Sept. 17.*

**Howard Taubman**
*Critic, "The New York Times"*

Now I'm not squeamish. I'm a big boy. I've been in the Army, I've heard four-letter words and I've read gamey books. I don't mind if some of the words and descriptions we are seeing today are used IF they serve a purpose in moving the story along. But I get the feeling a lot of them are being used today only because the writer and publisher think they are commercial. And, heaven help us, they are.

*At Town Hall, Oklahoma City, March 20.*

**Mark Van Doren**
*Author*

I think the reason people read detective stories today is because they are desperately in search of a story. Non-fiction has become very popular because fiction has lost touch with reality, it no longer gives a true account of life.

*Interview, New York, pub. June 11.*

Humor is the greatest quality a human being can have. No poet is great without it. Milton had no humor. Shakespeare had all the humor in the world, and he's hundreds of times greater than Milton.

(MARK VAN DOREN)

Shelley had no humor, and what a terrible ass he was. You can't take seriously anybody who lacks a sense of humor. It's what made (Robert) Frost a fine poet. Humorists are serious. They're the only people who are.

*Interview, Falls Village, Conn.,*
*pub. June 13.*

**Irving Wallace**
*Author*

Everyone likes critics—as long as they are nice.

*Interview, Los Angeles, pub. March 16.*

**Robert Penn Warren**
*Poet*

Lines, verses, even stanzas, come to me at odd moments—perhaps the best when I'm swimming. Swimming frees the mind. There's something about the rhythm of swimming—or running . . . the body is occupied, the mind is free.

*Interview, Fairfield, Conn.,*
*pub. Dec. 16.*

**John Adriani**
*Professor of Medicine,*
*Tulane University*

The situation (in the pharmaceutical industry) can now be described as nearly chaotic. No semblance of order can be made of the existing chaos until all drugs and combinations thereof are designated by given, common, or generic names and not by proprietary or brand names. Brand names should be abolished.
*Testimony before House subcommittee,*
*Washington, May 20.*

**Charles Althafer**
*Director, Smoking Research*

These guys (cigarette addicts) climb the walls, beat their wives, kick their dogs, and turn into tyrants when deprived of cigarettes. But once an addict quits, he won't go through that hell again. He has had a love affair with his cigarettes, and he'll be able to tell you to the hour when he gave them up.
*Pub. Feb. 10.*

**Lord Amulree**
*London Physician*

It (euthanasia) could completely undermine the confidence of patients in their doctors. We don't want them feeling that the man with the syringe is going to be a killer.

*Pub. March 30.*

**Christiaan Barnard**
*Heart Transplant Surgeon*

I think it is more immoral to bury a heart for the worms to devour than to use it to save the life of a human being.
*University of Witwatersrand,*
*Johannesburg, pub. April 20.*

We're going to continue with heart transplantations. We're certainly not going to slow down. In fact, we will probably do more. I think there's no doubt about it, this operation is worthwhile. We have been able to prolong life and relieve suffering. Things are not perfect yet. We've done much better than we expected, but we're sad that he (Dr. Philip) Blaiberg has gone . . . If I had a patient tonight and a donor tonight, I'd do a heart transplant tonight.
*News conference, Cape Town, Aug. 18.*

We were able to give 19 months of life to a man (Philip Blaiberg) who might long ago have been dead. Would anyone say this was too little to be worth it . . . I can only say that I am glad we were able to give Dr. Blaiberg as much extra life as we did. If nothing else, this tells us to go on with our work.
*Telephone interview, Cape Town,*
*pub. Sept. 28.*

**Larry Alan Bear**
*Commissioner, Addictions Services*
*Agency, New York City*
*Human Resources Administration*

I can truly say that in all my experience with drug abusers, I have never seen a single case where marijuana use has been responsible for producing a more mature, well-balanced, productive or even happier human being.
*Before Senate Special Subcommittee*
*on Alcoholism and Narcotics,*
*Washington, Aug. 6.*

**Philip Blaiberg**
*World's first heart*
*transplant patient*

There is a terrific suspense. You go through three hurdles. That's another thing about a transplant—it's full of hur-

(PHILIP BLAIBERG)

dles. The first is being selected for a transplant. Then, you wait for a donor—will you live long enough to get a donor? When you finally get one, they have to find out if your tissue is compatible with that of the donor—hurdle number three. When that is cleared, only then can you go to the table—that's why I welcome the idea of an artificial heart to do away with the pre-period of suspense.

*Interview, May 24.*

**Henry Brill**
*Director, Pilgrim State Mental*
*Hospital, Brentwood, N.Y.*

I am strongly against the legalization of marijuana and I am strongly against the message it would carry to the public—that this is a harmless or relatively harmless drug. It isn't. *Pub. March 11.*

. . . Like sex, there may be a lot of boasting talk about marijuana rather than actual indulgence in it. On the other hand, marijuana is coming to be regarded by many students as a badge of youth, like taking a drink or smoking a regular cigarette.

*Pub. March 14.*

**Victor Buhler**
*Pathologist, St. Joseph Hospital,*
*Kansas City, Mo.*

The cause of cancer in humans, including the cause of cancer of the lung, is unknown. No amount of speculation, no amount of suspicion, no amount of repetition of now familiar findings and no amount of emotion can alter this fact. The cause of cancer of the lung is not known.

*Before House Commerce Committee,*
*Washington, April 28.*

**Dale C. Cameron**
*Chief, Drug Dependence Unit,*
*World Health Organization*

I am not much impressed by the argument that marijuana is no worse than alcohol.

*Pub. Jan. 26.*

**Martin Cherkasky**
*Director, Montefiore Hospital,*
*New York*

This (doctor) shortage makes it im-

possible to deal with the medical profession. You're at their mercy.

*Pub. Feb. 21.*

**Charlotte Coggin**
*Cardiologist*

My feeling is this about heart transplants . . . I think that to give a kid more time to live is fantastic; but to give just a few months to the head of a family? Think of it: the emotional upheaval for everyone concerned, the creating of an enormous debt that will take years to pay off. Somehow, I'm not keen on this . . .

*Interview, pub. March 3.*

**Sidney Cohen**
*Director, Division of Narcotics*
*Addiction and Drug Abuse,*
*National Institute of Mental Health*

Liquor is a part of our culture. People weren't about to give up their booze. But amphetamines are not part of our culture. Prohibition might have some effect.

*Pub. Feb. 2.*

**Denton A. Cooley**
*Heart Transplant Surgeon*

I must repeat, to whom will we deny a (heart) transplant? More people have died from lack of a transplant than they have because of a transplant.

*News conference, Houston, Jan. 25.*

**Eliot Corday**
*Chairman, American College*
*of Cardiology*

Until we can overcome rejection, there is little place for (heart) transplantation. In time, we expect that scientists will come up with ways to overcome rejection. If they do, this would solve the donor shortage problem because it would then be possible to use hearts from animals raised especially for this purpose.

*Pub. April 28.*

**Robert G. Denewalter**
*Vice president for Development*
*Research, Merck, Sharp & Dohme*
*Research Laboratories*

It is glaringly clear that we haven't made the progress in cancer studies that we expected over the past decade . . . I don't see any alternative but to continue research in the field. It won't do any good to scold the scientists or to take the money away from them. This won't produce a cancer cure.

*At Science Writers Seminar of American Cancer Society, New Orleans, April 2.*

**Gerald D. Dorman**
*President, American Medical Association*

There is a crisis in medical care, but it's probably an overstatement to call it "massive." It's been a growing crisis due to misuse of medical facilities by patients as much as to shortage of all kinds of medical help—M.D.'s, nurses and other help in rural areas and ghettos. Coupled with this is an increased demand for everything everybody has read about as "the miracles of medical science." Everyone expects those miracles.

The medical profession can no longer tolerate a medical society that concentrates on the private interests of itself and its members.

*At AMA Convention, New York, pub. July 28.*

**Roger O. Egeberg**
*Assistant Secretary for Health and Scientific Affairs, Department of Health, Education and Welfare of the United States*

I don't personally think marijuana leads to heroin. I feel pretty strongly that it should be placed in a different category from barbiturates, heroin, amphetamines and LSD.

*Interview, pub. Sept. 9.*

**Philip Elman**
*Commissioner, Federal Trade Commission*

Cigarette smoking is, without question, the greatest single public health problem this nation has ever faced.

*Pub. April 25.*

**Dana L. Farnsworth**
*Director of Health Services, Harvard University*

No evidence has yet demonstrated that extensive use of marijuana for self-realization or increased creativity or attainments of mystical states of consciousness has been beneficial for more than a few isolated individuals. Pot smokers work out great philosophical theories, but fail to record them. Great paintings are envisioned, but nothing gets on canvas. With pot, everything draws to a halt.

*Pub. December.*

Both young people and adults are bombarded by advertising that displays the magical power of drugs . . . With this background, it is easy to see how today's young people grow up with the general conviction that drugs can solve anything, given the right prescription and the right dosage.

*At Conference on Drug Usage and Abuse, East Lansing, Mich., Dec. 8.*

**Mia Farrow**
*Actress*

I know too many people who use it (psychiatry) as a crutch: "Give us this day our daily analyst."

*Interview, New York, pub. Feb. 7.*

**Peter D. Fleming**
*Senior Consultant, Menninger Foundation*

I think too many psychiatrists, who are very competent and know a great deal about the treatment of people, too easily consider themselves experts on "the sick society." Our basic undertstanding is in the area of sickness, and we should always cling to that kind of expertise. There are people who can help a lot of people, but I'm not sure they're psychiatrists. They're sociologists, and a variety of others.

*Interview, Topeka, Kans., pub. April 7.*

**Lawrence J. Friedman**
*Senior Faculty Member, Los Angeles Psychoanalytic Society & Institute*

If a child watches enough television he will automatically become violent because he has nowhere to go with his normal aggressive energy that he should be working off in creative activity.

*Interview, New York, pub. March 2.*

**Walter B. Frommeyer, Jr.**
*President, American Heart Association*

Paradoxically . . . retrenchments (in federal funds for health research and services) are taking effect at a time when we are preparing for a second landing on the moon. It is incredible that we should be more interested in the conquest of space than the conquest of disease . . . I shudder to anticipate what will happen . . . if we decide to land on Mars.

*Dallas, Nov. 16.*

**Haim Ginott**
*Child Psychologist*

There are two kinds of criticism: constructive and destructive. Truthfully, with children I have discovered that there is no such thing as constructive criticism. With adults it's different. They can defend themselves; an adult can deal with it. But I look at kids as wet cement—if you hit them with something, it makes an impression.

*Los Angeles, March 17.*

**Martin Ginsberg**
*New York State Assemblyman*

If we are prepared to say that a life should not come into this world malformed or abnormal, then tomorrow we should be prepared to say that a life already in this world which becomes malformed or abnormal should not be permitted to live.

*Before New York State Assembly,*
*Albany, April 17.*

**James L. Goddard**
*Former Commissioner,*
*Food and Drug Administration*
*of the United States*

Anyone who plays with LSD deserves whatever spanking society has ordained. LSD is the most dangerous drug I've ever studied.

*Mankato, Minn., pub. Jan. 27.*

**Clyde C. Greene**
*President, American Society*
*of Internal Medicine*

Time will not answer America's need for 50,000 more physicians. The Ameri-can medical profession is nearing a confrontation (with the public) and may soon become a public utility, with all the accompanying regulations, unless physicians become very much more aware of the public's demand and expectation for health care.

*Pub. May 4.*

**Sir Harry Greenfield**
*President, International Narcotics*
*Control Board*

The main concern today is not with opium but with the lesser drugs—cannabis (marijuana, or hashish) and the psychotropic drugs. They are very difficult to control because so many are in daily and necessary use. In today's society, we must have tranquilizers.

*New York, pub. May 25.*

**Emanuel Hallowitz**
*President-elect, American*
*Group Psychotherapy Association*

Some of them (group therapy sessions) do a great deal of harm. We don't know the limits of tolerance for these techniques, and often defenses necessary to a person's survival are broken down prematurely. The next day, or next week, the person may find he can't sleep or can't fulfill most of his functions.

*New York, Feb. 8.*

**Philip Handler**
*Chairman, National Science Board*

It remains a scientific problem to decide whether or not marijuana is or is not dangerous in our society. The evidence of the harm that it does is not very clear at all. . . . But persons under the influence of marijuana are as mentally unreliable as those who drink to excess.

*Before House appropriations*
*subcommittee, Washington, June 6.*

**Harry J. Johnson**
*Chairman, Medical Board,*
*Life Extension Institute*

The trouble with our way of life is that most Americans no longer have to exercise to get sustenance, and all our technological conveniences encourage us to be passive—to ride in cars and elevators. The result is that few of us get the exercise we need for the efficient operation of the human machine. This is the first time in the history of the world that this situation has existed.

*Interview, pub. Aug. 11.*

**Rodney Hewitson**
*Senior Physician, Groote Schuur*
*Hospital, Cape Town, South Africa*

The life expectancy of heart transplant patients is based on the experience in kidney transplants, where all have been rejected within five years. The operation on Philip Blaiberg has cost a total of $21,426. An overseas expert has estimated that for this money he could have kept alive in one year 200 sick and malnourished babies.

*Before South African Academy*
*for Science and Art,*
*Cape Town, March 12.*

**Robert F. Horan, Jr.**
*Chief Criminal Prosecutor,*
*Fairfax County, Virginia*

The average parent knows little or nothing about the subject (drugs and narcotics), the average teacher in our schools today has never had a course on drug abuse, and, most unusual of all, the average physician has never had a course on the drugs that constitute the main problem.
*Pub. April 10.*

**Harold E. Hughes**
*United States Senator, D-Iowa*

We must have effective enforcement as well as good laws. But we must recognize that (drug) addiction is a sickness, not a crime. And we must understand the social and symbolic significance of youthful drug use.

*Washington, Sept. 3.*

That's what people don't realize about an alcoholic: When he says he quits, he really does mean it. Just the way you'd mean it if you said, "I want to quit having cancer or quit being a diabetic." The reason so many alcoholics relapse so often is because society gives them practically no support. Not only are treatment facilities rare or non-existent, but alcohol

has become so much a part of our culture that the diseased man can hardly get away from what makes him sick.
*Pub. Dec. 28.*

**Jack Hurst**
*President, Synanon Foundation*

Synanon is not in the rehabilitation business. We have less in common with rehabilitation centers than we do with the Los Angeles *Dodgers*. You won't find talk here about drug addiction. We're a social movement. We're in a sense a small model for a better world. We absorb people into a responsible community. It's a way of life. Synanon's goal goes far beyond getting a man off dope. The goal is social rehabilitation—moral, spiritual rehabilitation.
*Pub. Dec. 15.*

**John E. Ingersoll**
*Director, Bureau of Narcotics*
*and Dangerous Drugs,*
*Department of Justice*
*of the United States*

We are not preventing enough drug abuse; we are not apprehending enough peddlers; we are not rehabilitating enough users . . . My guess is that the number (of drug users) is far greater than we would care, or dare, to think.
*Washington, Feb. 11.*

**Allan K. Jones**
*President, California Chapter,*
*American Cancer Society*

Lung cancer is a rare disease among non-smokers. The facts are clear, but it's hard to get boys in search for manhood to exchange the prospect of longer life, 30 or 40 years from now, for the feeling of being grown-up today.
*News conference, Los Angeles, July 23.*

**Kenneth Keniston**
*Member of Faculty,*
*Yale Medical School*

Those of us who are critical of student drug abuse must demonstrate to our students that there are better and more lasting ways to experience the fullness, the depth, the variety and the richness of life

(KENNETH KENISTON)

than that of ingesting psychoactive chemicals.

*Pub. March 19.*

### John H. Knowles
*Director, Massachusetts*
*General Hospital*

Anyone who is qualified for the job (U.S. Assistant Secretary for Health, HEW) would be opposed (by American Medical Association). And I would worry about the qualifications of anyone who isn't opposed.

Whatever socialized medicine is—and I'm not altogether sure I know—I'm firmly against it.

*News conference, Boston, June 27.*

Any practical, reasonable man would agree that the costs of medical care are prohibitive today for 99 per cent of the American people. There must be an insurance mechanism to protect people against this kind of economic ruin.

*Pub. June 30.*

Medicaid is the lousiest waste of taxpayers' money and the most ill-conceived program which ever came down the chute.

*Television interview, Boston, July 6.*

### Otto N. Larsen
*Professor of Sociology,*
*University of Washington*

We do have more conclusive evidence about the effects of media violence than some media spokesmen would have us believe. In my judgment, social science knowledge about the effects of media violence resembles medical knowledge about the effects of cigarette smoking . . . the weight of the evidence designates televised violence as a national health problem.

*Pub. May 15.*

### Herbert L. Ley, Jr.
*Commissioner, Food and Drug*
*Administration of the United States*

The use of two or more active ingredients in the treatment of a patient who can be cured by (only) one is irrational therapy . . . It exposes the patient to an unnecessary risk. Antibiotics should be used like a rifle rather than a shotgun.

*Washington, April 1.*

### John V. Lindsay
*Mayor of New York*

Far too much time has been lost in trying to analyze, rationalize or ignore the steady introduction of drugs into the lives of our young people. The time now has come to move against this problem with every workable resource we have.

*New York, March 7.*

### Art Linkletter
*Television Entertainer*

Almost every time a top-40 record is played on the radio, it is an ad for acid, marijuana and trips. The lyrics of the popular songs and the jackets on the albums . . . are all a complete, total campaign for the fun and thrill of trips. If you don't believe it, you ought to take a good, long look at some of the lyrics and some of the albums with the hidden symbols, with the language that the kids know. They have words for trips and marijuana and speed that you have never even heard of. When those lyrics are sung, the kids are all rapping, as they call it, talking, rapping with each other on the subject.

*Washington, Oct. 23.*

### Donald Luria
*President, New York State Council*
*on Drug Addiction*

Five years ago, when people said marijuana led to heroin, I would leap to my feet and say "that's a lie." It was a lie then, but not now. We're now seeing kids literally dying in our schools—they're not addicted, just willing to take a crack at anything for fun.

*Pub. July 7.*

### V. D. Mattie
*President, Hoffman-La Roche*

I can't honestly say that drug prices are cheap. I think they're reasonable for those who can afford to pay the price.

*Pub. March 7.*

### D. M. F. McDonald
*Mental Hospital Superintendent*

About one-third of all New Zealand

goes to sleep on pills.

*Before Medical Association of*
*New Zealand, Auckland,*
*pub. March 23.*

## Margaret Mead
*Anthropologist*

There should be no more restrictions on smoking marijuana than on smoking cigarettes or drinking beer . . . Marijuana is not harmful unless it is taken in enormous and excessive amounts. We are damaging our nation, damaging our laws, damaging the relationship between young and old by this prohibition.

*Before Senate Small Business Monopoly*
*Subcommittee, Washington, Oct. 27.*

## Richard M. Nixon
*President of the United States*

We face a massive crisis in this area (health care), and unless action is taken—both administratively and legislatively—to meet that crisis within the next two to three years, we will have a breakdown in our medical-care system which could have consequences affecting millions of people throughout this country. I don't think I'm overstating the case.

*Washington, July 10.*

## Robert Osnos
*Director of Psychiatry,*
*New York City Department*
*of Hospitals*

Most psychiatrists do not like the field of forensic psychiatry because they do not like to have their opinions challenged in court.

*Pub. March 10.*

## Irvine H. Page
*Senior Consultant, Research Division,*
*Cleveland Clinic Foundation*

Heart transplantation and artificial hearts will not be the answer to coronary vascular disease for many years. We announce bravely through the news media that we will be doing it in the year 2000, knowing full well many of us won't be around to take the responsibility. This may keep the research dollars rolling in, but it deflects from the real problem, loath as we are to admit it. It is no fun to tell an eager congressional committee how much we don't know and even less rewarding to give a panting reporter the reasons why the role cholesterol plays is unclear. Especially is this so when dashing surgeons have just put the heart of a young girl into a man twice her age.

*Before Council on Arteriosclerosis,*
*American Heart Association,*
*Miami, pub. April 21.*

## Malcolm Peterson
*Chief of Medical Services,*
*St. Louis City Hospital*

. . . the wide disparity between the medicine that we know how to give and what we actually give—they're miles apart.

*Pub. Feb. 21.*

## Robert C. Peterson
*Chief, Center for Studies*
*of Narcotic and Drug Abuse,*
*National Institute of Mental Health*

The chances are there are some adverse effects from marijuana—as there are from most everything in life. The social effects —copping out, and loss of motivation among kids—are probably the worst.

*Pub. Feb. 4.*

## Jerome Pollack
*Professor of Medical Economics,*
*Harvard Medical School*

All, or virtually all, Americans are now medically indigent. Health insurance for all has become a necessity.

*Pub. Feb. 21.*

## Alan Sieroty
*California State Assemblyman*

The chronic alcoholic is a sick person who must be treated with a medical approach rather than being subjected to the revolving door of the drunk tank and the repeated jail sentences that are now imposed under our criminal laws.

*Sacramento, March 10.*

## Norman E. Shumway
*Heart Transplant Surgeon,*
*Stanford University*

. . . I think we'll probably be able to

(NORMAN E. SHUMWAY)

do about 2,000 to 3,000 heart transplants annually in America 10 years from now. For the recipients who would die otherwise, this is a meaningful number. But obviously, when 500,000 are dying annually of cardiac failure, it is only one answer. The technique clearly won't be applicable in most cases, such as your classic driving young executive who collapses in the cafeteria line and dies before he arrives at the hospital.

*Interview, Stanford University,*
*pub. March 16.*

**Charles W. Socarides**
*Psychiatrist, Albert Einstein*
*College of Medicine*

We believe that homosexuality is a form of emotional illness and that any attempt to glamorize it or elevate it or to condemn it as a moral offense is entirely beside the point and only clouds the issue.

*New York, pub. March 16.*

**Wendell M. Stanley**
*Director, Virus Laboratory,*
*University of California at Berkeley*

As to . . . just what cancer is, I'm leaning toward the virus theory, and I feel that the research into the vast forms of viruses themselves will probably provide the most information about the cancer.

*At Science Writers Seminar,*
*American Cancer Society,*
*New Orleans, pub. April 2.*

**William H. Stewart**
*Surgeon General, United States*
*Public Health Services*

If even one American doesn't have access to a reasonable level of (medical) care, there's something wrong. And when millions don't, there's obviously something wrong.

*Pub. Feb. 21*

**Kenneth O. A. Vickery**
*Medical Officer of Health,*
*City of Eastbourne, England*

. . . to a Christian nation serious consideration of euthanasia would be unthinkable. But in a community which can no

longer adequately nurse all its chronic sick, and where beds are so blocked by the aged that younger people requiring surgical and medical treatment cannot be admitted, we can no longer avoid the issue of medicated survival, which, as so successfully manifested in current medical practice, is surely one of the cruelest hazards to which we can be subjected.

*Before Royal Society of Health,*
*Eastbourne, April 29.*

**Dwight L. Wilbur**
*President, American*
*Medical Association*

Medicine and society have become so intertwined, they are inseparable. As one changes, so does the other . . . We live in an era of national commitment to health —a phenomenon of the 1960s . . . There is no turning back. There is further commitment ahead . . . Today, and even more in the future, health and medicine are not matters just for physicians and patients—they are matters of total public concern.

*At AMA Convention,*
*New York, pub. July 21.*

**John J. Williams**
*United States Senator, R-Del.*

The only way to end this sort of thing (abuses by physicians in Medicare and Medicaid) is to name names and sums of money and put it on front pages all over the country.

*Washington, pub. Feb. 20.*

**Irving S. Wright**
*Professor of Medicine,*
*Cornell University*

Today, interest at all levels of medical practice seems to decrease with the increased age of the patient. This may be an early manifestation of a faceless medicine of the future, or it may represent the deep-rooted tradition of our tribal past, when the aged were cast out to be devoured by animals or to freeze in the snow. We cannot accept this attitude as worthy of this affluent and generally compassionate society.

*Before International Congress of*
*Gerontology, Washington, pub. Sept. 9.*

**Jack Webb**
*Actor, Television Producer*

I feel like I've been witnessing the last act of a tragedy. Not so long ago, flower children used to stroll barefoot here (San Francisco's Haight-Ashbury District) and offer you a daisy . . . but then something happened. You'd hardly recognize the Haight anymore. Shops are boarded up. Windows broken . . . What happened? Drugs happened.

*Anti-drug television commercial,
Sept. 19.*

**Stanley F. Yolles**
*Director, National Institute of
Mental Health*

The problem (of marijuana) is growing much more serious. It would be serious enough if it were only the college student using it, because it is another intoxicant they are using. But when you get down into the junior high schools and into the upper grades of grammar schools, I become very, very much concerned. It is just at that age level that the personality is being molded and formed through an interaction of the individual with the society around him. The effect of these drugs—marijuana, LSD, etc.—is to reduce the interaction between the person and his environment. It removes him from that. The effects on the personality can, for long-continued use in a child of this age, be devastating.

*Interview, Washington, pub. July 14.*

I would like to make my professional position very clear . . . I do not, at this time, advocate the removal of all restrictions on the use of marijuana. I believe that, until we know more than we now do about the long-term effects of marijuana and other forms of Cannabis, use of the drug should continue to be controlled. Medically speaking, I cannot give it a clean bill of health. But penalties for its use should be lowered in proportion to the danger and risk to the individual and society of this drug.

*Before Senate Judiciary Subcommittee
on Juvenile Delinquency,
Washington, Sept. 17.*

# The Performing Arts

## MOTION PICTURES

**Renata Adler.**
*Former Critic, "The New York Times"*

Two months ago, I thought that very soon I was going to run out of anything to say. Frequently, it seemed as though the same movie was coming out again and again under a different title.
*Pub. March 10.*

**Jack Albertson**
*Actor*

Ninety per cent of the things you do in this business are crap.
*Interview, Los Angeles, April 15.*

**Ken Annakin**
*Director*

I believe in making a film for the family unit, so that people of all ages can enjoy it and get something from it. I believe that the film screen should be used as an entertainment medium to bring families closer together instead of keeping them apart. Even husbands and wives are sometimes embarrassed to be seen together at some of today's pornographic films.
*Interview, Hollywood, pub. Sept. 14.*

**Samuel Z. Arkoff**
*Chairman,*
*American-International Pictures*

If I were addressing all the exhibitors of America in the vernacular of my professional background as an attorney on motion picture affairs, I might point a meaningful finger and exclaim, "I accuse." I accuse you of permitting a theatre shortage, just as you accused the film producers of a product shortage a short time ago. It's a matter of simple mathe-

matics that more costly pictures have to play longer and if there are more pictures there must be more theatres, and there aren't. When gas stations sell more gas and oil, there are more gas stations. This happens to be the case, so there is a gas station on almost every corner.
*Dallas, pub. Feb. 6.*

**James T. Aubrey**
*President, Metro-Goldwyn-Mayer*

There are customers waiting to see pictures, but you can't give them what they don't want to see. You can't sell a bad picture, and you don't have to sell a good one. I am the last person to attempt to draw an analogy between TV and movies, but I found out in TV that you never have problems with a hit. I'm sure as hell going to try. We are going to cut the waste and make pictures.
*Pub. Nov. 10.*

**Warren Beatty**
*Actor, Producer*

Pictures are made by groups of people. When one guy does everything, it takes the fun out of it for everyone else.
*Interview, Los Angeles, pub. Feb. 28.*

**Joan Blondell**
*Actress*

Oh, the kids (young actors) today are fine. I just don't get the thrill I used to when I looked into Spencer Tracy's or Jimmy Cagney's eyes. They really had it. Feeling. And timing. Oh, the timing. They had all the magic. Not many of them have that today.
*Interview, Los Angeles, pub. July 23.*

**Claire Bloom**
*Actress*

I like to work in Hollywood, but I don't

like to live there. I'm too young to die.
*Interview, New York, pub. July 22.*

## John Boulting
*Producer, Director*

Now everything goes—far too much. It becomes a first-class—or is it a third-class?—bore. We are going through a phase to gratify a long-desired wish to deal with sexuality. In three, four, five years, we'll return to the ultimately rewarding drama of life.

*Pub. May 26.*

## Leslie Bricusse
*Composer*

I'm very happy if one of my songs turns out to be great; but it's more important that a song serve a function than that it be memorable by itself. A song can't just be thrown in (in a motion picture), nor can it just sit there and do nothing. It has to advance the drama.

*Interview, pub. Dec. 14.*

## Albert Broccoli
*Producer*

We've gone too far afield in making our pictures. Once the ban was lifted, everyone rushed in, to one side of the boat—and it can tip over . . . There was an industry explosion after the lifting of censorship. But they've gone too far the other way. I'm afraid we'll set the kids in another direction . . . It could split the business wide open.

*Pub. May 26.*

## Jim Brown
*Actor*

The black man will have arrived in the movies when they cast him as a villain. Black can be good and bad as well as beautiful. We just ask that you make us human.

*Interview, pub. July 10.*

## Michael Caine
*Actor*

The best kind of picture to be in for winning an Academy Award is a picture that looks like it should have lost money and makes a fortune . . .

*Interview, Subic Bay, Philippines, pub. April 20.*

## Art Carney
*Actor*

An actor can survive a bad play, particularly if his performance is well received. But a bad movie . . .

*Interview, Los Angeles, pub. Feb. 14.*

## John Cassavetes
*Actor, Director*

If an actor thinks he can help the truthful expression of emotion by saying something other than the line in the script, I tell him to go ahead with it. I believe in my players having complete emotional rights—after all, they're the only ones around working from pure emotion. I can help stimulate those emotions, but not tell them how to depict them.

I like to have fun, to fight and to swing. I like a "noisy" set. I yell, and they (the cast) yell back, especially my wife. What a wonder that camera is, what a way to tell a story! I'm like a kid with a toy pistol with it; I just run around, shooting everything.

*Interview, Los Angeles, pub. Feb. 16.*

## Henri-George Clouzot
*Director*

There is too much sex films. I've seen too many erotic pictures. Nude scenes are made for audiences; it is most boring for a director. If he cares for beauty, then it is most difficult. To show perversion is a tough job for an audience. Either they stand it or they don't stand it. They have to be involved. If someone stands up and says "Enough," I'll be glad.

*Pub. May 26.*

## James Coburn
*Actor*

Sidney (Lumet) is the only director I've ever worked with who makes me feel like I'm working toward a totality instead of a piece of nothing. I was reaching a point in my career where nothing meant anything any more. I've been through so many movies where you go through so much bull just to find out your best scene has been destroyed by some inept director who blew it for some crazy angle of a chandelier on the ceiling, or by some ac-

(JAMES COBURN)

tress who'se been making it with some-body in the front office.

*Interview, Baton Rouge, La.,*
*pub. June 8.*

**Francis Ford Coppola**
*Director*

Movies will be an integral part of life in 10 years, comprising all kinds of informa-tion and entertainment. You'll be able to buy a $2 film in the drugstore, just as you buy a paperback book today, take it home, shove it in a slot, and see it on the wall.

Movies are the art form most like man's imagination.

*Pub. Sept. 22.*

**Ann Corio**
*Burlesque entertainer*

I worked for years to make burlesque acceptable and respectable, but now the movies are doing it for me. What do you see now when you go to the movies? A terrified girl being raped by four or five idiots on a beach. They make bur-lesque look like "Rebecca of Sunny-brook Farm."

*Interview, Washington, pub. Sept. 24.*

**Sherrill C. Corwin**
*Chairman, National Association*
*of Theatre Owners*

In any classification (rating) system, there are bound to be some loopholes caused by carelessness or negligence. But, by and large, we feel the rules are being observed. I know that it is a prime topic whenever exhibitors get together . . . to discuss ways and means of policing the ratings system so that we can get the results we originally set. We recognized from the outset we wouldn't have 100% compliance, but the exhibitor who isn't following the rules is merely going to cause himself embarrassment in his own community—and I think that's the key.

*Interview, Hollywood, pub. Sept. 16.*

**Joseph Cotten**
*Actor*

I used to read scripts . . . and I would decide whether to do them or not. To-day, I've stopped reading them be-cause I can't understand them. But I do ask two questions: Do I have to take off my clothes, (and) Do I have to say THAT word? If the answer to both is No, then I say I'll do it.

*Interview, Hollywood, pub. Oct. 26.*

**Joan Crawford**
*Actress*

Gable the King could leer at you in a movie and it was ten times more sexy than a whole soundstage of nudes.

*Hollywood, pub. Nov. 18.*

**Judith Crist**
*Critic, "New York Magazine"*

When it comes to children's films, we are indeed an underdeveloped country—our children underprivileged and our film-makers uninterested.

*Pub. Feb. 22.*

It was the ambition of my life to see a stag film, but I never did until they started playing the art houses.

*Before Women's National Democratic*
*Club, Washington, May 15.*

**George Cukor**
*Director*

. . . life changes and the public taste changes. I remember when Hollywood censorship made it impossible to show a bedroom scene, unless one person had his feet on the floor. Nonetheless, we had frightfully exciting performers who could generate eroticism without uncovering much flesh. Now that there's full license, I think sex has become rather ugly, de-grading, humorless and, worst of all, un-romantic . . . It's unfortunate. Yet I'm not against sex, nudity, or anything else that might be ticklish, so long as it's necessary to the plot and it can be presented with some degree of quality.

*Interview, San Francisco, pub. Sept. 28.*

**Bernard Delfont**
*Chairman, Electric &*
*Musical Industries, Ltd.*

It's quite wrong that the British film industry should be so dependent on Amer-ica. What happens if they (the Americans)

pull out, leaving us simply with studios? Take a film like "Oliver," or "Alfie," both of which were big hits. We call them British films, because all the talent in them was British. But where did the money go? Mostly to the (United) States.
*Interview, London, Jan. 20.*

**Robert Evans**
*Vice president for world production, Paramount Pictures Corporation*

We won't pay the money up front in huge salaries. We'll give small percentages of the gross from the first dollar. If an actor doesn't want to take the picture, we'll get someone else. The agents can scream all they want. I don't care what the agents say. No one will get six figure salaries any more. If an actor doesn't like the deal and doesn't want to take the picture, we'll get someone else. That's it.
*Los Angeles, pub. Nov. 17.*

**Federico Fellini**
*Director*

There are three things Americans don't like to do in Italy. First, they don't like to give money to Italians. Second, they like even less to give money to Italian movie producers. Third, they like least of all to give money to Federico Fellini . . .
*Interview, Rome, pub. March 2.*

When I choose someone for a role in my film, it doesn't matter to me whether he is an actor or not . . . The criterion I follow . . . has nothing to do with acting ability, past experience or fame of a person. I choose an actor because of his eyes, the way he looks, and because there is "something" about him—something that makes him the character in my film. After I have chosen him, anything he does, goes. He can't help but be right. Because he is the character.
*Interview, Rome, pub. Sept. 21.*

**Richard Fleischer**
*Director*

. . . (I am) definitely against censorship. It is indefensible because there is no way to define pornography . . . After all, who censors the censors? . . . Pornography is supposed to arouse sexual desires. If por-

nography is a crime, when will they arrest makers of perfume?
*Los Angeles, pub. Aug. 12.*

**Rhonda Fleming**
*Actress*

Most of the people in this business have backgrounds in which they craved attention and didn't get it. You stand in front of the camera and bare your soul and give everything you've got so you'll be loved and applauded.
*Interview, Los Angeles, pub. April 13.*

**Henry Fonda**
*Actor*

If people stop going to these (nudie) pictures, they (the producers) are going to stop making them. You can hardly blame the bastards making them—and they are bastards—because they're doing it for their own reasons. But if they make a pot, if people want to pay money to come to see this trash, you can't blame some people for wanting to make it and giving it to them.
*Hollywood, pub. Sept. 19.*

**John Fowles**
*Author*

It is axiomatic that movie actors never understand parts they are playing. They are highly artificial people, full of masks.
*Interview, Majorca, pub. Jan. 19.*

**James Franciscus**
*Actor*

There's no reason for actors appearing nude on the screen. I wouldn't agree to that under any circumstances. It doesn't prove anything. I'm not objecting to subject matter in movies. Nothing under the sun should be taboo. Puritanical thinking can ruin any art form. But delicate subjects should be treated with good taste.
*Interview, Los Angeles, pub. April 4.*

**John Frankenheimer**
*Director*

No one wants to lose money, but if I made a movie that everyone liked, I'd be in trouble. A film is a personalized thing. I ask myself, "Did I make this film for

(JOHN FRANKENHEIMER)

me or a commercial audience?". If the answer is in favor of the audience, then I'm in trouble.

*Interview, Los Angeles, pub. Feb. 10.*

## Mike Frankovich
*Producer*

Nobody can make a picture great—if it's not written on the page, it won't be on the screen. The real guts is in the writing. It's one thing you can't computerize; if you could, IBM would be the greatest producer in the business . . . What concerns me most . . . is that the motion picture business is being taken over by conglomerates; it's the greatest danger the business faces. What happens to the creative people?

*Interview, Los Angeles, pub. Feb. 23.*

The trouble with the business right now is that so many bad pictures have been made. The big problem is that picture-makers are not deciding what pictures to make . . . Jules Stein and Lew Wasserman are probably the smartest businessmen around. Yet somehow or other they've never found the right guys to decide what pictures are going to be made. Consequently, Universal hasn't done too well. Everyone should take a lesson from United Artists. They were taken over by Transamerica, but Transamerica had the good sense to let the movie-makers decide what to do. That's the secret right there.

*Interview, Los Angeles, pub. Aug. 10.*

## Ruth Gordon
*Actress*

They (movies) are coming to their new peak. They're getting with it. Take "Petulia." Knocked everybody for sixes. Fantastic. People ask me, "Did you understand it?" Silly question. I don't understand a telephone, but I enjoy it and use it.

*Interview, Beverely Hills, Calif., pub. Jan. 23.*

## Princess Grace of Monaco
*Formerly Grace Kelly, Actress*

I'm tired of seeing people take their clothes off. Too many films are made for the sophisticated city audience, and this makes up a very small percentage of people who see films.

*News conference, Quebec City, Feb. 9.*

## Lee Grant
*Actress*

I don't want a quickie love affair with the public. I want to keep working until I end up in the home for old actors with my friends . . . Those actresses who are "stars" and have their names above the title can get talked into a corner waiting out the right part and the right billing. It's idiocy sitting around waiting to be a star again, afraid of a come-down. By the time they have the part and billing they demand, all they care is how their hair was set and their mouth was shaped the particular year they last worked.

*Interview, Los Angeles, pub. Feb. 12.*

## Ralph R. Greenson
*Psychiatrist*

Actors for the most part make poor patients. *All* artists are difficult, but actors, and particularly successful ones, are almost impossible. When they work, their *hours* are impossible and when they *don't* work, *they* are impossible. I had one who said to me, "Well, you know, Doctor, if I get the Academy Award I'm not coming back."

*Interview, Beverly Hills, Calif., pub. Jan. 23.*

## Richard Harris
*Actor*

No actor—I don't care whether he's Richard Burton or Laurence Olivier—can act pain. You have to actually suffer it to make it look authentic.

*Interview, Los Angeles, pub. Feb. 20.*

## Anthony Harvey
*Director*

If the American film industry withdrew, there would be no film industry in England. I think there is every chance that they (U.S. film makers) will withdraw in five years. That is a grave danger.

*Interview, Los Angeles, Feb. 27.*

The best kind of film is the one that has been cut to the bone with not a single ounce of spare flesh on it.
*Interview, pub. March 16.*

. . . I think that the longer actors are in the profession, the more they value the traditional roles of the actor and director —in which the director directs and the actor takes direction. I think the more professional actors are, the more they want direction.
*Interview, Los Angeles, pub. April 16.*

### Edith Head
*Costume Designer*

Back in the thirties, if the star of the movie played a waitress, we had to dress her like a queen. Today, we would dress her like a waitress.
*Pub. March 18.*

### David Hemmings
*Actor*

The day of the million-dollar-per picture star is waning. Too many unknowns are making their presence felt, and for far less money. If the old type stars want to talk million dollar salaries, they should put their money where their mouth is and take a gamble along with the producers.
*Interview, Hollywood, pub. Oct. 26.*

### Charlton Heston
*Actor*

I am privately convinced that unless production costs are in some way held back, Hollywood's position as the leader of the international film making community is in jeopardy. I think it's an on-going and increasing problem.
*Interview, Los Angeles, July 15.*

It's important for an actor not to be associated with big losers. When you're in a picture that is budgeted at 7½ million and comes in at 9 or 10, that means a helluva lot of difference in what you have to bring in at the box office. To pay off a 7½ million picture requires a 15 million gross, and I can tell you there are damn few pictures that draw 15 million. And, if you are the star of a picture that lays a big bomb, that's when your collar gets tight. The bankers start saying, "Oh yes, he's the guy in the picture that lost all that money."
*Lihue, Hawaii, pub. Sept. 17.*

I don't agree with this new freedom in movies. I think it results in more freedom than art.
*Before House Communications Subcommittee, Washington, Nov. 24.*

### Alfred Hitchcock
*Director*

The root of the problem today is that telling a story on the screen is considered old hat among some prominent writers. Comedies still get stories. Drama, no. In its heyday, the power of our films reached the world. Now it has shrunk to special audiences. We're not really developing talent or people to handle films. We're making photographs of people talking.
*Interview, Los Angeles, pub. April 21.*

Some say that it's the dearth of big stars that is hurting the Hollywood film industry. I don't think so. It's rather a dearth of good plots. Writers now seem to think it's a sin to have a good story line, but I'm of the opinion that no plot means no film. Most of my films have been rattling good yarns.
*Interview, pub. Sept. 27.*

Violence on the screen increases violence in people only if those people already have sick minds. I once read somewhere that a man admitted killing three women, and he said he had killed the third woman after having seen "Psycho." Well, I wanted to ask him what movie he had seen before he killed the *second* woman. And then we'd ban that movie, don't you see? And then, if we found out that he'd had a glass of milk before he killed the *first* woman, why then we'd have to outlaw milk, too, wouldn't we? At the screening of "Psycho" a young boy came up to me—he was about 9 or 10—and he said to me, "What did you use for blood —chicken soup?" And I said, "No, I used chocolate sauce." And he said, "Thank you." The point is that he said what did you *use*. He knew it was a movie, that it was pretend.
*Interview, pub. Dec. 14.*

**Mort Hock**
*Vice president for advertising
and publicity,
Paramount Pictures Corporation*

The big change over the past three to five years has been bringing kids to American films . . . Today, when kids like a film, they over-buy . . . They repeat. They go back. They don't mind standing in line in rain or snow. When they want a picture, you can machine-gun them down and you can't keep them away.
*Interview, Los Angeles, pub. March 13.*

**Dustin Hoffman**
*Actor*

Movie stars affect everyone's lives in ways they don't even know. They even affect people who don't go to the movies. They set styles in clothes. They affect all sorts of behavior. They set life-style patterns. The "Hollywood Film" is probably the leading factor in the distortion of values this country has and is now looking at with some perspective. That's dangerous.
*Interview, Hollywood, pub. Oct. 26.*

**Rock Hudson**
*Actor*

What do I think of dirty pictures? Well, I better think pretty well of at least one of them—"The Hornet's Nest," which I made in Italy. In it I use four-letter words, beat up and rape my co-star, Sylva Koscina, and generally behave like any good World War II soldier shouldn't. It's like Doris Day going into the cast of "Oh! Calcutta!"
*Interview, Beverly Hills, Calif.,
pub. Dec. 14.*

**Ross Hunter**
*Producer*

There has been an influx of pornography, sex and nudity (in motion pictures). They were dragged in by the heels. Stay away from those pictures. If the buyer isn't there, the picture won't stay. I'm on a soap box about good, clean, wholesome entertainment. Down with the other sort of stuff, I say. Up with good films.
*At Celebrity Luncheon of Stagehands,
Minneapolis, pub. March 5.*

**George Hurrell**
*Motion Picture Still Photographer*

Working on a movie now is like being a combat photographer. In the old days, stars *liked* to have their pictures taken. The studio had a regular portrait gallery and it took hours to make six or seven great shots. Now you run around with a camera and take what you can get.
*Interview, Los Angeles, pub. June 1.*

**Kenneth Hyman**
*Executive vice president
in charge of world-wide production,
Warner Bros.-Seven Arts*

People who claim to know say that it's easier and cheaper working abroad. It is cheaper, but it takes longer and in the end the cost evens out. The only difference is some governments subsidize a film. We are also told that shooting far away from the home office makes it easier for a producer to rob us blind on the budget. Frankly, I don't think most producers are bright enough to steal. Half of them don't even know how to produce. What we need—and Hollywood needs most of all—are men who know how to make films.
*Interview, Hollywood, pub. Aug. 3.*

**William Inge**
*Playwright*

The American writer is the least respected member of the movie producing unit. When "Come Back Little Sheba" was turned into a film and premiered in New York, there was a party. This was in 1951. My agent insisted that I take her; I didn't want to go myself. But we went. Well, you know I couldn't find a place to sit at that party. The cameras were flashing, but no one took a picture of me. I could hear my agent saying quietly to people, "He's the writer; he wrote the play." But no one was interested . . . And in Hollywood they all want to have a feeling of creation. Everyone involved in a successful film wants part of the success. It hurts them to think a play had a success before it came to Hollywood. A big name writer frightens them in Hollywood.
*At Pacific Coast Writers conference,
Los Angeles, pub. Aug. 24.*

I think there is one basic thing that accounts for a good successful film, and that's a story that the writer and director believe in . . . I think it's the faith in what you're doing that makes successes.

*Interview, pub. Dec. 30.*

**Anne Jackson**
*Actress*

I don't know whether they'll sell the studios, but it looks that way. And it's sad. The other day I said to this darling little driver I have at MGM, "Do you want to go somewhere with me?" We toured the lot, and I saw the house Scarlett lived in. I saw the little cottage Garbo lived in. I saw the house Andy Hardy lived in. And I cried . . .

*Interview, Beverly Hills, Calif.,*
*pub. Nov. 9.*

**Allen Jenkins**
*Actor*

I don't want to sound like a crotchity old man, but I refuse to pay $4 or $5 to look at films showing unpleasant people doing unpleasant things. The theatre and the movies should be places of illusion.

*Pub. March 30.*

**David N. Judelson**
*President, Gulf & Western Industries*

Let me put to rest once and for all some recent rumors and speculation: Gulf and Western is not—I repeat not—going to sell Paramount . . . The movie business is undergoing rapid and revolutionary change, and we intend that Paramount will be in the vanguard of that revolution.

*Before stockholders,*
*South Bend, Ind., Dec. 9.*

**Garson Kanin**
*Playwright*

(Movies)—they've become more dissociated from show business and more a part of the life of the audience. I think, honestly, the most important thing that's happened to change the whole climate and empathy of film-making is that the audience has become more sophisticated, knowledgeable and imaginative . . . The change in the audience has made it far more interesting to work in films.

*Interview, Beverly Hills, Calif.,*
*pub. Oct. 5.*

**Elia Kazan**
*Director, Author*

When I wrote the book ("The Arrangement") I thought it couldn't be filmed. After substantial financial offers, I decided it could be filmed.

*News conference, New York,*
*pub. Dec. 7.*

**Shirley Knight**
*Actress*

I've been sent five or six scripts in the past month—and every single one of them has had the same distinguishing features. First, it is required that you appear in the nude. This is, without question, essential. Secondly, you must perform, on stage or screen, some sort of equivalent to the sex act. And thirdly, you must use quite a few dirty words. I'm not a prude, but I just don't want to do any of this. I don't understand what it's all supposed to mean, and I begin to think that everyone has gone a bit mad.

*Interview, New York, pub. Nov. 23.*

**Stanley Kramer**
*Producer, Director*

Frankly, the people in the (Motion Picture) Academy don't know what the hell they're voting for. Not any more than a clothing salesman from Dayton, Ohio.

*Pub. April 15.*

As for many of the new films, my feeling is that technique covers a multitude of sins. I don't think they're any nearer the truth than any of the rest of us have been . . . Walking out of some pictures today, one has odd feelings. You ask yourself, "Is there something in this we can believe in, have faith in?" It's an emotional thing, but I think too many pictures today fail to give us something to reach for.

*Interview, Los Angeles, pub. Oct. 19.*

**Burt Lancaster**
*Actor*

I think the concern about violence (in motion pictures) is absurd. Violence is an innate part of man. I think the movies are another way to let off steam.

*New York, pub. Sept. 9.*

**Fritz Lang**
*Director*

In Europe, where there may be an emperor, a king or a Hitler, the hero may be a superman, but in a democracy he must be John Doe. You have got to have the audience identify with the plight of the hero—make it feel, "Here but for the grace of God, go I."
*Interview, Beverly Hills, Calif., pub. Feb. 27.*

**Sergio Leone**
*Director*

The western setting presents characters and society in their most primitive form. Westerns will always be popular. They'll be making them 50 years from now.
*Pub. April 2.*

**Jerry Lewis**
*Actor-Comedian-Director*

Critics? If I was making films for them I'd be playing to empty houses. The fans are my critics. They don't have typewriters, but they're the ones I work for.
*Interview, London, pub. Oct. 26.*

Every night I say a special prayer to Captain Kangaroo—because the people who watch him are my audience, too.
*Pub. Dec. 14.*

**Sidney Lumet**
*Director*

It's the unions that are killing (this) business. I wanted to bring Carlo di Palma, the man who shot "Blow-Up" and "Red Desert," over from Italy for a picture, but the unions wouldn't allow it. In the East, we have to hire a New York stand-by for James Wong Howe because he's a member of the California union. Here in Louisiana, Howe has to have a stand-by from the Chicago union. Each stand-by costs a *minimum* of $625 a week just to stand around. The insanity of unions is going to have to be challenged in court. They've made it impossible for me to make any movie for less than three-quarters of a million dollars. It's death for the cameraman and agony for the director. The only thing you can do is have a sense of humor.
*Interview, Baton Rouge, La., pub. June 8.*

**Joseph L. Mankiewicz**
*Writer-Director-Producer*

A film academy that includes financiers and publicity men and does not include Fellini, Bergman and Truffaut can hardly be called an academy. Somewhere there should be a place where film creators decide for themselves matters of merit.
*Pub. April 25.*

Most of the screenwriting today could very well be written on a fence. I think it's a pity that a certain wit and a certain indirection and a certain style of writing have gone. Audiences have been conditioned no longer to listen to the screen but merely to look at it. The screenplay today has to be constructed to assault the eyes . . . I believe in the word and the realities of the word and the power of the word and the suggestion of the word. I can't tell you how many women look better with sweaters on than they do with sweaters off. And I think that the same can be said of a lot of scenes in scripts.
*Interview, pub. Dec. 30.*

**Delbert Mann**
*Director*

Great European actors have a much more healthy attitude than ours. They've no hesitancy about appearing in a small but juicy part in a TV film, while our big-name actors feel insulted if you offer them such a part. They haven't our star-status pretensions.
*Interview, Los Angeles, pub. March 20.*

**Walter Matthau**
*Actor*

Producers are creatures of whatever happened yesterday. When they try films with unknowns and lose $50 million, they'll go back to using good actors.
*Interview, Los Angeles, pub. Dec. 22.*

**Albert McCleery**
*Television producer*

Every time you read a book on the history of films, they go back and talk about the wonderful days when Mack Sennett turned out a comedy a week. One way to stop the present cost squeeze is to let someone else do it again.

*Interview, pub. Nov. 21.*

**John L. McClellan**
*United States Senator, D-Ark.*

It has been said that movies merely reflect our current morality and values, but I believe they also strongly influence it. Casual infidelity, couples living together outside marriage, and unnatural personal relationships are depicted sympathetically while the spiritual values and traditions cherished by most of our citizens are ignored or not infrequently portrayed in a manner likely to promote doubts as to their creditability . . . The widespread presentation of such themes may well exert a more insidious influence on the development of young people than the more discussed shock films with graphic scenes of sexual activity, or unnecessary violence.

*Before the Senate, Washington, Sept. 22.*

**Roddy McDowall**
*Actor*

I absolutely adore movies. Even bad ones. I don't like pretentious ones, but a good bad movie, you must admit, is great.

*London, pub. Sept. 16.*

**Patrick McGoohan**
*Actor*

This pornography stuff is for the birds. There'll be a return to stories that have real adventure, or we're all finished.

*Interview, Culver City, Calif., pub. Nov. 14.*

**Steve McQueen**
*Actor*

This is the end of an era, the beginning of the end of movie stars. The people of our time are going to be the people of the future—heroes, not stars . . . Stars sell tickets now only when they're in good pictures. The visual experience is the thing, and reality is absolutely necessary.

*Interview, Los Angeles, pub. Sept. 21.*

**Russ Meyer**
*Producer, Director*

The name of the game is box-office—

getting as many fannies on the seats as possible. All I have to sell is my name. People see it and know what to expect. At "The Killing of Sister George," people sat through 80 minutes of boredom to see one very erotic scene at the end. In my films, they don't have to wait.

*Interview, Los Angeles, pub. Dec. 21.*

**Yvette Mimieux**
*Actress*

The cornerstone of a good film is and always has been a good script, then finding the right director for it. What sometimes happens with potentially good properties is that the filmmakers get so involved with the financing that they have no recourse but to push it through to completion even though added work on the script or necessary retakes are indicated.

*Interview, New York, pub. Feb. 5.*

**Liza Minnelli**
*Actress, Singer*

(Otto Preminger's) theory is that an actor is hired to act and must be ready at all times. He wants the work done immediately and perfectly. You get the impression with Otto that you don't have time to ask questions; and you come in and don't ask, and if you do it wrong you get yelled at. It's like teachers. There are some who correct you by saying, "It would be better this way," and others who just say, "That's *wrong!*" And Otto is, uh, the latter. But now, when it's over, you forget that. You just think, "I have made a picture with Otto Preminger."

*Interview, New York, pub. Dec. 7.*

**Vincente Minnelli**
*Director*

I approach every picture as if I had never done one before. I think of what is good only for that picture and nothing else in the world.

*Interview, Los Angeles, pub. Feb. 14.*

**Walter M. Mirisch**
*President, The Mirisch Company*

Just putting big stars into pictures doesn't mean automatic success. On the other hand, putting big stars into quality

(WALTER M. MIRISCH)

films may mean added value. Those stars got where they are because they could deliver a performance, and if you need the quality they can offer, then you'd better hire them.

*Interview, Los Angeles, pub. Nov. 17.*

**George Murphy**
*United States Senator, R-Calif.*

Consider that on an average day, 10.5 million people in foreign countries see an American film. There are 3.7 billion admissions to foreign theatres to see such films each year. These motion pictures clearly rise above barriers of languages and nationality in showing America to the world, and they occupy more than half the screen time in foreign theatres. No other American medium or industry reaches so many persons abroad.

*Before the Senate, Washington,*
*pub. March 17.*

**Don Murray**
*Actor*

I won't do any of that James Bond sort of thing—those dopey spies. And I won't do any of those "Our Man Flint" kind of pictures. Those heroes are sick; they're crazy; the values are insane; *the pictures are crazy.* I don't see how anyone can stand to make them. They're just . . . a combination of masochism and fake sex; ersatz sex. We're afraid of real sex. A movie about real sex would be great. But what passes for sex is really just down-home-Yankee business sense. They know the kind of peep show the public will pay to see and they give it to them. And the less real it is, the better.

*Interview, pub. Aug. 9.*

**Paul Newman**
*Actor*

There must be something wrong with a group (the Motion Picture Academy) that hands out awards and then has to send telegrams saying, please come.

*Pub. April 25.*

**Mike Nichols**
*Director*

When I direct, I always keep in mind what happens in real life, not what it will look like on the screen. Tell life as it is, or make fun of life as it is. That's all there is to it.

*Interview, Los Angeles, pub. Jan. 16.*

. . . more and more I believe that talents and abilities, gifts of this kind, are just given—and not earned or bought. They're just given for a short time and then taken away. You see it with actors all the time. You tell an actor to play a scene and he'll bring tears to your eyes . . . And in another ten years he may not be able to do anything like it again. It comes and it goes. And I think that movie directors may have their gifts for a shorter span than most.

*Interview, Guayamas, Mexico,*
*pub. April 7.*

It seems to me that the highest achievement in a film is for no technique to be visible at all.

*Pub. July 4.*

I'm not aware of belonging to any school or category of directing. I don't think any director has been. It's the news magazines who like to lump actors, writers, directors and even industries into categories. People aren't abstractions. Directors don't represent the young, the old, the poor, black humor and all the rest. Sometimes critics and others think of directors as ball teams, rooting for one or against the other as if we were in competition. It's ridiculous.

*Interview, Los Angeles, pub. July 27.*

The hardest thing about making movies is getting up in the morning.

*Pub. Aug. 24.*

**James H. Nicholson**
*President, American-International Pictures*

We operate under what you could call the Woolworth Doctrine. We're the dime store operators of the movie business.

*Interview, Los Angeles, pub. Dec. 14.*

**George Pal**
*Writer, Producer*

There are a lot of jokes about rigid story formulas—jokes about the story conference table and how every idea has to fit the formula of all other pictures. This is not true, and, if it were, Hollywood would never have to pay the salaries it does for writers and other creative people.

*Los Angeles, pub. Jan. 31.*

**Sam Peckinpah**
*Director*

I got sick and tired of people talking about violence who knew nothing about it. It's ugly and revolting and yet strangely beautiful. I wished (in "The Wild Bunch") to draw the audience in with this strange kind of beauty, get them hooked on it, make them realize that they were enjoying it and make them realize, too, this frighteningly real aspect of their own nature.

*pub. Dec. 14.*

**Eric Pleskow**
*Vice president,*
*United Artists Corporation*

The Italians and the French don't want to be confined to seeing a film at a specific time on a specific date. They're impulse buyers. An Italian, on his way to a movie, may see a pretty girl and never get to the theatre.

*Interview, New York, pub. Jan. 22.*

**Sidney Poitier**
*Actor*

The films are finding it necessary to stay on their toes because the audience is 13 to 25 years old and it's hip. They're not going to be had by old 1940s and 1950s ideas. If they're going to be won, it's going to be by exciting reflections of the world they live in. They're not going to be sold the impression that they live in anything but a multi-racial society . . . The kids say you have to make the world spiritually, morally and ethically better. With that transfer of values, it forces on the motion picture industry a new code of ethics.

*Interview, Hollywood, pub. Feb. 2.*

**Roman Polanski**
*Director*

. . . but how is the censor going to protect people against all the things they might find kinky? Some people find shoes stimulating. Do the censors want actors to work in their (bare) feet?

*Interview, London, Jan. 13.*

**Louis H. Polk, Jr.**
*President, Metro-Goldwyn-Mayer*

. . . I believe that film—or the fluid medium, as Marshall McLuhan calls it—is one of the most exciting communications methods in the world today. Its impact reaches not only throughout this country, but throughout the world, and its impact on the value structures of our societies is immense. While I have a great respect for the printed word, no medium has the power to move its audience so immediately and so completely as film.

*New York, Jan. 14.*

A great film with values has an impact on society more significant than another box of Wheaties—however sacrilegious that sounds to the flour industry.

*Interview, Culver City, Calif.,*
*pub. Feb. 23.*

The movie companies have lost control of their product. They don't develop their own actors any more, don't develop directors, don't develop writers. Instead of using packagers, they're at the packagers' mercy.

*Pub. June 30.*

**Michael J. Pollard**
*Actor*

. . . When I got into acting, Rock Hudson was a leading man. Now Dusty (Hoffman) doesn't look like Rock Hudson. And I don't look like Doris Day.

*Interview, New York, pub. March 16.*

**Stefanie Powers**
*Actress*

. . . the politics in this business, all the garbage that goes on . . . girls sleeping with producers, being seen at the right parties with the right people at the right time . . . I'm not a part of all that; I can't play those games. Maybe I don't get as many parts as I would if I did go along with them, but at least I can say that nobody owes me any favors, and I don't owe any, either.

*Interview, London, pub. Sept. 14.*

**Otto Preminger**
*Producer, Director*

Young people liked my film ("Skidoo").

(OTTO PREMINGER)

It's old people who didn't like it—and they'll die soon.
*Interview, Manchester, Mass., pub. Aug. 17.*

## Vincent Price
*Actor*

I take the making of pictures seriously. It's hard to make the unbelievable believable, and that's what we have to do. It's also hard not to break up while you're doing it. When Herbert Marshall and I were filming "The Fly," we had to do one of the scenes back to back, because every time we looked at each we fell apart. It was about this fly, you see, with a human head. Well, I *ask* you . . .
*Interview, London, pub. Nov. 30.*

## Robert Radnitz
*Producer*

. . . we have an obligation to provide movies for all segments of the population . . . In time, they (filmmakers) will exhaust their audiences because people will tire of films. What's happened is that none of the studios, except Disney, is equipped to market a family picture.
*Interview, New York, pub. Feb. 5.*

I'm convinced that even with the best will imaginable, the motion picture companies prefer not to get into the area of family films . . .
*Interview, Los Angeles, pub. May 25.*

Many people look at the MPAA rating code as a blanket under which dirty films can be made, and I believe that's true . . . If the purpose of the code was to obviate censorship legislation, it's a failure. We are closer to government intervention than we've ever been.
*Pub. June 18.*

## Martin Ransohoff
*Chairman, Filmways, Inc.*

The industry has to be overhauled, and not just by firing secretaries, closing executive dining rooms and throwing out pencil sharpeners—the whole damn industry . . . Everybody has to sit down and be-come realistic, because it isn't any single thing you can point to. It's just plain that the goddamn pictures cost too much, and some means has to be found to come to grips with that. The whole industry has to be restructured.
*Los Angeles, pub. Oct. 30.*

## Ronald Reagan
*Governor of California*

I think the motion picture business is killing itself off . . . What writing does it take to simply have two people undress and get into bed? Call me a square if you want to, but I think the business has degenerated.
*Interview, Sacramento, pub. Oct. 4.*

## Lee Remick
*Actress*

. . . technique is when you can look at the rushes and say to yourself that you've maintained the mood of the character for three days before the camera, while you yourself have felt three different ways.
*Interview, Los Angeles, pub. March 2.*

## Jean Renoir
*Director*

They (the French intellectual film makers) are always talking about "culture." What do they mean by culture? Films are made for people, not college professors. A film's first duty has always been, and still remains, to tell a story. All the rest is window trimming.
*Interview, Paris, Jan. 7.*

## Debbie Reynolds
*Actress*

I don't want to do the movies they're doing these days. Maybe it's realism but, in my opinion, it's utter filth. I even have my own production company and I looked for properties to buy. I wouldn't waste my money on such garbage.
*Interview, Culver City, Calif., pub. June 2.*

## Julian S. Rifkin
*President, National Association of Theatre Owners*

I'm not saying they (motion pictures) shouldn't have nudity. I think realistic pictures are our only hope of continuance of living as an industry. The excesses are what I'm afraid of—the gratuitous ones where they put them in just to have them. When they (sex scenes) are part of the story, part of the action, I think it's great. I'm just against anything that's put in for sensationalism.

*Interview, Hollywood, June 11.*

If a picture is successful, it is a false presumption that this is probably the prototype of what our public has been waiting for and (that) many more of that ilk should be made.

*Washington, pub. Nov. 10.*

**Cliff Robertson**
*Actor*

When you've been in the business as long as I have, you believe every award is an award for all your efforts, not just one picture. It makes you think that maybe you've been doing something right all these years.

*Interview, Los Angeles, pub. March 11.*

**George Sanders**
*Actor*

It really makes no difference nowadays what role one plays. Modern pictures in general are very difficult to understand for old timers. It is a question of going from one incomprehensible picture to another.

*Rome, pub. May 31.*

**Maximilian Schell**
*Actor*

. . . I think a good producer's job ends the first day of shooting. He should gather the property, the talent, and take care of financial details, but then leave the filmmaking to the filmmakers . . .

*Interview, New York, pub. March 12.*

**Lalo Schifrin**
*Composer*

. . . in movies, the music is very important. It is not true that the best film music you don't hear. What is on film is one part, one entity; the music is another entity. When you put the two of them together, you have something that is more than their sum. It is—what's the word?—alchemy.

*Interview, Los Angeles, pub. March 14.*

**John Schlesinger**
*Director*

. . . the majority of films still are made by people who are asked to do them. It's not so easy to go into some companies and say, "Look, I've got a great idea; will you do it?" But they are doing it more, because they're finding that the old theories don't quite work. There is a growing audience for something that deals more truthfully with life.

*Pub. Sept. 22.*

**Ronald Shedlo**
*Producer*

The obligation nowadays is to keep the film business alive. I think that is the foremost obligation. The film business is going to stay alive only as long as we can control costs. Hollywood technicians and their unions are going to have to work out some basis by which films can be made reasonably. And agents, producers, actors, directors—everybody down the line —are going to have to cut their costs.

*Hollywood, pub. Aug. 26.*

**William Shiffrin**
*Talent Agent*

If it's a good picture with a star, you'll make more money. If it's a bad picture with unknowns, you're dead. With a star, you might conceivably recoup your costs. Exhibitors say, first, "Who's in it?"

*Los Angeles, pub. Sept. 20.*

**Don Siegel**
*Director*

I don't make my pictures for the young or the old or the studio. I make them for myself. Fortunately, what I like seems to appeal to audiences and the studio. When the day dawns that the films I make for myself don't, then I'm out of business.

*Interview, pub. Dec. 14.*

**Sterling Silliphant**
*Writer, Producer*

God knows we neglected the Negro for

(STERLING SILLIPHANT)

so many years in our films—unless we showed him carrying in our bourbon or his knees knocking as he passed a cemetery—that we have every reason now to smother him in the rush to compensate and atone. If only that's what it was—compassion and atonement. But, instead, I fear, there's more tokenism than atonement, more exploitation than compensation.

*Interview, Los Angeles, pub. Jan. 23.*

## Milton Sperling
*Producer*

It's becoming increasingly clear that the star system has virtually disappeared, and that, whereas before, major studios would go into a deal if a star were connected with a picture, today their tendency is to go into a deal if a director is connected with it. In other words, the director has become a key ingredient in insuring the studio of its investment . . . Today, the kids who go to the theatres not only know Fellini and Antonioni, but they know Schlesinger and Arthur Penn and a handful of others. The directors' names are becoming star names to the audiences in America. The director, in the minds of the public, is an important creative ingredient in the picture. And since there are no stars in the film, the director is the star.

*Hollywood, pub. Sept. 23.*

## Blaze Starr
*Exotic Dancer*

There was a day when a man could get a thrill watching a pretty girl go through her dance routine in a g-string. Now a stripper in a g-string stirs the blood about as much as a mid-Victorian dame in five layers of petticoats. Why should you come to a strip joint to get a suggestion of sex when you can go to a movie down the street and see the whole thing in the raw?

*Pub. Oct. 19.*

## Rod Steiger
*Actor*

I think some of the people who go to movies are more intelligent than the people who make them.

*Interview, Los Angeles, pub. April 2.*

## Raymond Stross
*Producer*

If it weren't for the film editors, I'd be in an awful mess.

*At American Cinema Editors Awards, Los Angeles, March 15.*

## Lawrence Turman
*Producer*

I'm a nervous filmmaker, full of second thoughts. A film is rather like a color television set: You've got to fiddle with it until it's right.

*Interview, Los Angeles, pub. Nov. 9.*

## Oliver Unger
*Vice chairman,*
*Commonwealth United Corporation*

The production of motion pictures is a risk endeavor. That risk should now be shared. We share our profit via release terms. Perhaps the time has arrived that you should cushion our risk, share our losses as you participate in our gains . . . Perhaps it is time for all of us to realize that popcorn is as much a negotiable commodity as the admission paid at the box-office.

*Before National Association of Theatre Owners, Washington, Nov. 12.*

## Peter Ustinov
*Actor*

The things that really make money are pictures that start trends—trend setters. The people who lose money are the trend followers, because they can't find the formula. They know the ingredients, but they can't find the formula . . . I actually heard an executive say the other day that what we're looking for now is the ugly leading man. The idea of searching for an ugly leading man because of the success of one or two is so absurd—as if ugliness itself is a virtue. They're all searching for ugly leading men or dirty clean pictures.

*Interview, Los Angeles, pub. Dec. 11.*

## Jack Valenti
*President, Motion Picture*
*Association of America*

If censors should be set loose upon the land to curb the freedom of the motion picture, can anyone seriously believe that any medium—newspaper or magazine, radio or tv—could much longer be safe? Or any individual?

*Before Inland Daily Press Association,*
*Chicago, Feb. 24.*

There is no shortage of so-called family films—merely a shortage of family audiences . . . People who complain most about sex and violence in films rarely if ever go to the movies.

*London, pub. May 2.*

Our research makes clear that there is a correlation between education and those who go to the movies. The more a man is educated, the more he sees movies as an alternative to television.

*Before National Film Carriers,*
*New York, May 15.*

In movies, for the first time, there is an exploration of human aberrations—homosexuality, lesbianism, and even sodomy—there's an audience for that. Some of this is being done by genuine artists eager to explore what was previously forbidden, and others are just out to hoke up the box office.

*Before Foreign Correspondents Club*
*of Japan, Tokyo, pub. June 11.*

(The rating system's) sole reason for being is to inform parents about the kind of movie playing in their community (and) about the acceptability of the content of the movie as it concerns children. Nothing else. We don't rate for quality or lack of it. We don't rate for adults. We don't censor and we don't ban, because to do either would be contrary to constitutional safeguards as well as common sense.

*At annual meeting, MPAA,*
*Phoenix, July 1.*

The producer or director who inserts senseless violence and useless sex in his film so that he can hoke up the box office is a faker and a fraud and he ought to be

so labled in print and out of print. The critic who pillages every crevice of his integrity so that he may be accounted intellectually "with it," and who describes as art what ought to be quarantined, is surely part of the general air of hypocrisy . . . Blood and brutality, nudity that gets entwined—like fornication on the screen—foul language . . . these are the last, gasping cries of the inept filmmaker as he drowns, talentless, in a sea of mediocrity.

*Before Los Angeles Press Club,*
*pub. Aug. 26.*

There is no persuasive evidence that movies cause juvenile delinquency. Young people whose parents have given them solid, deep-rooted values . . . will never be corrupted by anybody or anything. More of life, good and bad, is to be learned on the playground and in the schoolyard than in the theatre. If my own son goes wrong, it will be my fault, not the Bijou Theatre.

*Before Los Angeles Press Club,*
*pub. Sept. 1.*

## Luchino Visconti
*Director*

I was very happy going to Hollywood. It was like going into a pavilion at a world's fair—it was such a different world. I said then I could never work there, and I still couldn't. In Hollywood, filming is a group effort; here it is individual. We have our Hollywood-style producers here—DeLaurentiis and Ponti—but I couldn't work with them either. Neither can Fellini. He tried. He told me that every morning, as he drove to DeLaurentii's office, he would reach a certain turn in the road and would be so terrorized that he wanted to turn around and run. He never finished the picture.

*Interview, Rome, pub. June 8.*

## Ray Wagner
*Producer*

Whatever the myth is, making a movie is not a joy. It's miserable. It's awful . . . Doing a film is like being in love. The pain must be worth it, or it must be worth the pain. If you're going to com-

(RAY WAGNER)

mit two years of your life, or more, you'd better care going in, really care.

*Interview, Los Angeles, pub. Jan. 21.*

## Ron Waller
*Producer, Director*

I firmly believe that in order to get anywhere in this town (Hollywood) you HAVE to start at the top.

*Pub. Jan. 7.*

## Lew R. Wasserman
*President,*
*Music Corporation of America*

I don't think it is a fair statement to say that the star thing is knocked down at all. That's what's wrong with Hollywood. People are always talking in bunches. "They" say this. "They" say that. Who is "they?" They say you don't need studios. They say you don't need stars. They say all you have to do is give a man a camera and he can make a picture. I don't know what they mean.

*Interview, Hollywood,*
*pub. Nov. 26.*

## John Wayne
*Actor*

When people say, "A John Wayne picture got bad reviews," I always wonder if they know it's a redundant sentence. Hell, I don't care. People like my pictures, and that's all that counts.

*Interview, Durango, Mexico,*
*pub. April 13.*

All the *real* motion picture people have always made *family* pictures. But the downbeats and the so-called intelligentsia got in when the government stupidly split up the production companies and the theatres. The old giants—Mayer, Thalberg, even Harry Cohn (despite the fact that personally I couldn't stand him)—were good for this industry. Now the goddamned stock manipulators have taken over. They don't know a goddamned thing about making movies. They make something dirty, and it makes money, and they say, "Jesus, let's make one a little dirtier, maybe it'll make more money." And now

even the bankers are getting their noses into it.

*Interview, Newport Beach, Calif.,*
*pub. June 29.*

## Dennis Weaver
*Actor*

Actors are going to have to prove themselves to be as individual and creative as new producers and directors are . . . The day is past when even a successful stage, screen or TV personality can expect to be carried along on the strength of what he has done in the past. The business is growing more intimate. The hits are being made by the people doing their own thing.

*Interview, Beverly Hills, Calif.,*
*pub. Sept. 21.*

## Raquel Welch
*Actress*

The whole sex goddess thing and glamour image is a bit of an anachronism—because we don't make movies about sex goddesses anymore. It almost doesn't apply to what the film industry is today. We just don't have Harlows, Garbos, Dietrichs and women who were in films almost primarily for the way they looked. And there's no call for it. I think the audiences today are far too sophisticated for it. Yes, they like to see attractive people in their films; but they also want to see humanity and be able to identify with them in some degree.

*Pub. November.*

## Jesse White
*Actor*

Jack Albertson has opened the door for all of us. Jack, when he won that Oscar, did more to convince producers in town that comedy supporting actors can really act. It takes an earthquake sometimes before these guys will take a chance on us.

*Interview, Los Angeles, April 28.*

## Stuart Whitman
*Actor*

The hardest thing about being a star is that you feel one step apart from humanity. You walk into a restaurant and get the best table—that's beautiful. But to walk down the street and not be able to be part of the crowd—man, that can really drive you up the wall!

*Interview, London, pub. Dec. 21.*

**Michael Winner**
*Director*

I discovered in Austria that filmmakers should always go to a country with a proud people in it. You can always use that pride because they're ashamed to refuse to do something. You say, "You fall down that mountainside" . . . and the fact that when they've finished falling they're carried off in an ambulance doesn't really worry them.

*Interview, London, pub. March 30.*

**Robert Wise**
*Producer, Director*

The important thing to me is to get as large an audience as I can. Not just for the commercial reasons. Those are important, obviously, because if we don't pay for our negatives we don't keep on making films. But even more so, if you have some message or a theme that you feel is important, that you feel audiences should get, it's only as good as the number of people that see it. And if you make something that is so small and personal that 200 people rather than 200,000 are going to be interested, then I don't think it's worthwhile. I think you've failed somehow.

*Interview, pub. Dec. 30.*

**Natalie Wood**
*Actress*

I think what's happening in Hollywood is terrific. I think it's in its healthiest phase. Once we're over this slight hurdle, this preoccupation with nudity, everything will be fine. Even that's curved around: You used to read about who would do a nude scene, and now you read about who doesn't do them.

*Interview, Los Angeles, pub. Oct. 30.*

**William Wyler**
*Director*

When a director is showing off, it's lousy. When they try to attract attention to themselves at the expense of the story and acting by camera tricks, it's lousy . . . I know the temptations, because I was a young director, myself, and tried to attract attention to myself. If you're a pro, you exercise discipline and don't try to distract attention from the story. Get it?

It's important for pictures, like the press, to make a comment on social issues of the times we live in, but only in the form of entertainment . . . Everything comes down to how it is done. If one feels the propaganda, it's no good.

*Interview, Los Angeles, pub. Dec. 17.*

**Bud Yorkin**
*Producer*

I think you're doomed as a motion picture maker if the only reason you go into a picture is that you think it will do well. You might as well get out of the business . . . Our point of view is, (1) we want to do it and, (2) we hope it will make money.

*Los Angeles, pub. Aug. 4.*

**Darryl F. Zanuck**
*President, 20th Century-Fox*
*Film Corporation*

. . . the cinema has not yet reached the age of reason. When the craze for monotonous eroticism overshoots the mark, we shall go back to the Bible or to pure romantic love, or even to a new version of Cleopatra . . .

*Interview, Paris, pub. May 14.*

**Richard Zanuck**
*President, 20th Century-Fox*
*Film Corporation*

If you look at some of the pictures this year, and last, that really cleaned up, you'll note that they're not by the big stars, for the most part. "Bonnie and Clyde"—nobody'd heard of Warren Beatty, really. He'd made a few flops before. Nobody'd heard of Faye Dunaway. Big hit. "Rosemary's Baby" had Mia Farrow. She'd been in 500 episodes of "Peyton Place," but nobody was that excited. It's the picture. Look at "Goodbye, Columbus." Nobody's in it; it's a big hit. Look at "The Graduate," a fantastic hit. Nobody ever

(RICHARD ZANUCK)

heard of Dustin Hoffman before. So when you're planning a picture you can say, "Wait a minute. I think this subject is as good as "The Graduate" or "Bonnie and Clyde," we don't have to spend a million dollars for so-and-so. Let's find our own Dustin Hoffman.

We've all had our flops. But the interesting thing that's always baffled me is if you make a lot of little flops you can get run out of the business. If you make big, smashing flops, you can keep going longer. A big flop creates more waves. Your name is in the limelight, but a little tiny flop gets buried. The most successful failures in the business have made millions. The key has been that they made gigantic flops. They've always been associated with big stars, big projects.

*Interview, Hollywood, pub. Aug. 24.*

## MUSIC

**Claudio Abbado**
*Conductor*

. . . it is nonsense to think that the orchestra will become an archive; composers, bad and good, are always producing. And, since the public is always slower in its development, the orchestra will always be 50 years ahead of public taste. Works by Hindemith, Webern and Alban Berg are still strange to today's concert audience.

*Pub. Feb. 21.*

**Ed Ames**
*Singer*

What I object to in rock is the monotony; every group copies every other group. I gag on the sameness. My personal taste is classical; it takes genius and discipline to write. Rock, an off-shoot of jazz, is instinctive expression, totally devoid of discipline. But then, today it's not the music, but the words, that are important.

*Interview, San Francisco, pub. Oct. 26.*

**Harry Belafonte**
*Singer*

I hold an audience to be a performer's greatest strength and ego-builder. A composer or painter can be discovered a hundred years from now and live on in memory. A live entertainer has only the now, and an audience by which to gauge his successes and failures.

*Interview, Las Vegas, pub. Sept. 14.*

**Marilyn Bergman**
*Music Lyricist*

Up until recently, almost every song dealt in one variation or another with love. Today, one can write about eyebrows if he pleases, that's how open the music industry is. The fences are down, anything and everything goes.

*Interview, Los Angeles, pub. Feb. 3.*

**Leonard Bernstein**
*Musical Director,*
*New York Philharmonic Orchestra*

. . . when I was growing up and observing conductors like Koussevitzky at their prime, there was still the last vestige of some kind of symphonic bloodstream flowing. There was still Copland's "Third Symphony," and Stravinsky and Shostakovich and Prokofiev. And then, suddenly, by the end of the war, it was all over. There is nothing left now, there is nobody to champion. The music director of a symphonic orchestra organization has nothing to do but guard the masterpieces of the past.

*Interview, Berlin, pub. Feb. 21.*

**Leonard Bernstein**
*Former Musical Director,*
*New York Philharmonic Orchestra*

I don't think there's any lack of musical talent among black people. But many young blacks, musically gifted, still to this day demur at the prospect of what lies ahead—the long, hard years of study coupled with a defeatist notion, "I'll never make it anyway and some people are against me."

*Before New York City Commission on Human Rights, Sept. 29.*

**Pierre Boulez**
*Incoming Musical Director,*
*New York Philharmonic Orchestra*

The idea of electronics as the big future of music is just an American trick of fashion . . . Playing Bach on the computer doesn't interest me at all because it's artistically irrelevant. All this indicates a simplistic way of thinking—an appallingly low level of thinking . . .

*Interview, pub. March 9.*

There are a lot of young people who are not attracted by concerts. I have ideas

(PIERRE BOULEZ)

but no ready solutions. I know that the main thing to attract a new audience is a new approach to performance. One of my aims is to make people aware that there is no new music, and no classical music, but only music.

*Interview, Vienna, pub. June 23.*

A symphony orchestra is not a delicatessen where you can get some of this and some of that. There should be a planned program.

*Pub. July 27.*

**Mary Bran**
*Impresario*

A real impresario must be one who wholly understands the psychology of artists; he must know their needs and ways; he must stand behind them when their spirits are low and must encourage and support them. He must be a considerate friend and an appreciative audience. He must not regard them as mere sources of income, but as friends whose talents are part of their natures. He must watch over them as a gardener watches over his flowers, to make them grow and develop and enrich the world . . . for one cannot exist without the other.

*Interview, Los Angeles,*
*pub. Feb. 27.*

**James Brown**
*Singer*

When I'm not working, I never listen to rock. How can you advance when all you hear is just three chords? A lot of what I hear today in these raggedy, undisciplined groups ain't nothing but an excuse for not being able to play.

*Los Angeles, pub. Dec. 28.*

**Glen Campbell**
*Singer*

If you've got a good song, a well-written song, there's nothing you can do to mess it up . . . The treatment you give it determines the style. I can turn "The Impossible Dream" into a country song.

*Interview, Los Angeles,*
*pub. Dec. 19.*

**Tito Capobianco**
*Stage director,*
*New York City Opera Company*

Opera uses music. Opera uses literature. Opera uses painting, architecture, the dance. Opera is where all the arts converge, where they break their own rules and each other's. always through beauty.

The art of directing is like giving birth, the joyful and painful delivery of a baby. Directing is like making love. There are rituals: a whiskey before, a cigarette after.

*Interview, New York, pub. Nov. 16.*

**Hoagy Carmichael**
*Composer*

If I were an unknown, and if I brought "Stardust" or "Georgia" or "Lazy River" or "Rockin' Chair" to a record company today, as unfamiliar material, I wouldn't get past the front door.

*Interview, pub. Sept. 14.*

**Pablo Casals**
*Cellist*

The great music of today is the great music of the past and they (the young people) know it. To say that young people are drawing away from it is poppycock.

*Interview, San Juan, P.R., pub. June 23.*

**William Chapman**
*Opera Singer*

My thesis is that opera, such as presented by the New York City Opera Company, is one of the only forms of theatrical endeavor in this country that has remained true to the tenets of the entertainment profession—projecting beauty of sight and song, genius of composition, unfailing delineation of emotional values and . . . a thoroughly professional integration of all the theatrical properties—in other words, complete theatre.

*San Marino, Calif., pub. Nov. 14.*

**Ray Charles**
*Singer, Musician*

When I was a youngster, what we now call soul music was known as race music, and you didn't hear it on the radio. Some black people felt they were on the bottom of the pile anyhow; and, since blues

singers were looked down upon—this was as low as you could get in the music field —by associating with it they would identify with the bottom of that bottom. But that's not a general rule—there are plenty of colored people who have followed my career for years and years and who certainly wouldn't qualify for the poverty program.
*Interview, Los Angeles, pub. Aug. 24.*

**Petula Clark**
*Singer, Actress*

The music we're making today, and the lyrics, are trying to get deeper, to touch people. The beat can touch a person physically and in that way open up the mind. I love the beat. It's a wonderful thing to lean on. You can sing with it or around it or against it. But all that is really a technical bit. What makes a singer is interpretation.
*Interview, Los Angeles, pub. April 2.*

**Willis Conover**
*Director, "Music, U.S.A.,"*
*Voice of America*

Jazz is more than a kind of music, a way of sharing the act of musical creation, the inheriting of materials and then reshaping and revitalizing them. It is the musical manifestation of the American spirit—a little loud, perhaps, sometimes a little rude, but optimistic and forward-looking, with the expanding energy of self-disciplined freedom.
*Interview, Washington, pub. Sept. 21.*

**Hal David**
*Song Writer*

I'm convinced that today's songs are ahead of other facets of show business in discussing the world's problems (and), at times, its uncertainties. The universal acceptance of good songs, even by people who don't get along with one another, gives me proof of this.
*Interview, Los Angeles, pub. March 18.*

**Colin R. Davis**
*Conductor, Royal Opera, London*

The conductor is one of the most privileged of people. Nothing you are as human being is not used—maybe this is why we tend to live so long. A conductor has to be completely fearless about what he is—performer, producer, teacher, conscience. A conductor should possess an overwhelming emotional response and a desire to show it off. Few conductors are dull as people. They may be sons of bitches, but they all have power in them, a pressure building up which spills out wonderfully through music.
*Pub. Feb. 21.*

**Lukas Foss**
*Former Conductor,*
*Buffalo Philharmonic Orchestra*

My own goal as conductor is to have a purely musical authority, not a schoolmaster's authority. I want the authority that flows from the score, based on the fact that I have a full score in front of me, and no one else does. Only the conductor has the duties of detection, diagnosis and remedy, which comes from knowledge of the totality of the score—that's what conducting is about.
*Interview, New York, pub. May 18.*

**Ernie Freeman**
*Conductor*

Inspiration is not the primary function. The job comes first. Bach had to eat, had to support his family. As a good craftsman, he could turn out whatever music was demanded of him and however many compositions were required. Wagner wasn't just a composer, he was a supervisor of performances—a sort of Noel Coward of his day. He put on those big German spectacles not just because he was inspired, but because they sold.
*Interview, Los Angeles, pub. Feb. 3.*

**Rudolf Friml**
*Composer*

The operetta is dead. It was replaced by the musical and the show, which are only spectacles for the eyes, without any musical value.
*Prague, pub. Oct. 3.*

**Richard Franko Goldman**
*Director and President,*
*Peabody Conservatory of Music, Baltimore*

Both jazz and rock bring back to music

(RICHARD FRANKO GOLDMAN)

the element of improvisation, which has been practically lost since the 18th century. This, in itself, makes them important and even necessary.

*Baltimore, Oct. 3.*

**Lionel Hampton**
*Musician*

Today's young don't have the magnetism we did. I guess they don't have to fight and struggle like we did. There doesn't seem to be the imagination put into music. Everything today is a mixture of the old—jazz, blues and classical —updated or sometimes even the same. There's very little experimenting or trying to find something new.

*Interview, pub. Sept. 16.*

**August Heckscher**
*Administrator of Recreation
and Cultural Affairs,
City of New York*

At the time we had expected to gather in a vast new audience, we find the audiences perplexed by the contemporary composers and ready to fill the hall only when the museum pieces of opera and symphony are wheeled out.

*Before National Music Council,
New York, pub. June.*

**Lorin Hollander**
*Pianist*

At a rock concert, the atmosphere is love. The rock groups talk their language. But at a classical concert, all they see is a guy in white tie and tails coming out very up-tight on a platform. That's a plastic mannequin—society's little machine running up there. If live concerts are going to survive, the artists themselves are going to have to change.

*Pub. Feb. 7.*

**John A. Howard**
*President, Rockford College*

In times gone by, there were those who thought that great art should ennoble or exalt. Now, many prize that art which "tells it like it is," not like it could be. We are raising whole nations of young people whose steady musical diet has been the complaints and the protest and the focus on physical gratification of rock music and never even exposed to the exhilaration of Beethoven, or the tranquillity of Mendelssohn, or the shear joy of Mozart.

*Rockford, Ill., pub. Oct. 9.*

**Sal Iannucci**
*President, Capitol Records*

The recording industry is the fountainhead of the entire entertainment business. It's that simple.

*Interview, Los Angeles, pub. Dec. 10.*

**Mahalia Jackson**
*Gospel Singer*

When I started singing the real Negro music, the Negro himself turned up his nose at me; they wanted me to sing opera. What do I know about opera? The only thing I know is what I heard down South, and the music wasn't a specialty; they just stood on the corner singing it and playing their guitars. I've heard better voices in the cottonfields than Columbia's got records. That's the truth!

*Interview, Los Angeles, pub. March 9.*

**Tom Jones**
*Singer*

Every Welshman can sing, y'know. It's in the blood. The love of music—all music, from the blues to Beethoven—is born in a Welsh lad. Do you know Ferndell? It's where the great Welsh Chorus is, and every manjack in town is a member of that chorus . . . I used to play the pubs in Ferndell, doing rock 'n roll, and at the end of an evening all the customers would stand up and sing. Just for the joy of it. Well, I'd be there with that glorious music flowing over me—God, how they could sing!—just listening to it and thinking to myself: What in hell are they paying *me* for?

*Interview, Hollywood, pub. Oct. 25.*

**Istvan Kertesz**
*Director, Cologne Opera*

Ours is perhaps the one branch of musical performance in which a man can rise the highest with the least ability. Our fingers cannot slip as those of a pianist or a violinist, nor do our voices crack. Any good orchestra can help a conductor past difficulties without destroying him.

*Pub. Feb. 21.*

**Dorothy Kirsten**
*Opera Singer*

Do I *care* if they (the audiences) interrupt the music? Heavens, no! Let them applaud in the middle of it.

*Interview, Los Angeles, pub. March 27.*

**Siegfried Landau**
*Conductor,*
*Brooklyn Philharmonic Orchestra*

Those people who predict the death of music have little faith in the ingenuity of man . . . The orchestra will change in a coloristic sense, as a result of the present electronic experimentation. But all the obituary notices are absurd. They will dissolve in the face of one composer who wields the new tools into a persuasive human language. It is for his music that we must keep the institutions alive.

*Interview, New York, pub. Nov. 9.*

**Eric Leinsdorf**
*Conductor*

. . . I may write a book. I already have the opening sentence, which is my wife's description of a conductor: "A conductor is a man who stands in front of an orchestra slicing up air."

*Interview, New York, pub. Feb. 16.*

I genuinely welcome the booing. I am as grateful for it as I am for applause. Anything but indifference.

*New York, pub. March 31.*

**Guy Lombardo**
*Band leader*

It takes no musicianship to play rock-and-roll. You just get a big drum, a big guitar and a big amplifier, and you beat the hell out of them.

*Interview, pub. Dec. 28.*

**Lorin Maazel**
*Director, Berlin Opera*

The only thing that counts in musicianship is passionate love for what the composer has written down and the knowledge of how best to interpret it.

*Pub. Feb. 21.*

**Mantovani**
*Conductor*

I owe my continued success to the Beatles and other groups. They are all alike and sound more or less the same. They are so loud that anything I play is like a breath of fresh air.

*London, May 22.*

**Zubin Mehta**
*Conductor, Los Angeles*
*Philharmonic Orchestra*

The conductor must be calm on the inside and excited on the outside. Showmanship is very important, especially to the orchestra. They want to be inspired. But you don't have to perform acrobatics to the public.

*Pub. Feb. 21.*

**Yehudi Menuhin**
*Violinist*

There has been a tremendous increase in the knowledgeability of audiences. There has never been a younger generation as informed, as aware, not only of contemporary trends but also very often of archaic music and medieval music. I only wonder if the leaders of our society are sufficiently aware of this and realize that an important part of the community wants its music and must be given help to get it.

*Interview, San Juan, P.R.,*
*pub. June 23.*

**Nathaniel Merrill**
*Resident Stage Director,*
*Metropolitan Opera Company*
*New York*

. . . I love animals on stage; they're more predictable than humans.

*Pub. March 14.*

**Robert Merrill**
*Opera Singer*

Most of it (modern serious art music) I don't like. It's too mechanically minded. Like an IBM machine. If music doesn't touch the soul and have melodies that haunt you, it isn't right.

*Interview, pub. April 28.*

**Darius Milhaud**
*Composer*

. . . why should you write long symphonies? It is so boring. I dislike what I must call "boring music." People seem to think that the longer the work is, and the more deep it is, that that is good. Terrible! They begin to look very serious and somber, and the music continues and continues and continues . . . ahh! . . . and when it is finished, they are very miserable people. No, no, I don't like that. I don't mean they are not beautiful works because they are very long. Mahler symphonies are not boring for one minute—but Bruckner is . . . All right, my friend, it is a question of taste. You like pancakes or you don't.
*Interview, London, pub. Nov. 7.*

**Richard M. Nixon**
*President of the United States*

In the royalty of American music, no man swings more or stands higher than Duke (Ellington).
*Bestowing the Presidential Medal of Freedom, Washington, April 29.*

**Seiji Ozawa**
*Incoming Conductor,*
*San Francisco Symphony Orchestra*

The first quarter hour of rehearsal with an unfamiliar orchestra is like a cold war. The musicians don't want to kill you exactly—but they are wary, watching and waiting. If you can get through this 15 minutes without serious trouble, you don't have to worry about the concert.
*Pub. Feb. 21.*

**Jan Peerce**
*Opera Singer*

As long as you can breathe, you should be able to keep singing . . . The other night in Utica I sang a full program that included two arias, besides more than a dozen songs by Bach, Handel, Schubert, Turina and Rachmaninoff. Then I sang five encores. When I got through, I was still pretty fresh. The pianist was tired, though.
*Telephone interview, New York,*
*pub. Nov. 26.*

**Krzysztof Penderecki**
*Composer*

Poland is the land of musical snobbery. But you must remember that these snobs also chased out Chopin.
*Interview, New York, pub. March 17.*

**Artur Rubinstein**
*Pianist*

All my life I have been on my knees before the art of music. I adored it. I lived for it. It has made me the happiest of men, for my work is the greatest privilege and the greatest joy in the world.
*Television broadcast, Sept. 5.*

**George Shearing**
*Pianist*

There are certain similarities between rock and jazz, and they have become more positive in recent years. Today, there is a closer meeting of the musical minds since each form of music has drifted closer to the other, and each has acquired some of the finer points of the other. I believe that people today can better accept, understand and relate to many of the characteristics of both. It is my hope that the public taste will be big enough to permit all types and trends of music to co-exist.
*Interview, Los Angeles, pub. June 21.*

**Beverly Sills**
*Opera Singer*

I want meaty characters. I don't want people to tell me after a performance how beautifully I sang. If that's what I did, then I failed. I'm prepared to sacrifice the beautiful note for the meaningful sound anytime. Rossini said opera was voice, voice, voice. He was wrong. Who cares if you can produce three hours of beautiful singing? Take Tosca. In the first act she's consumed by jealousy and in the second by loathing. If it's the same voice, then it's just 4,000 notes, getting paid and going home.
*Interview, pub. April 21.*

The emotional singer sings every role as if it were her last, and it might be. The intellectual singer knows every grunt and groan she's going to produce. She never lets go of technique, never gives a spontaneous performance, which is where the excitement is. I heard (Maria) Callas sing "Tosca" after her voice was gone, and in 20 minutes you weren't aware of it. If I had a choice, I'd take ten years as Callas rather than 30 years as somebody else.

*Pub. October.*

**Richard H. Wagerin**
*President, American*
*Symphony Orchestra League*

The orchestral development of this country has been made possible through the federal government's traditional tax policy of aiding and encouraging private citizens to support cultural organizations voluntarily. Should this private support be reduced, the orchestras would have no choice but to seek aid directly from government sources, or to abandon their operations—and their music.

*Before House Ways and Means Committee, Washington, pub. March 5.*

**Dionne Warwick**
*Singer*

. . . the acid scene is going to fade away, and the music with it. As soon as today's twelve-year-olds become 21 and are married, with kids of their own, it'll all be passe and another way of thinking will prevail. In fact, the appreciation for good music is already growing. You don't hear as much of that bang-bang-bang stuff on the radio as you did three years ago.

*Interview, Los Angeles,*
*pub. Jan. 12.*

**Frank Zappa**
*Rock singer*

I don't think the typical rock fan is smart enough to know he's being dumped on . . . These kids wouldn't know music if it came up and bit 'em on the ass.

*Pub. Dec. 15.*

## THE STAGE

**Richard Adler**
*Composer*

To me, it is a disgrace when people present a musical on Broadway and don't know how to end Act One. So they decide to have everybody take his clothes off . . . I couldn't have written "Hair" or had anything to do with it. I would have been ashamed and embarrassed.

*Before Minneapolis Women's Club,*
*March 16.*

**Edward Albee**
*Playwright*

. . . American critics are like American universities. They both have dull and half-dead faculties.

*Before Cultural League of New York,*
*May 5.*

**Dame Judith Anderson**
*Actress*

There isn't anything that I want to see today (on the stage). You hear about "Hair" and "Oh Calcutta!", and it's all disgusting to me. There is no quality or imagination in the theatre today. I object to the nudity . . . When I go to the theatre, I want to cry, be entertained, enlightened and enriched . . .

*Interview, New York, pub. Nov. 19.*

**Arthur Ballet**
*Professor of Theatre Arts,*
*University of Minnesota*

I can't put up with the playwright who says he can't write because he's got to work eight hours a day. You want to write that play, you'll write it. Foundations may have been a bit guilty in encouraging that attitude. But the starving-in-a-garret theory is sheer nonsense. Shakespeare was well fed, owned his tenement houses, collected his rents very carefully, kept the plumbing in repair—and wrote "Lear."

*Pub. Dec. 21.*

**Julian Beck**
*Founder, The Living Theatre*

The theatre exists to discuss the nature of man, the nature of politics. Yet when one comes out and talks about these things directly, one hears, "That isn't THEATRE," as if the theatre was some kind of amorphous, vague, colorless fabric—as if it was necessarily limited to discussing certain psychological issues within a fictional framework.

*Interview, Portland, Ore., pub. Feb. 23.*

**Milton Berle**
*Actor, Comedian*

The theatre is my first love; that's where I started. I know that sounds like Wampas baby stuff, but it's the truth.

*Telephone interview, pub. Dec. 14.*

**David Black**
*Producer*

One result of the flight from Broadway may be that the unions are going to come to their senses about Broadway rules. Oh sure, I'll produce there again, if I've got a property with some built-in hedges against failure . . . But you need a special reason to want to work there today.

*New York, pub. Oct. 19.*

**Douglas Campbell**
*Actor*

None of these big theatres and cultural centers can hope to have a real theatre company until they can support one over a long period of time. Theatre is an art form, not a play-by-play business enterprise. Financial success today is based on one show. This sort of thinking has either got to be altered or suppressed. Suppressed, I think.

*Interview, Los Angeles, pub. March 16.*

**Morris Carnovsky**
*Actor, Director*

This age of technology is a very difficult

one in which to be living. It tends to suppress emotion and that's hard on actors. Some will try tricks and other substitute effects rather than commit themselves to passion. And, sadly, audiences will often accept a dispassionate performance.

*Interview, pub. April 6.*

### Gower Champion
*Choreographer, Director*

The musical-comedy is at a dead-end at this point. It has become banal, everyone has seen it. Musicals all have the same form, with a ballad at the same point 10 minutes into the first act. I'm bored with them. Audiences are getting bored with them.

*Interview, San Francisco, pub. Feb. 14.*

### Carol Channing
*Actress*

Laughter is much more important than . . . applause. Applause is almost a duty. Laughter is a reward. Laughter means they trust you and like you.

*Pub. Dec. 28.*

### Harold Clurman
*Director; drama critic, "The Nation"*

The director won't always help you. Very often, the director only knows that something is wrong, but he doesn't know what; or he doesn't know how to talk. A director once said to an actor, "Ah . . . um . . . it's no good." So the actor said, "What should I do?" And the director said, "Ah . . . um . . . make it good."

I never, never bawl out a talentless actor. He's already cursed.

*Los Angeles, pub. Aug. 17.*

### Gordon Davidson
*Director*

Who really knows what people want? In any case, I refuse to get trapped in the quantity theory of art as exemplified by the way programs on TV are eliminated by ratings. If I do a play that pleases 80 to 85 per cent of an audience, that in itself makes the undertaking valid. No one judges the success of a symphony by the number of people who've heard it. A painting is not evaluated on the basis of how many people come to a museum to see it. The trouble is that the theatre is equated with show business, which is judged by financial success.

*New York, pub. March 6.*

### Henry Fonda
*Actor*

If you've ever been in the theatre, that's where you get your real kicks as an actor. You feel like a race horse chomping at the bit. You have the feeling you're really creating something. In pictures it's always somebody else putting your bits and pieces together. All these are cliches, but they're true.

*Interview, Hollywood, pub. Sept. 14.*

### Glenn Ford
*Actor*

Americans playing Shakespeare are really ridiculous.

*Pub. Aug. 28.*

### Ruth Gordon
*Actress*

You know why a lot of the great playwrights aren't writing these days? There are still a lot of them around, you know. Some of them, like Tennessee (Williams), have been sick. But a lot of them are just plain lazy. You know what I mean? Why, Garson (Kanin, her husband) and I would be successful even if we had no talent at all. Because we work all the time.

*Interview, Beverly Hills, Calif.,
pub. Dec. 29.*

### Rex Harrison
*Actor*

The American theatre scene has changed very much since I was last on stage here. It's an American America, very different from the days when (Maxwell) Anderson was writing, and (Robert) Sherwood. It was influenced by the British at that time. Very good to have come out of it, I say. But not good for me . . .

*Interview, New York, pub. Feb. 24.*

I never feel my age. And I'm fascinated by everything that's going on. In New York I even went to see a play, "Geese," in which the cast strip naked. I wanted to see if one acts any better with one's clothes off. After seeing it, I decided they

(REX HARRISON)

couldn't act even with their clothes on. But I had to see it. It is theatre.

*Interview, pub. July 27.*

**Helen Hayes**
*Actress*

We had nudity on the stage in my youth . . . In the Ziegfeld Follies. But it was beautiful nudity. Now, it's sort of grubby.

*New York, Aug. 27.*

**Lillian Hellman**
*Playwright*

The theatre is very, very bad, for a number of reasons. It gets a bad audience— to coin a phrase, an expense account audience—and a bad audience gets bad plays.

*Interview, Beverly Hills, Calif.,*
*pub. Nov. 2.*

**Sol Hurok**
*Impresario*

. . . that's the way things are today in films, the theatre, Broadway. We sell sex now . . . more blood, more sex . . . dirt and filth. How many nude girls . . . How many nude men can we get on stage? This is the "art" for now. It is too vulgar, too cheap. And I try to fight all this . . . because it affects the entire moral standards of the world.

*Interview, New York, pub. July 2.*

**William Inge**
*Playwright*

The theatre generally is very dead. The most alive theatre is happening to audiences of 100 in little barns in New York and around the country. The Ford Foundation, or some other group, gives them a grant and away they go.

*At Pacific Coast Writers' Conference,*
*Los Angeles, pub. Aug. 24.*

**Garson Kanin**
*Playwright*

I don't know to what extent the general public is interested in the theatre world or in that curious race of people that are called show people, but I see it very much as a world of its own. Things happen in that world that couldn't happen outside. All of the people in it are larger than life. If they have a failure, it's not just a failure; it's a cause for suicide. If they have a success, nobody ever had as big a hit. We live in a vocabulary of fantastics, sensations, terrifics, or the-worst-thing-I-ever-saw. From that point of view, I find it enchanting. For myself, I have enjoyed living in that world.

In the theatre of ideas, writing is easier now, because you can address yourself to a much more knowledgeable audience. Any theatre of feeling is hard writing, because that's not fashionable now. I come from a background where people went to the threatre to cry. Today, you can sit in front of a television set for 15 straight hours and you'll never see 10 seconds of human feeling.

*Interview, New York, pub. Aug. 11.*

**Alan Jay Lerner**
*Author, Composer*

. . . the theatre is very snobbish. You can win four Pulitzers for novels and poetry and an Academy Award or two—and then come back to the theatre and they'll ask if you've done anything lately.

*Hollywood, pub. Nov. 24.*

**Gina Lollobrigida**
*Actress*

I saw the Broadway musical, "Hair," and I think it is against sex, against love, against everything. There is nothing left to the imagination. Men and women stand naked on the stage in it. Even in the worst nightclub in Paris, men and women would never be completely naked. This is the opposite of sex.

*Interview, New York, pub. Jan. 23.*

**Theodore Mann**
*Producer, Director*

You have to begin with the basic premise that the theatre, even bad theatre, is an art form and not a business, as most people seem to think. The theatre has been mediocratized as fluff. To me, it can and should be a revelatory experience.

*Interview, New York, pub. Dec. 14.*

**Fredric March**
*Actor*

We did "Long Day's Journey" for two

years—that was enough! I've had the theatre. It becomes a damn bore night after night.

*Pub. June 9.*

### Groucho Marx
*Actor, Comedian*

When I heard about "Hair" I was kind of curious about the six naked primates on stage. So I called up the box office, and they said the tickets were $11 apiece. That's an awful price to pay. I went into my bathroom at home and took off all my clothes and looked at the mirror for five minutes, and I said this isn't worth $11.

*Interview, Beverly Hills, Calif., April 5.*

### David Merrick
*Producer*

Critics are going to learn to praise high-grade mediocrity. You're going to have to settle for it because that's all you're going to get. It's not going to get any better. Next season is not going to be much better than this season. Pretty good should be good enough. After all, critics are mediocre talents, themselves. They're not great journalists. In fact, I don't know any high-grade journalists.

. . . films are respected by the young today. I just don't know how to interest young people in the theatre. I think it's archaic, like opera. I don't think it's the price of the tickets. They have enough money. I've told them they don't need to dress up, that they can come any way they want. But it's films they pop into, not the theatre.

There's a lack of material for the theatre. The critics have driven the playwrights to films. What writer wants to gamble a year to write a play that is murdered overnight?

*Interview, New York, pub. May 25.*

### Arthur Miller
*Playwright, Author*

. . . Broadway hasn't come to terms with the present. There are now two audiences, the majority audience and the alienated audience. The basic economic fact is that our drama is not mass entertainment any longer. Broadway cannot exist as it has.

*Interview, pub. Oct. 26.*

### Mike Nichols
*Director*

You've got a situation today where everybody knows everything about the movies. You get into a cab and the driver starts talking to you about jump cuts and montages. There's too much awareness of the technical side of films, from the directors right on through to the audience. This can only be a healthy thing for the theatre. Maybe, while everybody is concentrating on movies, the theatre can lose a little of its self-consciousness and find its own way.

*Pub. Oct. 20.*

### Sir Laurence Olivier
*Actor*

What is the main problem of the actor? It is to keep the audience awake, and not let them go to sleep, then wake up and go home feeling they've wasted their money.

*Interview, pub. March 2.*

If you wish to create a national or community theatre, *begin* by assembling your company, work with it, find out what's wrong and what's right, and *then*—and *only* then—build a new building for it.

*Interview, London, pub. May 20.*

### Terence Rattigan
*Playwright*

There's an enormous amount of sensationalism in all this sexual activity on stage. And very little talent . . . I've seen other fashions come and go. The wheel will eventually come around full circle. And we'll have actors wearing clothes again and a curtain that opens and closes. When the maid answers the telephone, everyone will be terribly moved because it will look new.

All my life I've fought against a committed theatre. If you insist on a political point of view, you split your audience immediately. I don't see why a playwright needs a cause. To me, people have always been more important than ideology.

*Hollywood, pub. Nov. 20.*

**Jerome Robbins**
*Choreographer*

In today's world, you've got to have some real magic in the theatre, some real fantasy in the theatre. People go to the movies because that's such a fantastic medium—one of the few places your mind can take off, be provoked and have evocations. This is also true of dance, because although it is so non-specific, there is an intense emotional reality underneath it. But the theatre bores me, for the most part, and it bores the public, too.

*Interview, New York, pub. April 25.*

**Estelle Parsons**
*Actress*

I hate the theatre. That whole thing about the theatre being sacred is ridiculous —it's full of boring, unimaginative, third-rate people. Every good actor I know has moved to Hollywood.

*Interview, New York, pub. July 27.*

**Robert Ryan**
*Actor*

I'm for any theatre that keeps theatre existing in New York; what bothers me about some of this new stuff is it doesn't give young actors the kind of training they should have. Hell! *Anybody* can stand naked in front of an audience and shout Holy! Holy! But *anybody can't* perform Shakespeare or Shaw or Neil Simon.

*Interview, New York, pub. June 1.*

**Barbra Streisand**
*Singer, Actress*

The audience is the best judge of any-
thing. They cannot be lied to . . . after almost two years on the stage, one learns that. The slightest tinge of falseness, they go back from you; they retreat. The truth brings them closer. A moment that lags . . . they're gonna cough. A moment that is held, they're not gonna cough. They don't know why, they can't intellectualize it, but they know it's right or wrong. Individually, they may be a bunch of asses, but together as a whole they are the . . . wisest thing.

*Interview, pub. December.*

**Howard Taubman**
*Critic, "The New York Times"*

Producers today are unlike those in the twenties who read a lot and put up their own money on a play. Today they are gamblers. Few have real taste. It costs a lot to produce plays, so they are busy finding angels to finance the venture.

*At Town Hall, Oklahoma City, March 20.*

I have no moral objection to nudity on the stage. (But) it is only justifiable when it offers an artistic point. If it is pandering, I loathe it. And most of it today is pandering.

*Before Women's Club,
Minneapolis, pub. Dec. 1.*

**Peter Ustinov**
*Actor*

Working in the theatre you see few people and they are always the same. Once I went to Albania and people said, "Why on earth did you do that?" I couldn't very well say, "To get away from you," but there it was . . .

*Interview, Paris, pub. March 9.*

## TELEVISION AND RADIO

**Harry Ackerman**
*Vice president and executive producer,*
*Screen Gems, Inc.*

Eight to ten years ago, there was an intoxicating excitement in television, with an occasional "hell" and "damn." Suddenly, it's like Czechoslovakia. Everything's changed. Are the networks going to knuckle in to (Senator John O.) Pastore and institute a new dark age of censorship?
*Before Hollywood Radio and*
*Television Society, pub. Sept. 22.*

**Steve Allen**
*Television Entertainer-*
*Song Writer-Author*

Everybody (on TV talk shows) starts out wanting to get Cary Grant and the return of Christ. But soon they settle for Morey Amsterdam. It's not a serious problem.
*Pub. Sept. 1.*

**Woody Allen**
*Actor-Writer-Comedian*

You don't know what makes a man funny. That's the point. There are comedians with funny material you see on the (Ed) Sullivan show, but you never want to see them again. Then there are comedians like (Jack) Benny or (Bob) Hope or Jonathan Winters who can say the same lines, but you do want to see them again. It's inborn, in the same sense that Picasso can draw a rabbit and there's something great about it.

TV is . . . a mass medium and so it's a shame it is run in so complete disregard for a large segment of the country . . . those with IQs of over 100.
*Interview, New York, pub. Sept. 19.*

**Henry Alter**
*Director of education services,*
*National Educational Television*

U.S. television started out with nary a thought to the medium's potential for public enlightenment and, in some quarters, the notion that selling detergents is somehow more important than promoting literacy. The right of people to see serious, sustained coverage of public issues without fear or favor, to see a wide range of creative expression, to see programs that engage the minds of the young, all of it free from the pressures of the marketplace—that right was the cornerstone of television in all the western nations but ours.
*Washington, Dec. 8.*

**Fred Astaire**
*Actor, Dancer*

What bothers me (about television) is all these mountains of entertainment that we produce and that are shown once or twice and then forgotten. I was a juror for the TV Academy last spring, and I saw so many wonderful shows that I didn't even know existed. Such great talent went into them. And what happens to the shows? They sit rotting in vaults.
*Interview, Los Angeles, pub. Oct. 16.*

**Clive Barnes**
*Drama critic, "The New York Times"*

One thing that is fascinating is that for really 20 years we have seen popular culture on a scale we have never had. For the first time, we have a scientific experiment in popular culture called television. Television is the first truly democratic culture—the first culture available to everyone and entirely governed by what the people want. The most terrifying thing is what people do want.
*Panel discussion, New York,*
*pub. Dec. 30.*

**Arthur Barron**
*Producer*

The (television) networks concentrate

(ARTHUR BARRON)

on issues rather than events, on masses rather than on the individual, on information rather than emotion, on balance rather than passionate personal commitment.

*Pub. March 17.*

## Joey Bishop
*Television Entertainer*

I don't fancy myself as an interviewer. If we get something running, I let it go. I saw Gene Tunney and Jack Dempsey on one (talk) show recently, and the host kept butting in. I wanted to hear about that great fight from them, but the host told the whole damn story.

A late-night (TV) show should never be heard. It should be overheard.

*Pub. Sept. 1.*

I have a fine setup (with his ABC-TV show). I'm not about to walk out on it. But I'm of an explosive nature and one night might tell them, "You can take this network and—"

*Interview, Los Angeles, pub. Nov. 13.*

## Jimmy Breslin
*Author, Newspaper Columnist*

The country is insane. Our people are in such good shape that the only way they can communicate with each other is to call a television station and talk to some creep on the phone.

*Pub. Nov. 30.*

## Dean Burch
*Chairman, Federal
Communications Commission*

We've always understood that free speech is a modified right . . . Because a person can't use four-letter words on radio isn't a violation of free speech. I think you've got to come to the conclusion that it's a different problem when you're dealing with material that is coming into the home.

*News conference, Washington, Dec. 2.*

. . . there are some agile minds at work . . . who like to speculate . . . that some terrible cabal is being created to destroy the networks. And I think that this is a bunch of hooey.

*Interview, pub. Dec. 26.*

## Johnny Carson
*Television Entertainer*

Money isn't bad in itself. I don't know why people resent it. I see nothing wrong with a fair profit for something you create. When I was making a new NBC contract, million dollar figures were thrown around . . . Nobody says it's wrong for Liz Taylor to get $1,250,000 and 15 per cent of the gross for a picture. She must bring it in at the box office. I remember when Humphrey Bogart got $250,000 for a picture. Somebody asked him, "What makes you think you're worth $250,000?" He said, "Because I can get it!"

*Interview, New York, pub. April 15.*

## Dick Cavett
*Television Entertainer*

If you did a show with the thought that "We're on in the daytime," I don't see how you could show up for work. Everything connected with the idea of daytime television is nauseating. And so is daytime television.

*Interview, New York, pub. May 26.*

## Dick Clark
*President, Dick Clark
Television Productions*

Youth is a minority audience for TV. They don't watch it even though they were raised on it. They'll look at selected programs like "Laugh-In," for instance, or contemporary music and comedy. But, on the whole, TV is for middle-aged, funky thinking.

*Hollywood, pub. July 7.*

## Fairfax M. Cone
*Former Chairman,
Foote, Cone & Belding*

Radio put advertising people into show business for the first time, and they wanted to get out of it . . . Television has endangered the future of the business because the opportunity of mini-showmanship is not one that many people can resist.

*Interview, New York, pub. Nov. 2.*

## Mike Connors
*Actor*

Senator Pastore and a few others are

really censoring what you and I are going to see on our television screens. I just don't think that people want it that way. We have the very best censoring devices in our own homes. If we don't like what we see on television we can turn off the set. What I don't like is having someone saying ahead of time what I can see and what I can't.

*Interview, Hollywood, pub. Aug. 25.*

**Bob Crane**
*Actor*

I wish I could find some way to solve the economics of our business—26 weeks a year you're out of work. I've been offered several movies this year and each one of them has conflicted with the shooting of the (TV) show ("Hogan's Heroes"), so I've had to turn them down. The economics dictate that you've got to make up your mind that you're either going to stick with a hit show until it expires or quit TV entirely and concentrate on a movie career.

*Interview, Los Angeles, pub. Jan. 24.*

**Walter Cronkite**
*News Commentator,*
*Columbia Broadcasting System*

We must get away from under this outmoded concept that because we use the people's air the Government can say what goes over it. This is no longer valid; it is clearly a restriction of free speech.

*Before Association of Industrial*
*Advertisers, New York, pub. May 6.*

**Michael Dann**
*Senior vice president in charge of*
*TV programming,*
*Columbia Broadcasting System*

Television is most successful when it's an attendance form, when it takes you some place. Horowitz at Carnegie Hall or Joe Namath at the Super Bowl, or, unfortunately, sometimes a tragedy— maybe the slaying of a Presidential candidate. If we can go to Moscow to hear a concert, it would be that much more powerful than if someone came here and played in a 57th Street studio.

*Interview, New York, pub. July 12.*

**Sammy Davis, Jr.**
*Entertainer*

. . . I think acting is the way for me to go—acting in television, not movies. The way they make movies, with all that wasted time, drives me up the wall. With television, you get in there and do it.

*Interview, Burbank, Calif., pub. Nov. 4.*

**David Dortort**
*Producer*

Really, the essential basis of the Western is classic drama. The lines are simple but not simplistic. Good struggles with evil. A man shows courage by standing up to the elements and to fate. He defies the gods and the gods strike back . . . It's a mistake to change the Western. I try to keep it pure. It's there for you to take. You have to be careful not to foul it up with too much sophistication. The deep psychological or Freudian approach prevents people from relating to it.

*Interview, Los Angeles, pub. Jan. 23.*

**Mike Douglas**
*Television Entertainer*

. . . I don't think I'd want to be doing a talk show late at night, such as Johnny (Carson), Merv (Griffin) and Joey (Bishop). I have a feeling that some day the entire American audience is going to rise up as one entity and yell at their TV sets, "Shut up!" And that'll be it for the yak shows.

*Television interview, Philadelphia,*
*pub. Dec. 10.*

**James Farentino**
*Actor*

You just can't do the things today in TV that you can do in motion pictures. One thing that really bugs me is the violence and sex that TV has veered away from. It just isn't honest. The same people the networks are "protecting" are lining up and paying $3 a head to see "Curious Yellow" and "The Wild Bunch."

*Interview, Los Angeles, pub. Sept. 21.*

**Reuven Frank**
*President, National*
*Broadcasting Company-News*

Young people don't question the exis-

(REUVEN FRANK)

tence of TV anymore than any of us question the existence of the auto . . . They may be bored by TV or criticize it or like it. But they don't question that it should exist. Some older people can't assimilate it. Most people who talk of investigating it belong to that group.

*Interview, pub. Jan. 7.*

## Lewis Freedman
*Director*

The trouble with educational television is that it's been too esoteric, too academic, too dry, too dull. The first test of a play is not whether it's significant, meaningful or pertinent, but whether it's theatrical. If it's not theatrical, nothing else matters, because nobody watches it.

*Interview, Los Angeles, pub. Nov. 17.*

## Bruce Geller
*Producer*

A TV commercial in one minute must get your attention, tell an involved story, give you the message and getoff. The message may be hooey, but the technique is masterful.

*Interview, Los Angeles, pub. Jan. 21.*

## Arthur Godfrey
*Radio, Television Entertainer*

We who work in TV and radio have a special cause for involvement and a very special responsibility. Of all the media, radio is the most accessible to our young people. And never before in history have young people been more exciting, more creative, more questioning, more doubting, more exasperating than right now. We are the command generation. We own the tools and hold the license. It behooves us to understand what is happening.

*Interview, pub. May 28.*

## Lorne Greene
*Actor*

"Bonanza" was never a violent show, yet it is set in an era when men wore guns and violence was a fact of life. Now, when we shoot a man off a horse, we have to show him getting back on the horse and riding away again. It's idiotic. It's like

Hamlet stabbing Polonius, and then you part the curtains and Polonius comes back to life.

*Pub. Oct. 27.*

## Robert P. Griffin
*United States Senator, R-Mich.*

I think the (television) industry ought to show a little more interest in policing itself or they're going to drive us into passing some of these bills we have no business passing.

*Before Senate communications sub-committee, Washington, March 12.*

## Eugene Hallman
*Vice president,*
*Canadian Broadcasting Company*

We (in television) present hour upon hour of low-grade serial fiction . . . hour upon hour of daytime quiz and game shows and interviews and cartoons and old movies. And then there are the commercial messages, by the dozen, the hundred, the thousand, interrupting programs, dividing programs, surrounding and sometimes burying programs. Altogether, the dominant message we deliver in television goes something like this: Canada, like the United States, is a white, middle-class, affluent society, made up mainly by happy, gay, young suburban couples and families, and contented, irascible, lovable old codgers.

*Interview, Toronto, pub. Nov. 2.*

## S. I. Hayakawa
*Acting President,*
*San Francisco State College*

. . . Television doesn't teach us how democracy works . . . its commercials proclaim instant solutions for upset stomachs, neuralgia or bad breath, and its news reporting sums up even complex events in half-hour programs with a neat wrap-up at the end. The boring details of the democratic process . . . these you seldom learn on television.

*Interview, Washington, pub. Feb. 24.*

The world makes all sorts of demands the television set never told you about—such as study, patience, hard work and a long apprenticeship in a trade or profession before you may enjoy what the world has to offer.

*Before American Psychological Association, pub. Sept. 21.*

**Louis Hayward**
*Actor*

I'm back working again so I can live in the approximate style I was used to before I took a financial bath in television in England. Want to hear that sad tale? Roughly—and that's the right word—I co-produced, financed and starred in 39 segments of a series titled, "The Pursuers." As series go, it wasn't bad. But my partners insisted it be done in black and white instead of color. We wound up in color all right—all red!

*Hollywood, pub. Oct. 9.*

**Hugh M. Hefner**
*Publisher, "Playboy Magazine"*

Television is the *Reader's Digest* of mass communication. Certainly, compared with books, magazines, plays and films, there's a lamentable lack of sex. I think it should be otherwise.

*Interview, Nov. 23.*

**Alfred Hitchcock**
*Motion Picture Director*

I made a remark a long time ago. I said I was very pleased that television was now showing murder stories, because it's bringing murder back into its rightful setting . . . in the home.

*Pub. Sept. 4.*

**Richard W. Jencks**
*President, Broadcast Group,*
*Columbia Broadcasting System*

In the final analysis, we have no choice but to exercise our responsibility as we see it. This means resisting those on the left who tell us that our proper role is to grant license to whoever wishes to say or do anything. It means resisting those on the right who would have us turn our backs on the revolution in mores and morals that modern life has brought about.

*At CBS Affiliates convention, New York, May 20.*

**Nicholas Johnson**
*Commissioner, Federal*
*Communications Commission*

I have argued that the real threat of censorship over television's programming content comes not from the government but from networks themselves—that they have been all too eager to keep off the nation's television screens anything they find inconsistent with their own personal philosophies or corporate profits.

*Pub. June 4.*

Our concern ought to be with the possible domination of the content of the mass media by self-serving economic interests —the censorship, not by government, but by private corporations.

*Testimony before House Banking and Currency Committee, Washington, April 21.*

**Tom Jones**
*Singer*

. . . I think I hate television. With a live audience you can have a ball. But when a camera is on, you know you've got to prove something to people turning a knob somewhere and saying to their wives, "Let's see if this guy is any good." I don't like those buggy-eye cameras.

*Interview, pub. Jan. 20.*

**Bob Keeshan**
*Actor, Producer*

No doubt a tremendous diet of violence on television does tend to be dangerous to the child. But it isn't necessarily that it triggers or teaches the employment of violence. It probably won't often do that. No, I don't believe that's the big threat. The real threat is that seeing all this cruelty immunizes a child to violence. He grows callous. He isn't shocked at it in actual life. Growing older, he doesn't rise up in anger over a crime.

*Interview, Los Angeles, pub. April 3.*

**Alan King**
*Comedian*

We comedians have a terrific responsibility. We have to keep up with the people, doing something timely, saying what we feel, but also speaking for all. Some of

(ALAN KING)

us, Bill Cosby and Don Rickles for instance, go to extremes, but I deal with subjects that affect most people. I have to. There are no small towns. Television has made everything equal.

*Interview, Las Vegas, pub. Oct. 4.*

**Perry Lafferty**
*Vice president for programming,*
*Columbia Broadcasting System-TV*

Conflict is the essence of all drama. If you take the physical conflict out of Westerns and detective or police shows, you have nothing left.

*Interview, Los Angeles, pub. Jan. 25.*

**Michael Landon**
*Actor*

I don't believe it is a question of censorship (on television). It is a question of abiding by the rules under which we work and which we accept when we accept the work itself . . . I don't believe I have the right to say, "what I write is the way it will be," and then accuse the network of censorship if they don't agree. I do have one alternative—I can start my own network.

*Pub. May 21.*

**Hope Lange**
*Actress*

I think of the networks and the vast power of the medium, and I wonder why they haven't taken the lead in education. I think they could do so much for children . . . Saturday morning they watch cartoons. I think, "Damn, why isn't something else on?"

*Interview, Los Angeles, pub. Feb. 16.*

**Liberace**
*Entertainer, Pianist*

In America, if you're not on TV, you're not in show business—or so most people think.

*Interview, London, pub. Aug. 9.*

**Carl Lindemann**
*Vice president,*
*National Broadcasting Company-Sports*

It must be evident that sports are in big trouble when we can't sell the World Series, traditionally the Number One attraction . . . We're caught in a vicious circle of network competition and prestige. We've had the series for 30 years and it's an article of faith that we must keep it. I suppose CBS feels the same way about college football. One of these days, though, a top executive will look at the balance sheet and say the hell with competing for losses. When that happens, you'll see what John Foster Dulles called an agonizing reappraisal of the situation.

*Pub. Aug. 9.*

**Walter Lippmann**
*Author, Newspaper Columnist*

Television is guilty of an awful lot of things in our lives, and it's adding to the irrationality of the world, I think. There's no doubt of that, because it makes everything simpler or more dramatic or more immediate than it is. You really, if you listen to television, can't find out what's going on in the world.

*Interview, Seal Harbor, Me.,*
*pub. Sept. 14.*

**Ida Lupino**
*Actress-Director-Producer*

. . . if you could have imagined, years ago, seeing all the horrifying and great things that happen in that tube, people would have thought you were crazy. It's a marvelous medium. It has put a lot of people to work. It can also be misused, but as yet I haven't seen it misused. I find it curious, slamming at TV as a cause of teen-age unrest, campus riots and crime. A lot of things are being blamed on that box.

*Interview, Los Angeles, pub. Aug. 24.*

**William C. MacPhail**
*Vice president,*
*Columbia Broadcasting System-Sports*

In any other business we'd be arrested for throwing money away . . . To give you an idea of the crazy inflation in sports, we paid the Green Bay *Packers* $35,000 for all TV rights in 1956. Today, each of the 16 teams in the NFL gets a million and a half bucks a year from us. Costs to sponsors have gone up correspondingly, and the blunt truth is they're not getting their money's worth.

*Pub. Aug. 9.*

**Martin Manulis**
*Producer*

In this country, live TV had one great advantage. By the time they knew what they were doing it was too late to do anything about it. Plays would be in rehearsal for two weeks and some sponsor or network officials would yell: "You can't do that!" We'd say we either do it or you have no show Thursday night, you have 90 minutes of empty air . . . With tape or film, you don't have that advantage. It can be cut and changed and fussed with and reshot or even discarded, and, by the time they're through, most of the guts are gone.

*Interview, Hollywood,*
*pub. Aug. 22.*

**Donald H. McGannon**
*Chairman, Westinghouse*
*Broadcasting Company*

I have deep concern over the viewer's interest in television. Television is not doing enough for the sustenance of its viewers. Programming of the 1960's has rested heavily on growth during the 1950's. There is such a sameness to it. The hang-up is a lack of diversity of program originations. Most comes from the three networks (ABC, CBS, NBC) and from stockpiles of feature film occupying huge blocks of time in two-hour bunches. How to alleviate this? We attack it with our own programming. We must do our own. We must capture, find and produce our own offbeat, different and compelling programming.

*New York, pub. Aug. 23.*

**Darren McGavin**
*Actor*

Television has got worse and worse. The medium is all boxed in. There's no freedom in it. Look at the new shows this season—no originality and few, if any, fresh ideas for anyone to work with . . . The three networks seem to be doing everything possible to hurry the day of pay television. The comedy shows are

pap, and the other stuff is ineffectual drama—fairy tales for adults.

*Interview, Los Angeles, pub. December.*

**Ed McMahon**
*Television Announcer*

From years of having everything go wrong, I've reached the point where, if a fire's burning the set down all around me, *first,* I'll finish the commercial, *then* I'll put out the fire.

*Pub. Dec. 13.*

**Ashley Montagu**
*Anthropologist*

They (talk-show guests) are good soporifics. They put a lot of people to sleep. From my point of view, most are in horrible taste. But television people have got their audiences measured, and, as H. L. Mencken once said, "No one ever went broke underestimating the taste of the American public."

*Pub. Sept. 1.*

**Robert Montgomery**
*Actor*

No one in his right mind can say that the wholesale diet of idiocy in the entertainment sphere being foisted on the American public today by the three major (television) networks can deserve a better rating than that of mass mediocrity.

*Before Federal Communications*
*Commission, Washington,*
*pub. July 27.*

**Garry Moore**
*Television Entertainer*

There's an entertainment or diversion television, and then there's the real television. I was in the diversion business and I'm not ashamed of it. People need that, too. But then, the real television . . . the look of panic in a politician's eye on "Meet the Press" before he goes to his pat answer, which really doesn't answer the question. That's high drama. That's what I'd like to be a part of.

*Interview, Rye, N.Y., pub. April 12.*

**Henry Morgan**
*Television and Radio Entertainer*

I can't bear to watch it (television). It's

(HENRY MORGAN)

not cool. It's dull; it's boring; it's vapid; it's empty; it's *jejune*. I have quite a large vocabulary, and I can't use that on television, either. But there's no acting on television; it's not really necessary to act now. They do 96 takes and cut them together, and it looks like the actor is doing something. He's not doing anything. Go sit on the set and see if he's doing anything. All the perspiration is from the heat, certainly not from the effort.

Any medium is a reflection, not a leader. Maybe that's one of television's problems. It's a reflection of what people want. Television is governed by 1,100 morons who allow some company to attach a box (rating meter) to their sets. They're not a cross-section. They're only a cross-section of the kind of people who'd let somebody attach a box to their sets. And I'm not interested, anyway, in the opinion of somebody from Iowa.
*Interview, Los Angeles, pub. Sept. 21.*

**Bill D. Moyers**
*Former Press Secretary for
President Lyndon B. Johnson*

To give a President, who remains a politician at all times, 30 minutes of uninterrupted and unanswered (television) access to 60 million Americans, is too great a power to give one man, no matter how honest his motives.
*Television interview, New York, Nov. 25.*

**Leslie Nielsen**
*Actor*

Playing one character over and over again is not my notion of being an actor. It's like a painter having a five-year contract with the Hilton Hotel chain. He paints the same picture in every room of every hotel for five years. He will make a lot of money. But what kind of satisfaction would that be for a genuine painter?
*Interview, Los Angeles, pub. June 23.*

**John E. O'Toole**
*President, Foote, Cone & Belding*

. . . I sincerely believe that (television) commercials are getting better. The new-

wave advertising is more interesting, more fun to watch, and brings the viewer better film and editorial devices, better music, better photography and better talent . . . Many commercials, to damn with faint praise, are more rewarding than the programs surrounding them.
*Before National Academy of Television
Arts and Sciences,
Chicago, pub. May 21.*

**John O. Pastore**
*United States Senator, D-R.I.*

You don't serve the public by putting (broadcast station) licensees on the griddle every three years, but by encouraging those who are in the business to do their job right.
*At Senate communications
subcommittee hearing,
Washington, March 5.*

The American people are not all that naive and stupid. Does everything have to turn on sex when it comes to shaving cream (in television commercials)?
*At Senate communications
subcommittee hearing,
Washington, March 12.*

To me it's a matter of guts . . . if a broadcaster is not living up to the law, then refuse to renew the license . . . We are losing sight of common sense. We all know what obscenity is. When we have a station which broadcasts four-letter words again and again—and yet, to renew its license and grant it a new one, that to me is permissiveness on the part of the (Federal Communications) Commission. And that frightens me . . . You haven't got the guts to take away the license of a violator.
*At Senate communications
subcommittee hearing,
Washington, Dec. 3.*

**Harold Robbins**
*Author*

TV censorship is censorship by intimidation. No one *says* what you can or cannot do.
*Interview, Los Angeles, pub. April 15.*

**Elton Rule**
*President,
American Broadcasting Company-TV*

The big danger is that we in television

don't overreact to such an extent that we water down meaningful material until it is worthless. These movements against violence and against sex are very popular causes, but you cannot remove violence or sex and present anything remotely representative of human behavior. No matter how much we howl, we're not going to eliminate sex or violence from the life pattern of modern man.

*Interview, Los Angeles, pub. April 22.*

**Aline Saarinen**
*Commentator,*
*National Broadcasting Company*

I don't like the term "educational television." TV should move you, get you off balance. That's all it can do. It's a medium that's based on the public and it can't get too far ahead . . . When I come home tired, I don't turn on ballet; I look at an old movie. I don't use television for education and I don't think that's its primary purpose. I think that some of the dullest shows on television are the do-good shows that don't have sponsors.

*Interview, New York, pub. March 30.*

**William Sackheim**
*Producer*

The director comes in and works with the producer and writer on refining a script and, in many cases, to mold it to his needs. He works long hours, is on his feet all day. The entire film is up to him, and, if he folds, it folds. It's difficult work. He has to fight the clock, the budget and, in many cases, the producer. He is trying to tell the writer's story without being intrusive. If he is a good director, he will be faithful to the script—not a fancy dancer who is concerned for himself at the sacrifice of the story. The director's work is very creative, but his is a social job; he is constantly surrounded by people.

*Interview, Los Angeles, pub. Dec. 24.*

**Walter D. Scott**
*Chairman,*
*National Broadcasting Company*

Even though this is a time when our critics have never been more vocal and adamant, it seems to me . . . that we must be doing something right. We must be satisfying somebody, even if it only happens to be the overwhelming majority of the people who own television sets.

*At NBC Affiliates convention,*
*Los Angeles, pub. May 14.*

**Melville Shavelson**
*Writer*

That's the trouble with TV today. Too much comedy and not enough humor.

*Interview, Los Angeles, pub. March 3.*

**Barry Shear**
*Director*

Pressure groups are ruining TV. One crank letter from Minneapolis can dictate what goes on the air.

*Interview, Los Angles, pub. Jan. 8.*

**Sid Sheinberg**
*Vice president in charge of production,*
*Universal Television*

The one discernible trend I see is the developing of a variety of new forms for television. The only rules I find are that there are no rules. I think we'll break the nonsense of the half-hour, hour or two-hour show into programs of varying lengths—based on the time you need to tell the story. The medium has to accommodate the message, not vice-versa.

*Interview, Los Angeles, pub. Jan. 9.*

**Sidney Sheldon**
*Producer*

. . . a lot of guys doing TV are dying to get into pictures. I've had all that. TV is as challenging as any other medium, and I don't look down on it.

*Interview, Los Angeles, pub. March 5.*

**Penny Singleton**
· *Executive president,*
*American Guild of Variety Artists*

. . . subscription TV is just what they (the audiences) are looking for—family entertainment and special events at prices they can afford. To deny subscription television an opportunity to find that audience would . . . be to deny the American public a service they need and want very much. To deny it would continue to penalize tens of thousands of workers in the entertain-

(PENNY SINGLETON)

ment industries who find their jobs slipping away year by year.

*Before House communications subcommittee, Washington, Nov. 24.*

**Herbert F. Solow**
*Vice president in charge of production,*
*Metro-Goldwyn-Mayer Television*

Most of the shows winning Emmys don't jibe with those shows which are most popular. There has to be a reason and it's snob appeal . . . There is a condescending attitude by everyone but the buyers. We are always knocking, knocking, knocking. I don't understand it. You would need a psychiatrist to explain it.

*Interview, Los Angeles, pub. Jan. 21.*

**Charles Sopkin**
*Author*

. . . at the *New Yorker Magazine*, you can't—literally can't—get from the business floor to the editorial floor. There's no connecting staircase; they had it sealed up years ago, and there's a reason. They keep the business people out of the editorial department—and I think this is the problem with television.

*Radio discussion, New York, pub. Feb. 2.*

**Aaron Spelling**
*Producer*

You can say "hell" sometimes on NBC but never on ABC. We do a lot of horse-trading with them, one "hell" for two "damns," that sort of thing . . . But, so far as I'm concerned, they can take away all my "damns" and "hells" if they just leave my subject matter alone.

*Interview, Los Angeles, pub. Dec. 13.*

**Frank Stanton**
*President,*
*Columbia Broadcasting System*

I get very nervous when I see a med-ium that has the power and reach and impact of television passing through one or two or three men to make a (censorship) judgment on it. I would rather spread the responsibility and fix it at the local level.

*Pub. March 31.*

**Arthur Treacher**
*Television Personality*

It (the TV talk show) is the easiest work in the world. It's marvelous. You say the words, get the money and go home.

*Pub. Sept. 1.*

**Richard Widmark**
*Actor*

I don't like television. I don't like to work in the medium, and I don't like to watch it . . . Television was not meant for drama. It's all right for news, sports and documentaries. But that's it.

*Interview, Los Angeles, pub. Nov. 12.*

**Mason Williams**
*Writer*

People in the network are the most tasteless I know. They're in it for the money and nothing more. They want to make a million on every special. A show should be fun, but any time money contacts fun, it's not fun anymore. And I don't think things will get any better.

*Interview, Los Angeles, pub. Feb. 28.*

**William Windom**
*Actor*

I did 110 "Farmer's Daughters" and about six of them were really first-rate shows. That's 5%, and that's about all you can really expect out of this world. If 5% of the people you meet, the books you read, the haircuts you get are really memorable experiences, you're getting your full share, you've no complaints.

*Interview, Los Angeles, pub. April 1.*

**Giovanni Agnelli**
*Chairman, Fiat Company of Italy*

I obtained this position because I was appointed by myself and my brothers.

*At International Industrial Conference,*
*San Francisco, Sept. 17.*

**Spiro T. Agnew**
*Vice President-elect*
*of the United States*

I think the worst mistake I could make would be to attempt to placate and satisfy my critics. I think I have enough intelligence to know that I could do this, I could say exactly what certain people wanted me to say with a contrived purpose in making them happy. But I can't do that. I've got myself to live with and my convictions.

*Television interview,*
*New York, telecast Jan. 7.*

**Spiro T. Agnew**
*Vice President of the United States*

I don't think it's fair to say that (referring to criticism of himself) suddenly a yokel has descended upon the national government.

*Television interview,*
*pub. Jan. 27.*

I didn't come to this office unsophisticated, even though my image may have arrived that way.

*Pub. March 28.*

**Eddie Albert**
*Actor*

Happiness to me means constant growth. If I see a chance to do something, even if it stinks, I do it. I'm always on the side of action—I just can't sit on my butt and do "Green Acres."

*Interview, pub. Sept. 6.*

**Jack Albertson**
*Actor*

Do you know what I felt like doing (on winning an *Oscar* for best supporting actor)? If I had followed my immediate impulse, I would have done a soft-shoe dance. I'm sure I could have expressed my appreciation at that instant more with my feet than with my tongue.

*Interview, Los Angeles, pub. April 24.*

I started out in vaudeville, and vaudeville died. I hit the burlesque houses, and they padlocked 'em. I tried radio, and you know what happened to radio. Then live TV, and it vanished. Now that I've finally got a toehold in movies, look what's happening to them.

*Interview, Hollywood,*
*pub. Nov. 27.*

**Muhammed Ali (Cassius Clay)**
*Former World Heavyweight*
*Boxing Champion*

Even to this day, women are after me—white and black and brown and yellow. Airline stewardesses and waitresses and others ask if they can come up to my hotel. But my religion has made 'me strong. When a man can fight sex, you know he's strong. I am the cleanest champion ever produced.

*Las Vegas, pub. Oct. 26.*

**Woody Allen**
*Actor-Writer-Comedia*

I hate all critics. To me, they only serve a destructive function . . . I never read criticism of any kind, never look at a review of my own work, even if I know it's a smashing review. Hemingway said . . . that if you believe critics when they say you're good, you have to believe

(WOODY ALLEN)

them when they say you're bad. Who would ever want to believe that?

*Interview, pub. June 29.*

**Ursula Andress**
*Actress*

Acting is agony for me. It's wonderful to have done a film, but while I'm making it I feel like I'm diving into cold water every time I step in front of the camera . . . I don't like the nightclub routine or parties. I like to stay in my shell. It embarrasses me to talk about myself, and I give very few interviews.

*Interview, London, pub. Dec. 7.*

**Princess Anne**
*of the United Kingdom*

Princesses are getting a bit short on the market. I'll soon be next, but they'll have a job marrying me off to somebody I don't want.

*London, pub. Aug. 24.*

**Walter H. Annenberg**
*United States Ambassador*
*to the United Kingdom*

I started with an awful lot handed to me.

*Washington, pub. Feb. 24.*

**Michael Ansara**
*Actor*

Actors have ego problems, and acting gives them a release for those problems. Take me. I was shy, felt inferior, thought everybody was better than I was. When I acted, I wasn't Michael Ansara alone. I was Michael Ansara and a great talent. I was announcing, "Look at me. I'm good. I'm great." It was making people admire and love me. This is a generalization. Some actors are exceptions to the rule. But I haven't met any.

*Interview, Los Angeles, pub. Dec. 15.*

**Arthur Ashe**
*Tennis Player*

We (tennis players) are all egotists; we're all prima donnas.

*New York, pub. Feb. 8.*

**Elizabeth Ashley**
*Actress*

I was much, much too successful much, much too soon. I was a star at 21. I was the youngest person to ever win the *Tony*. Acting was my whole life. I was THE actress. Nothing else mattered. No outside relationship was important. I threw my whole life into everything I did. If that sounds arrogant, you have to be arrogant to get up there night after night and tell people: "Love me, love me, love me! . . ." Now I think I'm free of that . . . I'm having fun acting. I never did before.

*Pub. Nov. 16.*

**Sir Frederick Ashton**
*Choreographer*

I think I should like to be remembered as a significant creator of my time . . . I would like to feel that I had extended the idiom and the vocabulary of the classic dance, that I had taken it a step further. But the future is not a thing that preoccupies me. I don't worry about whether my ballets are going to live on or not. In years to come, though, I wouldn't like to be treated too lightly, or to be fobbed off as a somebody-somebody of my time, choreographically speaking. As long as I'm treated seriously, I'll be perfectly happy. Pavlova once took my hand and said, "Fred, you have a great future. It will come slowly, but it will come." She's always in the back of my mind, and I would like to think I haven't disappointed her.

*Interview, London, Sept. 25.*

**Isaac Asimov**
*Author*

My wife hates my life. When she says, "Let's go to the movies," I protest, but go. When she says we have to take a vacation, I kick and scream. I think 10 mistresses are better than one wife. Since I'm a good husband, I can only dream.

*Interview, West Newton, Mass.,*
*pub. Oct. 18.*

**Frankie Avalon**
*Actor, Singer*

It was murder being a teen-age idol. You couldn't do anything (without being mobbed). If I had a night off on the road and wanted to see a movie, I'd have to

have my manager buy out the balcony.
*Interview, Los Angeles, pub. Dec. 14.*

## Joan Baez
*Folk Singer*

People have tried to say I'm square because I cut my hair, but I'm more radical than ever. I feel I'm behind musically because I'm ahead politically. What's finally happened in the newspapers has been one of my goals. Now they call me a pacifist folk singer instead of a folksinger pacifist. At the least, they call me controversial. No one considers me just a girl with a pretty voice anymore.
*Interview, San Francisco, pub. Jan. 26.*

## Pearl Bailey
*Singer, Actress*

I never really look for anything. What God throws my way comes. I wake up in the morning and whichever way God turns my feet, I go.
*Interview, pub. July 6.*

## Brigitte Bardot
*Actress*

First I am a woman, then an actress. I'm not like some actresses who only come alive when they are in front of a camera. I live when I'm not filming.
*Interview, pub. Jan. 8.*

## Jack Benny
*Entertainer*

I don't like to look back. I never was crazy about radio. Some fans always want to go back, but I'm not interested anymore. I'm looking ahead to the next stage show. It's how I keep young.
*Pub. July 27.*

. . . retire? I couldn't retire; I just couldn't. I'm too much of a ham.
*Interview, Chicago, pub. Dec. 3.*

## Thomas Hart Benton
*Artist*

I'm trying to get rid of that stare that all self-portraits have when they're painted off a mirror. Only fellow that got rid of that was Rembrandt. How he managed, I'll never know. I don't really have a concept of myself. I'll just look into the mirror and paint whatever comes out. It's a portrait of an old man, that's all. An old man at work, that's probably what I'll call it. Now, let's get to something serious. Look at that sun . . .
*Interview, pub. Oct. 3.*

## Polly Bergen
*Actress*

Self-approval is the most necessary and yet the most hard to come by thing there is. But I finally got it. For years I thought of myself as a jack-of-all-trades-and-master-of-none. I held this against myself. I felt I was acceptable in many things but never really great in anything. I was always displeased with myself. People always say to me, "You're so competitive." That's true. What they didn't realize was that I was competing only with one person—myself. I was always trying to do better and better than I was.
*Interview, Beverly Hills, Calif.,*
*pub. June 19.*

## Georgie Best
*Soccer Player*

There are a few people who think I'm one of the best soccer players in the world, but I won't be happy until everyone does.
*Pub. Feb. 24.*

## Philip Blaiberg
*World's first heart transplant patient*

It (receiving a new heart) taught me to live each day, and to hell with the tears and worries it all has been—let it be. I don't know how much longer I will live —who does?—but I do know this: I'm going to enjoy every day that is left to me before the last hour comes.
*Interview, May 24.*

## Claire Bloom
*Actress*

The things I like? People who are aware of what happens around them, who are open to anything, and who are good at their jobs; the color yellow, because it's like the sun and makes me happy; mornings, before you start going downhill; reading, the greatest pleasure in life; baroque

(CLAIRE BLOOM)

music; just plain quiet, the sound of silence; placid waters; the smell of herbs growing wild in Sardinia; the taste of white truffles cooked in Italy; shopping for soft, casual, comfortable clothes; the gleam of mellow gold jewelry; and men who are brighter and quicker than I am.

*Interview, New York,*
*pub. July 22.*

### Winton M. Blount
*Postmaster General*
*of the United States*

When I was a little boy in Alabama, I was taught by my father to hate Yankees, Republicans and sin, in that order. Since then I have found that each could be nice on occasion.

*Washington, pub. Feb. 22.*

### Pearl S. Buck
*Author*

I am old, of course, but I am not vain about it. I was brought up in China, where age is honorable. And as long as I can work, I'm happy. As for being lonely, in the conventional sense, let me merely say that I have nine adopted children, plus 12 grandchildren, and they all live nearby. I also have four Korean girls who live at my house while being educated in this country. My house is full all the time, and so is my life.

*Interview, Philadelphia,*
*pub. July 28.*

### Carol Burnett
*Television Entertainer*

You know, I'm really a very square person. I've never smoked pot or seen a stag film. I've never even seen "Hair." I'm really out of it. Last month, at a party, this brooding man was staring at me, so I gave him my big, phoney smile, and he came over and said he always watched the show and laughed, but that the sketch endings weren't always sharp enough. He'd said his name was Edward, so I said, "Look, Ed, if you could write brilliant endings every week you'd own the network." Told him off for about ten minutes. When Joe (Hamilton, her husband)

came to get me, I said, "Ed what?" He said, "Edward Albee." I didn't even recognize him! See how square I am?

*Interview, Los Angeles, pub. June 1.*

### Abe Burrows
*Playwright, Director*

Everything I write is serious. It just comes out funny. Making jokes was my adjustment to life. Most kids have a sense of rebellion. Some kids throw rocks. I make jokes. Someone once defined humor as a way to keep from killing yourself. I keep my sense of humor and I stay alive.

*Interview, Chicago, pub. Oct. 12.*

### Richard Burton
*Actor*

She (Elizabeth Taylor) is the best. The Champ. And one of the nicest things about our marriage is that I don't have to lie any more about where I've been. There's no need to. She knows she can trust me absolutely. If she thinks I'm looking at a girl she'll say, "Watch it—!", mentioning a certain playboy who was caught by a husband in *flagrante delicto* and shot, very accurately, in the midsection.

*Interview, Shepperton Studios,*
*London, pub. Oct. 18.*

### Petula Clark
*Singer, Actress*

. . . I won't be put in a box or bag . . . I got one foot in reality and the other in fantasy. That's very close to my bag.

*Interview, Los Angeles, pub. April 17.*

I undergo a physical release in singing; my complexes vanish. On stage, I feel rather wanton, even abandoned. Well, I'm not married—I'm having an affair with the audience . . . And I'm six feet tall.

*Interview, Pub. Oct. 7.*

### Eldridge Cleaver
*Information Minister,*
*Black Panther Party*

I want to come back to San Francisco with all my heart. I miss everything: the noise of the city, the familiar sight of people I know, even that pig (Mayor Joseph) Alioto.

*Telephone interview, while fleeing from criminal prosecution in the U.S.; Algiers, July 17.*

**Sean Connery**
*Actor*

You know, even when I had no money I used to go to Harrod's to buy jars of caviar, which I love. The guilt I felt just going up to the counter—that was terrible. Now I've got a sauna bath in the basement, and next to it I installed an expensive German shower, one that shoots hot and cold water at you at the same time. It cost £299, and I thought: "What am I doing? What's wrong with the shower in the bathroom upstairs?" No, you never lose your guilt complex; never.

*Interview, London, pub. April 18.*

**Chuck Connors**
*Actor*

In baseball, I was starving. Among other reasons, as a batter I hit three ways —right-handed, left-handed and seldom. I had to find myself another racket. As a salesman of products, I was a flop. I'd wind up giving away my wares to some poor schmuck who couldn't afford to pay. I couldn't become a bank robber, because I was too tall and obvious. The only talent I had was a big mouth and a reputation as a baseball comedian who ran backward around the bases when I hit a home run and did cartwheels in front of the dugout. Oh yes, I had one other thing: I considered myself the greatest undiscovered actor in the country.

*Interview, pub. Sept. 14.*

**Joseph Cotten**
*Actor*

I'm always working. I love my wife. She loves me. My agent still calls me . . . so what's my problem, Mr. Anthony?

*Interview, Hollywood, pub. Oct. 26.*

**Tom Courtenay**
*Actor*

I don't want to write. I don't want to direct. I'm not smart enough for either. I just want to act.

*Interview, pub. March 1.*

**Noel Coward**
*Actor, Playwright*

I'm a chocolate milkshake with just a little vodka at the bottom.

*Television interview, pub. December.*

It will be a week of hell (celebrating his 70th birthday), not only for me but also for the people who have to sing my praises. I'll be sitting there wearing my tribute-accepting face, which shows me proud but unspoiled by my own success. It is a face I have used since 1920.

*Interview, pub. Dec. 26.*

I always talked as I talk now and always liked to wear nice clothes. I like being . . . chic. The young enchanters of today may have talent but why must they look so grubby? I think you should always look your best. I know it's not important, but it's silly to be deliberately grubby. I've always had a feeling for being an attractive public figure. I would do nothing to spoil it.

*Interview, Montreux, Switzerland, pub. Dec. 28.*

**Bob Crane**
*Actor*

I don't want to be put in a groove. Soon people (will) know me as the hat and jacket (in the TV show, "Hogan's Heroes") and won't recognize me otherwise. That's why I take all those guest shots. I don't want to be a hat and jacket.

*Interview, Los Angeles, pub. Jan. 28.*

**Joan Crawford**
*Actress*

I don't know anyone who isn't lonely. I didn't have much chance to be lonely during my marriage, but I've been pretty darned lonely since then. You just learn to live with it. You don't dwell on it. That's the only way to handle it. I've never had an ounce of self-pity in my life, and I'm not about to start now.

. . . I like to work. Inactivity is one of the great indignities of life. Through inactivity, people lose their self-respect, their integrity. The need to work is always there, bugging me.

*Interview, London, pub. Aug. 24.*

**Michael Dann**
*Senior vice president*
*for TV programming,*
*Columbia Broadcasting System*

I am not a very creative man. My whole strength and success is the people around me. Most of them are junior Phi Betas, hostile people who work around the clock with total dedication. They're all sort of paranoid—but the most wonderful people in the world. I'm the best listener in the business. I rob from everyone all day long. I sit here like a fox terrier snapping at their heels, trying to make things work.
*Interview, New York, pub. July 12.*

**Sammy Davis, Jr.**
*Entertainer*

There's no place in America where I can find a way just to live as a human being.
*Pub. Aug. 10.*

**Jimmy Dean**
*Singer*

For the right price I would do anything that's decent and legal—and a lot of things that ain't.
*Interview, Los Angeles, pub. Dec. 3.*

**Hubert De Givenchy**
*Fashion Designer*

The important thing in life is to have liberty. I'm 42 and I've fought to have this liberty, of creation and expression, for myself. But perhaps someday, if someone offers me X million . . .
*Interview, New York, Sept. 15.*

**Catherine Deneuve**
*Actress*

I like people who don't convey the air of what they really are inside, people who give the impression of a very private domain deep within themselves that they are determined never to reveal. And that's the kind of role I like to play in films. My theory of acting, to the extent that I have one, is to communicate through nuances—by keeping things very natural, simple, hidden, dissimulated.

I live a lot in the present, a little in the past and *never* in the future.
*Interview, Paris, pub. August.*

**Bernadette Devlin**
*Member of British Parliament*
*from Northern Ireland*

I'm not good enough to be a saint and not bad enough to be interesting.
*New York, Aug. 29.*

**Jimmy Durante**
*Entertainer*

I hope to live till CeCe (his daughter) marries. I don't want anything else. I've got my family, my health. I thank God every morning for both. I like to make people laugh. Dey like me. What could I want? I don't want all da money in da world.
*Interview, pub. March 4.*

I been asked why I don't retire. Retire? What for? D'ya think I'm crazy? A guy can only go to look at Niagara Falls so many times. I don't wanna be a vegetable.
*Interview, Los Angeles, pub. March 11.*

When you retire, all you can do is deteriorate. You gotta get on your hands and knees and thank God the people still want you—and that you got your health. I'm never going to retire.
*Interview, Los Angeles, pub. Oct. 19.*

**Clint Eastwood**
*Actor*

People who go to movies like me. I haven't had a special push or a big studio build-up. I never get my picture taken kissing my dog when I get off a plane—that sort of thing. There are stars who are produced by the press. I'm not one of them. Bogart once said he owed it to the moviegoing public—and to them alone—to do his best. I feel that way, too.
*Interview, Los Angeles, pub. June 22.*

**Samantha Eggar**
*Actress*

Marriage ain't easy, baby, as someone said. You go from independence to dependence to independence so you don't become a *nebbish*.
*Interview, Los Angeles, pub. Feb. 23.*

**Hillard Elkins**
*Motion Picture and Stage Producer*

I am egotistical and conceited and rude,

but I make up for it by being charming and amusing.

*Interview, pub. Sept. 14.*

**"Duke" Ellington**
*Musician*

I'm not in politics; I'm in the realm of art. As long as I stay in the realm of art, I'm welcome in the White House no matter who's living there.

*Pub. Aug. 5.*

**Robert Evans**
*Vice president in charge
of production,
Paramount Pictures Corporation*

Basically, I'm a gambler. To me, life is a gamble. And the picture business for me is the biggest gamble of all. It's not the money I'm playing for. It's way, way more than money. It's success and wanting to win. And because everyone says I can't do it. Because everyone said I was going to fall flat on my ass. Well, I can hold my own in any jungle, and, if I lose, it'll be the first time I ever lost at anything this important to me. I never lose, because I give everything to what I'm doing. I have no other interests but Paramount. I'm not that much more talented than the next guy, but I give more of myself, which counts. In the long run, it counts a lot.

*Pub. March 7.*

**Mia Farrow**
*Actress*

If I weren't doing what I'm doing now, the actress thing, the star business if you want to call it that, whatever it is, I'd be in an asylum. I'm sure of it.

*Interview, Los Angeles, pub. Jan. 26.*

**Jane Fonda**
*Actress*

I always said I would never get married until someone gave me one good reason for marriage, aside from the social, conventional one. Nobody ever did, but I married anyway, for social, conventional reasons—and my father.

*Interview, pub. Aug. 24.*

**Dame Margot Fonteyn**
*Ballet Dancer*

I said at one time I planned to retire at 35, and didn't, so I do not plan any more. I'll just take every day as it comes. Sure it is hard work. But it's the only life I've known for 35 years and I have no complaints about it. I'm delighted and astounded that it has lasted so long.

*Interview, London, March 25.*

**John Fowles**
*Author*

I'm very rich. I'm rich in a minor financial way—rich enough never to buy new clothes, never to want to go abroad, rich enough not to like spending money any more. I'm also rich in having many interests. I always have a backlog of books to read, there's the garden, nature, walking . . .

*Interview, Dorset, England, pub. Nov. 9.*

**David Frost**
*Television Commentator*

I love that moment when the band starts up and I'm on my way on stage. I really have great hopes that in those 90 moments something unpredictable and marvelous will happen each time. That's the unpredictability which can exalt television. I'm always watching for those moments, they're what I live for.

*Interview, New York, pub. Dec. 7.*

**Venkatagiri Varaha Giri**
*President of India*

Those who say I am too old, let them have the benefit of my fist.

*New Delhi, pub. Aug. 21.*

**Arthur Godfrey**
*Radio and Television Entertainer*

It has been said, rather wistfully, that any man who says he can still do at 50 what he did when he was 25, didn't do very much at 25. Well, it's been fifteen years since I was 50 and the only thing I've given up since then are cigarettes and tap dancing.

*Before National Association
of Broadcasters,
Washington, pub. May 28.*

**Barry M. Goldwater**
*United States Senator, R-Ariz.*

I feel like the only kamikaze pilot who

ever made a round trip. Just yesterday, a lady came up to me on the street, looked me over carefully, and said, "Say, weren't you Barry Goldwater?"

> *On being elected to the Senate,*
> *Washington, pub. Jan. 20.*

## Ruth Gordon
*Actress*

Always strict discipline. Every morning at work by eight, stop at 12:30. Nothing interferes. I walk three miles. Nothing interferes. After that, I do whatever I feel spunky about. Gay as a bird am I, after I do what I set about to do.

> *Interview, Beverly Hills, Calif.,*
> *pub. Jan. 23.*

## Frank Gorshin
*Entertainer*

I never have been able to get interested in golf or other games. When I have time to relax. I just sit around and read and think and worry. When I'm not doing anything, I worry why I'm not doing something.

> *Interview, New York, pub. Sept. 21.*

## Elliott Gould
*Actor*

I was about 22 when I first met Barbra (Streisand, his wife) during the rehearsals in New York for a Broadway musical, "I Can Get It For You Wholesale." I was hired before she was. I remember seeing her audition. She was fantastic. Stunning. Even then, I could recognize her as an extraordinarily talented, sensitive girl, with a cunning facade. She was aloof and confident, but in a blase way. She even conned herself into believing her facade. When we talked about it, she didn't even know it herself. What is appealing about Barbra is that, underneath that facade, is the most child-girl I have ever met.

> *Interview, pub. August.*

## Cary Grant
*Actor*

I often think my life has been a failure. But whenever I drop into a theatre and hear women laughing at one of my films,

I think, well, if I brightened their day before they went home and did the dishes, maybe my life wasn't wasted after all.

> *Pub. Nov. 16.*

## Stanley Myron Handleman
*Comedian*

To hang around—that's my goal in life. I want a quiet life—anything to keep my mind off work. I just hate working. It's not that I'm lazy; I just have a natural inclination toward inactivity.

> *Interview, Las Vegas, pub. Sept. 17.*

## Richard Harris
*Actor*

You can sum up my life and my acting in one sentence right now: "I want to play all the strings in the bow, because I want to find out how many strings there are . . ." I have this great zest for life and freedom. I want to be marvelously wild and Rabelaisian . . . but I also hope that people will say: "I think there's something going on under Harris's wildness."

> *Interview, London, pub. Aug. 24.*

## Rex Harrison
*Actor*

. . . I have never regretted the choice of any parts I have done. Because you get involved in the part, you grow to love the character, and you can never regret something you love.

> *Interview, Paris, pub. Jan. 26.*

## Elizabeth Hartman
*Actress*

The real me, I guess, is the shy, up-against-the-wall person. I like sympathy. I like people to feel sorry for me . . . You can tell from your fans what you are. I've got the adolescent crowd and the poetic boys. Those are the kind who write to me and stop me on the street. It's certainly not the lusty men.

> *Interview, New York, pub. Dec. 21.*

## Laurence Harvey
*Actor*

I am a flamboyant character, an extrovert who doesn't want to reveal his feelings. To bare your soul to the world I find un-

utterably boring, and I think that part of our profession is to have an air of mystery —to have a quixotic personality so that no one can put a finger on you and say you are this or this.
*Interview, Paris, pub. Oct. 5.*

It's in my nature to be unsettled, and I'll always be a nomad. I'm perfectly at home wherever I am—in a hotel in Rome or a tent in the Sahara.
*Interview, Rome, pub. Dec. 28.*

**Paul Hasluck**
*Governor-General of Australia*

Just because I don't giggle or dig people in the ribs all the time, outsiders say I haven't got a sense of humor. You go around my electorate and you'll find out what a warmhearted old fellow I am. I've put up with this sort of character assassination for years, often from people who have never met me.
*Interview, Sydney, Feb. 11.*

**Richard G. Hatcher**
*Mayor, Gary, Ind.*

In the past I've visited white areas where people almost spat on me. Today, I hear some mothers say to their children, "There is the Mayor; get his autograph."
*Pub. Feb. 28.*

**S. I. Hayakawa**
*President, San Francisco State College*

I've been, all my life, the kind of intellectual highbrow I disapprove of.
*Pub. Oct. 6.*

. . . many people expect me to be an English-speaking Toshiro Mifune in a tam o' shanter, wildly swinging a Samurai sword and lopping off the heads of radical students and faculty.
*Columbia University, pub. Dec. 21.*

**Hugh M. Hefner**
*Publisher, "Playboy Magazine"*

I'm sure that I will be remembered as one significant part of our time. We live in a period of rapid sociological change, and I am on the side of the angels.

. . . you know, in the next ten years I would rather meet a girl and have her fall in love with me than make another hundred million dollars.
*Interview, pub. Feb. 14.*

**Jascha Heifetz**
*Violinist*

Here is my biography: I played the violin at 3 and gave my first concert at 7. I have been playing ever since.
*Interview, Beverly Hills, Calif., pub. Oct. 31.*

**Gustav Heinemann**
*President of West Germany*

I love no states. I love my wife, and that's enough.
*Pub. March 6.*

**Katharine Hepburn**
*Actress*

. . . the thing that always intrigues me—the saddest thing with human beings —is the moment of giving up. I find the swim upstream stimulating business, though I know I was luckily endowed and have been pretty damn spoiled.
*Hollywood, pub. Sept. 18.*

**Alfred Hitchcock**
*Motion Picture Director*

I've been called a ghoul, but I know when an audience is going to scream. I enjoy it and I have to smile to myself in anticipation of what I'm doing to them.
*Interview, Hollywood, pub. Sept. 13.*

I want to be remembered as a man who entertained millions through the technique of film. I'm satisfied with life, and what the years have brought me. I wouldn't dream of retiring; the figure of a birthday is something one ignores. I sometimes think, though, I would have liked to have been a criminal lawyer. Think of the opportunity I would have had to be a great man in court.
*Interview, pub. Sept. 27.*

As for the purpose of life, I'd say it is to lead the good life. My greatest pleasure is to arrive at home at 6 o'clock, with my wife waiting, and we have a drink together, and I sit in the kitchen while she makes us some supper.
*Interview, pub. Dec. 14.*

**Dustin Hoffman**
*Actor*

I'm an actor, and that's all I am, aside from being a human being with feelings. I resist the temptation to be seduced by the press, which wants to put me in the avant-garde of acting. Youths laugh to think that I represent them.
*Interview, Los Angeles, pub. Dec. 21.*

**Bob Hope**
*Actor, Comedian*

I'm the all-weather comedian.
*Interview, Los Angeles, pub. Jan. 8.*

**Israel Horowitz**
*Playwright*

When I die, I don't want anyone to make a big deal over me. I just want a couple of friends to come around and try to bring me back.
*Interview, Boston, pub. Aug. 22.*

**Hubert H. Humphrey**
*Former Vice President
of the United States*

As I approach my new career as university professor and author, I am beginning to feel a new sense of freedom. I think I shall enjoy being a free spirit again—for, as they say, I've been a captive of the White House long enough.
*New York, Jan. 13.*

I'm a free man. It's wonderful to be a free man. But I want you to know I'd rather have been a captive of the White House.
*Washington, pub. Jan. 20.*

. . . this (running for the presidency) was the great opportunity, the ` grand prize, and a man would be less than honest with himself if he didn't say that, when he's reaching for that prize and comes so close that his fingertips could almost touch it, you feel the sense of disappointment, the deep disappointment . . .
*Interview, Washington, Jan. 25.*

I have never believed in the politics of criticism. I am an advocate.
*Pub. April 21.*

. . . what do I want to do with my life? I'm here now. I like my work (as a college professor) and I'm beginning to enjoy it more and more. I have a chance to make some money. I have a chance to live my own life. I don't have to answer everybody that makes a line of criticism. I can ignore a good deal of it. And maybe, after 25 years of public life, that ought to be a luxury that I'm entitled to.
*Interview, MacAlester College,
St. Paul, Minn., July 5.*

**Chester (Chet) R. Huntley**
*News Commentator,
National Broadcasting Company*

I've killed more good jokes than any man alive. David (Brinkley) could read the dictionary and it would be light and frothy.
*Pub. March 14.*

**John Huston**
*Motion Picture Director*

The only time I act is when I can't get anyone else for the role. And as an actor I'm always in accord with the director— when I'm the director.
*Interview, pub. June 16.*

**Nate Jacobson**
*Chairman, Caesar's Palace Hotel,
Las Vegas, Nevada*

When you live in this town (Las Vegas), you give up gambling for two reasons: it takes up a lot of your time, and it takes a lot of your money.
*Las Vegas, pub. March 2.*

**Lyndon B. Johnson**
*Former President of the United States*

I'm sure any person who has been active as I have for 38 years in public affairs will notice when the role is called and his name is not there. But I want to miss it. It hurts good.
*News conference, Johnson City, Tex.,
pub. Feb. 3.*

I don't think I can ever explain . . . to the American people something that's so deeply embedded in their beliefs as the fact that Lyndon Johnson was an extremely ambitious man who sought power, who enjoyed using it and whose greatest desire was to occupy the top job in American political life. That has never been my feeling.

*Television interview, Dec. 27.*

**Mrs. Lyndon B. Johnson**
*Wife of the*
*President of the United States*

Actually, the First Lady has an advantage over the President. He has all the hard decisions to make. She has the glamor and excitement.

*Interview, pub. Jan. 3.*

**Tom Jones**
*Singer*

I can't imagine being a man past 50, when you can't do everything you want. Then it's all downhill. The one thing that gives me consolation is money. Being old and poor is miserable. Having money, maybe it's not so bad.

*Interview, pub. Nov. 4.*

**Garson Kanin**
*Playwright*

Jean Renoir once told us that when his father's friends used to come to the house —all the distinguished French painters of the time—they never talked about grand theories of painting; they talked about where to get the best turpentine.

*Interview, Beverly Hills, Calif.,*
*pub. Oct. 5.*

**Kurt Kaszner**
*Actor*

I like to paint, but I have no time. So I take out my artistic frustrations in food. I eat my art, you might say.

*Interview, Los Angeles, pub. Feb. 20.*

**Kirk Kerkorian**
*Financier*

I'm just a small-town boy who got lucky. Gosh, to compare me with (Howard) Hughes is like the difference between a BB gun and a shotgun.

If there's a good deal, I'll go anywhere.
*Interview, Las Vegas, pub. Oct. 25.*

**Virginia H. Knauer**
*Assistant to the President*
*of the United States*
*for Consumer Affairs*

I am an activist. I act as a catalyst to the people around me, and if it can't be done today, it had better be done tomorrow.
*Pub. April 21.*

**Mrs. Nguyen Cao Ky**
*Wife of the Vice President*
*of South Vietnam*

My country has never known peace in my lifetime. A journalist in Paris asked me what peace was and I said it must be something quiet and happy.
*Washington, April 2.*

**Frankie Laine**
*Singer*

. . . those lean years taught me a lot. It taught me, among other things, the value of always giving a little more than you're asked. When I had all those big hits and could virtually dictate my own terms to nightclub owners, I felt I should give them my best at all times. I don't think I was ever temperamental. I've always found it easy to be nice to people—something a lot of the younger performers in the business today fail to understand.
*Pub. Sept. 2.*

**Burt Lancaster**
*Actor*

(Things he likes) . . . Jogging a couple of miles every morning, sirloin steaks and martinis, walking down Fifth Avenue here at 4 o'clock in the afternoon, wearing an old jacket and a $5 pair of pants, opera, ballet and pro football, reading and listening to music, pungent odors, such as cigar smoke, and people with the courage to be themselves, even if they're snotty.

(Things he dislikes) . . . Starchy foods, purple colors, the bleak look of winter in a big city, because it accents man's natural loneliness, cocktail parties, sweet smells, the sound of ambulance sirens, women who try to mold a man into something other than himself and people

(BURT LANCASTER)

who try to use you to satisfy some neurotic need in themselves.

*Interview, New York, pub. July 25.*

## Paul Laxalt
*Governor of Nevada*

I yearn for private life—the privacy, independence and the time for contemplation that each of us needs. I view public office as an honorable but temporary privilege.

*Carson City, pub. Oct. 6.*

## William P. Lear
*President, Lear Jet Corporation*

You know what I would like? I want my youth back. Not for the reason you think. I really want my youth back so I can mis-spend it again.

*Interview, Reno, pub. March 31.*

## Sam Levenson
*Writer, Humorist*

Don't try to tell me I don't understand kids. I've been 14 three times already.

*Interview, Washington, pub. Nov. 4.*

## Jerry Lewis
*Actor-Comedian-
Motion Picture Director*

I'm too busy working today and thinking about tomorrow to worry about the past.

*Interview, London, pub. Oct. 26.*

## John V. Lindsay
*Mayor of New York*

As I always say when I get applause in New York: "They must be out-of-towners."

*New York, April 20.*

## Mickey Lolich
*Baseball Player, Detroit "Tigers"*

There's something I heard someone say once and I can't remember how it went exactly: "Most people pass in the parade of life, and when they die they are forgotten." I'm passing in the parade of life, and now at least I've made a mark. Someone will know who Mickey Lolich was. He wasn't just a person who was on this earth and then passed away. I have a name now—and I know they'll be looking for new heroes as soon as this season starts—but I might be remembered by someone some day.

*Interview, Lakeland, Fla.,
pub. March 22.*

## Gina Lollobrigida
*Actress*

Today, sex comes from the personality and how you look at a man. The bust is not so important any more. But, of course, I'm not bad.

*New York, pub. Jan. 31.*

## Guy Lombardo
*Band Leader*

Why do I keep doing it (working)? Why do Jack Benny, Red Skelton, Bob Hope, Jimmy Durante keep doing it? What would they do if they quit? What would I do? It's beautiful, beautiful, and I wouldn't change a minute of it. Listen, doctors and lawyers see people when they're in trouble or sick or dying. We see them at happy times—anniversaries, weddings, birthdays, when they're on dates. Or on New Year's. Sure it's a gag; but when people say, "When Guy Lombardo goes, New Year's Eve goes with him"—well, I just love it.

*Interview, pub. Dec. 28.*

## Bryce Mackasey
*Minister of Labor of Canada*

. . . there's just no feeling like it. There it is—quarter to five in the morning. You have a two-day growth of beard. You've bullied and pressured and seduced the (labor) unions and management into a settlement. And suddenly you realize it's over. It's signed. You've won . . It's a tremendous feeling. Like winning a football championship. I have a grin from ear to ear because there's such a sense of satisfaction. Oh, I love it.

*Interview, Ottawa,
pub. Aug. 30.*

## Shirley MacLaine
*Actress*

I really *am* a flower-soul, *des*perately a part of today. I'm also a specialist in victimization. I'm the prize doormat. Name me a victim, I've played her, or I can, especially if she has a few laughs. On screen or off, I'm a victim . . . I'm an Oreo cookie, sort of crunchy on the outside and mushy-soft on the inside.

You don't *know* how it feels like to have a good picture for a change. The sheer ex*quis*iteness of it. It can only be fully enjoyed when you've had a run of bad ones, and, Cripes, I've had 'em.
*Interview, Los Angeles, pub. March 16.*

. . . I smoke pot, but I'm not addicted to it. I'm not addicted to anything except being alive. I can get high on a sunset . . .
*London, pub. May 9.*

**Anna Magnani**
*Actress*

The scripts come pouring in, they keep on coming. But unless I find something exciting, really exciting, I don't do any-thing . . . I might never do anything again. It is lovely to be lazy. It gives one time to catch up with oneself. I take care of my business; I go to the sea; I lounge around with friends. It is really divine.

Whom do I admire? You want names? No, it is better if I tell you *what* I admire. I respect talent, real talent as against bluff; loyalty, real loyalty as against light, once-over friendship; honesty, even cruel honesty, as against hypocrisy. That is what I admire.
*Interview, Rome, pub. Nov. 16.*

**Edgar F. Magnin**
*Rabbi, Wilshire Boulevard Temple,*
*Los Angeles*

I am turning 80. Not a day passes that I don't try to increase my vocabulary, read something worthwhile, listen to good music and keep growing.
*Los Angeles, Dec. 11.*

**Marvin Mandel**
*Governor of Maryland*

I've been in public office since 1952, and I learned, very early in the game, that, when you're besieged by reporters, you have to have time to think. So, every time they put a question, I put the pipe in my mouth, take out a match and light the pipe.

By the time I puff on it a couple of times, I have the answers.
*Before the Lions Club,*
*Hagerstown, Md., Sept. 10.*

**Dean Martin**
*Actor, Singer*

Playing Vegas has become a vacation for me. I love the atmosphere, the people I see and my daily golf game. I think I take better care of myself in Vegas than I do anywhere else I go. It's the time-table I keep in Hollywood that gives me ulcers—the TV show, recording sessions, guest shots, movies and other career things that tie me in knots.
*Las Vegas, pub. Sept. 27.*

**James Mason**
*Actor*

I'm tired of playing the lecherous, mid-dle-aged chap who is forever vaulting the generation gap.
*Interview, pub. May 1.*

**Jean Mayer**
*Special Consultant on Food,*
*Nutrition and Health to the*
*President of the United States*

My biggest problem is that I'm very underexercised right now, and, while I'm worrying about the fitness of the nation, I've never been so unfit in my life.
*Pub. December.*

**Mercedes McCambridge**
*Actress*

One of the most destructive things in my life was the kind of parts I played in pictures. I studied Shakespeare and the classics, and I end up shooting Joan Craw-ford and killing a horse that Elizabeth Taylor was in love with! I'm serious. I played the worst harridans, the most hard-bitten women, the absolute heavies, and it just about did me in.
*Interview, Los Angeles, pub. Nov. 12.*

**Barbara McNair**
*Singer*

I got contact lenses when I first started singing, but with them I could see people eating, drinking and talking. It added to

(BARBARA MC NAIR)

my frustration. Without glasses, the audience is just a nice, friendly blur, and that's the way I like it.

*Interview, Los Angeles, pub. April 12.*

**Lauritz Melchior**
*Former Opera Singer*

There has been no one to replace me . . . the breed has practically vanished.

*Pub. Feb. 28.*

**Melina Mercouri**
*Actress*

I adore ze young people. I understand zem. I think I am a part of zem because of my political views. I hated all my life ze Establishment. Everything zat is established I hate. I hate properties. I hate to be proprietaire. Zat is all. I have nothing. I have 4 icons zat were given me by friends. All ze other things I have are clothes.

*Interview, Los Angeles, pub. March 9.*

All this talk about sex, all this worry about sex—big deal. The sun makes me happy. I eat a good fish, he makes me happy. I sleep with a good man, *he* makes me happy . . .

*Interview, pub. June 15.*

**Darius Milhaud**
*Composer*

You know, I am 77 years old, and I have written 131 works, and if you remember that Mozart and Schubert, who each died before they were 40, wrote 600 works each . . . well, by comparison, I am a lazy composer.

*Interview, London, pub. Nov. 7.*

**Henry Miller**
*Author*

People come here to discuss metaphysics with me, but personally I'd rather take them to the ping-pong table and discover their metaphysics there.

*Big Sur, Calif., pub. Feb. 24.*

. . . when you arrive at my age, and have money that you never had before, you choose the greatest luxury of all: to do what you want, when you want! Half of my life I have had to get up early, be

somewhere in order to survive. Now, I stay in bed until noon, maybe later. Even at home I live like that. No plans, no appointments, no pressure. This is the loveliest aspect of being rich.

*Interview, Paris, pub. Sept. 28.*

**Liza Minnelli**
*Singer, Actress*

My private life is nobody's business. Besides, I lead a very routine, normal, boring life.

*Pub. Aug. 18.*

**Ron Moody**
*Actor*

I became an actor because I wanted to be an actor. At one time, though, I was a sociology teacher. You know why I gave up teaching? Because teaching gave me up. I absolutely couldn't maintain discipline. I was told off more than the kids. If the kids were reading horror comics, there I'd be sitting in the middle of them, reading along . . .

*Interview, Beverly Hills, Calif., pub. Jan. 25.*

**Garry Moore**
*Television Entertainer*

You come to my time in life and you want to do things significant. So this or that organization wants me on their board to help feed hungry children. And I'm hot for it. I'm ready to go. Put "T. G. Morfit (his real name) on the letterhead," I tell them, "and give me a job to do." They agree. The letterhead comes out—"Garry Moore." And no work. Frankly, I'm tired of seeing my name on letterheads.

*Interview, Rye, N.Y., pub. April 12.*

**Henry Morgan**
*Television and Radio Entertainer*

I guess all I am is a mess of opinions.

*Interview, Los Angeles, pub. Sept. 21.*

**Edmund Muskie**
*United States Senator, D-Me.*

. . . (running for Vice President in 1968) was a strange experience. For the first time in my life I was beginning to think of political success for the sake of political success. Always before, I was relaxed. I enjoyed the contest. If I won, fine. If I lost, too bad . . .

*Interview, Washington, pub. March 17.*

**Vladimir Nabokov**
*Author*

I have never seen a more lucid, more lonely, better balanced mad mind than mine . . .

*Interview, Montreux, Switzerland, pub. May 23.*

**Jim Nabors**
*Actor, Singer*

I don't think I'm much of an actor. The only part I've ever played was Gomer (in the "Gomer Pyle" TV Show). I'm the most surprised person around that I'm successful. I haven't got much voice, I can't really sing that well. I can't act much . . . I shave this face every morning and I sure know I'm not getting by on looks.

*Interview, Los Angeles, pub. Jan. 31.*

**Ralph Nader**
*Lawyer; Consumer Rights Advocate*

I don't like to think of myself as an idealist. If you define an idealist as someone who recedes from the real world because he wants his own world to be pure, then I'm not an idealist. I think of myself as being very practical because I want to be effective. One of the reasons I do what I do is that I feel very strongly the inadequacies of the traditional reformers. They don't do their homework. They get all involved with status, egotism and the rituals of publicity. Even the great old muckrakers like Upton Sinclair and Lincoln Steffens only did 20% of the job. They stopped with exposure. They didn't follow through by politically mobilizing a concerned constituency.

*Pub. Oct. 3.*

**Joe Namath**
*Football Player, New York "Jets"*

I belong to the "Now" people. Not the people with the view that hair is bad or not shaving is bad. I went out to the hospitals in Japan and Okinawa and this old Army nurse said: "Why don't you get a haircut?" and I said: "Look at these guys—do they care?" And you'd talk to the guys and they didn't care if you wore long curls. They just said: "What's it like back in the world?"

*Rancho La Costa, Calif., pub. Feb. 16.*

**Bob Newhart**
*Comedian*

I go off stage and always return after counting to four. Some comedians count to seven, but I won't do that. I tried it once, and when I came back the busboys were clearing off the tables.

*Interview, pub. June 7.*

**David Niven**
*Actor*

I used to work a lot in westerns. For some strange reason, directors always thought my Scottish face had a western look to it. When I auditioned for Hoppy (Hopalong Cassidy), I had only to open my mouth to lose the part.

*Pub. Feb. 27.*

**Richard M. Nixon**
*President of the United States*

I like to work in a relatively small room, with papers all around and that sort of thing . . . I'm a creature of habit.

*Press conference, Washington, Jan. 21*

I like the job I have now, but, if I had my life to live over again, I'd like to have ended up as a sports writer.

*Washington, July 22.*

It so happens that (former) President Johnson and I have a lot of things in common. We were both born in small towns. We both served in the Senate and in the House. We both served as Vice President. And we're both fortunate in the fact that we think we married above ourselves.

*Arcata, Calif., pub. Sept. 5.*

**Merle Oberon**
*Actress*

Even when I was single, I owned homes and gardens. I buy beauty where other women buy jewels . . . Land is security to me. I need gardens that are mine to walk on . . .

*Interview, pub. March 2.*

**Sir Leslie O'Brien**
*Governor, Bank of England*

I apparently provided some sorely needed material recently by being, it was said, nearly run over by a Basel tram. News of this non-event quickly circled the civilized world. I cannot undertake to provide this mild human interest each month.

*London, Feb. 3.*

**John O'Hara**
*Author*

Why should I give a damn, as I did for a long time, about not being elected to the National Institute of Arts and Letters? Because I saw the kind of people who were getting in. What the hell was Ogden Nash doing in there?

*Interview, pub. July 21.*

**Gustavo Diaz Ordaz**
*President of Mexico*

I like to operate like a submarine on sonar: When I am picking up noise from both the left and the right, I know my course is correct.

*Pub. Sept. 8.*

**Jack Palance**
*Actor*

I'm playing the role (as Fidel Castro in "Che") because my children are hungry ... At this stage in my career I don't formulate reasons why I take roles; the price was right.

*Interview, Los Angeles, pub. Jan. 3.*

**Gordon Parks**
*Photographer-Author-Motion Picture Director*

I'm extremely militant—with my camera, with my pen.

*Interview, New York, pub. Aug. 17.*

**Estelle Parsons**
*Actress*

People say I should never invite agents or interviewers to my apartment, that I should move to the East Side, get a fancy address, keep up appearances. But I have this whole idea that you have to live a certain way because you're who you are (Academy Award winner) and you've done all these *things*! I don't think of myself as a popular actress. I never do anything for anyone but me.

*Interview, New York, pub. July 27.*

**Tigran Vartonovich Petrosian**
*World Chess Champion*

The first move I make is always a good one.

*Pub. March 2.*

**Prince Philip**
*Husband of Queen Elizabeth II*

I am one of those stupid bums that never went to a university—and a fat lot of harm it did me.

*To students at Royal College of Science, London, pub. May 16.*

**Gary Player**
*Golfer*

People say I earn $500,000 a year, and they may be right. But they forget that I have to leave my family and chase all over the world for it. Last week I was walking with my son in Johannesburg and he said he hoped it would rain so that I wouldn't have to go away. What sort of price do you put on that sacrifice?

*Pub. Oct. 20.*

**Adam Clayton Powell**
*United States Representative, D-N.Y.*

What have I done that's been proven?

*Interview, Washington, Jan. 3.*

**Elvis Presley**
*Actor, Singer*

Sometimes when I walk into a room at home and see all those gold records hanging around the walls, I think they must belong to another person. Not me. I just can't believe it's me.

*Pub. Aug. 23.*

**Anthony Quinn**
*Actor*

I'm half Irish and half Mexican, born in Chihuahua, Mexico. The Quinn side of me from my Irish father was to be aggressive about my goals, set them high. The Mexican side of me kept whispering, "You

can't make it. It can't happen to you."
*Interview, Beverly Hills, Calif.,*
*pub. Nov. 2.*

**Rex Reed**
*Film Critic, Writer*

People think I live in some sort of weird, perpetual orgy of my own up here in the Hollywood hills. Actually, I'm a very simple person, really; I don't take drugs, I don't own a Rolls Royce, and I'm simply terrified of vegetarians. Actually—and this is strictly off the record, you understand —I'm really very shy.
*Interview, Hollywood, pub. Nov. 23.*

**Don Rickles**
*Actor, Comedian*

My big problem is that I've built up such a strong image of being a wise guy that, every time I go to a party, I'm in the firing line. A lot of people would love to get away with the murder I get away with. But I know the fine line to draw . . . I look on myself as the guy who insults his boss at the office party and comes in the next day to find he's still got his job. I don't say everybody loves me. They don't. But most people don't mind being ribbed. I enjoy being rude to people; but mostly I enjoy the success that goes with it.
*Interview, Umag, Yugoslavia,*
*pub. Oct. 19.*

**Warren Rogers**
*Washington Editor, "Look" Magazine*

When you interview a Kennedy, you have to be ready for a chase on land, sea and in the air.
*Pub. March 4.*

**Jerry Rubin**
*Organizer, Youth International Party*

This is the greatest honor of my life. It is with sincere humility that I accept this Federal indictment (of conspiracy to incite to riot at the Democratic National Convention in Chicago). It is the fulfillment of childhood dreams, climaxing years of hard work and fun. I wish to thank all those who made it possible: my mother, my father, brother, wife Nancy, Stew and Gumbo, Spartacus, Tom Paine, the Boston Tea Party, Ho (Chi Minh), Che (Guevara), Fidel (Castro), Huey (Long), Eldridge (Cleaver), Lenny Bruce, Walter Cronkite, and last, but not least, Richard J. Daley (Mayor of Chicago).
*News conference, New York, March 21.*

**Mrs. Artur Rubinstein**
*Wife of the Pianist*

We are married for 37 years and I am so content. It has been hectic, happy, interesting, sometimes strenuous, sometimes tiring—but never boring. No, never boring.
*Interview, New York, pub. Sept. 6.*

**Dean Rusk**
*Former Secretary of State*
*of the United States*

While I was Secretary of State, some 2,100,000 cables went out of the Department . . . signed "Rusk." My guess is that if I were doing all those cables over again, with hindsight some of them would be different. I'm going to let the historians figure out which ones those are.
*Pub. March 31.*

**Irene Ryan**
*Actress*

I was never a beauty, but I never wanted for boyfriends because they said I was fun to be with. As for the pretty girls who were impressed with their beauty, you can sit and look for just so long and then it becomes a bore.
*Interview, Los Angeles, pub. April 20.*

**George Sanders**
*Actor*

. . . I have no friends, I have no interests, I have no plans. I already wrote my life story called *Memoirs of a Professional Cad,* so I have nothing left to say. I won't be bored, because I'm bored already. I just want to be left alone.
*Interview, New York, pub. July 6.*

**Maximilian Schell**
*Actor*

I always said I won't marry until I go to Japan and see the beautiful women there. I've been to Japan now and I have to have another excuse.
*Interview, New York, pub. Feb. 7.*

**Fulton J. Sheen**
*Bishop of Rochester, N.Y.*

I am not resigning work; I am resigning the diocese. I am not retiring; I am regenerating.

*News conference, Rochester, Oct. 5.*

**Charlie Sifford**
*Professional Golfer*

I don't want to be the best *Negro* golfer in the world. I want to the best *golfer—* period.

*Pub. March 31.*

**Beverly Sills**
*Opera Singer*

I can't tell you what a good time I have onstage. Everything sparkles. I glow. I love being able to sing well, to have it just pour out of me. I'm happy onstage. I'm greedy for those three hours. They're hours of pure joy. People should go to the opera and have a good time. I do.

*Interview, pub. April 21.*

**O. J. Simpson**
*Football player*

Money never inspired me; prestige did. I always wanted to be known. I wanted people to say, "That's O.J. I like him. He's a great football player." I used to get autographs and envy the guys giving them. Now I know too much is too much. I sign autographs until the last one. I give the press whatever they want. Writers made me; I owe that. It's a price I have to pay. But it wears me down. I'm tired of being famous. I'd like to be just me. Sometimes, anyway.

*Interview, pub. August.*

**Frank Sinatra, Jr.**
*Singer*

I did a lot of crazy things when I was a kid; the usual, I guess, but you can't learn from anybody else's experiences. You have to learn from your own mistakes, and I've made plenty. My father always wanted to direct me, every inch of the way. He'd call me on the phone and try to give me advice, and more than not I'd say, "Sorry, I don't see it," and then he'd get mad at me. I used to get more

wires from him, never signed, with just a message: "Are you sure you know what you're doing?"

Happiness is a lot of different things. Who is ever happy all the time? I'm pleased with what I'm doing right now. Things seem to be working out. I don't need all the fame in the world. I don't need all the money there is. I just want to lead a nice, quiet, happy life. I want to be left alone, to work my own way.

*Interview, New York, pub. Oct. 19.*

**Sirhan Bishara Sirhan**
*Accused Killer of*
*Senator Robert F. Kennedy*

I loved him (Robert F. Kennedy) . . . I loved him more than any American could have.

*Testimony at his trial,*
*Los Angeles, March 4.*

**Bishara Sirhan**
*Father of Sirhan Bishara Sirhan*

I accept the fact that my son killed Senator (Robert F.) Kennedy. But Senator Kennedy was to blame. He provoked my son by threatening to supply arms to the Middle East, which would have caused the death of thousands and the displacement of many more . . . My son did well.

*Taiyebeh, Occupied Jordan,*
*April 18.*

**Robert F. Six**
*President, Continental Airlines*

My wife comes first, airplanes come second, guns come third and my ranch in Ridgeway, Colorado, comes fourth . . . I've learned that the love of a good woman, a really good woman, is just about the best riches a guy can acquire in this life.

*Interview, Honolulu, pub. Oct. 12.*

**Spyros P. Skouras**
*Chairman,*
*20th Century-Fox Film Corp.*

If I had it to do all over again, as a young immigrant from Greece, my choice would be—no. Not with all the struggles and problems of the (movie) industry. It has been my life, but it's time now to give my voice—and Greek accent—a rest.

*Announcing his retirement,*
*before the Metropolitan Club,*
*New York, March 12.*

**Ringo Starr**
*Member of Beatles Singing Group*

I've got a kit of drums, but I'm not the greatest player in the world and I've got just a fair voice. So what have I done to deserve it (success and fame)? I've given myself a few pushes, I'll admit. (But) if I hadn't . . . joined the Beatles, I'd still be on the shop floor as a fitter; I know that. But what I mean is, I didn't do anything to make all this happen. It just happened. And if I eventually get pushed out, then I'll agree with that as well. I'm a slight fatalist, you see.

*Interview, London,*
*pub. April 28.*

**Connie Stevens**
*Actress, Singer*

I do not believe in divorce; I'm not a prude, either. People can live together in today's world but marriage is another thing. If it doesn't work, there's a failing on both people's parts. I have a feeling I've been a failure.

*Interview, Hollywood,*
*pub. Aug. 21.*

**Rex Stout**
*Author*

If you would ask me what, looking back, I would like to have changed about my life, I'd say this: that I would like to have learned to play the piano well and play Chopin, and I wish that every morning of my life between May and October I had got out of bed to see the summer dawn. What a beautiful thing to see and be with . . .

*Interview, Fairfield County, Conn.,*
*pub. Oct. 5.*

**Barbra Streisand**
*Singer, Actress*

I don't enjoy performing before a bunch of strangers; I don't care about pleasing a group. Some performers get a thrill out of winning over a cold audience . . . I don't. It turns me off. My work now is making

movies. I enjoy it; I understand it. And you can work a normal day and have your weekends.

Real life is more important to me than performing. I get a pleasure you wouldn't believe from scrubbing my pantry.

*Interview, Las Vegas, July 30.*

I want to play all different kinds of parts—you know, from bitches to sweet girls to stupid girls to bright girls, to every kind of girl. 'Cause I have all these possibilities. I'm slightly dumb, I'm very smart. I'm many things, you know? I want to use them, want to express them. It's kind of funny, because I'm in all these sort of big pictures, and yet . . . I'm an odd ball. I mean, I'm not a Doris Day or a Julie Andrews. That's what's weird about it. I don't know how I got into these things. Honestly.

*Interview, pub. December.*

**Ed Sullivan**
*Television Emcee,*
*Newspaper Columnist*

They tell me I'm expressionless. They're right. I can't argue with it. All I have to do is look in the mirror. But the public knows I'm not the kind of MC who smiles a lot and gives it nothing . . . Each week the electricity still turns on for me. This is where I like to be. This is what I like to do. Why should I stop?

*Interview, Los Angeles, pub. Jan. 20.*

**Jacqueline Susann**
*Author*

I'm a very unmaterialistic girl . . . I'd like to be rich enough to own an ocean-going yacht and invite my friends to go to the Greek Islands. Otherwise I haven't thought about it (money) much. I'm not a poor little girl; my husband always did well as a TV producer . . . I mean, how many mink coats can a girl wear?

*Interview, Washington, May 25.*

**James W. Symington**
*United States Representative, D-Mo.*

My dad (Sen. Stuart Symington) is ever young and he's always growing, but there's a 30-year difference between us, and,

(JAMES W. SYMINGTON)

naturally, we don't look at things the same way. He's of one generation. I'm of another. He's his own man and so am I. I've learned plenty from him and his teachings, but I follow the beat of my own drum, the dictates of my own judgments. In Congress I am not about to let myself become labeled as Stuart Symington's little Sir Echo.

*Interview, pub. Oct. 19.*

**Elizabeth Taylor**
*Actress*

. . . unless something comes along that absolutely captivates me, the life of leisure is for me—if you call being married to Richard Burton and the mother of four leisure.

*London, Aug. 26.*

**U Thant**
*Secretary-General of the
United Nations*

I don't like to be disturbed at home. I tell the cable office not to call me before 6:30 A.M., unless there's a war.

*Interview, New York,
pub. Nov. 3.*

**Nguyen Van Thieu**
*President of South Vietnam*

Don't think that being President is a sinecure. I have been President for the last two years, and all I know is that my hair has turned gray.

*Saigon, July 22.*

**Danny Thomas**
*Entertainer*

The great green god Money. I hate it. I'm not pursuing money; it has pursued me.

*Interview, Los Angeles,
pub. March 25.*

**Strom Thurmond**
*United States Senator, R-S.C.*

I've been asked why I married a girl that young (22). In old age I would rather smell perfume than liniment.

*Pub. May 12.*

**Lee Trevino**
*Golfer*

Three years ago I had no car. Now I have five. I used to live in a two-bed trailer. Now I have a five-bedroom Spanish home. I didn't used to have a phone. Now I have an unlisted number.

*Pub. May 30.*

Arnold Palmer is the king of golf. Bill Casper is the best golfer in the world. Gary Player is the toughest competitor I ever saw. He never loses his concentration. And Old-Man-River Julius Boros just keeps rolling along . . . They're all tough, but I can't worry about them. I'm not nervous. Somebody else bigger than me is pulling the strings.

*Before start of annual
U.S. Open Golf Tournament,
Houston, Tex., June 10.*

**Lana Turner**
*Actress*

. . . to love and to be loved are two very different things. I always thought I was being loved for myself. It was only later I found out I wasn't. If they're clever, and if they give me the right story, I take the bait. Then I get kicked in the teeth again. I'm so gullible; I'm so goddamn gullible; and I'm so *sick* of me being gullible.

You know why I've been married so many times? Take the seven men. I could have lived with any of them, other than the father of my daughter, without that piece of paper. But I want it right on the table; I want it legal. I gotta marry 'em. Better I shouldn't, maybe, but I did.

*Interview, pub. Sept. 26.*

**Peter Ustinov**
*Actor*

In every country people have a different concept of me. I seem to have a different image. Some of the best acting I do is living up to my images.

*Interview, Los Angeles, pub. Nov. 28.*

**Roger Vadim**
*Motion Picture Director*

Fortunately, Jane (Fonda, his wife) has

some money . . . Without her, I could not have paid my taxes—and certainly not lived in this luxurious style to which I have become accustomed for some time.

*London, pub. Dec. 1.*

**Mamie Van Doren**
*Actress*

That's my new hobby, collecting diamonds. You know, like Carol Channing says, they're a girl's best friend; and I like to be friendly.

*Interview, Los Angeles, pub. Feb. 4.*

**Gore Vidal**
*Author*

Truman Capote—another survivor of our literary generation—with whom I am often confused, once said he wanted to be rich. He's spent his life, with some success, climbing into the life I was born into and with some success have been escaping—the world of the rich, the owners of the republic.

*Interview, New York, pub. July 29.*

**Edward Vilella**
*Dancer, New York City Ballet*

. . . It's so goddamn easy when I'm dancing to my full potential. It's so easy to be fantastic, to be great.

*Interview, pub. June 6.*

**Barbara Walters**
*Television Commentator,*
*National Broadcasting Company*

. . . it's too wonderful. It's the only job like it on TV (NBC's "Today Show"). I know the hours are difficult—it affects every aspect of my life—but so far I've been able to keep a balance . . . What else would I do? I don't sing, and I don't dance.

*Interview, New York, pub. Nov. 17.*

**Rudolph Wanderone ("Minnesota Fats")**
*Pool Player*

When I was a kid, I remember everybody would scramble into the bathroom, scuffle into the subway and go downtown and work all day long for nuthin'. Everybody was always broke. I seen all that scramblin' around and all that scufflin'

and I told my mother I was never going to work. And I didn't. I never worked a day in my life.

*Interview, San Francisco, pub. Aug. 24.*

**William Warwick**
*Captain, "Queen Elizabeth II"*

Don't talk to me about the romance of the sea. The only romantic thing about it is my paycheck.

*Interview aboard the "QE II" on maiden voyage, May 5.*

**Ethel Waters**
*Singer*

God is also my banker. I may not have everything I want but I have everything I need.

*Interview, Los Angeles, pub. Oct. 6.*

**John Wayne**
*Actor*

They can stop hiring this old horse and put him out to pasture—but I'll never go of my own accord.

*Interview, Durango, Mexico, pub. April 7.*

I thought of three things when I had the cancer operation—my wife, my kids and death . . . I was lucky; I beat it. In four months it will be five years since the operation and the doctors say I no longer have cancer. Now all I can feel is life.

*Interview, Durango, Mexico, pub. April 13.*

When (Ronald) Reagan was running for Governor (of California) I really got mad. All those actors making television commercials demeaning actors running for governor, and at the same time demeaning their own profession. Kirk Douglas and I were making "War Wagon" at the time, and he made an anti-Reagan spot. I like Kirk very much, but I got angry. Well, I fixed old cleft-chin. I halted the production on the picture while I made a trailer for Reagan, and Kirk had to stay on the set to wait for his call.

*Interview, Durango, Mexico, pub. April 24.*

**Raquel Welch**
*Actress*

People think of me as some *zaftig* lady with two stereo nose cones staring everyone in the face. The American idea of sex is two outsized mammary glands . . . I know the whole idea of a sex goddess wanting to be an actress is camp, but that is what I want to be . . .

*Interview, Beverly Hills, Calif., pub. April 4.*

Even if it sounds gunky, here I am, this very insecure lady, still putting up too many guards; on one side, sensitive and generous; on the other, stingy and selfish. I'm ambitious, but it's not money that drives me. I want to do solid work that will win me the respect of my peers. Like all actresses, I'm a shattered personality, with lots and lots of people inside of me crying to get out . . .

*Interview, Los Angeles, pub. April 15.*

**Mae West**
*Actress*

It isn't what I do, but how I do it. It isn't what I say, but how I say it—and how I look when I do it and say it.

*Pub. Sept. 7.*

. . . I've sat on more laps than a napkin.

*Hollywood, pub. Oct. 5.*

**E. B. White**
*Writer*

I was a flop as a daily reporter. Every piece had to be a masterpiece—and, before you knew it, Tuesday was Wednesday. My deadline now is death.

*Interview, North Brooklin, Me., pub. July 11.*

**John J. Williams**
*United States Senator, R-Del.*

I respectfully suggest that a man can learn more through his ears than through his mouth.

*Washington, Feb. 4.*

**Ted Williams**
*Manager, Washington "Senators"*

I never did particulary think that I could be a manager, but the circumstances were right, the timing was right to induce me to take the job. I had had eight or nine years of fishing all over the world and it wasn't quite as much fun anymore. Call it my real love and guts for baseball and money.

*Pompano Beach, Fla., Feb. 25.*

I don't feel 50, that's for sure, although I'm sure I'll feel my age by the time I'm 51.

*Interview, Pompano Beach, Fla., pub. March 10.*

**Nicol Williamson**
*Actor*

I never degrade or demean myself. "Please" is a word I have never used, and I never will.

*Interview, London, pub. April 27.*

**Shelley Winters**
*Actress*

Well, I'll tell you about my sex life. I haven't got time for it. I'm thinking about getting married so I can work it in.

*Interview, Los Angeles, pub. May 7.*

**Cale Yarborough**
*Auto Racing Driver*

During a race, particularly the long ones like the Southern 500, I spend a lot of time just talking to the race car—like it was a human. Sometimes I scold it for not handling right. Sometimes I scold myself for not doing a better job of driving it. Other times I pray . . . not necessarily for myself, that the car and I will react quickly to a dangerous situation that needs a split-second decision. I also talk to the other drivers during a race, although they can't hear me. Things like "stay in the groove, baby," or, to a slower car, "get out of the groove, get out of the groove." Sometimes I catch myself yelling, particularly to the slower cars . . . But, mostly, I talk to myself. I try to convince one Cale Yarborough that he's not as tired as he feels. I count the laps, much like I used to count the cows that we saw in the fields during a trip to the mountains . . .

*Darlington, S.C., Aug. 20.*

# Philosophy

**Joseph Agassi**
*Professor of Philosophy,*
*Boston University*

It is still the tradition to divide people into scientists and priests. I divide people into knowers and seekers. I find that knowers oppose speculation both in science and religion, and the seekers love it. The seekers are actually disappointed by knowledge.
*Interview, pub. Dec. 30.*

**Spiro T. Agnew**
*Vice President of the United States*

Instead of looking to Washington, perhaps we should be looking within ourselves. It is not government but the initiative of people acting on their own that makes a better world and, in so doing, makes better people.
*Cincinnati, Feb. 11.*

When Americans allow guilt to replace purpose as a primary motivating force, a malignancy is born. When Americans allow introspection to supersede obligation, our vigor is sapped . . . It is time for Americans to return to the hard, fresh realism and to the unique mix of optimism and pragmatism that made America a great power.
*Loyola College, Baltimore,*
*June 8.*

Should the establishments of this country—industrial, business, educational and governmental—cringe and wring their hands before a small group of misfits seeking to discredit a free system because they can't effectively compete and find success anywhere? I find it hard to believe that the way to run the world has been revealed to a minority of pushy youngsters and middle aged malcontents.
*Dallas, Oct. 9.*

We have among us a glib, activist element who would tell us our values are lies; and I call them impudent . . . I call them snobs, for most of them disdain to mingle with the masses who work for a living . . . America cannot afford to divide over their demagoguery or to be deceived by their duplicity or to let their license destroy liberty. We can, however, afford to separate them from our society —with no more regret than we should feel over discarding rotten apples from a barrel.
*Harrisburg, Pa., Oct. 30.*

People in the establishment don't want to say "No" to young people, even if they are wrong. Some self-serving politicians see our huge youth population as a volatile political commodity available for the plucking. Youth should challenge the adult generation and put its ideas to the test. But they must reason their way, not jump to what they feel is right.
*Pub. Nov. 2.*

We know that there is a silent majority in this country. This is the majority that President Nixon addressed on his Vietnam policy last week, and the majority which responded with such resounding support. There is also a silent young majority who go to school, and to work—and to war, if necessary. There are the non-shouting concerned; the non-radical responsible; the non-complacent constructive activists of the under-thirty generation. Their idealism is disciplined by reason. The presence, integrity and commitment of the silent young majority is overshadowed by the strident minority who arrogate unto themselves voice, virtue and power out of proportion to their numbers and even more out of proportion to their abilities. The silent young majority must be recognized.

373

(SPIRO T. AGNEW)

They must be given outlets for their concern, opportunities for their ideas, and responsibilities equal to their capabilities. The silent young majority is challenged to make itself heard, to come to its own defense. And we—the older majority—are challenged to accommodate them within all our institutions.

*Before National Municipal League, Philadelphia, Nov. 10.*

### Richard Armour
*Author, Humorist*

Adolescence is a disease. Put clinically, it is one of the longest-lasting diseases there is and one that has never been fatal to those so afflicted. Just think, if a doctor ever discovered a cure for it, he would be awarded the Nobel Prize. My only question is: Would it be for medicine or for peace?

The hope of the human race lies in its intelligence and its dispassionate use of the brain. I say dispassionate. I have a reason for not saying compassionate: for I think, take the college campuses, for example, that when compassion becomes passion, thinking stops.

*Los Angeles, pub. Jan. 21.*

### Neil A. Armstrong
*United States Astronaut; first man on Moon*

We, citizens of the world, who can solve the problems of leaving earth, can also solve the problems of staying on it.

*At United Nations, New York, Aug. 13.*

### John Astin
*Actor*

It would be a waste of time to attain total sanity. I don't even have an image of sanity. It's a mistake to have one. This madness isn't confined to actors and show business. Plumbing contractors and insurance salesmen, for instance, are faking sanity. The whole world is a collective maniac acting out a charade or pretending to an image of sanity.

*Interview, pub. Dec. 17.*

### Barbara Bain
*Actress*

Every bride should know the answer to this important question: "Do I care for him enough to put his interests first, to find pleasure in pleasing him?" Too many girls think about what they are going to receive rather than what they are going to give . . . It's a case that when love flows thick, faults flow thin.

*Interview, Los Angeles, pub. Jan. 12.*

### William Banowsky
*Executive vice president, Pepperdine College*

. . . Sex without commitment is merely another name for man's inhumanity to man.

*Santa Barbara, Calif., pub. Jan. 13.*

Persons are to be loved and things are to be used. The most immoral thing you can do is switch these factors—to love things and use persons.

*Abilene, Tex., Feb. 23.*

### Christiaan Barnard
*Heart Transplant Surgeon*

. . . I don't believe medical discoveries are doing much to advance human life. As fast as we create ways to extend it we are inventing ways to shorten it.

*Before Foreign Correspondents Club, Tokyo, Sept. 23.*

### Frank Baxter
*Professor Emeritus, University of Southern California*

The great demand today is for the expert, not the true intellectual. America remains an illiterate, nonintellectual society.

*Pub. July 21.*

### Betty Beale
*Society Columnist, "The Washington Star"*

There is no appeal like snob appeal and the greatest snobs are men. They relegate society and snobbishness to women, but I've found the people most concerned about where they play their golf, and with whom, are men.

*Interview, pub. Feb. 28.*

**Anthony Wedgwood Benn**
*Minister of Technology*
*of the United Kingdom*

Engineers have great respect for each other. The sooner engineers start manning the diplomatic corps, the better.
*Pub. March 14.*

**Thomas Hart Benton**
*Artist*

Samuel Butler once said that train engineers looked alike the world over, regardless of where they were. And I have begun to seriously wonder whether this applies to all machines and whether machines can actually change the physiognomy of those who tend them. We are all growing to look so much the same I wonder whether we are growing up a race of machine-tenders.
*Interview, pub. Oct. 3.*

**Shelley Berman**
*Entertainer*

The words of our times are "Burn, baby, burn," and "Hell, no, we won't go." When you have ferment and rebellion, your art forms invariably reflect it. When you get to specific symptoms, you invariably will find individual artists who reflect those symptoms best.
*Interview, pub. Jan. 26.*

**Bruno Bettelheim**
*Professor of Psychology and*
*Psychiatry, University of Chicago*

Deep down, what youth is fighting against is not so much the war in Vietnam or the global balance, but an America whose technology seems to have robbed them of any place in the real work of the world.
*Pub. Oct. 8.*

**Bruce Bliven**
*Lecturer in Communication and*
*Journalism, Stanford University*

I'm startled by the naivete of the young radicals. I've spent my life with revolutionists. I knew all the young American revolutionists in the twenties and they had studied the history of revolution. These kids take my breath away. They think they can tear everything down and some-how it will magically put itself back together. I've seen revolutions in operation in many countries and, believe me, it doesn't put itself back together.
*Interview, Palo Alto, Calif.,*
*July 26.*

**Julius Bloom**
*Executive Director,*
*Carnegie Hall, New York*

. . . You can't get away with some of the things now that used to be done in the name of culture. You no longer have yokels out there in Kansas. You have people of taste.
*Interview, New York, pub. March 20.*

**Shirley Booth**
*Actress*

Acting is a way to overcome your own inhibitions and shyness. The writer creates a strong, confident personality, and that's what you become—unfortunately, only for the moment.
*Pub. Oct. 10.*

**Victor Borge**
*Entertainer*

Humor has many departments. With humor you can create wars, cause governments to fall. You can destroy or you can create. For me, the object of humor is to bring happiness, to have people depart in a lifted mood . . . When I was a child, I was the center of parties because I could entertain. I played Mozart and Chopin and was also very witty. If somebody got sick, I was sent for to cheer him up. It's better to die laughing than just to die.
*Interview, Los Angeles, pub. Feb. 18.*

**Frank Borman**
*United States Astronaut*

Earth looks so peaceful floating against its pitch black backdrop. So quiet, completely unique among all the heavenly bodies. It's hard to believe, when you see it from a distance, that people not only live on earth but are generally at war, and full of hatreds, jealousies, larceny.
*New York, pub. Jan. 13.*

**Omar N. Bradley**
*General, United States Army (Ret.);*
*former chairman,*
*Joint Chiefs of Staff*

A man must know his business. He must have mental and physical energy. (You never hear of a lazy man getting very far.) He must have character. He must have the courage of his convictions. He must have human understanding and consideration for others. Usually, leaders have all these qualities . . .
*Interview, Beverly Hills, Calif.,*
*pub. April.*

**Willy Brandt**
*Chancellor of West Germany*

National consciousness is something different from arrogance, or overestimating one's worth as to other people. It rests on a confident evaluation of one's own strength, achievement and virtue—and of one's own limitations.
*Bonn, Oct. 21.*

**Jimmy Breslin**
*Author, Newspaper Columnist*

You've got to understand the "drink." In a world where there is a law against people ever showing their emotions, or ever releasing themselves from the greyness of their days, a drink is not a social tool. It is a thing you need in order to live.
*Pub. Feb. 28.*

**Kingman Brewster, Jr.**
*President, Yale University*

With all the mass media concentrated in a few hands, the ancient faith in the competition of ideas in the free market place seems like a hollow echo of a much simpler day.
*Pub. Sept. 21.*

**William R. Bright**
*President-founder, Campus Crusade*
*for Christ International*

The objective of the far left is complete moral breakdown. By destroying us morally, they can affect a takeover of our country without destroying our technology and industry. But the frightening thing is, history shows us it took 400 years in China

to reach the point of moral decay to which we've fallen in just four years.
*Arrowhead Springs, Calif., pub. July 5.*

**Michael Butler**
*Stage Producer*

The hippies ask searching questions— questions that search for the truth. Like, "Why make war in the name of love?" Like, "What is original sin?" Like, "If it's wrong, what's wrong about it?" Like, "In the midst of all the plenty, why do people starve?" Like, "If the tenets of the American Revolution are beautiful, why don't we follow them?" Like, "If we're all created equal, why are some of us more equal than others?"
*Interview, Los Angeles, pub. March 9.*

**Mary S. Calderone**
*Executive Director,*
*Sex Information & Education*
*Council of the United States*

A baby is not born a man or a woman. He is assigned to one sex or the other because of his physical organs. But these do not make him one or the other. He is made a man or a woman, to have the feelings and emotions of a man or a woman, by the way his parents and other adults deal with him. This is sexualization; it does not come from birth, but it begins with birth.
*Los Angeles, pub. Feb. 11.*

Our children need people they can look up to and model themselves on. They need heroes—not football heroes who announce in public print that they take a bottle and a girl to bed before every game; not paper heroes or heroines whose sex conquests are made possible only by purchase of a certain product . . . Do we really want our 14- and 15-year-olds to believe the message we beam to them continually —that you're not with it until you've had it?
*Pub. Sept. 21.*

**Millard F. Caldwell**
*Former Governor of Florida*

As we contemplate the future of mankind and appraise the astounding progress made in recent years in material endeavors, it is disconcerting to have to acknowledge the human mind is basically unchanged from the days of Plato and Aristotle. We all know war is destructive, unnecessary and futile, but none can say why the human race refuses to live in peace. We all know there is no such phenomenon as "something for nothing," but we tolerate and often accept the giveaway nostrums of the demagogue. Transportation has moved from the sled to the jet, warfare from the club to nuclear fission, communications from the smoke signal to the airways—but our minds continue to walk on foot.

*Before Louisiana Judiciary,*
*New Orleans, Oct. 6.*

**Erwin D. Canham**
*Editor-in-Chief, "The*
*Christian Science Monitor"*

The exposure of evil and the application of regenerative measures are forms of unrest which we should certainly support. Unrest against injustice. Unrest against outdated and hidebound forms of organization and controversy. Unrest against hypocrisy. Unrest against gross materialism.

*Boston, pub. Sept. 4.*

**Al Capp**
*Cartoonist*

Show me a young idealist who wants to change a world he hasn't been in long enough to know what's wrong with it, and I'll show you a pest.

*Before Young Americans for Freedom,*
*St. Louis, Aug. 31.*

**Frank Carlson**
*Former United States Senator*
*from Kansas*

I would most fervently hope that the free world has learned one major lesson since the end of World War II—that is the fact that we cannot defeat Communism **by** force of arms alone—or even primarily. For Communism is not simply a nation. It is not simply an army. It is not simply a nationalistic or political force. Rather, it is a system of ideas—an ideology —a philosophy of history.

*Commencement address,*
*Marymount College, Salina, Kans., June 1.*

**Emanuel Celler**
*United States Representative, D-N.Y.*

We can only live our lives forward; but we can only understand our lives backward. We can only understand what goes on before us if we understand history.

*Washington, pub. Sept. 21.*

**Marc Chagall**
*Artist*

Young people are a little astray these days because there is really a crisis in religion, in social life—a moral crisis. But I don't feel this crisis. I was a child of poor people. I had 125 francs in my pocket to live on in Paris. But our ideal was our work. You do your job and you do it well and your work is your ideal. The crisis among young people is that work doesn't interest them. I've worked all my life. I'm never without it. There's love, and work, and your wife. Work isn't to make money; you work to justify life. Those are small actions and simple truths.

*Interview, St. Paul de Vence, France,*
*pub. Dec. 5.*

**Geraldine Chaplin**
*Actress*

Drugs are marvelous if you want to escape, but reality is so rich, why escape? There are so many things happening, so many things to learn, to be conscious of —it's immoral to hide yourself in a world of drugs. I had that dream world when I was a child. That's over.

*Interview, Madrid, pub. March.*

**Leonard F. Chapman, Jr.**
*General and Commandant,*
*United States Marine Corps*

The well-intentioned Americans who think they can stop war and tyranny by destroying their own strengths are unknowing allies of the enemy (the North Vietnamese). The enemy has another ally in this country. This one is not a dove— or a peacenik—though he has made some success in identifying with the sincere antiwar groups. He is a veteran fighter, and a veteran hater. He is not tired of war. In fact, he preaches war, and he waves the flag of the Viet Cong. He is against

(LEONARD F. CHAPMAN, JR.)

this war (in Vietnam) only because he is in accord with the principles of the enemy. He employs the weapons of words in mass. His proven theory is: if something is said loud enough, and often enough, some of it will be accepted as truth. It has worked—now some of their words and phrases have found their way into the national vocabulary: "imperialism," "militarism," "the American military machine." Is it necessary to deny that this country is not imperialistic? Must it be said that Americans are not a militaristic people? How many seek victory for the enemy? I don't know. I know they are a minority. But because this noisy minority effects a bizarre appearance, because they offer instant and theatrical violence, they are news. Their images march across television screens throughout the nation. Their slogans and actions are chronicled in every newspaper and magazine. They have identified with youth, but they are not young because their ideas are old; Destroy the nation's defenses, destroy the nation's educational institutions, polarize the races.

*Before Combat Correspondents' Association, Chicago, Sept. 20.*

## Cyd Charisse
*Actress*

I don't want to sound like a know-it-all, but I feel strongly that a marriage is like a car: if you want to keep it on the road, you can't take your hands off the wheel.

*Interview, Hollywood, pub. June 15.*

## William Sloane Coffin
*Chaplain, Yale University*

Insurrection says that we must become twice as militant, to which resurrection says yes, and twice as non-violent. In short, I guess the order for the day reads twice as tough and twice as tender, as only the truly strong can be tender.

*Pub. June 15.*

Hate evil, hate evil twice as much and never stop. But love the good twice as much, too, or all you will be is damn good haters.

*Graduation exercises, Radcliffe College, pub. June 17.*

## Barry Commoner
*Chairman, Department of Botany, Washington University, St. Louis*

. . . the proper use of science is not to conquer nature but to live with it . . . to discover how to devote the wisdom of science and the power of technology to the welfare, the survival, of man.

*Los Angeles, pub. Nov. 25.*

## Mike Connors
*Actor*

. . . I don't want my kids to grow up believing that there is nothing destructive in the world. I want them to know that there is good and bad in the world, that you can be hurt physically, that guns can kill you, that drugs are bad for you, that not everyone means well.

*Interview, Hollywood, pub. Aug. 25.*

## Terence Cardinal Cooke
*Archbishop of New York*

The courageous man in space unquestionably has the right perspective when he looks down from above and sees one world. This—whether or not we all recognize it—is exactly what we are. We live in one world! We are united in our weaknesses; in sickness, suffering, death, in the social ills that plague us.

*Washington, May 25.*

## Robert W. Corrigan
*President, California Institute of the Arts*

The two greatest achievements of this century are going to the moon and the heart transplants. Both were team achievements, not possible by the individual . . . Charles A. Lindbergh was the last lone hero.

*Los Angeles, June 10.*

## Louise Cowan
*Chairman, English Department, University of Dallas*

We see best in the arts the nasty, filthy, violent and angry. Artists are trying to show us all the evil man is capable of. The artists in any age are to be listened to because they are telling the truth.

*Dallas, Feb. 27.*

**Harvey G. Cox**
*Associate Professor of Church
and Society, Harvard University*

It's a little silly to be in awe of a gothic cathedral if you've flown from across the Atlantic to see it.

*Pub. July 26.*

**F. Melvin Cratsley**
*Former College Basketball Coach*

Athletics are the last stronghold of discipline on the campus. It may be that they are in a life-or-death struggle of their own. I read somewhere . . . that the aim of the New Left is to replace the athlete with the hippie as the idol of kids. I don't know if it can be done, but it seems society is intent on destroying Horatio Alger. The oddball is getting control. The good guy is outnumbered. America seems interested only in glorifying the loser.

*Pub. Aug. 25.*

**George Cukor**
*Motion Picture Director*

There are no ugly women any more, no rejected old maids, as we used to know them. The cult of beauty is so accessible that any plain woman who is clever can become attractive. A woman who is born beautiful is very foolish to be so impressed with this gift that she offers little else and finds herself an empty egotist when time takes her good looks away.

*Interview, Los Angeles, pub. Nov. 10.*

**Nathan Cummings**
*Philanthropist*

The arts play a significant role in making this country great. They are important to our spirit, they are part of the solution to our problems. The arts are a major and effective weapon in any effort to improve the human condition. Art can stimulate and reinforce the human spirit. For the ghetto dweller, the arts can nourish and sustain values that might otherwise be coarsened or dehumanized by harsh reality. I have been told that no program dealing with urban blight can be successful unless opportunity to savor the arts in one form or another is provided.

*Stanford University, May 12.*

**Jean Dalrymple**
*General Director, New York City
Center Drama and Light Opera
Companies; executive director,
American National Theatre and Academy*

If you have the heart, the guts, and the talent . . . the world of the performing arts is not only the most fascinating but the most rewarding place to be. Art endures. Its creators and co-workers are not forgotten. There is a special kind of immortality in having been part of it.

*Interview, New York, pub. Oct. 7.*

**Hubert De Givenchy**
*Fashion designer*

Fill a house with animals, and you fill it with life.

*Pub. Nov. 15.*

**Babette Deutsch**
*Poet, Author*

Please don't misunderstand me. Sending those men to the moon was a unique and immense technological achievement; but I hope it won't divert poets from writing poetry, painters from painting and composers from composing. I believe, with all my heart, that mankind will continue to crave emotional satisfaction from the arts. That, I hope, will never end.

*Interview, pub. Sept. 14.*

**John Diefenbaker**
*Former Prime Minister of Canada*

Freedom is the right to be wrong, not the right to do wrong.

*Before Canadian Circulation Managers'
Association, Ottawa, Aug. 26.*

**Milorad M. Drachkovitch**
*Lecturer in Political Science,
Stanford University*

To be a Communist is to have the greatest self-discipline. The individual must be submerged. Most of the youngsters cannot accept this. And if the drug problem didn't enter in, their problem would be much simpler. Communists are Puritans. The most super-Victorian countries are the Soviet Union and Communist China.

*Interview, Palo Alto, Calif., pub. April 6.*

**James Elliott**
*Director, Wadsworth Athenium*
*Museum, Hartford, Conn.*

The role of the museum is to make art as available as possible, physically and psychologically, to the largest number of people who want it . . . The museum has a responsibility to the underprivileged. That, however, includes not only the economically underprivileged, but the culturally underprivileged—which includes many of the economically advantaged.

*Pub. Feb. 24.*

**Armand G. Erpf**
*Senior partner,*
*Loeb, Rhoades & Company*

Bureaucracy operates under certain principles. First: Never do anything the first time. Second: Establish rules and regulations and have a sanctimonious air of complete justice. So you say all people are equal before the law. That sounds great. Then you say all people are identical before the law. Third, you say all people are actuarial statistics before the law. So, from being the miracle of a human being, you become equal, identical and then a statistical abstract. In other words, you become nothing. And that is what bureaucracy is —inhuman.

*Interview, New York, pub. Dec. 27.*

**Edwin D. Etherington**
*President, Wesleyan University*
*of Connecticut*

Experience tells us that young people are usually right in central ways. More than ever, they are the activated conscience of the United States.

*Pub. Feb. 14.*

**James L. Farmer**
*Assistant Secretary for Administration,*
*Department of Health, Education and*
*Welfare of the United States*

A man has to decide one of two things. Either he is going to be a revolutionary and try to destroy the system, or he is going to make it work. I reject the notion that the way to progress is to make things as bad as possible.

*Pub. Feb. 21.*

**Richard E. Farson**
*Vice president of Ecological Affairs,*
*California Institute of the Arts*

It's probably true that women do not want dominence over men. Probably they mainly want access to leadership in professions, equal opportunities for jobs now held by men, freedom from chastity as the fundamental virtue, and both marriage and a career. Mostly, they'll probably want to be what they naturally are . . . and we don't really know what that is.

*Los Angeles, June 5.*

**Leonard Fein**
*Political Sociologist*

. . . Jews, in a perverse kind of way, *need* anti-Semites. Jews in this country are in fairly serious trouble spiritually and ideologically, and it is very comforting to come once again to an old and familiar problem. By confronting others, you can avoid the much more challenging confrontation with yourself.

*Interview, New York, pub. Jan. 31.*

**Harvey S. Firestone, Jr.**
*Former Chairman,*
*Firestone Tire & Rubber Company*

I have always felt . . . that you owe a great deal to your fellow man, because what you can do by yourself is nothing particularly important; but what you can help others to do is very important.

*Interview, pub. August.*

**Henry Ford II**
*Chairman, Ford Motor Company*

Modern industrial society is based on the assumption that it is both possible and desirable to go on forever providing more and more goods for more and more people. Today, that assumption is being seriously challenged. The industrial nations have come far enough down the road to affluence to recognize that more goods do not necessarily mean more happiness. They are also recognizing that more goods eventually mean more junk, and that the junk in the air, in the water and on the land could make the earth unfit for human habitation before we reach the 21st Century.

*Harvard Business School, Dec. 2.*

**Sergio Franchi**
*Singer*

Even before World War II, the image of the Continental man who courts a woman with serenades, flowers, etc., was passee. In Italy today it's the same as in the United States. We just call up a girl and ask, "Are you free tomorrow?" The great courtship is considered a waste of time. Isn't it terrible?

*Interview, pub. June 24.*

**David Frost**
*Television Commentator*

Having traveled around the world, I find it incredibly civilized, for instance, to buy a package of cigarettes and be given a packet of matches along with them.

*Interview, New York, pub. Sept. 14.*

**Zsa Zsa Gabor**
*Actress*

Darling, the only way to make the body more beautiful is to get a good man.

*Interview, New York, pub. Jan. 29.*

**John W. Gardner**
*Chairman, Urban Coalition*

We must dispose of the notion that social change is a process that alters a tranquil *status quo*. Today there is no tranquility to alter. The rush of change brings a kind of instant antiquity.

*Harvard University, pub. April 11.*

(I would cite) the "average citizens" who fatten on the yield of this prosperous society but will not turn a hand or make a sacrifice or risk discomfort to help solve its problems. They are earning higher wages or salaries than ever before, buying more consumer goods, enjoying longer and more elaborate vacations—yet they vote down school bond issues, neglect elementary civic duties, allow their local government to fall into disrepair, nurse their prejudices and complain. And grow fatter. They are angry at the way things are going, but they will not help to make them go better. Their apathy is the heaviest burden that this free society must carry.

. . . Every step toward the removal of arbitrary constraints on individual behavior must be accompanied by increments in self-imposed discipline. Self-discipline is the free man's yoke.

*Stanford University, pub. July 6.*

**Ralph Gerard**
*Professor of Biology,
University of California at Davis*

In the case of evolution, I know of no responsible person who has examined the evidence who questions that species arose by a continuing series of changes from ancestral ones. This is the essence of evolution, and is as much a fact as atoms and gravity.

*Nov. 22.*

**Alberto Giovannetti**
*Diplomat of the Holy See
at the United Nations*

Brotherly dialogue among men does not reach its perfection on the level of technical progress, but on the deeper level of interpersonal relationships.

*New York, Feb. 14.*

**Mills E. Godwin**
*Governor of Virginia*

I think today we are reaping the harvest in some of our student unrest of a generation raised on the theory of permissiveness, which began as a school of educational thought and reached its zenith, perhaps, with the childcare books of Dr. Benjamin Spock.

*Fredericksburg, Va.,
Sept. 29.*

**Harry Golden**
*Author*

The kids are very smart today—much smarter than we were at their age. When I was a kid in school, and the teacher mentioned France, it meant only Joan of Arc. England? Henry VIII and his wives. Today, they know all about Europe, Asia and Africa. They know the names of leaders I can't even pronounce. They're aware and they're committed; and these are the two most important things in life. There are a lot of hitchhiker hippies, of course— people who will hitch a ride on any movement that comes along. But the majority

(HARRY GOLDEN)

are sincere, and I believe they're right on
the mark.

*Interview, Beverly Hills, Calif.,*
*pub. Aug. 16.*

**Barry Goldwater, Jr.**
*United States Representative, R-Calif.*

. . . I think early marriages are a waste
of a person's life. When you're single,
you're mobile. That is when you are
learning the most. Life expectancy is
what—70? Some people get married at
20. Can you imagine being married to
the same person for 50 years?

*Interview, Washington, pub. Sept. 17.*

**Elliott Gould**
*Actor*

I love to use profanity because I just
don't think there are any dirty words in
the English language.

*Interview, New York, pub. Oct. 5.*

**Billy Graham**
*Evangelist*

Now, sex is a gift from God. We went
too far in the Victorian period. We hushed
it up. It should never have been suppressed. It's something that God gave us.
We should talk about it. It shouldn't be in
the back alleys in the dirt and trash. Young
people are getting the wrong idea about
sex. Within marriage, it's the most wonderful of relationships. It's more than a propa-
gation of the race. This is where I disagree with the Pope. Sex is more than just
to produce children. Sex is for enjoyment
within the confines of marriage. Sex is
also for the fulfillment of a couple. It's
the ultimate in fulfillment.

*Interview, pub. July 11.*

I believe that unless America has a moral
and spiritual awakening, we are heading
for a revolution one one hand or a dictatorship on the other.

*Television interview, New York, Aug. 24.*

**William Guy**
*Governor of North Dakota*

. . . I am amazed that Congress has
escaped the protest of youth so long, for

there is the key to the remedy of this
country's grave social and economic
problems.

*Pub. June 21.*

**Richard Harris**
*Actor*

We're all searching for paradise, but it's
something you remember having once—
and never realizing you had it then.

*Interview, London, pub. Aug. 24.*

**Mark O. Hatfield**
*United States Senator, R-Ore.*

Until I, as an individual, can relate to
the cleaning woman who comes to my
house in Washington two or three times
a week from the ghetto, I don't think we're
going to be able to solve our (social)
problems. No amount of money itself
can solve what actually is a problem in
human relationships. If man can be recon-
ciled with God, he can come to love his
brother and truly have compassion for his
fellow man on a sustained basis.

*Minneapolis, Sept. 12.*

**Enid A. Haupt**
*Editor-in-Chief, "Seventeen" Magazine*

I've never met anyone who wanted to
be a teenager again.

*Pub. Aug. 18.*

**S. I. Hayakawa**
*Acting President,*
*San Francisco State College*

Hell hath no fury like the frustrated
intellectual.

*San Diego, pub. March 22.*

**S. I. Hayakawa**
*President, San Francisco State College*

Every child should learn to read the
landscape so that he can interpret how the
terrain around him came to be what it is,
how it is changing and what part man
plays in it. He should know something
about the weather and the stars. He
should learn to look at the plants which
grow around him, even if they are only
plants growing in the cracks of an urban
sidewalk. He should know about the animals of his region. He should begin to get

an understanding of how plants and animals depend on each other and are determined by soil and climate. Most people go through life unaware of the fascinating complex of interrelated natural events which surround them.

*Columbia University,*
*pub. Dec. 21.*

### Will Heberg
*Graduate Professor of Philosophy and*
*Culture, Drew University*

The really serious threat to morality in our time consists not in the multiplying violations of an accepted moral code, but in the fact that the very notion of morality itself seems to be losing its meaning for increasing numbers of men and women in our society. To violate moral standards while at the same time acknowledging their authority is one thing. To lose all sense of the moral claim, to repudiate all moral authority and every moral standard as such, is something far more serious.

*Pub. Dec. 21.*

### Katharine Hepburn
*Actress*

I think the kids of today are sad and tragic. They're digging a hole they'll never get out of . . . I think people of today are just desperate to be noticed. That may be why they dress like freaks. So do I. But I'm clean. Being dirty never did anyone any good.

*Hollywood, pub. Sept. 18.*

### Alfred Hitchcock
*Motion Picture Director*

The world is confusing. Look at the men in politics and business who are doublecrossing each other. It's just like studio politics. On Wall Street, they're all robbing each other. Heroes are no longer heroes.

*Interview, Los Angeles, pub.*
*Nov. 16*

### Eric Hoffer
*Author*

We are told we have to feel guilty. We've been poor all our lives and now we're being preached to by every son of a bitch who comes along. The ethnics are discovering that you can't trust those *Mayflower* boys.

*Pub. Oct. 6.*

### Bob Hope
*Actor, Comedian*

. . . the real challenge of today is to achieve balance, to give recognition to equitable ground rules for this changing world . . . Take heed, because dissent destroys itself when it destroys the system that allows it to function.

*Miami University, Oxford, Ohio,*
*April 27.*

With today's kids wearing beards, looking dirty, fighting cops, dropping out, being hippies and taking drugs . . . it's a great thrill to be Father of the Year. It's like being promoted to captain just before the iceberg hit the *Titanic*.

*Accepting Father-of-the-Year Award,*
*New York, pub. May 24.*

### John A. Howard
*President, Rockford College*

The history of man's rise from caveman to civilized community has been the history of our institutions of self-restraint: law, marriage, morality and religion. They provide the only way we can live together. When you start tearing them down, you inevitably move into the coercive, chaotic society into which we are now plunging so rapidly. Without self-discipline, then some other force is going to have to impose restraint, such as the police. And that leads to totalitarianism. It always has, without fail. It always has to.

*Interview, New York, Feb. 1.*

Philosophy used to aspire to provide understanding so that man could climb toward the heights. Some large portion of current philosophers, having rejected the concepts of good and evil, of heights and depths, simply assert the flatness of life and analyze man's permanent state of nausea or despair, or else have abandoned the concern for man altogether and have wandered off into semantics.

*Rockford, Ill., pub. Oct. 9.*

**Hubert H. Humphrey**
*Former Vice President*
*of the United States*

We must come to see that our security is threatened more immediately and more directly by the missiles of hate and bigotry and injustice and violence that are loose within our own borders, rather than the nuclear missiles of the Soviet Union that are checked by the policy of mutual deterrence. And we must set our priorities accordingly.
*Williamsburg, Va., pub. Sept. 8.*

**Sol Hurok**
*Impresario*

Don't plan for two years from now . . . you'll end up losing those years. Think only of today and tomorrow. At the end of each day say, "It's been a good day today, and tomorrow is going to be a better day." Get pleasure out of life . . . as much as you can. No one ever died from pleasure. That's my philosophy.
*Interview, New York,*
*pub. July 6.*

**Gustav Husak**
*First Secretary,*
*Czechoslovak Communist Party*

There is an old joke about the ideal life being "to work in Socialism and to live in Capitalism."
*Pub. July 6.*

**Charles C. Johnson, Jr.**
*Administrator, Consumer Protection and*
*Environmental Health Service, United*
*States Department of Health,*
*Education and Welfare*

In . . . 1969, the greatest nation on earth must face a harsh and frightening fact: that in spite of unparalleled advances in medicine, science, engineering and technology; in spite of a lengthening span of human life through improved health services and victories over communicable diseases; in spite of unprecedented affluence and high standards of living; in spite of all these things—perhaps even because of these things—we have not succeeded in creating a physical, social and cultural environment in which we can find that satisfaction for the "whole man" which was surely the purpose of all our strivings.
*Washington, pub. Aug. 26.*

**Nicholas Johnson**
*Commissioner, Federal*
*Communications Commission*

There is a growing malaise in this country about the quality of life. It relates not so much to facts as to feel. People do not need scientific indicators to tell them that New York City's air doesn't feel good in their lungs. An economist's analysis is not much help to someone whose personal emptiness and frustrations increase in direct proportion to his material possessions. It doesn't feel good to talk to tape-recorded messages over the telephone and get mail written and addressed by computers . . . People are tired of everything breaking down and having to take it back to the store. Someday, sombody is going to get up from his three-martini lunch to discover that this is the day the world wouldn't work. Everything will break down at once.
*Before Senate Subcommittee on Economy in Government, Washington, pub. Sept. 19.*

**Wallace E. Johnson**
*President, Holiday Inns of America*

. . . God was smart when he made man. He made four holes in the head for information to go in, and only one for it to come out.
*Interview, Memphis, Tenn., pub. March.*

**Jenkin Lloyd Jones**
*President, Chamber of Commerce*
*of the United States*

The essence of free enterprise is that it has provided more people with more options than any other system. The Achilles heel of socialism is that, by its very nature, it diminishes options. The average man behind the Iron Curtain cannot buy an automobile. If he could buy one, it would be only one type. He has few options . . . We have to make the point that we are against socialism. Not because our control over our businesses or industries would be destroyed under a socialist system. We must be against socialism because under that system life becomes a drab and dirty gray.
*Interview, pub. May.*

**Herman Kahn**
*Director, Hudson Institute*

In 1930 a man who worked too hard and got an ulcer was regarded as a hero wounded in the war for material success. In 1969 the same man is looked on as a compulsive neurotic with twisted values.
*London, pub. May 18.*

**Sister Helen Kelley**
*President, Immaculate Heart College*

It is excruciatingly painful for men not to deceive themselves, particularly in a generation in which their comfort, their security, the best part of their value systems will almost certainly collapse under an honest gaze. But the honest gaze—to which rage and despair can be a prelude—has the power to give us back to ourselves.
*Los Angeles, pub. Aug. 31.*

**Alexander F. Kerensky**
*Former Premier of Russia*

Criticism in America is mostly negative, not positive. It is against things. It tends to be destructive, not creative. It seeks to destroy the old and not to preserve what is worthwhile in the old. History is ignored, discounted. New values are sought simply because they are new.
*Interview, pub. Nov. 9.*

**Michael Klonsky**
*National Secretary, Students for a Democratic Society*

We've come to understand that the university is very much a part of this system that we live under—a system that is based on racism, the capitalist system, exploitation of people's labor . . . This whole system of exploitation has been reinforced by the university . . . We all see ourselves fighting a common struggle . . . (by) oppressed peoples all over the world . . . because the system we are up against is an international system . . . the system of exploitation of capitalism.
*Television interview, May 11.*

**John S. Knight**
*Editorial Chairman,
Knight Newspapers, Inc.*

History has been filled with attacks on dissenters, but also with moments when dissent led to change and where speaking out on an unpopular cause has shifted that nation's course by changing the persuasion of its citizens. If the debate between dissenters and their government has been more acrimonious than normal, in large part it is because the first casualty of war is truth.
*Pub. Nov. 23.*

**Jerry Kosinski**
*Author*

. . . I, perhaps more than others, saw America as a free country. I still see it that way—but it is a different America now. It has become polarized, as Europe has been for centuries. Americans are no longer the same. They are less anonymous. They wrest freedom from each other. They clearly delineate their places in society. They are angry, violent and abusive. They have become political. And the system responds in turn and invades their freedom.
*At National Book Awards,
New York, March 12.*

**Nancy Kovack**
*Actress*

It is character, individuality, inner beauty —call it what you like—that makes a person memorable. Sometimes, too much accent is placed on what you want people to see and not enough on what you want them to feel.
*Interview, Los Angeles, pub. Aug. 18.*

**Herman Warden Lay**
*Chairman, PepsiCo., Inc.*

Some of the books I have read, some of the things I see on TV . . . imply that people who have achieved wealth have done it mainly by inheritance; that there is a narrow hierarchy in this country and that the opportunity to invade that hierarchy and become wealthy does not exist. I don't think the facts bear that out. Opportunity is just as great today—and even greater—than when I started out. I think it is important that the business schools and, of course, even liberal arts courses, get this philosophy across.
*Interview, pub. September.*

**Ralph Lazarus**
*Chairman, Federated Department Stores*

When people are put off, treated like

(RALPH LAZARUS)

numbers, excluded from the decisions that affect their lives and feel that they cannot influence the bureaucracy that is running things, they no longer count as individuals. They lose their self-respect. In the past 50 years this suffocating way of life has closed in on masses of people; witness the Soviet Union, Nazi Germany and China. I am glad to see that a larger number of Americans would rather fight the machine than be smothered by it. That is why I am optimistic about the future.

*University of Southern California,*
*pub. Sept. 8.*

**Sherman E. Lee**
*Director, Cleveland Museum of Art*

The art museum is not fundamentally concerned with therapy, illustrating history, social action, entertainment or scientific research . . . The museum is . . . a primary source of wonder and delight for mind and heart. In this, the art museum is comparable to a permanent storage battery, or to a library of original manuscripts.

*Dayton, Ohio, Feb. 28.*

**Sam Levenson**
*Writer, Humorist*

Lots of kids today seem to want the happiness without bothering about the pursuit . . . It's a hard life. Life is a practical joke. I understand. And if a hippie wants to get along on nothing, that's all right. But he should remember, while he sits there and drinks a cup of coffee, that some square made the coffee for him. For every hippie there is some schmuck making his coffee, washing his shirt, sending him $60 that was earned by the hard work he won't do. He should at least thank the squares before he goes out to do his thing.

*Interview, Washington,*
*pub. Nov. 4.*

I believe in love. The kid who is lucky enough to be loved has the best sex education in the world. The kid who isn't loved —learning mechanics won't make up for it. It's all in the heart—not in the plumbing.

*New York, pub. Nov. 30.*

**C. Eric Lincoln**
*Professor of Religion and Sociology,*
*Union Theological Seminary, New York*

Soul is the essence of blackness. It is the creative genius of the liberated men and women who have come to terms with themselves and with their heritage. If black is beautiful, it is soul that makes it so.

*Black Academy of Arts and Letters,*
*Boston, March 27.*

**James Ling**
*Chairman, Ling-Temco-Vought*

Don't tell me how hard you work. Tell me how much you get done.

*Pub. March 7.*

**Sol M. Linowitz**
*United States Ambassador to the*
*Organization of American States*

There is no such thing as a little bit of extremism.

*Yeshiva University, New York, April 20.*

**Walter Lippmann**
*Author, Newspaper Columnist*

Some problems are not soluble by living people. They can get on; they can compose their differences a little, but they can't solve them. People die off, and they outlive their problems. One of the great solvers of problems in history is death.

*Interview, Seal Harbor, Me.,*
*pub. Sept. 21.*

Believing as I do that we're in the age —I'm not talking about the next six months —of the decline of very great, very large powers in influence, I expect to see the breakup of the Soviet empire in Asia and possibly the breakup of the Chinese empire. They're too big to govern. I think those will go along with the deflation of the American ambition . . . the American theory that we are the guardians of the world.

*Pub. Sept. 28.*

**Gina Lollobrigida**
*Actress*

In America, women are so important and so selfish that they can almost live without men. They become so powerful that they're actually the equals of men. In Europe, the man is god. And when the man has the power, the women are more feminine. We don't destroy his image. We act small and unimportant—and even stupid—in front of him. And that makes us appealing to him . . . I think you are destroying sex here.

*Interview, New York, pub. Jan. 23.*

**Anita Loos**
*Author*

The European woman is happy. The American woman is frustrated, unhappy and bitchy. Because it's in the nature of women to give, and American women have always gone against their natures . . . They're takers.

*Interview, New York, pub. Aug. 29.*

**Robert Lowell**
*Poet*

The world is absolutely out of control now, and it's not going to be saved by reason or unreason.

*New York, pub. March 14.*

**Allard K. Lowenstein**
*United States Representative, D-N.Y.*

I think the world is getting tired of people being clubbed for no reason except that they want an opportunity to speak freely, whether it is in Madrid, Prague, or Berkeley.

*Prague, Czechoslovakia, Aug. 22.*

**Claire Boothe Luce**
*Playwright; former politician-diplomat*

The impact of the contraceptive revolution on the psyche of young American women has been shattering . . . challenging the most ancient concepts of the very nature of woman herself—and has left her in a state of bewilderment about her proper role in society . . . Fortunately for women, her body is still a trap—if no longer a baby trap, a man-trap. Young men still desire women as much as ever, even though they don't want to marry them as much.

*Chicago, Feb. 26.*

A young woman with matrimony in mind must put far, far more emphasis on her "sexiness" than her grandmothers did.

The first thing she must learn is to make her person glamorous, and, these days, to show as much of it as possible. The miniskirt and the plunging neckline are responses to the tightening up of the husband market.

*Before Chicago Women's Athletic Club, pub. March 10.*

**Thomas C. Lynch**
*Attorney General of California*

It (youth) is not an easy society to understand. In some ways it is an intensely materialistic society . . . in some ways it is an intensely moralistic society . . . on the whole, it is a rebellious, oppositional society, dedicated to the proposition that the grown-up world is a sham.

*Los Angeles, Sept. 23.*

**Milan Machovec**
*Professor of Philosophy,*
*Charles University, Prague*

It has been my experience that those who cannot talk with others because of their "principles" are people who in fact have no principles.

*Claremont College School of Theology, pub. March 9.*

**Archibald MacLeish**
*Poet, Playwright*

Nothing can be worse in a democracy than to have the conscience of the people or any part of the people silenced. Nothing can be worse for the country, and nothing can be worse for the human beings who compose the country. Silenced citizens—citizens silenced in their most profound convictions—are not free men, and a country with a censored conscience is not a country conscience-free.

*Pub. Nov. 23.*

**Charles Maechling, Jr.**
*Former special assistant to United States Ambassador-at-large Averell W. Harriman*

We must liberate ourselves from the delusion that the beloved cliche of the last Administration—that all the United States seeks is a free community of independent nations, each pursuing its own destiny—represents a policy or even a statement

(CHARLES MAECHLING, JR.)

of the national interest. There are no longer any independent nations in the world—only interdependent ones—and only a tiny minority of the world's people have ever been free.

*Pub. July 14.*

### Edgar F. Magnin
*Rabbi, Wilshire Boulevard Temple,*
*Los Angeles*

I prefer well-groomed people, but if you must let your hair grow long, it's no sin, so long as you keep it clean and have something under the hair that's worthwhile. In the last analysis, it is not the hair but what's inside the head that counts . . . brains, judgment, insight, understanding, love, friendliness, faith, reverence, loyalty and, not least of all, common sense.

*Address to the Confirmation Class,*
*Los Angeles, May 25.*

Life is not all rotten. You can't tell it all in terms of things stupid, vile, silly. I can see the faults in our society, but I don't shut my eyes to the good things—the beauty, freedom, glory of this country. With faith in Almighty God, you don't have to go backward; but you can go forward toward the pillar of cloud by day and pillar of fire by night. If we do that, we can't go wrong.

*Los Angeles, Dec. 11.*

### Thurgood Marshall
*Associate Justice, Supreme Court*
*of the United States*

I think we Negro Americans have just as many beautiful people in mind and body, as well as skin, as any other group—and that we have just as many stinkers as any other group.

*Dillard University, New Orleans, May 4.*

### Rod McKuen
*Poet, Songwriter*

You only really dig the country (United States) when you come back to it. You realize that *New York* is the art capital of the world, *our* actors and actresses are the roaming royalty of Europe, *our* poets and writers sell better and they (the Europeans) are going for *our* culture.

*Interview, Washington, June 4.*

### Yvette Mimieux
*Actress*

I resent the whole message of that magazine (*Playboy*). It promotes false, adolescent views of sex. They could never get away with the philosophy in Europe where people are more mature about such things. Men who believe in indiscriminate scoring with girls will never find a deep, lasting relationship. Hugh Hefner (publisher of *Playboy*) must be the most anti-female man in America.

*Interview, Los Angeles, pub. Feb. 10.*

### Ashley Montagu
*Anthropologist*

My discipline of anthropology is a very broad one, embracing virtually everything the human race is involved in. So many academics specialize in one narrow segment of knowledge. I range over the entire spectrum of human behavior, and in the course of my life I've accumulated a meaningful body of knowledge. It often amazes me how I, as a generalist, can see meanings where specialists see nothing.

*New York, pub. Sept. 28.*

### Malcolm C. Moos
*President, University of Minnesota*

What is most important for the future well-being of our communities, however we accomplish it, is that we learn to listen to what young people are saying. When we do listen, we discover quickly that our youth are at war with hypocrisy—that this is, in fact, an honest generation.

*Before American Newspaper Publishers*
*Association, New York, April 25.*

### Henry Morgan
*Television and Radio Entertainer*

A friend of mine, who should know better, moved to Sausalito (Calif.) and wrote me that the hippies really have something to say. I wrote back and asked: a) In what language? and b) What are they going to tell a 58-year-old man that he didn't know before? So he wrote me a disgusted letter saying they have a whole new point of view, that the world has changed. The world has changed while I was out of town, right? So what does he write me is the big problem? Well, they have no guarantee. We have children in college taking post-post-graduate courses. In what? In non-productivity. Milking their parents to death. And what is their beef? They have no guarantee that the world will endure. I have a small bulletin that just came in: Nobody ever did.

*Interview, Los Angeles, pub. Sept. 21.*

## Rogers C. B. Morton
*United States Representative, R-Md.*

I feel very, very strongly that the world is not going to hell in a handbasket, that we are just on the verge of a new plateau of civilization.

*Washington, pub. November.*

## Malcolm Muggeridge
*Author, Editor*

Let a collection of yahoos but take off their clothes, cavort about the stage and yell obscenities, and a great breakthrough in dramatic art is announced and applauded . . . (future generations would be astonished) at our crime-ridden, sex-ridden, fear-ridden, lawless, neurotic and unstable way of life.

*At International Festival of the Arts, Edinburgh, Scotland, Aug. 24.*

If the purpose of pornography is to excite sexual desire, it is unnecessary for the young, inconvenient for the middle-aged and unseemly for the old.

*Pub. Sept. 17.*

## Vladimir Nabokov
*Author*

My protest against protestors in America and elsewhere is that the greatest conformists and philistines are young people, especially hippies and their group protests. For me *they* are squares. I think all young people are conservatives—even if they're revolutionaries. It is the ripe man who knows what a revolution is—who changes things. You have to know the world before you can change it.

*Interview, Montreux, Switzerland, April 17.*

## Barnett Newman
*Artist*

Art should be ethics and not esthetics.
*Interview, New York, pub. April 14.*

## Gerard Nierenberg
*Lawyer*

In a successful negotiation, everybody wins. If you make the other party lose, it won't last. This is true in industry, unions, international politics, boss-employe, and certain personal relations . . . Man is supreme because, above all the other animals, he has learned to cooperate.
*Interview, Los Angeles, pub. Feb. 9.*

## Richard M. Nixon
*President of the United States*

The young people abroad, it seems, have somewhat the same problems of many young people here: They know what they are against, but they find difficulty in knowing what they are for.
*News conference, Washington, March 4.*

Some see America's vast wealth and protest that this has made us "materalistic." But we should not be apologetic about our abundance. We should not fall into the easy trap of confusing the production of things with the worship of things. We produce abundantly. But our values turn not on what we have but on what we believe.
*General Beadle State College, Madison, S.D., June 3.*

I believe that if human beings can reach the moon, human beings can reach an understanding with each other on earth. If we are to make progress in this lifetime effort we must see the world as it is, a world of different races, of different social systems; the real world, where many interests divide men and many interests unite them.
*Bucharest, Romania, Aug. 2.*

I think all these could happen: the end of the war (in Vietnam), stopping inflation, reducing crime, building more houses and feeding people better, the farmers happier, the wagging tongues shorter and all the rest, and still . . . it wouldn't be enough. It wouldn't be enough, because

(RICHARD M. NIXON)

some way we have to understand that this country can be the best-fed, best-housed, best-clothed nation in the world—which it is—and still be the unhappiest nation in the world—which it might become. It is this that the editorials must be written about. It is this that the speeches must be made about. It is this that in some way our young people must get a new vision of our country.

*Before Board of Directors,*
*Associated Press,*
*Washington, pub. Oct. 19.*

## Mrs. Richard M. Nixon
*Wife of the President of the United States*

I've seen it come true in my own lifetime. If people work, they can have what they want. People dream what they can achieve. It is possible.

*Washington, pub. June 2.*

## Kim Novak
*Actress*

Storms come, houses are wiped out, people drown, but every last little palm is there after the storm. Man is always saying, "I will overwhelm." Why can't he bend like the little palms? And rise again. Isn't that better than being broken and washed away?

*Pub. Nov. 4.*

## Paul VI
*Pope*

We have become used to this great phenomenon of transformation. It is affecting everything, every means of power, every person, every institution—and in a way so rapid and universal that everyone has the impression of being dragged away and overcome by an irresistible current as though by a river that hits us and carries us away.

One speaks always of revolution. Thus there is raised today, in every sphere, contestation—often without justifying either motive or scope. Novelty, novelty—everything is put in question.

*Vatican City, Jan. 15.*

The overriding need of novelty, originality and liberty propels the youthful spirit, and today even often in a rebellious way. The vitality of the young is expressed in a negative way, and it is almost pleased with the disorders it knows how to provoke and the problems it knows how to arouse.

*Vatican City, March 30.*

We see that the immodesty of fashions, the provoking and pornographic illustrations of some of the press, the publicity and the representation of many shows tend purposely to stimulate low passions. All this puts dirty fantasies and immoral and depraved thoughts in the hearts of mankind, sometimes provoking shameful crimes.

*Castel Gandolfo, Italy, Sept. 14.*

## Linus C. Pauling
*Professor of Chemistry,*
*University of California at San Diego*

I am disturbed when I see a cigaret between the lips or fingers of some important person upon whose intelligence and judgment the welfare of the world in part depends.

*Before International Congress of Social*
*Psychiatry, London, Aug. 4.*

## Mrs. Norman Vincent Peale
*Wife of the Clergyman*

One of the greatest things a wife can do is listen. I've spent years of my life listening. When Dr. Peale wanted to talk to me, whatever I was doing, I stopped. It isn't easy; this is an art, and there aren't enough women who have learned it.

*Interview, New York, pub. April 6.*

## Lester B. Pearson
*Former Prime Minister of Canada*

The seventies offer us crisis, no doubt, but also vast opportunities for creative action . . . We are at a moment in human destiny when the door can swing open to new opportunities and new hopes for the submerged 2 billion. The gates of the future are not closed. They are ajar. They *will* respond to a determined push . . .

*Racine, Wis., pub. Oct. 22.*

## Sam Peckinpah
*Motion Picture Director*

I have a 20-year-old daughter who is a

very strong pacifist and who believes that people are born without sin and without anger, which (are) not necessarily the same, and without violence. I totally disagree with her. People are born to survive. They have instincts that go back millions of years. Unfortunately, some of those instincts are based on violence. There is a great streak of violence in every human being. If it is not channeled and understood, it will break out in war or in madness.

*Interview, Hollywood, pub. Aug. 31.*

### S. J. Perelman
*Author*

. . . generally speaking, I don't believe in kindly humor. I don't think it exists. One of the most shameful utterances to stem from the human mouth is Will Rogers' "I never met a man I didn't like." The absolute antithesis was Oscar Wilde on the foxhunting Englishman: "The unspeakable in full pursuit of the unseatable." The two examples sum up for me the distinction. Wilde's remark contains, in the briefest span, the truth; whereas Rogers' is pure flatulence, crowd-pleasing and fake humility.

*Interview, Erwinna, Pa., pub. Jan. 26.*

### William Pfaff
*Political analyst*

Nothing seems to work properly any more. Industry makes cheap goods, but wrecks the landscape and pollutes the air and rivers. Technocrats tell us all problems are soluble, but their submarines sink at the dock and scientific administrators spill nerve gas onto grazing lands and then lie about it. Bureaucracies make the system function, but they meddle in private lives.

*Pub. December.*

### Prince Philip
*Husband of Queen Elizabeth II*

I want to make one point clear. This business of free speech has not been invented in the last five years. People have been arguing and dying for freedom of speech for a great deal longer than that . . . But freedom is not license. You can destroy freedom as successfully by making a mockery of it as you can by repression.

*Edinburgh University, Scotland, May 24.*

No matter what the material condition of our environment, people remain people, and the fight against prejudice, intolerance, injustice, oppression and hate must go on. The eternal principles of compassion, affection and liberty must still be the foundation of our modern philosophy.

*Before Canadian Council of Christians and Jews, Vancouver, Oct. 28.*

### James A. Pike
*Former Bishop, Protestant Episcopal Diocese of California*

To me, this talk about having someone else decide for you, at any age, is copping out of what a person is. A person is to be the subject of his own sentence. He is to be responsible for his own decisions.

*Santa Barbara, pub. Jan. 13.*

### Kenneth S. Pitzer
*President, Stanford University*

The dangers and difficulties arising from new technologies (in nuclear development), ranging from possible nuclear war to major pollution of water and air, are forcing us to abandon the *laissez faire* viewpoint that the natural result of scientific discoveries will be desirable improvements in our conditions of life.

*Before American Chemical Society, Minneapolis, April 14.*

### Mario A. Procaccino
*Controller, and candidate for Mayor of New York*

Unbridled pornography is a disease that can ravage a nation, rob it of its strength, dissipate its talent and lay waste its national heritage. History itself proves that either we must destroy it or it will destroy us.

*Washington, Oct. 22.*

### Louis T. Rader
*Division General Manager, General Electric Company*

. . . it is important to eliminate the man as a cog in the machine. Instead, we must use him in the system where his inductive reasoning and ability to design experiments, analyze data and determine courses of action are of greatest value.

*Los Angeles, March 10.*

**Ronald Reagan**
*Governor of California*

The too-prevalent fad of trying to act like the young people, the mod generation —rather than trying to get young people to act more like adults—is a disservice to the students. Young people are eager to move up to adulthood. When there seems nothing to move up to, they lose an important drive to grow up, to mature and share in the prerequisites of maturity.
*Los Angeles, Sept. 24.*

**Tom Reddin**
*Television News Commentator; former Chief of Police of Los Angeles*

The price of freedom still is what it always has been: willingness to submit to the rule of reason.
*Interview, Los Angeles, pub. May 9.*

**Ira L. Reiss**
*Director, Family Study Center, University of Minnesota*

Today's more permissive sexual standards represent not revolution but evolution.
*Before Illinois Social Hygiene League, Chicago, Oct. 10.*

**Mitja Ribicio**
*Premier of Yugoslavia*

In the past turbulent years, nonaligned policy has experienced many trials and tribulations. It has been exposed to various forms of pressure. In spite of everything, it has proved its vitality and asserted itself as a constructive moral-political force in international relations and as a realistic course for many countries in their efforts to preserve their independence, sovereignty and autonomous development.
*At conference of 51 nonaligned countries, Belgrade, July 8.*

**Abraham Ribicoff**
*United States Senator, D-Conn.*

. . . the youth of America has given this nation a heart transplant. We needed one badly. They are the ideas Americans have been professing for generations. But the difference is that this generation wants to put our principles into practice. They had the courage of our convictions.
*Claremont Men's College, Claremont, Calif., June 8.*

**Edward G. Robinson**
*Actor*

An audience identifies with the actors of flesh and blood and heartbeat, as no reader or beholder can identify with even the most artful paragraphs in books or the most inspiring paintings. There, says the watcher, but for some small difference in time or costume or inflection or gait, go I . . . And so, the actor becomes a catalyst; he brings to bright ignition that spark in every human being that longs for the miracle of transformation.
*Before the Masquers, Los Angeles, March 14.*

**Norman Rockwell**
*Artist*

The Romans didn't like the way the Christians dressed or wore their hair or the way they smelled, so they threw them to the lions. There are a lot of people who want to throw these (hippie) kids to the lions. But I think that out of them will come the leaders—if the atomic bombs don't blow the world to bits first.
*Interview, Los Angeles, pub. Nov. 12.*

**Willie Mae Rogers**
*Director, Good Housekeeping Institute*

I think it vital to give a family more than the physical attributes of a home. Fine as these things are, they are not enough to create the spirit of a home, a fortress in which family ties can develop. This fortress is the most important factor in children's lives. It is the source of psychic security.
*Pub. Jan. 30.*

**Victor G. Rosenblum**
*President, Reed College*

What is remarkable about this generation of students is not that it has its quota of cynics and cop-outs, but that it has so much idealism and faith in man's capacity to surmount the turbulence of the irrational and to find ways toward fulfillment and peace.
*Urban School of San Francisco, May 30.*

**Jonas Salk**
*Director, Salk Institute for*
*Biological Studies*

This is perhaps the most beautiful time in human history; it is really pregnant with all kinds of creative possibilities made possible by science and technology which now constitute the slave of man—if man is not enslaved by it.

*Interview, pub. Dec. 28.*

**Harland Sanders**
*Founder, Kentucky Fried Chicken*
*Corporation*

Work keeps a man alive. I been working since I was ten years old. That's what's wrong with this country: too many people don't care about work any more . . . A man'll rust out faster than he'll wear out. Hard work never hurt anybody.

*Interview, pub. Oct. 12.*

**Arthur M. Schlesinger, Jr.**
*Professor of Humanities,*
*City University of New York*

On the whole, I would say this generation is rather non-knowledgeable. I don't think they know much about history or particularly care to know about it. And I don't think they are being nearly as persecuted as they would have you believe. Each young generation feels it is being uniquely persecuted.

*News conference, Cincinnati, Ohio,*
*pub. April 24.*

**Karl Otto Schmid**
*Deputy Chief Planner,*
*Zurich, Switzerland*

A human city is a livable one . . . Livability reflects a state of mind. The environment, particularly the urban environment, is increasingly man-made, and therefore definitely mirrors the collective state of mind of the people. It also reflects the ambitions of a society just as it reflects the failures of societal values . . .

*Zurich, pub. Sept. 27.*

**William Schuman**
*Former President, Lincoln Center for*
*the Performing Arts, New York*

The arts gain from the presence of businessmen. But what art needs is a dreamer. A dreamer is the only practical answer in the arts. You can't solve artistic problems by balancing the budget.

*Pub. Jan. 27.*

**Glenn T. Seaborg**
*Chairman, Atomic Energy Commission*
*of the United States*

Today we are still going through the stage where, while we may marvel at many of the things the computer can do, many of us still fear it, resent it and are only too happy when we can catch it in error. But in a world of many more people, far more complicated than it is today, we are going to be vitally dependent on the computer, and learn, soon, that its benefits will far outweigh its drawbacks and that it will grant this greater freedom, not become a tool of restriction and repression.

*At Nobel symposium, Stockholm,*
*pub. Nov. 18.*

**Eric Sevareid**
*News Commentator,*
*Columbia Broadcasting System*

True pacifists aside, the young militants claim they hate war and love peace. They hate this particular war in Asia (Vietnam), but they love their own substitute wars on campuses and elsewhere. They are, in fact, warriors, containing within their breasts all the hate, fear, envy, aggression and boredom out of which so many wars have been born. They assume the right to commit acts of common criminality, but demand exceptions from the common penalties. One of the basic complaints of young revolutionaries is that adult society is full of hypocrisy. But it appears that hypocrisy is one phenomenon that has managed to bridge the generation gap.

*Pub. Nov. 4.*

**Joseph Sittler**
*Professor of Theology,*
*University of Chicago*

Man's brazen stupidity and hardness of heart in the realm of the human is the crucial challenge. Man on the moon is a less significant fact of our time than man in poverty when plenty is available, man at mass murder when alternatives are envisionable, and man yelling "Nigger!" at his fellow man.

*Pub. July 13.*

**Page Smith**
*Provost, Cowell College,*
*University of California at Santa Cruz*

Rational argument and naive goodwill have never proved effective in changing the world. It is changed by passion.
*Pub. Nov. 23.*

**Tommy Smothers**
*Entertainer*

The only valid censorship of ideas is the right of people not to listen.
*Before Commonwealth Club,*
*San Francisco, Aug. 22.*

**Johannes F. Spreen**
*Police Commissioner of Detroit*

If you care about your fellow citizens, no matter what their hue, that's love. If you do your thing well within the law and within the bounds of propriety, that's love. If you have faith in people and your police, that's love.
*Pub. March 28.*

**Connie Stevens**
*Actress, Singer*

In California, I find people have the same psychology about marriage as they have about buying a house. They buy a house to live in five years and then get another one. When they go into a house, they're already thinking of the next one.
*Interview, Hollywood,*
*pub. Aug. 21.*

**Roger L. Stevens**
*Chairman, National Council on the Arts*

I will readily admit that the formidable advance of modern science and technology, especially to business and industry, are essential elements required for progress, expansion and profits. I have no argument whatsoever with that. I'm all for it. But what I do not believe, the premise I cannot accept, is that we as the leading nation in the world, as reflected in the Federal budget, consider science to be 1,000 times more important than the arts—unless we have already resigned ourselves to a world of technocracy . . .
*Before Business Committee for the*
*Arts, New York, pub. Feb. 4.*

**Leopold Stokowski**
*Orchestra Conductor*

The youth in America makes the America of tomorrow. Therefore, they are very important to the cultural life and conditions of the United States. We hear much about youth in protest. I hear nothing about the great youth of today which is not in protest but which is educating itself both in the material side of life and also the cultural side.
*Interview, New York, pub. March 19.*

**W. Clement Stone**
*Chairman, Combined Insurance*
*Company of America*

Wealth is our power. Wealth is good. With money you can do good—your whole horizon changes.
*Interview, Chicago, pub. Feb. 7.*

**C. L. Sulzberger**
*Correspondent, "The New York Times"*

Students have rioted in England, France, Spain, Greece, Poland, Yugoslavia and Egypt and in very few countries is Vietnam a word of importance. We must not blame student rioting on the war. We take a confused and distorted view of the problem if we do. This is a problem of our moment in history.
*Interview, Los Angeles, pub. June 6.*

**Goh Keng Swee**
*Finance Minister of Singapore*

Universal franchise is ineffective where the majority of the electorate consists of peasants.
*Pub. Feb. 10.*

**U Thant**
*Secretary-General of the United Nations*

I do not wish to seem overdramatic, but I can only conclude from information that is available to me as Secretary-General that the members of the United Nations have perhaps 10 years left in which to subordinate their ancient quarrels and launch a global partnership to curb the arms race, to improve the human environment, to defuse the population explosion and to supply the required momentum to world development efforts. If such a global partnership is not formed within the next decade, then I very much fear that the problems I have mentioned will have reached such staggering proportions that they will be beyond our capacity to control.

*United Nations, N.Y., May 9.*

Wise men have little to fear from the surging ebullience of the young but will, on the contrary, welcome their energy, vitality and honesty. Let us first try to hear, then to listen, then to understand—and, finally, to use. Let the voice and passion of youth be part of our work for peace. Let those of us who are older strive to understand youth's concern and priorities. Let us make new plans in the light of an eloquent new reality.

Perhaps the most important thing we can say to the young of today is that the emotions that move them—the hatred of war, the thrust for equality of opportunity, the passion for building a more equitable society, the cry for tolerance and justice— are the very foundations upon which the U.N. was built.

*United Nations, N.Y., Oct. 24.*

**Ruth Tibbits Tooze**
*National President, Women's
Christian Temperance Union*

Nations that have died have died drunk, and, unless we wake up, ours is going to go the same way.

*Pub. Feb. 3.*

**Arnold J. Toynbee**
*Historian*

. . . I do think that you must have some code about sex, and I think from the extremely stiff 19th-century code, which was very hypocritically disobeyed in secret by many people, the younger generation has come to the opposite extreme—extreme license. There will probably be a reaction against this—their children will probably be extremely prim.

*Interview, London,
pub. March 18.*

What strikes the European is that it is thought almost anti-American, or un-American, to have tragedies. If your son is killed in Vietnam, you mustn't mourn

because this makes it look as if America isn't the ideal place . . . If I did have a tragedy in my personal life, I would rather have it in Europe or Asia than in America . . .

. . . you have to shoot somebody, burn yourself alive, do something violent, in order to get any attention at all, however good your cause or causes, however patient you have been, however well you have put your case. There is an absolute stone wall of indifference. All over the world.

*Interview, London, pub. April 2.*

If we're clever enough to reach the moon, don't we feel rather foolish in our mismanagement of human affairs?

*Pub. July 21.*

**Arthur Treacher**
*Television Personality*

Discipline means ethics. It means esthetics. It means style. It means elegance. It means manners. It means don't lose your temper. It means being on time to work. It means consideration for others. It means efficiency. It means giving a damn for the job you do. Half the people today would *die* if they had to toe the line.

*Interview, pub. Dec. 6.*

**Pierre Elliott Trudeau**
*Prime Minister of Canada*

It is a constant hazard of democracy that the loudest and most determined group is often that which holds the most extreme and reactionary views.

*University of Moncton, Canada, May 18.*

**Gabriel Valdes**
*Foreign Minister of Chile*

The idea (of a single international community, with common goals of security and development) is a myth which can be seen in this and other forums with speeches by prominent leaders who promise, with beautiful phrasing, what we know they are not willing to put into practice.

*United Nations, N.Y., pub. Oct. 5.*

**Jack Valenti**
*President, Motion Picture
Association of America*

No matter what the age or the era, the society that endures is the society that be-

(JACK VALENTI)

wares extremes. Total freedom is as awful as total repression.

*Before San Francisco Commonwealth Club, Oct. 10.*

**Tarjei Vessas**
*Author*

Of course man needs computers and machines. But he also needs dreams in order to live a full life. Cold death gushes out of computers. How man is to solve this dilemma, I can't tell. But his dreams are priceless.

*Interview, Vinja, Norway, pub. March 10.*

**George Wald**
*Professor of Biology, Harvard University*

We have desperately to find our way back to human values. I would even say to religion. There's nothing supernatural in my mind. Nature is my religion, and it's enough for me. I stack it up against any man's. For its awesomeness, and for the sense of the sanctity of man that it provides. What I mean is: we need some widely shared view of the place of man in the universe, some even tentative idea of the long-term needs and goals of human society.

*Interview, Cambridge, Mass., pub. Aug. 17.*

**Barbara Walters**
*Television Commentator,*
*National Broadcasting Company*

I know I'm not everyone's cup of tea. I'm not the girl next door. But you know something? The girl next door is becoming more like me. We used to think of her as blonde, freckled and maybe a little silly. Now she's intelligent, involved, complicated—and much more interesting.

*Interview, New York, pub. May 19.*

**Rudolph Wanderone ("Minnesota Fats")**
*Pool Player*

Where you come from don't mean nothin'. You can be born in an ash can so long as you're not there when you're thirty.

*Interview, San Francisco, pub. Aug. 24.*

**Earl Warren**
*Chief Justice of the United States*

Of all the revolutions that have marked the course of this century, perhaps the most fundamental and most enduring in its effects may turn out to be the emancipation of youth.

*Jewish Theological Seminary, New York, pub. May 26.*

One thing I will do (upon retirement from the Court) is keep busy. That I must do. I'm not leaving to just go fishing or something of that kind, but there's so many things that can be done, there are so many causes in the world today, that one need never lack one that he can really work on.

*Interview, Washington, pub. June 27.*

**Raquel Welch**
*Actress*

Any girl who desires to be popular must learn to listen. You hear a great deal about women gabbing all the time; but men, less publicized, love to talk. And they like to feel that the girl to whom they are talking is actively interested in what they have to say. You can't fake listening. It shows.

*Interview, Los Angeles, pub. Nov. 9.*

**Jacqueline Grennan Wexler**
*President-designate,*
*Hunter College, New York*

Social change does not mean a change of identity. Growth is an assertion of identity. There should be merging of rugged individualism and social consciousness. We have got to combine, somehow, a reverence for authority and the questioning of authority. These are not contradictory.

*Interview, New York, Dec. 19.*

**Jonathan Winters**
*Actor, Comedian*

. . . I don't buy this "Love" facade. I'm afraid of those flower children. Under those bouquets are grenades with the pins pulled.

*Interview, Los Angeles, pub. Jan. 6.*

**C. Vann Woodward**
*Professor of History, Yale University*

So long as man remains recognizably

human, he will remain a creature with both a past and a future. A creature so long described as earthbound and so newly transcending these bounds, so giddy over his spectacular innovations, so guilt-ridden about his past and so anxiety-ridden about the present and the future is not a creature who can safely turn away from history.

*Interview, pub. Dec. 30.*

**Joanne Woodward**
*Actress*

I was a rebel, and my idea of expressing this was to look a mess. Our whole group tried to shock people by going around like the hippies do today, but there was no name for us. We were really conforming,

and one only sees this with the eyes of maturity.

*Interview, Los Angeles, pub. April 11.*

**Dana Wynter**
*Actress*

Today, there is too much concentration on externals. The things that really count are the ones that stay with you when your flamboyant period of youth has passed. The older women who do not realize this have sad-looking faces because the things they depended on so are no longer there. They make an effort to appear young, but what imbalance there is when not a line of living is left in the face, and their eyes are old, old.

*Interview, Los Angeles, pub. Aug. 17.*

# Religion

### Robert N. Bellah
*Sociologist,*
*University of California*

The modern world is as alive with religious possibility as any epoch in human history.

*Rome, pub. April 4.*

### Eugene Carson Blake
*General Secretary,*
*World Council of Churches*

A government with mounting problems cannot be expected to keep its hands off the wealth of a rich church forever.

*Pub. May 5.*

When one remembers that churches pay no inheritance tax, may own and operate businesses and be exempt from the 52 per cent corporate income tax, and that real property used for church purposes is tax exempt, it is not unreasonable to prophesy that, with reasonably prudent management, the churches ought to be able to control the whole economy of the nation within the predictable future.

*Pub. May 26.*

. . . the ecumenical movement must not be confined to a mystical vision of God. The movement is important only if it makes itself felt in problems of justice and peace, hunger and race. Yet it must not go so far in dealing with these problems that the Christian church merely becomes a second class United Nations.

*Geneva, pub. June 15.*

### Frank Borman
*United States Astronaut*

I didn't see God (in space) . . . But I saw the evidence that God lives.

*Interview, pub. Feb. 23.*

### Balfour Brickner
*Director, Interfaith Activities, Union of American Hebrew Congregations*

People want to be lifted, not just analyzed . . . Most guys in the pulpit are too stiff. They have no humor. They're just speaking. You have to do more. You have to have fire. But most people think that's too pretentious.

*Pub. June 2.*

### Harvey G. Cox
*Associate Professor*
*of Church and Society,*
*Harvard University*

It may be that the major reason for nonbelief is not that people find the Gospels incredible, but that they find the churches incredible.

*Rome, pub. April 7.*

### Richard Cardinal Cushing
*Archbishop of Boston*

There has been, and let us acknowledge it, a spiritual flabbiness from which our fathers would have fled. We have become in some measure "fat" Christians whose religion does not overmuch interfere with our comfort.

*Pub. March 24.*

### Dalai Lama
*Former Ruler of Tibet*

The Marxist accusation that "religion is the opiate of the people" may have been right insofar as the way religions are practiced. But if a religion is truly practiced I think even a Communist, if he were honest, would have difficulty in making that charge.

*Interview, Dharamsala, India,*
*pub. April 13.*

**Robert M. Donihi**
*Former Director, Office of Information,*
*United States Catholic Conference*

The P. R. (public relations) image of the bishops is not good. Many—possibly most —religion news writers confide the belief that a great many Catholic bishops are arrogant, unapproachable, removed from the mainstream of humanity, living in their own exclusive club-like atmosphere made up almost exclusively of brother bishops . . .
*Before Religious Public Relations*
*Council, Washington, pub. April 19.*

**James Forman**
*Founder-Director, National Black*
*Economic Development Conference*

Anytime a Catholic Church, through one of its branches, the Jesuits, owns 51% of the Bank of America, it is a financial entity, man. It is more than just a religious institution.
*News conference,*
*Los Angeles, May 19.*

**C. C. Goen**
*Professor of Church History, Wesley*
*Theological Seminary, Washington*

One of the most obvious aspects of American religious life is that the churches are notably lacking in discipline . . . According to reported statistics, we now have around 125,000,000 members—for bragging purposes; we cannot begin to locate all of them . . . Of those whom we can locate, we cannot count on more than half to be in public worship on any given Sunday morning. Of these "Sunday morning Christians," fewer than 50 per cent will be active in the program of the local church, and, of those who are active, a painfully small fraction will be living disciplined lives of Christian obedience in home and office, market and factory, school and play. My judgment as an historian is that authentic Christianity has always been a minority movement; and, to use the name "Christian" for the undisciplined masses who are little more than practitioners of culture and religion, is to confuse the meaning of the term.
*Bridgewater (Virginia) College,*
*pub. April 21.*

**Billy Graham**
*Evangelist*

It is a matter of concern to some of our religious leaders that present trends indicate that by the year 2000 most religious worship will be conducted in the home. I don't know whether their concern is justified, but it is there and may help explain the criticism of anything that takes worship out of our churches.
*Pub. April 28.*

An evangelist is the man who stands at the gates of the Kingdom of Heaven and says, "Come in."
*Interview, pub. June 14.*

There is so much hell in the country because there is not more hell in the pulpit.
*Television address, New York, Aug. 24.*

**James E. Groppi**
*Militant Milwaukee Priest*

The church is a white racist institution. The people who shout, "Black Bastards, go back to Africa," go to church on Sunday. The church should teach revolution.
*Before World Council of Churches,*
*London, May 21.*

**James Gunther**
*President, Ministerial Interfaith Association*

The white church puts an emphasis on property. The black churches have always been poor, so they concentrate on people. We don't talk theology, we do it.
*New York, pub. May 31.*

**John C. Harper**
*Rector, St. John's Episcopal Church,*
*Washington, D.C.*

. . . if we are permitted to make the Christian Church as a whole a collection of people who are too comfortable with each other, who are unwilling to accept the stranger in whatever form his strangeness may take, then we are dead—dead to the world and dead inside.
*Washington, May 25.*

**Kirby James Hensley**
*Founder, Universal Life Church*

Every man who feels a desire to preach

(KIRBY JAMES HENSLEY)

is a preacher. And I never met anyone who wasn't a preacher.

*Pub. Feb. 21.*

The thing that's putting America in the graveyard is a little black book called the *Holy Bible,* because it says that one man's good and another man's bad.

*Pub. May 5.*

**Robert Jones**
*Unitarian All Souls Church,*
*Washington, D.C.*

Ever since Ike (Dwight D. Eisenhower), Presidents have been forced to account for their Sundays. If they didn't go to church, they had to have a good excuse. I admit to be looking forward to the day when a President will tell us all: "I didn't go to church this morning because I didn't feel like it."

*Pub. Feb. 7.*

**Freda Magid**
*Consultant on Interreligious Action,*
*Commission on Interfaith Activities,*
*Union of American Hebrew Congregations*

The church is more of a country club than a house of worship; and while many are open at all times for prayer and meditation, most of the congregations in the last 15 or 20 years have been caught up in the "edifice complex." They have beautiful buildings, large mortgages and so many financial projects that there is little energy left over for worship and social concern.

*Los Angeles, pub. Dec. 21.*

**Edgar F. Magnin**
*Rabbi, Wilshire Boulevard Temple,*
*Los Angeles*

To paraphrase Mark Twain, the reports of religion's death are greatly exaggerated. Pews in churchs and synogogues are well filled, even when the ritual is performed with dignity, solemnity and the aesthetic quality that comes with centuries of hallowed tradition.

*Pub. Feb. 12.*

**Martin E. Marty**
*Associate Professor, Divinity School,*
*University of Chicago*

In the new age of technology and urban living, churches are experimenting to find a new role for themselves . . . Today's religious experiments are following a course that could have been programmed on a computer. There is restlessness with intellectualism, a desire for "feeling," a dissatisfaction with authority—the same things you find on the campus.

*Pub. April 14.*

**Carl McIntire**
*Evangelist*

The "Black Manifesto" is the voice of hell. It is the evidence of Communist participation in the internal life of the churches in the United States of America. It is the fruit of the social gospel. It will destroy the United States.

*Riverside Church, New York, Sept. 14.*

**Arch A. Moore**
*Governor of West Virginia*

I sometimes fear that in the extreme restlessness of some of our youth today and their disrespect for the so-called establishment is but the reaping of the harvest of the seeds we sowed when we took the prayer from our schoolhouses across this land.

*Dover, Del., April 24.*

**Casimiro Morcillo**
*Archbishop of Madrid*

Let me tell you that all this talk about prophecy is a lot of hogwash. The prophet is a man who speaks in the name of God. Nothing else. And to be a prophet you have to be called by God. I don't know if there could be anybody nowadays who can say that God has inspired him to say this or that. Since the Apostles, prophecy in the church has been restricted exclusively to explaining the Gospels.

*Interview, Madrid, pub. Sept. 28.*

**James A. Pike**
*Former Bishop, Protestant Episcopal*
*Diocese of California*

The poor may inherit the earth, but it would appear that the rich—or at least the rigid, respectable and safe—will inherit the church.

*Pub. April 20.*

**Daniel Poling**
*President, Christian Herald Association*

(Today) we are watching the collapse of an historic profession—the clergy. It is a very rapid collapse. This is one of the reasons for the tremendous erosion of authority. A young priest no longer lives in fear of his bishop. He will accept a certain amount of discipline, but only if it appears to him to be just and wise discipline.

*Interview, Los Angeles,*
*pub. April 27.*

**Paul VI**
*Pope*

The church suffers above all from the restless, critical, unruly and demolishing rebellion of so many of its children—priests, teachers, laymen, those devoted to the service and testimony of Christ in the Living Church—against its intimate and indispensable communion, against its institutional existence, against its canon rule, its tradition, its interior cohesion, against its authority, the unchangeable principle of truth, unity and charity, against its very requirements of sanctity and sacrifice. It suffers from the defection and the scandal of certain priests and religions who today crucify the Church.

*Vatican City, March 2.*

Many said: It (religion) is finished. But others say: No, it is not only not finished, but it prevails . . . Religion returns, and even if it is not professed, at least it is discussed, and sometimes, in the light of violent and irrational acts or of anguished states of mind, religion imposes itself in terms so appealing and desperate that . . . it is desired.

*Vatican City, May 28.*

One cannot invent a new church according to his own judgment or personal tastes. To be truly faithful to the church today, we must guard against the dangers that derive from this proposition, from temptations, perhaps, to renew the church with radical intent or drastic methods, subverting it.

*Vatican City, pub. Sept. 25.*

The church is like a musical concert. And no instrument, however good it

sounds in the orchestra, can play as it pleases.

*Rome, Nov. 5.*

**Ronald Reagan**
*Governor of California*

People have become so concerned with church-state separation that we have interpreted freedom *of* religion into freedom *from* religion. There is no need greater in our land today than to rediscover our spiritual heritage.

*Anaheim, Calif., Sept. 26.*

**Vance D. Rogers**
*President, Nebraska Wesleyan University*

Science will be more and more concerned with creation and all it has wrought. Religion will continue to study the Creator. Science will work on the world without, religion with the world within men.

*Los Angeles, Feb. 23.*

**Jose Maria Gonzalez Ruiz**
*Canon of Malaga, Spain*

. . . I do believe in celibacy. Celibacy is prophetic. But celibacy is more than not going to bed with a woman: It is not going to bed with anyone or anything—total celibacy. I never understood those priests who called themselves celibate but, nevertheless, went to bed with money, with honors, with social position, with luxuries. I never understood it. Sometimes I learned later, in fact, that they also went to bed with women. If not always literally, at least in an imaginary, poorly-sublimated fashion. In any case, they were repressed men. The true prophet goes to bed with nobody and nothing.

*Interview, pub. Sept. 28.*

**Zev Segal**
*President, Rabbinical*
*Council of America*

The classic anti-Semite has now put on a new uniform more in keeping with modern times and the present situation. He refuses to be identified as an anti-Semite and declares fervently that he has no prejudice against the Jews. Instead, he has now become an anti-Zionist—a posi-

(ZEV SEGAL)

tion from which he attacks both the Jews and "Israeli imperialism" as part of a nefarious worldwide conspiracy from which he must save peace-loving humanity.

*New York, Feb. 8.*

### George Gaylord Simpson
*Professor of Paleontology,*
*Harvard University*

If in some madhouse there is a lunatic who still believes the old churchly tenet that heaven is up above, even this (the first manned landing on the moon) probably will not disabuse him. Surely those of us still sane enough to be at large realize that this event will have no more to do with theology, God, or self-knowledge than any flower we pluck or any hand we press—in fact, much less.

*Pub. July 13.*

### Leon-Joseph Cardinal Suenens
*Primate of Belgium*

It is not the authority of the Pope which is in doubt among faithful sons of the church, but the system which holds him prisoner . . . What is wanted is to liberate everyone, even the Holy Father himself, from the system—which has been the subject of complaint for several centuries, and yet we have not succeeded in loosening its grip or reshaping it. For, while the Popes come and go, the Curia remains . . . Nothing can be achieved if every honest criticism, every desire to question, is seen as arising out of pride or ill will . . . At present, if any group of bishops decide to confer together, they are seen as conspirators.

*Interview, pub. May 18.*

The institution of the Papacy today needs credibility, and the first step to achieve it would be for the Pope to be elected by representatives of the universal church—not only cardinals and bishops, for I would gladly see the laity adequately included among the electors. The Pope today does not give the general impression of being Peter's successor, but rather the successor of Emperors and political sovereigns.

*Interview, pub. June 24.*

There are some who insist on the primacy of the Roman pontiff to the extent that it resembles the absolute monarchism of the time before the French Revolution. We (the Bishops) are not only under the Pope, but we exercise our power *with* him.

*Rome, pub. Oct. 19.*

### John H. Thomas
*Professor of Biology, Stanford University*

The population problem will be solved one way or another—either in a humane and Christian way, or an inhumane and un-Christian way. The humane and Christian way is through birth control. The inhumane and un-Christian way is through war, famine and disease. It would seem that the Roman Catholic Church has chosen in favor of an inhumane and un-Christian way.

*Pub. Dec. 14.*

### F. Thomas Trotter
*Dean, School of Theology,*
*Claremont College*

The problem of religion basically is not cosmic. Basically, it is the human problem, and very earthy. The church historically has always fought against a theology that tried to translate human religion into cosmic religion. Christianity has always argued that the payoff is personal—the way one expresses love for his neighbor. This is where the action is—not out in space.

*Claremont, Calif., pub. July 13.*

### Wernher von Braun
*Director, George C. Marshall Space*
*Flight Center, National Aeronautics*
*and Space Administration*

There certainly is no scientific reason why God cannot retain the same position in our modern world that He held before we began probing His creation with telescope and cyclotron . . . Manned space flight is an amazing achievement, but it has opened for us thus far only a tiny door for viewing the awesome reaches of space. Our outlook through this peephole at the vast mysteries of the universe only confirms our belief in the Creator.

*Interview, pub. July 5.*

**Ralph D. Abernathy**
*President, Southern Christian
Leadership Conference*

It is so exciting a thing to see, that I forgot for a moment why I was here . . .
*At launching of Apollo 11, first manned
moon flight, Cape Kennedy, Fla.,
July 16.*

**Spiro T. Agnew**
*Vice President
of the United States*

It is my individual feeling that we should articulate a simple, ambitious, optimistic goal of a manned flight to Mars by the end of this century. Whether we say it or not, someone's going to do it.
*Interview, Cape Kennedy,
Fla., July 16.*

We can, as the song goes, dream the impossible dream and reach the unreachable star. The danger lies not in daring to dream or to reach, but in dreaming timid dreams and making feeble grasps. There remain those who say we cannot afford to venture into space . . . they equate progress to comfort and would limit life to drab dimensions . . .
*At Western Governors Conference,
Seattle, July 28.*

. . . we will have space programs because we are ambitious. Why space? Because it is in our blood as Americans. Because we believe that a better life lies beyond the horizon. Because we are citizens not of the Old World but of the new one. Because ours is the heritage of those who broke the barriers of Gibraltar and entrusted to us their legacy of eternal hope—"plus ultra" —"more beyond."
*Before The Executive Club,
Chicago, Sept. 30.*

**Edwin E. Aldrin**
*United States Astronaut*

This is far more than the voyage of three men to the moon. We feel this stands as the symbol of the insatiable curiosity of all mankind to explore the unknown.
*Aboard Apollo 11 flight to moon, July 23.*

We accepted the challenge of going to the moon. The acceptance of this challenge was inevitable. The relative ease with which we carried out our mission, I believe, is a tribute to the timeliness of that acceptance.
*Pub. July 28.*

This medal (the Medal of Freedom) is not only for the crew, but for the countless thousands of others who strived for eight long years over the Apollo project. It is an honor to all Americans who believed and persevered with us. The footprints on the moon belong to all of you. They are a symbol of the true human spirit.
*At dinner honoring Apollo 11 astronauts,
Los Angeles, Aug. 13.*

The Apollo lesson is that national goals can be met where there is a strong enough will to do so. A small step for a man was a statement of fact. A giant leap for mankind is the hope for the future.
*Washington, Sept. 16.*

**Neil A. Armstrong**
*United States Astronaut;
first man to set foot on moon*

I wouldn't say that fear is an unknown emotion to us. Fear is characteristic particularly of a knowledge that there may be something that you haven't thought of and feel that you might be unable to cope with. I think our training and all the work that goes into the preparation for a flight does everything it can toward erasing those

(NEIL A. ARMSTRONG)

kinds of possibilities, and I would say that as a crew we, among the three of us, have no fear of launching out on this expedition.

*News conference prior to launching first manned flight to moon; Cape Kennedy, Fla., July 14.*

That's one small step for a man, one giant leap for mankind.

*First words upon setting foot on moon, July 20.*

Today, we saw a sign carefully scribbled: "Through You We Touched The Moon." Today, it was our privilege across the nation to touch America.

*At dinner honoring Apollo 11 astronauts, Los Angeles, Aug. 13.*

### Bernard H. Baumrin
*Associate Professor of Philosophy, City University of New York*

It is true that, despite the expenditure of about $50 billion, the Apollo program could have failed, as of course many voyages before have (though few were covered by television). But what must occur to the reasonable man is that an expenditure on the scale of the Marshall Plan could have gone a great distance in the creation of a livable world. We are $50 billion further behind, and 10 more years.

*Before American Psychological Association, Washington, pub. Sept. 7.*

### Alan L. Bean
*United States Astronaut*

Hey, it's real nice moving around up here. You don't seem to get tired. You really hop like a bunny. Where is earth? There it is.

*On moon, Nov. 19.*

### Anatoly A. Blagonravov
*Member, Soviet Academy of Sciences*

The exploration of the cosmos—the moon and the planets—is a noble aim. Our generation has the right to be proud of the fact that it has opened the space era of mankind . . . In the future, there is no doubt that space exploration will become a general task for all humanity and not only for individual countries.

*Interview, Moscow, pub. June 22.*

### Frank Borman
*United States Astronaut*

. . . why do this? Why spend all this money (on space exploration) when our cities are decaying, when people are hungry and we have all these miseries here on earth? In my seven years with NASA, the Apollo has come from a nothing concept to the most miraculous machine that has ever been built. The genius that produced it is essentially American. That technology and that capability is transferable into every phase of our life . . . And I go to bed periodically and remember that probably the one greatest force and stability for freedom in this world right now is the combined might of this country. And I think a lot of people have forgotten it.

*Before American Newspaper Publishers Association, New York, April 23.*

Our flight to the moon was an American achievement and we are proud of it. But, in a broader sense, it was an achievement of all great scientists of the past, of all the past minds of history. We took the accumulated knowledge of all time and applied it to our machine.

*News conference, Bonn, Germany, Feb. 11.*

### Ray Bradbury
*Science-fiction Writer*

Once we make it to the moon, once we touch down on Mars, once we move on out to the stars and go to planets revolving around stars so far away we can't even imagine it—once we do this, we become the thing that we've always wanted to be, and that is immortal . . . The whole race goes on then, and the gift of life passes from hand to hand. We don't have to stay here. The race doesn't have to die. It doesn't have to be destroyed by the dying of the sun, or the super-explosion of the sun. And, in future generations, other races of people, other generations of people will look back to this summer and say, "Oh, how wonderful it must have been to have been alive then when this huge step which insures the victory over time and space and eternity for all of us, how wonderful to have been alive when that happened."

*Radio interview, on eve of first manned flight to moon, July 19.*

## Leonid I. Brezhnev
*General Secretary, Communist Party of Union of Soviet Socialist Republics*

Soviet-made spaceships are ships of science. They are traveling to outer space to conduct scientific and technical experiments. We are following our road, advancing consistently and purposefully.

*Moscow, Oct. 22.*

## David Brinkley
*News Commentator, National Broadcasting Company*

This will be remembered as long as man remembers anything. To land on the moon and to walk around on it—I almost don't believe it.

*Commenting on launching of Apollo 11, first manned moon flight, July 16.*

## Eldridge Cleaver
*Information Minister, Black Panther Party*

The moon shot is out of this world. It is irrelevant to what is happening here and now. The world is not sitting on a powder keg—it *is* a powder keg, and the pigs in Washington, D.C., who control the government use the space program as a circus to distract people's minds from the real problems, which are here on the ground. The time for the moon is later . . . What we need is an earth program, not a space program. We need rockets on Washington, South Africa, Mozambique, etc. I don't applaud the space shot. I would only applaud if the U.S. would commit suicide.

*Telephone interview, Algiers, July 17.*

## Michael Collins
*United States Astronaut*

Many years before there was a space program, my father had a favorite quotation: "He who would bring back the wealth of the Indies must take the wealth of the Indies with him." This we have done. We have taken to the moon the wealth of this nation, the vision of its political leaders, the intelligence of its

scientists, the dedication of its engineers, the careful craftsmanship of its workers and the enthusiastic support of its people. We have brought back rocks and I think it's a fair trade. For just as the Rosetta Stone revealed the language of ancient Egypt, so may these rocks unlock the mystery of the origin of the moon, of our earth, and even of our solar system.

*Before Joint Session of Congress, Washington, Sept. 16.*

I think a future flight should include a poet, a priest and a philosopher. From these people we might get a much better idea of what we saw.

*Pub. Nov. 9.*

## Jose Maria Otero de Navascues
*Director General, Spanish Nuclear Energy Commission*

I would compare the event (landing on the moon) with the only one which is comparable in history—the discovery of America. But in that event there was much improvisation, where today everything is super-prepared.

*Madrid, July 21.*

## Lee A. DuBridge
*Science Advisor to the President of the United States*

A dozen years ago public opinion was galvanized into action by the Russian Sputnik, and science support took a sudden upward burst. No Sputnik is in sight now, and public interest is lagging. Maybe we should have let the Russians beat us to the moon.

*News conference, New York, Dec. 3.*

## Konstantin Feoktistov
*Soviet Cosmonaut*

I think the military use of space is not practical. I think the idea of space ships armed with machine guns is ridiculous.

*At American Institute of Aeronautics and Astronautics, Anaheim, Calif., Oct. 23.*

## Franco Ferrarotti
*Professor of Sociology, University of Rome*

The Americans got there (to the moon)

(FRANCO FERRAROTTI)

first because of their superior ability to organize men and resources. What amazes people most is this knack of harnessing and coordinating so effectively the efforts of thousands of industrial and scientific groups and concerns.

*Rome, July 21.*

**Donald P. Hearth**
*Director, Planetary Programs,*
*National Aeronautics and Space*
*Administration of the United States*

Jupiter! Now *there's* a great planet! It has 12 moons, a completely unknown atmosphere, those radio emissions, and that crazy red spot that's as big as Mars. I think the 1980s are going to be the decade of Jupiter.

*Washington, pub. Feb. 20.*

**Lyndon B. Johnson**
*Former President*
*of the United States*

I don't believe there is a single thing that our country does, that our government does, that our people do, that has greater potential for peace than the space effort.

*Television interview, Cape Kennedy,*
*Fla., July 16.*

**Edward M. Kennedy**
*United States Senator,*
*D-Mass.*

We need not try to get to Mars or Venus merely because the Russians might get there first. We need not pay the overtime and the costs necessarily involved in a program with an urgent deadline . . . I am for the space program. But I want to see it in its right priority, one which will let it continue into the future and not have to be cut back or abandoned . . .

*Clark University, Worcester, Mass.,*
*May 19.*

**Sir Bernard Lovell**
*Astronomer*

This (landing on the moon by Apollo 11) is the first time the United States has been demonstrably superior in a vital part of the space program. American approaches for collaboration may be received with sympathy in the Soviet Union, as they (the

Russians) can no longer regard themselves as masters.

*Jodrell Bank Observatory, England,*
*July 22.*

**James McDivitt**
*United States Astronaut*

You know, the kind of man the space agency is looking for is impossible. They want a man who has a master's degree in science or engineering, with 5,000 hours flying time and not over 25 years old. There's no one like this around, so they have to be satisfied with someone like me.

*Pub. March 25.*

**George E. Mueller**
*Associate Administrator for Manned*
*Space Flight, National Aeronautics*
*and Space Administration*
*of the United States*

Four billion years ago, the earth was formed. Four hundred million years ago, life moved to the land. Four million years ago, man appeared on the earth. One hundred years ago the technological revolution that led to this day (the moon landing) began. All of these events were important, yet in none of them did man make a conscious decision to follow a path that would change all mankind. The will of the people of this nation, and of the world, will determine whether mankind will make the great leap to the planets.

*Houston, July 24.*

**John Naugle**
*Assistant Administrator for Space Science*
*and Applications, National Aeronautics*
*and Space Administration*
*of the United States*

Automated spacecrafts are powerful tools for exploration of space; but it is clear there are limits to what they can do. For example, suppose we put a package in orbit today to conduct a series of experiments. Next week we make some great advance in science or technology. We can't change that spacecraft; we're stuck with it. So we have to design a new package based on our new knowledge. But with men, if we discover something new, we can take immediate advantage of our evolving technology. Man in space brings into being

a tremendous new capability for research in exploration of other bodies. This is where man really comes into his own.
*Interview, Los Angeles, pub. Aug. 7.*

### Richard M. Nixon
*President of the United States*

, I can't tell you how proud we all are of what you have done for every American. This has to be the proudest day of our lives. For people all over the world I am sure that they, too, join with Americans in recognizing what an immense feat this is. Because of what you have done, the heavens have become part of man's world. For one priceless moment in the whole history of man, all of the people on this earth are truly one.
*Speaking to Apollo 11 astronauts on moon, Washington, July 20.*

I hope that when the next great adventure into space takes place that it will be one in which Americans will be joined by representatives of other countries so that we can go together. That is why, as we look at the future adventures, let them not be adventures of conquest, but adventures of exploration which tend to unite us all into one people, which we truly are.
*Washington, July 22.*

This is the greatest week in the history of the world since the Creation.
*Describing Apollo 11 manned moon landing, aboard U.S.S. Hornet, July 24.*

On my recent trip around the world, I visited countries in all stages of economic development; countries with different social systems, different economic systems, different political systems. In all of them, however, I found that one event had caught their imagination and lifted their spirits almost beyond measure: The trip of Apollo (11) to the Moon and back. On that historic day, when the astronauts set foot on the Moon, the Spirit of Apollo 11 truly swept the world—a spirit of peace and brotherhood and adventure, and a spirit that thrilled to the knowledge that man had dreamed the impossible, dared the impossible and done the impossible.
*Television address, Washington, Aug. 8.*

For years, politicians have promised the moon. I'm the first one to be able to deliver it.
*Washington, Dec. 3.*

### Thomas O. Paine
*Administrator, National Aeronautics and Space Administration of the United States*

. . . while the moon has been the focus of our effort, the true goal is far more than being first to land men on the moon as though it were a celestial Mount Everest to be climbed. The real goal is to develop and demonstrate the capability for interplanetary travel . . . With some awe we contemplate that men can now walk on extra-terrestrial shores.
*News conference, Houston, May 26.*

We don't know all the ways in which space technology may affect future defense postures. We do know that, in the past, wherever man has flown farther and higher and faster, wherever he has developed new capability to observe from higher areas, to carry out operations in new media, this has had a major effect on the equations of international power. We're quite confident that this will probably be true again in space.
*Interview, Washington, pub. July 7.*

At the time the Soviet Union orbited Sputnik, Nikita Krushchev said that the achievement proved their way of life, but, by reaching the moon, we proved that our way of life could do it, too.
*News conference, Los Angeles, July 31.*

It seems to me we ought to now have a national debate about this (the space program). If we were not going to consider bold new goals, then we might just go willy-nilly into the 1970's. There are people who think we ought to be talking softly and letting this go on in the backrooms at NASA; but I don't think so. I think we ought to tell the country. Win or lose, it's a debate we ought to have.
*Interview, pub. Aug. 13.*

### John O. Pastore
*United States Senator, D-R.I.*

I asked him (Dr. Thomas O. Paine, NASA Administrator): Why do we have to go up there 10 times? We have been

(JOHN O. PASTORE)

there; we did it. He said: "*It is like everything else; if a man lands on Cape Cod, he knows about the Atlantic Ocean. But does he know about the wheat fields in Kansas? Does he know the topography of Kansas because he landed on Cape Cod?*" What we are trying to do is continue our research. Maybe we will find nothing—but who knows? Maybe the next set of rocks will be diamonds—who knows? Would that not be wonderful?

*Before the Senate, Washington, Nov. 10.*

### Lester B. Pearson
*Former Prime Minister of Canada*

It is likely that the historians of the future will see the experience of space as humanity's chief insight of the '60s. Gradually entering the world's consciousness, like a silent and rising tide within the human imagination, are those pictures taken from interstellar space, where our bright planet, Earth, full of life and light, hangs small, single and alone in the cold void . . .

*Racine, Wis., pub. Oct. 22.*

### William H. Pickering
*Director, Jet Propulsion Laboratory*

There is a lot of talk about exploring the universe, but the solar system is only a small part and it's going to be a long time before we venture out. We are making a very local exploration . . . I sometimes think of the first decade—nineteen-sixties—as one in which we learned to operate in space. The next decade should be devoted to the exploration of the solar system.

*Interview, Pasadena, Calif., July 26.*

### Walter O. Roberts
*President, American Association for the Advancement of Science*

The next step in space must be directed towards the earth. We must turn our newly-discovered skills toward the construction of world systems that make the planet earth even better than it is now for its burgeoning numbers of people. We must invent new world technologies. We must commit the resources of space science, directly and indirectly, to the achievement of an optimum balance of man and nature on this magnificent, but imperiled, planet.

*Before American Association for the Advancement of Science, Boston, Dec. 28.*

### Eric Sevareid
*News Commentator, Columbia Broadcasting System*

This is not a romantic era, not a poetic era. We have not the words to describe what is happening here. Our very language needs overhauling. How can you say as high as the sky anymore? Or the sky's the limit?

*Commenting on launching of Apollo 11 first manned moon flight, Cape Kennedy, Fla., July 16.*

### R. Sargent Shriver
*United States Ambassador to France*

How beautiful it is. The red of the flames, the blue of the sky, the white fumes—those colors! Think of the guys in there getting that incredible ride!

*Describing take-off of Apollo 11, first manned moon flight, Cape Kennedy, Fla., July 16.*

### Bradford Smith
*Astronomer, New Mexico State University*

The only way the human race can survive is to extend the range of man's habitat to Mars. The sooner that man gets there, the better—for his own survival.

*At Jet Propulsion Laboratory, Pasadena, Calif., pub. Aug. 27.*

### Harold Urey
*Consultant to National Aeronautics and Space Administration of the United States*

I am so proud of the United States for telling the world exactly what we tried to do (in landing a man on the moon). It shows an enormous self-confidence in our effort. If it fails, we say it did. I do wish our Russian friends would come out and tell us what they are trying to do.

*Houston, July 21.*

### Wernher von Braun
*Director, George C. Marshall Space Center, National Aeronautics and Space Administration*

A couple of years ago you could answer

the question, "Are we ahead of the Russians or are they ahead of us (in the space race)?" in very simple terms. For example, right after Sputnik it was pretty clear they had something in orbit and we didn't . . . But today the space program has so many facets that it may be impossible for all eternity from now on to be ahead in all fields. And, equally, it will be impossible for them to be ahead of us in all fields.
*Interview, Huntsville, Ala., June 4.*

**Edward C. Walsh**
*Former First Executive Secretary,*
*National Aeronautics and Space Council*

We are not going to make just one trip to the moon and then stop. The moon may become an excellent place for a joint international venture, something like Antarctica, which the nations have by treaty reserved for scientific research. Discoveries made on the moon properly belong to the world. Consider the moon as a space station, a kick-off point for travel to the planets. There it is. It's in orbit. Why not use it?
*Washington, pub. Feb. 16.*

**John Young**
*United States Astronaut*

Portugal is clear. Italy is clear south of Rome . . . Bulgaria is clear, but the rest of Europe is mostly under the clouds . . . Arabia appears clear. Israel clear. Jordan clear . . . that's your morning weather report from 100,000 miles.
*Aboard Apollo 10, in flight, May 19.*

# Sports

## BASEBALL

**Hank Aaron**
*Player, Atlanta "Braves"*

The big thing now is concentrating on pitching, and I mean all the way down to the Babe Ruth leagues. No one worries about a kid hitting. All they want to know is how many games a kid wins and how many batters he strikes out. I think there should be a lot more concentration on teaching hitting.
*West Palm Beach, Fla., March 17.*

**Richie Allen**
*Player, Philadelphia "Phillies"*

They say I have a direct line to the front office. They say I call my own shots. How can they say that when all I want to do is get the hell out of Philadelphia?
*Pub. Aug. 30.*

**Arthur Allyn**
*Owner, Chicago "White Sox"*

The fans will be looking at you this year more closely than ever before to see whether or not you are really giving the 110 per cent they expect. I am not asking you to do it for me. I'm asking you to do it for your fans. If we don't have the right attitudes, if we don't give everything we've got to those who pay their way into the park, then you can be sure they'll know it and we'll know it.
*Addressing the team, Sarasota, Fla., pub. April 12.*

**Ernie Banks**
*Player, Chicago "Cubs"*

I can't remember ever stepping into the batter's box and swinging for the fences, although there must have been times in the late innings when a homer would win a game. If so, I don't remember trying. Instead, I always caution myself, "Just meet the ball." I say to myself, "If you hit it right, it will go far."
*Interview, New York, pub. Feb. 2.*

**Mario Biaggi**
*United States Representative, D-N.Y.*

Baseball is no longer the sport we all knew it was. Baseball has been reduced to a fiscal asset like any other business. Conglomerates have bought teams. Gambling interests have become involved. It is no longer acceptable to the public as it was when it was in its pure form.
*News conference, Washington, Aug. 7.*

**Jim Brosnan**
*Former Pitcher*

On-the-job training is essential under the circumstances of modern ball, but it is the current batter's bugaboo. The death of the minor leagues, where the fittest survived and advanced to the majors, has hindered the average hitter's development. There is no adequate substitute for proper apprenticeship.
*Pub. May 13.*

**Michael Burke**
*President, New York "Yankees"*

The business of baseball and football has grown so complex that you need people running these enterprises with a breadth of background and a breadth of vision.
*Pub. Feb. 9.*

**August A. Busch, Jr.**
*President, St. Louis "Cardinals"*

. . . we are told that many ballplayers have begun to ignore the fans. We are told that too many ballplayers are refusing to sign autographs. We are told that some ballplayers fail to show up for scheduled appointments. We are told that some ball-players push kids aside when they try to take their pictures . . . I plead with you not to kill the enthusiasm of the fans and the kids for whom you have become such idols.

*Address to the team,*
*St. Petersburg, Fla., March 22.*

**Roy Campanella**
*Former Player*

I have always believed that any professional athlete, to be good, has to have a little bit of boy in him. When you see Willie Mays and Ted Williams jumping up and hopping around the bases after hitting a home run, and you see the kissing and the hugging that goes on at home plate, you realize they have to be little boys.

*At induction to Baseball Hall of Fame,*
*Cooperstown, N.Y., July 28.*

**Norm Cash**
*Player, Detroit "Tigers"*

I'm not going to quit a $60,000 to $70,000 job to go to work.

*Published July 28.*

**Jocko Conlan**
*Retired National League Umpire*

I know a lot of players complain about night games, long (airplane) flights and that stuff. I grant you that it's not easy, but it's not too hard either. There is no flight that takes longer than five hours. I wonder what some of those guys would say if they traveled by train the old days. I can still feel those cinders and smell the smoke that came pouring in the open windows of those old Pullman cars.

*Interview, Scottsdale, Ariz., pub. Feb. 15.*

**Willie Crawford**
*Player, Los Angeles "Dodgers"*

Base running is a science that takes time to learn. In fact, let's face it, this whole game is a science, including hitting and playing the outfield. You should know the game like a manager. If you take anything for granted, someone will come along and replace you.

*Interview, Los Angeles, pub. April 15.*

**Bob Dailey**
*Player, Montreal "Expos"*

I didn't believe in striking for what we wanted. It was not good for the game—the image ball players have with the kids. When I was a kid, I thought ball players played for nothing.

*Interview, West Palm Beach, Fla.,*
*pub. March 22.*

**Alvin Dark**
*Manager, Cleveland "Indians"*

I've always said the managers and umpires and team captains should get together in the winter and discuss the rules. But they never do. So the umpires are still saying, "I'm going to call it my way," and managers are being thrown out of ball games because of misunderstandings.

*Tucson, Ariz., March 10.*

**Willie Davis**
*Player, Los Angeles "Dodgers"*

Guys in baseball are crazy. They don't understand the consequences of hitting a man with a ball. They don't know the pain and discomfort and downright danger to his life. This is apart from what you do to a team when you knock a starting player out. Naturally, they would prefer not to hit you. But there are two kinds of inside pitches. One is inside and the other is very inside. When you throw very inside, you are a potential killer, and I have lost all feeling for this kind of person.

*Interview, Los Angeles, pub. July 23.*

**Joe DiMaggio**
*Former Player*

It's the *structure* of baseball today that's killing off the hitters, not the pitchers. What hitters need is more minor league experience, and they can't get it anymore.

*Interview, Rancho La Costa, Calif.,*
*pub. Feb. 14.*

**Don Drysdale**
*Player, Los Angeles "Dodgers"*

My first day at Vero Beach (Fla.) this spring, I started to put on my uniform and look around. I had to get a stool and sit down because I never felt so old in my life. Here were all these kids, and most of them

(DON DRYSDALE)

I had never seen before. Lord! Were they ever young-looking!

*Pub. May 19.*

I deeply regret having to retire, but, like they say, some things are inevitable, like death, taxes and retirement from professional sports . . . I owe a lot to baseball. Baseball has given me everything I have, including my wife, my daughter and everything else.

*News conference, Los Angeles, Aug. 11.*

### Ron Fairly
*Player, Los Angeles "Dodgers"*

If I had to name the number one asset you could have for any sport, I'd say speed. In baseball, all a guy with speed has to do is make contact.

*Interview, pub. June 3.*

### John Fetzer
*President, Detroit "Tigers"*

The under-30s tend to be more attracted by pro football, but once they're 32 or so they start to become interested in baseball, because it's more of a thinking man's game; and when they're 40, they're hooked; and, by the time they've reached 50, they're dyed-in-the-wool fans.

*Pub. Dec. 22.*

### Curt Flood
*Player, St. Louis "Cardinals"*

At this moment, I would not consider taking even $99,999. I think I deserve to be in the $100,000 category.

*St. Petersburg, Fla., March 1.*

### Joe Garagiola
*Commentator, National Broadcasting Company*

I certainly don't want to sound bitter, but I think maybe there is too much emphasis on pension plans and retirement at 45 . . . It seems the baseball player of today will not be satisfied until he plays two weeks in the big league and is able to retire at 22. That's the only criticism I have, and I sure hope you don't think it is sour grapes; but I just wish they would worry more about bats and balls.

*Television interview, St. Louis, pub. June 21.*

### Lefty Gomez
*Former Pitcher, New York "Yankees"*

I personally don't think it makes any difference how high or low the mound is. The pitchers are going to adjust anyway. When I was pitching, we had mounds from park-to-park that varied at least five inches in height. We adjusted from one part to the next. I think a club should build its mound to suit its pitching staff, anyway.

*Interview, Omaha, pub. June 15.*

### Joe Gordon
*Manager, Kansas City "Royals"*

I don't like helmet throwing, bat throwing or swearing in front of the stands. If you pop up with the bases loaded, you are going to be mad, but Babe Ruth and Lou Gehrig did the same thing and they didn't throw things.

*Addressing the team, Fort Myers, Fla., pub. March 8.*

### Hank Greenberg
*Former Player*

Let's not kid ourselves. There are too many factions in the game that are competing against one another. The American League owners don't trust the National League owners, and vice versa. They have always operated as individuals. They don't think of the welfare of the game as a whole.

*Interview, Chicago, Jan. 16.*

### Ken Harrelson
*Player, Cleveland "Indians"*

Baseball is a sport, but it's more of a business. It's simply a matter of money.

*Pub. August.*

### Ralph Houk
*Manager, New York "Yankees"*

. . . you have to remember one thing about inspiration—you can only inspire a man who has talent to begin with. Hell, I was the most inspired ballplayer I ever saw. Go look up my batting average some time.

*New York, April 20.*

A good athlete with a strong arm can be taught how to pitch, but I guess hitters are born that way. They can develop their natural talent and we can help them a little; but you're not going to teach anyone from scratch how to be a great hitter.

*Pub. April 23.*

The truth is that there really isn't much difference between winning and losing. One man, two men can make all the difference—and not always the men with the best statistics. It's the way things fit together, the way a few games can be turned around, the way momentum builds up when you start winning.

*Pub. July 3.*

**Reggie Jackson**
*Player, Oakland "Athletics"*

My salary is based on production, not gate receipts. The biggest disappointment I've had as a major leaguer was not that I failed to break the home-run record but that, when I looked up at the stands in Oakland, I saw so many empty seats.

*Interview, Oakland, pub. Dec. 6.*

**Dave Johnson**
*Player, Baltimore "Orioles"*

I don't know how to program myself. I just hit the ball and run like hell.

*Baltimore, pub. Feb. 16.*

**Bowie Kuhn**
*Commissioner of Baseball*

The important thing is that Denny Mc-Lain and Bob Gibson be household words, not Bowie Kuhn. The players are the game. The focus has to be on them. If the commissioner becomes better known, that's well and good, but it's the public's interest in our players and our game that really counts.

*News conference, New York, Feb. 5.*

I don't think the players want a union. I heard George Meany say he doesn't believe in a union for ball players. A normal union relationship is not appropriate for baseball.

*Interview, Clearwater, Fla., pub. March 15.*

Baseball's problem isn't that there has been a loss of interest in it, but rather that as the amount of money that goes to recreation has increased, baseball has not gotten the percentage share of the increase that it should have expected. There has been increased support for baseball, but not at a rate that I'm altogether happy with . . .

*Interview, New York, pub. March 31.*

. . . I see baseball as something which I can have a dream the way Martin (Luther) King had a dream about America . . . I can see it build a bridge between people of all colors. I think it's gone a long way in that direction; I think it has done, and will do more in the future, as it has built bridges to Canada, Japan, to Mexico, to Latin America and the Caribbean countries. It will do more of this, and I think this is a wonderful contribution to America and the world.

. . . if baseball doesn't face the fact . . . that it has a lot of competition on the scene—and I'm not talking just about other professional sports, but I mean a whole array of recreational activities that people can turn to—if baseball does not face the fact that they are there, baseball will make a grievous mistake. So long as I'm commissioner, we're not going to make that mistake if I can help it.

*Television interview, pub. April 26.*

The astronauts have spanned the cosmic and we feel that baseball, too, over 100 years, has made cosmic contributions. It has provided untold hours of pleasure and entertainment and it has been a major force in the area of human relations and human dignity.

*At baseball centennial ceremony, Washington, July 21.*

I see in Japan an enormous enthusiasm (for baseball). Perhaps that enthusiasm pales that in America. I see it also in South and Central America. I also see it in Europe, although I don't think it rivals cricket or soccer in England. But it's there in the Netherlands, France, Germany and Italy. The game is developing and making its mark.

*National Press Club, Washington, July 22.*

**Mickey Mantle**
*Player, New York "Yankees"*

I can't play anymore. I've had three bad years in a row. I don't hit the ball anymore

(MICKEY MANTLE)

when I need to. I can't steal when I need to. I can't score from second on a hit when I need to . . . I had a wonderful time playing ball.

*Announcing his retirement from baseball, Fort Lauderdale, Fla., March 1.*

As far as I'm concerned, (Hank) Aaron is the best ball player of my era. He is to baseball of the last 15 years what Joe DiMaggio was before him. And you know what? Nobody would recognize him if he walked through that door this minute. It's tragic. He's never received the credit he's due.

*New York, Dec. 9.*

**Billy Martin**
*Manager, Minnesota "Twins"*

Baseball is a hard game. It's not as easy as people think . . . Leo Durocher once said that nice guys finish last. There's a lot of truth to it, whether people admit it or not. The idea in this game isn't to win popularity polls or to be a good guy to everyone. The name of the game is win . . . The best way to play is hard and clean. Don't expect any favors; don't give any . . .

I don't care what it takes to win . . . I'll cheat if I have to.

*Pub. May 24.*

Everybody judges players different. I judge a player by what he does for his ball club and not what he does for himself. I think the name of the game is self-sacrifice.

*Washington, May 28.*

**Gene Mauch**
*Manager, Montreal "Expos"*

Branch Rickey said there were five ingredients that make up a ballplayer. I know you've heard them before—run, field, throw, hit and hit with power. If you have three of them you can play; four, you excel; and all five, you're a superstar.

*Interview, Montreal, pub. May 17.*

I'm not the manager because I'm always right, but I'm always right because I'm the manager.

*Philadelphia, pub. Sept. 15.*

**Willie Mays**
*Player, San Francisco "Giants"*

I have a kid. I know how it is. I'll sign as many (autographs) as I can. Kids have their idols. That's a part of baseball. I guess you'll have to say I'm one of their idols.

*Interview, Phoenix, Ariz., March 6.*

**Willie McCovey**
*Player, San Francisco "Giants"*

Gimmicks and rules aren't going to get more runs in baseball. The guys who make the rules should realize that hopped-up baseballs, lower mounds and smaller strike zones won't change anything. A good pitcher will get you out on any kind of ground. The guys who make the rules must think the players are dumb.

*Interview, pub. March 29.*

**Denny McLain**
*Pitcher, Detroit "Tigers"*

The lower mounds are going to shorten a lot of pitching careers.

*Rancho La Costa, Calif., pub. Feb. 17.*

**David Merrick**
*Stage Producer*

There's not enough showmanship in baseball. It *is* show business, isn't it? It's entertainment . . . In the theatre, we're always thinking of the audience. When we put the show together, when we cast it, when we rehearse it, we're thinking of the audience. But in baseball they're unmindful of the audience. I find it appalling that they forget about the fans. You almost think they should build a fence around the diamond and play with no spectators. They've forgotten it's entertainment.

*New York, pub. July 27.*

**Marvin Miller**
*Director,*
*Baseball Players' Association*

Now that sports are becoming bigger business, they are adopting the problems of big business. Any affluent society makes people more security-conscious, and it's happening in sports . . . Baseball has a pretty good lobby. The railroads and airlines get privileges, too, but they also get regulations. Some congressmen still think baseball is apple pie, but it's a profitable business and bears examination.

*Pub. Feb. 9.*

Labor relations-wise, the (baseball) owners have not yet reached the 19th century. This business of owning people is the worst form of slavery I've seen. I thought slavery was abolished; but not in baseball.

*Interview, New York, pub. Feb. 15.*

## Wilmer Mizell
*United States Representative, R-N.C.; former major league pitcher*

I'm anxious to see the moon rock samples the astronauts brought back. I'm sure there are a few of my home run balls in that crowd.

*Pub. Aug. 30.*

## Stan Musial
*Former Player*

When I came up in the majors, there were some great ball parks to hit in. I have loved every minute in St. Louis, but what I would have given to hit every day in that band box in Brooklyn! And the Polo Grounds! What targets they were! Now, most of the parks are big ones. You can't hit the ball out every time you swing. You have to adjust. And a lot of hitters haven't adjusted. They're still trying to pull everything, and all they are doing is hitting long outs.

*Interview, St. Louis, pub. Feb. 8.*

## Johnny Neun
*Former Manager*

Rookies of today are pampered and coddled and helped. It wasn't that way when I broke in with the Detroit *Tigers* in 1923. They called the rookies "yannigans," and we were a species apart.

*Fort Lauderdale, Fla., March 11.*

## Jim Odom
*Umpire*

No manager ever thinks he got a break. I call them like I see them, and I don't care what the team is. If I'm right only half the time, I'm batting .500—and I never saw a ball player bat .500.

*Boston, Aug. 20.*

## Walter F. O'Malley
*Owner, Los Angeles "Dodgers"*

What other American sport has been played under the same rules by your father and his father before him? Oh, I know a lot of so-called experts think they know what's wrong with baseball. They want to speed up the game, they want to do this, do that. They want to imitate other sports, completely overlooking the fact that baseball is *the* traditional American sport, and I am convinced that the fans don't want to see this game tampered with—they don't want to see changes. They want records that mean something . . . They don't like to see a lot of asterisks in the record book indicating, well, this was done prior to 1969, and so forth.

*Interview, pub. April 6.*

I would say that radio created our first serious problem. When radio started carrying the first big-league games to the country, it made people too much aware of the majors and it hurt the minors. Farm teams began to die. I also would say that air conditioning hurt baseball. In the East and Midwest, people used to come to the park to escape the horrible heat of summer. Today, they can sit home in comfort. Then, air travel hurt us indirectly. When planes made it easy to get from coast to coast, it led to expansion, and expansion may have led to more baseball than is advisable . . . Baseball today is merely going through the change of life. But the old gal still has plenty of sock left. The game will ride out this present cycle of boat-rocking. Some changes will be required, but they will come.

*Interview, Los Angeles, pub. April 24.*

Is baseball on the spot? I would say yes; but then, religion is on the spot, government is on the spot, the integrity of treaties is on the spot. These are times when people spit on the flag, when priests go over the fence. You have to understand the pattern of things today. There is rebellion against the Establishment, and baseball is linked to the Establishment.

*Pub. June 2.*

Most clubs are trying to look good before the public. A manager has a decent season

(WALTER F. O'MALLEY)

and the club gives him a three-year contract to show the public it is generous. If the guy has a bad season, the club fires him to show the public it is working all-out in its behalf, trying to bring the fans a winner. I'm not trying to impress the public. I don't give three-year contracts—and I don't fire my manager.

*Los Angeles, pub. Oct. 5.*

An old friend of mine used to say, "Radio whets the appetite for baseball, and television satiates it." We televised nearly every home game in Brooklyn, and we'd have gone bankrupt if we stayed. But TV, properly applied, is splendid for baseball. My goodness, without our national "Game of the Week" program on NBC, many of our teams would be running in the red.

*Pub. Dec. 22.*

**Wes Parker**
*Player, Los Angeles "Dodgers"*

. . . it would be a great idea for baseball to take off each Monday. It would restore a lot of players physically, and . . . it would mean better baseball the other six days. Personally, I'm not concerned with the physical fatigue as I am the mental tiredness, being one of the those unfortunate players who just can't leave the game at the ball park.

*Interview, Los Angeles,*
*pub. Feb. 21.*

**Red Patterson**
*Vice president, Los Angeles "Dodgers"*

To the baseball fan, strategy IS baseball. The score is 3-2 in the seventh. What should the manager do? Will his mistake cost the game? He talks to the pitcher—and some people in the pressbox say the game is too slow. But in the stands, the fans are asking themselves: Will he knock the batter down this time? Will he walk him? If I were the manager, I'd throw him three bad ones. Or I'd throw the ball down his throat. Things like that. Baseball is a game of strategic situations. It is a game that can't be rushed too much—and there are a lot of people who like it.

*Interview, Los Angeles,*
*pub. Feb. 11.*

**Joe Pepitone**
*Player, New York "Yankees"*

The outfield was a pain. You're running in; you're running out. You sit down and get up . . . In center field, you got too much time to think about everything but baseball.

*Pub. March 22.*

**Hank Peters**
*Director of Player Personnel,*
*Cleveland "Indians"*

Baseball is moving toward a new era of specialization. The designated pinch-runner, the designated pinch-hitting specialist are just around the corner.

*Interview, Cleveland, pub. March 8.*

**Beans Reardon**
*Former Umpire*

It will never happen (replacing umpires with electronic devices), because when you do that you've taken away all the alibis. Who can the managers blame losses on? Who can pitchers and hitters blame their troubles on? Believe me, the umpire will always be with us.

*Pub. June 9.*

**Paul Richards**
*Vice president, Atlanta "Braves"*

All this fussing and tinkering around with the rules in order to get more action into the game is just ridiculous . . . They have to do everything in the most devious and roundabout way, like reducing the height of the mound, shrinking the strike zone, hurrying the pitcher with the 20-second rule—and all that stuff.

*Interview, Sarasota, Fla., pub. March 23.*

**Phil Rizzuto**
*Former Player*

Only three infielders have been elected (to the Hall of Fame) in the last 13 years. What does a guy have to do?

*Pub. Jan. 23.*

**Frank Robinson**
*Player, Baltimore "Orioles"*

What baseball is missing . . . is guys who battle to get on base. Slap. Punch. Bunt. Anything to get on . . . Base runners make for excitement, so there should be more of the kind of guys who just try to get on. But even though you can teach a hitter how to control the bat, how to slap for base hits, what good is it to him when he goes in to talk contract in the Spring? The Man gives you a lot of jazz about sacrificing yourself, being a team man and all that. Then he turns around and gives the big money to the guy who hits 30 out. You'd see a lot more guys with higher averages from slap-hitting if those guys got paid for it. It's probably coming.

*Pub. May 13.*

I think baseball has been ready for a Negro manager for a long time. It is my belief that the fans are ready. And as for the players, they certainly are ready.

*Interview, Anaheim, Calif., pub. June 1.*

**Ray Sadecki**
*Pitcher, San Francisco "Giants"*

Wait until those hitters come in to the owners at the end of the season and ask for big salaries based on their fat averages. Then the owners will be sorry they lowered the mounds, shortened the fences and narrowed the strike zone. They'll change everything back, and then the pitchers can ask for the money they rightfully deserve.

*Pub. May 12.*

**Joe Schultz**
*Manager, Seattle "Pilots"*

We should have interleague play. It's got to come to that. We have great competition to sell—between the two leagues —but we don't do it.

*Pub. June 14.*

**Vin Scully**
*Sports Announcer*

I really love baseball. The guys and the game. And I love the challenge of describing things. The only thing I hate—and I know you have to be realistic and pay the bills in this life—is the loneliness on the road.

*Interview, Los Angeles, pub. Feb. 11.*

**Mayo Smith**
*Manager, Detroit "Tigers"*

The thought hit me last spring that we

may have been the last true champions. We won in a one-league race. But now we have divisions and it's conceivable that a great Baltimore team might not even get into the World Series. I'd hate to be in Earl Weaver's shoes when the *Orioles* meet the (Minnesota) *Twins* in a three-of-five preliminary series. Baltimore is a better team, but a ball can bounce funny ways in a short series.

*Pub. Oct. 4.*

**Albert Henry (Hank) Soar**
*Senior Umpire, American League*

I've always worked under the theory that the greatest compliment an umpire can be paid is obscurity. When the fans leave the park, I want them to have no idea who the umpire was. Some of the best umpires in baseball today are almost unknown to the fans, even if they've been in the big leagues for 10 years or more. They're not the showboaters.

*Interview, pub. Oct. 10.*

**Warren Spahn**
*Manager, Tulsa "Oilers"*

A manager has to live with his club, feel the pulse, be the appeaser, the consultant and father . . . Some players need a kick in the fanny, others a pat on the back. Your shoulder has to be the one they cry on.

*Tulsa, Aug. 15.*

**Harry Walker**
*Manager, Houston "Astros"*

If you're looking for the primary reason for a lack of action in the games, where would you have to go? To the plate, because that's where everything in the game begins. And what's the deadest thing in baseball, insofar as action is concerned? The strikeout. Nothing happens. Nobody moves. And there have been more strikeouts with each passing season.

*Interview, Sarasota, Fla.,*
*pub. March 23.*

The game has been too good for too long. Why change it? (the rules). We're making a gamble that could destroy all of baseball's beautiful checks and balances. Is the game slipping? I insist it isn't.

*Interview, Cocoa, Fla., March 25.*

## Steve Whitaker
*Player, Kansas City "Royals"*

A ball player has to let his emotions out some way. He's got to yell or do something. If he didn't, he wouldn't be human. Maybe there are people who can keep everything inside. If a guy can do that, beautiful. But not many can. The big thing is not to put on a temper display in front of the fans. That looks bush. But if you want to go down in the runway and hit the wall, I don't see that you're embarrassing anybody.

*Interview, Fort Myers, Fla., pub. March 22.*

## Hoyt Wilhelm
*Pitcher, California "Angels"*

There is no art to it (the knuckleball). It's just like any other pitch. When you're getting the ball over, then it's artistic. When you're not, it's not . . . You can take a kid who can throw hard and teach him a curve or slider. But a knuckleball pitcher is born, not made.

*Pub. April 21.*

## Ted Williams
*Manager, Washington "Senators"*

What's wrong with hitting today? I'll tell you what's wrong with hitting today. First of all, the hardest thing to do in sports is to hit a baseball. If this is true, and it is, then it takes more hours of practice, more hours of dedication, more hours of desire to hit a baseball than it does to do anything else . . .

*Interview, Big Rapids, Mich., pub. Feb. 8.*

When you are the manager, there is nothing you can do to compensate for the fact that you have lost. It stays with you and you can't shake it. When you are a player, the loss is of concern, but you rationalize some of it with the home run you hit or the fine defensive play you made.

*News conference, Anaheim, Calif., May 12.*

I can't honestly tell you that I love managing . . . I hate all of the dinners. I hate all of the television interviews and I hate having all of the writers on your neck.

*Interview, Bloomington, Ind., June 6.*

People always told me that my natural ability and good eyesight were the reasons for my success as a hitter. They never talk about the practice, practice, practice! Dammit, you *gotta* practice!

*Pub. July.*

I'm thoroughly convinced about one thing in baseball. If you get to a guy the right way, surround him with the guys who do things right, he can't do anything but improve. I don't believe there has been any player in baseball, with the exception of Ty Cobb, who, when he finished, looked back over what he accomplished and said, "I did it all."

*Washington, pub. Aug. 24.*

## Maury Wills
*Player, Los Angeles "Dodgers"*

A man should never try to steal unless the odds are 80 per cent in his favor. He sizes up the situation. If it looks like 80 per cent for him, he goes. Well, you can find such things stealing second and third, but trying to make it home, there's no way. You're lucky if the odds are 50 per cent— and that isn't enough.

*Pub. June 20.*

## Thomas Yawkey
*Owner, Boston "Red Sox"*

I wouldn't want a dome (stadium). To me, baseball was meant to be played and enjoyed in the outdoors. People like home runs, and my understanding is that you don't get nearly as many in a closed stadium. If I were a ballplayer, I wouldn't like the idea of all that air-conditioning, either . . . But I do like the idea of a completely synthetic playing surface . . . More teams are installing synthetic turf all the time. It has the . . . appeal of cutting maintenance costs. In anything as large as a baseball or football stadium, this is important.

*Interview, Boston, pub. June 19.*

# BASKETBALL

**Sig Borgia**
*Supervisor of Officials,*
*American Basketball Association*

A referee must accept the gripes and abuse. If he can't accept it, he can't be an official. He must understand the positions of the players and coaches. They disagree, and must argue. I wouldn't give a nickel for a player or coach who didn't gripe when he felt he had one coming. The referee must listen awhile, then walk away from the scene and get on with the game. A good pro referee will know when the player or coach has had his say, and will know when to walk away. An average one won't.

*Interview, Twin Cities, Minn.,*
*pub. April 12.*

**Lou Carnesecca**
*Coach, St. John's University*

I'm involved. I know I'm a madman, but I'm in a different world during a game. The players say I do those things and I say they're crazy. If I ever saw myself on a replay, I'd probably be shell-shocked. But I seldom berate officials and I never swear at them. I'm yelling at my kids. That's just me. If I sat there with my arms folded, it would be pure purgatory.

*Pub. Jan. 27.*

**Wilt Chamberlain**
*Player, Los Angeles "Lakers"*

Many people think statistics are important. I'm sure that's why most players don't think they are making a contribution to the teams unless they score points. But an example is the guy who comes down on a three-on-one break. He may not even touch the ball, but just by being in the right spot he has enabled us to score. He has made a contribution. I've scored all the points I ever care about scoring, but if it is the thing that will help the club, I'm all for it. I'm only interested in winning. I don't care about the points.

*Interview, Los Angeles, pub. March 15.*

. . . I have a great deal more respect for someone who keeps coming back after losing heartbreaker after heartbreaker than I do for the winner who has everything going for him. Basketball, as you know, is the game of variables.

*Interview, Los Angeles, April 22.*

**Bob Cousy**
*Coach, Cincinnati "Royals"*

I'm a great believer in a running game and in every player knowing exactly what his job is before he goes on the floor . . . We're not going to have one man handling the ball all the time . . . When you have that, you have four other guys standing around doing nothing. I want total involvement by all players and I intend to get it.

*Interview, Worcester, Mass.,*
*pub. May 31.*

**F. Melvin Cratsley**
*Former College Basketball Coach*

I wanted my players to wear blazers, get haircuts, wear a tie, take a bath once in a while, be on time. They didn't want to do these things. I object to players telling me they want beards, long hair and all the rest, because the next thing they want to do is run the team. More important than the beard is what it represents—rebellion. If you can't tell them what to do, they don't need a coach.

*Pub. Aug. 25.*

**Larry Fleisher**
*Counsel for Players Association,*
*National Basketball Association*

The merger of the leagues would be clear violation of antitrust laws. The owners have told us time and again that the sole purpose of the merger was to limit salaries, and that is a restraint of the players' individual rights to bargain.

*News conference, Monticello, N.Y., Aug. 19.*

**Bobby Hunter**
*Player, Harlem "Globetrotters"*

The smartest thing I ever did was to spend a full season playing in the minors.
*Interview, San Antonio, pub. Jan. 30.*

**Sam Jones**
*Player, Boston "Celtics"*

As a man gets older, I think he probably gets smarter. He knows what things work for him, so he relies primarily on them. Take me, for example. I shoot exactly the same against Los Angeles as I do against the rest of the teams in the league. If I change my style against Wilt Chamberlain, then I'm giving up something I do best for something I don't do as well . . . Look, I know Chamberlain is going to block some shots on me. But I also know he isn't going to do it enough times a game to make any real difference. If I can get to the spot I like on the floor before the man who is guarding me, I'm going to score.
*Interview, Boston, pub. Feb. 15.*

**Pete Maravich**
*Player, Louisiana State University*

The fans go crazy over what I do, because I can do these things well. What's more exciting: Wrapping the ball around my back and bouncing it through my legs to a guy for an assist, or just handing off the ball to a guy? The fans want to see you win, sure. But they want to be entertained, too. Why not try to do both?
*Interview, Baton Rouge, La., pub. Dec. 22.*

**John Vallely**
*Player, UCLA "Bruins"*

Basketball is a game that nobody can play perfectly. I guess that's what is so interesting about it. You can never play a perfect game. Even if you hit 100 per cent of your shots, somebody might beat you on defense, or you might throw the ball away . . . It's a game that will always put you in your place. You can never get a fat head, because the next day some guy next to you can make you look pretty bad.
*Interview, Los Angeles, pub. Jan. 23.*

**Lon Varnell**
*Coach, University of the South*

The only really free enterprise left is athletics. Everything else is turning to politics and apple-polishing. But when a basketball player steps out on the floor, it's just him and the Great White Father.
*University of the South, pub. Feb. 24.*

**John Robert Wooden**
*Coach, UCLA "Bruins"*

A lot of people think I'm rather peculiar for a coach. Why, just the other day a man came to me and said, "You don't like to recruit, is that right?" And I said, "That's right." "You don't do very much scouting, either. Is that right?" "That's right." "And you don't worry very much about the other team?" "That's right." "Well, then, you certainly must be nuts." "That's right, I am."
*Interview, Los Angeles, pub. Feb. 4.*

An Alcindor comes along only once in a great, great while. And one like that is always going to command a tremendous amount of money. But to offer three and a quarter million for someone who has just stepped out of college is unrealistic. It's just out of line to offer that much money to any person just coming out of school—a doctor, a lawyer, whatever he might be.

Just being there, just standing there is enough, even if he (Lew Alcindor) doesn't do anything at all.
*Interview, Los Angeles, pub. April 4.*

I'm not saying there's no finesse in the pro game; but the college game is mainly finesse, the pro game mainly brute strength.
*Darlington, S.C., Aug. 29.*

# FOOTBALL

## Sammy Baugh
*Former Player*

. . . the ability to call the right plays at the right time—that's all there is to quarterbacking. But wrapped up in that short answer are so many thousands of things, that nobody has ever mastered them all. For example, you have to know every weakness of every player in the league—and the exact strength of each of your teammates in relation to all those defensive weaknesses. There's no sport in the world that's anywhere near as involved as football. Automatically, just by living, a quarterback with ten years' experience is a better man than he was the previous year.

*Interview, Los Angeles, pub. July 19.*

## Tommy Bell
*Referee, National Football League*

The ball must cross the goal line for a touchdown. Nothing else counts, only the ball. I tell my fellow officials never to place the ball closer than six inches from the goal line if the ball carrier just misses going over. If they place it one inch away, the ball carrier will never believe he came that close and didn't score.

*Pub. Nov. 15.*

## Frank Broyles
*Coach, University of Arkansas*

We coaches feel football is being made the whipping boy for all the increased costs of athletics . . . Educators think nothing about doubling tuition or room and board, but when athletic budget costs are doubled, they view the soaring costs with alarm and immediately there's a demand to get the athletic budget in line. It makes me boil when schools drop football or curtail their football programs because someone thinks football costs are upsetting the entire athletic budget.

*Before Football Writers Association of America, Chicago, pub. Sept. 14.*

## Paul W. (Bear) Bryant
*Coach, University of Alabama*

We think TV exposure is so important to our program and so important to this university that we will schedule ourselves to fit the medium. I'll play at midnight, if that's what TV wants.

*Pub. Dec. 22.*

## Mike Curtis
*Player, Baltimore "Colts"*

It's a good thing I am a football player. I'm naturally aggressive. I like body contact. I need to hit people. And football is one area where you're not criticized for having a good time, because you're expected to play rough. If I tried to satisfy that need off the football field, I'd be locked up.

*Interview, pub. October.*

## Al Davis
*Managing partner, Oakland "Raiders"*

The problem with today's draft choices is so simple. I don't even like to waste time explaining it. You have a business. You are trying to operate it with sound principles. Say you pay an O.J. Simpson $130,000 a year or a Leroy Keyes $100,000. It isn't going to bust you; but the problems resulting are so obvious. At contract time, what do you tell a quarterback who is making maybe $60,000? What do you say to your fullback who is earning $35,000? They aren't asking for a hundred grand, but they are going to want $10,000 more, or $20,000 more. And this attitude will be felt through the whole lineup. There is no way you can fight it. What you are doing is changing the whole payroll structure.

*Interview, pub. Aug. 6.*

## Frank Deford
*Associate Editor, "Sports Illustrated"*

I like professional football, but I do find annoying the false complexity and sacro-

(FRANK DEFORD)

sanctity that has been built around the game. There are hordes of writers willing to dig at baseball for being old-fashioned or at basketball for being small-time, but they shy away from football as if they'd be poking at the fourth person of the Blessed Trinity.

*Pub. Jan. 27.*

**Mike Ditka**
*Player, Dallas "Cowboys"*

Guys are losing their loyalty to the sport. The first reason they got into that restaurant business—or any other business—is that they made a name in professional football. And, as long as a guy is going to put a football uniform on, I think he owes it to himself, to the coaches, to his teammates and to their fans to go out there and play football and forget about the other crap.

*Interview, pub. Oct. 21.*

**Dan W. Dodson**
*Professor of Education,*
*New York University*

The black players in professional football in the past have held the beef and brawn jobs, like being linemen, and now they want to demonstrate intelligence and nimbleness. And, they are doing it in the name of race . . . To some Negroes, it has become a symbol for them to have a quarterback of consequence.

*New York, Sept. 13.*

**Otto Graham**
*Coach, Washington "Redskins"*

In my first public statement, when I came into the NFL three years ago, I said the top teams in the AFL could give any team in the NFL a battle. A couple of guys almost shot me for saying that. But the Super Bowl was no upset. There's very little difference between the leagues. I coached many of the top players in the College All-Star Game. If a player went into the NFL, they said he was great. If he went into the AFL, they said he was not so hot.

*Pub. Jan. 27.*

**Bud Grant**
*Coach, Minnesota "Vikings"*

A good coach needs a patient wife, a loyal dog and a great quarterback—but not necessarily in that order.

*Pub. Dec. 7.*

**Eugene V. Klein**
*President, San Diego "Chargers"*

It (football) is a game of refined violence. And it gets more violent every year —and more refined.

*Los Angeles, pub. Aug. 28.*

**Joe Knapp**
*Player, Minnesota "Vikings"*

Everyone ought to get a chance to play in Canada for a while, if only to understand how rough football can be.

*Pub. Nov. 29.*

**Edward ("Moose") Krause**
*Director of Athletics,*
*Notre Dame University*

College football, as played today, is highly exciting. We have high scoring games, plenty of wide-open action, and that is what the people want . . . The modern spectator is no longer satisfied with the three-yards-and-a-cloud-of-dust theory . . .

*Interview, Los Angeles, Jan. 7.*

**Vince Lombardi**
*Coach, Washington "Redskins"*

Football is a pressure business, and on my teams I put on most of the pressure . . .
*Telephone interview, Potomac, Md.,*
*pub. March 11.*

Considering the money involved, we do have to put forth some cooperation with television. If they ask to start a little later so more people can see the game, we have to cooperate . . . Given today's budgets, there wouldn't be a single franchise left in the National Football League without television . . .

*Pub. Dec. 22.*

**Arthur Modell**
*Principal Owner, Cleveland "Browns"*

The future of our game (football) lies in television. The way operating costs are growing, we can't make a go of it at the boxoffice alone.

*Interview, pub. March 27.*

Pro football is not a prudent business investment. It is too unpredictable. Operating profits never justify your investment. The only way to make money is to sell your club at a profit—and at a capital-gains tax rate. But there is no room in pro football for the smart businessman who is looking to turn his money over in a year or two for a quick profit. He'll get hurt.

*Pub. Sept. 22.*

**Clint W. Murchison, Jr.**
*Owner, Dallas "Cowboys"*

You could make more money investing in government bonds. But football is more fun.

*Pub. Sept. 22.*

**Joe Namath**
*Player, New York "Jets"*

I'm 190 per cent against them (All Star Games) . . . Why should anybody be for them? One slip, and your career could be ruined . . . all for nothing.

*Interview, Jacksonville, Fla., pub. Jan. 16.*

I've done nothing wrong, but because of the way some of the people have written and some of the things that have been said in the past, and because of the public reading these things, because this has caused so much trouble for football and me, we feel we should divorce ourselves of the restaurant (Bachelors III in New York) at this time, and play football even though everything that's been said about myself having dice games is wrong. And the magazines writing what they have, and the newspapers, about undesirables in Bachelors III and all that, I've still done nothing wrong. I still want to play football and we are back in football.

*News conference, New York, July 18.*

**Chuck Noll**
*Coach, Pittsburgh "Steelers"*

If you mean, do I believe in running a football game like the Marine Corps, the answer is no. I believe in dealing with mature men on a mature basis. If they want to drink a few beers—well, after all, beer is one way to replace body fluids. I'll be guided only on what's good for the team. I don't want a team whose players are more afraid of the coach than they are of their opponents.

*News conference, Pittsburgh, pub. Feb. 15.*

**Merlin Olsen**
*Player, Los Angeles "Rams"*

You take the best team and the worst team and line them up and you would find very little physical difference. You would find an emotional difference. The winning team has a dedication. It will have at its core a group of veteran players who set the standards. They will not accept defeat.

*Interview, Fullerton, Calif., Aug. 2.*

**Joe Paterno**
*Coach, Pennsylvania State University*

I enjoy the day-in and day-out work with young men. You work with them, they have confidence in you and you in them, and all of a sudden on a Saturday afternoon you look up and there are 40,000 people. Then the whistle blows and you're in the middle of things. It's great excitement—a great feeling of pride when the players and coaches get the job done. Of course, you're frustrated when you don't, but this, too, is exciting.

*Interview, University Park, Pa., pub. Dec. 27.*

**Max Rafferty**
*Superintendent of Public Instruction, State of California*

(Critics of college football) are kooks, crumbums and commies . . . hairy, loudmouthed beatniks . . . Football is war without killing. Football players are the custodians of the concepts of the past. They possess a clear, bright fighting spirit which is America itself.

*Pub. Nov. 2.*

**Joe Robbie**
*Owner, Miami "Dolphins"*

I had all my fun on the first play the *Dolphins* ever ran. It was the opening kickoff, and I ran 50 yards for a score. Imagine, no other owner ever ran for a touchdown. This kid, Joe Auer, took it back 95 yards. I'm on the bench, and I pick him up on the 45, me and my cigar. Yelling, I go the rest of the way. I fall

(JOE ROBBIE)

flat on my face, right in the end zone. What an opening!

*Pub. Dec. 15.*

## Dave Robinson
*Player, Green Bay "Packers"*

I love to hit people, and I admit it—blockers as well as ball carriers. Defensive football players are innate hitters. It's a joy to me. I tell people it's how I work off my daily hostilities. During the week I'm as gentle as anybody. Sunday is my time to hit.

*Interview, pub. Oct. 25.*

## Alvin (Pete) Rozelle
*Commissioner of Football*

I think that so-called "violence" has been a factor in the popularity of pro football, but I think a better word would be "action." I think that we deliver high action in the games, and it's because football has a very fast pace. I think we're fortunate that it's apparently attuned to the times. We just hope that the times don't change without us changing with them.

*Interview, pub. October.*

## Tex Schramm
*President, Dallas "Cowboys"*

I think the public today is taking more of a jaundiced look at teams that don't perform well. In the old days, it used to be that, when teams didn't do well on the field, the fan would say, "By God, at least the boys were trying." Today, when a team goofs, the fan is prone to shout, "Why, you lousy bums . . . making all that money and playing like that!"

*Interview, pub. Oct. 21.*

## O. J. Simpson
*Player, Buffalo "Bills"*

I know that if I become just a real good pro football player, I'll be considered a bust. I won't be able to get by if I'm ordinary and maybe not even if I'm just sort of outstanding. I've gotten so much publicity and I've asked so much money for myself that, if I'm not super-something, I'll be like nothing.

*Pub. August.*

## Billy Ray Smith
*Player, Baltimore "Colts"*

If I can get the quarterback rattled and nervous, that's fine. I may not land on him every time, but I do want to make him "Smith conscious." My tastes are simple. I like to crack those rich guys who play quarterback.

*Pub. Nov. 8.*

## Hank Stram
*Coach, Kansas City "Chiefs"*

Every football team, whether it plays in the grade-school league or the Super Bowl, is an expression of its coach's philosophy.

*Pub. Aug. 23.*

The main difference between the rookies of this year and those who came to us in the early days of the AFL is that the new crop has a much greater awareness of what is involved in being a pro football player. I think this stems from the tremendous increase in the number of hours of televised pro football. They get to see all the great pros, and, of course, they try to emulate them. They may even pick up little aspects of technique, just as a golfer like me tries to do when he watches an Arnold Palmer on television.

*Pub. Oct. 20.*

## Harland Svare
*Defensive coach, Washington "Redskins"*

. . . the more I see of football, the surer I am that, when a man becomes an owner, he only has two choices. He can bow out of management and put his coach in charge. Or, he can run the club himself and make up his mind that he is going to enjoy running the club—and losing games.

*Interview, Washington, pub. Aug. 21.*

## Jim Sweeney
*Coach, Washington State "Cougars"*

Speed is a relative factor in football, relative to endurance and effort. Speed is a football weapon only insofar as the athlete is willing to sacrifice and to be in condition. When I come off the line with great acceleration, I've still got to be doing that in the fourth quarter to be an effective football player, and that means endurance. So the good Lord endows you with speed . . . somewhere else along the line you've got to pick up courage and the right attitude.

*Pub. Oct. 8.*

**Ralph C. Wilson**
*Owner, Buffalo "Bills"*

Players asking exorbitant bonuses threaten us in four ways. One, they will go to Canada. Two, they will make a deal with Indianapolis or Orlando. Three, they will skip football and enter private business. Or four, they will challenge the draft in court. The next time a rookie asks $500,000 from me, I'm going to give him his choice of any of the four.

*Interview, pub. Nov. 29.*

## SPORTS—MISCELLANEOUS

**Muhammed Ali (Cassius Clay)**
*Former World Heavyweight*
*Boxing Champion*

You're the champion until somebody beats you—and nobody has beaten me.
*Interview, Chicago, pub. April 7.*

He'll (Joe Frazier) be the toughest guy I ever met, and I know I'll never be as sharp as I once was. I'm actually pooped, and Frazier is a big risk. Without him, I could have stayed in retirement and been unbeaten, like Rocky Marciano. But I know the world is waiting. I have to take the chance.

*Dec. 9.*

**George Allen**
*Coach, Los Angeles "Rams"*

As far as I'm concerned, the key to competitive sports is what you do in an unfriendly stadium. Anybody can win at home. The street to obscurity is paved with athletes who performed great feats before friendly crowds. Greatness in major league sports is the ability to win in a stadium filled with people who are pulling for you to lose.

*Pub. Nov. 15.*

**Eddie Arcaro**
*Jockey*

How can you educate people to horse racing if children are banned from the tracks? There's no reason in the world why children shouldn't be allowed to come out. Not to bet, but to watch the racing as a colorful and exciting sport. When they're old enough to bet, you'd have some new faces at the tracks. That's what racing needs.
*Interview, Fort Lauderdale, Fla.,*
*pub. March 2.*

**Roone Arledge**
*President, American*
*Broadcasting Company-Sports*

Sport is a set of created circumstances —artificial circumstances—set up to frustrate a man in pursuit of a goal. He has to have certain skills to overcome those obstacles—or even to challenge them. And people who don't have those skills cheer him and admire him. It is that simple.
*Pub. Dec. 22.*

**Arthur Ashe**
*Tennis Player*

. . . tennis has been content to present the product for the most part in upper-middle class settings—private clubs—and hasn't done much to attract the general public. The average sports fan feels he's an intruder. The game can't develop at places like Southampton on Long Island, but it can at public arenas. Putting an open tournament in Madison Square Garden, for example, was a good move. Tennis is an exciting game with potential to become a spectator sport at least on a par with golf; and I think, with the right direction, it will.
*Interview, pub. August.*

**Robert Briner**
*Executive Director,*
*World Championship Tennis*

There is still a shortage of promotional expertise (in tennis), a shortage of real leadership around the world. There are still too many amateur people walking around in blazers and keeping the sport for themselves. There's too much time spent protecting club tournaments at the expense of building the game in great public areas. The sport still has not proved itself to television.
*Pub. Sept. 14.*

**Clarence S. Campbell**
*President, National Hockey League*

In the past 10 years, more than a thousand boys have come down from Canada to play hockey in American colleges. Those who have gone on to careers in the NHL can be counted on one hand. A college hockey player should be able to look forward to a career in pro hockey just as much as his classmates can look forward to one in pro football, basketball or baseball. But, because of the difference in rules and lack of programs extensive and intensive enough to develop his potential, the odds are stacked against the college hockey player.

*Pub. March 24.*

**John F. X. Condon**
*Public Relations Director, Madison Square Garden Boxing Club*

It (boxing) needs a national commissioner, so that the rules in New York are the same as those in Boise, Idaho. It needs to get a lot of the delicatessen owners out of it, and to put qualified people in it who know the sport . . . It needs to get rid of the politicians—they're the ruination of boxing—politicians have to pay off favors. And it needs to be taught in the elementary schools. Every kid gets into a fight once in a while. Every kid should be instructed on how to defend himself. Boxing is required in Russia in their elementary schools, and it should be required here, and it should be a sport in high schools and colleges.

*Interview, Grossinger, N.Y., April 12.*

**Jack Kent Cooke**
*Part Owner, Washington "Redskins"*

It (TV) is making instant heroes of athletes. Whereas in the old days you had to go to the newsreels to see Red Grange and Babe Ruth, television is bringing athletes into every home and giving them greater stature. And, feeling their power, they are rubbing the owners' noses in it.

*Pub. Feb. 15.*

**Diane Crump**
*Jockey*

A horse doesn't know whether the rider on his back wears a dress or pants away from the track.

*Pub. April 4.*

**Joseph C. Dey, Jr.**
*Commissioner of Golf*

It is astonishing to me sometimes that golf has remained as untouched by scandal

as it has, when you consider the scope of it . . . Golf isn't like football or baseball, played on a field so many yards long and so many yards wide where thousands of people can witness almost every move. The opportunities to cheat in golf are limitless . . . The greatest stop-gap is the game's integrity. It has always been a game of honor . . .

*Interview, New York, pub. April 6.*

I hate to compare my job with those of the other (sports) commissioners, but perhaps mine is easier. Take the baseball commissioner, for example. He deals with people who own ball clubs. I do not. I deal primarily with the players, and players in golf have an entirely different status than those in baseball, football and basketball. They don't have to depend on anyone for their living except themselves. They're completely independent, whereas baseball, basketball and football players are not.

*Interview, New York, pub. May 29.*

**Joe Frazier**
*Boxer*

All this hollerin' he (Cassius Clay) is doing about not wanting to fight is just a defense. He knows I can beat him . . . knock him out. I'd like to button his big mouth once and for all, knock him out and get rid of him. I think the public is fed up with his fussin' and fumin'.

*Telephone interview, Kiamesha Lake, N.Y., June 4.*

It isn't so much the running and sparring and exercises I have to do that bother me. That's part of my job. That's part of what I do for a living. I must do these things if I want to be a fighter. What bothers me most are the incessant questions by reporters, and the TV and radio interviews. It seems like everybody asks the same questions all the time and I get sick listening to myself answer them. And the photographers—wow! Some day I'm going to write about them and I'm going to title it, "Just One More."

There's one thing I don't ever think about—losing. A fighter who thinks about

(JOE FRAZIER)

losing is a born loser. Instead, I think about how I'm going to win, how I can do it the quickest way.

*Interview, Kiamesha Lake, N.Y.,*
*June 14.*

### Leonard Gardner
*Author*

Boxing is a difficult subject. It is easy for it to go wrong. There have been so many cliches connected with boxing that it is difficult for people to think of boxing without the cliches. I wanted (in his book, *Fat City*) to show boxing as it really is—not an exciting piece of entertainment but as the sport of the poorest element of our society. Two guys climb into a ring and beat each other up, while a few others pay to watch. I wanted to tell about these guys who muddle around, get beat up, perhaps drop out and start up again, the guys who never become champions.

*Interview, Paris, pub. Aug. 29.*

### Mike Gibson
*Referee,*
*Wimbledon Tennis Tournament*

Let's face it. We've had nearly 300,000 people at this year's Wimbledon, and how many of them came solely for the tennis? Wimbledon is a social event, and people don't like to stay away because they think their absence will be noted. We thrive on snob appeal here, and I think it's what we must aim for at Forest Hills. We want more people to buy subscription tickets because it is the "fashionable" thing to do.

*Interview, Wimbledon, England, July 6.*

### Bill Hartack
*Jockey*

If I was an owner or trainer, you know who I'd want riding my horse? Me. I want me because I want my jock, when he loses, to come back mad. I don't care who he's mad at. I want him to be mad. That's the kind of guy I want riding for me. I don't want a guy coming back to me, patting me on the back and saying, "Oh, I got into a little trouble today. Better luck next time . . ." I don't want

this guy riding for me if he's gonna pat me on the back and speak nice to me and tell me my horse should have won . . . That's why I want me.

*Interview, Louisville, Ky., May 2.*

### George (Punch) Imlach
*General Manager and Coach,*
*Toronto "Maple Leafs"*

. . . I'm the type of guy who thinks hockey is a war. A war against the other clubs . . . In a war, you don't say we'll call a ceasefire and then all the guys from both sides will get together and have a big party and start the war again the next morning. I don't like fraternizing.

*Interview, Toronto, pub. March 6.*

### Nick Jemas
*Managing Director, Jockey's Guild*

They (female jockeys) won't last. They're not strong enough to become good race riders. They'll freeze. They'll panic. Wait till they start riding horses that can really run but won't extend themselves unless they're forced to by the jockey. That's the real test.

*Interview, pub. Feb. 16.*

### Claude Kirk
*Governor of Florida*

It comes as a surprise to me that a man (Muhammed Ali) who lacks the courage to fight for his country could have the guts to get in the ring. Any claim he might have to the title ought to be taken away from him in the ring by someone worthy to wear the title.

*Dec. 12.*

### Eugene V. Klein
*President, San Diego "Chargers"*

It is far easier to deal with people in the business world because they have an understanding of values. There will be differences of opinion, but the differences won't be absurd. In the cases of many athletes, they don't understand business principles and they develop grandiose ideas. They become confused and often unreasonable. I will never again deal with a player.

*Pub. Feb. 7.*

**Arthur G. Lentz**
*Executive Director,*
*U.S. Olympic Association*

Our challenge (for the 1972 Olympic Games) is to raise all teams to the level of our basketball, track and field and swimming teams. We cannot risk going into competition now and not doing well. International prestige is at stake. The world judges a country's vitality by how well it does in competition . . . We need a dedication of purpose. We need more than weekend athletes.

*Denver, pub. April 27.*

**Gene Littler**
*Golfer*

. . . Golf is not a game of great shots. It's a game of the most accurate misses. The people who win make the smallest mistakes . . .

*Interview, San Diego, pub. March 22.*

**Tommy Loughran**
*Former World Light-Heavyweight*
*Boxing Champion*

People ask if the boxers of today are less than their predecessors and I say no. But, of course, we had a greater opportunity for training and fighting, and it was more of a sport then. I recall having cut one opponent over the eye with a jab. I assured him not to worry, I would not hit him on that cut again. I didn't, hitting him everywhere else—and winning, too.

*Interview, Spring Valley, N.Y., Jan. 15.*

**Rene Maheu**
*Director-General, United Nations*
*Educational, Scientific and Cultural*
*Organization*

. . . young people are so little concerned about sports. But is this not because both players and spectators see in it a means of distracting man from his problems? Although sports, in fact, has a vital part to play, through character training and the balanced development of the personality, in defending human values against the inroads of an increasingly oppressive mechanistic civilization, it is chiefly valued today for the opportunities it provides for escape and diversion. It is high time we reacted against this situation and helped sports to return to its rightful place and rank in man's self-development.

*Paris, pub. Nov. 3.*

**Alastair B. Martin**
*President, United States Lawn*
*Tennis Association*

Tennis has two courses of action. We can pull in the horns and remain amateur, or widen our view and let all of tennis work together under one umbrella . . . We're moving into tennis as a big business. It's too much for part-time officials to administrate. We have to professionalize and streamline, or we'll lose certain aspects of the game.

*Interview, New York, pub. Jan. 19.*

**Frank McMahon**
*Race Horse Owner*

A Triple Crown is one of my ambitions, but I don't want to see a "Cripple Crown" . . . They (the Triple Crown races) are too close together . . . The Belmont should be run a month farther on. (But it is on the seventh of June) and you can hardly get the horses cooled down. Yes, they should rename it the "Cripple Crown."

*May 20.*

**Horace McMahon**
*Actor*

You know why show people love sports and are always around it? Almost any sport is dramatic. You do a movie, a TV show or a play and you follow a script that was written in advance. You know the finish. A game . . . all you know is the start. You don't know the finish. Sure, any theatrical event is dramatic. But when a cellar team beats the champion, in any sport, there's nothing more dramatic than that.

*Pub. Oct. 18.*

**Stirling Moss**
*Former Auto Racing Driver*

Any true racing driver is almost certain to have at least one major accident during his career. I use the word "true" with intent. I realize it is possible for a man to drive continually to within nine-tenths of his limit and never have a really bad moment. By

(STIRLING MOSS)

so doing, he might even achieve a certain reputation among his friends, but he will never be a "true" racing driver. To achieve anything in this game, you must be prepared to dabble on the boundary of disaster.

*Pub. July 13.*

### Joe Pignatano
*Baseball Coach, New York "Mets"*

Everybody takes this game (golf) too serious. Some day some guy on the pro tour is going to come along swinging his way through tournaments and running right up to hit the ball without studying his shot for five minutes—and the whole game of golf will be turned around.

*Memphis, pub. June 7.*

### Jerry Quarry
*Boxer*

I'm not a nice guy when I climb into the ring. They don't pay nice guys. I didn't state I would knock out Joe (Frazier) in five rounds to get a psychological edge. I stated it because I believed it. Guys who talk about psychological edges are whistling past the grave yard. They're usually scared to death.

*New York, May 19.*

This (the impending championship bout with Joe Frazier) has to be one of the greatest fights in a long while. Boxing genius, no. This is going to be out and out brawling, which is what the people want to see. People want to see two guys beat each other's brains out. This is what they're going to get.

*In training, Grossinger, N.Y., June 17.*

I want to leave boxing with a little bit of looks and the ability to talk.

*Interview, Los Angeles, Aug. 6.*

I blew my chance against (Joe) Frazier because I did a lot of things I shouldn't have. I said I was going to meet him in the middle of the ring and it would be me or him. That was mistake number 1. I had him hurt in the first round, and I let him get away. That was mistake number 2. I listened to a lot of people who had

ideas about how I could beat Frazier. That was mistake number 3.

*Pub. Nov. 30.*

### Sammy Renick
*Jockey*

Ladies just don't belong on a race track as jockeys . . . this isn't any giddyap through Central Park. Nor is it the same as looking cute in derby hats in a horseshow . . . But no one knows what pro-riding is unless you've ridden as a pro. No one else knows what it means to leave the gate and hustle a horse through heavy traffic into a turn to get position or to be on a horse that wants to lug in or bear out. No one else realizes the danger involved . . . Women riders? The only one I ever heard of to make a historical contribution was Lady Godiva.

*Interview, New York, pub. Jan. 26.*

### Charlie Sifford
*Golfer*

The Negroes in golf can't be compared with the Negroes in baseball, football, track and boxing. We've been playing those sports all our lives. It's not like that in golf. White golfers learn to play in country clubs and even on their fathers' courses. We blacks had to learn it as caddies. That's as far as the door opened.

*Interview, Pebble Beach, Calif., pub. Feb. 15.*

### Harry Sinden
*Coach, Boston "Bruins"*

Our game (hockey) is thump. We play our best when we're hitting people.

*Boston, pub. Feb. 15.*

### David A. Werblin
*Former President, New York "Jets"*

In football, your inventory can cause you trouble overnight. Players can have a fight with their wives or their girl friends. They can stay out late, drinking. They can feud with each other. They can pop-off and make controversial headlines. Silent Screen (his race horse)—he gets to bed early, gets up early, drinks water, keeps his mouth shut and does his work.

*Pub. Oct. 20.*

**Cale Yarborough**
*Auto Racing Driver*

Racing fans used to be kind of blood-thirsty. People would come out because of the possibility of accidents. And with tires and brakes the way they were, accidents happened. All of racing had a kind of unsavory reputation, when some of the drivers were whiskey runners, and so forth. But now the fan comes for competition, to root for his man or his car, and the drivers are professional athletes.

*Interview, Darlington, S.C.,*
*pub. May 5.*

# Tributes

## EVERETT M. DIRKSEN

**Frank Annunzio**
*United States Representative, D-Ill.*

Senator Dirksen was one of the most skilled legislators of our time, a great statesman, and a great American. Even those who disagreed with his thinking on the issues of the day could not help but admire and respect the eloquence, the wisdom, the showmanship, the strength and resolute commitment to our democracy that characterized the Senator from Illinois.
> *Before the House, Washington, Sept. 8.*

**Howard H. Baker**
*United States Senator, R-Tenn.*

A man of imposing presence and bearing, Everett McKinley Dirksen was, nonetheless, a man of eminent wit, humor and perspective, who kept himself and others constantly on guard against taking themselves too seriously. He was guided by a simple religious faith, carrying through life a sense of the creator's presence and doing homage to the small, frail spark of immortality which defines the human spirit. But perhaps, most of all, his hero was the people. He was of the people.
> *Washington, Sept. 8.*

**John Dellenback**
*United States Representative, R-Ore.*

He is one of those few men of whom it may in truth be said, "He changed the path of history."
> *Before the House, Washington, Sept. 8.*

**John J. Flynt, Jr.**
*United States Representative, D-Ga.*

Everett Dirksen practiced what he preached. He was one of the greatest orators that this country has produced and he spoke words of wisdom as well as words of eloquence. The Senate of the United States listened attentively when he spoke—and, indeed, the people of all America listened when Everett Dirksen spoke.
> *Before the House, Washington, Sept. 8.*

**Gerald R. Ford**
*United States Representative, R-Mich.*

(Everett M. Dirksen was the) kind ot man who not only filled the canvas, but spilled over from it. There was nobody like him before. There will be nobody like him again.
> *Pub. Sept. 9.*

**Charles E. Goodell**
*United States Senator, R-N.Y.*

No one of us agreed with him on every issue. And so we would drift into opposing camps for a time. But it was his style, and ultimately his strength, to never oppose so vigorously as to lose a friend.
> *Before the Senate, Washington, Oct. 29.*

**Ernest F. Hollings**
*United States Representative, D-S.C.*

Everett Dirksen . . . was a Senator's Senator and, as such, was respected by everyone who met him. Senator Dirksen's mark on history will be recorded not so much for his stand as an unflinching Republican leader, but as a man who was able to see needs and fulfill them, see trends and interpret them, see humor in serious problems and lighten our load with his quick smile and ready wit. As a politician, he was without peer. But I think what endeared him to most of us was his humanity, his gentleness and his everlasting spirit.

*Before the House, Washington, Sept. 9.*

**Mike Mansfield**
*United States Senator, D-Mont.*

A great chair across the aisle stands empty. The Senate has lost a Senate man. Yet, his death does not diminish the Senate. His uniqueness is the stuff of legends, and he leaves here a permanent imprint and an enduring echo.

*Washington, Sept. 8.*

**Richard M. Nixon**
*President of the United States*

Two thousand years ago the poet Sophocles wrote: "One must wait until the evening to see how splendid the day has been." We who were privileged to be his friends can take comfort in the fact that Everett Dirksen, in the rich evening of his life, his leadership unchallenged, his mind clear, his great voice still powerful across the land, could look back upon his life and say: "The day has indeed been splendid."

*Washington, Sept. 9.*

**John O. Pastore**
*United States Senator, D-R.I.*

Many voices in many tongues will speak the eulogy of Everett McKinley Dirksen, and history will write the epitaph for this powerful figure of his times. So, humbly, we shall speak of him as an old-fashioned American, with a love of family that inspired decency, a love of country that inspired dedication, grateful for freedom's blessings—concerned that these blessings might be preserved and shared by all —an able advocate of the American dream and the American destiny.

*Before the House, Washington, Sept. 9.*

**Charles H. Percy**
*United States Senator, R-Ill.*

Seated, standing or pacing before this chamber; whispering, rumbling, advocating, embellishing, pleading, cajoling and frequently persuading—each of us retains his distinct and private memories of our departed leader.

*Before the Senate, Washington, Oct. 29.*

**Robert D. Price**
*United States Representative, R-Tex.*

Everett Dirksen was more than a political craftsman of the first order; he was a political personality which had no equal since the days of Daniel Webster. His colorful personality, his engaging air and his bombastic colloquies, delivered in a rich baritone, set a style in the Senate that may never be recaptured.

*Before the House, Washington, Sept. 8.*

**Winston L. Prouty**
*United States Senator, R-Vt.*

Never doubt that Everett Dirksen loved life. It seemed to love him, too. He was enthralled by the beauty of the flower and the spoken word. He cultivated them as few could do. As raconteur, gardener and orator, he brought us joy. The flowers continue to grow. His words still echo.

*Before the Senate, Washington, Oct. 29.*

**Roman C. Pucinski**
*United States Representative, D-Ill.*

Ev Dirksen disagreed often, but he symbolized the highest tradition of this Congress by never being disagreeable. In debate he was a strong foe, but, above all, he was always a gentleman.

*Before the House, Washington, Sept. 8.*

**Howard W. Robison**
*United States Representative, R-N.Y.*

Everett M. Dirksen was the very epitome of a U.S. Senator. He looked like one; he acted like one—and enjoyed every dramatic moment of it. He spoke like one, loving words as much as he did the flowers he grew, cherishing the proper placement of each and nourishing both with the same tender, loving care. But, most of all, he served his nation and his people in that effective, dedicated, and always-faithful manner that typifies the height of legislative service in (what) we believe to be the greatest legislative body in the world.

*Before the House, Washington, Sept. 8.*

**Richard B. Russell**
*United States Senator, D-Ga.*

Few Senators have been more universally loved by the American people. When

(RICHARD B. RUSSELL)

he spoke, the nation listened, and his eloquence on the issues of our day was a source of national strength.

*Published Sept. 9.*

**Ted Stevens**
*United States Senator,*
*R-Alaska*

. . . the moment I shall not forget was that moment when I was first on this floor—a newly appointed Senator—and he said to me, "Let me walk you down the aisle."

*Before the Senate,*
*Washington, Oct. 29.*

**Robert Taft, Jr.**
*United States Representative, R-Ohio*

He was, above all, a legislator of great skill and wisdom. At times this led some, without justification, to question his consistency and his dedication to principle. It was rather that he knew and practiced well the necessary lubricant of the law-making process, the art of compromise.

*Before the House, Washington, Sept. 8.*

**Lawrence G. Williams**
*United States Representative, R-Pa.*

Senator Dirksen was a great man but, more importantly, he was a *good* great man.

*Before the House, Washington, Sept. 8.*

## DWIGHT D. EISENHOWER

**Mark W. Clark**
*General, United States Army (Ret.)*

I looked on Ike as one of the greatest human beings I have ever met, a man you would be proud to call your friend. When I heard the news (of his death), I stood at attention for a minute, reflected on our 50-odd years of friendship and said, "Well done, Ike, be thou at rest."

*March 29.*

**Charles de Gaulle**
*President of France*

For me, I see disappear with much sadness a dear companion in arms and a friend. I will keep forever the memory of him—(he) who was a great soldier, an eminent statesman, a sincere friend of France and for whom I had a deep affection.

*Paris, March 28.*

**Elizabeth II**
*Queen of the United Kingdom*

He will always be warmly remembered here for his presence among us in the war years as a great soldier and leader of the Allied Forces and later, especially during his two terms as President of the United States . . . for his statesmanship which did much to further the cause of understanding between our two countries.

*London, March 28.*

**Gerald R. Ford**
*United States Senator, R-Mich.*

He wielded with decision and laid down with dignity the most awesome power ever entrusted to a man, and kept only the admiration and affection of all who love freedom.

*Washington, March 28.*

**Adolph Geusinger**
*Chief of German Army Operations in Eastern Europe, World War II*

General Eisenhower was the first Wes-

tern Commander-in-Chief who held out a hand to conquered Germany.

*March 29.*

**Hubert H. Humphrey**
*Former Vice President of the United States*

As General and President, he unified the Free World's efforts to end World War II. He worked with dedication and patience to bring a truce to Korea, and he recognized early that the cold war must give way to peaceful coexistence. Though trained as a warrior, he was one of our nation's greatest peacemakers.

*March 28.*

**Sidney Hyman**
*Historian, University of Chicago*

Marshall Joffre once said that it takes 16,000 men to train one major general. And it often takes many more casualties to train a President. But when you look at Ike's personality from the perspective of time, lots of things the days hide are revealed by the years. You see that there were surprisingly few casualties required to train Eisenhower. There's nothing dramatic about the kind of work that (he) did, so he suffers by comparison with the trombones-and-drums kind of President. But, in terms of what service he performed, I would give him a B-plus.

*Interview, pub. April 4.*

**Lyndon B. Johnson**
*Former President of the United States*

I was proud to serve with him when he was President. I respected him as a wise and valued commander during my own days in the White House. I treasured him always as my close and lasting friend. His death leaves an empty place in my heart, as it will in the hearts of men and women everywhere. America will be a lonely land without him, but America will always be

(LYNDON B. JOHNSON)

a better nation—stronger, safer, more conscious of its heritage, more certain of its destiny—because Ike was with us when America needed him.

*Johnson City, Tex.,*
*March 28.*

**Bernard Law Montgomery**
*Commander-in-Chief, British*
*Occupation Forces in Germany,*
*World War II*

He had only to smile at you, and there was nothing you could not do for him.

*March 29.*

**Richard M. Nixon**
*President of the United States*

Many men are known and respected outside their own countries. Very few are loved outside their own countries. Dwight Eisenhower was one of those few. He was probably loved by more people in more parts of the world than any President America has ever had. He captured the deepest feelings of free men everywhere . . . He remained, through his final days, the world's most admired and respected man, truly the first citizen of the world.

*Eulogy, Washington,*
*March 30.*

**Lauris Norstad**
*Supreme Allied Commander in Europe*
*during Eisenhower Administration*

History is going to be kind to General Eisenhower's record, as his country has been to him. No man in his lifetime has been loved by so many people in the world and has been the recipient of so much great affection and respect.

*Toledo, Ohio, March 28.*

**Ivy Baker Priest**
*Treasurer of the United States*
*in Eisenhower Administration*

I have lost a dear friend. The nation has lost an historic leader. The world has lost a man of great integrity, honor and ideals.

*March 28.*

**Clinton Rossiter**
*Professor of American Institutions,*
*Cornell University*

I think Eisenhower will not be remembered as a great President. He will be remembered as a great person. I don't think Eisenhower intended to be a great President because he didn't believe in the exercise of presidential power. The country needed him in a deep-down peace-serenity-virtue kind of way, but it was a four-year, not an eight-year, need. Still, for the first time since Jack Kennedy, I shed tears.

*Interview, pub. April 4.*

## ROCKY MARCIANO

**James A. Burke**
*United States Representative, D-Mass.*

Those who followed the champ's career marveled at the gentleness of the "Brockton Blockbuster" outside the ring, and it was often said that he seemed somehow out of place in the boxing world. He brought to boxing a fresh, clean wind and added a sense of honor and dignity to the profession. For millions of Americans he became an unfaltering hero—one they could identify with—and his life gave credence to the Horatio Alger myth . . . Who can say how many he touched, how many he influenced, how many imaginations he fired? The Marciano legend will not die, it will live in the imagination of every young boy it touches, as fathers will tell it to sons and they to their sons.
*Before the House, Washington, Sept. 3.*

**Thomas J. Dodd**
*United States Senator,*
*D-Conn.*

. . . earlier this month, Rocky Marciano was laid to rest after a tragic plane crash . . . claimed his life. I am deeply saddened by the loss of this man, who was a hero to millions throughout the world. Rocky Marciano was a fighter whose success was nonpareil. He climbed through the ropes 49 times and emerged each time wearing the victor's laurel, having won in a style that was never elegant or classic, but always courageous. He was a gentle man and an acutely sensitive one. His opponents were amazed at his gentleness outside the ring. He was respected by all of them and loved by many of them . . . Rocky Marciano exemplified all that is best about sports. He translated all the painfully learned lessons of courage, respect and perseverance to a code of conduct which made him admired and honored among men.
*Before the Senate, Washington, Sept. 18.*

**Emile Griffith**
*Former World Middleweight and*
*Welterweight Boxing Champion*

I came back from the movies and heard the news; my friend asked me, "Emile, why are you crying?" And how could I explain? Rocky and myself were always good friends—that's what hurts me, and why I'm crying; because this man was a gentleman with me, a great champion . . .
*Weehawken, N.J., Sept. 1.*

**Hastings Keith**
*United States Representative, R-Mass.*

In the world of professional boxing, Rocky stood out like a beacon on a foggy shore. As his hometown paper put it in their eulogy, "Rocky was clean." Not one whisper of anything contrary to good conduct ever touched the champ during his distinguished career at the apex of professional boxing.
*Before the House, Washington, Sept. 3.*

**Joe Louis**
*Former World Heavyweight*
*Boxing Champion*

Everything I remember about him is good.
*Sept. 1.*

**Peter W. Rodino, Jr.**
*United States Representative, D-N.J.*

Rocky Marciano was not only a great pugilist and an excellent professional athlete, but, even more importantly, he was an outstanding human being. His qualities as heavyweight champion of the world were outshone by his qualities as a compassionate concerned man who loved and cared about his family and his fellow man. His attitude about people endeared him to all and made him the best possible example to the youth who looked up to him.
*Before the House, Washington, Sept. 3.*

**Sam Silverman**
*Former Boxing Promoter*

Rocky might be the best heavyweight who ever lived. You don't know how good a fighter is until he gets licked. He'd never been beaten. Rocky was an inspiration to kids who wanted to become fighters. He had a clear background. He came up the hard way. Boxing gave Rocky a lot and he gave boxing a lot. He's one of the all-time greats.

*New York, Sept. 1.*

## DREW PEARSON

**Jack Anderson**
*Newspaper Columnist*

There are no words that, in two minutes, can capture the past 22 years, no words that can describe my deep feelings for Drew Pearson. To me, he was a giant, a man of courage and conviction, yet never without compassion. He who believes is strong; he who doubts is weak. Drew had the strong convictions that made him a master of those who were weak and wavering.

*At memorial services, Washington Cathedral, Sept. 4.*

**Don Edwards**
*United States Representative, R-Calif.*

The role Drew Pearson played was a harsh one, one which stung men and institutions to the quick. However, he was a far different man in private than he was in public, and I would like to pay tribute to the warm and gracious man who was hidden behind the public mask. I knew him as a friend and as a gracious human being, as well as the public man who would criticize if he felt it necessary. Both the public and the private Drew Pearson will be missed. For many years he served as the conscience of America, and it is a tribute to him that a new breed of reporters has grown up to follow in his tradition. We will not have another Drew Pearson, but his works, both public and private, will live on as a lasting monument to the complex and vital man he was.

*Before the House, Washington, Sept. 18.*

**Robert Sherrill**
*Magazine Editor*

Drew Pearson was no gentleman, and that was his great strength . . . You could always see him perfectly willing to say to a man's face what he said in his columns.

*Pub. Sept. 15.*

# War and Peace

**Dean Acheson**
*Former Secretary of State
of the United States*

I think less of the capabilities of the United Nations now than I did when I was Secretary (of State), and I thought little enough of them then.
*Interview, Washington, Sept. 24.*

**Spiro T. Agnew**
*Vice President of the United States*

We cannot withdraw from our position of world leadership and assume, by turning our backs, that our burdens will lessen. When our citizens question why we defend the integrity of free nations in Southeast Asia, the answer is that we are defending not only their integrity, but ours. If we allow the small and the weak to be devoured, the larger and stronger will infallibly become the prey.
*Arlington National Cemetery, May 30.*

**Raymond Aron**
*Professor of Faculty Letters,
Paris University*

The sort of stability we have had for the last 10, 20 or 25 years in the world is based, not only on American power, but on the American political will to use that power.
*Interview, Paris, pub. Dec. 1.*

**Charles E. Bennett**
*United States Representative, D-Fla.*

Nobody wants wars, but if we must fight to preserve our national security, let us fight to win at the lowest level of intensity. Let us successfully conclude the small wars before they become big ones. Let us demonstrate by our resolve and strength that we are willing to protect ourselves by force of arms. Then we will avoid the big war against a sophisticated enemy such as Russia, China, or the Warsaw Pact.
*Before the House, Washington, Oct. 3.*

**Kirti Nidhi Bista**
*Prime Minister of Nepal*

We have no doubt, if peace is to be maintained in the world, there is no alternative except coexistence.
*Radio broadcast,
Katmandu, April 9.*

**Winton M. Blount**
*Postmaster General
of the United States*

No soldier, whether he is a private or the Commander-in-Chief, prefers war. No President sees the fathers and sons and husbands of this nation sent to their death with anything but the most bitter pain in his heart. And who can truly know that pain but the man who bears it. General Eisenhower commanded four million men, and said: "Every one of those men is precious to me." As war material? No. As human beings. Who, in all decency, can pretend to desire peace more profoundly than the man who bears the final responsibility for war?
*Abilene, Kans., Oct. 14.*

**Angie E. Brooks**
*Ambassador to the United Nations from Liberia; president, 24th General Assembly of the United Nations*

(The United Nations) could and should remain the best means of international cooperation that has been at mankind's disposal since the beginning of its history, and we have to nurse and cherish and cultivate it—or else we shall one day perish, and not even the moon or the knowledge of space will save us.
*United Nations, N.Y., Sept. 16.*

440

**Leonard F. Chapman, Jr.**
*General, and Commandant,*
*United States Marine Corps*

I believe that the true "dove" is born of battle. No one wants peace more than that young Marine rifleman on his 50th patrol or the Marine aviator flying his third helicopter medical evacuation mission in one day.

*Pub. Oct. 8.*

**Clark M. Clifford**
*Former Secretary of Defense*
*of the United States*

Intelligence collection stabilizes the relationships among nations. Intelligence gathering is an aid toward peace and not a hindrance toward peace. It is a step in the direction that ultimately leads to a better world than we have now. If a nation is getting reasonably accurate intelligence, it is less likely blindly to strike out at some country it thinks is its enemy. It is less likely to be disturbed by rumors and guess work and so, in a moment of hysteria or deep concern, launch an all-out effort.

*Washington, April 24.*

**Norman Cousins**
*Editor, "Saturday Review"*

Nobody has much hope that the arms limitation talks will accomplish much. The approach has seemed to be that only when a country has fully developed its weaponry—systems such as the ABM and MIRV—will it be the right moment to sit down and talk sanity. The United States, the Soviet Union, Great Britain, France and Communist China are now engaged in a competition to which there can only be one outcome—the use of these weapons.

*Beverly Hills, Calif., Nov. 3.*

**Edward J. Derwinski**
*United States Representative, R-Ill.*

. . . I am convinced we will have peace in Southeast Asia, we will have peace in the Middle East only when the Communists recognize that aggression does not pay. Anything short of that is to have impossible dreams.

*Before the House, Washington, Oct. 14.*

**Jack Edwards**
*United States Representative, R-Ala.*

There is not one American who wants war at any cost, just as there should not be one American who wants peace at any cost. An unjust peace is just as bad as, if not worse than, an unjust war.

*Before the House, Washington, Oct. 3.*

**Sam J. Ervin, Jr.**
*United States Senator, D-N.C.*

We are impatient people who demand immediate solutions of our problems, no matter how difficult and enduring they might be . . . Moreover, the hunger for peace in our time, which sent Chamberlain to Munich and our world to its unhappy state, still tempts multitudes to conjure up utopias and fantasies.

*Pub. Aug. 11.*

**James M. Gavin**
*Lt. Gen., United States Army (Ret.);*
*former United States Ambassador*
*to France*

We're extremely venturesome in war, and we ought to be as venturesome in peace. The rewards are greater.

*Interview, pub. Nov. 19.*

**Bernard Gert**
*Professor of Philosophy,*
*Dartmouth College*

National self-interest, except for self-defense, does not justify violence, nor does national honor. To use violence to defend honor is to do such violence to the concept of honor that it will never survive the defense.

*Interview, pub. Dec. 30.*

**Andrei Grechko**
*Minister of Defense of the*
*Union of Soviet Socialist Republics*

Imperialism, with U.S. imperialism in the lead, continues to step up international tension, to increase the arms race, to make aggressive blocs more active. The continued aggression by the United States in Vietnam, armed provocations staged by the Israeli extremists against the Arab peoples, revenge-seeking aspirations of the West German militarists are fraught

(ANDREI GRECHKO)

with dangerous consequences . . . (Russia will continue) raising the military might of (its) Army and Navy.

*Moscow, pub. July 28.*

**Andrei A. Gromyko**
*Foreign Minister of the Union of*
*Soviet Socialist Republics*

The idea of passing from war to peace without negotiation is far less realistic than that of flying to the moon. The fact is that the moon has been attained by mortal men, whereas peace without negotiation has never in all history been achieved at all.

*United Nations, N.Y., Sept. 19.*

**Seymour Halpern**
*United States Representative, R-N.Y.*

Peace is everyone's concern and nobody's job, which may explain why we have failed to convert a peace-keeping intent into a peace-keeping capability.

*Before the House, Washington,*
*pub. Sept. 30.*

**Gustav Heinemann**
*President of West Germany*

It is not *war* that is the emergency in which one must prove oneself, as any generation was told at the school desks of imperial days. Today, *peace* is the emergency in which we must all prove ourselves. Beyond peace, there can be no existence.

*Inaugural address, Bonn, July 1.*

**Hubert H. Humphrey**
*Former Vice President*
*of the United States*

The danger to peace in the world is not the confrontation openly between the United States and the Soviet Union. That's very remote. But the danger is that you get sucked in by your little brother. Your cousin or the kids get in a street fight, and pretty soon you've got the whole town in conflagration.

*MacAlester College, St. Paul, Minn.,*
*Feb. 4.*

**Daniel K. Inouye**
*United States Senator, D-Hawaii*

If we are to have peace, we must think the unthinkable—a Red Chinese ambassador in Washington and a Red Chinese representative at the United Nations.

*New Orleans, March 31.*

**Lyndon B. Johnson**
*President of the United States*

There are many critical issues facing the people of the world. But none of them—except the quest for peace—is more important than the problem of rising population. Indeed, world peace will probably never be possible if this problem goes unsolved.

*Washington, Jan. 7.*

**Edward M. Kennedy**
*United States Senator, D-Mass.*

It takes two sides to make a lasting peace, but it only takes one to make the first step.

*Pub. Jan. 26.*

**Melvin R. Laird**
*Secretary of Defense of the United States*

The (Safeguard anti-ballistic missile) system we are proposing is the best kind of people-protection, because it strengthens our ability to deter nuclear war. To the extent that it does that, it can truly be called a building block for peace.

*Before Senate Armed Services*
*Committee, Washington, March 20.*

**Alfred M. Landon**
*Former Governor of Kansas*

The United Nations has been oversold. Established to achieve world peace, the United Nations—after 24 years—is far from realizing its purpose; and its goal will remain a distant dream so long as the major powers—including the United States—act unilaterally on major world issues, and so long as Communist China—representing one-fourth of humanity—is unrepresented in that body.

*At Kansas State University, Manhattan,*
*Kans., June 24.*

**L.S.B. Leakey**
*Archaeologist*

We can, should, must sit down tonight —every one of us—and say to someone else, "War is impossible. War is insane."

That would snowball a wall of public opinion right across the world, and then we'd look around for other, sensible ways to solve our disagreements. Man can reason . . . It would be far more effective than burning draft cards, waving banners in the streets. Just make war unreasonable.

*Interview, Los Angeles, pub. March 16.*

**Lyman L. Lemnitzer**
*General, United States Army;*
*Supreme Allied Commander, Europe*

There is an unsound belief that wars can be fought with nuclear weapons alone. This is not so. You must have the means and the forces to employ them effectively, and they have to be employed together with conventional forces to make them really effective. Nuclear forces require the same high degree of training, the same high degree of leadership and organization to fit into the total military picture, or they cannot be employed effectively against an enemy.

*Interview, Mons, Belgium, pub. May 12.*

**Walter Lippmann**
*Author, Newspaper Columnist*

After World War II, Britain having exhausted itself and America becoming very strong, the theory was propagated—foremost of all by Churchill himself after World War II—that from now (on) we would have a *Pax Americana* in the world. Now, that proved to be an illusion. We're living in the aftermath of that. There is no such thing as a *Pax Americana*. There won't be a *Pax Sovietica* or anything like it, because the world is too big to be governed by anybody. There will be no central place—not London, not Washington, not the United Nations—to which you can go and resolve every problem.

. . . our nuclear power is good only as a balance and deterrent to the nuclear power of the Soviet Union. Their's, vice versa. We can't use nuclear power in Viet Nam; they can't use it in Czechoslovakia; they can't use it in Romania; they can't use it anywhere where they are in trouble.

*Interview, Seal Harbor, Me.,*
*pub. Sept. 14.*

**Glenard P. Lipscomb**
*United States Representative, R-Calif.*

. . . in a world where peace still depends upon a balance of power, antimilitaristic emotion is as bad a guide to policy as militaristic emotion.

*Before the House, Washington, Nov. 6.*

**George S. McGovern**
*United States Senator, D-S.D.*

If, in view of the enormous striking power we have in our Polaris missile system and our land-based missiles, we have not developed the capacity to convince an enemy aggressor that his society will be destroyed in the event of an attack on the United States, then we must assume that sheer madness and a determination for mutual suicide have taken over in a potential enemy capital. That being the case, one wonders if there is anything that can be done to save the human race. In the last analysis, I think that all of these (missile) systems depend on some assumption, however low their intentions might be, that the rational factor, the desire for survival, still exists on the part of the nuclear powers. If that factor ever breaks up, then one wonders if any amount of expenditure on military purposes can save any of us.

*Before the Senate, Washington, Sept. 15.*

**Hans J. Morgenthau**
*Professor of political science and*
*modern history, University of Chicago*

Within the framework of conventional war, the arms race was a perfectly rational instrument of national policy. The more machine guns you had, compared with your enemy, the better off you were in this particular department. However, when it comes to nuclear weapons, the arms race becomes a complete absurdity once you have reached the optimum of being able to destroy your enemy a couple of times over, even under the worst of circumstances. Yet, we are still practicing the arms race with regard to nuclear weapons, unable to understand this basic difference between nuclear and conventional weapons.

*At Congressional Conference on the*
*Military Budget and National Priorities,*
*pub. May 25.*

**Wayne L. Morse**
*Former United States Senator, D-Ore.*

No power in the world is a greater threat to peace than the United States.
*Cleveland, Feb. 17.*

**Daniel P. Moynihan**
*Assistant to the President of the United States for Urban Affairs*

The U.S. is for peace in the world, but that doesn't necessarily tell the Secretary of State what to do when he gets up in the morning.
*Pub. Jan. 31.*

**Richard M. Nixon**
*President of the United States*

The greatest honor history can bestow is the title of peacemaker. This honor now beckons America—the chance to help lead the world out of the valley of turmoil and onto the high ground of peace man has dreamed of since the dawn of civilization.
*Inauguration speech, Washington, Jan. 20.*

I consider the Department of State to be a department of peace; I consider the Department of Defense to be a department of peace; and I can assure you that, at the White House level, in the National Security Council, *that* is where we coordinate all of our efforts toward peace.
*News conference, Washington, Feb. 6.*

I believe . . . that we can bring about a durable peace in our time; but it cannot come to those who seek it frantically, with overnight deals or drastic gestures; It cannot come to those who pursue it casually, without real hope or genuine idealism.
*London, Feb. 25.*

When you hear the criticism of the military complex in this country, when you hear what is wrong with the United States and our armed forces, of what we are necessarily doing in the cause of peace and freedom in Vietnam—just remember that history will record that never has a great nation had military forces which were more dedicated and whose activity made a greater contribution to peace than the United States.
*Aboard U.S.S. "Saratoga," near Norfolk, Va., May 17.*

The adversaries of the world are not in conflict because they are armed. They are armed because they are in conflict and have not yet learned peaceful ways to resolve their conflicting national interests.
*U.S. Air Force Academy, Colorado Springs, Colo., June 4.*

There are differences between the nations and differences between the leaders and differences between the peoples in this world. But, based on my own experience, of this one thing I am sure: the people of the world, wherever they are, want peace, and those of us who have the responsibilities for leadership in the world have an overwhelming world mandate from the people of the nations we represent to bring peace, to keep the peace and to build the peace.

We should be under no illusion . . . that arms control will itself bring peace. Wars are fought by soldiers, but they are declared by politicians. Peace also requires progress on those stubbornly persistent political questions—questions that are considered in this room—questions that still divide the world. And it requires other exchanges, not only of words but of deeds, that can gradually weave a fabric of mutual trust among the nations and the peoples of the world.

It is no longer enough to restrain war. Peace must also embrace progress—both in satisfying man's material needs and in fulfilling his spiritual needs.
*United Nations, N.Y., Sept. 18.*

**Paul VI**
*Pope*

We all desire that conflicts should be resolved no longer by trails of murderous brute force, blind and ruinous, but through rational procedures . . . Peace is necessary; peace is difficult; peace is fragile.
*Rome, Jan. 1.*

**I. I. Rabi**
*Professor of Physics, Columbia University*

When you look at the proposition inherent in a nuclear exchange, you realize that even minimal losses—such as taking out New York, Chicago and Los Angeles— would spell the end of the American dream as we know it.

*At Center for the Study of Democratic Institutions, Santa Barbara, Calif., pub. Feb. 10.*

### Gideon Rafael
*Director-General, Ministry of Foreign Affairs of Israel*

Optimism is for diplomats, and realism is for soldiers.

*Los Angeles, June 18.*

### David C. Richardson
*Commander, United States Sixth Fleet*

I think that should another war come, and should that war be conventional and involve major powers, the ability of a nation to control the electronic environment will have a great deal to do with the outcome. I believe that a third world war at sea, should it ever materialize, will be an "electronized" war, as the second was an air war and the first a battleship war. That is the kind of war which all powers concerned are learning about right now.

*Aboard U.S.S. "Little Rock," pub. July 21.*

### Carlos P. Romulo
*Foreign Secretary of the Philippines*

It (the United Nations) has not been a spectacular success. But neither has it been a dismal failure, as some would say. And isn't it wonderful that you can bring together diplomats from 126 countries under one roof? Where else but here can you see the whole world?

*United Nations, N.Y., Sept. 21.*

### Dean Rusk
*Former Secretary of State of the United States*

If the idea of collective security is not the answer, find a better one. But let's not stumble on a worse one—there will be no lessons to be drawn from World War III.

*Granville, Ohio, pub. March 17.*

### Mitchell Sharp
*Secretary of State for External Affairs of Canada*

. . . the world body (the United Nations) is drowning in a sea of words . . . This has led governments to attach less importance to the United Nations' activities and efforts. The credibility of the United Nations as a negotiating forum and an instrument for resolving the world's problems is wasting away. Public confidence in the organization is being weakened and public support is being undermined.

*Pub. Oct. 4.*

### John Stennis
*United States Senator, D-Miss.*

Even though modern weapons are not cheap, they are bargains even at today's prices, if they accomplish the purpose of deterring aggression and preventing war.

*Pub. Nov. 23.*

### U Thant
*Secretary-General of the United Nations*

. . . the peoples of the world, in whose name the United Nations claims to speak, tend to regard the United Nations as a kind of supranational authority, and to blame the UN for every failure of the system of collective international security which is envisaged in the charter. In actual fact, the UN is not a supranational authority, and, while the General Assembly . . . is in a sense the parliament of mankind, it does not have the legislative authority with which national parliaments are endowed. . . . the real issue is the willingness of the member states to uphold the charter of principles and abide by them.

*United Nations, N.Y., pub. Sept. 16.*

### Cyrus Vance
*Former deputy Secretary of Defense of the United States*

We must face the reality that until we succeed in developing a stronger U.N., the world community and all its members —strong and weak alike—will remain dangerously insecure.

*Des Moines, Ia., Oct. 25.*

**William C. Westmoreland**
*General, and Chief of Staff,*
*United States Army*

All of us—you and I—wish within our hearts that armies could be forever eliminated . . . Only a fool would ever hope for war . . . Yet . . . violence between men and violence between nations are harsh realities with which we must be able to cope.
*Kansas State University, April 9.*

(Until the time when) all armed forces can be banished from the face of the earth, most assuredly international peace must be armed peace.
*Virginia Institute of Technology,*
*Blacksburg, Va., June 7.*

**Earle G. Wheeler**
*General, United States Army;*
*Chairman, Joint Chiefs of Staff*

I put little equity in such sweeping insights as "the atmosphere has changed in Eastern Europe," or, "the Soviet Union has a vested interest in peace," or, perhaps the granddaddy of them all, "if we undertake a significant, unilateral measure of 'demonstrative' disarmament, the Soviets will be 'shamed' into a like measure." I wouldn't try any of these statements on the unfortunate Mr. Dubceck.
*Pensacola, Fla., Sept. 29.*

**Adam Yarmolinsky**
*Professor of Law,*
*Harvard University*

The (SALT) talks may not produce agreement, and they can even be used as an excuse to build new weapons—so we can bargain from strength. But if one believes, as I do, that enough is enough, then it may be possible even for Americans and Russians, if they both work at it, to agree on how much is enough. It will still take patience on both sides and a willingness to confine the discussions to our one undoubted area of common concern—not to be blown up together.
*Interview, pub. Nov. 19.*

**Charles W. Yost**
*United States Ambassador*
*to the United Nations*

. . . If, as we review the record of the United Nations, we find that the efforts made in that organization are not good enough, let us not forget that the responsibility for that state of affairs lies with us, the members. As Adlai Stevenson once said, it is a bad idea to mock the UN's weakness, for when we do we are mocking ourselves.
*Before Cincinnati*
*World Affairs Council,*
*Oct. 21.*

# The Indexes

# Index to Speakers

## Mc

## M

**T**

**U**

**V**

**W**

# Index to Subjects

## A

"A Horse's Head," 298
Aaron, Hank, 414
ABM (see missile, antiballistic)
Academic freedom, 50, 54, 59, 61, 70, 71, 73, 132
    profession, 62
    standards, 69
Academics, 51
Academy Awards, 311, 314, 366
Academy for Educational Development, 47
Academy of Motion Picture Arts and Sciences, 317, 320
Accounting gymnastics, 16
Acquisition, 16, 21
Activism, 63-64
Activist, 2, 62, 67, 73, 121
Actors, 100, 352
Addicts, 41
Adolescence, 374
Adriatic, 255
Adversary system, 113
Advertising, 16-17, 19, 22-23
    agencies, boutique, 22
    cigarette, 26
AEC (see Atomic Energy Commission)
Affluence, 4, 84, 116
AFL-CIO (see American Federation of Labor-Congress of Industrial Organizations)
Africa, 10, 116, 195-199
Afro-American, 8, 10, 49
Agency for International Development (AID), 251
Aggression, 79, 81, 247
Agitators, 68, 72
Agnew, Spiro T., 3, 159, 164, 291
Agricultural revolution, 173
AID (see Agency for International Development)
Air, 27, 30-32, 187
Air field, floating, 147
Air Force Association, 138
Air Line Pilots Association, 186
Air Resources Board, 29
Air space, international, 141
Aircraft carriers, 128, 132, 139, 146, 150, 174
Alabama, 74
Alaska, 98, 127
Albee, Edward, 354
Albert Einstein College of Medicine, 56, 308
Albertson, Jack, 326
Alcindor, Lew, 420
Alcoholic, 305, 307
"Alfie," 313
Alfred P. Sloan Foundation, 52
Algebra, 57
Alger, Horatio, 19, 379, 437
Algeria, 274
Alien and Sedition Acts, 295

Alienation, 49
All deliberate speed, 2
Allegiance, mindless, 153
Alliance for Progress, 201-203, 205
Alliances, 82
Allies, 76-78, 83-84
Aluminum Company of America, 49
Ambassador, 5, 77-79
America, down with, 155
    hunger in, 166
    peace and freedom in, 152
American, anti-, 218
American Association for the Advancement of Science, 408
American Association of Advertising Agencies, 17
American Association of Junior Colleges, 49
American Association of School Administrators, 55
American Association of State Colleges, 54
American Bankers Association, 104, 183
American Bar Association, 18, 20, 34, 36, 72, 110, 112, 114, 117-119
American Baseball League, 412
American Basketball Association, 419
American Booksellers Association, 299
American Broadcasting Company, 290, 293, 295, 347, 350, 426
American Cancer Society, 303, 305, 308
American Cinema Editors, 324
American Civil Liberties Union, 68, 153, 161
American College of Cardiology, 302
American College Public Relations Association, 70
American Council on Education, 61, 74
American dream, 154, 170, 173
American enterprise, 25
American-European Community, 82
American Farm Bureau Federation, 191
American Federation of Labor-Congress of Industrial Organizations (AFL-CIO), 10, 12, 100, 103, 105, 159, 239, 246
American Federation of Teachers, 56
American Fighter Pilots Association, 130
American Football League (AFL), 422, 424
American Group Psychotherapy Association, 304
American Guild of Variety Artists, 349
American Heart Association, 304, 307
American Institute of Aeronautics and Astronautics, 405
American Institute of Architects, 190
American Institute of Certified Public Accountants, 30
American Institute of Graphic Arts, 2
American-International Pictures, 310, 320
American Iron and Steel Institute, 108
American Jewish Committee, 72
American Jewish Congress, 9
American Legion, 150, 155
American Management Association, 16
American Medical Association, 303, 306, 308
American National Theatre and Academy, 379

# B

# C

# I

# O

# P

# Q

# R

# S

## DATE DUE

| APR 1 0 1989 | | | |
|---|---|---|---|
| | | | |
| | | | |
| | | | |
| | | | |
| | | | |
| | | | |
| | | | |
| | | | |
| | | | |
| | | | |
| | | | |
| | | | |